Model Perspectives

Structure, Architecture and Culture

This book contains a unique collection of various perspectives on the relationship between structures and the forms and spaces of architecture. As such it provides students and professionals alike with an essential sourcebook that can be mined for visual inspiration as well as for textually rich and authoritative insight into the links between structure, architecture and cultural context.

The chapters address fundamental structural elements and systems: columns, walls, beams, trusses, frames, tensile structures, arches, domes and shells. Each chapter is subdivided into two parts:

• The essays – introduce the chapters with the reprinting of a curated set of essays and excerpts by various authors that uniquely address how particular structural elements or systems relate in essential fashion to architectural design concepts.

• The model studies – physical models of the overall structural systems of several notable contemporary buildings from Europe, North and South America, Africa and Asia are illustrated with large photographs, detail close-ups and views of their external forms and internal spaces that establish the exceptional qualities of these projects in connecting structural form to architectural design objectives. Mosaic layouts complete the chapters with a collection of photographs of yet more models whose particular details and unique features serve to extend the visual repertoire of the structural type being considered.

The combination, juxtaposition and mutual positive reinforcement of these two collections, one largely textual and the other image-based, provides the reader with unique and multifaceted insights into how structural forms and systems can be related to architectural design intentions. Conveyed by a strong and deliberate graphical design format, this assembly of materials gets to the very essence of structures within the context of architecture, and will inspire students and practitioners alike to make strategic design decisions for their own projects.

Mark R. Cruvellier is the Nathaniel and Margaret Owings Professor and Chair of the Department of Architecture at Cornell University, USA. He teaches and conducts research in the area of structural form and behavior considered within the context of architecture.
Bjørn N. Sandaker is Professor of Architectural Technology at The Oslo School of Architecture and Design (AHO), Norway, and Adjunct Professor at the Norwegian University of Science and Technology (NTNU) in Trondheim, Norway. His particular academic interest focuses on the borderline between architecture and structural engineering.
Luben Dimcheff is the Richard Meier Assistant Professor in the Department of Architecture at Cornell University, USA, where he teaches studio as well as courses that are focused on the visualization and analysis of space. He leads a design and architectural practice based in New York City with projects built internationally.

Some books are treasure troves – ensembles of deep human experiential research – which need to be kept close to hand. This book is one such treasure. The combination of selected texts with the constructed models becomes the thoughtfully constructed intellectual structure within which to navigate these essential topics.
– Yvonne Farrell & Shelley McNamara, Directors, Grafton Architects

During the past decades, architecture has been dominated by an interest in expressive singular forms, often facilitated by computerized design and methods of calculation, novel material technologies, and robotic methods of production. The book Model Perspectives: Structure, Architecture and Culture returns architectural thinking back to its tectonic principles and elementary syntax. It also emphasizes the essential cultural connectedness of the art of building; architectural meaning cannot be invented, as it is bound to reflect the human existential and mental reality. All true architectural meaning echoes tradition, and the most radical artistic innovations become part of this esteemed continuum of tradition.
– Juhani Pallasmaa, architect, writer, professor emeritus, Helsinki University of Technology (Aalto University, School of Art, Design and Architecture), Finland

Model Perspectives

Structure, Architecture and Culture

Mark R. Cruvellier
Bjørn N. Sandaker
Luben Dimcheff

Routledge
Taylor & Francis Group
LONDON AND NEW YORK

First published 2017
by Routledge
2 Park Square, Milton Park, Abingdon, Oxon OX14 4RN

and by Routledge
711 Third Avenue, New York, NY 10017

Routledge is an imprint of the Taylor & Francis Group, an informa business

Publisher's Note:
This book has been prepared from camera-ready copy provided by the authors.

British Library Cataloguing-in-Publication Data
A catalogue record for this book is available from the British Library

Library of Congress Cataloging-in-Publication Data
Names: Cruvellier, Mark, author. | Sandaker, Bjørn Normann, 1954- author. |
Dimcheff, Luben, author.
Title: Model perspectives : structure, architecture and culture / Mark R. Cruvellier,
Bjørn N. Sandaker and Luben Dimcheff.
Description: New York : Routledge, 2016. | Includes bibliographical
references and index.
Identifiers: LCCN 2016003816| ISBN 9780415731935 (hb : alk. paper) | ISBN
9780415731942 (pb : alk. paper)
Subjects: LCSH: Architecture--Themes, motives.
Classification: LCC NA2540 .C78 2016 | DDC 720--dc23
LC record available at http://lccn.loc.gov/2016003816

ISBN: 978-0-415-73193-5 (hbk)
ISBN: 978-0-415-73194-2 (pbk)

Typeset in Adobe Garamond

Printed and bound in India by Replika Press Pvt. Ltd.

Contents

Preface

A passion for structure – from its overall forms and physical behaviors to material choices and connection details. A passion for architecture – from its external shapes and interior spaces to conceptual inspirations and aesthetic preferences. A passion for culture – from the artistic and literary to the social and technological. These are the things that have motivated this book – especially when considered as closely intertwined topics. Other passions are behind it as well: for the written word, for the photographic image, and for *making*, whether at full scale or one much reduced.

Structure, architecture and culture; these topics can be considered in relation to one another in multiple ways, but two perspectives in particular are used here: one is a collection of essays/text extracts, and the other an archive of photographs of models. For the first, text is premiated for inherent quality and embedded message; for the latter, the image is the focus. In both cases, the intention is to dwell on things for a while, to contemplate them, to luxuriate in generous treatment. Furthermore, this book is organized into seven chapters that each covers a quintessential structural element or basic system type; columns start things out, followed by walls, beams, trusses and so on. These fundamental building blocks of structure have already been well covered in books elsewhere, including by two of the present authors in *The Structural Basis of Architecture, 2nd ed.*, but here they are considered afresh in what is regarded as a mutually productive and complementary manner. Whereas structures textbooks generally approach the topic through explanations of systems of forces and analytical descriptions of responsive behaviors (i.e., the "*how things work*" aspect of the subject), here broader cultural themes are fleshed out and considered equally relevant to address the "*why things are the way they are*" facet of the argument. Moreover, photographs of three-dimensional systems demonstrate in ways that words simply can't the "*how do these things look?*" aspect that is so critical to being able to appreciate – and incorporate – structures as an integral part of architectural design.

With regard to the collection of essays/extracts: each one addresses, in a way that we feel strikes a resonant chord, the interconnections between the topics of central concern here. Sometimes this has been done intentionally by the author, as in the case of Peter Collins' description of the dilemma Auguste Perret confronted when columns had to be fashioned from the newly developed material of reinforced concrete. In other cases, the idea of addressing the topic of *structure* may not have been there to begin with, but when read with this in mind the words take on new relevance; Gottfried Böhm's text about the deeply sensed impact of Richard Serra's sculptures, for instance, could not better embody the essence of walls in architecture. Other entries address familiar buildings, but in perhaps unexpected ways, such as the Munich Olympic Stadium, Miami's 1111 Lincoln Road, or the Sendai Mediatheque. Several of the authors might be anticipated: Cecil Balmond is here *informally* as is Robert Silman recounting his experiences in strengthening Fallingwater; Colin Rowe and Roland Barthes are present with their respective essays *The Chicago Frame* and *La Tour Eiffel*, which are included for their eloquence and engagement of structure alike. Other writers will likely be more unexpected in the present context, such as

Donald Ingber with his description of living cells' cytoskeletal structures and their tensegrity characteristics, or installation artist Sanjeev Shankar's recounting of the communal building project for a suspended canopy made using discarded cooking-oil cans. The list of entries on the preceding four pages indicates the range of what has been collected in this book; but this is not to imply that this is *the* definitive collection of such essays/extracts. Rather, it is hoped that it will act as more of a prompt for other such texts to be researched, gathered, shared – and written too!

The collection of images of models forms the complementary lens through which the topics of structure, architecture and culture are here explored. This is derived from a collection of well over 750 unique and often exquisite models that have been built by architecture students at Cornell University for over the past twenty years. This approach to the teaching of structures was in part inspired by the earlier work of Professor Steinar Eriksrud and his students at The Oslo School of Architecture and Design (AHO) who built up a unique model culture there. Among other things, this led to the substantial collection of stave church models that still exists at the school today, inspired by the interests of Professor and colleague Arne Eggen.

So why this particular focus on models? Because they are a highly effective and engaging way of teaching and conveying the subject matter of structures when considered in the context of architecture's conceptual ideas and design objectives. Certainly the models' conception is in and of itself an artistic/creative act. And with their assembly there are plenty of "Ah-hah!" moments that signal critical understanding; when a diagonal brace all of a sudden "locks" into place a previously flimsy frame, for example, or when the anchoring of a tension ring enables a set of radial ribs previously lying flat and without purpose to form into a dome and hold it in place. In models' final realization space and form are created and the sense of "inhabiting" such space comes to life. Moreover, how the structural skeleton is modeled relates in fundamental ways to the conceptual, formal, spatial and material ideas that are embodied in the "real" structure from which the lessons are being learned. But also, at some point these projects take on a life of their own; not as precious miniatures of the actual buildings but as their own entities – no less real, no less "accurate" for the translation of authorship; the lessons are still embedded, and often self-created. And finally, if many of the essays/extracts are inherently more historical in character, the complementary models are purposefully mostly of contemporary structures – thus emphasizing the ongoing and ever-present relevance of the theme of this book.

The late architect Sverre Fehn liked to read novels collected here and there, perhaps received as gifts or picked up at a bookstore on his way home; in these he found particular sentences or phrases on which he reflected deeply, becoming engrossed in them before eventually turning the words into architectural content.[1] That is the analogous objective here as well. Each of the text entries or model studies can be approached individually and at random. Or they can be gone through in sequence, as the introductory paragraphs connect and put them into context with each other. One could instead start by just deciding to read the essay introductions and model study texts to get an overall sense of what is contained in this book and then decide what to come back to, but it is likely that along the way one would have become engrossed in something, akin to Fehn's approach for broadening his intellectual horizons and inspirational repertoire – which is, of course, just the intent.

1. Fjeld, Per Olaf. *Sverre Fehn: The Pattern of Thoughts.*

Acknowledgments

A book like this does not come together without significant and critical assistance. The following individuals have all been key contributors: Mia Kang, who lent this project her keen design skills from the start; Katayoun Amirmoeini and Cora Visnick, who with great care and patience waded through a permissions process that was as extensive as it was complicated; also, Michael Babcock and Ethan Davis whose help with text transcriptions and proofreading was both essential and timely. Others have also contributed in various ways: Juan Carlos Artolozaga, Nicholas Cassab-Gheta, Alberto Embriz de Salatierra, Iroha Ito, Daniel Toretsky and Mariya Tsvetkova. Too many to name are the structures teaching assistants at Cornell over the years, whose overall support and photographic expertise have made this project come to life. And clearly this book would not have been possible without the many former students who have so effectively contributed to it through their model building skills, creativity, ambition and perseverance; it is to them, therefore, that we dedicate this work.

We also wish to recognize the creative flair and contribution of faculty colleague Mark Morris, whose final essay *A Model Curriculum* so ably helps tie together some of the many threads of this endeavor, both in spirit and over time.

To the many authors, publishers, photographers, architects, engineers, librarians, curators, archivists, etc. who either individually or on behalf of their respective practices/institutions provided the permissions necessary to reproduce the various texts and images contained herein, we express our sincere gratitude.

The support of the many dedicated staff members, faculty colleagues and administrators alike at our "home" institutions of Cornell University's College of Architecture, Art, and Planning and The Oslo School of Architecture and Design (AHO) is gratefully acknowledged, as is these institutions' generous financial support for the endeavor.

And lastly, at Routledge publishers, we are very grateful for the support and encouragement of Editor Fran Ford, Editorial Assistant Trudy Varcianna, and Production Editor Christina O'Brien for seeing this project through to being realized in the way that we had envisioned it at the start.

CHAPTER ONE

Columns

Consider … the momentous event in architecture when the wall parted and the column became.

Louis I. Kahn

2

Musée des Travaux Publics, exhibition hall

The column is commonly understood to be a structural element that is subject to compressive load – perhaps caused by the weight of a roof held aloft, or other story levels and occupants in a multi-story building. As such, columns are essential to the creation of occupiable space; moreover, the details of their design have varied greatly over time according to changing architectural styles and material advancements. One such notable material development in the early 20th century was the widespread introduction of reinforced concrete construction, leading to the struggle of architects and engineers of that era to adapt not only to its load-bearing capabilities but also to the new possibilities it provided for form-making – whether for its base, shaft or capital. As described in the following extract written by Peter Collins in his seminal book *Concrete: The Vision of a New Architecture*, Auguste Perret was a Parisian architect who took this challenge to heart with his innovative and evolving designs for columns in such notable buildings as Notre Dame de Raincy and, of primary focus here, the Musée des Travaux Publics.

Auguste Perret and the Concrete Column

from *Concrete: The Vision of a New Architecture*
Peter Collins

In examining Perret's doctrine in detail, it will be convenient to begin with his attitude towards the design of columns, the element in his vocabulary to which he attached the most importance. Columns have traditionally been regarded as the very symbol of architecture, since they express more forcibly than any other element the peculiar dignity of the architect's achievement, and it is only within recent years, mainly as a result of their abuse in the nineteenth century, that their use on façades and in interiors has been looked upon with mistrust. As we have seen, Perret's substitution of reinforced concrete columns for load-bearing partition walls at 25b rue Franklin was interpreted by the younger generation as an invitation to do away with visible supports altogether, and this attitude became more and more pronounced as the new concepts of spatial integration spread, and the desire to exploit the slenderness of new structural materials increased. The traditional idea of a colonnade, with its rhythm of vertical supports forming imposing perspectives throughout interiors and across façades, was discarded as both structurally unnecessary and inappropriate to modern planning, so that the columns themselves, which at the beginning of the century were already being disguised by Art Nouveau decorators as naturalistic stems, were now reduced to their minimum frequency and dimension so as to be as unobtrusive as possible, if not completely unseen.

Auguste Perret liked columns, and proliferated them with all the enthusiasm of the architects of the past. It was not only the inherent structural dignity of the column itself which captured his imagination but the powerful emotional effect created by receding ranks of columns, and the optical function fulfilled by such rhythmic sequences in creating an awareness of scale beyond the effective bounds of stereoscopic sight. However much the Renaissance principles of perspective might be outmoded as a means of pictorial representation, the abiding reality of its laws as a means of apprehending spatial relationships seemed to him incontestable, and instead of diminishing or camouflaging his structural supports, he sought every means at his disposal to isolate them in space, and make their rhythm provide the dominant unifying element of his designs. This did not mean that he limited himself on principle to spans only possible in older types of construction, or multiplied columns unnecessarily where they were not structurally required; but it did mean that instead of feeling morally bound always to use the maximum spans obtainable by civil engineering, he considered himself free to use intermediate supports whenever desirable, and saw no objection to dividing a large hall with interior colonnades, provided that these were not in any way detrimental to its use.

In order that full aesthetic advantage could be taken of these structural columns, it was necessary to ensure that each would be a pleasing object in itself. Pride in his new material, and a growing contempt for veneers and renderings, made him seek beauties inherent in concrete, but unlike most of the early theorists, he was not rash enough to assume that the resultant shapes must be of a kind never seen before. On the contrary, he based his researches on those inalienable characteristics, derived from structural and optical laws, which all vertical supports must have in common, and being a building contractor, he perceived that it would be the methods of casting the material, rather than the nature of the material itself or any presupposed theoretical analyses and calculations, which would be the cause of such modifications as might distinguish concrete from worked stone.

The engineers of the period, who had had no reason to abandon the conventional theoretical assumptions of steel frame construction, designed each stanchion as one continuous support rising from floor to floor, and considered the most distinctive characteristic of reinforced concrete frames to be the 'haunches' of the beams, namely the flared ends of the beams which increased the area of concrete under compression near the vertical supports. It soon became apparent to Perret, however, that despite the effective continuity of such columns from the point of view of theoretical calculations, they were not in fact constructed continuously, but were cast independently in sections one storey high. Similarly, though the beam might be conceded theoretically as requiring an increased amount of concrete at its extremities, it was in practice more efficient to make the form-work completely regular, and hence horizontal at its lower edge. In consequence, Perret reversed the normal conception of a reinforced concrete frame. The columns now butted into the beams, and the latter formed a simple grid pattern on a level plane, so that henceforth continuity was horizontal and hence also visible, and each internal column appeared as a distinct element, expressing the way it was cast. It was as if the standard Hennebique diagram had been turned on its side.

The next stage was to consider the character which the form-work should take. In Hennebique's earliest industrial buildings, the columns had been of simple rectangular section, which was logical enough, since this was the cheapest way of assembling timber planks, and Perret himself had used a similar method in the garage in the rue de Ponthieu, where the only major modification was the introduction of diminution and entasis in the columns of the façade. He did not have any occasion to experiment with the shape of vertical supports in monumental buildings during the ensuing twenty years, for the columns of the Théâtre des Champs-Elysées had had to be veneered with marble or plaster, and his other private commissions were mainly for the most utilitarian kind of industrial building, where such refinements would have been extravagant, if not out of place. In 1922, however, an unexpectedly favourable opportunity presented itself when he was commissioned to build the church of Notre Dame du Raincy, for the propaganda of Viollet-le-Duc had disposed the public to accept the idea of ecclesiastical architecture as structure unadorned, and it was thus possible to concentrate here on the refinement of bold and original structural methods without the risk of outraging popular taste, or inviting unfavourable comparisons with the processes of factory design.

The result was undoubtedly the most revolutionary building constructed in the first quarter of the present century, and it justly occupied the place of honour in the first issue of the first magazine specifically devoted to the New Architecture: *L' Architecture Vivante.* The design comprised four rows of free-standing columns 37 ft. high, spaced 33 ft. apart along the length of the nave, and diminished from 17 in. at the foot to 14 in. at the summit. Being free-standing, and thus unaffected by the normal need to receive the abutment of intermediate beams or partitions, there was no practical obligation to make the columns rectangular in section, and therefore, despite the increased cost of the form-work, Perret made them round. This shape was preferred for two reasons; firstly, because it was most economical (in the structural sense of the word), in that it provided constant rigidity from every angle, like a tree trunk, and was, as he himself pointed out, 'best adapted for a member subjected to compression'[1]; secondly, because it was more satisfactory optically as a result of the gradations of shadow and constancy of silhouette. The architects of the eighteenth century, like those of antiquity, had studiously avoided free-standing square columns (or 'pilasters' to give them their correct, though now misapplied name), because apart from their clumsiness, their apparent width varied according to whether they were seen diagonally or from the front. As geometric projections or drawings, a series of pilasters might well appear similar in appearance to columns, but when viewed in perspective, the width of each pilaster would seem to increase as the angle of vision became more oblique. It was thus not merely in obedience to Platonic ideals (whereby the circle was regarded as the configuration of perfection), or in obedience to the belief that the most 'natural' architectural forms were those found in natural organisms such as trees, that the Greeks used cylindrical columns; it was also in obedience to visual experience and optical laws, which demonstrated that rhythms discernible on plan did not necessarily produce the same rhythmic effects when projected into three-dimensional space.

To give greater elegance to the columns of Notre Dame du Raincy, and also (since this was his first attempt to give entasis to round columns) to make provision for any inaccuracies in casting, Perret modelled the surface of the form-work with a series of flutings. These were not regular segmental grooves, as in antique columns, but an alternation of curved projections and angular fillets more suggestive of Gothic composite piers. Similarly, by applying diminution and entasis to columns twenty-three diameters high, Perret showed that the forms were in no sense dictated by a subservience to either Greek or Gothic prototypes, but were on the contrary an attempt to extract the most rational elements from both. Nevertheless, it is clear that although he scrupulously observed the structural characteristics of the new material as he then understood them, Perret was still, like Labrouste before him, unable to free his mind entirely from standard historical conventions, and although he must have known, from reading Choisy, that Mycaenean columns tapered in the opposite direction,* he as yet saw no cause to modify the traditional assumption that a column must always derive its stability from being narrower at the summit than at the base.

It is not known precisely when he first began to question this assumption, but his first radical modification of the traditional lithic shape seems to have been introduced when designing the new Palais de Chaillot in 1934 for the 1937 Paris Exhibition. The authorities had decided to demolish the old Trocadéro Palace, built by Davioud as a temporary centre-piece for the 1878 exhibition, and to substitute a new monumental group of permanent buildings on the same site (the Mont de Chaillot) which would fulfill the same function of housing exhibition and concert halls, and would also terminate effectively the splendid axial vista extending through the Eiffel tower from Gabriel's École Militaire. Perret, who had been entrusted with the commission, abandoned the earlier Baroque composition, with its dominating central structure and curved concatenated wings, and substituted two symmetrical groups of museum buildings linked by an open colonnade. The resultant composition was, in character, reminiscent of Jules Hardouin-Mansart's Grand Trianon at Versailles, but the difficulty here was to design a colonnade appropriate both to the new material and the vastly increased scale. Perret finally decided to arrange giant columns, 83 ft. high, in four rows, making a hundred and four in all, across the whole width of the Place du Trocadéro, and roof them at the same height as the four-storey museum blocks on each side.

The task of designing an open colonnade 17 ft. higher than that of the Madeleine presented aesthetic problems of the greatest delicacy, since the whole visual effect of the *ensemble* depended on the success of this focal element of the design. The columns could conceivably have been designed as simple cylinders, like those of the nearby Musée d'Art Moderne to be built contemporaneously as part of a similar though much smaller composition, but the harshness of such a rigid silhouette would, at this scale, have created an effect so brutal that even the most uncompromising advocates of elemental geometric forms might have hesitated before taking such a drastic step. Alternatively, they could have been tapered and fluted in the traditional manner to produce a solution which, provided that the columns were proportionately as slender as at Notre Dame du Raincy, would have had the advantage of combining classical precedents with the expression of a new structural technique. It had become apparent to Perret, however, that in spite of the elegance and apparent rationalism of the columns at Notre Dame du Raincy, there was a fundamental illogicality in monolithic columns which tapered upwards, since although the convention was justifiable enough in Greek architecture, where the shafts were composed of isolated drums, and even in Roman architecture, where the columns, though monolithic, were unsecured at the ends, the laws of gravity did not apply in the same manner to columns of reinforced concrete, which were rigidly secured at the top by a monolithic framework of interlocking beams, and could, if necessary, be free at the base. The proper analogy, if analogy were needed, was thus not with stone trabeated structures, such as Doric temples, but with timber trabeated structures, such as tables and chairs. Just as table legs, deriving their stability from the rigidity of the upper joint, were traditionally considered more elegant when tapered towards the bottom, so concrete columns might logically be shaped in a similar way; an argument which was especially valid when the columns did not form part of a continuous frame, but were, as in this instance, only one storey high.

Another justification for this shape was that it also corresponded more accurately to the system of reinforcement. In the 40 ft. high free-standing columns supporting the roof of Perret's Musée des Travaux Publics, the reinforcing rods gradually increase in number upwards, so that there are six times as many in the top sixth, where the diameter is 3 ft. 5 in., than at the bottom, where the diameter is 9 in. less. Indeed, the logicality of the shape was so apparent that it soon became an accepted form for reinforced concrete *pilotis*, even though most architects still preferred cylindrical columns for the intermediate floors of a multi-storey frame. There is however no reason why a multi-storey building should not be considered as a series of single-storey structures stacked one on top of the other, unless there are over-riding reasons for expressing the invisible continuity of the internal vertical supports.

Once Perret had accepted a general shape for his columns in principle, the next step was to determine the profiles they could most logically be given. Until that time, it had generally been assumed by classical architects that the basic plan of a column was a circle, since the stonemason's method of carving each drum was to inscribe a circle on the lower bed, and then cut back to form a rough cylinder before finally making it polygonal so as to carve the fluting. Perret perceived, however, that the most logical way of casting a reinforced concrete column was to make it polygonal in the first place, since the most direct way of creating the form-work would be to assemble flat strips of planking, in the same way that staves are assembled to form a barrel. It was not feasible to shape the form-work in such a way as to produce classical fluting, for without using plaster of Paris moulds … it would have been necessary to carve each plank at enormous expense. However, neither process would have produced any real advantage, since it would not have been possible to remove the cement film by bush-hammering without at the same time destroying the precision of the lines. To obtain the optical advantages of fluting, Perret therefore considered it sufficient and more logical merely to remove the cement film from the centre of each face, and leave the arrises untouched,

* No archaeologist, as far as I know, has ever given solid reasons why the shaft should have been thus inverted. I suspect, for reasons which will be clear later, that the original timber prototypes, though standing freely in the normal way on stone discs, were rigidly tenoned or pegged to the wooden architraves at the top.

thus producing slight concavities which, though not possessing the accuracy of Greek fluting, seemed more in keeping with modern reinforced concrete techniques.

The problem of deciding whether or not to give entasis to these new forms was more delicate. Perret felt very deeply the inconsistency of paying lip service to Greek optical refinements whilst at the same time disregarding them in contemporary design, and considered that if a slight curve was necessary to correct the illusion of attenuation in the silhouette of Greek columns, it must be equally necessary in those built today. He therefore designed his columns so that instead of diminishing regularly, their silhouette deviated imperceptibly from a straight line by an amount comparable to that of the Parthenon, i.e. a radius of about half a mile. In concrete this can be achieved with the greatest simplicity, since the form-work is built by nailing tapered boards to the inside of stiffening rings placed at regular intervals along its length. Thus instead of diminishing the diameters of these rings by equal amounts, the diminution is varied to produce the curvature desired. 'It is not to be supposed that the architects ever troubled to calculate the radius or to establish the form of an arc of such a theoretical circle,' wrote Professor Dinsmoor, with reference to the entasis in the Parthenon. 'Their system consisted rather in deciding first the maximum increment of curvature desired, and then selecting any convenient arbitrary number of equal intervals between the beginning and apex of the proposed curve. The maximum increment of curvature was then divided by the square of the above-mentioned number of intervals, thus determining the size of the fractional parts.'[2] The same method was pursued by Perret, with even greater constructional logic, since the 'convenient number of equal intervals' was already constituted by the stiffening rings which kept the form-work in place. Expert craftsmanship was indeed demanded in tapering each plank or stave to ensure that it curved regularly, but this, far from being regarded by him as a demerit of the system, was the guarantee that he was pursuing the right path.

In practice, the number of facets and the amount of entasis varied according to the position occupied by each colonnade, the size of each column, and the incidence of light. These variations are not obvious, simply because we are not trained to look for such minutiae today, but if evidence were needed of Perret's complete integrity in the pursuit of classical ideals, nothing could be more conclusive than his tireless search for perfection in these elemental forms, and the care with which he adjusted his standard elements to accord with each individual design.

In addition to determining the correct form and most effective silhouette for the shafts of his columns, it was necessary to decide how they should terminate at each end. A base could be readily dispensed with, as in Greek Doric architecture, but it seemed clear that some change of shape at the top was desirable if the transfer of reinforcement was to be effected smoothly between the round columns and rectangular beams. Perret had at first avoided this problem altogether; at the Théâtre des Champs-Elysées he had merely emphasized the upper termination by a narrow decorative band, whilst in the church of Notre Dame du Raincy he achieved a similar effect by placing the consecration crosses in the spandrels of the shell vaulting immediately above the shafts. Yet even at that time, he realized that such decorative expedients could not be resorted to indefinitely, and publicly stated his intention of seeking the logical transition from a circle to a square appropriate to reinforced concrete as soon as time and money would permit.[3]

Little guidance as to the correct means of terminating the shafts of a monolithic frame was offered by historical precedents, whilst even carpentry techniques offered few hints apart from a general indication of what to avoid. In trabeated masonry construction, the problem of transferring the load from a square beam to a circular shaft was solved by separate blocks of stone, which also had the function of minimizing the span. In mediaeval timber construction, as in furniture design, no termination was considered necessary (apart from carved or applied ornament), since both the posts and beams were usually square in section. Perret never regarded the need for some visible token of transition as absolutely essential, and frequently, even in his later works, butted shafts directly against the rectangular beams above, as in the colonnade of the Mobilier National, or the interior of the Musée des Travaux Publics. But he felt that if there was in fact some way of creating a transition which would be both structurally logical and aesthetically advantageous, he was under a moral obligation to find it, and there is no clearer evidence of his painstaking and idealistic intellectualism than in the way he devoted his time and energy to this abstract geometric task.

His first executed attempt to achieve a satisfactory transition may be seen in the monumental façade of the Musée des Travaux Publics, built just before the second world war, where the shafts were gradually widened and transformed to a square by an imbrication of leaf-like or scale-like projections. Technically, the method was perfectly justifiable, since the form-work could be assembled like roof shingles, and overlapped to form a kind of hollow cone; but in appearance the result was too reminiscent of conventionalized plant forms such as we find in Egyptian architecture, and as a result it did not affirm sufficiently clearly the essential qualities of the material employed. The method was therefore superseded by a more geometric solution, developed after the war when making studies for the reconstruction of Le Havre, whereby the transition was effected by a series of prismatic modulations developed progressively from the faces of the polygonal shafts direct. Thus, since the 'capital' was composed entirely of plane surfaces, the form-work could be built as an assemblage of flat pieces of wood, and once the minimum number of facets had been determined mathematically, the only arbitrary choice left to the designer consisted in determining the most suitable proportions for each particular case.

It was a solution as absolute and inevitable as the Romanesque cushion capital or the Doric echinus.

The theoretical basis of this 'capital' may be explained quite simply. It will be evident that the easiest way of supporting a square above a circle (which is the essence of the problem) is by means of four inverted triangles, whereby the points of the triangle rest on equally spaced points on that circle – in this case the upper perimeter of a shaft. If the shaft were in fact a circle, the spandrels remaining between each triangle would form conical or spherical surfaces, but since, in this instance, polygonal shafts are used, the problem of filling the spandrels is best solved by a transitional series of triangular planes. Their number and arrangement will depend on the number of sides to the polygon, but if these are always in multiples of four, and if the points of the main supporting triangles are placed above the arrises of the shaft, rather than above the centres of facets, the most economical geometric arrangement for eight-, twelve-, sixteen- and twenty-sided shafts can be determined quite easily, so that the architect's task is limited to deciding dimensions, as it always was in the past.

In view of Perret's enthusiasm for columns, it may be wondered why he never followed, or even started, the current fashion of placing buildings on *pilotis*. The reason is probably that whereas so many of the younger architects of his day regarded buildings as plastic objects standing isolated in space, he himself took the more orthodox view of regarding architecture as essentially a means by which space is enclosed. We shall have cause to consider this important distinction in more detail later, but it may be observed here that although many functional and economic justifications have been given for the practice of standing a building on stilts, the real motive (except when it is merely adopted as a *cliché*) has usually been purely aesthetic. In 1928 Le Corbusier claimed that the purpose of *pilotis*, which he had just started using, was to allow cars to circulate freely beneath the building, and to permit the lady of the house to wash her laundry under shelter in the open air.[4] In 1930, he asserted that *pilotis* were the 'consequence of calculation and the elegant outcome of the modern tendency towards economy'.[5] In his description of his Centrosoyus building in Moscow, however, he justified the decision to raise the entire structure on columns by saying that 'the building presents itself to the observer like an object in a show-case supported on a stand; it can thus be read in its entirety',[6] and it may confidently be asserted that this has been the over-riding motive in every other instance. Had Perret wished to raise his buildings on *pilotis* in the more traditional way, so as to form part of an enclosure, he would not have found Classical precedents lacking. Gondouin, a pupil of Jacques François Blondel, had raised the entrance block of the Paris École de Médecine on a colonnade in 1771, so as to allow an uninterrupted view of the main building at the back of the courtyard round which the composition was designed. Yet for various reasons Perret seems to have avoided this motif, and even when, as at the Mobilier National, he felt the need for an enclosing colonnade across the front of a similar courtyard, he preferred to make it a purely decorative feature rather than build, like Gondouin, an elevated structure linking the two lateral wings. Whether or not his colonnade would have been any more useful structurally if it had in fact supported such a link is a matter of opinion, but it seems clear from both his work and utterances that, in general, Perret considered any aesthetic advantages derived from raising an entire building in the air more than offset by the economic disadvantages of depriving himself of ground floor accommodation. He was entirely in favour of the mediaeval practice of raising façades on columns to provide shelter in front of a recessed line of shops, as had long been traditional in Paris, and as he himself was to introduce at Le Havre. Moreover, he had proposed that the whole of Le Havre, including, that is to say, the roadways, should be raised on piles above the previous level, as the town was sited on marshy subsoil (a project eventually rejected because of the prohibitive cost). But airborne buildings were anathema to him, and whilst he was fully aware of the effectiveness of *pilotis* as an expression of reinforced concrete frame construction, he considered that this effect could be less extravagantly obtained by articulated façades rising directly from the ground.

Photo: doublespace photography

The details of columns' design as well as their locations in the plan of a building (and, thus, the relationships that they may have with other vertical elements such as wall surfaces or glass enclosures) have been described as being instrumental to the changes in the conceptualization of space that are associated with Modern architecture. Kenneth Frampton, in his book *Studies in Tectonic Culture: The Poetics of Construction in Nineteenth and Twentieth Century Architecture* discusses this topic, first with respect to Mies van der Rohe's Barcelona Pavilion, in which eight cruciform columns are physically disengaged from the enclosing walls; further along he cites Colin Rowe's observations on how Mies changed his design approach for the shape of columns and how he then incorporated them into the exterior curtain wall – in what would became iconic Miesian fashion.

Mies' Columns: Barcelona and Beyond

from *Studies in Tectonic Culture: The Poetics of Construction in Nineteenth and Twentieth Century Architecture*
Kenneth Frampton

Mies saw glass as embodying a new challenge, as it were, to the fundamental tectonic elements of the wall, the floor, and the ceiling. He was to state as much in his contribution to a prospectus written for the Union of German Plate Glass Manufacturers in 1933 wherein he stressed the symbiotic impact of glass on modern form.

> *What would concrete be, what steel without plate glass? The ability of both to transform space would be limited, even lost altogether, it would remain only a vague promise. Only a glass skin and glass walls can reveal the simple structural form of the skeletal frame and ensure its architectonic possibilities. And this is true not only of large utilitarian buildings. To be sure, it was with them that a line of development based on function (Zweck) and necessity began that needs no further justification; it will not end there, however, but will find its fulfillment in the realm of residential building. Only here, in a field offering greater freedom, one not so bound by narrower objectives, can the architectural potential of these technical methods be fully realized. These are truly architectural elements forming the basis for a new art of building. They permit us a degree of freedom in the creation of space that we will no longer deny ourselves. Only now can we give shape to space, open it, and link it to the landscape. It now becomes clear once more just what walls and openings are, and floors and ceilings. Simplicity of construction, clarity of tectonic means, and purity of materials have about them the glow of pristine beauty.*[1]

Such a programmatic view of modern transparency was surely already evident in the Barcelona Pavilion of 1929, where tectonic value is unequivocally asserted in the eight freestanding cruciform columns, and where the space field is framed by the freestanding planes that bypass these supports. Aside from this patent opposition between columnar and planar form, it is possible to break down the Barcelona Pavilion into a series of polarities; tectonic versus stereotomic, still versus agitated, open versus closed, and above all, perhaps, traditional material versus space endlessness. The first dyad is tectonically self-evident, the second and third are related to the surfaces and the contents of the open and enclosed pools, while the last is evident in the opposition between the marble-faced pinwheeling planes and the symmetrical placement of the eight columns in relation to the roof. This pinwheel organization may also be read as a planimetric allusion to the Arts and Crafts asymmetrical plan form and hence to building, while the columnar peristyle recalls classical architecture. This last, reinforced by the particular treatment of the column casings, is further evidence of Mies's capacity to integrate tectonic meaning with abstract form.

Mies's Barcelona column is a dematerialized cruciform point support, and yet at the same time it is altogether more planar than the half-round cruciform column casings employed in the later Tugendhat House. The planar character of the Barcelona column derives from the orthogonal profile adopted by the bent, chromium-plated, sheet steel case covering the built-up steel core. Like Le Corbusier's *pilotis* in his Purist *plan libre*, this column has neither base nor capital. Both column types are, in fact, abstractions of the idea of support, since, due to the fact that no beams are expressed in either instance, a somewhat insubstantial act of bearing is conveyed by the form. In both instances the ceiling is treated as a flat, continuous plane. Here we see how modern, beam-less construction favors the suppression of the frame; that is to say, it eliminates the very trabeation that for Perret was a prerequisite of tectonic culture. In this regard, both the Villa Savoye and the Barcelona Pavilion may be seen as atectonic...

While columnar support is patently a key element in the structuring of the Barcelona Pavilion both technically and phenomenologically, the ontological interaction between support and burden (Schopenhauer's *Stütze* and *Last*) is patently absent. One may argue that this absence is more categoric than in the Villa Savoye, since in the latter the monolithic appearance of the reinforced concrete structure permits the perception of a certain fixity between column and soffit, particularly since both are monolithically expressed by being plastered and painted white throughout. In Barcelona, on the other hand, the riveted steel frame supports a faired-out, plastered soffit that appears to float independently of the chromium columns. This illusion of levitation is strengthened by the uninterrupted planar continuity of the ceiling and the floor, white plaster above and travertine below; an effect that is partially countered by the free assembly of pinwheeling planes and screens rendered in heavier material, in vert antique marble, in onyx, and in various kinds of glass of a translucent or transparent nature, set in chromium-plated frames. These last also tend to make any sense of fixity uncertain due to their proliferation of highlights and reflections. No one has perhaps written more perceptively of the illusory, empty character of this spatial field than the Catalan critic José Quetglas.[2]

All of these vertiginous effects are emphasized, as Robin Evans would later observe, by the vertical mirroring of the volume about a horizon that happens to coincide not only with eye height but also with the central horizontal seam in the onyx plane, thereby suggesting a potential inversion of floor and ceiling that is paradoxically heightened rather than diminished by the differences in finish. As Evans remarks, since the floor reflects light and the ceiling receives it, the perceptual differences in the planar tone would have been greater had they been of the same material. Thus Mies would use "material asymmetry to create optical symmetry, rebounding the natural light to make the ceiling more sky-like and the ambience more expansive."[3] Traces of traditional value still remain, however, above all in the jointing of the travertine which tends not only to stress the tactility of the stone, as paving, but also to assert the presence of a stereotomic earthwork. Some vestige of the tectonic also remains in the columns, first, because the eight-column grid is perceivable as a peristyle, despite the asymmetrical freestanding planes, and second, because the reiterated highlights on the profiles of the casings effect a reference to classical fluting. Thus while the essential quality of chromium is its modernity, the form that

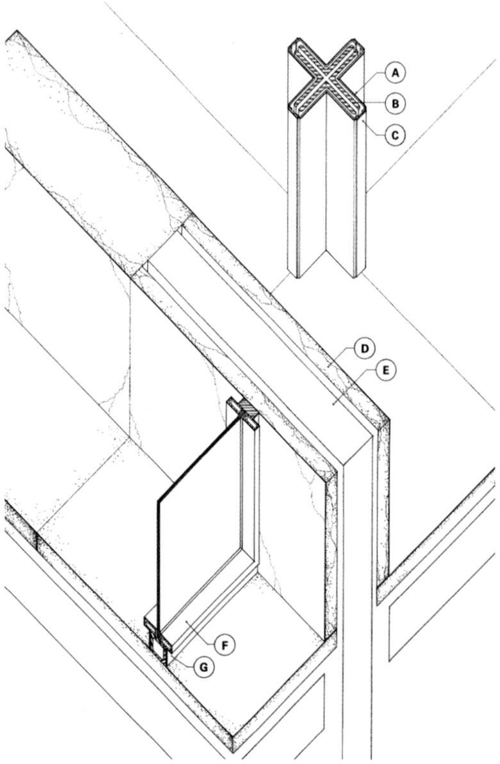

Barcelona Pavilion. Drawing by Edward R. Ford

it assumes in this instance also evokes a subtle traditional resonance....

While the Resor House projected for Wyoming in 1938 still employs the cruciform column, Mies will shortly abandon this element, along with the free plan. From now on, the tectonic focus shifts to the exposed steel frame with brick and glass infill. No one has written more cogently of the spatial consequences of this tectonic metamorphosis than Colin Rowe.

> *Mies's characteristic German column was circular or cruciform; but his new column became H-shaped, became that I-beam which is now almost a personal signature. Typically, his German column had been clearly distinguished from walls and windows, isolated from them in space; and typically, his new column became an element integral with the envelope of the building where it came to function as a kind of mullion or residue of wall. Thus the column section was not without some drastic effects on the entire space of the building. The circular or cruciform section had tended to push partitions away from the column. The new tectonic tended to drag them towards it. The old column had offered a minimum of obstruction to a horizontal movement of space; but the new column presents a distinctly more substantial stop. The old column had tended to cause space to gyrate around it, had been central to a rather tentatively defined volume; but the new column instead acts as the enclosure or the external definition of a major volume of space. The spatial functions of the two are thus completely differentiated.... As an International Style element, the column put in its last appearance in the museum project of 1942; while in the Library and Administration Building project of 1944, the effects of the H-shaped column are already apparent and are clearly exhibited in the published drawings of its plans. From these drawings it is evident that the column is no longer to be allowed to float ambiguously beneath a slab. It is now—apparently for the first time—tied to a network of beams, and these beams have appointed definite positions for the screens, and for the most part the screens have already leapt into these positions—in fact only the extra-thick walls around the lavatories seem to have been able to resist the new attraction.*[4]

As Rowe indicates, this change is of an epistemic nature, not only because the integration of frame and partition transforms the character of the space, but also because the revelation of the joint between column and beam represents a shift back toward the tectonic tradition, first manifest at IIT in the Minerals and Metals Building. Mies's general focus now begins to shift away from universal modernist space to the primacy of the frame and its joint. This change is fundamental, for it means that the opposition between modernity and tradition will now no longer be mediated by an elision between columnar support and the system of spatial enclosure.

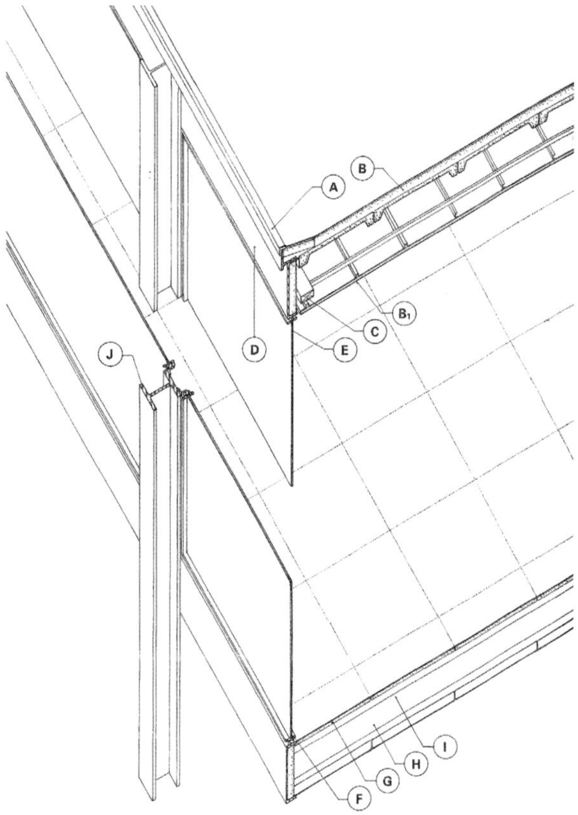

Farnsworth House. Drawing by Edward R. Ford

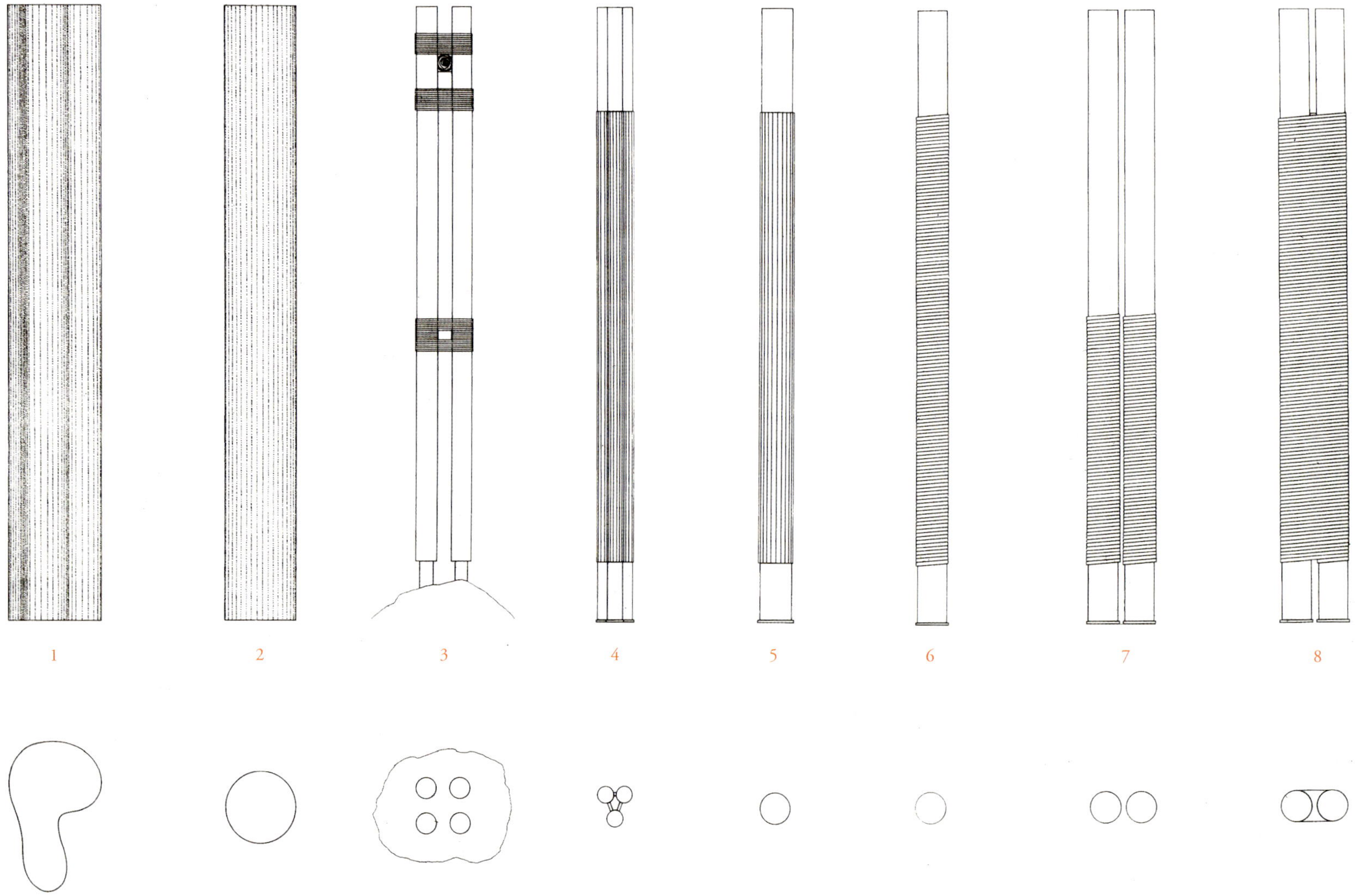

ARTICULATION OF COLUMNS
ELEVATIONS AND PLANS

1	Entrance canopy
2	Library
3	Sauna terrace
4	Music room
5	Music room
6	Living room
7	Living room
8	Music room

Drawing by Darren Stewart Capel

The regularity of identical columns and their gridded arrangements, reflecting early twentieth century developments in construction techniques, led to characteristics often associated with Modern architecture: uniformity and non-directionality of inhabited space. At the Villa Mairea built in 1939, however, the Finnish architect Alvar Aalto subtly but deliberately worked to "undo" such spatial qualities by incorporating eccentricities of material usage as well as irregular ways of perceiving and occupying space, yet without losing the advantages of a regularly arranged structural system. In the following extract, Juhani Pallasmaa describes how Aalto varied the detailed design of this guest house's many columns, with some made of steel, wood and concrete, some being single, paired or omitted altogether, some lashed together and others varying from one floor level to the next. The Modernist uniform three-dimensional grid, while still present, is undermined – to wondrous effect.

Villa Mairea's Columnar Variations

from *Alvar Aalto: Villa Mairea*
Juhani Pallasmaa

Modular Coincidences

The earliest sketches of the final version of the Villa Mairea show the idea of an all-purpose room, basically within a square volume. The square is articulated by a square grid suggesting a modular subdivision and flexible use of the space. In Aalto's three sketches the basic square volume is subdivided into 7 by 6, 9 by 10, and 8 by 8 square modular units. One of the earliest ruler-drawn sketches shows a regular spacing of columns in the southwest-northwest direction (4 by 4 modules), whereas the structural bays closest to the entrance road are only 3½ modules wide. A further development of the ground floor plan shows the overall dimensions of the building proper to be equal in both directions, ie, 2850 cm.

Later drawings do not reveal the application of any modular grid or regulating lines. On the contrary, further elaboration of the scheme, such as the articulation of the columns, walls and other items, seems to aim at confusing any reading of regularity or repetition. It is well known that later in his career, Aalto ridiculed the design approach based on modular or proportional co-ordination.[1]

In relation to Aalto's disrespect for modular co-ordination and the spontaneous, almost whimsical experiential impact of the Mairea, it is quite surprising to find that the executed design seems to follow a grid based on subdivisions of the initial 2850 x 2850 cm square. The sauna section resonates with the same grid, shifted half a unit to the west and a quarter of a unit to the north. Even the amoeba shape of the pool is balanced precisely on one corner of the square, and the skew lines of the studio and entrance canopy are oriented towards the corners of modular squares. The main staircase is located in the centre of this basic square. In addition, the actual spatial experience of the Villa revolves around the focus of the stair which is conceived as an object in space. It is the only vertical element that experientially relates the two floors to each other. The wooden decking between the sauna and the pool and diving board, introduce a 45-degree angle to the basic coordinates. There are also other concealed orientation lines between the elements of the design; the skew line of the wall of the entrance hall, for instance, points to the corner of the fireplace, the oblique line of the cloakroom nook points to the corner of the dining room, and the axis of the twisted outdoor fireplace points to the sauna door. The sauna door is placed opposite the glass door to the living room, but shifted roughly an equivalent of its width from the position of direct axiality. The placement of the sauna, however, connects its activities effectively to the living room. Consequently, the various phases of a social gathering are strongly integrated. The usual privacy of the sauna is reversed to face the living area, almost as if it were a stage.[2]

The most pronounced axiality in the floor plan, however, is the line that relates to the main entrance door, the dining table, and the combined fireplaces of the dining room and terrace. In one of the early sketches, this is expressed as a separate zone and in another the entrance is aligned with the main stair. Actual diagonal movement patterns in the house, however, completely annihilate the experience of this axiality. 'Aalto was masterful in destroying symmetry. He did not accept symmetry,' recalls Bernoulli.[3]

Violation of Simplistic Order

In 1926 Aalto wrote: ' ... the city of hills, that curving, living, unpredictable line which runs in dimensions unknown to mathematicians, is for me the incarnation of everything that forms a contrast in the modern world between brutal mechanicalness and religious beauty in life.'[4]

The actual spatial experience and situations of daily life in the house introduce diagonal movements, such as entry - fireplace, fireplace hall - music room, living room - dining room. The flower room and the library subdivide the square main space diagonally. Altogether, subtle twists, skews and curvilinear shapes create effective counter-points to the rectangular order, like eddies within a basic rectangularity. They also help to create a relaxed, informal atmosphere and a feeling of improvisation, as well as subtle ergonomic and emotional articulation. Some of these aspects are closely related to Asplund's designs of the Villa Snellman (1917-18) and particularly of his summer cottage Stennäs (1936) at Lisön, Sorunda, in the Swedish archipelago near Stockholm.

By means of slanting and curving the end wall of the studio, which had been pushed from the centre to the edge of the composition during the design process, the studio gently turns towards the centre of the courtyard so as to announce its being part of the cycle of normal daily life. The variously designed fireplaces in their corner locations also turn and open up towards the centre of the respective space and, consequently, project a socially uniting atmosphere. Various details in Asplund's Villa Snellman and his summer cottage make similar animistic gestural moves.

The structural identity of columns on the ground floor is weakened by grouping them singly, doubly and triply into a playful and rhythmic articulation by rattan bindings. The effect contradicts structural logic and confuses any sense of regularity. Replacement of some of the columns in the implied grid by load-bearing walls, as well as the strategic replacement of one of the steel columns in the library area and another on the sauna terrace by concrete columns, annihilates the possibility of reading a grid-like structural order to the plan. Incorporation of two of the columns into the built-in library cabinet-table and the window sill of the dining room, serves the same purpose of weakening the reading of structure. All beams within the main entrance-living-dining-area are concealed within suspended ceilings.[5]

The deliberate confusion of structural articulation serves the purpose of emphasizing the continuity of spatial flow, abstracting or poeticizing the structural elements freed of their prosaic load-bearing function, and maximizing the visual interplay of elements liberated from hierarchical categories. In other words, the columns, decorative poles, as well as the tree trunks outside the building, can be seen as equal elements within a rhythmic continuum of verticals; in the Paris Pavilion Aalto had even used birch trunks as actual columns. ...

The Independence of the Two Floors

The two floors are so independent of each other that it is very difficult to read the unity of the plans due to the lack of cues enabling one to mediate between them. Anyone interested in the detailed interaction of the floors is almost obliged to study the plans by means of superimposed transparencies. Beyond the tightly rectangular northern half of the service wing there is precious little similarity in the spatial subdivision or dynamics between the two floors. Even the character of the steel columns is completely different on the two levels. As a matter of fact, the columns do not structurally continue through the floor; the triple and double columns, as well as the concrete column in the library, are exchanged for single steel columns resting on the beams concealed within the false ceiling. In addition, the columns of the upper floor appear in a different context in their relationship to the walls and windows and this completely confuses their identity with their lower sections on the ground floor.

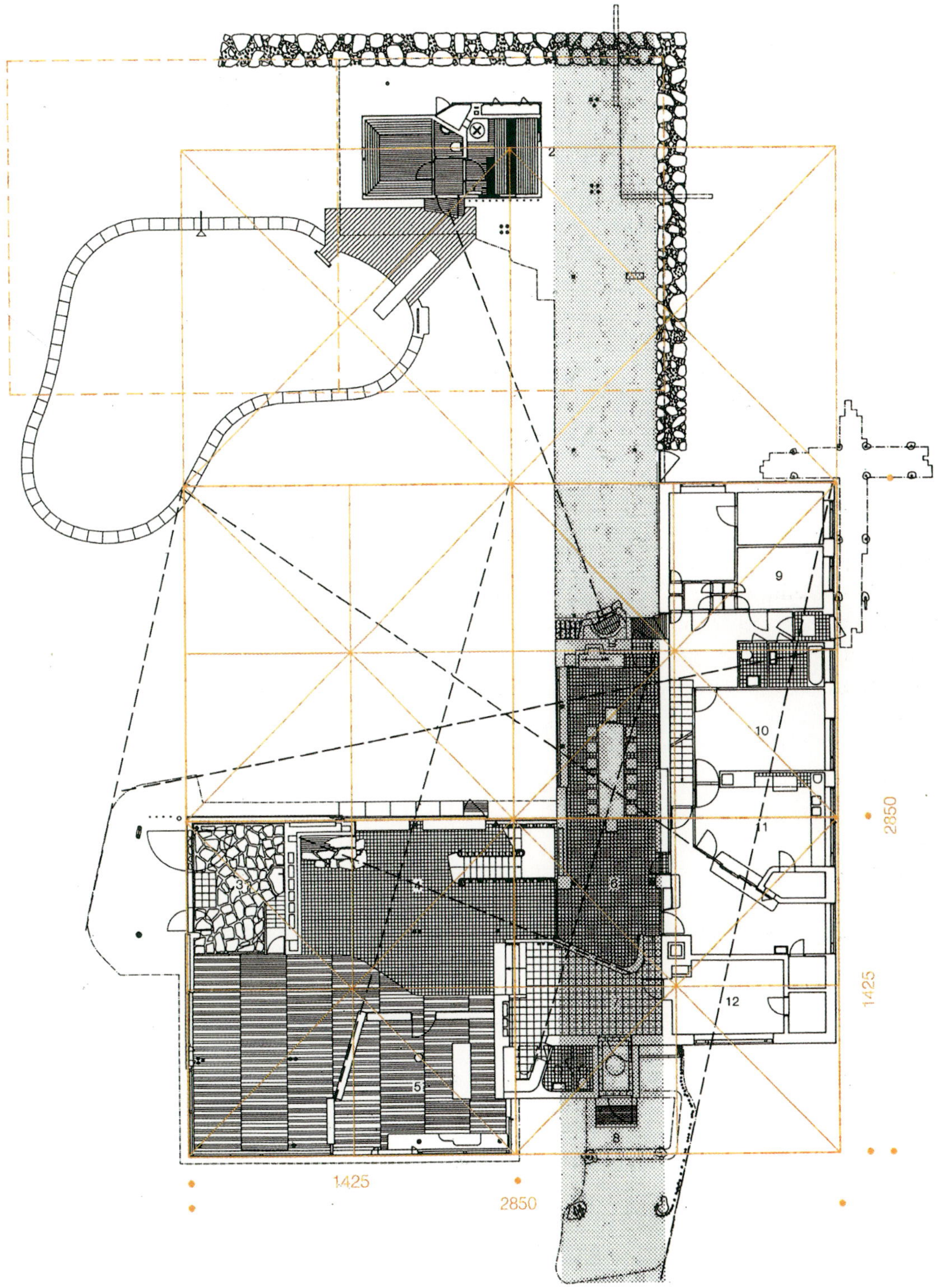

Drawing by Juhani Pallasmaa

Photo: Iwan Baan

Just as Aalto recognized the perceived structural advantages of a regular column grid and yet tried to undermine its Modernist uniformity at the Villa Mairea by dissembling this through his many column variations, several recent SANAA projects – and in particular their Serpentine Pavilion of 2009 – take an altogether different approach toward what is arguably a similar objective of disguising the benefits of particular columnar arrangements and variations thereof. Here the number of slender columns is multiplied many times over, so as to become omnipresent and/or at once invisible through such sheer and overwhelming numbers. The column grid of the Serpentine is also non-existent, with columns located here and there in a naturalist fashion, mimicking the randomness of trees in a forest; they even "grow" in this structure to different heights.

The two text extracts presented here address these SANAA Serpentine columns from different points of view. The Mark Wigley text evocatively relates the pavilion to its origins in the primordial house, and the columns to the surrounding trees. The second piece, by Giles Reid, is highly technical in nature (even poetically so?) and complements the first in being that way. The columns become mechanical, machine-like in their precision and even in their variation; for example, a gathering together of short ones becomes a stiff "core" for the pavilion's lateral stability. The "truth" of these alternate views lies perhaps somewhere in between them – or, undoubtedly and more appropriately – with both at the same time.

A Forest of Minimal Columns

from *Optical Acupuncture*
Mark Wigley

'The ponderous illusions of solidity, the non-existence of things, is what the artist takes for "materials". – Robert Smithson, 1969[1]

In the distance, a thin undulating line hovers among the trees, as if floating on the wind. Yet there is no wind. The seemingly delicate line is not drifting innocently across Kensington Gardens. Quite the opposite, it has been cut into the scene itself. The very thinness of the line marks a painless and almost imperceptible slice deep into the view of the park. The horizontal line is a seam in the view, the trace of an opening in the visual field. It quietly offers us a unique form of entrance into the scene. Instead of being invited into a traditional architectural space that is circumscribed by walls, we get to enter a line. In a very precise kind of optical surgery, the space of the park has been discretely opened up to forensic inspection. Oddly, we are offered the chance to see the view itself, to see what we are already seeing.

As we move closer, the line turns out to be the leading edge of a mirror suspended above the ground. The first clue to this comes when what we see above and below starts to multiply. The grass, trees and sky are more than doubled by reflections. Because the mirror dips down, our eyes can be simultaneously above parts of it and below others. Everything expands. With each step forward, the seam gets exponentially wider and we are drawn further and further into the opening. The world inside the mirror soon becomes larger than the world outside. If we move left and right, or simply turn our heads, the reflections spin and flare. In this expansion and multiplication of the view, the view itself becomes visible as such. Rippling in the smoothly polished aluminium plane, it floats in the mirror just as much as the mirror floats in the park, and the limit of each is confused. Any sense of a division between reflection and what is reflected is quickly lost. The role of the architects has simply been to craft a set of reflections that expand the park and the sky. The park is magnified, intensified as if the mirror allows the park to become more like itself. Perhaps no park can ever be a park without a pavilion. Yet this Pavilion is not simply placed inside the landscape completed when the Royal Gardener Charles Bridgeman created the Serpentine River in 1730. Rather, the whole park seems to be inside the Pavilion. More precisely, the hovering mirror turns the park into an interior, a single room. The expanded visual field is contained without being restrained.

This exploration of an expanded horizon without walls goes beyond the countless ongoing architectural experiments with glass that can be traced back to the largest pavilion of all, the vast 1851 Crystal Palace that sat for six months on the nearby bank of the Serpentine, with the full-size elm trees of the park growing inside it. Now, for a few summer months in 2009, even the river itself will be absorbed and reconfigured by a small serpentine pool hanging upside down in the air.

The 25mm thick undulating aluminium surface is held up, or perhaps held down, by an array of randomly scattered thin shiny stainless-steel rods that want to disappear into the reflections. The whole thing tries to be as little as it can be. It wants to swallow itself. There are no walls, doors, windows; just a light canopy that casts a kind of concrete shadow on the ground. And not by chance does its horizontal plane echo the canopy line of the surrounding trees. In the set of four drawings of the Pavilion that were the first public clues about the forthcoming Pavilion, the floating plane doesn't just meander among the trees like a plant. It echoes the form of the trees around it, with its own little forest of trunks propping it up. In a calculated blurring of identity, the trees are abstracted and the Pavilion is naturalised. What shelter it offers is meant to be something like that of a large tree, or what a group of trees could offer.

The relationship between architecture and trees is an old one. Indeed, much of the history of architectural theory has been devoted to saying that the architecture/tree relationship is the oldest of all. The endless stories of architecture's origin that have organised centuries of theory since Vitruvius, and were never fully abandoned, symptomatically begin with the tree. The first and most elemental shelter, which will then supposedly be echoed by all subsequent buildings, is taken from the tree. In the most famous image of the first architectural shelter, the frontispiece of Marc-Antoine Laugier's 1755 *Essai sur l'architecture*, the building is simply a roof added to the existing trees of a forest. Not by chance does the seated woman in the image, who represents architecture itself, look at the structure rather than occupy it, pointing it out to a child. In fact, this primitive hut doesn't give physical shelter. Rather, it gives the all-important image of shelter, of order, security, orientation, etc. Architecture begins as a kind of pavilion, a supplementary structure, something to be visited, looked at and looked out from, a viewing station. And the first view is that of the surrounding trees. The building learns from the tree and the tree is reconstructed in the image of the building. Architecture starts with the reconfiguration of trees. The way that architects draw trees reveals their design philosophy. One could do a very precise and surprisingly comprehensive history of architecture based only on the way in which each architect draws their trees. Each drawing unconsciously restages the beginning of the field.

SANAA's trees, like their Pavilion and the people encountering it, are drawn like those of a child, with elemental lines deployed for maximum effect and even a yellow circle for the benign sun beaming down on the scene. As the viewpoint in the first four drawings moves steadily downwards from the sky to the ground, the diagrammatic trees always look the same, but the Pavilion steadily condenses the form of the tree into a thin line hanging in the air. This kind of drawing, and the kind of architecture it incubates, is not minimalism in the sense of reducing everything down to the least elements. Rather, it is a matter of going back to the beginnings of things, the beginning of the beginning. SANAA's architecture is not about buildings and rooms, but that which comes just before a room. It is not about walls, but that which comes just before a wall, and so on. The physical fabric of a building becomes just a prop for modulations of the light, diffractions of the visual field, mirages of different kinds than can give birth to a sense of space. This mirage logic is taken to the extreme in the Pavilion in Kensington Gardens, which explores whatever might come just before a roof, the beginning of the simplest canopy. That is to say, it works on a subtle distortion of the view that might come just before the most basic idea of shelter. Conversation, music, drinking, reading, relaxing, playing and eating are to be nurtured in amorphous zones defined only by a kind of tent made entirely out of rippled reflections, an inverted pool in the air. To enter such a Pavilion is to swim in an expansion of the view at the threshold of architecture.

Like so many modern architects, SANAA treats the space between the canopy of the trees and the ground as the real site for core architectural experiments, but the project tries not to occupy that space with any building. It simply provides some kind of minimal lining to the dimension, inserting a reflective surface to the underside of the canopy above and a non-reflective surface to the ground below. In so doing, it stages a unique intersection of the history of the architect's tree and the history of reflectivity in architecture.

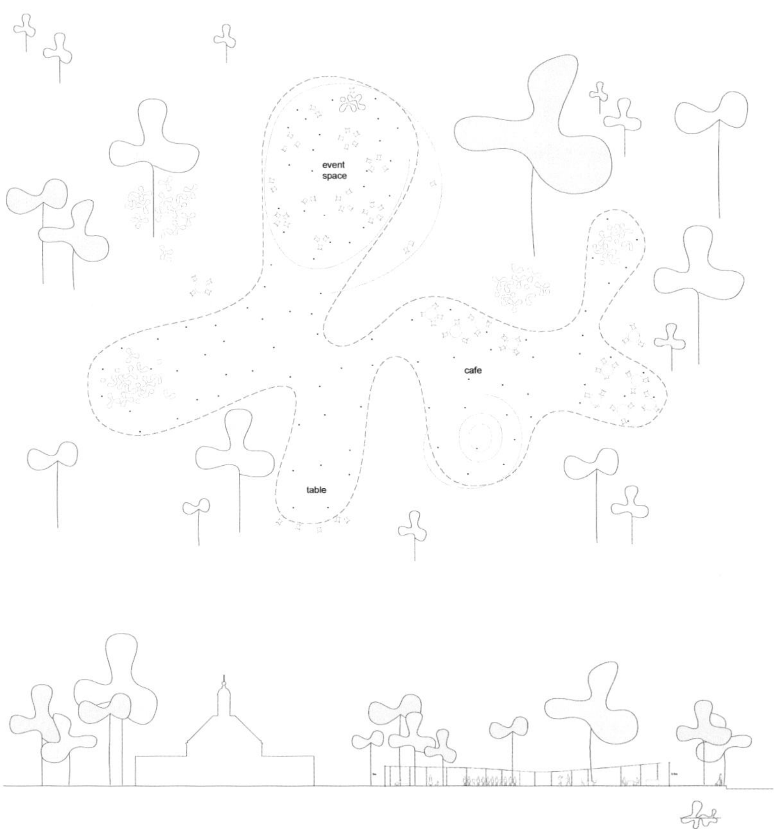

Drawing: ©SANAA

SANAA: 2009 Serpentine Pavilion, Kensington Gardens, London

Giles Reid

A more minimal or limpid structure than SANAA's Serpentine summer pavilion is hard to imagine. The roof is a Matisse-like 'painting with scissors', cut freehand out of mirror polished aluminium. Paper thin, it drifts through the trees supported atop 112 shining stainless steel columns, most 60mm diameter, some 40mm. The columns rise from a screed floor, bordered by pebbles and grass. Delicate plants, speakers, lights and pink and yellow SANAA 'rabbit' chairs are scattered throughout. There is almost no articulation or hierarchy to any of the detailing and seemingly no effort. However, behind such apparent randomness, there is a logic. The columns cantilever from two-metre-deep screw piles. These will be undrilled when the pavilion is dismantled three months hence. A base plate is bolted to the top of each pile head. This permitted plan and vertical adjustment. The builder located each column from a spreadsheet giving x, y and z co-ordinates and column lengths. The columns had to be positioned to within millimetres of the co-ordinate or the prefabricated roof panels would not fit on site.

The spreadsheet was generated from a parametric model used to develop the roof topography. The model also aided understanding of the effects of column positions on stress concentrations. For instance, a sub-rule was introduced to dictate that columns be set no closer than 300mm from each panel joint. The greatest stresses coincide with the longest spans—above the lecture area and where the roof crosses an existing footpath.

At the top of each column a small head is threaded. The tops of these heads are milled to set angles (five degrees, ten degrees and others) to adapt to the warp of the roof.

A stainless steel plate was bonded into the panel to spread the punching force of the column. The roof is bolted to the column head and plugged with a flush-fitting polished aluminium disc.

The panels themselves are made of 3mm aluminium top and bottom sheets bonded to an 18mm ply core. The 3 by 1.5 metre panel dimension was dictated by the largest available ply sheet. The edges of all outer sheets have an aluminium box section fascia, maintaining the illusion of all-metal construction.

The roof functions as a horizontal bracing plane, and the structure as a whole acts as a table. The ply extends beyond each aluminium sheet to form tongue and groove biscuits, distributing the load from one panel to the next. The tongue of one panel is screwed to its neighbour, creating an offset pattern of dots along all panel joints, top and bottom, like the fuselage of a plane. The screws are drilled to a gauged depth and capped with aluminium plugs.

The roof was assembled on adjustable scaffolding. Once it had been bolted to the columns and the panels screwed together, the scaffolding was dropped and the roof found its form. Where it bends down in one specific location, almost touching the ground, the increased curvature required the panels to be factory-formed on a mould.

Because this section is much lower than the rest of the roof, the columns are shorter and stiffer. This part of roof thus acts as a core, helping to anchor the whole pavilion. However, the structure does not have to resist direct wind loading so much as drag and the potential loads imposed by people climbing the roof, which seems likely.

If time and money had permitted, the architect's desire would have been for a seamless roof. However, a welded and ground finish might have created the very different feeling of arrested weight. Instead, such minimal details as do exist give the roof its visual ripple, adding to the mirror effect, the ethic of precision and a wondrous levity. They create a small puzzle: a structure which at first looks quite arbitrary, but on closer viewing reveals a field of logical decisions.

Photo: Luke Hayes

Sendai Mediatheque model. Photo: ©Tomio Ohashi

In architect Toyo Ito's innovative Sendai Mediatheque building, the traditional column is no more – it has become a spatial "tube-column" that can be occupied and services the many floor levels of the building, that shifts in plan location and size from one floor level to the next, seemingly "swaying" to and fro "like seaweed", and that in spite of the heavy gravity loads and large earthquake forces becomes "dematerialized" by having its tube "walls" made up of many smaller cylindrical elements that are spaced apart yet bound together to work as one. Andrea Maffei and Toyo Ito himself relate in their own separate ways how in this building the tube-columns directly support – literally and conceptually – the contemporary spatial notions of merging interior private space with that for the exterior public, and of the relative informality of occupation in today's interior spaces.

The Sendai Mediatheque and its Tube-Columns

from *Toyo Ito: Works Projects Writings*
Andrea Maffei

In 1994 an international competition was held for the design of a media library in the city of Sendai, in the north of Japan, about two hours by train from Tokyo. The structure was to be built on a site in the centre of the city, on one of the main streets and close to the Kotadai Park and the most important public buildings such as the theatre and the seats of local government. The functional programme called for a library, galleries for exhibitions and multimedia spaces ... On 22 March 1995, Toyo Ito's design ... was declared the winner ... The proposal submitted to the competition underwent no substantial changes during the drawing up of the executive plans, although there were a number of interesting evolutions in this passage. The basic idea remained that of a large volume of glass, with a square plan of 50 x 50 metres and a height of around 37 metres. The conception of the building is founded on three main elements of composition: six linear planes, thirteen reticular columns and an external skin. The "planes" present the appearance of thin square sheets, suspended in the void at different heights to meet the needs of the client and to avoid a "classic" and constant rhythm on the façade. The thirteen "columns" (there were twelve of them in the competition project), formed out of tubular steel structures, support all the floors, running vertically through the building from the basements to the roof. The columns permit natural illumination of the central parts of the various floors and contain all the systems of vertical circulation and the ducts of the plant. The skin is made up of four façades and a reticular flat roof. Each front is characterized by an architectural solution that accentuates its two-dimensional graphic quality and differentiates it from the others.

Each of the three elements is separated from the others, forming an almost self-sufficient system. In fact the designer did not want to propose a large and solid volume in which columns, floor slabs and façades would be fused together. He has avoided any formal or plastic compromise between the elements. This type of decomposition makes it possible to lighten the image of the building and bring it into line with Ito's research into an ephemeral and insubstantial architecture. His buildings are not designed to last, they are not "palaces" of masonry based on models from the past, but light, almost immaterial structures, resembling temporary installations that reflect the fragile dynamism of the great Japanese cities. The functions are located on different floors, whose interiors have been entrusted to different designers. Each level is characterized by different colours, forms and materials, creating an effect of stratification as if various fragments of the city had been laid one on top of the other.

Visitors enter the building through the large entrance hall on the ground floor, which has the appearance of a covered plaza, completely open onto the urban surroundings. In the competition project, Ito had proposed an authentic concave plaza sunken into the ground and with no outside walls, so as to create an open filter between the building and the city. Unfortunately, the client later decided to enclose the ground floor so that it could be used as an entrance hall, information area and cafeteria. In order to maintain, at least in part, the interaction with the world outside, the four boundary walls are made entirely of glass, with no frames and shutters. In addition, a portion of the glass wall on the main front can be opened totally, transforming part of the interior space into exterior space.

The upper levels are open plan, traversed solely by the reticular columns that act as conductors of natural light and contain the vertical links and plant. The position of the columns has been changed from the design submitted to the competition: instead they are arranged in three parallel strips to rationalize the spaces of distribution, especially in relation to the exhibition galleries on the fourth floor and the structural logic of the floor slabs. The parts at the rear are generally used for service functions and reserved for the staff, while the south side, completely glazed and facing onto the main street, is open to the urban landscape and houses the spaces for the public.

Any constraint of a formal character applied to the project as a whole has been set aside in favour of a neutral system, in which the various solutions are defined floor by floor. Just as in the Yatsushiro Museum, built in 1991, it was the roof that defined the building's architectural image while the spaces inside remained neutral, so that they could be adapted to the museum's requirements, in the Mediathèque the tubular columns, the building's most distinctive feature, permit the creation of *plans libres* in the manner of Le Corbusier that are perfectly adaptable—precisely because they are free of formal constraints—to functional requirements.

On this neutral base, Ito and others have designed the interiors as installations. While on the ground floor Karim Rashid has proposed pieces of furniture-sculpture with organic forms and strong colours, on the first floor the spaces are bounded by retractable synthetic white drapes, lightweight divisions that do not interfere with the perception of a single open plan. On the second and third floor, Ito has laid out the library as a two-storey-high volume, with reading rooms on the south and north sides. The space is characterized by a regular grid of ceiling lamps and the furnishings are designed by KTA.

There are two types of exhibition space: on the fourth floor there is a gallery subdivided by partition walls of full height, some of which can be moved along tracks on the ceiling, allowing the interior distribution to be varied according to need; on the fifth level an open plan can be adapted to any installation. The reticular columns can be left exposed to let in natural light, or covered up by [black] drapes...

The top floor houses the Mediatheque proper: a curved wall of translucent glass reaching all the way to the ceiling delimits a central volume containing an auditorium with seating for 180 people, meeting rooms, offices and a cafeteria. The outer walls of this floor are made entirely of glass. This creates a sort of belvedere with views onto the city in which the audiovisual spaces are concentrated, with video collectors and consulting tables designed by Ross Lovegrove.

The Sendai Mediatheque is a long way from the so-called high-tech style, in which technology determines the form of the building and is flaunted as the primary element of the architecture. Ito, by contrast, has been able to retain control of a technologically complex structure, placing the technical aspects at the service of his quest for a poetry of light and a dematerialization of the building. Special attention should be paid, in this connection, to the solutions adopted for the reticular columns. In the competition project, they had been faced with opaque glass which masked their internal structure. They had been conceived, in fact, as "columns resembling seaweeds". They were supposed to be solid, white and have the physical consistency of a homogeneous "material". Fascinated by the studies of Mutsuro Sasaki, who was responsible for the structural calculations and designs, Ito was drawn toward a progressive dematerialization of the originally solid form, eventually arriving at the final solution in which the tubular structure is left exposed, faced solely with transparent glass. Right from the start, it had been the intention to set skylights at the top of the columns in order to transform them into pillars of light. For this purpose, computerized systems of rotating mirrors have been installed in the upper part of the two central columns to reflect natural light down to the lower floors and permit automatic control of the internal illumination.

Mutsuro Sasaki designed the reticular columns in the form of hyperbolic paraboloids, with tubular steel elements reduced to the minimum possible thickness. The study of the form of the columns started out from the concept of a cylinder, subjected first to torsion and then deformed by oscillation. The torsion imparts greater stability to the structure. The diameter of the columns ranges from 2 to 9 metres, while the diameter of the tubes of which they are made up ranges from 140 to 240 millimetres and their thickness from 9 to 40 millimetres. The four reticular columns with the largest diameter have been designed as trusses with reinforced-concrete bases, to resist earthquakes. They are positioned at the four corners of the building so as to withstand any kind of eccentric torsion. The other nine, more slender columns make no contribution to the resistance to horizontal forces, but are located in positions where they are able to support only vertical forces. They are made out of bundles of tubes simply arranged in parallel to control the phenomenon of partial as well as total deformation, with the addition of a ring in the middle section to prevent compression.

The floors are designed as flat slabs of steel, as slender and light as possible, to improve the resistance to earthquakes. They have a sandwich structure, formed out of grids of beams covered with plates of steel above and below, using the same technique as in naval construction. The thickness of the floor slabs, with spans of up to 20 metres, has been reduced to just 40 centimetres, with frameworks of beams at a distance of 1 metre. The beams are welded together, with tubular components used for the most complex joints. The foundations have been designed to absorb shocks from earthquakes in the basement levels and leave the structures of the upper floors free. This has been achieved by setting the reinforced-concrete slab of the ground floor on the outer walls of the foundations, allowing horizontal movements of up to 100 millimetres. The reticular columns are transformed into frame structures in the sunken storeys, with rounded heads that allow them to rotate. The transverse beams of the frame structures at the base of the columns have been designed to give way immediately in an earthquake, permitting the tubular structures to rotate and the ground floor to move. The shocks are concentrated and dampened in the basement, making the upper structure lighter and allowing greater freedom in its design. The construction of such a complex structure has relied chiefly on prefabrication, as fabrication on site would have entailed much higher costs and less precision in the details. The steel sandwich slabs of the floors, along with the attachments and the base rings of the reticular columns, were prefabricated in modules of 3 x 10 metres and assembled on site. The structures of the columns were also broken down into modules the height of a single storey, and these in turn subdivided into prefabricated sub-modules. Before each module was brought to the construction site, it was pre-assembled in the factory so that the connections with adjoining modules and the floor slabs could be checked. Given the complexity of the design it would not have been possible to make corrections *in situ* and only prefabrication and checking in the factory could guarantee ... the result.

Separate mention must be made of the elevations. Starting out from the idea of a building-aquarium, Ito wanted the main façade to be completely transparent. The façade was designed as a thin and independent sheet of glass, merely set against the structure behind. This effect was obtained by means of a double, ventilated façade, with a slender and sophisticated internal structure of glass that accentuates its lightness. At the corners there is no connection with the adjacent façades but the panes of glass extend freely into empty space beyond the edges of the façade, underlining the two-dimensional effect. During the day, the façade reflects the sunlight and remains ambiguously transparent, creating a translucent filter between the inside and outside. At night, however, it almost seems to vanish so that the interior of the building is laid bare at every level. This produces an interesting effect of stratification, due to the different patterns adopted in the design of the internal lighting.

On the east and north sides, the internal floor slabs have been extended 50 centimetres outward solely for aesthetic reasons, so as to create the dark horizontal bands that characterize the lateral façades. The facing materials on each level are different—transparent glass, opaque glass, solid panels—to accentuate the effect of fragmentation that contributes to the abstraction of the building. In the competition design, the west front was the same as the other lateral elevations. While the executive plans were being drawn up, the need to add a series of fire escapes was exploited by the architect to create a façade that differed from the others, made up of a semitransparent structure in galvanized steel applied to the wall behind and faced with vertical slats running the full height of each floor: a sort of skin with a highly graphic effect.

from *ArchIdea Magazine, 31*
Edzard Mik interview with Toyo Ito

AM: Besides the transparency, the design of the columns is eye-catching. Why did you give them those strange, twisted forms?

> *If I'd made them orderly – all the same and in rows – I'd have created a strong order. But I didn't want order. I wanted each place to have a different atmosphere. So I positioned them randomly and gave them different shapes. It's also to orientate the visitors. Originally, I wanted the columns to be invisible – closed, covered. But in the process of construction I felt more and more attracted to the strength inherent to the structure. As a result, I used glass to expose the tubes. I discovered that I'd changed, that I'm very much attached to something strong, attached to exposing strength. After the competition, many politicians and journalists were against the tubes. I needed the strength of the columns, I needed something that was strong enough to fight their opposition.*

AM: At the same time you stressed the immateriality of the building. For instance, the floors seem to float.

> *The fluid nature of the floors is something I always aim at. But I didn't want the building to look immaterial, not at all. By exposing the materials and the structure I wanted to show people that these materials actually support the building. Architecture always has to deal with the challenge of gravity; that's something that hasn't changed in the course of history. However, by changing the structure we have to create a quality of space that matches the present times. Before, I tried to hide the price of withstanding gravity. Now I feel I can expose these materials, have them out in the open, and still create modernity that responds to what is going on today. That's a major change. We architects have to provide bodily experience through our creations. In the past I tried to construct something that's weightless. Like society itself becoming increasingly weightless. Nowadays, I feel that even in this information society we still have gravity, we still have to feel it, so we have to reopen and establish the awareness of gravity again.*

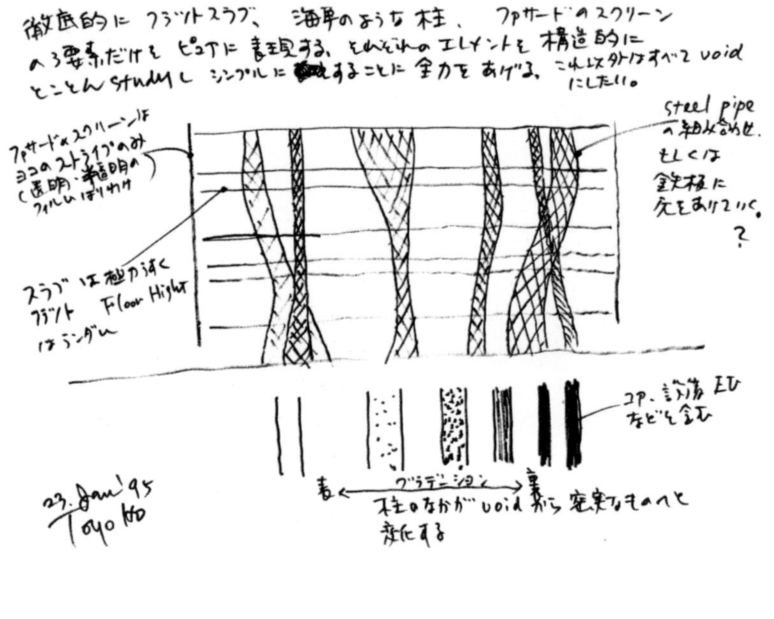

Tree-Columns

Lantern Pavilion, Sandnes, Norway (2010)
Architect: AWP + Atelier Oslo
Structural Engineer: Dr. techn. Kristoffer Apeland AS
Model: Sophia Buffara + Sarah Schwartz

www.jonasadlofsen.com

Intended to be seen from a distance, this open pavilion subtly protrudes out from a small public square into a busy pedestrian street; it has become both an iconic image for its city and an important informal public gathering place. It is its shape of an archetypical, traditional house with gable roof and side walls that at once gives this project its visual distinctiveness and suggests its fundamental mission of encouraging human gathering and providing shelter. In order to reinforce the form as that of a recognizable house, a homogeneous roof "shell" is created in which the typical physical and visual differences between various structural elements are consciously avoided – the result is that the roof and wall planes all have a uniform, double-layered grid character. This iconic form is lifted off the ground on four clusters of columns that have a visually contrasting and more organic, tree-like character. All structural components in the pavilion are made of wood: pine is used for the raised superstructure and oak for the columns, and the two are joined together by meticulous steel detailing. The upper parts of the columns fork out irregularly and their bases likewise spread out into stable tripod configurations. The tree-columns are somewhat randomly positioned, making the space between them quite versatile, while some column bases become benches or tables, thus enhancing the overall quality of informality and playfulness of the structure.

Åke e:Son Lindman

A Forest of Columns

El Bosque de Acero, Cuenca, Spain (2010)
Architect: Moneo Brock Studio
Structural Engineer: Jesús Jiménez, NB35, Cristina Alcazar
Model: Joshua Carrelo Mendez + Nicolas Dareau

To soften the transition from urban to green space this pavilion makes the forest's morphology its own: steel columns seem to grow like trees that branch out to carry, not leaves, but rather glass-covered angled roof planes. Each of the pavilion's 23 modules consists of a bundle of four steel tubes forming a composite column that forks out at a certain height in different directions to support part of a folded pentagonal roof segment. The roof beams also run in many different directions and at various angles, giving an overall impression of thin, quivering lines – not unlike tree-top leaves moving in the wind. [see also p. 163]

© Iwan Baan

Multi-Directional Plate Columns

White Forest Pavilion, KAIT, Atsugi, Japan (2007)
Architect: Junya Ishigami + Associates
Structural Engineer: Yasutaka Konishi
Model: Jordan Berta + Henry Gao

Designed as a workshop for students, this one-story building gives a free-flowing sense of space as well as an impression of structure that almost disappears into its surroundings: a roof and glass walls surrounding a forest of thin columns are all the eye can latch onto. From the outside, depending on the angle of view and time of day, trees are either mirrored off the glass walls or else a view is afforded deep into the interior space. A unified reading of this interior space is partially obstructed, however, by the large number of irregularly placed, randomly oriented planar columns that act as visual screens of variable densities. Furthermore, the interior space, while indeed one big room, is subdivided into many small local spaces by this irregular column arrangement, thus defying the idea of a uniform universal space in the Miesian tradition.

The varying location and orientation of the 305 steel plate columns not only invites ambiguity of circulation and perception of space, but also of load-carrying function. Purposefully enigmatic is the fact that 42 columns resist the roof's gravity loads while the rest are post-tensioned and brace the building against wind and earthquake forces, effectively acting as many small shear walls. A light steel beam grid, irregular in plan, is carried 5m (16ft) above the floor to form the roof; light filters deep into the workshop space through strips of glass. [see also p. 165]

Hiroyuki Oki

Tapered Column Masts

Bamboo Wing, Vinhphuc, Vietnam (2009)
Architect: Vo Trong Nghia Architects
Contractor: Hong Hac-Dai Lai JSC
Model: Lucia Lee + Patti Limansubroto

This building exploits locally sourced and ecologically sound bamboo as a structural material for an open-air restaurant. Pairs of outwardly curving sets of columns provide support at their upper ends for cable-stiffened roof beams that span the substantial 12m (40ft) distance between these points of support. The outwardly curved columns/masts are partly trussed to increase stiffness and prevent buckling, and their overall cross-sectional dimensions are tapered according to load-carrying demand and to provide rigidity toward the base. Stability against wind forces acting on the building is provided by angled tension rods that connect the column tips to the ground.

3D Matrix Column Grid

Bodegas Protos Winery, Peñafiel, Spain (2008)
Architect: Rogers Stirk Harbour + Partners, Alonso Balaguer & Associated Architects
Structural Engineer: Arup/BOMA/Agroindus
Model: Min Keun Park + Siying Lu

www.wenzel-fotografia.com

This contemporary winery is situated below the old Peñafiel Castle on the banks of the Duero River. The careful storage and fermentation of wines call for precise regulation of humidity and air temperature, conditions traditionally achieved by making use of the ground as a thermal mass. To that end and according to the age-old principle, the main spaces for this winery are built below ground and are thus naturally protected from the heat of the sun and from chilly weather. Moreover, the storage rooms are supported by a trabeated structure of reinforced concrete, a construction material that has its own significant thermal mass. Two story-levels constructed with precast columns and beams are arranged in a rectangular grid on a triangular site plan. At the top of the columns are cruciform precast concrete brackets designed to carry beams in all four directions. The completed beam configuration reads as a continuous system where the beam-to-bracket element connections form hinges at the point where bending moments are zero, while the bracket offers gradually increasing structural dimensions towards the columns in a logical response to increased bending moment and shear.

Atop this underground concrete structure rests the most recognizable and visible part of the actual building: its exterior terracotta-clad roof consisting of multiple barrel vaults carried on the inside by a series of distinctive parabolic glulam wooden arches.

Inclined & Multi-Story Columns

Fogo Island Inn, Newfoundland, Canada (2013)
Architect: Saunders Architecture
Structural Engineers: DBA Consulting Engineers Ltd
Model: Natalie Hemlick + Vinayak Portonovo

Alex Fradkin

The building of a distinctive inn on this remote, rugged island along the north Atlantic coast of Newfoundland was done to help establish a new economic base for a community that once depended on cod fishing and shipbuilding for survival. Organized as an X in plan, building volumes of two and four stories intersect and partly share the same footprint; where this is not the case they project outward, raised up on exposed columns to produce dramatic overhanging volumes.

The longest of these extends toward the open ocean and is carried on a set of 16.6 m (50 ft.) tall, slender steel tubular columns that in their disposition recall vernacular fishing piers, with several columns inclined this way and that in apparently erratic fashion but in so doing effectively resisting lateral forces as well as carrying gravity loads. These columns also touch the ground relatively lightly (vs. a continuous foundation wall, for example) so as to barely disturb a ground condition consisting only of rocks and slow-growing, delicate vegetation. A multi-story framed steel structure is hidden behind the wood cladding of the building. The two separate volumes of the building must be stabilized by appropriately positioned and oriented cross-bracing within the framework; notably, this bracing does not occupy every bay of the structure, as the floor systems effectively transfer lateral loads to where these can be resisted.

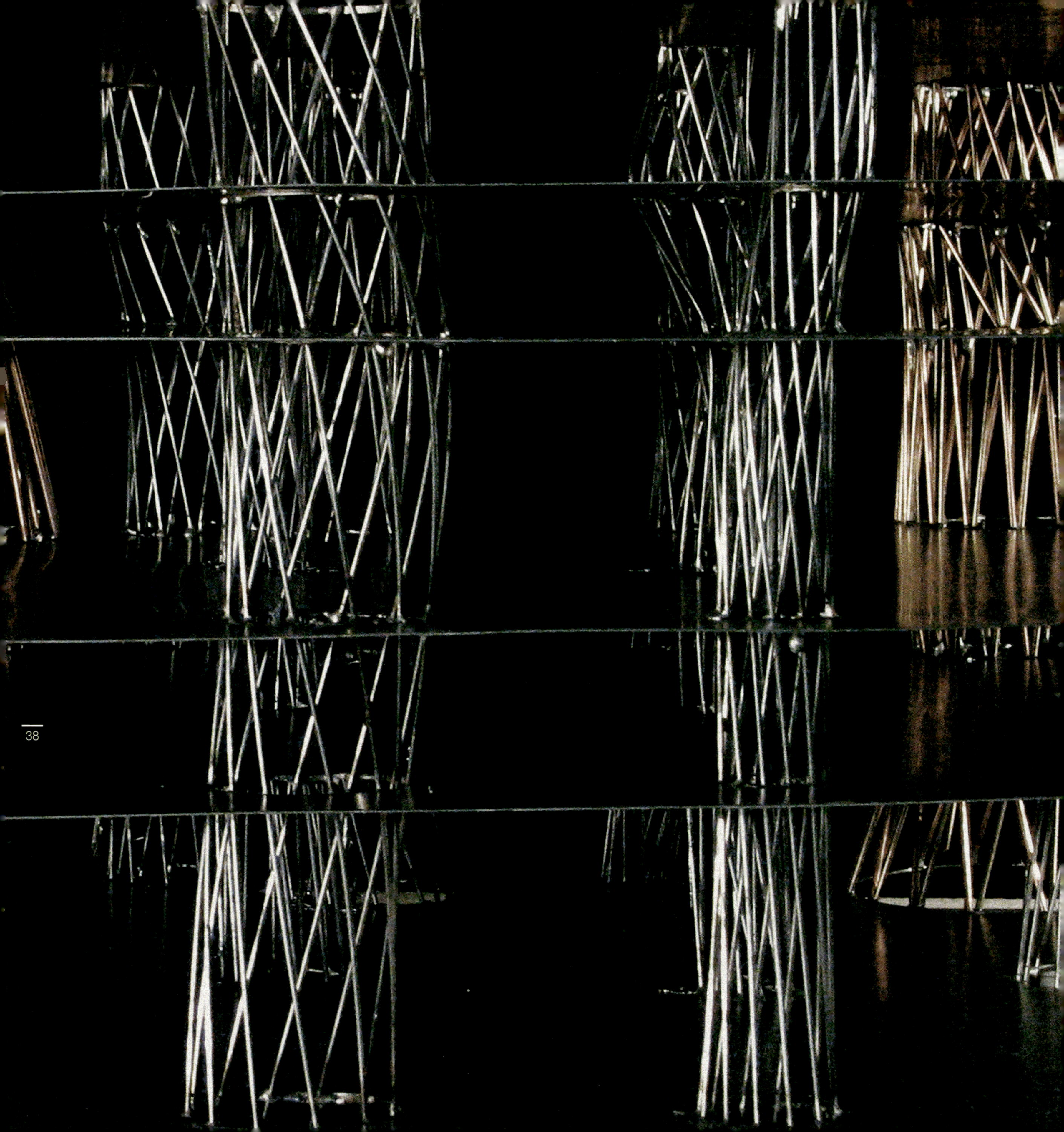

Organic Tube Columns

Sendai Mediatheque, Sendai, Japan (2001)
Architect: Toyo Ito & Associates
Structural Engineer: Sasaki Structural Consultants
Model: Sara Arfaian

William Veerbeen, Netherlands

The Sendai Mediatheque houses an art gallery, a library and a media centre for people with visual and hearing impairments. Likened to an "aquarium", it is designed to have an open, inviting interior that is considered an extension of the city into the building. Each of the seven levels has a different programmatic function and physical characteristics, including floor height, color scheme, furniture and structural configuration. Common, though, is the experience of spatial fluidity, whereby space extends horizontally, unobstructed by partition walls, and vertically through large openings in the floor slabs.

This aspect of "fluidity" extends to the structure, with vertical supports that look like "kelp dancing in the water"; the stem-like tubes bend and twist (but do not yield) to the forces applied to them. The building's thirteen tube-columns have diameters ranging from 2-9m (6-30ft) and shapes and inclinations that change with height; their "side-walls" are an open network of steel members welded together. The building's four corner tubes have diagonal bracing to withstand large wind and seismic forces, whereas the others that carry only gravity loads do not. In contrast to the typical strategy of minimizing structure, here "columns" are expanded to provide usable space for vertical circulation, light wells and service ducts – i.e., the tube-columns allow the building to live and breathe as well as stand up. [see also p. 23]

01

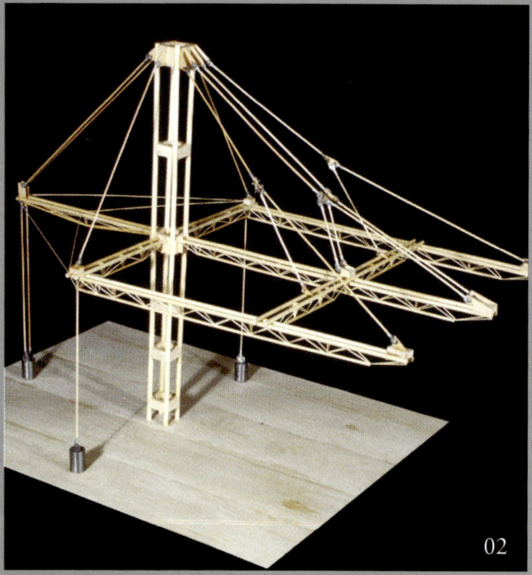
02

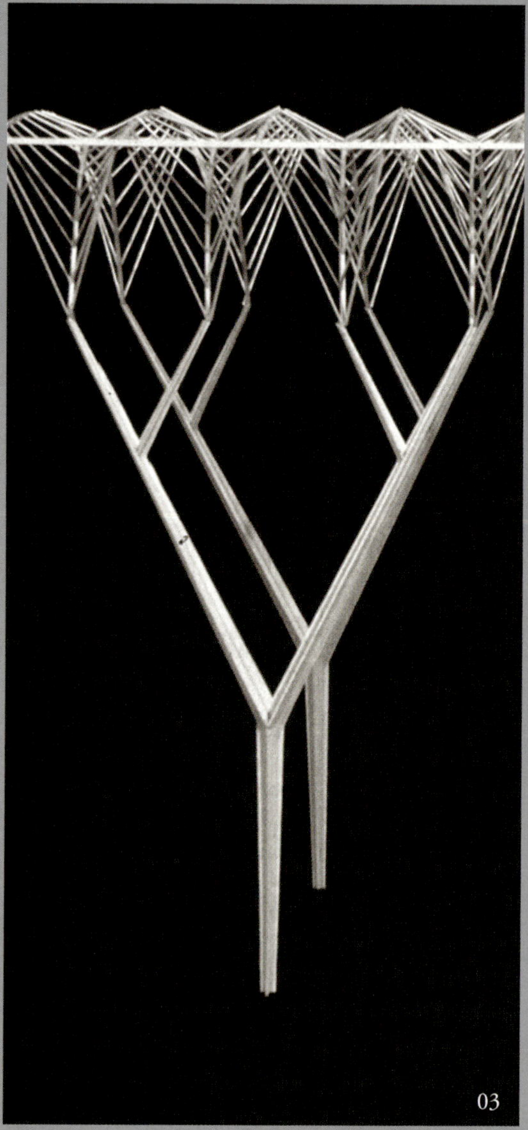
03

04

05

06

07

08

09

10

01. Riveted steel columns – La Maison de Verre; Paris, France; 1932; Pierre Chareau (furniture and interior designer), Bernard Bijvoet (arch.), Louis Dalbet (craftsman metalworker); model by Christopher King **02. Compression vs. tension member dimensions (mast & struts vs. cable stays)** – Sydney Exhibition Centre; Sydney, Australia; 1988 (demolished 2014); Philip Cox Richardson Taylor Partners (arch.); Arup (eng.); model by Bryant Lu **03. "Tree" column; load accumulation & member size** – Allan Lambert Galleria; Toronto, Canada; 1992; Santiago Calatrava (arch.); Yolles Partnership Limited (eng.); model by Carl Negin **04. Column expressing compression, tension and bending moment** – Lucerne Station Hall; Lucerne, Switzerland; 1989; Santiago Calatrava SA (arch., eng.); model by Chee Song Chern **05,06. Inverted tripod column supports – exposed and covered** – Burnham Pavilion; Chicago, USA; 2009; UNStudio (architect); Rockey Structures (eng.); model by Cole Phoenix Skaggs & Lisa Yun Zhu **07. Tension-cable-stabilized columns; tensegrity's "flying" columns** – Blur Building; Yverdon-les-Bains, Switzerland; 2002; Diller + Scofidio (arch.); Passera & Pedretti, Emch & Berger (eng); model by Juan Carlos Artolozaga & Mia Kang **08. Bracketing-beam column "capital"** Yusuhara Bridge Museum; Kochi Prefecture, Japan; 2011; Kengo Kuma & Associates (arch.); Katsuo, Nakata & Associates (eng.); model by Bradley Kinsey & Alison Nash **09. Material-varying columns** – Meadow House; Kirkland, WA, USA; 1993; Olson Kundig (arch.); John Brown Builder (contractor); model by Katherine Richardson **10. "Tree" column struts share load-carrying responsibility** – Sainokuni Chichibu Forest Lodge and Study Center; Saitama Prefecture, Japan; Kazutoshi Katayama / DIK Architects & Associates (arch.); Masuda Engineering Office (eng.); model by Joanna Wielock

11

12

13

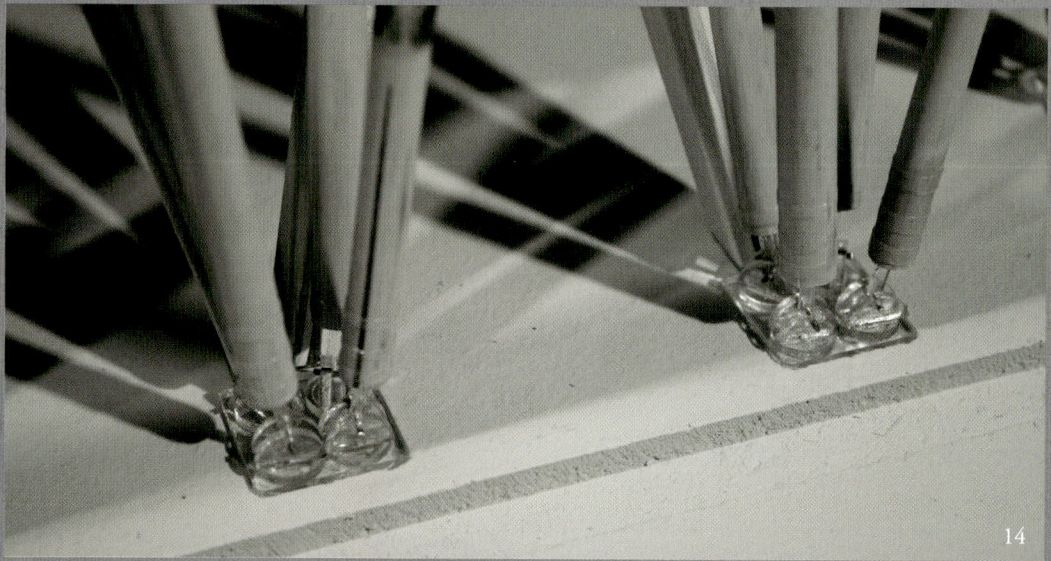

14

11. Occupiable tube-column; variable openness according to load-carrying demand – Jübergtower; Hemer, Germany; 2010; Birk Heilmeyer und Frenzel (arch.); Knippers Helbig Advanced Engineering (eng.); model by Jared Curtis & Steven Smolyn **12,14. Bamboo columns: articulated joint, base connections** – German-Chinese House, Shanghai, China, Expo 2010; Markus Heinsdorff (arch.); Mike Sieder/University of Technology, Munich (eng.); model by Jason Freedman & Elizabeth Saleh **13,16. Contrasting member dimensions: compression vs. tension** – PA Technologies Center, Princeton, NJ, USA, 1982; Richard Rogers and Partners (arch.); Arup (eng.); model by Sean J. Kim & Yen-Ju Timothy Tai **15. Contrasting member dimensions & materials: base supports vs roof ribs** – Brentwood Skytrain Station, Vancouver, BC, Canada, 2002; Busby + Associtcs (arch.); Fast & Epp Partners (eng.); model by Betty Huang & Xi Zhang **17. "Tree-column" struts share load-carrying responsibility** – Stuttgart Airport, Terminal 3, Germany, 1991; von Gerkan, Marg und Partner (arch.); Schlaich Bergermann und Partner (eng.); model by Christian A. Sandel **18. Countering buckling: built-up slender columns** – Waitomo Glowworm Caves Visitor Center, Waitomo, New Zealand, 2010; Architecture Workshop (arch.); Dunning Thornton Consultants (eng.); model by Michaela Delesanta & Jason Schwab **19. Base supports; temporary tower adjusts to differing conditions** – Scholzberg Tower, Liberec, Czech Republic, 2006; e-Mrak (arch.); model by Mariya Tsvetkova **20. Base support counters accumulating compression load carried by "column" within wood wall** – Swiss Pavilion, Hanover, Germany, Expo 2000; Peter Zumthor (arch.); Conzett, Bronzini, Gartmann (eng.); Garrett Knoll & Adrianne Ngam

15

16

17

18

20

19

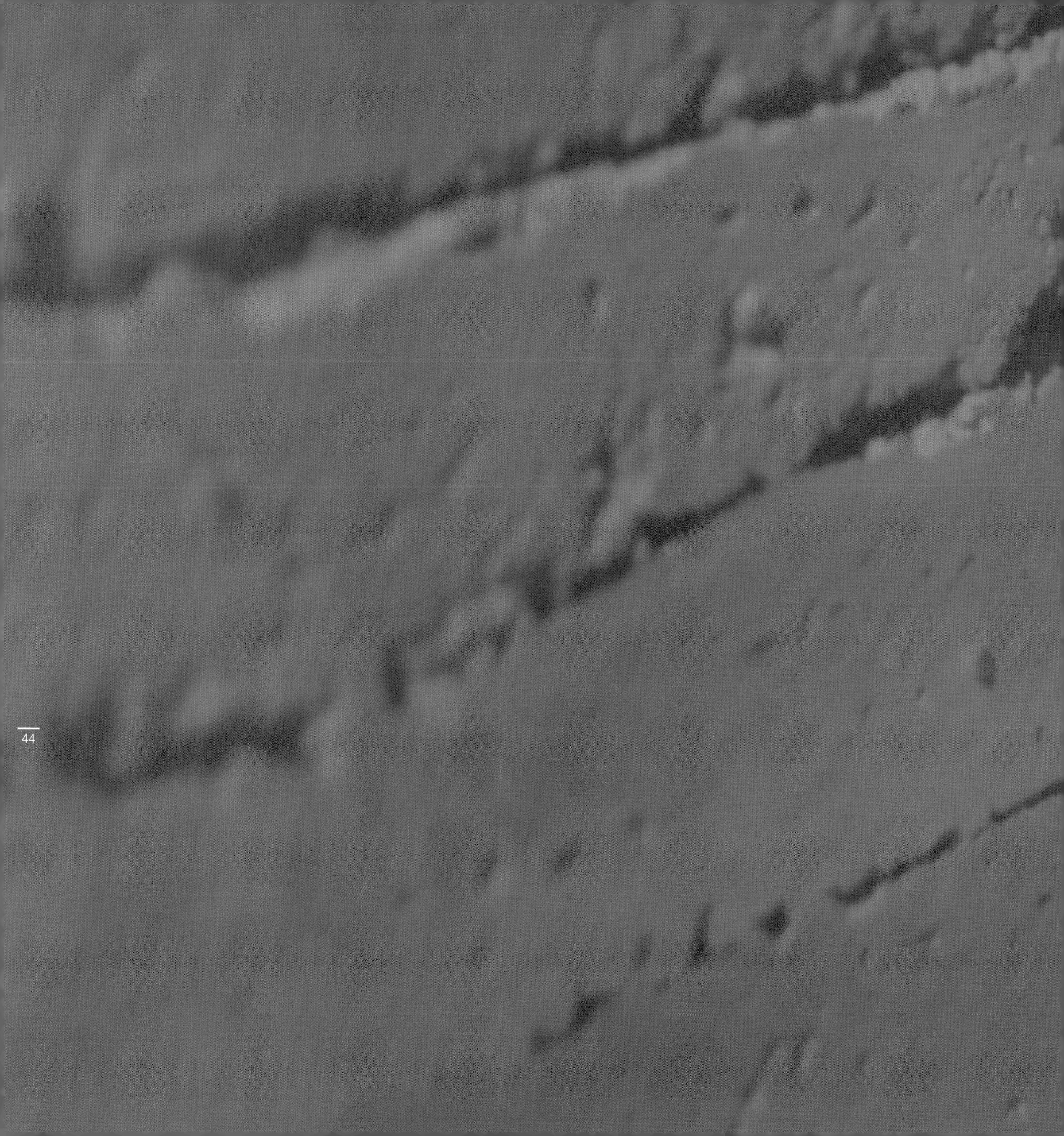

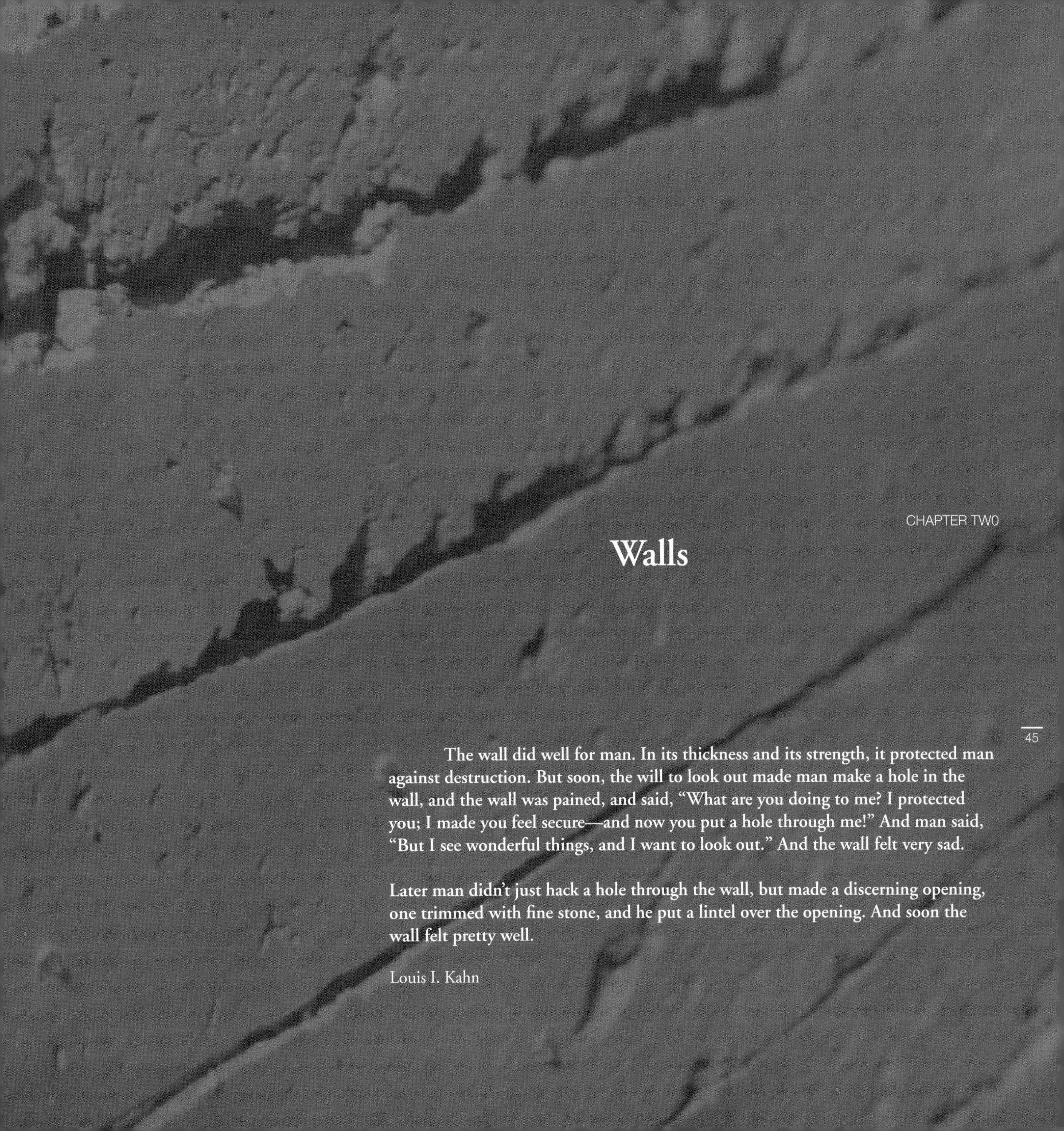

CHAPTER TWO

Walls

The wall did well for man. In its thickness and its strength, it protected man against destruction. But soon, the will to look out made man make a hole in the wall, and the wall was pained, and said, "What are you doing to me? I protected you; I made you feel secure—and now you put a hole through me!" And man said, "But I see wonderful things, and I want to look out." And the wall felt very sad.

Later man didn't just hack a hole through the wall, but made a discerning opening, one trimmed with fine stone, and he put a lintel over the opening. And soon the wall felt pretty well.

Louis I. Kahn

San Cristóbal stables – courtyard and pool

We have lived with walls since time immemorial, perhaps beginning with the caves of our distant ancestors. Walls can have many different structural functions in architecture and they take on various names according to those roles, from gravity load-bearing walls to earth-retaining walls to lateral force-resisting shear walls (that counter wind and earthquake forces). Of course, the design of walls in buildings also serves to create, enclose and form space while offering the opportunity to affect the perception and qualities of this same space – in various instances by directing views and circulation paths, or perhaps by blocking views and light if only to then selectively establish strategic openings, or by dramatically varying colors and textures through deliberate material choices and finishes, or by creating acoustical separation of adjacent spaces, or by providing the thermal mass that supports a (long-established) sustainable approach to heating and cooling or, on a more abstract level, by being considered as conceptually connected to the ground, at once rooted in it and an upward extension of it.

Many of these functions and qualities of walls are remarkably brought to life through the lifework of Luis Barragán, as described here by Danièle Pauly in a brief extract from her monograph on the celebrated Mexican architect, *Barragán: Space and Shadow, Walls and Colour*. Central to this discussion is the horse-bathing pool of the San Cristóbal Ranch (left – an image that in and of itself certainly has to be considered among those that best embody what the wall can be in architecture).

Barragán's Walls and Colour

from *Barragán: Space and Shadow, Walls and Colour*
Danièle Pauly

Walls and Colour

Walls are an essential tectonic feature of Barragánian architecture and are clearly distinguishable by their materials and colours. Not only do they mark out the spatial boundaries, providing scale and proportion, but they also bear the traces of time, for their aspect is altered by the shadows that are cast on them as the sun follows its course. Their strong presence is heightened by their colouring, which together with the sunlight, transforms spaces and softens the shadows. The surfaces of the walls are never smooth; rather, they are coated in thick plaster, giving rise to the solid, palpable texture that characterises Barragán's walls. When the coloured wall stands on its own, the hue that uniformly clads the sides and profile turns the wall into a near-abstract artefact. The effect is intensified in accordance with the sightlines produced.

Inside Barragán's buildings, colour is employed as an agent for metamorphosing spaces and creating different ambiences. Within the intermediary spaces (courtyards, patios and terraces), it provides a material link with the outside, delimits surface areas, picks out structural volumes, and binds the composition. Outside, the walls structure the site, orchestrate the spatial scenario and underline the geometric scheme, their colours contrasting sharply with those of the natural surroundings.

A Landscape Orchestrated by Coloured Walls

"But where does sculpture begin? Where does painting begin? Where does architecture begin?" So asked Le Corbusier in 1948, continuing his studies into a synthesis of the arts, begun a decade earlier: "In the very body of the artistic event, everything is one [...], that is, specific materials, amounts, and consistencies – assembled in ways that stir the senses".[1] The notion of an "artistic event" is skilfully echoed in Barragán's "landscape architecture",[2] as the architect himself termed his works set in natural surroundings. In these schemes – such as Las Arboledas, la Fuente de Los Amantes (the Lovers' Fountain) and the courtyard of San Cristóbal – colour, walls and water are brought together in a poetic ensemble that can be perceived as a total work of art, filled with the presence of horses.

Barragán sought the same introspective effect in his outdoor schemes as for the indoor ones. Within each work, the spatial concept is that of an enclosure, in which a route is laid out – like a ceremonial procession - and set around horses. These airy spaces serve as a protection from the hustle and bustle of the outside world, with the plain geometric forms and proportions of the coloured walls generating a monumental aura. Each wall structures the surrounding environment, acting as a screen that delineates or conceals a background setting, frames perspective views, ensnares the shadows, and sets the spatial score to music. It provides a focal point, whilst mapping out a pathway with several different sequences.

"The Bough of Tree [...] Behind a Wall"

On the site of Las Arboledas, a long wall – "el muro rojo" – outlines the whole scheme, like a ribbon billowing across the landscape.[3] It forms an enclosure that provides protection from the outside world and the traffic, enticing us to discover its secrets. "I think there's mystery when you see the top of a tree behind a wall," noted Barragán.[4] Bright orange tones contrast with the greenery and emphasise the character of the site.

Within this belt of land is a riding path lined with eucalyptus trees – the remains of an older track and a reminder of the family ranch at Corrales. The tree-lined path ("el Paseo de los Gigantes") crosses the terrain and constitutes the backbone of the scheme. Looking down this pathway, one's gaze is arrested by a high white wall, before being drawn up to the boughs of the trees. The wall is, in effect, a screen that depicts the outline of the horses and riders.

There are two clearly defined spaces at either end of the path, along which there are perspective views, hidden nooks and crannies, shadow-mantled walls and the constant gurgle of water. At one end there is a fountain ("el campanario"), designed for animals to bathe in; at the other end there is an expanse of water ("el bebedero"), intended as a drinking trough. Once again, then, the scheme contains a clear reference to the watering places that can be found on a ranch.

The Plaza del Campanario marks the entrance to the site. It is partially enclosed, wedged between two parallel L-shaped walls, one of which is made of logs and separates the square from the riding path, half concealing it. The fountain wall is painted orange, and juts out into the middle of the pool, its flow of water cascading onto the stone flags that clad the ground. At the other end of the site, there is the Plaza del Bebedero, which is structured by the long horizontal line of the pool of water and the high vertical line of the white wall; a low indigo blue wall[5] closes off the perspective view and dialogues with the shimmering reflections of the sky. The white wall is also reflected in the water, playing with the clouds and forming a screen onto which the foliage's ever-changing shadows are projected. In fact, the interplay of shadows is the very reason for the wall's existence, for it was built purely so that shadows could be cast onto it.

The Fuente de Los Amantes, which is located at one of the far ends of the residential area of Los Clubes,[6] is also intended as a stopping place for horses and riders. The scheme is laid out around a fountain, which stands in a large stretch of water, and two vertical blocks of wood – totemic outlines symbolising the Lovers. A large corner wall frames the mounted riders and delineates the field of vision. The wall is painted bright pink, contrasting with the boughs of the trees, and the space it veils seems to be excluded from the overall composition. Only two shafts of light filter through – one at the corner of the pink wall, and the other at the point where the wall intersects with the fountain, the narrow slits underscoring the screen-like appearance of the thin walls. The fountain, which is an over-flow shaped in the form of a long beam, extends out from a wall covered with brown plaster[7] and rests on another perpendicular wall of the same colour, texture and thickness. The water gushes onto the slightly sloping ground, laid with pebbles, creating a pool in which the animals can frisk and frolic. The pebble flooring offers a material texture that contrasts with the abstract coloured walls.

The wall at the back of the scheme and those of the fountain showcase the blocks of wood in the foreground (made from an old drinking trough, sawn in half), bestowing a monumental air upon them. Here, Barragán capitalised on the poetic value of an object stripped of its original use, and played on the contrast between organic forms and the abstract lines and surfaces of the fountain. The natural elements – water, wood and pebbles – are orchestrated by the geometric shapes of the coloured walls, and a strange metaphysical atmosphere shrouds the sculptural ensemble.

The design for the Los Amantes fountain fed that for the San Cristóbal fountain.[8] The original idea for the hollow raised beam derived from the architect's childhood memories, notably the wooden aqueducts that criss-cross Mexican villages, carrying water to the fountains. The same childhood reminiscences can be noted in the dark wooden gate that provides access to the service road of the residential quarter of Los Clubes. In addition, the small cubic pink building that adjoins the gate, and which serves as a security guard's hut, bears close similarities to a traditional house. The two pink walls that also stand at this entrance are rooted in the same reference points, as is the paving made up of small flat hewn stones. Barragán transposed the images he could recall (drinking troughs, aqueducts, gates, paved paths, and long blank walls), translating traditional features into contemporary language.

"Stables, Stretches of Water, Drinking Troughs, the Dwelling"

In the courtyard of the San Cristóbal Ranch, one can find the same values accorded to coloured walls as in Barragán's previous "landscape architectures". In particular, there is the same staging dedicated to the world of horses. "San Cristóbal [...] combines the elements I've always looked for: the stable, the pool, the drinking trough for the horses, the house".[9]

The whole scheme is organised around a horse-related layout, encompassing stables, water and a riding ring. The focal point is a fountain that stands in a pool devoted to bathing thoroughbreds, its torrent gushing forth from a double wall. The tethering posts form two parallel lines and guide perspective views of the courtyard, which is cast into shadow by a majestic tree.[10]

The courtyard is vast yet partially enclosed, the only vistas being side views of the surrounding landscape revealed through a long portico. A wall stands perpendicular to the portico, directing one's path towards the riding ring, while at the same time hiding it from view.[11] Three large coloured walls enclose the scheme. In the foreground, there is the bright orange aqueduct-fountain; looking sideways, one can see the long horizontal line of the portico; and at the back stand the high walls of the fodder barn. The latter two structures are covered with pink plaster and are linked by a low purple gate. The palette of colours – orange, magenta pink, and dark purple – contrasts yet complements the greenery, the yellow ochre ground and the blue water that shimmers with reflections from the sky.

The fourth side of the courtyard is taken up by the structure accommodating the stables, which gradually comes into sight as one walks on. It is a typical ranch building, with a wide overhang, and introduces a dash of reality that breaks with the scheme's abstract colouring. Within the geometric set formed by the coloured walls, there is a staging of natural elements – the tree, the pool and the flow of water – whose scale is established by the horses. The positioning of the walls tautens perspective views and creates a sequence of cut-out shapes, with the horses as the protagonists.

The proportions and bright colours of the walls, combined with their interstices and geometric features, generate an overall monumental aura. The huge courtyard, which seems empty when there are no horses in it, engenders a strange atmosphere that is not unlike some of Giorgio de Chirico's paintings, which Barragán often talked of. "In him I found the magic I've always sought", the architect confided to Elena Poniatowska. "When I saw his painting I thought: 'This is what I can also do in the architecture of landscape,' if you want to call it that, an architecture made with walls and ramparts and a series of spaces in which you pass from one grille to another grille, from one water feature to a patio where there's also water".[12]

In the scheme for San Cristóbal, as in those for Los Amantes and Las Arboledas, the wall sections are of differing heights and serve as screens. Their profiles (sometimes split in two) become lines, and their surfaces are shifted in three dimensions, resembling a compositional process theorised about by De Stijl.[13] Equally, the scheme's allusions to the Miesian framework are further evidence of how Barragán was influenced by the modern masters. Like them, he explored the notion of spatial geometry – and enriched it. Like them, he drew on arrangements of orthogonal lines, extending these beyond the point of intersection and underscoring the corner angle through which bright shafts of light could be channelled. He too played on the dynamics of spatial flows obtained by creating wide passageways, as well as on the tense pull engendered by slotting narrow slits between solid surfaces. The difference in Barragán's landscapes, however, is that the architectural matter is the colour scheme; the flooring is beaten earth, pebbles or roughly hewn stones; the sculptural component is bare timber; and water is not a glassy stretch, but a gurgling torrent.

Walls as Sculpture

Barragán's coloured walls finally became pieces of sculpture in the Ciudad Satélite scheme, which he designed in association with Mathias Goeritz.[14] The design of the high-rise buildings testifies to the close working relationship between the sculptor and the architect. Barragán, who claimed to be inspired by the outline of the San Gimignano Towers, also worked on the project with architect-planner Mario Pani. Similarly, Chucho Reyes provided input with respect to the colour scheme. Goeritz, who had previously explored the theme of tower structures,[15] produced an interlocking set of structural volumes, achieved via five prisms, for which several preparatory models were developed.

The scheme was designed on a monumental scale, in line with that of Mexico City itself. The towers were deliberately positioned in order to be seen from the motorway, and their colours energise the whole site. They seem to hover, breathtakingly high, and change aspect depending on the angle from which they are viewed. Close up, the walls look flat, with the marks from the formwork generating a textured effect. From a distance, however, they seem sturdily thick, especially when one's gaze falls on their flared edges. They are totemic outlines that dominate the site. They are at one with the flow of traffic; from one side they are as sharp as razor blades, enticing motorists to drive fast, whilst from the other side they seem to be hefty standing blocks, prompting vehicles to slow down. In this scheme, the coloured walls are in a constant state of metamorphosis, orchestrating the urban landscape. One's ever-changing perception of the whole scene gives rise to an illusion of ongoing transformation – the metaphor of the modern city. It is an architectonic and sculptural work, whose symbolic content is as much a translation of spiritual aspirations as a quest for the gigantic proportions of a megalopolis.

Coloured walls are thus an integral component of the Barraganian design process. Their underlying artistic essence, conveyed through their proportions, positioning, hues and texture, renders them pieces of sculpture that showcase the site and bestow a poetic dimension upon it. The overall ensemble produced by such an alliance between walls, matter, colour and water takes on an emotive quality that is specific to Barragan's design universe.

Inca wall at Cuzco. Photo: Gvillemin

The stone wall is primordial. It is simple, typically made of rocks taken from the very ground on which it sits; yet holding these together one on top of another in vertical, planar fashion is an ages-old challenge. From a spatial perspective, stone walls and their solid, linear, enclosing characteristics have long defined both the exterior forms and the quality of the interior spaces of buildings, or at least they did so until the advent of lighter, more efficient construction materials. The walls erected by the Inca in the southern Peruvian town of Ollantaytambo in the 16th century personify such qualities perhaps like no other. As recounted here by Jean-Pierre Protzen in his book *Inca Architecture and Construction at Ollantaytambo*, the stones of the walls in certain places spectacularly interlock without mortar, in others they define carefully choreographed spatial approach sequences and establish a gridded layout of urban blocks. Within a single town block, they establish the enclosed, double-courtyarded, multicellular, multilevel housing units called the *"kancha"*, whose details of design allow the walls to also take on the role of furniture, of stairway support, and more besides. Contemporary inhabitants of these buildings and spaces are found to have re-appropriated them to suit their own purposes. The stone wall lives on.

Inca Walls at Ollantaytambo

from *Inca Architecture and Construction at Ollantaytambo*
Jean-Pierre Protzen

The astonishing precision with which stone was fitted to stone is still what most defies the imagination of visitors to Inca ruins. How could a people who did not know the wheel and did not have iron tools build such artful walls? Was there magic involved? Several myths continue to be perpetuated, the most colorful of which has it that the Incas had an herb whose juice softened stone, so that the stone could be modeled, a motif derived from European folklore. As I have demonstrated elsewhere,[1] the Incas, in reality, were quite capable of fitting stones together with the tools at hand and without the help of an extraterrestrial race. At Ollantaytambo, the Inca stonemasons pushed their craft to its extremes: a tiny chink that broke off because of a cleavage plane at a corner of a stone was offset by a matching cut in the next stone. Here, the stonemasons so dominated their craft that it became art playfully applied.

The Approaches

Today's tourists, arriving at Machu Picchu by train and bus, miss one of the most important features of Inca site planning; they are deprived of the dramatic encounter with the site the ancient traveler experienced when coming through the Gate of *Intipunku*. That traveler encountered a succession of open spaces that are scaled from the vast horizons of the Andes to the intimate courtyard in town—spaces strung together by narrow passages over precipitous cliffs, steep staircases, alleyways, and gates. Along this pathway the site is veiled and unveiled in a sequence of vistas that reveal the lay of the land and the setting of the town, and that attract attention to details of nature or architecture framed by narrow passages or gates. The approaches to Ollantaytambo and its monuments are perhaps not as dazzling as the ones to Machu Picchu, but they, too, were designed for special effects.

The voyager approaching Ollantaytambo from the east followed the course of the river at the valley floor with a view of the snow-covered mountain range of Mount Verónica framed by the big V of the valley profile. Past the Fort of *'Inkapintay* the scenery became hidden from his view as he ascended to the Gate of *T'iyupunku* with no clue of what lay beyond it. From the Gate of *T'iyupunku* it is still more than half a kilometer before one reaches the town proper. What an Inca traveler would have encountered along this path cannot be reconstructed with much confidence, but Squier, coming from Cuzco and Urubamba, described his entrance to Ollantaytambo:

> *Soon we came to a massive crenated wall, pierced by two gate-ways with grooves in their piers, as if to receive a sliding porticullis. ... Beyond, the road led between two ancient stone buildings, still inhabited, which fill the space between the edge of the terrace and the cliffs, apparently designed as guard-houses, and between which the visitor to Ollantaytambo had to pass in the olden, as he has to do in modern time. Past these the road continued between a high niched wall, on the one hand, and the cliff with its gurgling azequia, on the other. Thus shut in betwixt wall and mountain side, and our view circumscribed, we jog on for half a mile. Then the wall ends.*[2]

Today's visitor follows roughly the same course, except for some details that since have been lost. Immediately past the gate, several terraces have been broken to accommodate a hairpin turn in the modern road. The defensive wall flanking the gate to the south has in part succumbed to the road construction, but its general layout can still be followed down over several terraces. A sketch map by Bingham's surveyors shows that the "guard-houses" were already destroyed to their present state in 1915.[3] En passant, I should note that the grooves Squier observed in the piers of the gate can no longer be seen, probably because part of the double jamb has been destroyed for no apparent reason, and that immediately to the west of the "guard-houses" there are the vestiges of yet another Inca building, which is not shown on Bingham's sketch.

Because the Wall of a Hundred Niches was not level but sloped up gently from the gate toward the town, the row of niches was stepped up at least four times over the wall's entire length. Today, the niches are buried under the modern roadbed, some up to their sills and others to their lintels, indicating that the Inca road, if it did run along the wall, is now covered with from 1.5 to 2.5 meters of new deposits. The wall is now only the shadow of "a high niched wall." Because niches were generally used only on the inside of buildings, Hemming suggested that the wall may have been the inside wall of one or several long barrackslike halls or that the road may have been roofed.[4] Although halls as proposed by Hemming are a distinct possibility, my guess is that the Inca road here was walled in between two walls, as was the road between *Choqana* and the bridge, and that the second wall was demolished to make room for the current access road. Excavation across the road could clarify this question. As to Hemming's other suggestion, there is no evidence, to my knowledge, that the Incas ever roofed their roads.

The *azequia* (canal) is still running, although its course, too, must have been altered since Squier's passage. It follows the current road right through the destroyed, southern "guard-house," but water flows through the original conduit in the bottom of the central pier of the double gateway.

As one progresses from the gate along the Wall of a Hundred Niches, one gets a first, distant view of the top of the Temple Hill. The niched wall is somewhat shorter than Squier estimated; it is just over 250 meters long. Where the wall actually began near the gate is difficult to ascertain, as it gets lost between newer buildings, but it ends precisely where Squier said it did. There, today's main road jogs before it continues along a massively built terrace wall, which follows exactly the prolongation of the niched wall but on the opposite side of the road. The traces of several ancient buildings neatly arranged in a row perfectly parallel to the terrace edge and the road are above this wall. Some 90 meters farther along the road, the massive terrace wall disappears behind a modern wall of carelessly stacked rocks. The latter joins an Inca wall of well-cut and well-fitted stones that forms the corner with Laris Calle, the street delimiting the town of Ollantaytambo to the east. Today, several doors cut into the wall lead to dwellings behind it. Whether the wall belonged to an ancient building or whether it was a terrace wall is not clear. A town block beyond Laris Calle, the main road emerges onto today's Plaza de Armas.

The Plaza de Armas occupies what I suspect to have been a large esplanade in Inca times, extending to Laris Calle. Thus the traveler would have come out from a narrow passage enclosed "betwixt wall and mountain side" onto a wide open space. Only here did he get a full view of the imposing Fortaleza and a glimpse of *Manyaraki* across the Patakancha River, and only here did he discover the town on the north side of the esplanade. ...

Looking at the plan of Ollantaytambo, one might be tempted to argue that the town block is derived from a grid cast onto the land, as it is in modern North American cities. But that is not the case: the blocks are the result of a particular building arrangement—a *kancha*—which will be discussed in the next section. The grid was a convenient way to accommodate the *kancha* on relatively flat land, such as at Ollantaytambo. Under somewhat less propitious conditions, the grid was modified to fit the particular terrain, as it was at Cuzco and Patallaqta. In more broken terrain, such as at Machu Picchu and Wiñay Wayna, the grid disappeared, but the *kancha* remained, even if it had to be altered and squeezed to fit into the limited space.

The Kancha

The unit of design for the blocks in the southern half of the town was the *kancha*. The *kancha* at Ollantaytambo was a walled compound with a central courtyard surrounded by four buildings, leaving small open courts in the four corners.[5] Two *kancha*, mirror images of each other, formed a block. There was no connection from one *kancha* to the other; each had its own and only entrance off the longitudinal street on which it bordered.

Bingham mapped the three southwestern blocks of the town and their six constituent *kancha*. I investigated five of these six *kancha*. What proved to be most perplexing about Bingham's plan is that several original Inca remains still visible today do not figure on that plan. I was further puzzled when I found a field sketch of blocks 7 and 10 made by Bingham's surveyors, in which block 7 differs significantly from the one in Bingham's map. This sketch is much closer to what I have observed. Block 7 is the best-preserved block in town, and so much is left of its eastern *kancha* that it leaves very few open questions about the original design of the block and the *kancha*. A reconstruction of this *kancha* is no longer hypothetical, and much of it could be authentically restored. Based on my observations and comparisons with corresponding elements preserved in other *kancha*, I am confident that the eastern *kancha* of block 7 is characteristic of all other *kancha* at Ollantaytambo and is representative of the standard design.

The *kancha* was entered through a double-jamb doorway, which meant prestige or high status,[6] leading into a porchlike building,[7] with one side open to the center courtyard. The main doorway was secured by a set of barholds, one on either side, which may have served to tie a rope across the opening to indicate that the place was off-limits to strangers. The Incas did not have doors as we know them.

Upon passing through the open-front building and entering the central courtyard, one faces a two-story building. With its gable roof extending into the next *kancha*, this building appears to straddle the wall separating the two *kancha* on the block, yet it is divided from the foundation up to the roof ridge into two unconnected halves, one in each *kancha*. The second floor of this building is reached by a stair of cantilevered steps in the courtyard to the left, as one faces the building. These stairs are the only element that is not mirrored across the wall dividing the two *kancha*. There is a structural reason for this asymmetry. The party wall would have had to be inordinately thick if projecting stone steps were to be tailed into it from both sides. To avoid a breach of customary standards, the stairs on different sides were built into the party wall of diagonally opposite courts. At the same time, this arrangement would have provided more privacy to each *kancha*, preventing one from climbing the stairs up on one side and down the other. The second floor has door-sized openings in both gable walls and seven niches on the back wall with protruding stone pegs about 15 centimeters in diameter set between them. How high the front wall stood above the floor could not be determined, but my guess is that there was no front wall above the second floor.

If we assume a slope in the roof of between 55° and 58°—the approximate slope of other gables in the *kancha*—and the eaves to be even with the second-floor level, the roof would have cleared the doorway and left enough headroom for a person to walk upright over two-thirds of the floor area. As a consequence, the back wall would have stood about 4.5 to 5 meters above the ledge on which the floor joist rested, which again is in line with examples at other sites. The room on the ground floor has eight niches in its back wall that, like the second-floor niches, have stone pegs set between them. The gable walls have two niches with a high window for ventilation placed just under the ceiling, and the front wall has three doorways with niches in the walls on either side.

On the north and south sides of the central court, two single-story buildings face each other, symmetrically opposed. These two are not covered by hip roofs, as suggested by Gasparini and Margolies,[8] but by gable roofs. On both buildings the original, somewhat eroded gables with their high windows are still standing. A last stone peg stuck in the west gable of the southern building is testimony to the fact that such stones, as is typical of so many Inca buildings, protruded all along the gable eves. The buildings were erected on a plan of six niches in the back wall, three niches in the gable walls, and two entryways flanked by niches in the front wall. Stone pegs, set level with the lintels of the niches, are found in the center of the gable walls and between the second and third and between the fourth and fifth niches in the back wall. These buildings also present some rather puzzling details. First are three small square holes or windows, about 30 centimeters on the side, placed just under the eaves in the center of the front wall. These holes are echoed, in the form of carefully built recesses of the same size, exactly opposite on the back wall. More of these recesses are disposed all around the inside of the buildings. They are built in between the large niches where there are no pegs, yet above the level of the lintel stones. As an intriguing variation, the second recess in the back and gable walls, counting from the nearest corner, is set lower—at the same level as the lintel stones. Although the location of these recesses shows a clear pattern, no obvious explanation for them imposes itself. The recesses do recall second-floor beam sockets found at the Fort of *Choqana*, but no plausible framing plan emerges from the utilization of the recesses. Today's inhabitants have built lofts and attics into these buildings without making use of the recesses. To date, further investigations into the purpose of the recesses and into whether these buildings had second floors in Inca times have been frustrated because the task cannot be achieved without invading the privacy of the inhabitants and disrupting their lives.

Not enough evidence has survived on any of the open-front buildings to be sure of how they were roofed. Since there is no indication that they had gables, I assume the open-front buildings were covered with a hip roof. The standard design of the open-front building called for six niches on the back wall with stone pegs set between them at the level of the lintels; a south wall with two niches and a narrow doorway leading into the adjoining corner courtyard; a front wall with two wide openings and just a pier between them, and a niche on either end of the wall; and, finally, a north wall with three niches. The open-front building also has its baffling peculiarities. A square hole, or window, as described earlier, was built above the lintel of the narrow doorway in the south wall, and two pairs of recesses, one on each wall, faced each other across the room at the northern end of the building. Two protruding flat stones with a hole pounded through them, so-called ring-stones, were set between and at about midheight of the niches in the north wall.

Ring-stones are plentiful throughout the *kancha* and are typically set at 1.80 to 2.00 meters above the ground. They occur between the niches of the corner courts flanking the open-front building and appear on the façades fronting onto the central court: one in the pier of the open-front building, one each in the center of the buildings to the north and to the south, and two between the doorways of the two-story building. The Peruvian archaeologists Nuñez del Prado[9] and Gibaja[10] believe the rings were used to hang looms. Today wires used as clotheslines are strung from ring-stone to ring-stone across the central court. There is no archaeological evidence to assign a specific function to the peg stones protruding from the walls inside the buildings. Based on today's usage, Nuñez del Prado suggested that the pegs may have served as supports for logs laid tight to the walls to serve as supports for second floor joists.[11] In my view, this is a modern, unintended adaptation of the pegs. Where the Inca wanted to build a second floor, they constructed a ledge to receive the floor joists, as in the two-story building described earlier. There, the ledge is at least half a meter above the row of seven pegs set into the back wall. More likely, the pegs served to hang household items and personal belongings. The Inca had no furniture to speak of.[12] Thus what needed to be stored was placed on the floor, put in the niches, or hung from the pegs. Guaman Poma de Ayala, a seventeenth-century chronicler, depicted items of clothing hanging from a peg.[13]

Who occupied the *kancha* at Ollantaytambo in Inca times and how they were used is not really known. To work his land, the *Inca* employed *yanakuna* (retainers). The *yanakuna* were exempt from taxes; they were settled on the Inca's estate and were given a plot of land to provide for their needs. In return, they had to cultivate other fields for the benefit of their master.[14] It seems unlikely that these simple farmers were housed in the *kancha*; more appropriately, perhaps, they were given modest quarters outside town, near their fields. The size of the *kancha*, its cut- and fitted-stone enclosure walls, and the double-jamb doorway indicate that the *kancha* was occupied by a social class with high status. It is, of course, probable that to run his estate the *Inca* required the services of retainers of a higher status,[15,16] such as administrators, accountants, and other specialists, and it is possible that these retainers were accommodated in the *kancha* with their families. Better yet, it is possible that *Pachakuti* built the *kancha* for the nobles of Cuzco, as his son *Thupa 'Inka Yupanki* did on his estate at Chinchero.[17] Cobo, indeed, stated that only the houses of the leaders had large patios, where people joined to drink at their festivals and celebrations, and had more (than one) living quarters.[18]

The present tenancy of the *kancha* is rather complicated. Three or more families claim scattered parts of one *kancha*. A family is not necessarily confined to one house, but may inhabit separate areas

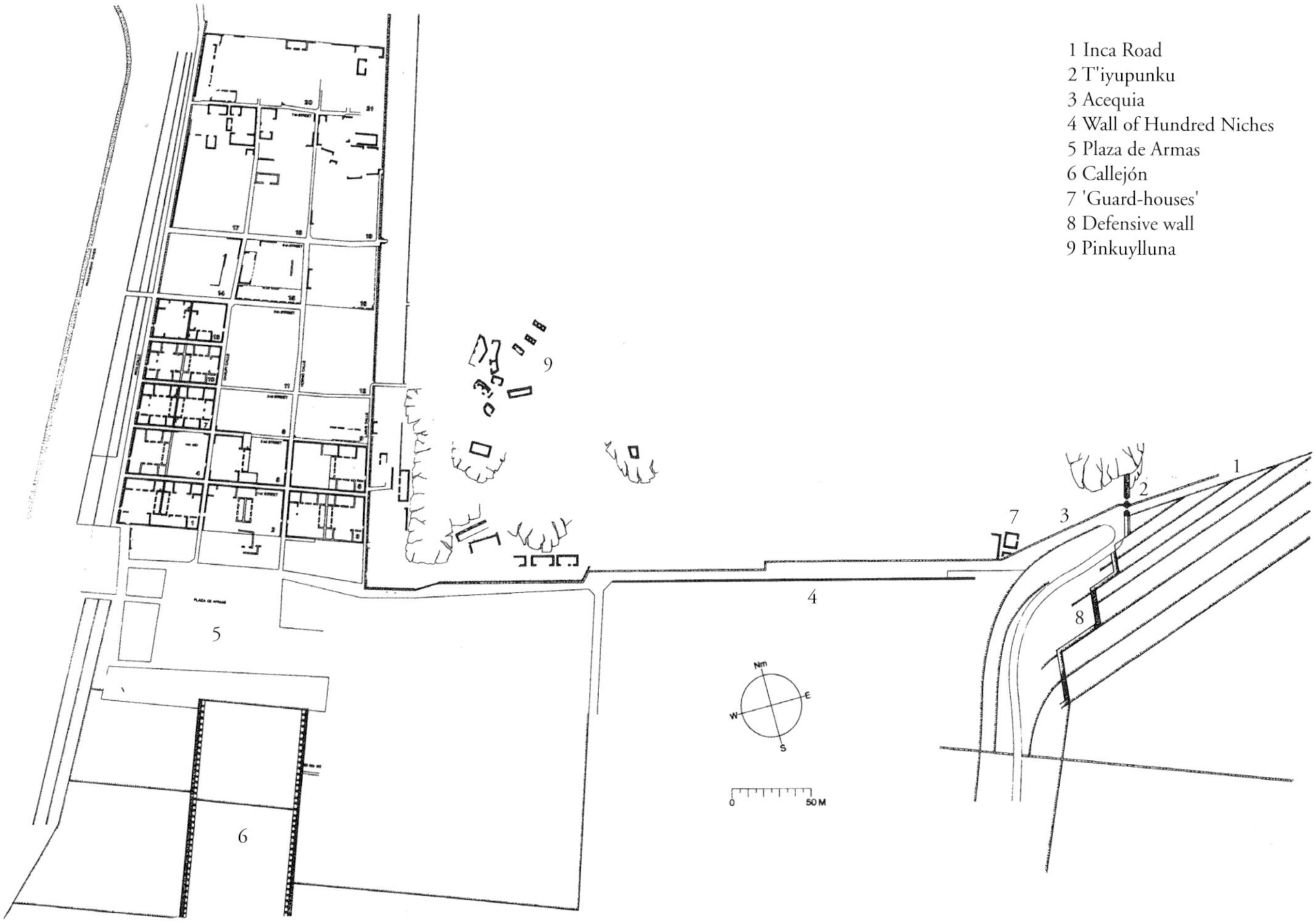

Approach to Ollantaytambo. Drawing by Jean-Pierre Protzen

in different buildings. In the better-preserved *kancha*, and where they still exist, the courtyards seem to serve the common good. The corner courtyards are used as midden and animal pens. The central courtyard mainly provides access to the different dwellings, but it is also used to spread and dry maize, to do and hang washing, and to perform other household tasks. Today's occupancy pattern would make the subject of a fascinating ethnographic study, but I doubt that much could be learned regarding the original uses of the *kancha*; modern living patterns and new construction have altered the original *kancha* too much.

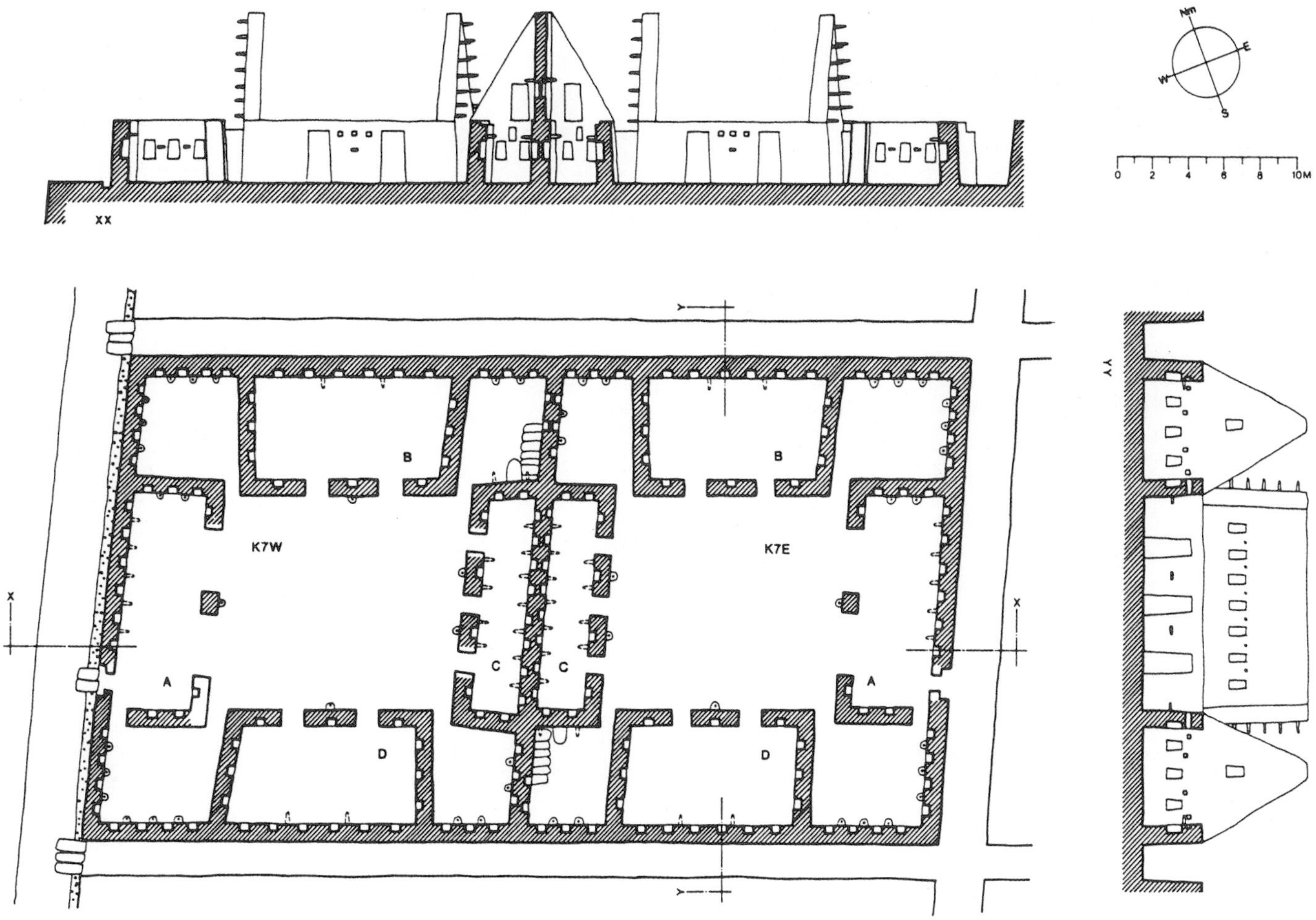

Town block composed of two *kancha*. Drawing by Jean-Pierre Protzen

Photo: Grant Mudford

The walls of R.M. Schindler's Kings Road House were highly innovative for their time (early 1920s), whether from the point of view of their tilt-up concrete-panel method of construction, their use in support of an experimental social living agenda and for their role in connecting and unifying interior and exterior spaces – the latter of which might seem counter to notions of walls' typical solidity and space-dividing form. As described below by Richard Guy Wilson in the monograph *The Architecture of R.M. Schindler*, this house was designed by Schindler for himself and his wife to live together with another professional couple; several living spaces were shared while others were privately assigned. Walls are strategically located and shaped in planar and pin-wheel forms, cut short in certain places only to be extended out into the garden in others, their panels detailed with a certain textural roughness and tapering profile as well as with small gaps in between, at once undermining their solidity yet also emphasizing their thickness – and all of this is unified by means of an overriding (and starkly contrasting) redwood roof-beam system. The Kings Road House and its garden thus embody the classic indoor/outdoor spaces and built forms of California Modernism, an architectural style – and a lifestyle – made possible by walls that are both literal and natural and, sometimes, are only implied.

Schindler's Metaphysical Walls

from *The Architecture of R.M. Schindler*
Richard Guy Wilson

An indication of Schindler's departure from orthodox modernism ... is his own dwelling, the Kings Road House (1921-22). The house is a "machine-made" house in the sense that concrete was used as a flat slab directly on the ground and for the solid enclosing walls. The walls were erected by using a tilt-slab or, as he termed it, a "SLABTILT" construction system that he derived from the designs of Irving Gill. The concrete wall slabs inclined from eight inches at the bottom to four inches at the top to create a battered appearance. Filled with several types of glazing, the thin three-inch spaces between the concrete wall units increased the sense of fortification. Untreated redwood employed in the roof, fascia, and sleeping baskets added an improvisational air to the public front. In its massing, Schindler's house might invoke a close analogy to an adobe house he had drawn while in New Mexico in 1915. Schindler would return in his various writings to the idea of the house made out of rock or earth—a sculptural mass, like the cave. And in a sense that is what Kings Road House embodies: the creation of a primitive cave merged with Schindler's new concept of space as the controlling medium. Behind the house's concrete walls, its rooms extended out through wide openings glazed with redwood mullions or covered by moveable screens onto various patios and gardens. Spatial flow was continuous between interior and exterior. He explained, "The shape of the rooms, their relation to the patios and the alternating roof levels, create an entirely new spatial interlock between the interior and the garden." To further the sense of spatial interpenetration, Schindler placed clerestory windows over many of the openings to create diverse levels of spatial movement and light. He described the Kings Road house as a "theme ... for a camper's shelter: a protected back, an open front, a fireplace and a roof." [1]

Schindler's vision of the house as a primitive shelter was intensified by the rough concrete, the untreated redwood, and the exposed timberwork of the ceiling. Instead of the flat, parallel planes of floor and ceiling beloved by modernists such as Le Corbusier or Neutra, Schindler's wooden joists stand out in relief, and ceiling heights shift to emphasize the variety of scale and the interplay of space. Large concrete fireplaces dominate one wall of most of the interior rooms, and two appear on the exterior patios. But instead of resembling typical raised hearths, where the fire is separated from the floor, Schindler's sit right on the slab or on the ground. Instead of the bright porcelain fixtures indicative of precise mechanical production, poured concrete appears in Schindler's bathroom to form the bathtub and countertop.

In its linear line and repeated geometrical motifs, the Kings Road house betrays the impact on Schindler of Frank Lloyd Wright, for whom he had worked. Some of its plain, unadorned quality might be traced to Irving Gill, whom Schindler admired. The blank frontage towards the street recalls Adolf Loos's dictum that anonymous character is appropriate to private dwellings. But other elements are purely Schindler's own. A few years after the construction of Kings Road, he explained in a newspaper column: "Our rooms will descend close to the ground and the garden will become an integral part of the house. The distinction between the indoors and the out-of-doors will disappear." He went on to claim that walls would be "few, thin, and removable," and "All rooms will become part of an organic unit, instead of being small separate boxes with peepholes."[2] The employment of modern technology with a rough edge was as Schindleresque as the harsh juxtaposition of parts. The inclined concrete walls of the entrance capped by wide redwood boards, the thin frame of the sleeping basket, and the thin slab of roof all allow for a variety of spatial inter-penetrations. Density contrasts with transparency, colors clash, and the forms appear additive, or even ad-hoc: a harsh resolution.

The Kings Road House was Schindler's manifesto about what the modern house should be. Ten years earlier he theorized that man's original home—the cave, a "timid retreat"—had, with the advent of mechanized civilization, given way to a new idea of a dwelling that conquered the elements. He wrote that the new power of the machine "has enabled him to return to nature." [3] The Kings Road House was an expression of this idea and also of how security and open space might be combined. …

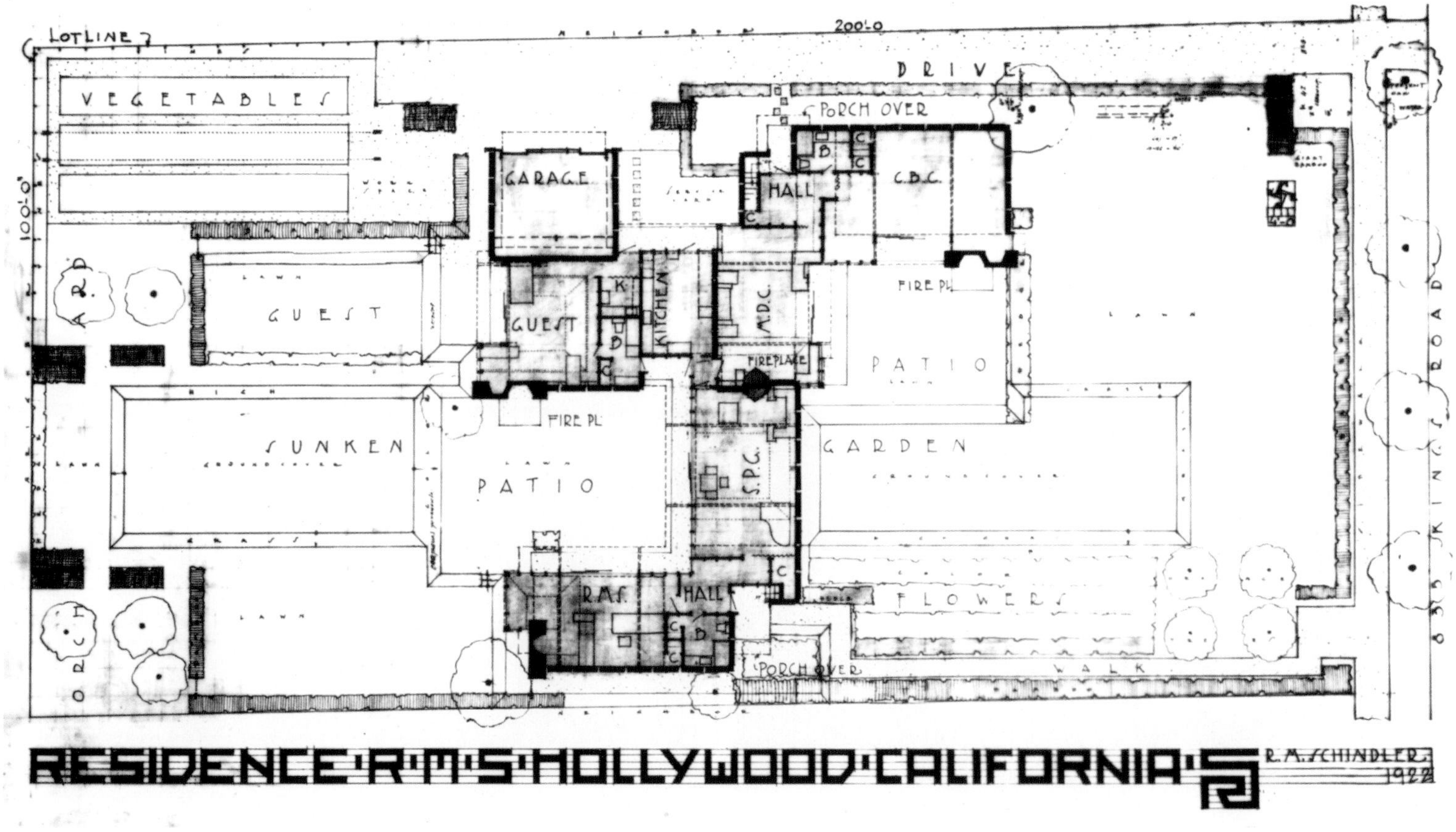

Floor plan of the Schindler House, including gardens

Church of the Cross. Photo: Mia Kang

The basic perimeter-wall form of the Inca *kancha* discussed in preceding pages is here again revisited, but this time in the context of the contemporary Church of the Cross, designed by Tadao Ando. Once again, spatial quality issues of seclusion and protection, of the careful control of light and organization of space are deliberately established by means of walls. In this instance, the walls are made of reinforced concrete – a material whose heaviness and solidity well support the contemplative program agenda as well as the gravity and lateral load-resisting functions that must be addressed. Yet, when considered from the different point of view as related here by Jin Baek in his book *Nothingness: Tadao Ando's Christian Sacred Space,* these very same concrete walls are rendered light and ephemeral through their careful detailing. Ando's precisely polished and finely finished concrete contrasts dramatically with the Inca's highly worked interlocking stones of the earlier text (as well as with, for that matter, the colors of Barragán's walls, seen earlier in this chapter). The fact that walls with very similar load-bearing and space-defining roles can be perceived so very differently is a testament to the remarkable potential of craft and detailing to transform and affect built form. Walls, when considered carefully, are most certainly not "just" walls.

Ando's Ephemeral Concrete Walls

from *Nothingness: Tadao Ando's Christian Sacred Space*
Jin Baek

> *My intent is not to express the nature of the material itself but to employ it to establish the single intent of the space. When light is drawn into it, cool, tranquil space surrounded by a clearly finished architectural element is liberated to become a soft, transparent area transcending materials. It becomes a living space that is one with the people inhabiting it. The actual walls cease to exist, and the body of the beholder is aware only of the surrounding space.*[1]

Emptiness and the Demise of Symbols

In his 1978 "The Wall as Territorial Delineation," [Ando] revealed a preference of walls over columns, with the reason that walls have no figurative quality, while columns are never completely free of the anthropomorphic connotation of the vertically standing body. The columns draw attention to themselves. In contrast, walls efface their presence and, because of this quality, are able to shape an enclosed space. He resisted the conception of the wall as the contradictory formal synthesis of the functional and symbolic demands from both inside and outside, as theorized by Robert Venturi in *Complexity and Contradiction in Architecture* (1966), and as the prop of a signboard in the everyday cityscape, a concept based on Venturi's fieldtrip to Las Vegas.[2] For Ando, when an architectural element is deprived of its signifying quality and is left with unadulterated materiality, it arouses a sense of simplicity. Giving account of his architecture of spatial emptiness with traditional Japanese architecture, Ando wrote in "From Self-Enclosed Modern Architecture towards Universality" in 1982 that:

> *In the traditional Japanese house, the wall does not actually exist. Of course walls were used. But the main aim was not to express the* simplicity *of the wood, paper, earth, and straw of which they were made. According to the traditional Japanese interpretation, architecture is always at one with nature and attempts to isolate and freeze at a point in time nature as it exists in its organic metamorphoses. In other words, it is an architecture reduced to the extremes of* simplicity *and an aesthetic devoid of actuality and attributes that it approaches theories of* Ma, *or nothingness. Further connections with nature are effected by the subtle transformations caused in part by delicate contrasts of light and shade. In all these connections it is the wall, made as light and thin as possible, that permits—or perhaps more accurately evokes—space.*[3]

Here, Ando used the term simplicity twice. In the first instance, simplicity comes from the removal of sign qualities from architectural elements, which are as a result left with pure materiality. In the second, another level of simplicity is acquired through bringing the former to extremity in which the materiality itself is transcended to almost nothing so that its actual presence is virtually negated.

Ando's comment on "the wall made as light and thin as possible" to suit "an aesthetic devoid of actuality and attributes" is somewhat apologetic of his treatment of the concrete wall. Ando's preference of the wall over the column for its lack of anthropomorphic figurative quality further leads to the process of removing materialistic sensuousness from the concrete wall. As this two-fold procedure of acquiring simplicity verifies, Ando appears to have considered the object quality of the concrete wall to be consisting in two layers: figurative quality and materiality. Ando seems to have believed that its material presence would attract as much attention as its signifying qualities. The attention aroused by an element's material appeal has somewhat the same effect as Michael Fried's critique of minimalism, the sensuous literal objecthood of the non-figurative elements.[4] The aesthetic effect brought about by elements that "do not represent, signify, or allude to anything," allowed such artists as Robert Morris to proclaim boldly "the death of author."[5] The viewer is set free from the mode of deciphering and association on account of the non-figurative quality of an element. According to Fried, however, the hollowness of the element—or meaninglessness as it has been liberated from the subjective intentions of the author—is now taken up by the sensuousness of the material itself. Put differently, materiality starts to attract one's attention to appear as the new subject matter, being encouraged by the thematic emptiness of the work. The beholder is now conversely fettered in an endless perception of the sensuousness of the element's materiality: from the rough steel meshes with tactile seduction to the reflectivity of the highly polished steel plates and to the gentle spreading of fluorescent lights into the real—not imaginary—space of gallery. In this theatrical situation, meaning never fixes itself, and the perceiver has to roam around the element as the object of inexhaustibility and indeterminacy.[6] This "presentment of endlessness" of the non-signifying element is as distractible a condition that renders the subject *attached* to the element, rather than liberated towards the world, as figurative signification.

Curiously enough, Ando's reductive path gives rise to a dilemma. The walls made of *shōji* paper in the tea room are flimsy; walls, especially load-bearing ones like the concrete walls favored by Ando himself, have thickness and heaviness, registering their recognizable presence. In his concrete construction, Ando preferred lower slump—around fifteen centimeters with thirty centimeters high slump cone, occasioning a compromise with workers who customarily demanded twenty centimeters—to secure strength of the wall. Then, Ando sought to transform contradictorily its solid presence into a self-effacing surface with a "concealed background of strength."[7] The pathos of Ando's surface thus emerges from this paradox of bringing together thinness and thickness, lightness and heaviness, and delicacy and strength.

Ando's interest in the finish quality of concrete dates back to his Tomishima House (1973). Here he first adopted exposed concrete almost solely for the matter of economy of the construction. He was not experienced enough to deal with the material under a certain architectural vision, yet this project initiated an attention to the material that persisted for the following decades. One exceptional aspect in Ando's continuous study of concrete is his interest in subtlety and smoothness of the surface. Ando did not follow the contemporaneous *béton brut* treatment. This treatment was already well-known to Japan. For instance, Antonin Raymond (1888-1976) designed in the pre-war period the Chapel of Tokyo Women's University (1934), an imitation of August Perret's (1874-1954) reinforced concrete Church of Notre Dame du Raincy (1922), and Le Corbusier designed in post-war Japan the National Museum of Western Art (1956-1965), a reinforced concrete building with a partial exposure of rough-hewn texture. This manner of treating concrete was also practiced by influential, local architects such as Kenzo Tange (1913-2005) and Kunio Maekawa (1905-1986).

In contrast with the uneven textural roughness of the surface in *béton brut* treatment, Ando sought to achieve smoothness. According to one writer, his dissatisfaction with the rough-hewn exposed concrete was partly a response to a Japanese ethos of subtlety.[8] In order to formulate an exquisitely refined surface, Ando forbade applying any release agent on the surface of wooden formwork for the reason that it could cause undesirable surface changes. He instead painted the surface of the shuttering to minimize the trace of wood grain on the concrete. He further gauged the positions of reinforcing bars as precisely as possible to have enough cover thickness between the line of the outermost bars and the shuttering. He maintained the planar quality of the shuttering as much as possible, and mixed concrete with well-rounded river pebbles, rather than rough and crude aggregates. Ando had assistants help in the vibrating process with manual rams on the day the concrete was poured in order to eliminate vapors, resulting in a smooth and non-porous solidity. The surface defects found after the shuttering was dismantled were not patched because, they would, as time passed, weather in a different phase from the remaining part of the wall and thus detract from the homogeneity of the surface. Constructed in this manner, Ando's concrete walls are rendered with homogeneously planar surfaces comprised of unpretentious rectangular grids based on the width of the shuttering boards (about ninety centimeters by one hundred and eighty centimeters). Regularly distributed holes mark the traces of cone nut separators, and horizontal seams reveal each batch of concrete pouring (about every three meters). This planarity transforms the "sculpturesque solidity and weight" of the concrete walls, which are already devoid of sign quality, so that "homogeneous surfaces" alone may truss up together to shape the space of inconspicuousness.[9]

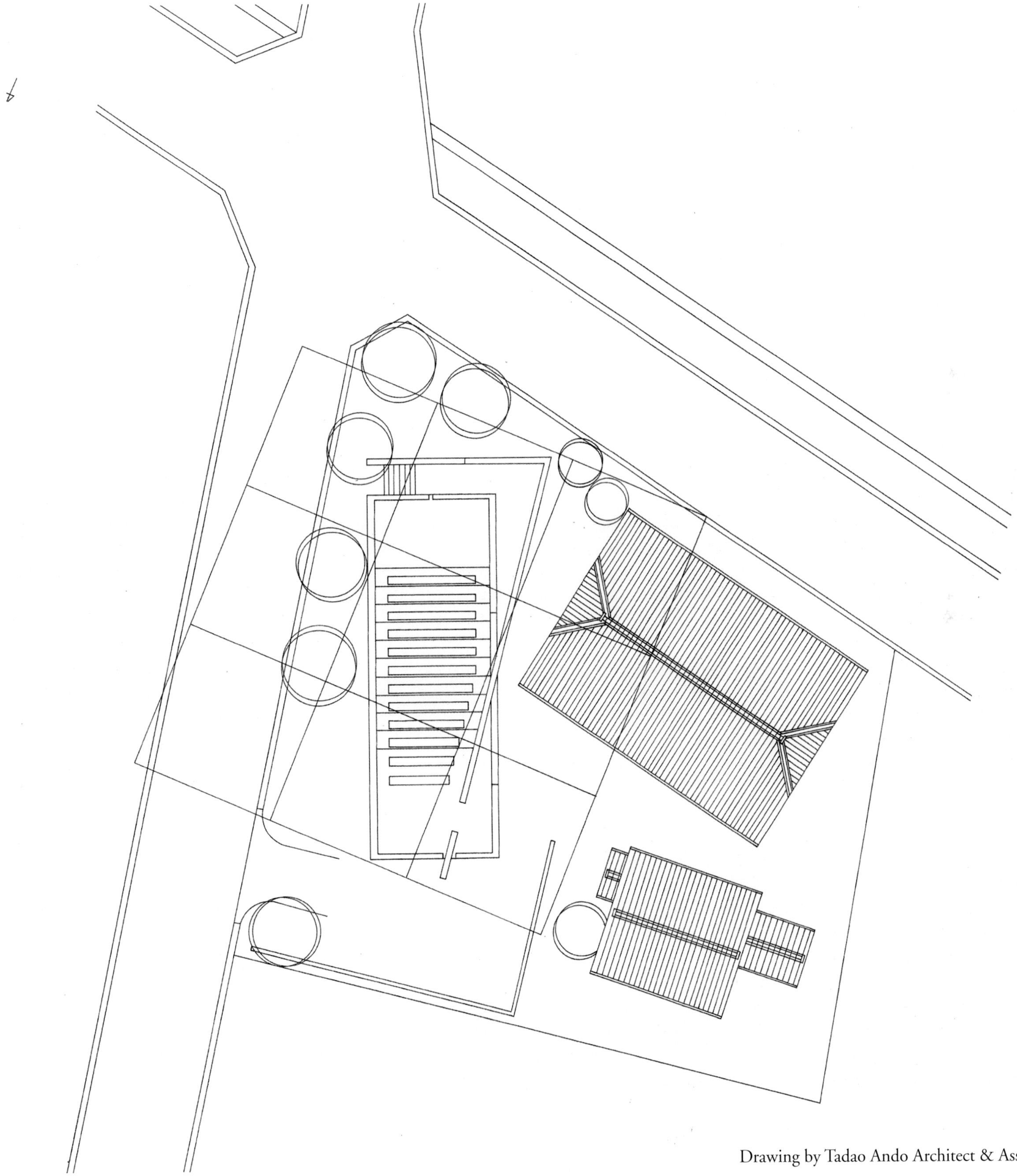

Drawing by Tadao Ando Architect & Associates

Richard Serra, "Strike: To Roberta and Rudy, 1969-1971". Photo by Peter Moore

The walls that are Richard Serra's iconic steel sculptures might be considered by some to be tangential to a discussion of architecture and structure, arguing that they really belong to the associated art of sculpture – but these two worlds overlap. Indeed, when it comes to these structures/installations, one can find in common the contemplative consideration and visceral experience of both functional and phenomenological aspects of walls: of their external form, of the view of them from a distance and upon approach, of occupied spaces, of visual perception of their internal spaces, of circulation, of "atmosphere", of material finishes, of mass and heaviness, of stability and arrested gravity, of relationship to the ground, and so on. Here, excerpted from the book *Intersection: Richard Serra*, Gottfried Böhm elaborates on these walls' remarkable qualities. His words serve well to describe what it is or, rather, what it can be to be Wall.

The Sculpted Walls of Richard Serra

from *Intersection: Richard Serra*
Gottfried Böhm

Opening Remarks

Richard Serra's works are surrounded by what can be called a *field of gravity*. We sense their gravitational pull quickly and unmistakably. To such an extent that our habitual reserve, our distance as observers are swallowed up. We in fact find ourselves going straight up to masses—often precariously rigged—that weigh several tons. No boundaries separate the work of art's space from day-to-day space here, unlike traditional art where the classical paradigms of the pedestal, the plinth and the frame distinguish between aesthetic reality and the reality of life. Serra's works inspire a direct, unprotected approach. Although we can walk into them like buildings, they still fall into the category of sculpture. Since ancient times, sculpture has always addressed itself to more than just the eye. Traditional three-dimensional works incite us to move around, appealing to our sense of touch, our physical sensibility. While carrying on from this, Serra's sculptures go much further. They engage us totally. More is involved here than a quantitative escalation that can mainly be attributed to the accumulation of great masses and weights. There is a *qualitative leap* that sets a *specific experience* in motion. It is of this experience that we shall be talking.

Our methodology is founded on the experience that viewers undergo, but we shall not dwell merely on subjective sensation. Analysis and reconstruction must seek to ascertain the *conditions* that underlie experiences. In order to cast light on what Serra's sculptures are, it is not enough solely to look at facts about the works. Their true meaning is manifested in the effect they have. Yet this is something that is difficult to talk about and that often occurs through an indirect speaking that must be constantly verified against the work.

It is therefore extremely fortunate that the three sculptures by Serra on public exhibition in Basel represent the full spectrum of his work since the late 1960s. These works are, in chronological order, *Inverted House of Cards* (1968/69), which is on permanent loan to the Museum für Gegenwartskunst from the Emanuel Hoffmann Foundation, *Open Field Vertical/Horizontal Elevations (for Breughel and Martin Schwander)* (1979/80) in the Wenken Park in Riehen, and *Intersection* (1992) on the plaza in front of the City Theatre.[1] As well as covering a period of more than twenty years, these three sculptures are representative of Serra's three most important types of work: indoor sculptures, sculptures in landscape and urban sculptures. A tour around Basel can also be a path for gaining a comprehensive insight into Serra's work. So let us take this tour—supplemented by references to works in other locations—while bearing in mind that it is far less helpful to emphasise Serra's *development* than to examine the *artistic questions* he asks. Those questions' richness is demonstrated by the fact that Serra does *not* definitively answer them when he addresses them, but often takes them up again years later, in a different, more highly developed form.

Distance and Proximity. Modes of Perception

How are we to obtain specific experiences from Serra's sculptures? Certainly only when we enter their field of gravity. We must, however, realise that the beginning of this path lies still at quite some *distance* from the work, but already in an excellent position for viewing it. For only from a distance, preferably from an elevated vantage point, do we see the sculpture as a *whole*, perceive it as a form. This vista is lost to us even as we take our next few steps. All we can see on drawing closer is a succession of *partial views*. This shift in visibility can also be reproduced on photos. It is only at a distance that the sculpture's *plan* emerges clearly, whereas from close up we see its *elevation* or, to be more precise, partial views of its upward-striving components.

It is generally also from a distance and from above that the logic of Serra's constructions is most clearly apparent. In the case of *Inverted House of Cards*, it consists of an interlocked joint forming an inaccessible centre where the four sheets of lead arranged at right angles all *touch one another* and, as a result of that touching, all *hold one another up*. What one sees *from above* is a star-shaped geometric arrangement that masks the minimal deviations created by the angles of incline. Yet it is only thanks to this slight incline from the perpendicular that the sheets of lead Serra has *propped up* against one another also *hold one another up*. They stand because they all *simultaneously tend to fall*. A single sheet of steel on its own, with no reciprocal relationship to others, would never remain upright unless it were secured by one technical device or another, for example were anchored in a foundation. Serra is, however, interested solely in the *apparent* logic of his constellations. As we have seen, he follows the laws of geometry and gravity sculpturally rather than mathematically or physically. He is therefore no more a constructive sculptor than he is a minimalist object artist who works with simple, straightforward cubes, like Donald Judd, or who spreads out a steel square composed of part-squares on the floor, like Carl Andre.

Rationality and clarity of construction are, however, also fundamental for Serra. Models of all his works could be built using the very simplest elements. This is suggested by some of Serra's titles, at least by that of *House of Cards*, which recalls a children's game. A game, moreover, that owes its fascination to the precariousness with which the cards are arranged, to the player's skill in averting collapse. Serra always works with simple components—rectangular or curved sheets of lead or steel, metal slabs, dense cubes that are exceptionally heavy for a given volume, cylinders, rods, rolled lead sheets, to name but some—arranging them in a constellation, in a relationship to one another that has sometimes also been described, by extension, as '*montage*'. There is a quality of the *haphazard*, the *provisional* that cannot be overlooked and that contrasts sharply with the materials' bulk and weight. Together, these two qualities create the precariousness that is characteristic of Serra's works and that is often associated with an impression of danger and menace. That impression sometimes results from only a very slight deviation from the horizontal or the vertical. This slight deviation is endowed with the very greatest artistic value. For it has a twofold effect: It ensures that the constellation stands up (or, in one-part works, is correctly positioned in relation to the ground) and it arouses strong feelings. It serves both the *construction* and *emotion*.[2]

As we have already said, a Serra sculpture shows itself as a *whole* when we look at it from a distance. But does the *sculpture*, too, reveal itself to our gaze? Or is it not rather its mere anatomy, a lifeless skeleton—and not yet that energy-charged construct whose powerful effect on us will be discussed subsequently. The generous distance from the work acts as a 'cordon sanitaire' that objectivises the sculpture, subduing its emotional qualities. Those qualities are submerged in a cognitive approach that recognises the work solely as a given fact with quantifiable characteristics (height, mass, shape, weight, and so on). The different experiences offered by distance and proximity correspond to characteristics possessed by the work. What are those characteristics? What turns a rational construct into a powerful work? Is it ultimately only our personal sensitivity that can be held responsible for it, do we act in a psychological drama that feeds on our need to project ourselves? Is sculpture's effect in fact open to rational analysis?[3]

As we draw close, we at first experience a *loss*: We cease to have an overall view, we can no longer perceive the form of the work. This is, however, offset by a significant *gain*, a gain in intensity. The quantitative totality of the overall view is replaced by a new quality which, paradoxically, results from partial views whose emotional power *maximises* our experience in a different way.

Proximity offers us a succession of sudden views. What we *know* about the sculpture can no longer be verified *visually*, particularly as the works can be entered, possess no intangible, sacrosanct sphere. Instead of what has been called the *aura* of a work (a certain proximity, remote as it may seem), another potential builds up: a *field of gravity* that penetrates us to the marrow.

It is impressive to see how Serra's works attain sensual fullness as we draw close to them. The long-distance supremacy of the *optical* gives way to a presence that, as we saw, has a direct effect on our entire body, touches our *physical sensibility*. Mere impressions of colour and shape materialise into the rusty, porous surface of metal, the stubborn indestructibility of steel, the downward-bearing heaviness of forged cubes, the matt but shimmering sheen of lead surfaces. We become sensitive to mass and heaviness, our sense of equilibrium reacts to the interlocked elements, we begin to feel vulnerable, we become aware of an imminent threat. We would, however, misunderstand Serra's sculptures if we were to attribute these feelings solely to their heightened quantum. While it is true that Serra generally works with weights and masses that far surpass a human being's physical strength, the intensity of his sculptures' effect results from an intentional artistic act, not from the work of a crane. *He raises up* in an act that catches us in its thrall.

Height and Heaviness. The Act of Raising Up

Only when Serra's sculptures are freestanding, attain their true height, interact with the *vertical* does their *impact* unfold. The height and other characteristics of the chosen elements, each work's intended location and the situation are meticulously calculated by Serra to achieve this impact. He aims not at absolute height but at giving his sculptures the possibility to *reveal* themselves—depending on the logic of the chosen constellation. This visual finding could also be paraphrased by the image '*downward momentum*' which, far from coincidentally, is also drawn from physics. In its basic meaning in that field, it signifies the level of kinetic energy resulting from the nature of the slope: the force experienced by a ball that rolls down it. In the case of sculpture, visual experiences stand in the foreground, with the psychic, the material and the non-material being closely interconnected. Downward momentum thus becomes a powerful artistic image. As well as describing a *distance travelled downwards* that has complex effects, it also emphasises the role of the vertical. *Height* and *weight* are correlated. Only because of this may we speak of a downward momentum, of a potential to fall. It is, as we saw, created through precarious relationships. They evoke those powerful impressions that affect us physically.

The act of raising up is a response, with the repertoire used by Serra, to a given situation. It is, in fact, an act through which Serra deals with some of the physical conditions of nature and human life: particularly the oppressive, binding impact of heaviness which, inherently invisible, is only *seen* when the earth's inertia meets a permanently exposed force. This occurs in the sculptural act I have mentioned. *Intersection, House of Cards* and *Open Field*, a low sculpture composed of ten steel cubes that follows the slope of the land, are each a very different expression of this. The most dramatic formulation of this primordial act of Serra's sculpture is to be found in *Delineator*, in which we enter the open space between a sheet of steel lying on the floor and a second, parallel one attached to the ceiling. The space is charged with great energy, turns into a danger zone that we need little imagination to experience.[4] We abruptly come up against powers that not only impress us but also affect us existentially, because they could lead to our certain death. Our sensations are less acute when a sculpture's potential is established in the horizontal. We find the simplest formulation of this possibility in *Strike*. One of the room's four corners contains a more than head-high rectangular wall of steel, rigged at an angle of 45° and pointing towards the centre. The density of the sculpture's space is experienced very differently, with the space seeming compressed where the sheet of steel touches the wall, open but threatening where it juts out into the room.

With his act of raising up, Serra carries on from age-old cultural traditions, in which the origin of sculpture may also be presumed to lie. Raising up stones (single ones or steeply layered piles), erecting menhirs or groups of monoliths (such as Stonehenge), putting up topping-out trees, hewn pillars or obelisks belong to the most ancient stratum of cultural activity, which continues to make its impact felt today. The purpose of this activity was, in particular, to give orientation (as in the case of signposts), to provide markings (as in the case of graves), to act as a memorial or cult object, and to create a sense of permanence.

The inherent power of what is raised up is one of man's primary cultural experiences and, as such, deeply rooted physically, psychically and anthropologically. Figurative statues and monuments mounted on pedestals carry on from this, if only because their fall prostrates the vertical and all its power, a significant, awe-inspiring implication. The work of art's fall also signifies the decline and death of what it represents.

This brief look at the historical background is intended to heighten our receptiveness to Serra's work with raised up elements. Not because he uses an archaic language, operates with cultural reminiscences or alludes to them.[5] His world is a modern one, a world of industry and its factories, of large cities, complex societies and their need for aesthetic direction—even if the titanic, fire-spewing, disruptive technology of heavy industry has in the meantime been supplanted by electronic machines with their subtle networks and bundled switches. Serra implants a downward momentum, a tendency to fall, a latency (that will in fact never be realised) in his heavy, industrially produced building components. What merely *exists* as a steel building component in, for example, a metalworks or a machine-shop takes on meaningful visual qualities, is endowed with *iconic power*, becomes a work of art through the calculated act of being raised up, through its artistically achieved eccentricity. Not only because it is thereby withdrawn from direct use but also because it gives visible form to the sculptural dimensions of mass, weight, tangibility and the *flow of energy* between above and below.

In everyday life these feelings have generally been lost. Even at the foot or on the roof of a skyscraper, we rarely have a sense of that Babylonian yearning for height which distinguishes human civilisation. When we do, however, it occurs not because of an intentional creation whose uselessness and artistic self-evidence are capable, first and foremost, of opening our eyes. Serra does not just extend elementary experiential spaces through his work: He shapes them, he gives them critical form.

The power of the vertical derives in each case from a meticulously formulated ambivalence. Each of the works possesses a *turning point* at which the rationality of the sculpture gives way to a direct emotional and physical impact. Serra uses gravity's natural downward-striving tendency to articulate this energisation, which embraces our eye, our emotions, our sense of balance and our physical sensibility. Gravity is *overcome not architectonically* (it is not neutralised through the stability of a building) but by being transferred *tectonically* or, to be more precise, *sculpturally* into a state where it can be experienced. Serra neither denies nor celebrates gravity. He makes it both the theme and the medium of a deliberate artistic act, which, because it counteracts gravity by raising up, simultaneously suspends its potential and makes it visible. …

Time and Intensity

The intertwining of a work of art's space and its viewer's movements is a general quality of sculpture. Ancient artefacts (menhirs, obelisks and so on) demonstrate this, as does the history of European sculpture. When we walk around Michelangelo's *David*, for example, we integrate the multiple views into a coherent whole. Our experience of the work's completeness is built up from partial perceptions, the figure's *spatial presence* is refined and heightened as we *walk around* it. What can be described as principal views or preferred directions of access certainly exist for both figurative and abstract sculptures. Accordingly, there are also subsidiary views that are less fertile or show the figure off to poor advantage. One can to this extent talk of visual hiatuses, observe discontinuity. Manneristic sculpture's maxim "Equally beautiful from all sides" can certainly not be historically generalised.[6] If we tried to focus on a centre in a Serra sculpture and to optimise it while we walked around, it would remain empty or indifferent. Serra has no interest in the harmonious integration of viewers' successive gazes. What we experience in time does not merge into a whole, it does not become a concept of balance (not even a fragile balance), harmony or beauty.[7] But what is the content of this experience in time that manifests itself in abrupt change?

An anecdote that Serra himself recounts from his early childhood comes to mind at this point. However much of a (legitimate) autobiographical stylisation it might be, it has the quality of a seminal scene, above all when we are seeking to understand the intertwining of sculptural spaces with specific temporal impulses. Serra tells how as a four year-old, in 1943, he was taken by his father to visit the shipyard where he worked. It was the day of the launching of a large ship that was still in drydock, a huge steel vessel that seemed to the child to resemble a skyscraper on its side. He and his father walked along the hull, overwhelmed by the steep metal walls and the towering masses. Suddenly the colossus started to move, sliding noisily and swayingly into the water before finding its new equilibrium there. In conclusion, Serra says: "All the raw material that I needed is contained in the reserve of this memory which has become a reoccurring dream."[8]

Raw material: It means not just industrial steel and factories (instead of the studio) but also the seminal role of the *situation* which, viewed literally, brings with it both a *spatial* and a *temporal* index. Situations are spaces in time. Raw material ultimately also means the dramatic nature of the event, the *disproportion* between the towering vastness of what has been made and the perspective of a child, with its sudden overwhelming quality that has remained unforgettable.

The point of this anecdote fits readily into our observations regarding Serra's works. At the centre lies a *shift* between what things are and the way we perceive them, a shift that can have various aspects but that is crucial to Serra's entire artistic concept. It is only through this discrepancy that the specific downward momentum between material and effect, between rational construct and its emotional consequences, can come into play. The sculptural elements become charged with a power to which we, as viewers, cannot relate if we keep our distance. This power touches, disturbs and upsets us. The dismantling of the boundary between the work's space and our space heightens the immediacy of the confrontation.

The content of this experience has to do with the act of raising up. The sculpture appears to be elevated, upward-striving. The translation of our visual findings back into Latin takes us a step further, for it brings us to 'sublimis', the Latin word for sublime. We would, however, achieve very little if we were merely to mention this word now or were simply to apply to Serra the sublimeness debate that was conducted in the 1980s, not least with respect to American postwar art.[9] It would soon be agreed that Serra's renunciation of a strategy that leads to contemplative peace in the face of an aesthetic totality has to do with the transition from an art of the beautiful to an art of the sublime. However, details about what this transition entails in Serra's case are hardly likely to be gleaned from texts by Burke, Kant or other theorists. The path that recommends itself is rather the reverse one of reviewing the works' structural characteristics and the way we experience them to identify sublime aspects.

Before we do so, however, it is worth taking a brief look at Barnett Newman who, with his postwar painting and his writings on art, particularly 'The Sublime is Now!', made a major contribution to the change of paradigm, in which Serra in his way also participates. There are startling analogies between Serra's works with large rectangular sheets of steel propped up at various angles against walls and certain paintings by Newman, for example *Vir heroicus sublimis*. The purpose of such a comparison is not to suggest any borrowing from earlier artists or the like. However, Newman's paintings, which he wanted viewers to see *close up*, were intended to overwhelm (as does proximity in the case of Serra's sculptures). Newman wanted viewers to experience a state of perceptive overload, he wanted the pictorial field and the viewer's perceptive capacity to be disproportionate to one another. The relationship between the sheer dimensional aspects of Newman's painting (the large canvases, the energy of the paint, the role of the vertical, the renunciation of an aesthetic of beauty and balance) and the sheer dimensional aspects of Serra's sculpture (the unworked sheets of steel, their materiality, their downward momentum, the importance of height and the vertical, the renunciation of aesthetic correspondences) makes it clear that Serra returns to artistic questions that had preoccupied Newman earlier. The two men certainly arrive at different solutions, but the maxim formulated by Newman also casts a certain amount of light on Serra's sculpture: "I became involved with the idea of making the viewer present: the idea that 'Man is Present'."[10]

The *upward-striving* (sublime) has specific qualities in Serra's work. Those qualities relate first and foremost to the sculptural medium, to the way Serra uses it. In traditional sculpture, the basic sculptural elements such as volume, weight, surface and touch were already confirmed and transformed in many different ways, not infrequently to the extent of their complete elimination, something to which, for example, Giacometti aspired when he combined the tangibility and heaviness of a standing figure with the quality of its appearance at an "absolute distance" (Sartre). Serra enriches the repertoire of sculpture's basic elements in a different way. First of all, he transfers the sculptural process from the realm of the hand (and its tools) to that of industrial technology. This results in a new spectrum of expression. The sculptor's traditional sublimation of his materials (stone, bronze, wood) is replaced by a process that imbues physical and material qualities with a direct and powerful presence, rather than altering them. Whatever it is that we now experience as sublime, as elevated, it is not an *aesthetic idea* but something that *happens to our senses* in the field of gravity. The sublime is bound up with intense sensations that are triggered physically and experienced emotionally. It is a *maximum* that is connected with time if for no other reason than because it cannot be perceived once and for all, cannot be brought under control. Our experience takes place interactively, abruptly, suddenly. It cannot be separated from our participation. For all the discontinuity to which it is subject, our experience does not occur just anywhere, but within the horizon of a given work. However much the disproportion that has been described isolates us, affects us existentially (as has sometimes been said), what happens takes one form in one place and another elsewhere, it possesses individual qualities that depend on the works' different features.[11] The debate about the sublime has all too often used art as a mere example to help elucidate a category or a conclusion. The specific characteristics and sensuous qualities of individual works are, however, crucial for the purposes of an interpretation. Their diversity must not be obscured or obliterated by conceptual considerations. In this sense the path of experience along which the three works exhibited in Basel have taken us has not been completed, but must be repeated.

Through Serra's accentuation of the intense, time acquires a crucial role in the sculptural process. Effects can neither be experienced nor described without temporal means. What seems from a distance to be a stable construct gains energy close up. There is a turning-point, a peripeteia. This turning-point is that not of a narrative but of a sculptural reality: It has to do with resistance, height, heaviness, denseness and so on. Serra's sculptures are spaces for human experience, they cause us to explore both them and ourselves, to probe the limits of our sensuous capacity, and, in the most pointed and dramatic works, to come face to face with the boundaries of our own finiteness. This is the significance of works like *Delineator* and *Tot.*[12] Serra does not thematise human beings in his sculptures. Quite the contrary: He does everything in his power to eradicate the very last thematic allusions, to counteract symbolic and narrative readability. Precisely because his works are totally naked, make no attempt to offer a mirror of human knowledge, recollection and events, because the mirror into which we look is quite blank, we find ourselves transferred to a state where the flow of everyday life seems interrupted. We have the chance to come face to face with ourselves, mortals whose *hope* lies in the fact of our being subject to definitive boundaries.[13]

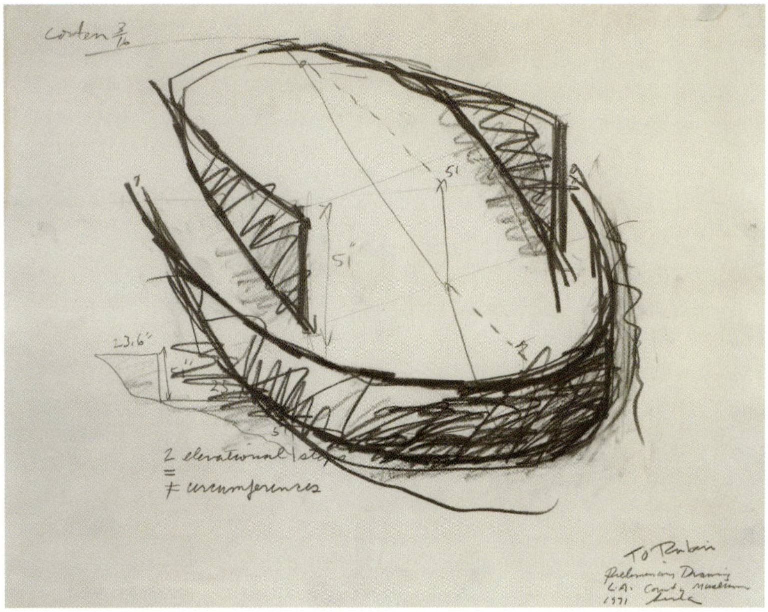

Richard Serra sketch

Walls That Divide and Connect

Palafolls Public Library, Catalonia, Spain (2007)
Architect: Miralles Tagliabue EMBT
Structural Engineer: STATIC, Gerardo González, Nilo Lletjós (IOC)
Model: Melissa Simonetti

Alex Gaultier

Sunk one meter into the ground in order to permit the neighboring houses to have an uninterrupted view of the surrounding mountains, the public library for the town of Palafolls is a modest but nonetheless highly expressive single-story building. Its chief organizing principle is established by an array of curved-in-plan walls that subdivide both the building's internal spaces and the adjacent grassed parkland; but these walls that spread out like tentacles also physically connect the building's interior rooms with their immediate exterior space and the more distant landscape views. The space of the building is thus not limited by its enclosed volume, but rather is established by the curved walls that run from the inside out, and vice versa.

There is no attempt here to hide the fact that the walls are actually roughly cast concrete; rather, their thin brick masonry facing is applied in irregular strips that clearly reveals the actual structural material. Propped up by these curved walls as well as by several free-standing columns are a number of steel beams that span the rooms of the library at unexpected, crisscrossing angles to support a vaulting, metal-clad roof. On the inside, the white-painted curved ceiling and light gray steel beams and columns contrast with the red, rustic walls. This non-linear and seemingly ad-hoc arrangement of walls, beams, columns and vaults offers an informal visual expression that is associated with the Deconstructivist movement in architecture.

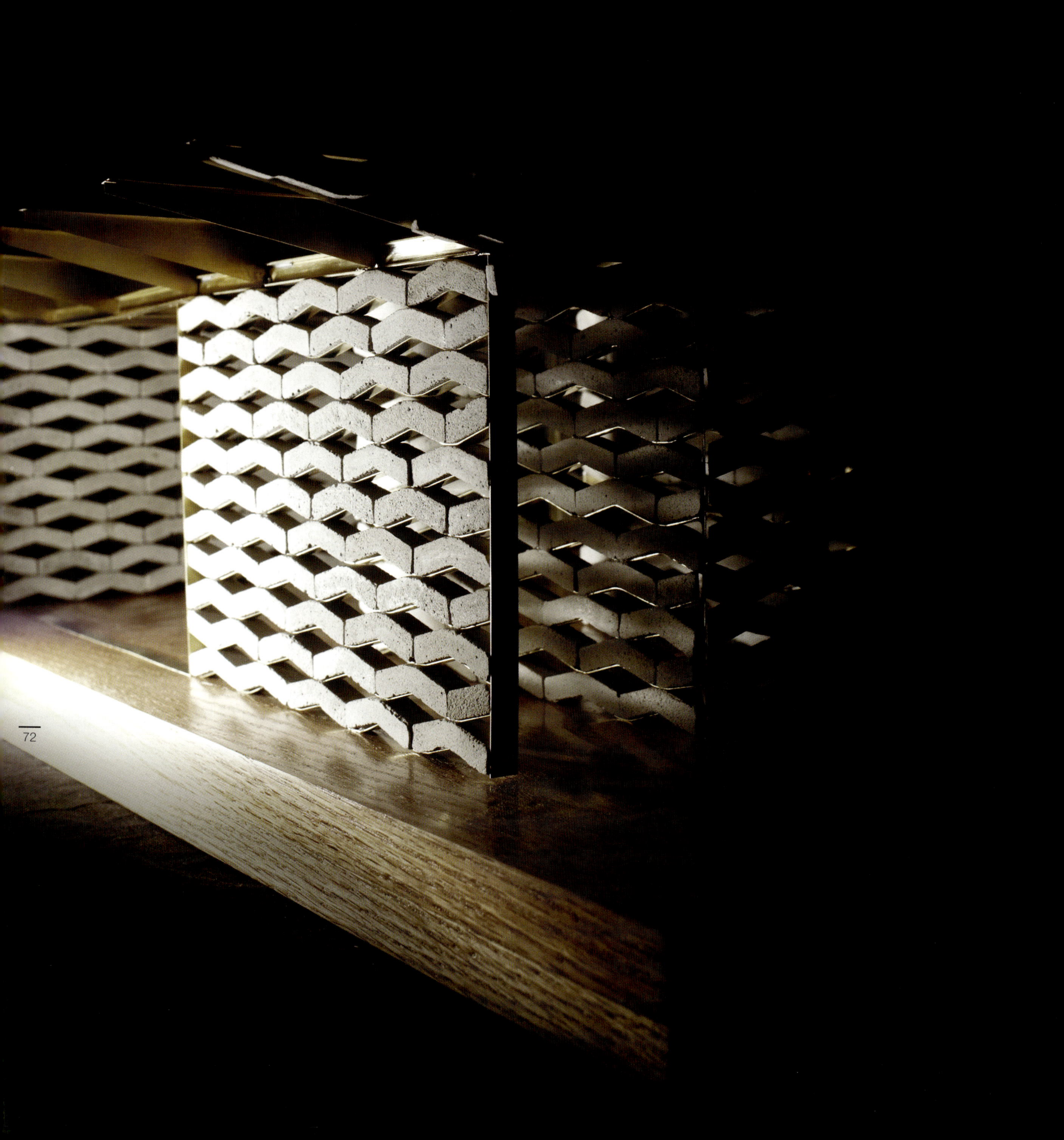

Daici Ano

Contemporary Masonry Wall

Chokkura Plaza and Shelter Community Center,
Takanezawa, Japan (2005)
Architect: Kengo Kuma & Associates
Structural Engineer: Oak Structural Design Office
Model: Prim Chanarat + Max Silverstein

Part of a town's urban renewal, this project comprises a community center situated in a former rice warehouse and a newly constructed gallery. The use in both buildings of the traditional Ooya stone, a soft and easily worked igneous rock that is quarried locally, connects the two parts. The gallery consists of several small pavilions unified under a single roof; supporting the roof are distinctive lattice-patterned stone walls. The Ooya stones are cut into angled shapes and stacked on a discreet bent steel plate armature; the resulting diamond-shaped openings at once allow for a degree of both transparency and privacy, and for a pleasant light to seep in.

Roland Halbe

Reusable Timber Walls

Swiss Sound Box, Hanover, Germany (2000)
Architect: Peter Zumthor Architect
Structural Engineer: Conzett, Bronzini Partner AG
Model: Garrett Knoll + Adrianne Ngam

Designed as a place to rest at the 2000 Hanover Expo, this temporary pavilion offered the public multiple secluded spaces in which to listen to music or enjoy refreshments. Its walls were configured into an orthogonal system of 12 modules that created a labyrinth of tall and narrow spaces. In certain places this arrangement was opened up to make "rooms" for relaxing and gathering. The nearly 9m (30ft) tall walls were made of horizontally stacked pieces of 100 x 200mm (4 x 8in) lumber spaced apart by 45 x 45mm (2 x 2in) cross-pieces, the whole given structural integrity by a finely detailed post-tensioning system of steel rods. The shrinkage and creep that occurs in green lumber, calculated here to be more than 200mm (8in), necessitated two re-tensioning operations during the Exposition, making the Swiss pavilion a truly "living" building. The walls were dismantled after the Expo and their timber reused. [see also pp. 43, 87, 338]

Bart van Hoek

A Solid Wall Volume

Bruder Klaus Field Chapel, Mechernich, Germany (2007)
Architect: Peter Zumthor Architect
Structural Engineers: Jurg Buchli, Claus Jung
Model: Luke Erickson + Apexa Patel

This rural chapel was built in honor of a 15th century hermit Saint Niklaus von Flüe, known as Bruder Klaus. It is set in the middle of a field as a monolithic block of reddish-yellow concrete with few exterior signs to reveal its sacred function. Indeed, it is only upon entering this stark prismatic volume that visitors encounter a spiritual atmosphere of seclusion and religious mysticism. A cave-like space lit from an opening high above is formed by casting concrete against 112 pine logs used as near-vertical shuttering, logs that were later burnt out to leave bas-relief projecting ribs between concave depressions in the charred concrete wall surface.

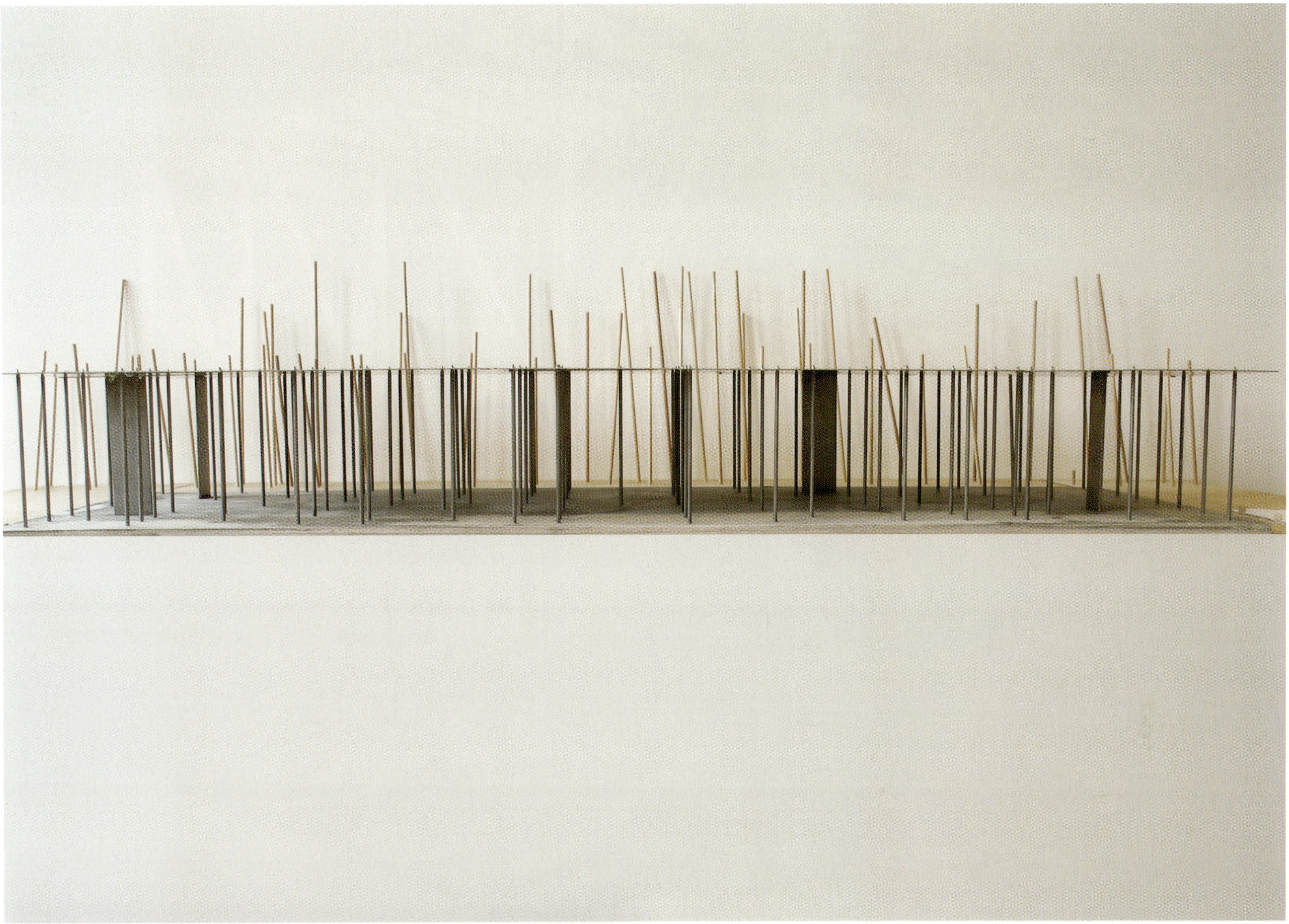

wakiiii

Minimalist Walls

Koga Park Café, Ibaraki, Japan (1998)
Architect: Kazuyo Sejima + Ryue Nishizawa & Associates
Structural Engineer: Sasaki Structural Consultants
Model: Victor Chea

This building subordinates its presence to the surrounding park: the café is enclosed in glass and the presence of structure is minimized. Ironically, the latter is achieved with a large number of slender, closely spaced steel columns that each only need to carry small gravity loads from the thin roof plate. Furthermore, the structure is stabilized against lateral loads by four steel plate shear walls; two are aligned in each of the orthogonal directions. These walls are barely visible in the finished building: their high material strength permits exceptionally small dimensions and the steel plates are clad with mirrored stainless steel that reflects the surroundings.

Paul Warchol

Combined System: Walls and Skeletal Frame

ArtsQuest Center at SteelStacks, Bethlehem, PA, USA (2010)
Architect: Spillman Farmer Architects, Structural Engineer: Barry Isett & Associates
Model: XiaoXiao Li + Ying Xu

Part of a plan to revitalize an abandoned steel plant in the American Rust Belt, this four-story building houses performance spaces and cinemas and is located directly across from the old blast furnaces of the historic Bethlehem Steel. Appropriately, steel is prominently expressed here as a building material, with a structural framework left exposed and painted bright orange. Service cores, in contrast, are made of reinforced concrete; these serve structurally to stabilize the building against lateral forces and in so doing allow the frame to be visually lighter and spatially more open than it otherwise could be. The concrete walls are made of precast panels; two-story high elements are stacked, one on top of another and connected to each other and to the steel framework – the composite system is thus made to work as one. The form and materiality of the concrete walls visually contrasts with the brightly painted steel and the precision of its section profiles. [see also p. 224]

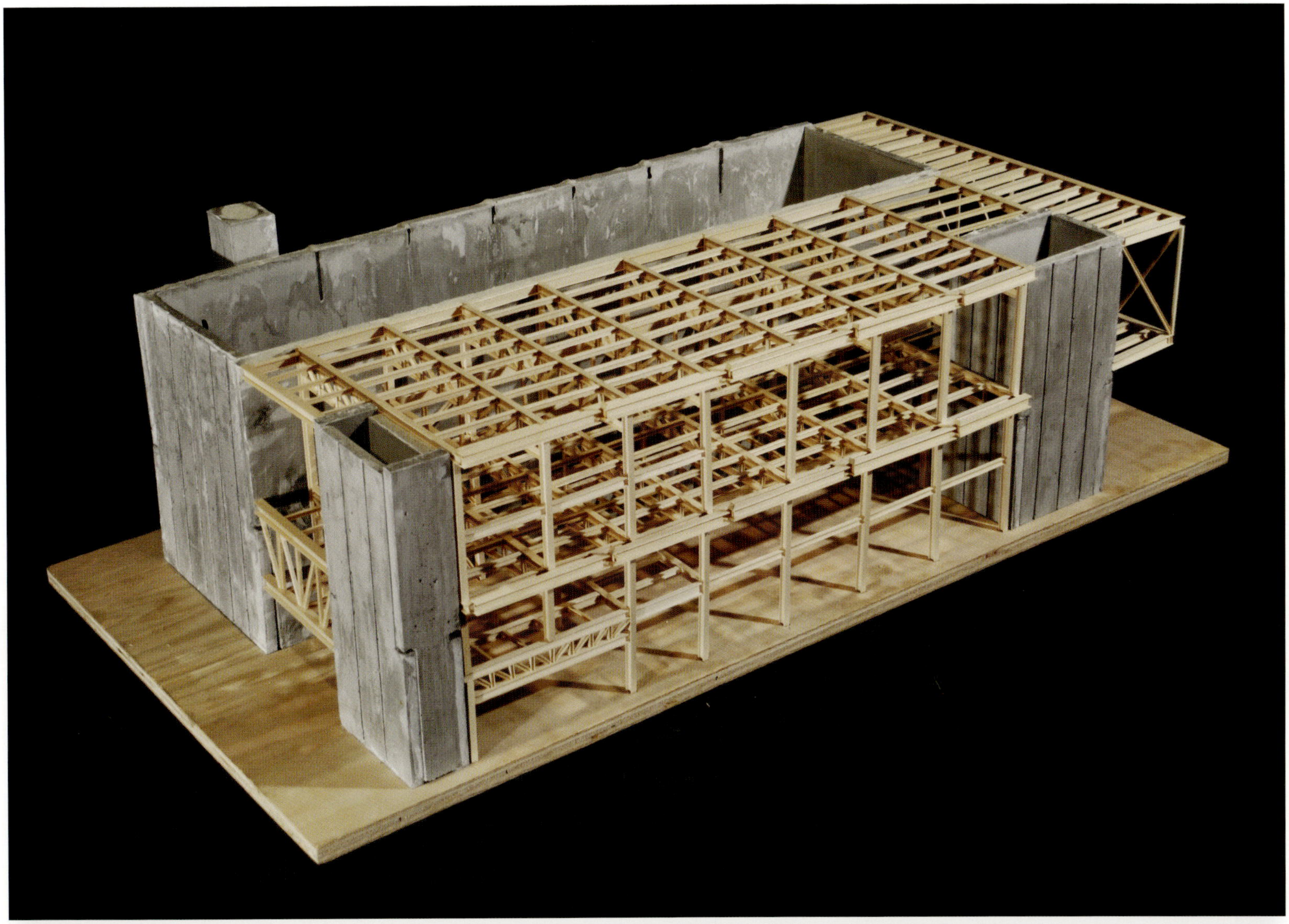

Richard Anderson

Wall Variations

Samitaur Tower, Culver City, CA, USA (2010)
Architect: Eric Owen Moss Architects, Structural Engineer: Arup
Model: Danica Davis + Lucy Márquez

The Samitaur Tower has multiple observation platforms looking out over an area of urban renewal. It is located next to a busy street intersection and a light rail line station connecting to downtown Los Angeles; as such, the tower is also designed to reflect the activities of and be viewed by many people who are in motion; several large curving screens display information about local events as well as film and video art.

Among the striking structural features of the tower is its angled wall assembly made of two 12.5mm (1/2") thick steel plates stiffened by rolled sections welded to their inside surface. These walls' irregular configurations support five circular floor plates that project outward in different directions, giving the tower its skewed exterior appearance. With its overall form and stark industrial materials and finishes the Samitaur Tower's structure is an unambiguous expression of its public function and cultural context.

01. Doubly-curved shell walls shelter space – Jubilee Church, Rome, Italy, 2003; Richard Meier & Partners (arch.); Arup, Italcementi (eng.); model by Timothy Liddell **02,03. Wall carries loads, provides stability, defines space** – Kunsthaus, Bregenz, Austria, 1997; Peter Zumthor (arch.); Robert Manahl (eng.); model by Luiz Arturo Corso & Erin Pellegrino **04. Wall carries loads, provides stability, defines space** – Rokko Housing I, Kobe, Japan, 1983; Tadao Ando (arch.); model by Yu-Liang Chen **05. Pre-existing gas-storage wall supports conical trussed roof** – The Round Building, Mellor Cutlery Factory, Hathersage, UK, 1989; Hopkins Architects; Whitby and Bird (eng.); model by Mike Pritchard **06,09. Meandering walls define lower level spaces; trussed structure overlaid on top** – Austrian Pavilion, Shanghai, China, Expo 2010; SPAN and Zeytinoglu Architects; Thomas Lorez ZT GmbH (eng.); model by Andres Romero Pompa & Daniel Tompkins **07. Earthbound foundation walls vs. steel framed structure above** – T-House, Wilton, NY, USA, 1992; Simon Ungers & Tom Kinslow (arch.); Ryan-Biggs Associates (eng.); model by Andre Guimond **08. Curved walls define lower level; shallow oval dome provides roof over main space** – Atsushi Imai Memorial Gymnasium, Odate, Japan, 2002; Shigeru Ban Architects; TIS & Partners (eng.); model by Olivia Cho & Ashley Mendelsohn **10. Diagrid structure makes for relatively open walls** – Francis Gregory Library, Washington, DC, USA, 2012; Adjaye Associates (arch.); ReStl Designers, Inc. (eng.); model by Iroha Ito & Whitney Liang **11. Walls allow museum to "inhabit" the earth** – The Museum of the Earth, Ithaca, NY, USA, 2003; Weiss/Manfredi (arch.); Weidlinger Associates (eng.); model by Lauren Bass **12. Wall acting as backdrop to inhabited space** – Meadow House, Kirkland, WA, USA, 1993; Olson Kundig (arch.); model by Katherine Richardson

07

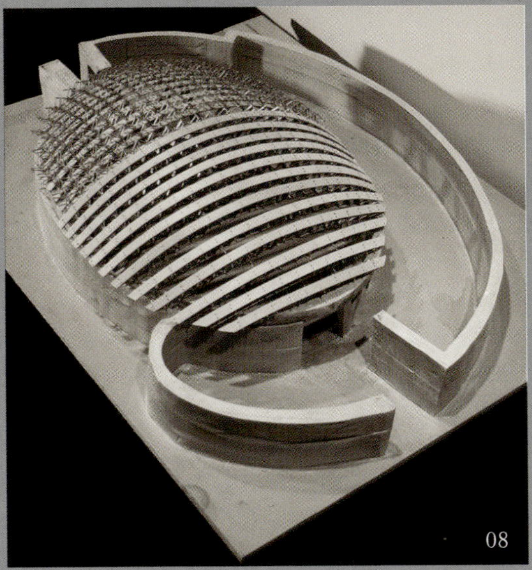
08

09

10

11

12

13

14

15

18

16

17

19

20

23

21

22

13,15. Precast concrete planking define perimeter walls; lighting effects and stair/furniture support ensue – Layer House, Kobe, Japan, 2003; Hiroaki Ohtani (arch.); Koichi Touki, Toshiro Hojo (eng.); model by Lisa Corkum & Gideon Stone **14. Shear wall helps stabilize skeletal steel framework** – Seattle Public Library, Seattle, WA, USA, 2004; OMA, LMN (arch.); Magnusson Klemencic Associates, Arup (eng.); model by Chris Leonberg **16. Space-defining walls topped with contrasting light roof structure** – Shima Art Museum, Shima, Japan, 1993; Naito Architects & Associates (arch.); Structural Design Group Co, Ltd. (eng.); model by Siobhan Rockcastle **17. Walls of conflicting geometry and materiality: contemporary vs. historical** – Bundeswehr Military History Museum, Dresden, Germany, 2011; Studio Libeskind (arch.); GSE Ingenieur-Gesselschaft mbh (eng.); model by Ngaire Stuart-Gorgora & Alexander Zink **18. Formwork-defined wall surface texture** – Bank of London and South America, Buenos Aires, Argentina, 1966; Clorindo Testa SEPRA (arch.); model by Evan Ahn & Michael Lee **19. Pinwheel wall arrangement in plan reorients spaces; roof beam overlay unifies the whole** – Schindler House, West Hollywood, CA, USA, 1922; Rudolf M. Schindler (arch.); model by Maria Gorodetskaya **20,21,22. Walls made from stacked wood planks post-tensioned together; anchorage details** – Swiss Pavilion, Hanover, Germany, Expo 2000; Peter Zumthor (arch.); Conzett, Bronzini, Gartmann (eng.); model by Garrett Knoll & Adrianne Ngam **23. Formwork-defined wall surface texture** – Bishop Edward King Chapel, Oxford, UK, 2013; Níall McLaughlin Architects; Price and Myers (eng.); model by Kate Kerbel & Siobhan Lee

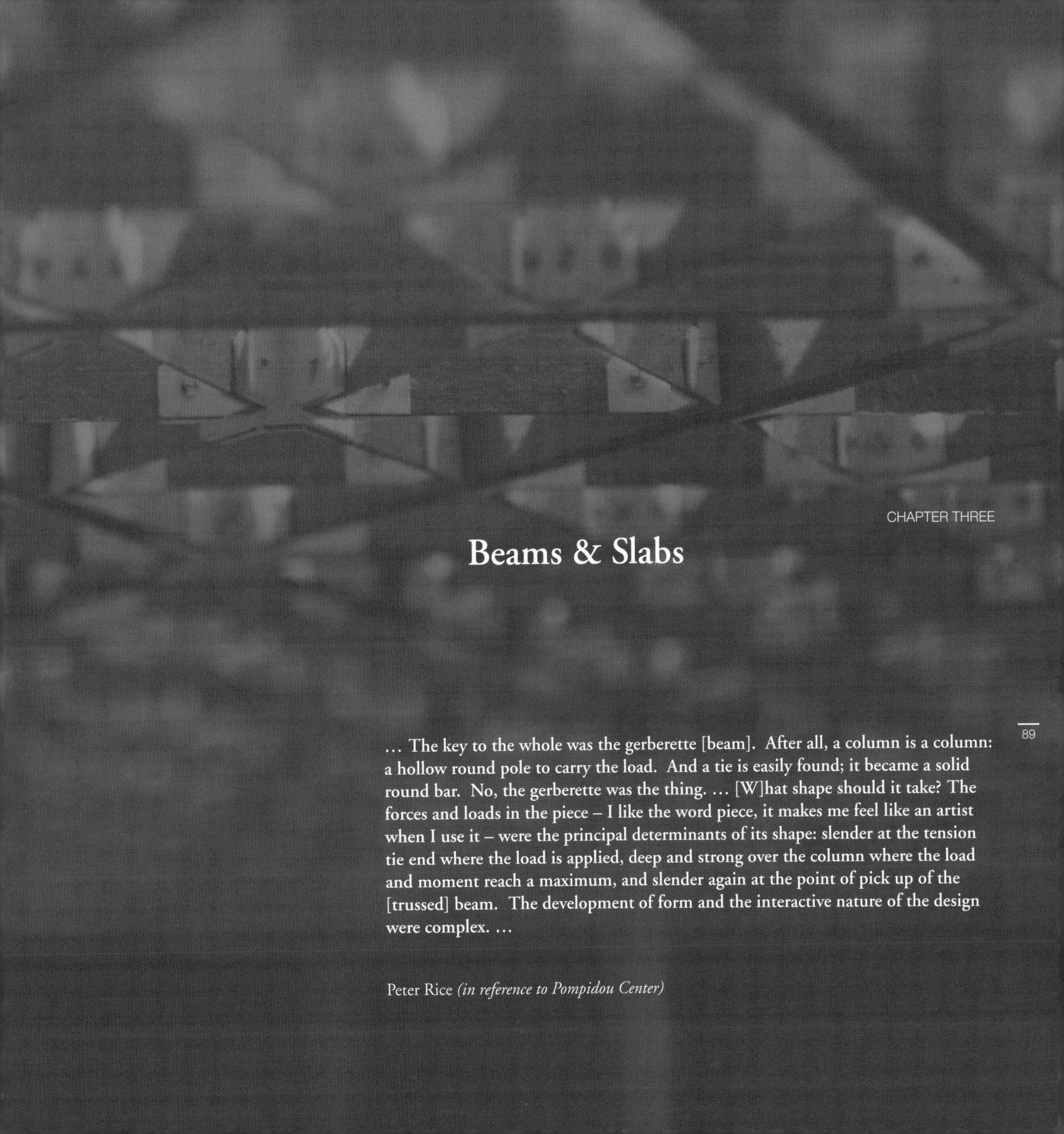

CHAPTER THREE

Beams & Slabs

… The key to the whole was the gerberette [beam]. After all, a column is a column: a hollow round pole to carry the load. And a tie is easily found; it became a solid round bar. No, the gerberette was the thing. … [W]hat shape should it take? The forces and loads in the piece – I like the word piece, it makes me feel like an artist when I use it – were the principal determinants of its shape: slender at the tension tie end where the load is applied, deep and strong over the column where the load and moment reach a maximum, and slender again at the point of pick up of the [trussed] beam. The development of form and the interactive nature of the design were complex. …

Peter Rice *(in reference to Pompidou Center)*

Photo: Peter Brian Klein

Beams span space; either singly or in groups they help support floor surfaces to walk on or roofs that provide shelter. Typically oriented horizontally, they can also be inclined or even vertical (e.g., roof rafters or curtain wall mullions). From a structural perspective, beams bend. In contrast to columns and hangers that are subject to axial loads *along* their main longitudinal axis, beams carry loads that are applied *transversely* to them, resulting in a fundamental state of bending at every cross-section whereby tension exists in the lower portion of a beam together with compression in the upper – or vice versa, depending on the situation. But there is so much more to beams than these introductory statements. They can cantilever, projecting space outward; several may span together in unison in one direction or else intersect in two, to various load-carrying, lighting and spatial effects; beams often span simply between supports but can also be run continuously over them, leading to variations in depth according to bending moment diagrams; moreover, differences in material properties and cross-sectional profiles can also have important implications for beams from both structural and visual perspectives. And somewhat perplexingly, beams can even be made to seemingly "disappear" into flat floor slabs.

Fallingwater, by Frank Lloyd Wright, is one of the world's most recognizable buildings. It can be argued that this is largely because of its spectacularly cantilevering terraces, which fundamentally embody bending behavior in order to seemingly hover unsupported directly above the waterfall. Just how they do so is made evident through this diary-like recounting by structural engineer Robert Silman about the repair strategy that was devised to stabilize the terraces' alarming downward deflections over the years. Moreover, the stabilization strategy itself ingeniously relies on a subtle reversal of the terraces' fundamental behavior; i.e., bending counters bending.

Arresting Cantilever Deflections

Strengthening Fallingwater
Robert Silman

On a quiet day in the summer of 1995 our office receptionist informed me that Lynda Waggoner, director of Fallingwater, was on the telephone. Lynda described the ongoing problem with cracking of the concrete parapets on the master bedroom terrace. She asked if we would be interested in coming out to take a look.

How could we say no? This, after all, was the number one building in the whole United States, voted the best all-time work of American architecture by the American Institute of Architects (AIA). Although the entire professions of architecture, engineering, and historic preservation would be following our every move, we relished the challenge and of course responded with an emphatic yes.

Our first site visit confirmed the suspicions. In a building of this age, cracks, once repaired, were not supposed to open at the same location each time they had been patched. Yet anecdotal evidence showed that the cantilevers were continuing to deflect. The top sides of the cantilever beams, at the point of maximum stress, were cracking and, even after being repaired and painted over, were cracking again at the same locations. The building was apparently moving.

Our first step was to monitor the building accurately in order to determine definitively that there was a long-term trend towards continuing deflection. So far, all that we had was subjective evidence.

First, there was the story of the removal of the formwork in 1935, after the concrete had gained sufficient strength to stand on its own. When Wright's on-site apprentice, Bob Mosher, witnessed the removal of the last prop under the cantilever of the living room he, like everyone else there, became alarmed when the entire structure deflected about 1¾ inches. Although this immediate deflection was easily predictable by advance calculations, apparently no one had thought to camber the formwork for the concrete upward by at least that amount so when it did deflect, the structure would come back to the level position. In addition, cracks opened in the master bedroom terrace concrete parapet beams. Bob Mosher immediately telephoned back to Wright's studio at Taliesin in Spring Green, Wisconsin, reporting the deflection and cracks; they in turn called the principal structural engineer, Mendel Glickman, in Madison. Glickman is reported to have asked for a moment to check his calculations and the drawings. Then he came back to the phone and said, "Oh my God, I forgot the negative reinforcing!" The negative reinforcing that he referred to would have been steel reinforcing bars placed in the top of the master bedroom terrace-level beams running north-south on each edge of the terrace. Instead, only very small, very short bars were placed here.

Knowing of that supposed interchange in 1935, we still needed to know about the history of the movements in the house from that time until the present. Our measurements at the site indicated that at some locations the main floor cantilever had deflected nearly 7 inches with respect to the support point of the cantilever some fifteen feet away. The master bedroom terrace had deflected similarly. These numbers were extremely large, more than ten to fifteen times what we would normally design for.

Checking through the archives at Fallingwater, we found that Edgar Kaufmann Sr. seemed to be only moderately concerned with these movements and cracks. Between the time that the house was completed in 1937 and 1945, he only had the deflections surveyed once. Thereafter until his death in 1955 he commissioned 16 visits by the surveyor. We could find no record of Edgar Kaufmann jr. ever commissioning such a survey after his father's death. Instead, he asked the chief of maintenance, Earl Friend, to keep his eye on things. Earl's method was simple: the first time he measured he cut a length of wood to fit exactly between the master bedroom terrace-level and the main-level parapets. Each time he went back to check—by inserting the wood in the same spot—there was no change. Of course what Earl did not realize was that the two cantilevers were moving together and were not changing relative to one another but were deflecting at the same rate!

Thus we discounted all previous surveys and designed a high-tech electronic monitoring system that would give us information on very small movements that could be recorded on a datalogger and downloaded onto a computer. Over a seventeen-month period, we found, as expected, that there was a definite trend toward ongoing downward deflection of the cantilevers.

How could this be? Reinforced concrete seems about as solid a material as one could want for building a house. It is likely that Edgar Kaufmann Sr. and jr. both agreed with this sentiment, even though they were aware that the house was still cracking each time they repaired it. But as engineers, we know that many solids, such as concrete, exhibit small movements under continuous loads, a phenomenon called plastic flow or "creep." The continuous load here is the heavy weight of the concrete house itself. In general we say that 90% of the plastic flow occurs in the first year after casting, and the remaining 10% continues in a gradually reducing quantity for about twenty years more until it ceases to move. But the house was now almost sixty years old and was still experiencing plastic flow. To an engineer this was very scary. It is almost never seen in an existing building and, ultimately, is an indication of impending failure.

During the seventeen months of monitoring, we also made calculations of the actual stresses and strains in the reinforced concrete of the structure. We could calculate the loads quite easily, and we knew the dimensions of all the members from the original drawings that we verified with site observations. One thing that we noticed in the original drawings was that the south end of the master bedroom terrace was shown to be supported on four very small structural steel T-shaped members, continuing below in the south wall of the living room. When we looked out the living room windows to the south, we saw that four of the mullions were larger, corresponding to the locations of the steel T-shaped supports. We removed a metal covering at one of these larger mullions and verified that it indeed contained a support of the dimension called for in the drawings. This confirmed our suspicion that Earl's measurements using the cut piece of wood were not meaningful. In addition, it caused us to shift our focus from the master bedroom terrace parapet beams where the cracking was most obvious to the main floor cantilever girders that were, in the end, supporting not only the main floor but also the master bedroom terrace.

The major stumbling block for our analysis occurred in trying to determine the amount of reinforcing in the main floor concrete girders. Once again the archives proved to be essential. A memo from Bob Mosher to Mr. Wright sent four days after the concrete for the living room and the terraces was poured stated, "I am enclosing some calculations made in Pittsburgh by engineers hired by Kaufmann: their contention was that more steel [was] necessary in beams because they discovered that the weight of [the] second floor transposed through T-iron window frames was not figured. Steel was sent out and put in at last moment. Our builder does not trust us ..." Mr. Wright's response to Mr. Kaufmann is one of the classics of the architect-client relationship. "If you are paying to have the concrete engineering done down there, there is no use whatever in our doing it here. I am willing you should take it over but I am not willing to be insulted. So we will send no more steel diagrams. I am unaccustomed to such treatment where I have built buildings before and do not intend to put up with it now ... I don't know what kind of architect you are familiar with but it apparently isn't the kind I think I am. You seem not to know how to treat a decent one. I have put so much more into this house than you or any other client has a right to expect that if I haven't your confidence—to hell with the whole thing."

The archives also revealed a report commissioned by Mr. Kaufmann nine months later from the firm of Pittsburgh engineers that Bob Mosher had referred to—Metzger-Richardson Co., Engineers & Fabricators, Steel for Concrete—stating that they had installed twice the amount of reinforcing in the main living room girders as had been shown on the original design drawings. They calculated the stresses in the concrete and the steel at the main floor girders and concluded, "These stresses are not satisfactory. ... [They] do not fall within the limits of those prescribed by accepted engineering practice. [T]herefore the structure does not have a satisfactory factor of safety, or what might be termed reserve strength."

We felt that it was crucial that we determine the exact amount of reinforcing steel in these girders. Although we had not yet prepared calculations, our instincts warned us that the stresses were very high in the concrete girders and we dared not cut into them significantly to expose the reinforcement. Any diminution of strength was a potential source of disaster. Instead we decided to use a technique called non-destructive evaluation in which a specialty contractor uses tools such as impulse radar and magnetic detection to find actual quantities, sizes and locations of reinforcing bars hidden in concrete. Their results confirmed that Metzger-Richardson had indeed inserted the extra bars referred to in their report.

At several locations where the levels of stress were not high, we recovered samples of the concrete and reinforcing steel and sent them to a laboratory for testing. The concrete proved to be of excellent quality. Although it was hand mixed on the job site using local aggregate, the ultimate compressive strength tested out at more than 5,000 psi (pounds per square inch), 30% more than anticipated. And the reinforcing met the chemical and physical requirements typical of steel for that period. We were now ready to accomplish the task of calculating the stresses in the actual structure. The tools available to us in the late 1990s were far more advanced than those in Mendel Glickman's arsenal in 1935. We utilized sophisticated computer programs using finite element methods and three-dimensional modeling that gave very accurate results for both stresses and movements of the structure. We were able to compare the calculated movements with the actual observed movements in the structure and then fine-tune the computer model until the two agreed. In the end, we found that the beams in the parapets of the master bedroom terrace were not able to carry any significant load (remember that the negative reinforcing had been omitted by mistake); all of the load of both the master bedroom terrace and the main level was being carried in the four main girders under the living room floor. It was these girders to which Metzger and Richardson had added reinforcing, but alas, they had not added enough. The easternmost of the four girders was supported on a slender steel post that was part of the stair going down to the stream below, so this member was not overstressed. However the other three girders showed alarming results. Both the concrete and the reinforcing steel were stressed way beyond their allowable limits—the former to 95% of its failure strength and the latter beyond its elastic limit. Normally we would limit these stresses to one-half or two-thirds of these values. In all of our years of practice, we had never seen an active, working building with such high levels of stress. All of the safety factors had been wiped out!

In 1935 the principles of reinforced concrete design were well known; every engineering student could calculate the required reinforcernent in a cantilever beam. Mendel Glickman, Wes Peters, and Metzger-Richardson were all accomplished engineers. How could they have missed this?

One explanation for the error in the original design might be the speed at which Fallingwater was designed. After Mr. Wright's initial visit to the site several months elapsed, and Mr. Kaufmann had heard nothing. According to a tale that I heard personally related several times during the 1990s by Edgar Tafel, the lead design apprentice on the house, Mr. Kaufmann called Taliesin early one morning to inform Mr. Wright that he was in Milwaukee and was going to drive over to Spring Green to look at the plans. Mr. Wright heartily invited him, saying that they would lunch together and after that they would go over the drawings.

Now at this time there was not yet a line on paper. Mr. Wright gathered the apprentices around him, overlaid the site survey with a piece of tracing paper, and began to draw. First, the foundation plan showing the bolsters, then the main floor, then the second floor with the master bedroom and terrace, then the third floor. As he finished, the butler announced Mr. Kaufmann's arrival and Mr. Wright hurriedly showed the apprentices what he wanted the elevations to look like, charging them to draw these during lunch.

When they came back to the studio after lunch Mr. Kaufmann was reportedly thrilled with the scheme that Mr. Wright showed him and wanted to start construction immediately. Thus the working drawings, including the calculations for the reinforcing steel in the concrete must have been produced exceedingly quickly. It is very possible that Glickman and Peters showed some reinforcing bars in the main floor girders as a "place holder," fully intending to go back later and perform a final design. But perhaps, in the rush to get the drawings out to the contractor in the field, this got overlooked.

We cannot, however, imagine why Metzger-Richardson did not supply the correct amount of steel when they increased the number of bars to twice the amount shown on the design drawings. Perhaps they too did not have time to perform an accurate calculation and were acting on instinct. When they went back nine months later and did precise calculations, they realized that the steel that they had put in was not adequate.

However, even armed with this information, Mr. Kaufmann elected to believe Mr. Wright that the house was perfectly safe for occupancy, for he never acted on any of the suggestions made by Metzger-Richardson to reduce the length of the cantilevers.

Immediately upon learning the results of our calculations, we notified Ms. Waggoner. Distressed and worried, she conveyed the information to the advisory committee. They shot back the crucial questions: Is the building safe? Can we continue to allow visitors and staff to enter into it?

The answers were not clear. The structure was no different from what it had been on day one of its existence. Its problems had nothing to do with aging, deterioration, corrosion, breakdown of the concrete, or stress due to occupancy loads. There was simply insufficient reinforcing in the three concrete girders in the living room floor—a deficiency had been built into the original structure.

In the end we did not answer their questions directly but rather convinced the advisory committee to agree to repair the problem, whatever it took. We then stated that, if they were going to undertake a repair campaign, we would need to shore the three concrete girders temporarily, so why not shore them immediately, even before we had decided on a repair scheme? They agreed, and a single line of shoring was installed under the cantilevers in 1997.

Even the shoring required an intricate design and installation. The stream had to be temporarily diverted, holes for anchor bolts carefully drilled into the stream's bedrock floor, the rock overhang of the waterfall temporarily shored up, and then the line of steel shoring erected.

While the shoring was being installed on site, we were working in the office to develop repair schemes. Even before we had established the full scope of the problem and completed the calculations, we had been thinking about possible alternative repair solutions. Several universities assigned the problem in their classes. Solutions came from all over the country, and we were ready to listen to anything that seemed a remote possibility.

One obvious choice was to strengthen the deficient concrete girders with new structural steel "sister" members that would be placed on each side of each girder. This would have required much more temporary shoring as each of the 4-inch-wide concrete joists would have to be cut free from the existing girders in order to install the sisters. Then the joists would have to be reconnected. This solution would do nothing to correct the existing level of stress in the concrete or the steel reinforcing bars. It would merely transfer the entire load onto the new sister girders.

Another solution would be to bond reinforcing plates made either of carbon fiber or steel to the top sides of the girders using epoxy adhesive, once the floor had been removed. If these could be made thin enough, then they could be buried in the eventual built-up finished flooring installation. This solution, too, did nothing to remedy the existing high level of stress.

Finally some hard-core preservationists suggested that in accordance with the strictest principles of historic preservation, no existing historic fabric be removed or disturbed and the shoring be left in place permanently. The reasons for such a solution would be explained to visitors and would be in any text that accompanied pictures of the stabilized structure.

But we were not happy with any of these proposed solutions. What our office envisioned was a fix that would not alter Fallingwater's unusual beauty, would retain the principle of the cantilever, and would utilize the existing concrete as much as possible.

Our office ultimately developed a repair scheme using a technique called post-tensioned concrete. In this procedure, very high-strength steel cables would be installed adjacent to both sides of each concrete girder. The cables would be placed in an inverted V configuration, anchored into a new block of concrete located some fifteen feet north of the supports for the girders, sloped over a diverter block at the support point, and threaded through a temporary hole cut into the south parapet wall. In order to install the tendons to their proper slope, a series of 4-inch-diameter holes would be drilled into the concrete joists, but otherwise the joists would remain fully attached to the girders. These cables or tendons would then be inserted into a hollow plastic tube and would be free to move during the construction phase.

Once all of the tendons were in place and anchored, a high-capacity hydraulic jack would be attached to the cables outside the south parapet, on temporary scaffolding rising up from the stream, and the tendons pulled with an enormous force—up to 390 tons in each girder. The tendons would then be wedged tight and permanently locked off to an anchorage block just beneath the surface of the face of the south parapet. The jacks could then be removed without losing the tension in the cables. The large tensile force in the cables induces an equally large and opposite compression force in the girders. Because the tendons are not horizontal but are rather sloped to a very carefully calculated alignment, the stress imparted to the existing girders actually reduces the existing very high compression in the concrete and tension in the reinforcing bars by introducing reverse forces. This solution required the least amount of intervention, was the only one that significantly reduced the existing overstresses, and was, in the end, the most cost-effective by far. Our projected schedule showed that the work could be accomplished over the winter when the house traditionally closes.

All of the work would be done from the top side of the slab, after the finished floor had been carefully removed. This would allow the work to proceed in all weather. Materials and manpower could be delivered from the exterior directly into the south end of the living room via the temporary scaffold built up from the streambed and concrete pumped from trucks parked on the other side of the stream. Repairs began in November 2001 and the house reopened on schedule in April 2002, a period of less than six months. There was no loss of a visitor season because of repairs.

In order to ensure that our solution was indeed the best possible one, we counseled the advisory committee to conduct a peer review among leading specialists in concrete and historic preservation throughout the world. The peer reviewers had several months to study our proposed solution and they presented their findings to a standing room-only audience in the Carnegie Museum of Art in Pittsburgh. They strongly endorsed the proposed repair as the most cost-effective and appropriate to the needs of the property.

The contractor selected to make the concrete repairs was VSL of Springfield, Virginia, a contractor specializing in post-tensioning. Their affiliated firm, Structural Preservation Systems of Baltimore, Maryland, assisted with concrete repairs.

Moving forward, the final step was to remove all the built-in furniture. Then the maintenance staff of Fallingwater carefully removed each of the stones from the finished floor, numbered them, and recorded their exact position. They were stored on site in temporary shelters. The existing wooden subfloor and its 2x4 wood purlins were removed and discarded. Removal of the stone flooring had been achieved previously by the maintenance staff in order to install new waterproofing on the terraces, so they were confident that this could be accomplished without incident.

Our office had prepared the initial calculations. We then retained a consultant who specialized in post-tensioning, Schupack Suarez/TDEG, with Mario Suarez leading their team. They verified and refined our calculation. VSL then made a third set of calculations to be sure that the geometry and the stresses were correct before they proceeded with the work.

The dead-end anchor blocks, central diverter blocks, and jacking-end anchorage blocks of concrete were first poured and clamped to each existing girder. On each side of two of the girders, wire bundles—composed of thirteen strands of 1/2-inch-diameter twisted steel wire—were threaded through the hollow tube and anchored to the dead-end block. At the easternmost girder to be reinforced, the bundle could only be placed on one side because of the presence of the stair going down to the stream; thus only 10 strands were placed on one side of this girder.

The worst deflection was noted at the tips of the east and west terraces, which are double cantilevers. The main girders were cantilevered in the north-south direction and the terrace cantilevered off of these in the east-west direction. We found it prudent to reduce the stresses in the terrace cantilevers as well and to do this we used smaller post-tensioning cables called monostrand. These were installed in advance of the post-tensioning of the main girders.

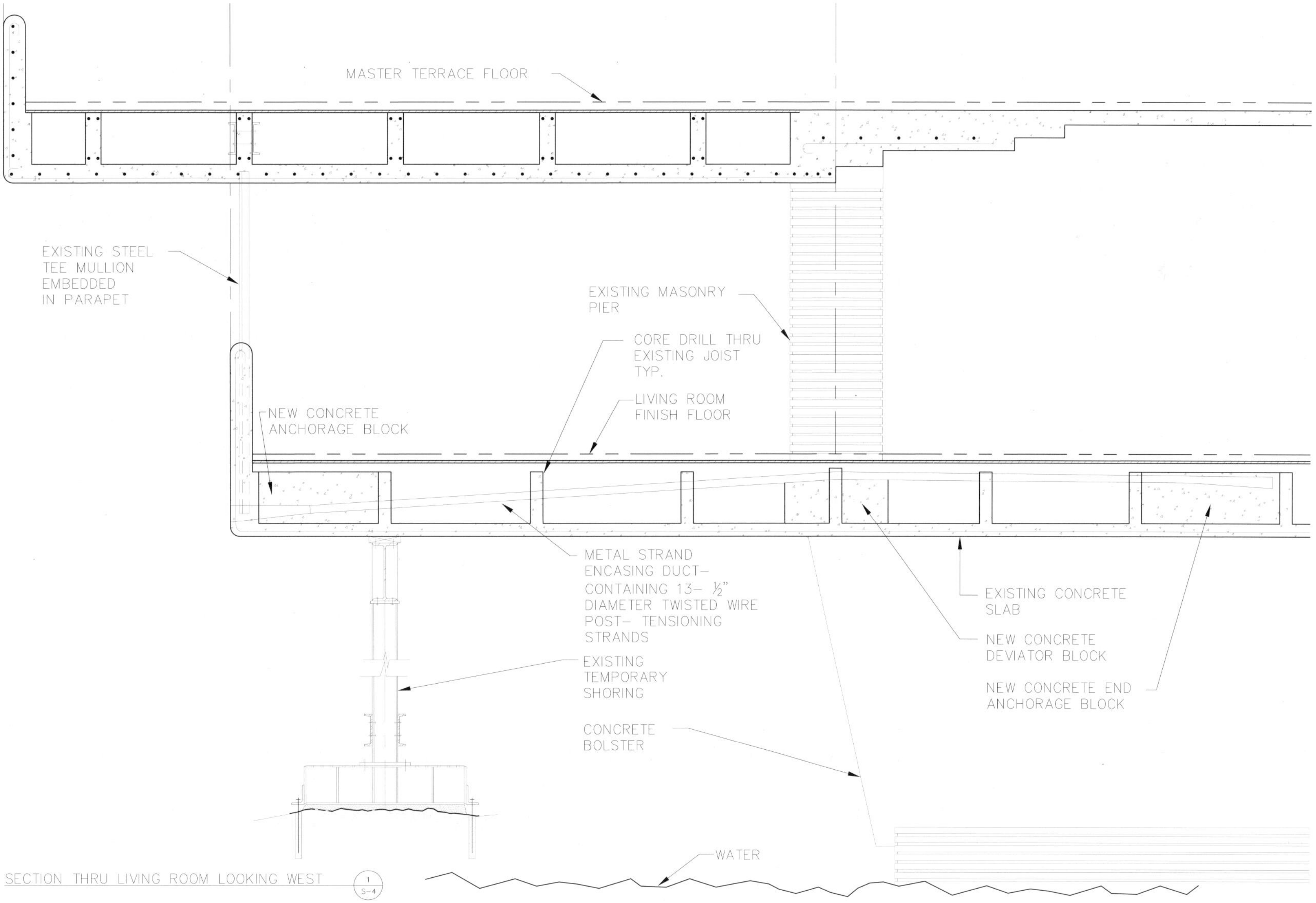

Each of the 1/2-inch diameter strands had a working strength capability of 40,000 pounds of tension. Calculations required that we use thirteen strands in a bundle on each side of the two western girders, one girder carrying a force of 780,000 pounds and the other 858,800 pounds. The remaining easternmost girder's ten strands carried a force of 330,400 pounds.

On a very pleasant day in February 2002, I flew to Pittsburgh with John Matteo, our project manager, and then drove to Fallingwater. On the drive, I felt myself growing anxious. I had recently finished a four-month tour working the twelve-hour night shift once a week at the World Trade Center site, helping the first responders place heavy equipment and evaluate stability of existing roadways, makeshift ramps, and access paths. The memory of whistles blowing while work stopped and a dead hero's body was lifted from the wreckage brought tears to my eyes, as it still does.

Then there was the worry of what we were about to attempt at Fallingwater. Post-tensioning had not been commonly used for making repairs to severely distressed concrete buildings. What if there were some obscure forces that we had not accounted for in our calculations? Might the application of the huge jacking force cause the concrete, already stressed to 95% of its capacity, to rupture? We had installed some shoring towers within the living room just in case. Still, I was worried.

The next morning, we began the delicate post-tensioning operation. Tension force was to be introduced in three stages. The first stage would be 20% of the force, sufficient to set the tendons. Then an additional 30% would be added and this was to be left overnight. Measurements were taken to record forces in the tendons as well as movements in the girders. Strain gauges in the four steel T-shaped supports at the south parapet indicated that there were unequal forces being transmitted up to the master bedroom terrace. In order to verify

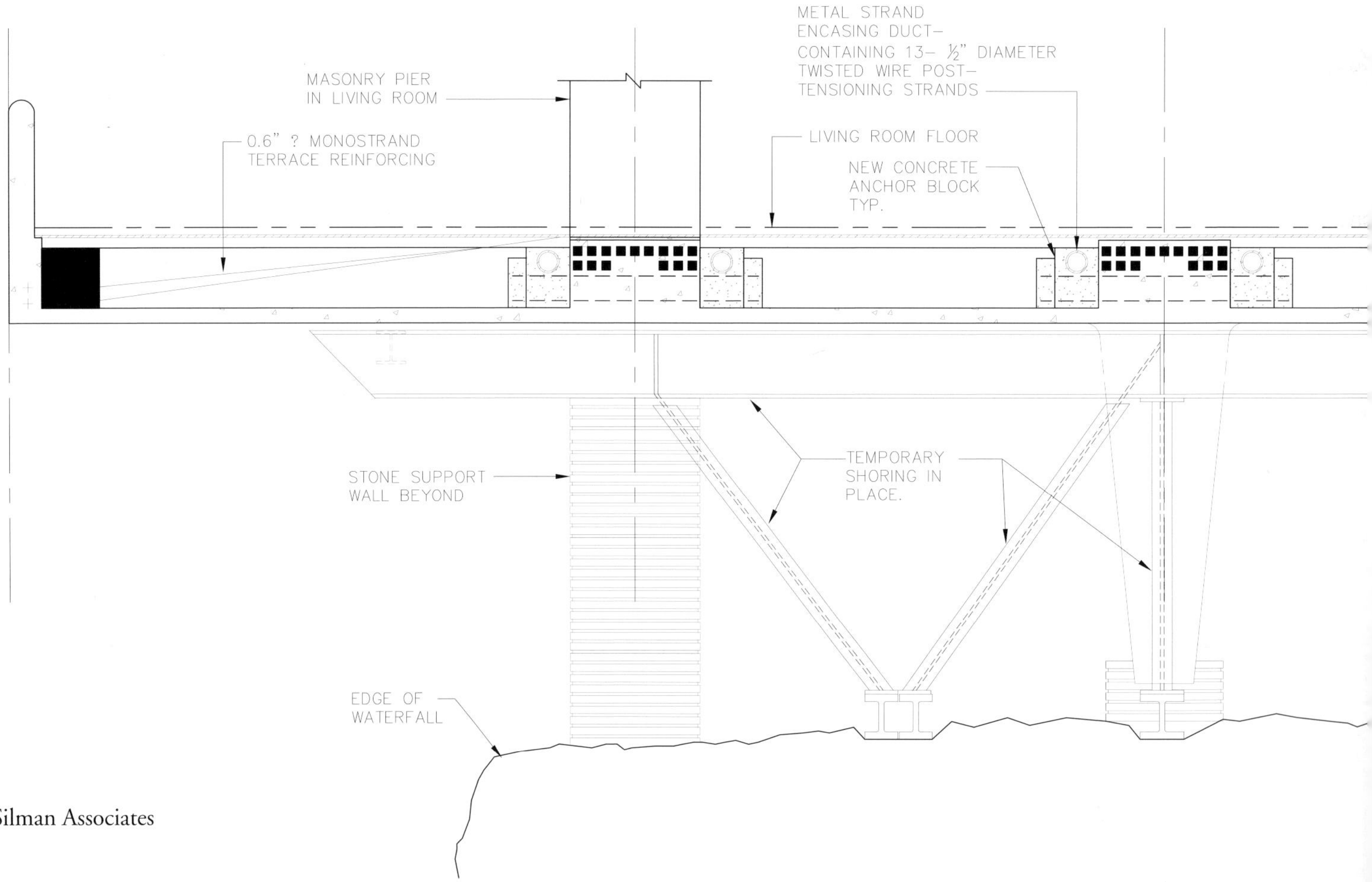

Drawings by Robert Silman Associates

this reading, Mario Suarez who was on site observing tapped each support with a steel hammer and noted the difference in pitch. Based on this he adjusted the final post-tensioning forces. He practiced the *art* of engineering as well as its *science!*

The next day VSL verified that there were no significant losses of pre-stress force, and they gave the thumbs-up to install the remaining 50%. Out on the scaffold platform, we collectively held our breath as we watched the needle of the gauge on the hydraulic jack climb to its design level. A united sigh was heard—nothing out of the ordinary had occurred. We had done it successfully.

Finally, the strands were locked off and cut, and the holes in the south parapet patched.

Although the edges of the doubly cantilevered terraces had deflected more than 7 inches and the ends of the single cantilevered girder more than 5 inches, we never intended to try to raise the building back up to the level position. Over its sixty-year life, the plaster on the walls and ceilings, as well as the glass and the window and door frames, had all adjusted to or been modified to accept these movements. Had we tried to straighten it, all of the brittle finishes would have suffered severe damage and required drastic repairs. Thus the ends of the girder picked up off the temporary shoring only about ¾ inch, exactly as calculated. These movements were carefully charted throughout the post-tensioning process using both electronic and visual monitors.

Other small supplementary repairs were made throughout the structure.

At the conclusion of the structural work, a new subflooring system of purlins and plywood was put down, over which the stone floor was carefully reinstalled. The built-in wooden furniture was returned to the house, the temporary shoring removed, the exterior repainted, and when all was done, the house looked as it always had.

Of course it was left in a permanently deflected position, but this is part of its story. However, it is now safe for future generations to enjoy and visit with no further structural maintenance required for the main cantilevers.

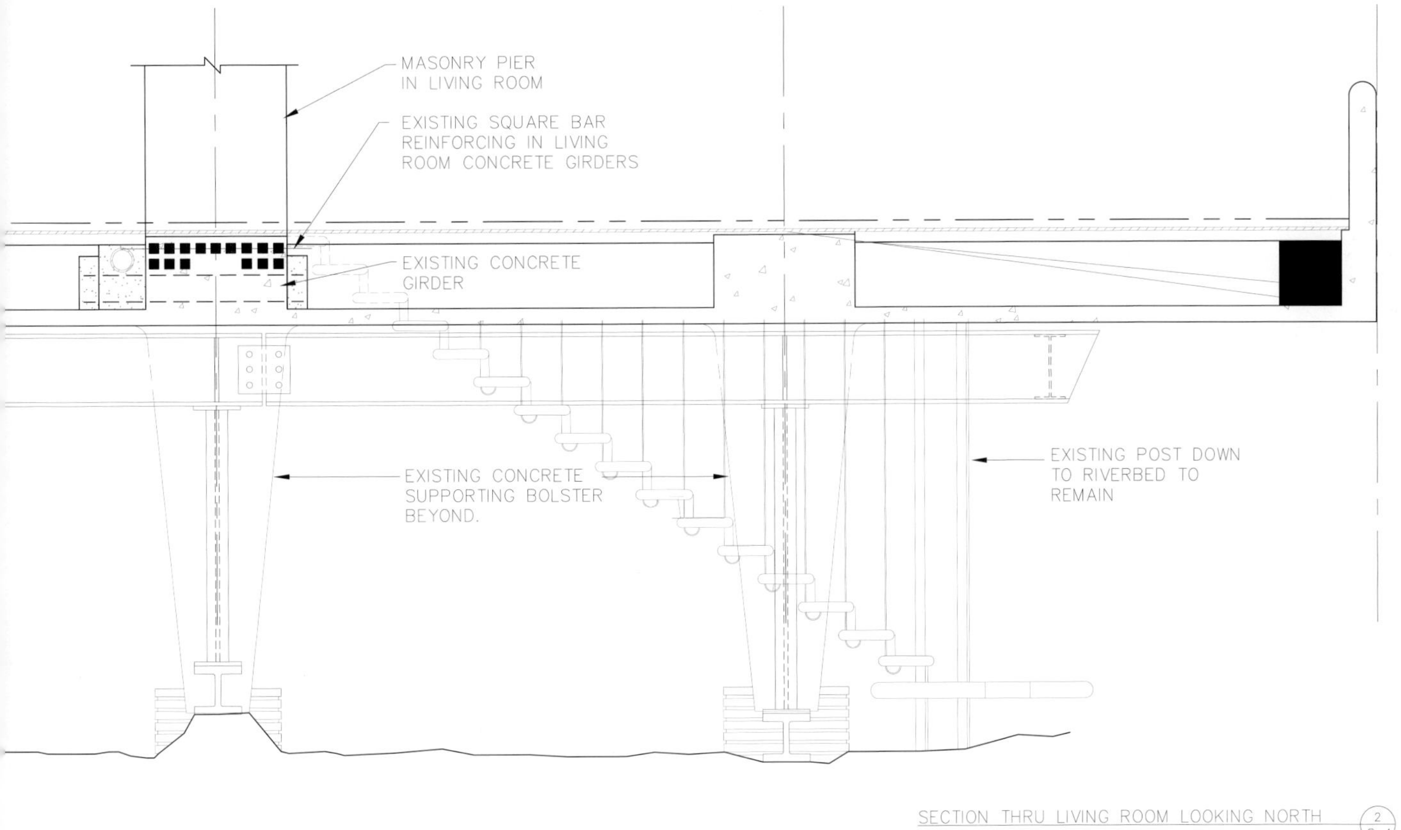

SECTION THRU LIVING ROOM LOOKING NORTH 2 S-4

Photo: Teigens Fotoatelier / DEXTRA Photo

Beams largely define Sverre Fehn's Nordic Pavilion in Venice. The two-layered, two-way orthogonal grid of exceptionally tall, thin and closely spaced reinforced concrete beams is certainly distinctive. Common experience and basic knowledge of bending-stress-calculation formulas dictate such a vertical orientation of the beams; their seeming exaggeration here emphatically drives home the point (there are other reasons for these proportions, as is discussed below). Likewise the advantages of an orthogonal beam grid are generally understood in terms of being better able to span space in column-free fashion, while limiting the depth of beams necessary to accomplish the task. Even so, the manner in which the beam grid is here accomplished is sublime, notwithstanding that many beams are on full display; indeed, it is because of this. The Scandinavian art exhibition program and the very particular light-quality design objectives associated with this, combined with a commitment to preserving any trees that previously existed on the site are both determining factors in establishing the unique grid system for the roof. Further reinforcing Fehn's mastery of and reliance on the beam for this project, a level of subtle detailing and "play" with the beam elements of the grid confounds initial expectations; also, and in contrast to such refinements, the robust edge support beams allow the interior space to be completely opened up to the outside by means of two fully glazed walls. In an exclamation point to the whole beam ensemble, one of the edge beams is forked into Y-configuration so as to preserve – and highlight – the largest tree on the site. At the Nordic Pavilion, the beam enables all.

Nordic Pavilion – An Illuminating Beam Matrix

from *On Span and Space: Exploring Structures in Architecture*
Bjørn Normann Sandaker

... 'Building a museum for the visual arts', Fehn says, 'is the story of the struggle with light.' [1]

The Nordic Pavilion is essentially a room of about 470 m^2 for displaying different kinds of art works. The room is without any intermediate support. On two adjacent sides there are concrete walls closing off a more or less square plan, while the other two permit an almost invisible transition between the interior and the exterior. This is achieved by sliding floor-to-ceiling glazing. This openness visually brings the surrounding park inside the building, the only element pointing out the boundary being the floor covering of slate tiles.

... one of the basic ideas of the roof structure design is to protect ... paintings from direct sunlight. This is done by devising a structure of two orthogonal layers, consisting of narrowly spaced, thin concrete girders that create an atmosphere of diffused light that recalls the light of 'the shadowless world of the Nordic countries'.[2] The art works are thus exhibited in an environment of light supposed to resemble that of the countries in which they were made. To keep as much of the intensity of the light as possible, the concrete is cast in a mixture of white cement, white sand and crushed white marble. The girders follow a structural module of 523 mm (an ancient Egyptian module, according to Fehn), while their height and thickness are 1000 by 60 mm. These figures relate exactly to the trajectory of the sun at the Venetian summer solstice (64 degrees), and ensure the blocking out of direct light. The span of the bottom layer girders is about 18 m, not counting the 4+ m cantilevering part. In between the upper layer of girders are hung translucent gutters of glass-fibre-reinforced plastic sheets.

The quality of the light is thus the key to our aesthetic appreciation of the structure. The spacing, heights and remarkably small thicknesses of the girders derive from the manipulation of the light. If such a conception escapes us, we will experience the structure differently; if mechanical constraints alone were decisive, the proportions and the structural module will not seem appropriate in relation to the span and the choice of material. We will wonder why a primary tier of girders is as narrowly spaced as the secondary tier of purlins. If we conceive the roof structure as a two-way grid of beams, we will question why the grid is made by placing one layer of beams or girders on top of the other (making a total structural height of 2 m). This would be a quite unusual solution when seeking two-way structural action, especially when constructing in reinforced concrete.

There are, then, different possible interpretations as well as a number of different perceptions, but not all of them induce an experience of intellectual coherence or appropriateness. A grasp of the relevant concept when experiencing structures (as well as other objects of aesthetic interest) is very important. In this case, the idea of the control of light very nearly (but not entirely) dominates the concept and hence the experience. Another factor informing the choice of structure and determining how that choice is experienced was the need to protect the trees on the site from being cut down, trees that are part of the only park in Venice. The highly appropriate two-way beam system controlling the interior light also seems right and fitting for making room for the trees. The trees actually penetrate the roof level by way of openings in the structure; this is made possible by the two-way structural action. From a mechanical, load-bearing point of view, then, the openings for the trees legitimate the structural system to a certain degree, although that particular two-layered form is not necessary for achieving this. Hence a richness of aesthetic experiences is possible because different ways of seeing sometimes harmonise and strengthen the feeling of appropriateness; sometimes they clash and make us wonder. Ambiguity – when a structure looks right from one point of view and strange from another – reveals the complexity of the work and thus contributes to our intellectual enjoyment.

The real highlight of our aesthetic attention is the areas around the openings. Here the experience of the structure and the light reaches a particular intensity, where the diffused light reflected by the surfaces of the girders mingles with the direct light that reaches us through the openings for the trees. These areas are 'packed' with perceptual tension related to the different possible ways of seeing the load path of the structure: the lower tier of girders (generally experienced as supporting the tier above) is in some places abruptly cut off to give room for the trees. Seemingly without support, the girders read as hovering in the air. We can enjoy the fascination of choosing between ways of seeing: lower tier as supporting, or lower tier as suspended from above. The two ends of the girders in question introduce additional ambiguity because they are very differently designed, with the opposite end from the openings firmly underpinned. Even if we know that the orthogonally-directed upper girders relieve the cut-off lower ones in these areas by 'pulling' the load upwards, a support from underneath is definitely easier to grasp perceptually than a device for suspending them from above.

The Nordic Pavilion by Sverre Fehn shows with great clarity the value of considering structures not merely as mechanical assemblages but also, as in the present case, as architectural compositions that affect natural light and thus qualitatively influence our experience of the structure and the architectural work as a whole. In a wider perspective, the discussion concerns the relationship between architectural tectonics and the corresponding architectural spaces, and our experience of enjoyment when confronted by both. Kenneth Frampton understands this relationship when he says of the Pavilion that 'the architectonic form of the structure was once more to reinforce the spatial system'.[3]

Sverre Fehn sketch by permission of Prof. Per Olaf Fjeld

Photo: Ferruzzi, 1962 by courtesy of the National Museum of Art, Architecture and Design, Norway

Kimbell Art Museum. Photo: Robert LaPrelle

The remarkable lighting and space-defining effects of the roof structure of Louis Kahn's Kimbell Art Museum are legendary; these qualities are well worth revisiting here though the words of Patricia Cummings Loud. Even so, the concrete roof structure of the Kimbell is perhaps not the most immediately obvious of "beam" structures to be included in this chapter; indeed, because of its form it is often categorized as a series of vaults or cylindrical shells. Yet when considered from a certain distance and vantage point as well as in terms of its overall structural behavior, each roof module clearly serves to span horizontally in beam-like fashion between pairs of distant columns. Indeed, the characteristic bending stresses that one expects to find within a beam exist here, varying from top to bottom over the depth of the concrete section and along the length according to bending moment demand. The unique aspect, of course, is that the cross-section of this "beam" is of cycloid profile (nearly semicircular) rather than of conventional rectangular or I-flanged shape. But then, such classic beam shapes themselves vary quite a lot, so it is really only a matter of degree of variation, with Kahn here having pushed the boundaries in order to achieve an exceptional result.

Built forty years later, Renzo Piano's Pavilion at the Kimbell faces off with Kahn's Museum in a remarkable dialogue between buildings. As Paula Deitz's text conveys, the roof structure of the addition is complementary to yet distinctive from that of the original museum: here pairs of rectangular, glu-laminated Douglas fir beams span the open spaces and support multiple layers of light-controlling materials. The means and forms are different, yet in the end both of these closely related buildings explore the quality of light and space that can be made possible by beam structures.

The Kimbell's Beam Variations

from *The Art Museums of Louis I. Kahn*
Patricia Cummings Loud

For the Kimbell's trustees, Kahn's concept of a villa in a garden, as he had explained it in his letter to Mrs. Kimbell, fit their idea of a traditional and classical art museum, even perhaps surpassing their expectations in its beauty and serenity. Kahn had appropriated sources from familiar historic American museums. The tripartite Beaux-Arts organization, for example, could be found on the west front with its advanced side wings and recessed center forecourt—the "court of honor"—recalling the museums in Philadelphia that Kahn visited as a youth and saw as a young architect. But he had transformed this concept of a museum building and its setting. One does not approach the Kimbell head-on and find a monumental entrance. Axial paths echoing the axis inside the building itself lead the visitor in toward the forecourt from the streets. Clearly expressed is the vault on four columns, the unit multiplied to form the entire upper floor, all of which can be read by the visitor in the porticos. Thus the museum's constructive means and its logical organization are visually comprehensible. The main west entrance is in the center of the museum's axis, and the gallery floor layout can be perceived directly or inferred. The interior seen upon entering confirms intuition and further reinforces the tradition of museums through our familiarity with the vaulted gallery illuminated from above. Location within the building is easily sensed even by the first-time visitor.

The Kimbell's exterior provides more than one inference. The entrance from the parking lot is sheltered in a shadowy void forming a recessed porch, equivalent in size and proportion to the porticos on the west but without the elegance of the vault. Windows are hardly apparent; indeed, the usual indications that communicate scale are nearly nonexistent. As a consequence, the building savors a certain tradition when seen from the east, north, or south: the tradition of warehouses or storage structures with low vaults, like those of ancient Egypt (the Ramesseum) or Rome (the Porticus Aemilia) or even of Auguste Perret (the docks warehouse in Casablanca, 1915). One could add—though his are not warehouses—Le Corbusier's Monol housing of 1919 and certain of his private houses in the 1950s and 1960s.[1] Many a contemporary observer, alternatively, has conjured up other contemporary images: large, modern industrial units such as aircraft hangers, even silos, quonset huts, or European railroad terminals.

At the same time we have classical Mediterranean allusions. The gravel paths approaching the museum from south and north (and paralleling the processional approaches to the Amon Carter Museum just up the hill) become sacred ways leading one beside dark pools of gray granite with waterfalls. At the forecourt they converge in a grove of uniform small trees spaced in rows and selected to canopy any visitor walking over the gravel toward the entrance portico.[2] Repeating that motif on the south is another small "sacred grove," this time of crape myrtle trees, which may be seen east of the path's entrance from West Lancaster Street. Each grove forms an outdoor room, as designated by George Patton. The grove sheltered by the building's wings, with its canopy of yaupon hollies, especially contributes to a quickening sense of place; this site is Parnassian, dedicated to the muses. Renaissance villas also consciously emulated such classical settings.[3]

At the Kimbell Museum, all is preparation for entering the building. The journey is made physical not only in distance but through the senses. One walks over grass, steps on crunching gravel, hears as well as sees water. Then the usually brilliant Texas light that Kahn thought silvery is relieved by the shadow of a portico or by the small trees in the court. Gravel gives way to firm aggregate under the entrance portico and, once inside, to travertine and wood. Like a classical villa, the gallery level is uplifted by the lower level and one looks outward onto the green space and trees: a park preserve, a museum sanctuary.

The Yale Art Gallery gave us Kahn's double-faced building with a street facade and a garden facade. So too does the Kimbell Art Museum. The difference is striking, however. At the Kimbell the street facade is austere. Only a few yards distant is the public parking area. This is the entrance thought of by both architect and patron as the "back door." At Yale the front of the building is the public face of the institution: closed, proper, and protective except for the glazed, angled entry wall with its slice of view to the inside. It is on the garden facade, sheltered and enclosed by surrounding college buildings, that a wide window wall reveals and lights the interior and opens onto terraces with sculpture and places for visitors to sit. In Fort Worth the garden facade is the true front of the building; opened by the porticos and forecourt, it extends a welcome to visitors who must make the transition by approaching over paths or across the broad lawn.

The Kimbell's handsome proportions, simplicity and elegance in details, clarity of plan, and repetition of the low, spreading vaults are the hallmarks of Kahn's design, his classical museum. An average visitor, however, perceives the museum's interior space and its special lighting as most definitive and idiosyncratic. In contrast to the Yale Art Gallery's continuous open space, concentrated natural light at the window walls, and tight service core, the Kimbell galleries' skylights disperse light throughout. Kahn often stated that light was central in his architecture. With the Kimbell he achieved an unsurpassed quality of light that bathes whole rooms and reveals works of art in their richness. Onto the underside of the vaults and down the side walls and partitions flows a silvery light channeled by pierced aluminum reflectors. Still more light is allowed through in the areas where there are completely transparent reflectors. (We are reminded of the "beam splitters" in Marshall Meyers's early description, when these were to be made of mirrored glass.) In galleries where solid aluminum is immediately below the skylights this effect is reduced, but reflectance is just as silvery.

As foreseen by the architect in his 1967 address in Boston, courtyards introduce a different type of light into the galleries, varying the intensity and sometimes introducing subtly differing colorations. Window slits on exterior walls and lunettes under the vaults create further variations of light within the building. Control of the strong, often glaring, Texas sunlight transforms it and makes it almost a part of the architecture, so essential is it to the character of the museum. Kahn called material "spent light" and defined structure as "the maker of light, because structure releases the spaces between and that is light giving." [4] Statements like these are invested with weight and substance in the context of the Kimbell Art Museum.

As we have seen, the galleries possess an open plan but convey the sense of individual, lofty rooms separated by low channels, which in their turn are spaces more compressed and slightly darker. The distinction in materials on the floor reinforces the pattern: under the large spaces, white oak; under the channels, travertine. The open space possesses a definite shape. As at Yale, where the ceiling is used for horizontal distribution of services, here the channels—cast U-shaped concrete elements with aluminum soffits—perform the role of service spaces for ducts and conduits and serve to distribute air. They also have been used effectively for art installations. Temporary panels placed at the outer edges have created a long, narrow space, open at the ends, for showing drawings related to paintings exhibited in the bigger area. The arrangement has worked well and offers the additional advantage of exhibiting light-sensitive works in reduced light. The architect may not have foreseen just this possibility, but it is consistent with his idea of the museum's space and his expectation that it would adapt to more varied use than originally planned. (Kahn once suggested that enclosures beneath the low spaces could be used to store paintings that related to others in the galleries, a suggestion probably stemming from the study gallery he designed for the Yale Center for British Art.)[5] Elsewhere on the gallery floor other service components are found beneath the channels: the main stairwell and fire stairs, the passenger elevator, entrance to the library, storage areas, an auditorium aisle, and even entrances to the building.

In the nonpublic areas—library, offices, and workshops—Kahn also controlled natural light through means derived from observations of indigenous architecture, going back to his 1961 design for the consulate in Luanda, Angola. Using walls outside windows to cut glare and soften light, he placed the glass end-walls of the library three feet away from the travertine diaphragm walls that terminate the adjoining vaulted units north and south. The west light wells for offices and shops act in much the same way. Before entering interior spaces, light is bounced off travertine or, as the case may be, architectural concrete. The quality of the concrete itself, with its V-shaped demarcations of formwork panels catching the light, provides a pleasure the architect foresaw for those who work there.

Each wing has its own courtyard. In fact, the plan represents a variation on the traditional museum double-court layout. The large square court in the north wing is immediately seen from the front entrance and is a part of the axial spine; the southern courtyard is smaller, a twenty-foot square, and lies a little to the west of the center axis. The larger has the Maillol sculpture, the other a travertine fountain with a small standing figure by Bourdelle. Both have plantings of vines (Kelly's idea) to reduce the intensity of sunlight…

Kahn explained that "the whole plan of Kimbell is based on the room-like quality; and the natural light as being the only acceptable light," These were the form, the inseparable parts of the design. He valued the changeability of natural light—its ability to convey mood, weather, and seasons and even to create associations with the artist. "A painting that you don't see as well one day as you do another has a quality which the painting itself wants you to realize. It doesn't want you to have a one-shot image of it. Even it was painted in moods." Rather than windows that would permit too much glare, he preferred light from above, which is the most "brilliant," modified by the "natural light fixture"—the reflector to filter sunlight.

The cycloid vault structure that could function like a beam spanning one hundred feet from column to column and the low space between vaults "gave the small room and the large room at play ... The vault defies division, [and] the room has this character of completion." That same vault formed the exterior porches "like a presentation, like a piece of sculpture outside." The portico was not merely an addition, he said, but the same as the interior "without any obligation of paintings on its walls" It was a place of rest, an architectural introduction not called for in the program, an "offering." It was typical of Kahn that he thought of architecture generally not as "the solution of a problem but [as] a presentation of its spirit ... an offering to architecture itself. ... So the porch is part of that. ... This is Kimbell," he summed up. "Kimbell stands as natural light, and the making of rooms which are really indivisible, you see, so that the room remains a room." [6]…

... a 1987 analysis also focused on the building's structure and its expression. Peter McCleary thought the vaults a structural hybrid, "neither pure vault nor pure shell," basing his evaluation on the use of both stiff edge-beams and cables within the concrete. The skylight at the apex removes material at the point of maximum compressive stress. "The structural behavior of the roof [is] beyond the intellectual and visual comprehension of most architects and engineers," said McCleary, rejecting published explanations. But he also reported Kahn's own priorities, conveyed to him in conversation between the two during construction. Kahn told him that "the quality of light and place in the then partially completed museum was sufficiently beautiful that, for the moment, he was willing to sacrifice the truth of the structural principle." [7] Most visitors are convinced by the beauty of these architectural spaces in light and accept their structural means unquestioningly as logical.

An interesting parallel can be drawn between the Yale Art Gallery and the Kimbell Art Museum in connection with this criticism concerning structure. Kahn's space-frame for the Yale gallery floor was modified so that it became a floor of braced beams that preserved the appearance of a space-frame because of the tetrahedral openings. Unlike some critics, Kahn never expressed much regret over the loss of opportunity to use the space-frame, and in fact found that the slab as constructed served the purposes for which he designed it. The Kimbell's vaults with skylights are not traditional but are made possible by Komendant's shell design; structurally they are closer to a bridge between columns. Nevertheless, they are visually convincing when read as vaults with skylights. Some concrete walls also contain structural beams that are not visible to the spectator. (Frank Sherwood has pointed out that there are distinctions in formwork patterns suggesting these, but one must be intimate with the structure to comprehend them.) Kahn's attitude toward this aspect of architecture was humanistic: he embraced the structuralist belief in honesty of structural expression, but realized that at times human interpretation of expression rules structure.

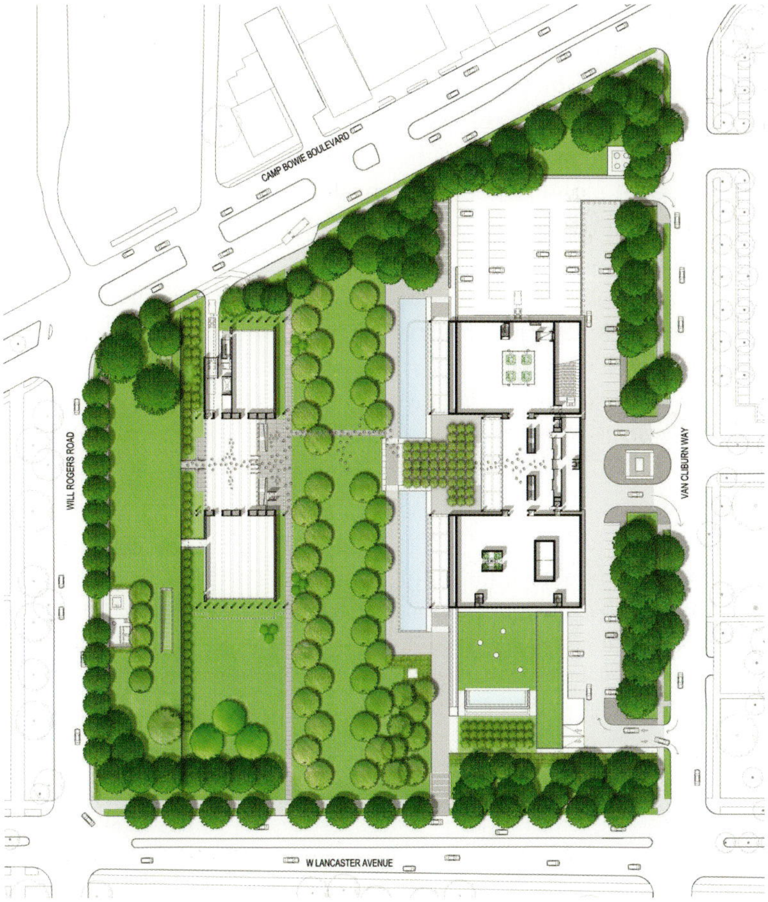

Drawing: © Renzo Piano Building Workshop

Extracts from *Renzo Piano as Light and Space Artist*
Paula Deitz

In the 1960s, Renzo Piano met Louis I. Kahn at the home of French structural designer Robert Le Ricolais on the campus of the University of Pennsylvania. Piano, the son of a builder from Genoa, was working as an assistant to Le Ricolais, who taught in the university's architecture department. At the time, Kahn was designing the Olivetti-Underwood Factory in Harrisburg, Pennsylvania, and needed someone to help him with drawings for the lighting of the open-plan factory. Within a week, Piano was installed making sketches for the project. Piano would work for Kahn intermittently for a few years before opening his own firm with Richard Rogers, with whom he won the competition to design Paris's iconic Centre Pompidou.

It was during the time that Piano worked for him that Kahn's firm began construction of the Kimbell Art Museum in Fort Worth, Texas (Kahn completed the building in 1972), a fact that became newly salient two years ago, when the Kimbell opened its Renzo Piano Pavilion, a freestanding glass, concrete, and wood addition. ...

More than anything else, it is his focus on light when designing the Kimbell pavilion that brings to mind Piano's history with Kahn. In his 1975 book *Light Is the Theme*, Kahn poetically describes his own use of natural light in the Kimbell, an approach that echoes his 1955 Trenton Bath House, in New Jersey, where sunlight slanting through clerestory bands and the central oculus in each pyramidal rooftop creates a luminous effect.

In the cycloid vaults of Kahn's Kimbell building, sunlight falling through slots running the length of their apexes is cast back upward by gull wing–shaped aluminum reflectors, imbuing the curved ceilings with a silvery glow that contrasts with the galleries' warm beige travertine walls. With eyebrow-shaped lunettes at the ends, and light slots along the bottom edges of each vault, the Kimbell is the Bath House squared. ...

Comparable to Kahn's Kimbell in size and proportion, Piano's pavilion consists of two separate, parallel buildings connected by two glass passageways, with the rear section underground, bermed over by a luscious green lawn of a roof. Like the Kahn building, the front section of the pavilion is divided into three spaces, with a gracious central glass-walled entrance lobby and café with white-oak floors that incorporate narrow slits as ventilation outlets.

In the south gallery one marvels at the soft light and silvery sheen of the smooth-as-silk concrete walls, constructed from architectural concrete mixed with titanium: without repeating Kahn's specific effect—that glow of dispersed light—Piano found an equivalent using contemporary materials. Running high overhead the length of the gallery, each of the roof's eight sections consists of three layers to regulate daylight: mechanical aluminum louvers above shade the sun's rays and function as photovoltaic cells; next, fritted glass diffuses light; and, finally, light is distributed evenly below through silky scrims stretched between pairs of laminated Douglas-fir beams. A gap between these ceiling elements and the wall creates a clerestory band of light not unlike Kahn's, and light also filters in through a glass wall at the gallery's end.

Outside the building, the wooden beams overhang a gallery supported by square white columns, an assemblage that resembles a classical colonnade but also suggests something of Japanese design. In the same way that Kahn extended his vaults into porticoes, Piano has created a starkly decorative exterior by converting his utilitarian materials into a canopy that also serves to shade light.

Piano Pavilion. Photo: © Nic Lehoux

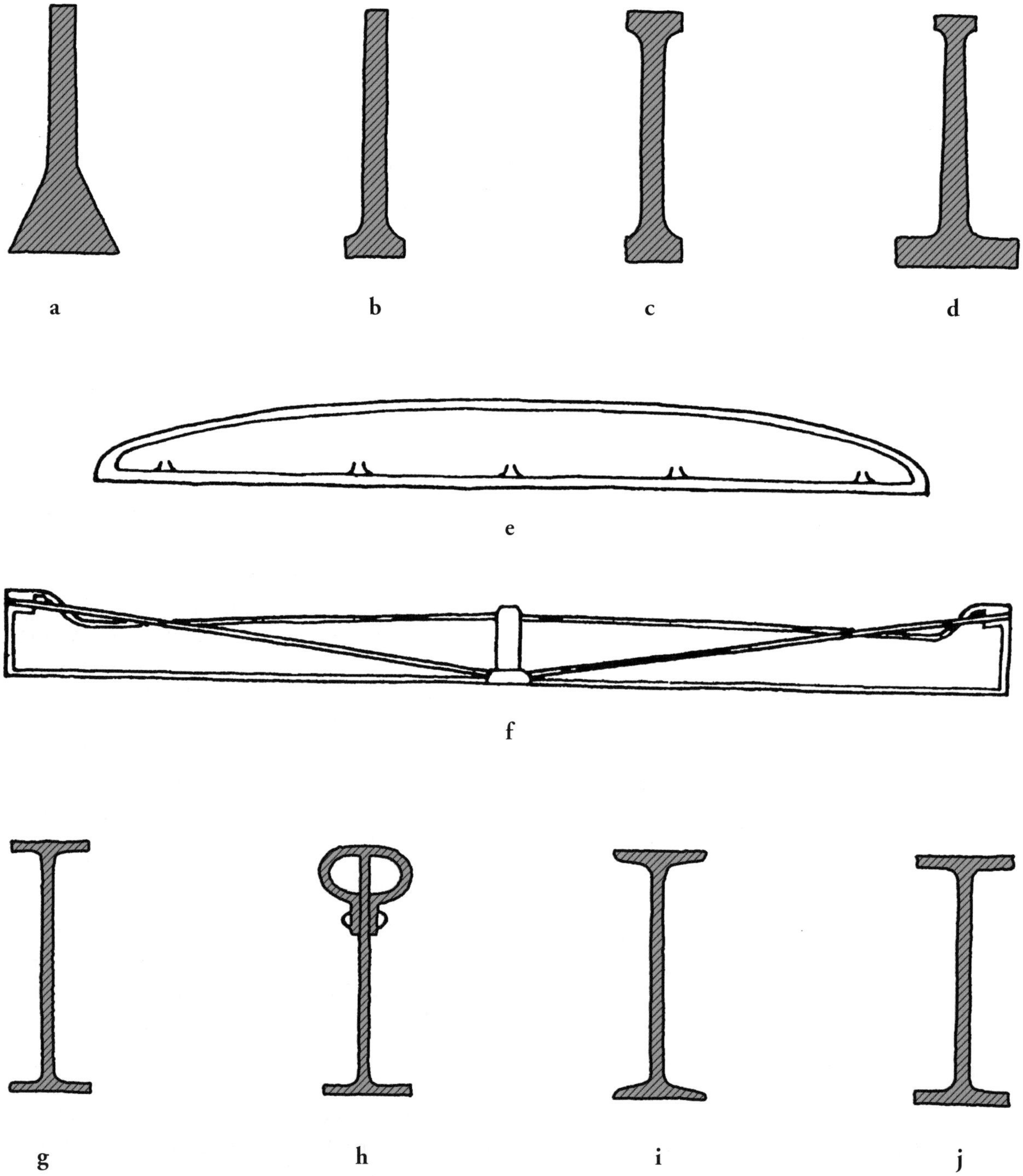

Adapted from drawing in *Developments in Structural Form, 2nd ed.*, by Rowland Mainstone

If the beam is well known and is effectively recognized as one of architecture's two primordial structural elements (together with the column), substantial and widespread refinements to the cross-sectional shape of the beam have been slower to occur, mostly dating from about a century ago. Be that as it may, the steel I-beam today holds symbolic status, often serving for the layperson as stand-in for all recent developments in structural engineering, indeed for the topic of structures itself. A short recounting of the evolution of this particular beam form is thus in order, presented here in an extract from Rowland Mainstone's seminal book, *Developments in Structural Form*, which is as equally wide-ranging in its topics covered as it is in historical and cultural breadth.

Roughly in concert with the evolution of this beam form, and taking full advantage of the element's symbolic, spatial and structural qualities, was the development in architecture of Modernism. From among the architects closely associated with this movement, Mies van der Rohe was one of the steel I-beam's most ardent adherents (and experimentors). Here, in a couple of passages about the Farnsworth House and the New National Gallery, the architect and critic Peter Blake recounts how Mies' design of these structures is dependent on and adapted to the use of steel beams, whether in the hierarchical, one-way beam system of the Farnsworth that (even if ultimately mostly hidden) is necessary to define continuous thin planes that "float" and suggest a direction of spatial "motion/direction" or – in the case of the Gallery – that maximize open space and provide a uniform visual foil in the form of an exposed two-way beam grid system. Moreover, close attention to the detailing of these elements is described as being integral to Mies' overall conceptual design intentions for these buildings.

The Iron and Steel Beam Evolves; Mies Follows Suit

from *Developments in Structural Form*
Rowland Mainstone

The iron beam had remained, until the end of the eighteenth century, of little importance structurally. Long before then it had been known as a bar of roughly square cross-section forged from pieces of soft blacksmith's iron welded together to build up the desired length and cross-section. Well-preserved examples even up to 10.6 m long and up to 280 mm square have survived from as early as the thirteenth century at Konarak on the north-east coast of India.[1] They were used to assist in bearing the weight of heavy masonry corbelled (or false-arch) ceilings. But they represented a prodigal waste of material and labour since the multiple welds were so defective that the finished beams can have had little useful strength. It has also been suggested that cuttings in the stone lintels of some Classical Greek temples originally housed similar, though smaller, beams.[2] But nothing has survived of these despite the good preservation of iron cramps and dowels in some of the same temples. It seems more probable that the insertions in the cuttings were of timber, perhaps sheathed in iron or sandwiched between thin iron plates.[3]

Towards the end of the eighteenth century, two factors led to the substitution of iron beams for the timber beams that had initially been used to carry the floors of the large new textile mills built to exploit the machines invented by men like Jedediah Strutt and Richard Arkwright. These were a desire to put an end to a series of disastrous fires in the original timber-framed buildings, and the general availability, by this time, of good cast iron as an obvious incombustible substitute for timber. The next fifty years saw an intensive development of 'fireproof' floors and of the iron beam as the major element of these floors.[4] 'Incombustible' would have been a more accurate description, since collapse could still result from the action of the heat of a severe fire, particularly in the case of the earlier floors in which shallow brick vaults spanned between the parallel beams and had their thrusts resisted by exposed or partly exposed wrought-iron tie rods.

[Drawing] (a) to (d) shows some typical cross-sections. In profile the depth was commonly increased towards the centre as in (e), correctly recognizing the increase in bending moment towards the centre when the ends were simply supported. The first cross-section (a), though much more slender, was otherwise closely modelled on a slightly earlier timber form in which triangular wooden skewbacks were attached to each side at the bottom to receive the shallow brick vaults spanning from beam to beam. It was soon altered to the (structurally) slightly more efficient form shown at (b). As yet, there was no top flange. But this was not a serious defect if the beam was simply supported, since the cast iron used was so much stronger in compression than in tension. It is, on the other hand, equally stiff under both. Therefore, when Tredgold first attempted to apply *a-priori* theoretical reasoning to the devising of the most efficient cross-section, he was correct in concluding that it was one with two equal flanges as at (c) if maximum stiffness (or least deflection at a given load) was taken as the criterion.[5] In practice though, there was usually ample stiffness whatever the cross-section; and maximum strength was more important, particularly since the brittleness of the material meant that any failure took place suddenly and without warning. Adopting, therefore, a criterion of maximum strength, Hodgkinson finally conducted a series of tests in which he progressively increased the width of the bottom flange of Tredgold's section in relation to that of the top flange until failure occurred in compression of the latter rather than in tension of the former. This gave the section shown at (d).[6]

A number of attempts followed to make good the tensile deficiencies of cast iron by the use of wrought-iron reinforcement. One expedient was the trussed beam shown in (f). ... The idea was very promising, being one of several early anticipations of modern prestressing techniques with the wrought-iron tie rods usually prestressed against the cast iron. But it fell into disrepute as a result of some serious collapses of beams that had been designed without adequate understanding of their behaviour, and was soon superseded by beams made wholly of wrought iron and then of steel.[7]

The wrought-iron and steel forms corresponding to those shown in (a) to (e) are parallel flanged ones with cross-sections such as those shown in (g) to (j). With no significant difference between the strengths in tension and compression, equal flanges at top and bottom become desirable for both maximum strength and maximum stiffness. The first two of these sections were early experimental ones; the other two are more recent ones produced in a wide variety of standard sizes for a variety of uses. The last section (j) has flanges of more uniform thickness which can be much broader if desired. It is therefore more efficient than (i), particularly where there may be bending about both axes of the section. All these sections have (or had) to be produced by passing white hot billets of the metal between a series of shaped rollers. A succession of opposed pairs of rollers is sufficient to produce (i). To produce (j) calls, on the other hand, for separate rollers for each face, suitably geared together. Development of suitable mills began around 1900 and sections of this form became more and more widely available from the 1930s onwards.[8]

The alternative to rolling single sections of the required shape and size in either wrought iron or steel was to build them up from simpler sections—usually flat plates and angles or Ts. These were riveted or bolted together and are now more frequently welded. All early large wrought-iron beams were, in fact, fabricated in this way, and the largest steel beams have continued to be so fabricated despite a progressive widening of the range of large sections available directly from the rolling mills.

from *The Master Builders*

Peter Blake

The house that Mies designed ... in Wyoming—and that was his immediate reason for coming to the U.S.—was never built. But shortly after the end of World War II, Mies began work on another house, which has probably had as great an influence on recent domestic architecture in America as any single work of the postwar years.

The client for this house was Dr. Edith Farnsworth, a brilliant Chicago physician who had been a close friend of Mies for several years. In 1946 she bought a piece of land on the Fox River in Plano, Illinois, about an hour's ride from Chicago, and Mies began to design a house for her to be built on that site.

The Farnsworth house is, in all likelihood, the most complete statement of glass-and-steel, skin-and-bones architecture Mies or anyone else will ever be able to make. It is, also, the ultimate in universality, the ultimate in precision and polish, the ultimate in the crystallization of an idea.

The house is a rectangular structure of eight steel columns, set in two parallel rows some twenty-eight feet apart. In the long direction of the plan the steel columns are spaced twenty-two feet apart. Between these eight columns there are held two slabs framed in steel—the floor and the roof. These slabs seem to float in the air (the floor slab is about four feet above the ground, and the ceiling plane is about nine feet above that), and they are held between the steel H columns as if by some magnetic force. At each end the floor and roof slabs cantilever out six feet beyond the last row of columns.

Between these two floating slabs there is a simple, glass-enclosed living space and porch. The living space is, to all intents and purposes, a single room, divided into sleeping, living, kitchen, and service areas. The floor throughout is of Italian travertine; the ceiling is white plaster; the few interior partitions are finished in natural primavera; the curtains inside the glass skin are of natural-colored, off-white shantung; and the steel frame itself is painted white.

As a matter of fact, the steel frame was carefully polished before the coats of white paint were applied: first, all the welding marks at the connections between columns and beams were ground down; next, Mies had the steel sand-blasted to get rid of the "rough" texture of the

Chicago History Museum. HB-13810-I. Photo: Hedrich-Blessing Collection

rolled, structural sections; then he had a coat of zinc sprayed over the sandblasted surface to prevent rust; and, finally, the white paint was applied with such care that the finished surfaces look almost baked on.

One reason for the elevation of the floor plane above the grade is that the Fox River tends to rise and overflow its banks in the spring, so that the house looks like a pier or a boat during those days. Another reason is that Mies wanted a quality of airiness, of space-in-motion, which an earth-bound house would not have had to the same degree.

It took Mies six years to design and build this perfect jewel of a house. During this period his disciple, Philip Johnson, went ahead and built his own famous glass-and-steel house in New Canaan, Connecticut. Johnson has always made a point of saying that his house was designed after Mies had first developed the Farnsworth concept and that it was, therefore, based upon the Farnsworth house, although the latter was not completed until two years after Johnson moved into his own home. Actually, Johnson is unnecessarily modest in crediting Mies with all the qualities of his own house, for the Johnson and the Farnsworth houses—apart from being all steel and glass—are completely different in character. Johnson's house is symmetrical in its elevations; the Farnsworth house has a porch and a lower deck at one end and is quite dynamically asymmetrical. Johnson's house sits on the ground like a delightful little classical temple; the Farnsworth house is virtually airborne. Johnson's house has dark gray steel columns at all corners, containing the volume within the glass shell; the Farnsworth house has open corners and cantilevered ends, so that the interior space is projected outward into the landscape as in any structure by Wright. Finally, the Johnson house has a strong post-and-beam look, a feeling of compression in the columns; whereas the Farnsworth house has a sense of tension, of steel being stretched out to its ultimate potentials. (The white steel columns of the Farnsworth house are so precisely welded to the horizontal steel fascias of floor and roof planes that the steel "sings" like a tuning fork when it is lightly tapped. ...)

These differences between Johnson's and Mies's glass houses are more significant than they might seem. For what they add up to is this: Mies's house was a very "American" sort of statement—dynamic, cantilevered, almost in motion; whereas Johnson (who was born in Ohio) had built a tiny, classical *palazzo*—a static, columnar, serene temple of a house. Mies's responsiveness to America—a continent of motion—began long before he came to Chicago; indeed, this quality of motion is already quite apparent in the Barcelona Pavilion (although the Pavilion did sit on a pedestal), and it is the quality Mies undoubtedly derived from Wright's Prairie houses. ...

Throughout most of the 1960's, Mies had worked on a scheme for a so-called New National Gallery (Neue Nationalgalerie) to be built in West Berlin, as part of a large cultural center going up in that city. On September 15th, 1968, the building was dedicated. It turned out to be one of his finest works—easily on a par with the Barcelona Pavilion and the Seagram tower.

Its basic scheme resembles that of the Bacardi Administration Building, designed by Mies for Santiago, Cuba, in 1958, but never built. It differs from the Bacardi Building in two essential respects: its great pavilion structure is of steel, rather than of concrete—and it is about fifty per cent larger in area. The huge steel-and-glass pavilion was designed to house temporary exhibitions (it is known as the Gallery of the Twentieth Century); and the pedestal on which the pavilion stands houses the permanent collection of the so-called Prussian Cultural Heritage Foundation. The two areas are administered as a single museum, but—initially, at least—the exhibition spaces were kept quite separate. As a result, exhibitions much more suitable for the low (thirteen foot) ceiling height of the galleries within the pedestal were shown under the huge (twenty-eight foot) ceiling height of the upper level, and dwarfed by it.

Apart from this, the building is a success in every respect. It has a grace, an attention to detail, a quiet repose that makes it one of the most completely self-assured structures of the century. When Dirk Lohan, Mies' grandson and close collaborator, inspected the finished building, he felt that the "grain" of the Greek marble used to clad the two vertical utility shafts within the upper floor might have been better matched. But that seemed to be the only flaw—and no one except Lohan or Mies would have noticed it.

The vital statistics are impressive: the prefabricated, steel roof measures about 215 feet square, and weighs 1,250 tons. It was raised hydraulically to a clear height of twenty-eight feet in a mere eight hours and fifty-seven minutes. (Mies was driven onto the site in a Mercedes convertible during the roof-hoisting operation, and stood under the roof as it went up, leaning against his car. Someone found him there, watching those 1,250 tons of steel poised over his head—while his chauffeur had taken cover in a safer precinct—and asked how it all looked to him. "Enormous!" he said, grinning, and puffing at his cigar.)

Like the Bacardi project, the glass pavilion of the New National Gallery is supported on eight cross-shaped steel columns, pin-connected to the roof. The roof framing consists of six foot deep welded steel girders, spaced twelve feet apart in both directions to form the grid. The frame, it was announced by the German structural engineers, was "statically indeterminate to the 36th degree," and could not have been designed without reference to computers. One major problem, in Mies' mind, at least, was how to determine the amount of camber (or upward curvature) required in the steel roof to counteract the downward deflection that occurs when the structure settles in place. This incredibly subtle balance between initial upward curvature and ultimate downward deflection was here achieved to perfection.

The roof grid contains elaborate downlights, designed to be as inconspicuous as possible. Within the egg-crate of structural steel, there are recessed grilles of black aluminum that keep the glare of spotlights out of the viewer's eyes.

The platform on which the steel-and-glass pavilion stands is more conventional in construction—reinforced concrete, clad in granite, and measuring roughly 350 by 340 feet in plan. A portion of this—a slice about sixty-six feet wide and a little more than 300 feet long—is a sculpture court, open to the sky. The rest of this handsome "basement" is a succession of spacious galleries, most of them artificially lit.

The site is next to one of West Berlin's characteristic canals—the Landwehrkanal—and has a slight slope to it; and the New National Gallery's pedestal almost touches the sidewalk on the east, and drops off toward the west so that the walled sculpture court, at the end of the building, is really on grade with its surroundings. The building not merely fits into its site—it helps define and organize it through its granite retaining walls, and the wide flights of stairs that rise to the upper level platform. That platform—the plaza on which the steel-and-glass pavilion stands—supports major works of sculpture as well.

When the New National Gallery was dedicated, Mies' doctors in Chicago pronounced him unfit to attend the ceremonies.

They were wrong, and he might have lived a little longer had he seen this splendid work. Museum directors from every part of the world attended the opening, and so did architects—including even Walter Gropius. He had not always seen eye-to-eye with Mies, nor Mies with him. An American friend who had gone to Berlin to attend the dedication talked to Mies upon his return. Mies was enormously excited: he did not care about the honors, the dignitaries who had attended (or what they had said); he wanted to know about the light and the space, and about the finish of the structure and the quality of the workmanship.

He had told the citizens of Berlin, three years earlier, during the groundbreaking ceremonies, that he hoped his Gallery would be "an adequate framework for a noble endeavor"; and a few days before the dedication he had sent word from Chicago that he hoped the New National Gallery would serve the happiness of mankind, man's spirit, and man's art. ...

New National Gallery. Photo: Andreas Levers

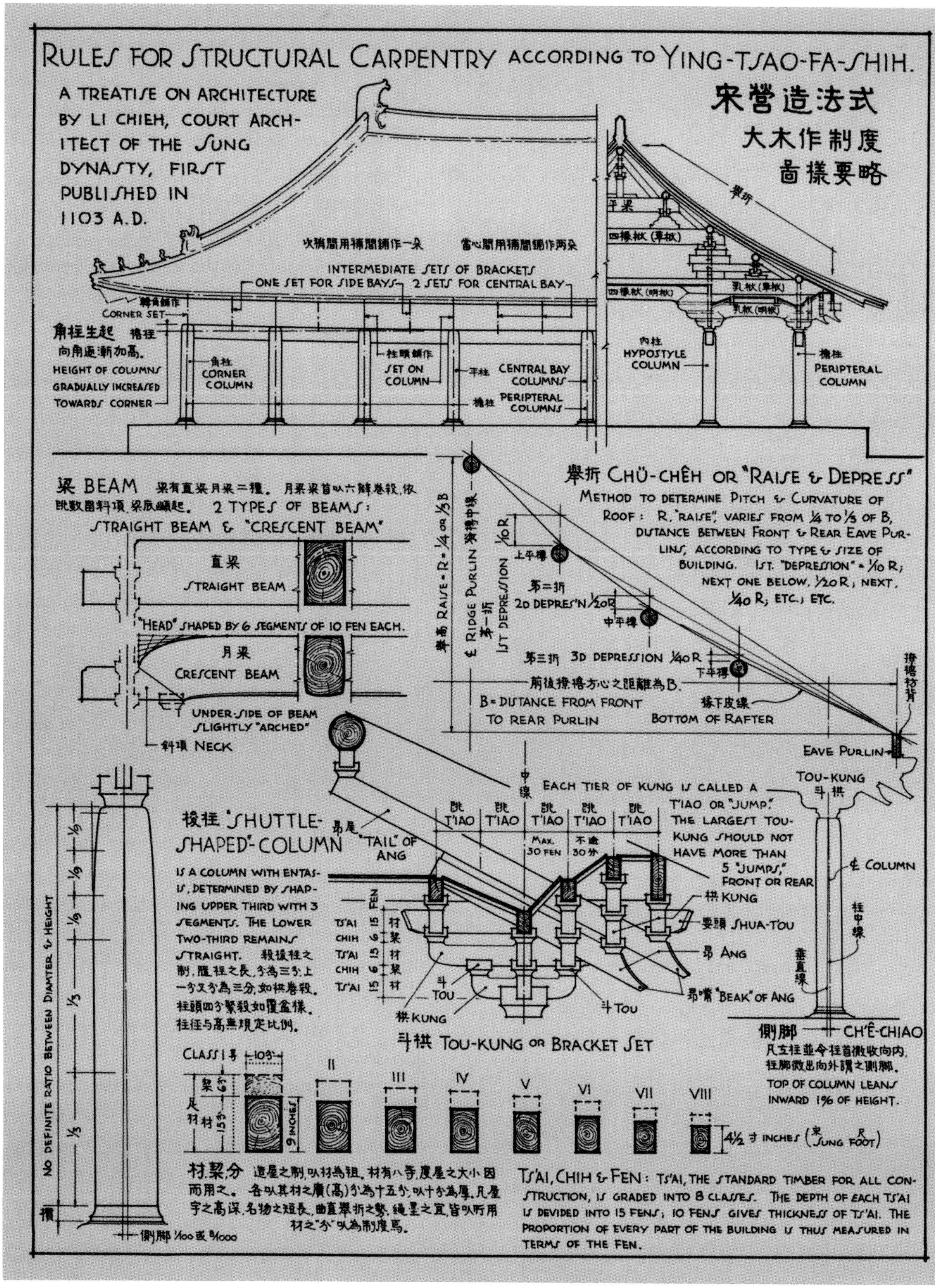

Drawing from *A Pictorial History of Chinese Architecture*. By courtesy of Mrs. Lin Zhou

It is, of course, not only the Miesian steel beam that can be associated with Modernism; for example, Auguste Perret, who as we saw in Chapter 1 experimented with adapting the design of reinforced concrete columns, was also concerned with the detailing of beams made of this "modern" material. The perennial struggle to adapt traditional built forms to new material developments and changing notions of space and program is a timeless story, and one that has played itself out in various cultural contexts. As a case in point, the architectural historian Delin Lai reveals here how, roughly a century ago, the Chinese architect and scholar Liang Sicheng sought to reconcile through the design of the Nanjing Museum (built as the National Central Museum) the forms and particular details of historical Chinese temples and palaces – e.g., their iconic roofs built up of stacked arrangements of wooden beams, exquisitely detailed and connected together – with the novel Modernist notions of form, space and material development emanating at that time from the West. This makes for a fascinating story about both cultural heritage adaptation and cross-cultural exchange, and Sicheng was particularly well suited to the task, having carefully catalogued many historical temples himself as well as having been educated at Ivy League architecture schools in the United States. And so while it is generally well established that Asian architecture strongly influenced the development of the Modernist movement due to eye-opening visits to Japan and China by several renowned architects from Europe and the United States, it should not be surprising to also find evidence that the cross-cultural influences on building forms occurred in both directions between East and West.

Chinese Building Traditions Meet Modernism

from *Idealizing a Chinese Style*
Delin Lai

In 1946, Liang Sicheng (1901-72), the most distinguished architectural historian of twentieth-century China, wrote:

> *The Chinese building is a highly "organic" structure. It is an indigenous growth that was conceived and born in the remote prehistoric past, reached its "adolescence" in the Han dynasty (around the beginning of the Christian era). Matured into full glory and vigor in the Tang dynasty (seventh and eighth centuries), mellowed with grace and elegance in the Sung (Song) dynasty (eleventh and twelfth centuries), then started to show signs of old age, feebleness, and rigidity, from the beginning of the Ming dynasty (fifteenth century). Now, with the coming of reinforced concrete and steel framing, Chinese architecture faces a grave situation. Indeed, there is a basic similarity between the ancient Chinese and the ultramodern. But can they be combined? Can the traditional Chinese structural system find a new expression in these new materials? Possibly. But it must not be the blind imitation of "periods." Something new must come out of it, or Chinese architecture will become extinct.* [1]

Did he have an answer, no matter how tentative, to this problem of style, new materials, and Chinese architecture? If so, it may lie in the National Central Museum in Nanjing, which was designed a decade before he posed the problem.

The National Central Museum was one of the most important buildings created in the early decades of Republican China.[2] The product of one of the few architectural competitions held during the period, it had a self-consciously Chinese design, modeled on that of the Liao and Song dynasties, and reflected the historicist thinking of its design advisor, Liang Sicheng. It was the first building design in which Liang participated, and it remains his most significant work because of the "big roof" *(da wuding)* controversy later in his life. [3]

Owing to the building's importance in the history of China's Republican period, its architectural style has prompted a number of scholarly speculations. Present day historians who try to explain the designers' seemingly thorough grounding in Liao and Song architecture tend to view the building's style as one with a revivalist underpinning. For example, *Zhongguo Jianzhu Shi* (History of Chinese architecture), the textbook of Chinese colleges, identifies the style of the museum as "Gongdian shi" (palatial style).[4] The author of the entry "The Central Museum in Nanjing" in the encyclopedic book *Ershi Shiji Zhongguo Jianzhu* (Architecture of twentieth-century China) labeled it "fanggu jianzhu" (architecture that imitates the ancient).[5] Although these characterizations effectively summarize a key approach to Chinese style architectural design in the twentieth century, they are also misleading. Not only do they imply that the design of the museum passively "imitated" traditional Chinese architecture, an assumption that leads them to a simplistic interpretation of this building, but, more important, they also overlook the efforts of Liang and his colleagues to pursue an architectural idiom that is simultaneously modern and uniquely national.

This study addresses two key questions. How did Liang cope with issues of national identity and modernity in architecture as a Chinese architectural historian and an architect trained in the Beaux-Arts tradition? And what was his conception of modern Chinese culture as a member of the elite during the early Republican period? By carefully identifying the sources of the museum's design and analyzing the relationship between the design and early writings on Chinese architecture, this article demonstrates the creativity of the design response, particularly in relation to Liang and the architects' ideal of a Chinese-style modern architecture. This ideal, I argue, is profoundly rooted in the expectation on the part of Chinese intellectuals in the early decades of the twentieth century of a Chinese cultural renaissance. To achieve that goal, they studied China's architectural past, evaluated it, and, more significant, redefined and justified it by putting it into a dialogue with contemporary architectural discourses and historiography formulated in the West, as well as with criticism of Chinese architecture by Western scholars and the contemporary Chinese public. Seen in this light, the National Central Museum in Nanjing, the most important building dedicated to a cultural institution in the first three decades of the Republic of China, emerges as the epitome of this ideal.

The Design of the National Central Museum

In July 1934 the Ministry of Education authorized the formation of the Preparatory Committee of the National Central Museum (PCNCM). The members of the committee included two geographers, an artist, a historian, a law professor, an economist, an archaeologist, and a physicist, as well as Liang Sicheng. [6] Liang, as the only architect and architectural historian, was appointed the "special member" *(zhuanmen weiyuan)* of the committee and the "project consultant" *(gongcheng guwen)*, responsible for "reviewing all the affairs associated with the project and drafting all the guidelines and contracts." [7] In June 1935 the committee held a limited competition for the design of the museum. Twelve of the thirteen renowned Chinese architects who were invited submitted a proposal. [8]

Liang had received his master of architecture degree from the School of Fine Arts at the University of Pennsylvania in 1927. He went on to Harvard University to study Chinese architectural history, planning to pursue a doctorate in art history. Dissatisfied with the contemporary treatment of the subject by Western scholars, however, he returned to China in 1928 and established the Department of Architectural Engineering at the National Northeastern University in Shenyang. In 1931 he moved to Beiping (now Beijing) to join the Society for Research in Chinese Architecture (Zhongguo Yingzao Xueshe, SRCA) with his wife, Lin Huiyin (Phyllis Whei-yin Lin, 1903-54), who in 1927 received a bachelor of fine arts degree from Penn as well. [9] The SRCA, established in 1929 by Zhu Qiqian (1872-1964), a retired scholar official in early Republican China, until the 1950s was the only institution in China that studied architectural history. To reform a methodology that had been grounded in the traditional compilation and interpretation of Chinese classical texts, Zhu asked Liang and Liu Dunzhen (Liu Tun-tseng, 1897-1968), an architect who had graduated from the Tokyo Polytechnic in 1921, to spearhead the work of the society by carrying out a series of field surveys to search for the remains of ancient Chinese structures. By the time of the museum competition, their investigation had covered about fifty counties in Hebei, Shanxi, Henan, Zhejiang, and Shandong provinces. In 1934 Liang published *Qingshi yingzao zeli*, a book on Qing dynasty construction methods. [10] Meanwhile, he had also been studying the Song-dynasty architectural manual *Yingzao fashi (YZFS)* during these years. [11] Another work that he had compiled with a student, titled *Jianzhu sheji cankao tuji* (Pictorial references for architectural design), a collection of details of historical buildings intended for use in the new Chinese-style architectural design, was to be published in November 1935. [12]

The competition guidelines written by Liang required that the museum "fully employ [the style of] Chinese architecture" "as long as doing so does not affect the function of a modern museum" and providing that it be "as simple and spacious as possible." [13] Implicit in these conditions was a concern that modern function and Chinese style might conflict. Designers were challenged to avoid that conflict.

The proposals were reviewed on 4 and 5 September by a jury consisting of the client's representative, the chairman of the PCNCM, a representative of the architectural committee, Liu Dunzhen, and Liang. The results of the competition were announced on 6 September. [14] None of the proposals dealt thoroughly with the issues of site, function, and architectural form that the committee had expected them to address. The committee reluctantly chose the design by the University of Michigan graduates Xu Jingzhi (Su Gin-Djih) and Li Huibo (Lei Wei-Paak), of the architectural firm Su, Yang & Lei Architects, who rendered the main hall of the museum as an eleven-bay corridor with a Qing-style hip roof. This design, as the report stated, was "the best one among all the proposals in meeting all the requirements and in showing the potential for revision." Liang, as the "special member" of the museum's construction committee, responsible for architectural affairs, was appointed architectural consultant, to guide further modification of the design. [15]

Liang's name appeared on major working drawings as the "consultant" *(guwen)*,[16] but he must have done more than offer suggestions. Chen Mingda (1915-97), a research assistant in the SRCA, recalled in 1988 that "the architect of the Nanjing Museum (originally the Central Museum) was Xu Jingzhi. Because the design had to include the big roof [of traditional Chinese architecture], and he was ignorant [of that tradition], he came to us. At that time, we as the consultants were very honest and did a lot of substantial work and quite a large number of drawings, unlike those nowadays who are called consultants but do nothing." [17] Chen's statement reveals the extent of Liang's involvement in developing the design, which is affirmed by analysis of its details, especially those of the main hall in the museum compound.

Liang's efforts were instrumental in changing the architects' design of the main hall. The new design, with nine bays, is in what Liang described as the "Liao and Song Style *(Liao Song xingshi)*" [18] and the architects called the "Liao or early Song style", [19] referring to the architecture of coexistent dynasties of the tenth to the twelfth century, Liao (907-1125) in the North and Song (960-1279) in the South. The construction of the reinforced-concrete structure started in June 1936. Interrupted by the Sino-Japanese War from 1937 to 1945, it was not completed until 1948. [20]

The style of the building deserves closer scrutiny, given that it was not adopted detail for detail from any historical structure. By the time Liang and his colleagues at the SRCA participated in designing the museum, they had carefully studied a substantial number of buildings dating from the mid-Song and Qing dynasties, as well as two famous construction manuals, the *YZFS* of the Song and the *Gongbu gongcheng zuofa zeli* of the Qing. The style of Liao and early Song dynasty architecture did not exist as a composite style historically but was assembled and classified by SRCA scholars from the historical structures they discovered and identified. Why did Liang and the architects invent a new style instead of simply using either the Qing or mid-Song style?

To answer this question I follow Liang's approach to architectural investigation, analyzing the characteristics of the composition and structural elements of the museum by re-examining the data on working drawings. I then compare this information with data on the ancient structures, especially those of the Liao and Song dynasties that Liang and the architectural historians who were his contemporaries investigated, to identify their approach to these models. ...

Guiding Principles behind the National Museum Design

The synthetic approach to the sources Liang and the architects explored for the museum would have been familiar to Liang as a student of the Beaux-Arts tradition. As Julien Guadet, the chair of the Theory of Architecture at the École des Beaux-Arts, wrote in his monumental work *Éléments et théories de l'architecture*, the two fundamental issues of architectural design are elements and composition. The elements include the walls, cornices, doors and windows, porticos, and especially the orders. Composition refers to the functional and spatial logic of the plans of different architectural types. Although many of Liang's contemporaries had attempted to create a Chinese-style modern architecture by combining the plan layout and compositional devices of Western architecture with such elements of Chinese architecture as the curved roof, bracket set, and sculptured plinth, Liang endeavored to define a "pure" language of Chinese architecture. His study of the two ancient architectural manuals and his compilation of ancient architectural details, which he later referred to as the "grammar" and "vocabularies" of Chinese architecture, [21] are evidence of this endeavor and of the Beaux-Arts notion of architecture on which it was premised.[22]

Even though it is clear that in general Liang resorted to what he considered an authentic language of Chinese architecture for the building's composition, namely, its plan, section, elevation, and structural elements, some crucial details have yet to be explained. What was the rationale for choosing elements from some buildings but not others? Why was a detail as important as the roof curve revised when other elements were not? And most significant, what were the principles that guided the selections and the modifications?

Undoubtedly, the authenticity or "Chineseness" of the design was the first concern of Liang and the architects. Yet further examination of the relationship between the elements they chose and Liang and Lin's historical writings reveals the link between the Liangs' writings on Chinese buildings, the design of the museum, and Western architectural preoccupations with an ideal of "classical" beauty and with structural and functional rationalism. In other words, the seemingly pure Chinese style of the museum was in fact shaped by Western aesthetics. To the Liangs, this was not a contradiction, for they understood that the style of the museum was not only Chinese but also universal and modern.

"Classical beauty" is visible in many subtle modifications and in the reference to the classical orders of Western architecture in the design of the corridor. The subtle modifications include the upturned roof ridge, the gradual rise in pillar heights toward the ends of the corridor *(shengqi)*, the outward-pushing ridge *(tuishan)*, as well as the entasis, or slight convexity, of the pillars, and the shape of the lintel (which is flattened on its top and bottom surfaces but has convex sides).These measures would certainly have increased the difficulty of construction. They were key markers, however, of the vigorous and elegant Liao and Song styles.

Liang associated the beauty of the curved lines in Chinese architecture with Greek architecture. For example, in discussing the lintels and beams of Dule Monastery, he said:

> *As to its delightfulness, a noteworthy point is the entasis that makes the central part of a lintel a convex surface. Although entasis does not change the static property of the lintel, the rigid line becomes rounded. This is the result of assiduous craftsmanship and should not be overlooked. The Parthenon in Athens, Greece, has similar subtle measures. To counterbalance vigor with elegance was a widely accepted principle in the past. So is the aforementioned batter [of the inward-leaning side columns of the Dule gate], which is also visible in Greek architecture. Is it because our ancestors learned from the Greeks?* [23]

... Liang, in his writings, regarded the combination of bracket and column in Chinese architecture as analogous to the role of an order in Greco-Roman architecture. [24] The increase in the museum's ratio of bracket to column height to 1:3 was hardly coincidental. According to Fletcher's *History of Architecture*, that is the ratio of entablature to a column of the Doric Order, the most masculine of the five orders of Western architecture. By drawing a mathematical connection with the most appropriate paradigmatic Greek order, Liang and the architects achieved a classical Chinese form that was analogous to its Western Greek counterpart.

Structural rationalism, in addition to its importance as a criterion for judging Chinese architecture of different periods, also served as a standard for Liang and the architects in their choice of the ideal forms of structural elements from existing Liao and Song buildings. For example, Liang and the architects referred to Sandashi Hall of Guangji Monastery in designing the interior beams and *dougong* brackets of the museum. Liang once enthusiastically praised the hall for employing the open-frame method *(cheshang luming zao)*, which, with no ceiling to conceal the structural features, "gives the architect a grand opportunity to display his ingenuity in handling major carpentry as an artistic creation." [25]

The use of brackets in the hall to replace small posts, he said, "though visible in later buildings, exhibits an unforeseen delicacy of workmanship". [26]

Structural rationalism seems also to have shaped their preference for a particular proportion for the section of the *lan'e* lintel of the corridor. Its height is 20.5 inches, equal to two *cai*. This measurement follows the prescriptions of *YZFS*, which specified that "the height of a lintel is twice that of a *cai*." Yet its width is not two-thirds of the height, as prescribed, but 10.25 inches, or half the height. This proportion recalls Liang's comment on the beams and lintels of Guanyin Pavilion and the Front Gate of Dule Monastery: "According to the modern science of beam making, the section should be about two to one in proportion. *YZFS's* prescription is three to two, more reasonable than the one based on the Qing method, which is almost a square, with a proportion of ten to eight or twelve to ten. Guanyin Pavilion's and the Front Gate's proportions are two to one, the same as the modern way. Is our scientific knowledge becoming backward?".[27]

The use of reinforced concrete raised the question whether it was still necessary and "reasonable" to design a structural element in the size and the proportions of wooden models. [28] But in this case aesthetic considerations, such as the stylistic authenticity and structural rationality exhibited in the design, led Liang and the architects to sacrifice material sincerity.

As a unique part of Chinese Order, *dougong* bracketing is clearly the key element in Liang's study of Chinese architectural history as well as the most characteristic feature of Chinese architecture. Structural rationalism, however, rendered *dougong* unnecessary in the modern era when reinforced concrete offered a much stronger support for cantilevering than the wooden arms of bracketing. Liang and the architects thus needed to balance contradictory pursuits, that is, to display unique Chinese architectural characteristics on the one hand, and to fulfill the imperative of modern structural rationalism on the other. To do so, they chose their models of pillar-top bracketing and corner-pillar bracketing from the Front Gate of Dule Monastery, a building that, as Liang put it, "is a masterpiece in the use of *dougong* brackets that meet the highest artistic structural standards," [29] as well as the use of intercolumnar bracketing from Haihui Hall of Huayan Monastery, the simplest of all the Liao and Song examples. The Front Gate of Dule Monastery is low-grade and only three bays wide, and Haihui Hall is also a low-grade building owing to the form of its

overhanging gable roof *(xuanshan)*. In adopting the bracketing from these buildings to the high-ranking, nine-bay-wide museum, Liang and the architects abandoned the hierarchical connotation of this traditional element while retaining its unique formal beauty. Furthermore, in a modern republican society, the repudiation of hierarchy could be seen as a modern and universalist choice. In using the gate's *dougong* as a model, Liang and the architects highlighted the bracket's structural-rational purpose over its decorative purpose, for the gate's *dougong* is a much simplified type of five-*puzuo* and *touxin*. It is made of horizontal load-bearing arms with neither an extra lateral bracket arm crossing through the first projected arm, as in the "added heart" *(jixin)* method, nor the *ang*, or lever, an element unnecessary in a concrete structure. For the same reason, it seems Liang and the architects eliminated both the diagonal arms, "a favorite of the Liao architects," [30] and also the diagonal arm cutting across the corner horizontally at a 45-degree angle in the corner-pillar bracketing of the Dule gate.

The irregularity of the pillar grid, another noteworthy feature visible in Liao buildings, gets reinterpreted in the museum as well. Although that irregularity may have been a result of using varied structural systems, as Chen later believed, [31] Liang named it the "column-eliminating method," meaning that the irregularity in column arrangement was not a consequence of using special structural systems but rather a measure taken to meet functional requirements or, in Vitruvian terms, "commodity"-appropriate spatial accommodation *(shiyong)*. As Liang wrote in a report of an investigation in 1933: "The most admirable parts of the plans of the aforementioned six buildings (the Daxiongbao Hall, Sutra Library, and Haihui Hall of Huayan Monastery and the Gate, Sansheng Hall, and Daxiongbao Hall of Shanhua Monastery] are the arrangements of columns. They varied according to practical needs, and maintained the architectural principle very well. ... [For example,] because the pedestals of statues are placed within the inner circle of columns in the central area of a hall, and worshipers are outside the circle, a big space is needed. Eliminating the columns at the center would satisfy the commodity." [32]

Liang had criticized the spatial arrangement of Ming and Qing architecture for maintaining a rigid column grid that lacked the flexibility needed for functional adjustments: "Judging by this single fact, we can see that the architecture of our country had been in decline since the Ming dynasty". [33] Accordingly, Liang and the architects working with him eliminated four central columns of the museum hall, so that the design would demonstrate the architects' functional orientation.

The great curvature of the roof demonstrates dramatically the effort to conform the design of the museum to the nature of a modern material, as part of the concern with function as well as rational structure. The upturned roof of Chinese architecture has prompted much speculation in the West. The German scholar Ernst Boerschmann wrote, "The impulse which drove the Chinese to use these curving forms came from their desire to express the movement of life ... By the curving of the roof, buildings are made to approach as nearly as possible the forms of nature—the varied outlines of rocks, trees, etc."[34] It is no surprise that Lin, who believed Chinese architecture was not only structurally rational but also functional, disagreed. She argued:

The roof is originally the most necessary part of a building ... From the beginning it is not merely the building's cover. Because of the real problems of rain and sunlight, the eave expands. It is not difficult to make a protruding eave, but the deeper the eave, the lower it is, preventing sunlight [from coming in]. Moreover, when rainwater runs down rapidly from the roof, it splashes [the wall] under the eave. To solve these problems, we create the "flying eave," namely the upturned roof edge with double layers of rafter, which forms a slight curve. For aesthetic reasons, the curvature of the corners of the roof is increased. This "flying eave," curved on the edge and raised at four corners, is a natural and reasonable structural method ... By and large, the curved roofline, which has long been regarded as a mystery, has no rationale beyond structural principles, unnatural or artificial. [But] it is also successful in both aesthetics and commodity ... Because the roof style developed by the Chinese is unique, distinct from various European traditions, foreigners noticed it from very early on and proposed different interpretations, all of which were quite imaginative. Some said that the Chinese roof was derived from the tents of nomadic times; some said that it symbolized the overhanging branches of the pine tree; some saw the Chinese flying eave as bizarre, some called it childish, some focused on its animal ornaments, uselessly studying their meanings. It is a waste of time to criticize their analyses of the curved roof or the reviews of its decorative principles. The curved roof argues for its own aesthetic and functional value. We can simply acknowledge the undeniable artistic success of our structure. [35]

To Lin, the "raise-depress" method of constructing a curved Chinese roofline also satisfied the functional point of view. She cited a sentence from *Kaogong ji* (Records of artificers)—a Chinese classic believed to have been compiled in the early Western Han dynasty (206 BCE-24 CE), based on the remaining text of the Spring and Autumn period (eighth to fifth century BCE)—that reads, "The craftsman who makes the canopy [of a cart] ... wants the top *zun* and the edge *bei*. Top *zun* and edge *bei* can help throw water quickly and far away." Although no evidence indicates that the curved roofline of Chinese architecture appeared as early as the Western Han dynasty, the precise meanings of the words *zun* and *bei* are "high" and "low," or "up" and "down," which in *Kaogon gji* could represent only a pitched roof. Lin, however, interpreted these terms as meaning "steep" and "flat." Hence, she said, this sentence, "clearly explained the actual function of this kind of roof [built according to the 'raise-depress' method]." Moreover, making the top *zun* can "correct the perspective that downplays the roof ridge, making the roof look lofty and enhancing its beauty in appearance and silhouette." [36]

Lin's view can be seen as the guiding principle in the roof design of the museum. Based on the Song method of "raise and depress," but exaggerated, this design was not modeled after any existing Liao and Song structure that Liang had investigated, nor did it follow precisely the prescriptions of the Song manual *YZFS*. Appropriately, the museum's reinforced-concrete roof appears both thinner and more graceful than its Liao and Song predecessors, which were made of timber and clay. Covered with the kind of yellow glazed tiles used to roof the Ming and Qing imperial palaces, this modern civic edifice had a light and lively visual effect never seen in the heavy and somber Liao and Song religious temples.

Conclusion

The National Central Museum opened to the public on 29 May 1948. Before the building was completed, Liang Sicheng included commentary on it in the last chapter of his book, *A History of Chinese Architecture*, the draft of which he finished in 1944. Without mentioning his own contribution, he wrote: "The Central Museum, designed by Xu Jingzhi and Li Huibo, has very simply and rationally reincarnated Liao and Song architectural form in a modern structure. It is also a significant example of modern Chinese architecture." [37] Xu, moreover, praised the museum in his own book *Chinese Architecture—Past and Contemporary*, published in 1964: "It was designed along the lines of Liao or early Sung [Song] style. The details are simple and bold. The bracket system is more functional than decorative. It was built in reinforced cement concrete with [*sic*] the consideration of [the] cantilever principle. The curve of the eave was plotted by increasing the length of the outer columns, and [that of] the roof by using the method of 'lifting and depressing' the positions of the purlins. The result was a light and buoyant-looking structure." [38]

The museum was a monument of the New Cultural Movement that began in 1916 and led to a fundamental change in Chinese society and culture. One of the leading figures of this movement, Hu Shi (Hu Shih, 1891-1962), called it a "Chinese renaissance" that aimed to re-create Chinese civilization by studying current problems in China, importing new methodologies and new ideas from the West, and "reorganizing the national heritage" *(zhengli guogu)* by systematically reevaluating and reforming Chinese indigenous civilization. In his *Plan for Reordering the National Heritage*, proposed in 1923, Hu elaborated a methodology that would make the enigmatic Chinese classics easier to read and apprehend by means of the strategies scholars commonly apply to produce authoritative new editions of important early Western writings: collating, annotating, and adding analytical introductions as well as organizing the text into paragraphs and inserting punctuation.[39]

The goal of research on traditional Chinese architecture and also of modern Chinese-style architecture designed and built by Chinese architects since the 1920s has resembled that of the New Cultural Movement. As proposed by Zhao Shen, chairman of the Society of Chinese Architects, it was to "synthesize the advantages of both Eastern and Western architecture, to develop the intrinsic beauty of our country."[40] The common approach in efforts to achieve this goal has been to use Chinese architectural motifs or forms with modern material and structures. Two efforts are of great significance. The first, proposed by Lü Yanzhi (Yen-chih Lu) and continued by Yang Tingbao (Ting-pao Yang), and the second, by Liang and Lin, aimed to provide rational principles to codify the Chinese-style designs. Lü and Yang employed Western compositional principles, trying to incorporate Chinese architecture into a universal plan type associated with the architectural doctrines of the Beaux-Arts school. [41]

Liang, Lin, and their colleagues at the SRCA achieved notable success in identifying the unique compositional principles of Chinese architecture by an in-depth study of the ancient manuals and a wide-ranging investigation of extant structures. [42] Liang's study of the Song manual *YZFS* and the Qing Gongbu *gongcheng zuofa zeli* enabled him to pursue *zhengli guogu* (reorganizing the national heritage) by providing the syntactic order, annotation, and analysis that Chinese traditional writing lacked. Liang thus was able to codify the classical language of Chinese architecture—the "grammars" of the two ancient manuals and the "vocabularies" of elements and motifs.

Like all great buildings, the National Central Museum has an inventive design that neither imitates the past nor represents a "conservative revivalism." Its idealized approach to a Chinese-style modern architecture could hardly have succeeded had the architects not had such a thorough knowledge of Chinese architecture, nor could this approach be applied to designs intended to serve more complicated functions. [43] This example demonstrates, however, the effort that Liang and the architects under his guidance made 'to "reorganize" the Chinese architectural heritage, to reevaluate it by the standards of modern science and aesthetics, and to create an ideal Chinese-style modern architecture. Made of modern materials, satisfying modern functional requirements, and sharing a similar sense of the nuances of Western classical architecture in composition and the rationalist imperative of modern architecture, the museum embodied the Chinese nationalist elite's expectations of a "renaissance" of Chinese culture that would originate in a vigorous Chinese tradition but be modified according to Western classical and modern standards.

National Central Museum, Nanjing. All photos this article: Delin Lai

Fig.1 Palace of Labor floor system, Turin. Photo: Courtesy of Pier Luigi Nervi Project Association

Images of the curvilinear patterns of the underside of Pier Luigi Nervi's reinforced concrete floor beam systems (such as that of the mezzanine of Palazzo del Lavoro in Turin, left) have long had iconic status in architecture and engineering circles alike – at once defining forms that reflect "pure" mathematical/physical analysis of structural behavior while also demonstrating a visual expressiveness that in no uncertain terms broke down the conventional straitjacket of the rectangular grid. What is much less well known are the cultural and economic conditions that led Nervi to experiment with concrete in such remarkable fashion, as is recounted here in the first half of a technical paper by Halpern, Billington and Adriaenssens. The latter part of the paper gets considerably more technical and esoteric in nature, and may not be easy reading for all; but for those who can persist, it does serve to demonstrate and compare Nervi's experimental stress analysis methods to mathematical theories of that era and then to a contemporary method developed by the authors for predicting these isostatically inspired ribbed floor patterns. What emerges is that there are still things to learn about these remarkable structures, even after more than a half century, and not least among them is that the apparently rigorously defined ribbed beam patterns are not without some remaining mysteries and/or that it seems Nervi also resorted to using some artistic license!

Nervi's Isostatically Inspired Ribbed Floors

The Ribbed Floor Slab Systems of Pier Luigi Nervi

Allison B. Halpern, David P. Billington, Sigrid Adriaenssens

HISTORICAL BACKGROUND

Evolution of Concrete Floor Systems

Prior to the 20th century, the prevalent materials used for floor systems were timber, masonry, brick, and tile. Safety concerns arising from several 19th century building fires and aspirations to construct taller buildings provided impetus for engineers to develop stronger, noncombustible floor systems. The absence of a universal system prompted the rapid filing of patents to protect the proprietary nature of these new systems. [1]

Despite the development of reinforced concrete in the latter half of the 19th century, concrete was first used for its fireproofing rather than its structural qualities. The 1844 Fox and Barrett floor system, patented in the UK by Fox, was the first to use concrete as a fireproof covering over timber planks and cast-iron joists. [2] Though the first floor system to use concrete in a structural capacity was patented in 1854 by Wilkinson in the UK, it was Monier's 1873 French patent that stimulated the spread of structural concrete floor systems. Monier experimented with the layout of iron reinforcement within concrete floors. The widespread use of the Monier system was due to the financial sponsorship of the German firm of Wayss and Freytag, who in 1885 obtained the rights to the Monier patent. [1]

The first reinforced concrete framing and floor system was patented by Hennebique in 1892. The success of this system in France provided his firm with the financial impetus to further develop and promote the system internationally. Although the Monier and Hennebique systems provided the fire resistance and structural capacity required for taller construction, the orthogonal arrangement of ribs essential to these systems produced an imitative timber joist and beam aesthetic. [2]

Cement-based Floor Developments in Italy

In 1883, Monier filed a series of Italian patents, which included applications for floor systems. However, the development of reinforced concrete floor systems in Italy was soon hindered by a nearly decade-long economic crisis. In 1892, Hennebique filed an Italian patent application for his reinforced concrete floor and framing system, followed five years later by an updated version with improvements for beam reinforcement. While the first major projects using this system could not begin until the start of the economic recovery in 1898, the spread of this system throughout Italy was largely due to Hennebique's marketing expertise. Not only did Hennebique promote the new system as immune to fire and both lighter and cheaper than a comparable iron system, he also appointed local engineers as agents of the patented system authorized to promote its use in new construction projects. [3]

The first native Italian patent related to reinforced concrete was filed by Carlo Poma in 1893, which improved upon the preexisting Monier patent by providing a cheaper, more workable alternative through modifications of the aggregate proportions.[4] The economic recession not only slowed cement sales but also deterred the industrialization of the construction site, which retained the "artisanal" masonry methods of construction. The rise of Hennebique's reinforced concrete system coupled with the artisanal construction site stimulated the integration of masonry elements into concrete floor systems. The combination of hollow bricks (*pignatta*) and cement in concrete floors resulted in a lighter structural system with improved material economy; the first patent for a *pignatta* and concrete floor system was filed by Sigismondo Ghilardi in 1902. [5]

Due to the destruction caused by the 1908 Messina and Reggio Calabria earthquake, an international competition was established by the Società Cooperativa Lombarda di Lavori Pubblici in 1909 to establish the best material for withstanding earthquakes. Arturo Danusso (1880-1968), a practicing Italian engineer and later a professor at the Polytechnic of Milan in strict relation with Nervi his entire life, received highest recognition in the competition. Danusso ascertained that reinforced concrete structures would provide the most reliable resistance to earthquakes, which established reinforced concrete as the preeminent construction material for Italy's seismically-active regions.[6] However, when Italy declared war in 1915 construction plummeted due to the ensuing supply and labor shortages. Postwar reconstruction saw reinforced concrete restored as the main construction material of Italy, [7] which led to the development of new building regulations in 1927. This first update in 20 years prompted the development of several references with practical calculation methods for designing and constructing reinforced concrete structures. [3]

After graduating from the University of Bologna in 1913, Pier Luigi Nervi worked for the Società Anonima per le Costruzioni Cementizie (SACC), which was owned by Attilio Muggia, one of Nervi's professors and mentors at the University. As Muggia had obtained the rights to the Hennebique patent for central Italy in 1895, Nervi was exposed to the *avant-garde* of reinforced concrete construction early in his career. [8] Excluding a hiatus during WWI, Nervi worked at SACC from 1913 to 1923, after which he founded his own firm, Soc. Ing. Nervi & Nebbiosi, with Rodolfo Nebbiosi. In 1932, Nervi transitioned Soc. Ing. Nervi & Nebbiosi into a second company, Soc. Ing. Nervi & Bartoli, which allowed Nervi to control both the design and construction of a project. [9] Shortly thereafter, the Italian Fascist political atmosphere shifted into a state of Autarchy, or self-sufficiency. As metal reinforcement was primarily imported from foreign manufacturers, reinforced concrete quickly became an Anti-Autarchic material. [10] This prohibitive designation was a radical change from reinforced concrete construction symbolizing the architecture of the regime. [3]

When reinforcement was first partially and then fully banned in 1935 and 1939, respectively, engineers were forced to use either traditional masonry arch systems or experiment with atypical reinforcement materials manufactured within the Kingdom of Italy. As cement was a material produced in mass quantities in Italy, this new research was characterized by cement-based floor systems with nominal reinforcement, no reinforcement, or reinforcement made with materials other than iron or steel, e.g., bamboo, aluminum. Patents of floor systems with a drastic reduction or complete elimination of reinforcement were filed throughout Italy. One of the most promising systems, the S.I.F. (*Senza Impiego di Ferro*, without the use of iron) floor, was patented by Eugenio Miozzi in 1937. To compensate for the absence of the required tensile capacity typically provided by reinforcement, the S.I.F. floor was composed of several layers of terracotta tile joined with high strength cement plaster and applied to the extrados and intrados of a traditional pignatta and concrete rib floor. While structurally sound, the S.I.F. floor was too time-consuming and labor-intensive for widespread use. [5]

During the partial reinforcement ban, Nervi started on a series of hangars for the Italian Air Force, the first series of which could only be made with timber formwork and concrete poured on-site. This expensive, time-consuming construction process provided impetus for Nervi's 1939 patent for an efficient, economical construction procedure, which used prefabricated concrete elements. Nervi also focused on developing a new material to facilitate the consideration of fluid structural forms. This material exploration resulted in the creation of ferrocement, which is comprised of layers of flexible wire mesh encased in sufficient cement to achieve complete coverage at a reduced thickness. [11] In the years prior to his 1949 isostatic ribbed floor patent, Nervi explored a means of using ferrocement in tandem with his 1939 patented construction procedure. [12] The extension of the 1939 patent to include mass-produced, reusable ferrocement forms on moveable scaffoldings made constructing large floors supported by evenly spaced columns fiscally possible.

Fig. 2 Tobacco Factory, Bologna, 1949. Photo: Fabio Mantovani

Nervi first tested this moveable formwork procedure (entitled the "Nervi System") with the construction of the Bologna Tobacco Factory in 1949 (Figure 2). While the formwork produced a pattern imitative of the traditional beam and joist systems, the successful implementation of this construction procedure inspired Nervi's departure from orthogonality to the curved forms of the isostatic ribs. Although the isostatic rib patterns are considered integral to the "Nervi System," the concept of aligning floor ribs along the isostatics of the principal bending moments is attributed to Aldo Arcangeli, a practicing engineer who worked in the office of Soc. Ing. Nervi & Bartoli. [12] Arcangeli is noted as the author of the invention listed in the corresponding 1949 patent (No. 455,678), filed by Soc. Ing. Nervi & Bartoli, which included the improvement in the construction of a variety of structures, e.g., floors, domes, by the arrangement of support ribs along the isostatics of bending moments or normal stresses. [14]

Arcangeli determined from classical plate theory that a 2D continuous body subjected to normal forces produces two families of orthogonal curves (isostatics), tangential to the principal bending moment trajectories, along which torsional moments are equal to zero. If this continuous body is replaced by ribs oriented along the isostatics, then the rib structure and the continuous body would have identical structural behavior under identical loading and support conditions.[14] Nervi drew inspiration from the patterns formed by the isostatics; he stated: "it was amazing to find that by thus limiting our task to the interpretation of a purely physical phenomenon, we were able to discover unexpected and expressive new forms"[12] and asserted that "in harmony with such inspiration, reinforced concrete beams lose the rigidity of wooden beams or of metal shapes and *ask* to be molded according to the line of the bending moments". [13]

NERVI'S METHOD FOR EVALUATING ISOSTATICS

While the structural behavior on which the isostatic rib patterns are based has been highlighted by Nervi, the manner in which these patterns have been generated has seen limited literary discussion. This section explores the experimental and theoretical analysis methods emphasized in Nervi's writings and the application of these analysis techniques to generating isostatics.

Strain Gauge Methods

In *Structures*, Nervi identifies two domains of experimental stress analysis: strain gauge methods and photoelasticity. Strain gauge methods rely on devices capable of measuring strain via mechanical, optical, electrical, acoustical, and pneumatic methods, to determine the displacements and stresses at points on a small-scale model.[15] Nervi first used mechanical strain gauges to determine the magnitude of the stresses in the ribs of a scale model for the 1935 Orvieto hangars.[13] In the late 1930s, Simmons and Ruge independently developed bonded-wire electrical-resistance strain gauges,[15] which permitted the calculation of principal stress directions.

To find the stress field on the surface of a flat slab, it is necessary to use three-element strain gauge rosettes. These rosettes include three strain-gauges, each oriented at a different angle relative to the two in-plane axes (x and y), which provide three strain measurements corresponding to the three orientation angles. Using strain-transformation equations, the three Cartesian components of strain (ε_{xx}, ε_{yy}, and γ_{xy}) can be calculated and can be used to find the principal strain direction at the measurement location.[15] While calculating the principal stress directions from the rosette readings is simple, the experimental preparations and procedure are costly and time-consuming. Several rosettes would be needed to obtain enough data to clearly represent the full field of principal stress trajectories. As this method does not provide a more accessible way to obtain isostatics than theoretical calculations, strain gauge methods could not have been Nervi's initial means of finding isostatics.

Photoelasticity

Nervi's fascination with stress visualization in photoelasticity experiments (led by Danusso at the Polytechnic of Milan) suggests Nervi's possible use of photoelasticity to generate isostatics.[12]

Photoelasticity is derived from the strain- and stress-optics laws (Neumann 1841, Maxwell 1852) on the theory of artificial double refraction (anisotropic birefringence) in a stressed isotropic, transparent solid. In 1816, Brewster coined the term photoelasticity due to the color pattern produced in clear glass when stressed and examined under polarized light. When certain transparent materials undergo stress, the material exhibits birefringence. As polarized light passes through the material, the rays refract and separate into two perpendicular components each parallel to the principal refractive indices of the material. A condition of the stress-optics laws states that these principal indices correspond to the principal stress directions.[16]

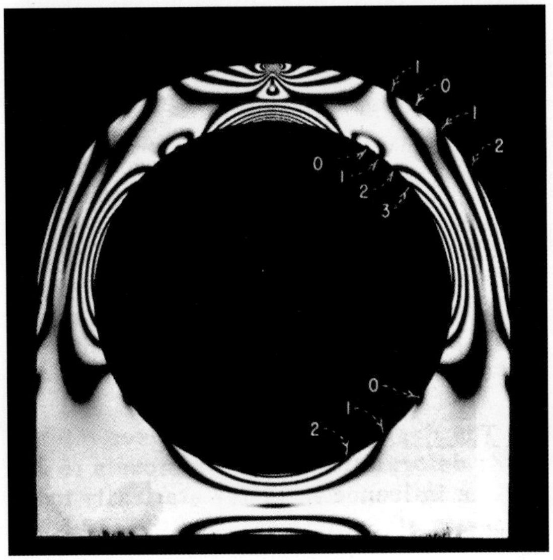

Fig. 3 Example photoelastic pattern

In 2D cases, small-scale models with plane stress conditions are placed in a polariscope, which allows analysis of a model under polarized light. There are two types of optical interference patterns, *isoclinics* and *isochromatics*. Isoclinics designate the locus of all points where the principal stress directions are parallel to the directions of the polarizing axes, appearing as black bands. Isochromatics define the locus of all points having equal difference between the two principal stresses (constant maximum shear stress) appearing either as a field of dark fringes or a continuous range of the visible spectrum, depending on the light source (Figure 3).[17]

Isoclinics allow the user to determine the principal stress directions at all points of the model, whereas the isochromatics indicate the differences in the principal stresses in the model and the stress at the free boundaries. As the isoclinics indicate the lines along which the directions of the principal stresses within the stressed model are constant, the isoclinics are not identical to the isostatics. Although isostatics can be drawn from the isoclinic diagram, the manual process is time-consuming to generate a full field of orthogonal isostatics.[18]

While plane stress is an assumption of thin plate theory, thin plates subjected to transverse bending cannot be observed solely using the aforementioned 2D photoelasticity method. As thin plates subjected to transverse loading experience tension on one side and compression of equal absolute value on the opposite side, any phase difference resulting from light passing through the first half of the plate thickness would be cancelled out when travelling through the second half of the plate thickness,[19] thus producing no photoelastic patterns. The first successful photoelasticity experiment to capture the principal stresses in plates subjected to transverse loading was documented by Goodier and Lee in 1941,[20] yet photographs of the optical interference patterns were not published. Based on the model discussed by Goodier and Lee, Kuske developed a "time-efficient" method using traditional 2D photoelasticity methods to view isoclinics occurring at the surface of the plate.[19] However, this method was not published until 1953, the same year as the completion of the Gatti Wool Factory [Figure 6] and four years after the submittal of the 1949 isostatic ribbed floor patent.

Although Nervi referred to the photoelastic phenomenon as "the beauty and poetry of this transmutation of stress into a play of light rays,"[13] photoelasticity experiments could not have been used to determine the ribbed floor slab patterns. Nervi asserted that photoelasticity was "more efficient in the study of local stresses in bodies of limited dimensions (crane hooks, chain links, and parts of machines), than in the analysis of entire structures."[12] Given this mindset, the authors assume that he would not have been inclined to use photoelasticity to evaluate the stresses present in a large flat slab. Despite his dedication to experimental methods, Nervi was cognizant of their time-consuming and costly aspects – the preparation, measurement, and analysis phases – and thus recommended that experimental modeling be reserved for structures of "special technical and architectural importance" and the analysis of structural problems unable to be solved theoretically.[12] The problem of determining the stresses in a thin plate subjected to transverse loading could be solved theoretically at the time of the patent submittal in 1949, indicating that the use of models to evaluate the stresses was not mandatory. This conclusion is substantiated by Iori[14] who asserted that the shape of the isostatics relating to the ribs of the Gatti Wool Factory must have been determined using calculations derived from thin plate theory.

Mathematical Theory

As no efficient experimental approach existed at the time, Arcangeli theoretically studied the concept of placing ribs along the isostatics of principal moments in proposing the idea to Nervi.[14] The two most commonly used plate theories are the Kirchoff-Love and Reisner-Mindlin plate theories. The Kirchoff-Love theory, applicable to thin plates, was developed by Love in 1888 using Kirchhoff's 1850 boundary condition assumptions.[21] Reissner-Mindlin plate theory, an extension of Kirchoff-Love plate theory and applicable to thick plates, takes into account shear deformations through the thickness of a plate and was proposed by Reissner in 1945, but not fully developed by Mindlin until 1951. Given this timeline, Arcangeli's theoretical calculations for the principal bending moment directions must have been based on Kirchoff-Love thin plate theory. Although thin plate theory involves high-order partial differential equations, numerous analytical (Navier, Lévy, Timoshenko,[22]) approximate (Ritz), and design solutions (Westergaard and Slater) for thin plate-bending theory were already well-established and in widespread use when the patent for isostatic rib floors was filed in 1949. Additional resources were developed in Italy, including the analytical solutions of Botasso[21] and the design solutions of Santarella, who wrote and edited a plethora of practical manuals and theoretical texts on reinforced concrete produced as a result of the 1927 updates to the building regulations.[3]

ISOSTATIC LINE TOOL

While Arcangeli and Nervi relied on theoretical calculations to determine the isostatics of principal moments for flat slabs, contemporary engineers can employ two manual methods. The first method includes theoretically calculating the principal bending moment directions at a selection of nodes, hand drawing lines at set lengths in the respective directions, recalculating the directions at the next nodes, and repeating the process until reaching a boundary.[16] This process is described in detail below and illustrated in Figure 4:

1) Select a start node (e.g., Node 0)
2) Calculate the maximum principal bending moment direction at that node
3) Draw a straight line of a set length in the calculated maximum principal bending moment direction (e.g., Segment a)
4) Recalculate the principal bending moment direction at the new node (e.g., Node 1)

5) Iterate through this method until crossing a boundary
6) Perform this method for a selection of start nodes to obtain a field of primary isostatics

To draw the secondary isostatics, one can simply use the minimum principal bending moments.

Alternatively, one can print out the principal bending moment trajectories displayed by commercially available Finite Element Software and manually draw the isostatics tangent to these trajectories or import a picture of the plot into a CAD or graphics editing program to draw the lines electronically. The main disadvantages of these methods are: 1) the plots produced by commercial FEM software are typically of low resolution, which complicates drawing lines at the accurate angles; 2) the principal bending moment directions are averaged to the center of the finite element, which leads to biased isostatics; and 3) the principal bending moment trajectories are displayed as arrows, rather than continuous lines, which forces the drawer to interpolate between elements.

As an alternative to these manual drawing options, an automatic, computational method of drawing the isostatics was developed using the FE Software SAP 2000v15 and MATLAB. First, a flat slab FE model is generated with the appropriate geometry, external loading, boundary conditions, and material properties. After running the analysis, the primary and secondary principal bending moment angles are obtained. The MATLAB algorithm follows the six-step procedure previously outlined. Termination of the algorithm occurs when the generated isostatic line has reached a slab boundary, resulting in a plot of the isostatic line (Figure 4).

ANALYSES OF THREE FLOOR SLABS

Three of Nervi's floor slabs are evaluated using the Isostatic Line Tool: 1) the Gatti Wool Factory warehouse floor (1953, Rome), 2) the Palace of Labor mezzanine floor (1961, Turin), and 3) the Large Sports Palace gallery floor (1957, Rome). As all of these floors were designed to support uniformly-distributed loading conditions, and as scaling the load does not alter the directions of the principal bending moments, each system is evaluated under equivalent uniformly distributed loads. This consistency in the applied loading patterns leaves the principal bending moments unbiased so as to highlight how alterations of the dimensions and boundary conditions influence the resulting isostatic rib patterns.

Gatti Wool Factory

The use of isostatics to inform the arrangement pattern for a ribbed floor system was first realized for the warehouse floor of the Gatti Wool Factory. Nervi and Arcangeli collaborated with architect Carlo Cestelli Guidi for the factory design, which required a wide-spanning floor system capable of supporting heavy wool-spinning machinery.[14] The curved isostatic pattern of the Gatti Wool Factory floors (Figure 6) fully exploited the moldable flexibility of Nervi's ferrocement forms.

Each 5m x 5m slab of the Gatti Wool Factory is supported by a central column. All slabs are monolithically joined along the perimeter edges.[14] A quarter of the slab is evaluated using the Isostatic Line Tool. To satisfy the one-eighth symmetry in each quarter slab, a sufficiently fine step size must be used. A relation between element length and step size was prescribed to evaluate symmetry convergence, as illustrated in Figure 5, with the chosen step size of one-sixty-fourth the element length yielding a symmetry error of only 0.31%.

The analysis of an upper-right quarter of a 5m x 5m Gatti Wool Factory slab, using the Isostatic Line Tool, is shown in Figure 6a. Symmetry conditions (axial rotation and orthogonal translation restrained) are applied to the right and top boundaries and monolithic perimeter conditions (full rotational fixity and in-plane translation restraints) are modeled on the bottom and left boundaries.

The red lines in Figure 6a represent the primary isostatics,

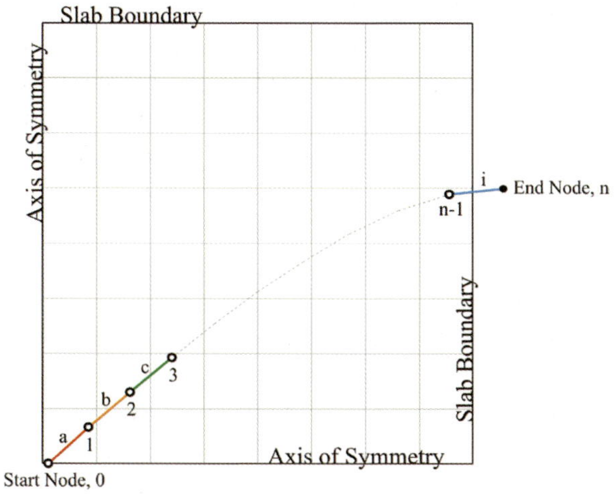

Fig. 4 Isostatic path determination

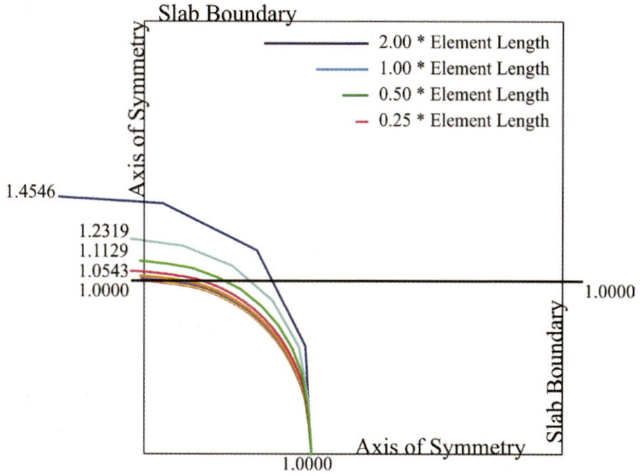

Fig. 5 Stepping procedure convergance

corresponding to the maximum principal bending moments, and the blue lines represent the secondary isostatics, corresponding to the minimum principal bending moments. Both pairs of lines were generated from start nodes set at increments equal to half of the finite element lengths and placed along all four boundaries. The concentrations of lines indicate convergence of the principal bending moment directions, highlighted by the prescribed method of starting node generation. The grey and white outline shows an approximate plan of the Gatti Wool Factory floor to illustrate the correlation between the theoretical isostatics and the as-built rib pattern. The concentric secondary isostatics produced around the column support at the top right of the quarter slab reflects the reasoning for placing concentric curves of reinforcement around the column head and verifies Nervi's placement of the rib encircling the column head. The ribs emanating from the central column also show close correlation to the generated primary isostatics.

Palace of Labor (Palazzo del Lavoro)

In 1961, a celebration was held in Turin for the centennial of Italy's unification, for which Nervi designed and constructed the Palace of Labor. [23] The interior border along the building perimeter is formed by the mezzanine, which has repeated reinforced concrete slabs with isostatic ribs (Figure 1, 7). Each 10m x 10m slab is supported by columns at the four corners and the isostatic patterns follow one-eighth symmetry.[13] The analysis of an upper-right quarter of a 10m x 10m Palace of Labor slab is shown in Figure 7a, with symmetry conditions at the left and bottom boundaries, monolithic perimeter conditions at the top and right boundaries, and a column support at the top right corner. The presented results show strong correlation exists between the theoretical primary and secondary isostatics and the as-built plan.

Large Sports Palace (Palazzo dello Sport)

The Large Sports Palace was designed by Nervi, with architect Marcello Piacentini, as one of three structures constructed for the 1960 Rome Summer Olympic Games. The intradoses of the perimeter gallery floor include isostatic rib patterns (Figure 8).[24] In contrast to the Gatti Wool Factory and Palace of Labor slabs, the Large Sports Palace slabs are rectangular. While these slabs are supported by columns at the four corners, the shift from a square to rectangular boundary shape induces different isostatic patterns.

The analysis of the Large Sports Palace floor required further evaluation as applying identical boundary conditions as the Palace of Labor case study yielded isostatics satisfying the assumed bounds of only two of the four outlined floor ribs (Figure 8a). Additional boundary conditions were evaluated to try to shift the isostatics towards the two disparate ribs, yet no combination yielded exact results for all ribs, as seen in the Gatti Wool Factory and Palace of Labor analyses. The analysis shown in Figure 8b removed the fixity of the top boundary and the Figure 8c analysis placed simply-supported conditions at the top and right boundaries. While the fully simply-supported conditions show close correlation between the topmost transverse rib and the neighboring secondary isostatics, the other three ribs lack correlation with the isostatics. The rib closest to the left boundary captures the strictly vertical portions of select primary isostatics, whose starting nodes start along the left axis of symmetry, yet they soon diverge towards the top-right corner support.

Despite this divergence, the two disparate ribs from Figure 8a appear to be offsets of the two curves closely correlated to the isostatics. This departure from pure conformity to the isostatics supports Nervi's statement of prescribing the design to an interpretation of the true static behavior. Naturally, the addition of the ribs dictates the structural behavior of the floor system, reorienting the isostatics along these predefined paths.

Conclusion

The successes of Nervi's isostatic floor systems and the discussed historical precedents highlight the catalysts for the widespread recognition of a reinforced concrete floor system: 1) the protection of patents; 2) the personal ownership or financial sponsorship of an established engineering firm; and 3) the connection to academic research and experimentation. In addition to these influential factors, the artisanal construction sites endemic to Italy and the political atmosphere at the time helped foster the construction and material innovations developed by Nervi related to floor system design. The elegant design of these floor systems is expressed by the rib patterns, which allude to the isostatics of the principal moments produced in a corresponding flat slab system. The experimental stress analysis methods (strain gauge and photoelasticity) referenced by Nervi and the mathematical analysis methods available at the time (pertaining to transversely loaded flat slabs) were discussed to evaluate the potential for these methods to have been used by Nervi to generate the isostatics. Although isostatics can be generated via these experimental and theoretical methods, it was determined that a theoretical approach was used by Nervi and Arcangeli.

The theoretical approach to generating isostatics has been implemented in a computational Isostatic Line Tool, the efficacy of which was proven in analyses of three of Nervi's floor systems. A modern designer can explore the efficiency of the Isostatic Line Tool to develop conceptual designs for ribbed floors according to new geometries, boundary conditions, and loading patterns. This tool provides designers with a visual method of automatically determining the primary and secondary isostatics in flat slabs, which provides an efficient alternative to the potentially biased, time-consuming FE-based drawing methods composed of centrally averaged principal bending moment trajectories. The close correlation between the theoretical isostatics and the as-built rib patterns for the evaluated floor slabs, as well as the artistic interpretation of the static theory, highlights Nervi's desire to construct correctly while expressing elegance.

Fig. 6 Gatti Wool Factory, Rome, 1951
Fig. 6a Quarter slab analysis

Fig. 7 Palace of Labor, Turin, 1961
Fig. 7a Quarter slab analysis

Fig. 8 Large Sports Palace, Rome, 1957
Fig. 8a, 8b, 8c Quarter slab analysis – full fixity, partial fixity, simply supported, respectively

Photos: Courtesy of Pier Luigi Nervi Project Association and MAXXI Museo nazionale delle arti del XXI secolo, Roma. MAXXI Architecture Collection

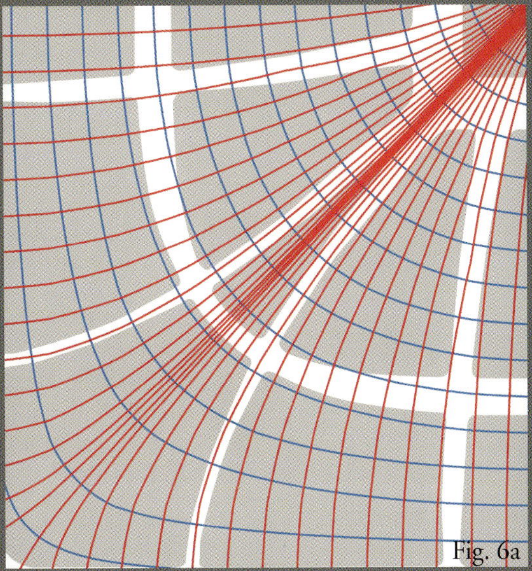
Fig. 6a

Fig. 6

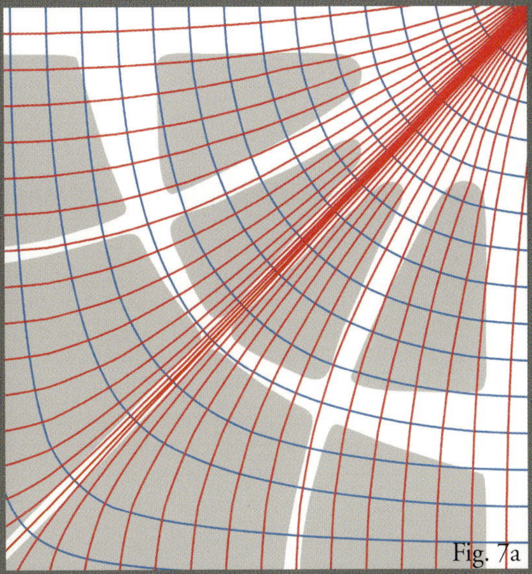
Fig. 7a

Fig. 7

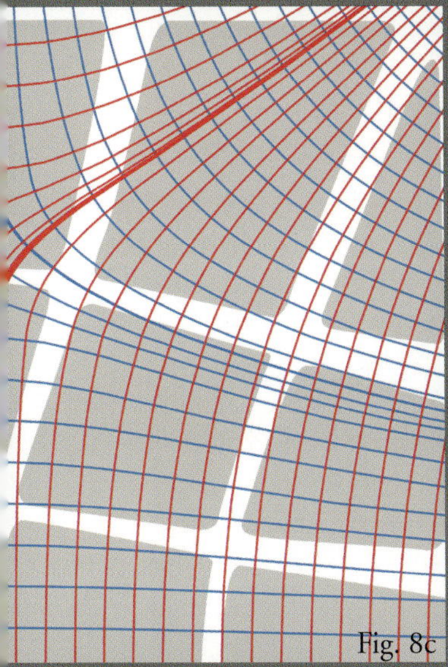
Fig. 8c

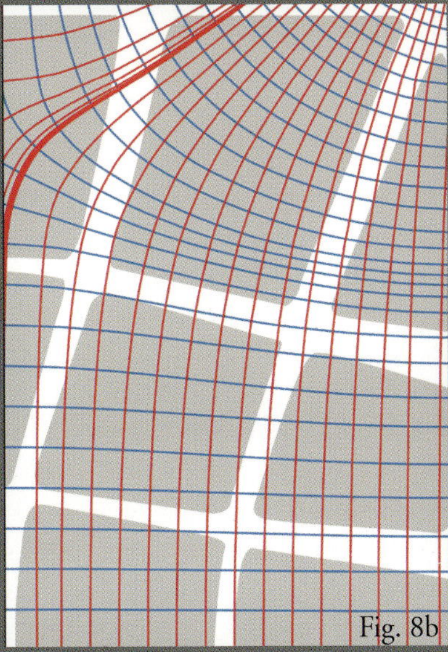
Fig. 8b

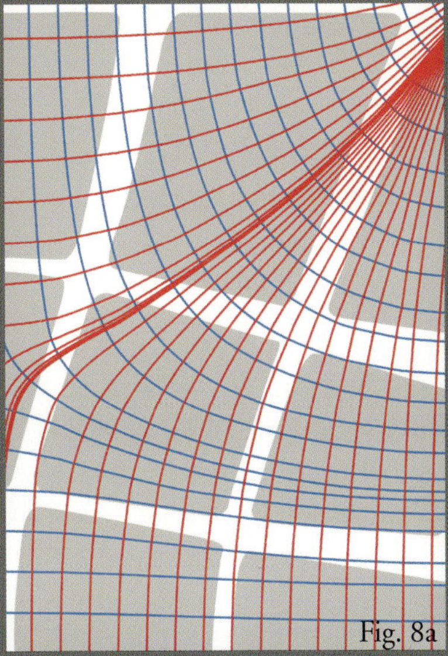
Fig. 8a

Fig. 8

Warehouse in St. Petersburg by Maillart & Co., 1912

Material innovations are frequently first incorporated into building structures in the familiar forms associated with the construction technologies that pre-date them; i.e., it takes some time for the implications of new developments to be realized, for conventional structural forms to evolve and for the often unfamiliar aesthetic results to be accepted by society. Reinforced concrete was no exception, including for the familiar slab-on-beam hierarchy of typical floor and roof construction. But at a certain point the structural possibilities and visual implications that result from the hidden steel reinforcing bars emerged, such that the beams themselves could effectively become hidden within a flat slab of uniform thickness – something that proved revolutionary not only in terms of built form but also of spatial reading and conceptual underpinning.

A century ago, the Swiss structural engineer Robert Maillart was at the forefront of such developments with his innovative designs for arched bridges and warehouse buildings alike. To this day images of his projects remain remarkably compelling; e.g., here of the St. Petersburg warehouse, left, as well as of the Schwandbach Bridge on the next page. The short text extract reprinted below is from the seminal book *Space, Time and Architecture: The Growth of a New Tradition*, written by the architectural historian and critic Sigfried Giedion; in it he focuses on the development of Maillart's work with concrete slabs through several projects. Furthermore, and in quintessential fashion, Giedion establishes a cultural context for these experiments in built form by drawing parallels between the slabs' articulated, geometric shapes and the simultaneous emergence of planar surface representations within Modern art.

Maillart Minimalism: The Flat Slab Emerges

from *Space, Time and Architecture: The Growth of a New Tradition*
Sigfried Giedion

... the methods of science and the methods of art came unconsciously to parallel each other about 1908. Among other more spectacular instances, ... construction and painting arrived at similar basic elements in their search for solutions to problems that had not previously been attempted. With the bridges of the Swiss engineer Robert Maillart we are brought ... to this topic. They offer us the chance to compare these basic elements and to investigate the way in which the aesthetic effect produced by a new type of construction arises.[1]

Those whose aesthetic sense has been formed or developed by the art of the present age can hardly fail to be stirred by Maillart's bridges, for their appearance may be trusted to arrest such observers before they can even ask themselves why. Maillart's surprising designs, which attract some as much as they repel others,[2] are the product of the uncompromising application of a new method of construction. They have almost as little in common with the solid arches, stout piers, and monumentally emphasized abutments of the usual "massive" type of bridge as an airplane has with a mail coach.

What, then, is the peculiarity of Maillart's methods of building?

In the early days of reinforced concrete the same methods of construction were used as were employed with timber and iron. Timber, being the trunks of trees, has length, just as iron has when rolled into long girders. One dimension always dominates, which is the one that transmits the load. As Maillart himself puts it: "The engineer was so accustomed to using those basic materials which provide only one-dimensional support that they became second nature to him, and restrained him from exploiting other possibilities. This was the state of affairs when reinforced concrete was introduced, and at first no change ensued."

Maillart was a pupil of Hennebique;[3] and Hennebique's reinforced concrete structures had beams and columns like timber-framed buildings. Following the model of timber construction, his beams reached from wall to wall and from column to column, the roof stretching across them in the form of a flat, inert slab.

In designing a bridge Maillart began by eliminating all that was nonfunctional; thus everything that remained was an immediate part of the structure. He hid this by improving the reinforced concrete slab until he had turned it into a new structural element. What Maillart achieved after that was based on one idea: that it is possible to reinforce a flat or curved concrete slab in such a manner as to dispense with the need for beams in flooring or solid arches in bridges. It is very difficult to determine the forces present in slabs of this nature by calculation alone. To obtain positive results entails a complicated process which cannot be entered into here, except to say that it is based partly on calculation and partly on experiment. The engineer's adoption of systems incapable of exact calculation is typical of the present day (as in shell concrete structures) and contrasts with the absolute, checked and proven calculations typical of Maillart's period.

Slabs had hitherto played a neutral or passive part in construction. Maillart transformed them into active bearing surfaces capable of absorbing all forms of stress, and he subsequently developed this principle into a comprehensive system of support able to be employed for tasks previously considered impossible for reinforced concrete. Whether engaged in perfecting a new form of flooring or in striking out new principles in bridge construction, he has always adhered to the same basic method of using reinforced concrete slabs as active structural elements.

Maillart's experiments with beamless flooring date from 1908. He treated a floor as a concrete slab, converting it into an actively coöperative structural member by distributing the reinforcement throughout its whole area. Since every part of the surface now became self-supporting, beams disappeared, their function being resolved into the floor itself. The heavier the load this homogeneous type of flooring is called upon to bear, the greater the practical inducement to adopt it. Consequently it is usually found in warehouses, factories, and other large, many-storied buildings.

The appearance of the branching columns which support this type of flooring somewhat recalls certain traditional styles, for in the basements of warehouses they resemble the heavy pillars of a Romanesque crypt and in the upper stories they suggest the slender palmlike columns of late Gothic. In point of fact, however, mushroom-headed columns have nothing beyond these superficial resemblances in common with either, since the peculiarity of the system resides neither in the formation of the shafts nor in the extruded corbeling of the capitals that crown them, but wholly in forces in the ceiling above, which do not meet the eye.

As floors of this type provide a uniform bearing surface throughout their length and breadth, their ends can be cantilevered out to carry supplementary loads. They are therefore ideal in combination with nonsupporting walls, such as continuous expanses of horizontal fenestration. It is hard to realize this in the obscurity of a warehouse, for the latent possibilities of mushroom slab construction can only find architectural vindication in buildings which are flooded with the light of day from all sides. [4] ...

Maillart had embodied this principle in a bridge as early as 1900; and in that over the Tavanasa (1905) he dared to strip his construction of all disguise. The Tavanasa bridge (span, 51 m.) represented a wholly unprecedented form, for in it Maillart discarded massive beams just as he was also shortly to eliminate the beams from floors. Instead, he employed a shallow, curved, reinforced concrete slab for the arch, which, with the horizontal slab of the platform and a series of stiffened vertical slabs used as ties to articulate them, constituted a monolith.

Thus Maillart resolved bridge-building into a system of flat and curved slabs so juxtaposed as to achieve a positively uncanny counterbalance of all stresses and strains arising between them. The first realization of a stiffened elliptical concrete bridge with an arch of eggshell thickness (his Valtschiel-Brücke) followed in 1925.

The elimination of all nonfunctional members has led Maillart during the last few years to dispense with the usual separate decking slab. In these later bridges trains and motor cars run directly upon their naked structural framework: that is to say, on the longitudinal slab of the platform itself.

In Maillart's hands the rigidity of the slab, hitherto an incalculable factor in construction, became an active bearing surface, which... opened up possibilities that had remained a closed book for reinforced concrete engineering. Thus the torsional strains that would have to be allowed for in a concrete bridge built on a curving alignment had previously been deemed to defy calculation.[5] Maillart's Schwandbach-Brücke in the Canton of Berne, opened in 1933, is the most beautiful example of a road bridge carried out in that material with a sickle-shaped platform. ...

Schwandbach Bridge by Robert Maillart. Photo: © Chriusha/Хрюша Media

... one or two striking features of Maillart's bridges may be touched on without entering into the technique of his structural methods:

One of the problems in art in which research has not yet made much headway is the relation between sculpture and nature—and, beyond this, the interrelations between sculpture, painting, and architecture. It is easier for the constructor to find a convincing solution than the artist, because physical factors (like the width of the interval to be spanned, the nature of the foundations, etc.) dictate its conditions. All the same, there is something altogether out of the ordinary in the way Maillart succeeds both in expressing and in sublimating the breadth of a chasm cleft between two walls of rock (i.e., in his Salginatobel-Brücke, 1929-30). His shapely bridges spring out of shapeless crags with the serene inevitability of Greek temples. The lithe, elastic resilience with which they leap their chasms, the attenuation of their dimensions, merges into the coördinated rhythms of arch, platform, and the upended slabs between them.

A bridge designed of slabs of various shapes no longer resembles the ordinary kind of bridge either in its form or in its proportions. To eyes that are blind to the vision of our own day, slanting columns with grotesquely splayed-out heads, like those of the approach viaducts of the Thur bridge—a form imposed by purely structural considerations that enabled Maillart to make two columns do the work of four—are bound to appear somewhat ugly; whereas eyes schooled by contemporary art recognize in these shapes an echo of those with which modern painting has already familiarized them.[6]

When Picasso paints half-geometric, half-organic plastic images on canvas—forms which in spite of their apparently capricious projection somehow achieve a singular degree of equipoise—and the constructor (proceeding from purely technical premises) arrives at similar absolute forms by substituting two vertical supports for four, there is a clear inference that mechanical shapes and the shapes evolved by art as the mirror of a higher reality rank *pari passu* in terms of development.

It is, of course, easy enough to retort that this is simply the result of chance, and that such resemblances are purely superficial. But we cannot afford to leave the matter there, for what concerns us is the question which must serve as our point of departure: Are the methods which underlie the artist's work related to those of the modern structural engineer? Is there in fact a direct affinity between the principles now current in painting and construction?

We know the great importance which *surface* has acquired in the composition of a picture, and the long road that had to be traversed—starting with Manet's light-fusion of paint, advancing by way of Cézanne's flat coloration and the work of Matisse, and ending with cubism—before this was finally recognized.

Surface, which was formerly held to possess no intrinsic capacity for expression, and so at best could only find decorative utilization, has now become the basis of composition, thereby supplanting perspective, which had triumphed over each successive change of style ever since the Renaissance.

With the cubist's conquest of space, and the abandonment of one predetermined angle of vision which went hand in hand with it, surface acquired a significance it had never known before. Our powers of perception became widened and sharpened in consequence. We discovered the interplay of imponderably floating elements irrationally penetrating or fusing with each other, as also the optical tensions which arise from the contrasts between various textural effects (the handling of color *qua* color, or the use of other media, such as sand, bits of dress fabrics, and scraps of paper, to supplement pigments). The human eye awoke to the spectacle of form, line, and color—that is, the whole grammar of composition—reacting to one another within an orbit of hovering planes, or, as J. J. Sweeney calls it, "the plastic organization of forms suggested by line and colour on a flat surface."

If Maillart, speaking as an engineer, could claim to have developed the slab into a basic element of construction, modern painters can answer with equal justice that they have made surface an essential factor in the composition of a picture. The slab long remained unheeded and unmastered: an inert inadaptable thing which defied calculation and so utilization. But just as a great constructor transformed it into a medium for solving structural problems that had always been considered insuperable, so the development of surface into a basic principle of composition in painting resulted in opening up untapped fields of optical expression.

This is no longer a fortuitous optical coincidence, as might be objected, but a definite parallelism of methods. By what mental processes the constructor and the painter arrived at it defies analysis. We can only authenticate a particular phenomenon in a particular case: a new method of construction found its simultaneous echo in a parallel method in art. But this proves that underlying the special power of visualization implicit in each of these fields similar elements have emerged which provide a creative impetus for both of them.

If the constructor, who necessarily proceeds from quite different considerations, finds he has to adopt substantially the same basic elements as the artist in order to solve his own technical problems, this signifies that in each case similar methods have informed optical imagination.

Contemporary artists continually reiterate the claim that their work forms part of Nature. This they explain as follows: "Modern art has reached the same results as modern science by entirely independent, intuitive steps. Like science it has resolved the shape of things into their basic elements with the object of reconstituting them in consonance with the universal laws of Nature." Now those forms in concrete which ignore former conventions in design are likewise the product of a process of "resolution into basic elements" (for a slab is an irreducible element) that uses reconstruction as a means of attaining a more rational synthesis.

In this connection mention should be made of the "eggshell" concrete vaulting which Freyssinet used for some locomotive sheds he built at Bagneux, outside Paris, in 1929, though since then that particular branch of reinforced concrete engineering has produced forms of almost fantastic daring. On the same principle of using the slab as an active structural member, the Finnish architect, Alvar Aalto, has struck out an entirely new line in furniture design. He uses thin sheets of plywood, which, like the concrete slab, was formerly regarded as useless for purposes of structural support.

In the community of method which now prevails in so many departments of human activity we may read a presage of far-reaching developments. The growth of this spontaneous identity of approach and its repercussions on society are being separately studied in every branch of knowledge. That there is a remarkable analogy between recent departures in philosophy, physics, literature, art, and music is a fact which has frequently been commented on. In the light of the particular case we have just examined, it is worth considering whether the field of structural engineering cannot be included as well. New methods are new tools for the creation of new types of reality. The greater the degree of identity in respect to what is fundamental to each of the creative spheres, and the closer the extent of their approximation to one another in terms of achievement, the sooner will the requisites for a new phase of culture be forthcoming.

Warehouse in Chiasso following Maillart slab design approach, by Bernasconi & Mascetti, 1924

Penguin Pool at London Zoo. Photo: © Crown copyright.EH

If Robert Maillart's warehouses and bridges were an early indication of the innovative possibilities of concrete slabs, the diminutive but no less spectacular spiraling ramps of the London Zoo's Penguin Pool built in 1934 have been widely regarded as having made the case for this type of structure's remarkable form-making potential, which was to be fully realized with the concrete shells in the decades that followed. Designed by the architect Berthold Lubetkin (as a member of the Tecton group) and the structural engineer Ove Arup (assisted by Felix Samuely), these remarkably thin, sharply curving, spectacularly cantilevering circulation ramps would have been quite unexpected to most of the general public attending the Zoo at the time, and in a sense they at once embodied as well as carried the promise of Modern architecture to largely transform the built/living environment. As is recounted here in an extract from an essay by the architectural historian Hadas A. Steiner, their structural and conceptually innovative qualities alike would have been made all the more noticeable given the adjacency of other quite traditional and sometimes heavy-handed approaches to representing an artificial "nature" elsewhere at the Zoo. Notwithstanding their demonstrably remarkable qualities, however, the notion of the Penguin Pool ramps' pointing the way forward with their seemingly effortless, weightless, free-form architecture is not without certain underlying ironies, in particular given the complicated formwork needed for construction as well as the exceptionally heavy reinforcing that ultimately remains hidden within the finished slabs; formal freedom coupled with apparent structural simplicity are evidently qualities not so easily achieved.

Concrete Takes Flight

from *For the Birds*
Hadas A. Steiner

Any illusion of a boundary-free environment was also one between inside and out.[1] Most massive but least architectonic of the pavilions, the exterior of the Mappin complex [open-air terraces housed various ruminants, pigs, bears, mountain goats, and waterfowl] tells the story of a remote natural environment. Internally, a dense forest of "elaborately latticed and trussed frames of crudely shuttered reinforced concrete posts, beam and braces" supports the rugged bareness of the irregularly finished slab and pebbledashed concrete.[2] ... Thus the surface naturalism of Mappin incrusted the archetypal machine of industrial production. ...

Some 600 feet to the southeast, by way of contrast, the diminutive Penguin Pool ... of the interwar period does not employ any such illusions of naturalism or boundary. The pool used the structural dynamics of concrete to demonstrate the opposite principle: nature, not as an environment, but as a system of geometric and physical order. Natural principle as truth to structure and the rejection of mimesis was at the root of theory at least since the widespread influence of the *Essai sur l'architecture*.[3] Structural inevitability was to modernism what the "State of Nature" had been to the Enlightenment philosopher: the equivalent of a vernacular essence for industrial times. In the modernist version of the primitive hut, however, structure had to support circulation as well as the roof.

Mitchell commissioned Tecton to design a penguin pool as a corollary to the success of its first commission, also for the London Zoo, the just completed Gorilla House (1932-3).[4] The most innovative structural engineering firm in London was also brought in on this project: Lubetkin hired Ove Arup; the contractors consulted with Arup's new assistant, Felix Samuely. Until penguins were designated their own home on a site that had been a paddock for geese, they had been squatting at the Mappin pond. Part of the brief was to accommodate the needs of this flightless seabird,[5] which primarily meant providing areas in which to swim and nest, as well as access for keepers to dispose of guano. At the same time, the pavilion had to enable the viewing of penguin activities.

Tecton proposed an elongated ellipse (36 x 118 feet), the dynamism of which was reinforced by two ramps that bisected it in plan and elevation. The elliptical enclosure clearly differentiated the space of the pavilion from that of the viewer, as opposed to the experience at Mappin where, once the viewer entered the space, the totality of a panorama saturated the cone of sight. Further, the curved perimeter wall, cut to create a viewing aperture, was to retain penguins, sound and water. There is no pedestrian intersection of animal space in this model: the ramps are not a human zone as they were in Picturesque park or at the Mappin Terraces but are rather a topographical feature of the penguins' abstract Antarctica. Emphasis is placed on the representational geography by the contrast of the glacier-white concrete with the azure tile mosaic that lends the underwater floor its hint of ocean. The visual sense of a continuous white surface, as if the curved upright perimeter folds into ramps, makes plain that circulatory infrastructure belongs to the natural order of things, not to the boundary condition between the feral and the cultivated.

Rationalism did away with the epistemology of Picturesque construction: that the fine line between elusive categories, such as nature and its cultural embellishments, is discovered by the mind through the spatial experience of the body. Here the stationary observer looks inward through the strip windows at the animated show, not unlike a viewer watching a film. The same bodies that traversed the heavy ranges of Mappin, their movement adding spatiality to a scenic vista, watched longingly and immobilized as the penguins milled about on light arcs. The pool is a stage for the exotic animals that perform their lives on it but is also, especially from an architectural point of view, a stage for structure. The whole exercise is a platform for circulatory spectacle, and the ramps are such a spectacle themselves.

To cantilever the interlocking ramps of the pool without intermediary supports, Tecton had to petition for an exemption from the city building code. The ramps are about 46 feet long, 4 feet wide, 3 to 6 inches thick, and can tolerate 240 pounds per linear foot of applied load.[6] At this point of equilibrium, solid form reduced to a minimum; material pressed to its limits. Since the structure aimed to calibrate the ideal engagement of its inhabitants, the circumscribed form, whole in and of itself, left no room for addition or alteration. One ramp spirals up from the nesting boxes to the top of the slate stairs that curve around the northern perimeter, the other leads to the top of diving tank with a plate-glass front that faces the public. Reflections of the ramps in the water below redouble the spiral effect. In the Mappin Terraces the mechanics of circulation were concealed. In the Penguin Pool circulation was the empirical means of revelation.

The shell was a display of material technology, what the Royal Commission called "the liberating possibilities of modernist architecture." But to be a harbinger of a truly modern lifestyle, the circulation of the penguins was required. The structure dictated that penguins, birds that move gracefully through water, awkwardly plod up and down ramps.[7] The shape of the penguins, often referred to as dumpy, as well as the clumsy engagement with the ramps provides a formal foil for the elegance of the structure. A forced contraposition, of the penguins in their "natural" watery state versus the state of zoological exhibitionism, exposes the dichotomies of technological impressionism.[8]

Penguin Pool ramps under construction

1111 Lincoln Road by Herzog & de Meuron. Photo: Cora Visnick

Miami's 1111 Lincoln Road parking/multi-use structure is the quintessential slab building: not only are the beam-less floors of necessity doing all the work of carrying the loads of its occupants (cars and people alike, in ever-changing fashion) as well as of its own self-weight, but these slabs are on full display. At 1111 there is no enclosure; i.e., the slabs are all there is to be seen of the structure and of the architecture – well, almost. There are indeed also many columns holding the concrete slabs apart, but these are also "slab-like" in quality – i.e., they are planar, polygonal shapes that are strategically arrayed to carry gravity and lateral loads alike, their constantly changing forms and orientations from one floor level to the next serving to accentuate the horizontal layering of the building. The edges of the floor slabs themselves also do not line up vertically, suggesting the variation of things that happen on one level of the building vs. those on the floor above or below. In fact, as Michael Holt and Marissa Looby argue in this extract from their longer essay about the ever-evolving body of work of 1111 Lincoln Road's architects, Herzog and de Meuron, the edge of slab here effectively defines this building's façade and volume, even though such a façade is completely absent; here the slab does all. Although built nearly a century apart, the connections between the concrete slabs of Maillart's warehouses (or of the London Zoo Penguin Pool) and those of Miami's 1111 Lincoln Road are not so hard to fathom, whether structurally or conceptually…

Floor Plate–Defined Façades

from *Beyond the Wall, the Floor*
Michael Holt and Marissa Looby

Simple adjustments, slight alterations, subtle illusions. These are not tagline descriptions of the 1111 Lincoln Road, Miami Beach project, or a synopsis for a body of work. Instead they operate as retroactively projecting the course of professional development in the works of Swiss architects Herzog & de Meuron. The practice is known, from its earliest built projects, as a firm who produced artistically driven façade treatments where the vertical plane — the 'nominal façade' — would define form through the visually stimulating *surface* or *skin*. As the practice has evolved, it is argued here, they have crafted a new strategy: the horizontal plane as vertical façade generator.

In its progression the practice has deviated from façade ornamentation and fabrication towards the removal of the façade altogether; allowing for the floor plate — as a visual element — to operate as inadvertent façade and thus doubling its structural and visual importance. The placing of floor plates becomes the force creating the form — the 'inverted structural skin'. The stripped back architectural form does not remove the façade, but removes the *idea* of a façade, paradoxically creating a building mass almost by default.

The floor plates at 1111 Lincoln Road are design generators in both programmatic and visual terms. The building is a mixed-use development comprising of four different parcels that predominantly functions as a parking facility. Floor-to-ceiling heights vary between standard parking heights, double or even triple height in order to accommodate other programs in an inventive twist on the underutilized programmatic constraint of the typical parking station. The site accommodates an existing building, the former Suntrust bank; 300 car multi-level parking facility; 40,000 sqft retail; four luxury private residences as well as a number of internal courtyards; and, a public promenade with a glass pavilion designed by the artist Dan Graham.

Here, the ornamentally reductive, yet visually apparent, car parking mass is formed through a number of striated, interlocking concrete slab floor plates which are carried by irregularly-spaced, shard-like columns with pedestrian and vehicular ramps. The structure seems strangely flimsy, mainly as a result of its multilateral columns that seem to bow and compress with the force applied by the floor plate above. Of course, the visual impact is achievable by the fact that there is no apparent façade.

The Miami Beach project marks a significant step in the evolution of the practice. Where previously Herzog & de Meuron initiated the idea of a layered building envelope through the use of gabion wall construction (e.g. Dominus Winery, California, 1998); furthered by a flattening into a planar surface perceivably acting as three-dimensional skin (e.g. Ricola-Europe, Mulhouse-Brunstatt, 1993); to the present incarnation with a project that sublimates — the façade appears visible in its actual non-visible state. 1111 Lincoln Road visually collapses the façade into a *figural sublimation* where it appears through the very fact it is illusory. This is not achieved through representation, nor through a naïve formal abstraction, it sublimates: where one component is taken as given, worked against another, producing something entirely different or subtly ambiguous, yet genealogically connected.

'Figural', in object terms, denotes the idea of comprehending an object through a process of association, where inflections give an idea of the object as opposed to its representable form. The act of 'sublimation,' in this analogy, would allow for the object to be identifiable as a more refined version of its original. Therefore, the figural sublimation of the façade is to define the vertical plane through a purified association of the basic components of construction. The same approach has been used in the marketing of the project with the design of the logo. The logo does not define the building's postal address solely; nor does it illustrate the building's aesthetics. Instead it collapses everything into a *figural sublimation* of what the building stands for in theoretical terms.

Herzog & de Meuron's use of artwork or their notable artistic collaborations with Michael Craig-Martin, Dan Graham, Karl Blossfeldt or Ai Weiwei are widely documented. Each collaboration has shifted the practice towards a new line of enquiry: whether it is the façade treatment of polycarbonate backlighting at the Laban Dance Centre, UK (Craig-Martin); the light filtration through replication of a photographic image at the Ricola-Europe factory, Switzerland (Blossfeldt); or, the instantly recognizable structural conglomeration of the Bird's Nest, China (Ai Weiwei). However, in projects designed since the turn of the century, Herzog & de Meuron has allowed the floor plate to become a defining element in the façade's visual appearance. ...

In their collaborations with notable artists, [Herzog & de Meuron] have previously cited figures from different fields believing that such a cross-contamination of discursive methods only adds to the richness of architectural production. Many of the terms at play in much of the earlier works are centered on terminology rooted in the late 1980's through to the mid-1990's, significantly impacting upon the architectural production of the practice. *Skin, surface, decoration, ornament, functionalism* and *cosmetics* are architecturally identifiable adjectives.

In the latter part of the 1990's, turning the corner into the twenty-first century, the practice speculated on the idea that the *skin* or *surface* could still operate as a decorative element, but significantly also begins to partially reveal the mechanics of the floor plates. Through varying façade treatments Herzog & de Meuron obscurely reveal the floor plates' simple form and strong visual impact. For instance, the Prada Aoyama (Tokyo, 2003) project with its rhomboid-shaped structural glazing façade creates a visual interactivity but also, ultimately, a transparency through the mixture of convex, concave or flat glass panels. Similarly, at the Laban Dance Centre (London, 2003) the use of colored, transparent polycarbonate panels mounted in front of the glazing system provides a visually engaging façade but virtually reveals the skeletal form of the building's frame.

Herzog & de Meuron hold a focus and importance on the façade, be it in aesthetic terms or solely functional. The façade would diffuse light through its gabion construction; or seductively shimmer in the moonlight; or its metal surface was figuratively perforated in its fabrication; or, its smooth, flatness collapsed images into a silk-screened two-dimensional image dually operating as a three-dimensional skin. One aspect remained constant: the façade was paramount; remaining as such for the fact that it concealed the mechanics of the building with the floor plate lying visually dormant. A non-visible, functional component in the construction process and a programmatic element.

As the body of work progressed, so does the concept of façade. In its various manifestations the façade has been a figurative description of a functionalist plane; with its overriding significance never in doubt, rather it has merely shifted from immediate view. Where once the façade — for Herzog & de Meuron — provided shelter, programmatic segregation or an aesthetic attraction to the viewer; the façade, skin or surface has now visually eroded into the *notion* of a façade. This is through the implementation of shifting, striated floor plates which passively project the notional façade and present the idea of a volumetric mass, minus façade treatment. It could be said that Herzog & de Meuron's work has encountered a complete reversal of aesthetics where solid becomes void, where ornamentation is paradoxically replaced by emptiness, and where three-dimensional form switched to the illusion of form — its figural sublimation.

Herzog & de Meuron's built resolution has, previously, proclaimed its arrival through a glamorous, aesthetically explicit façade; in a bid to present an inherent, figural expression the more recent projects rely not on a figurative representation but on the infinitely more gracious implicit notion of a façade resolutely sculpted by nothing yet announcing everything.

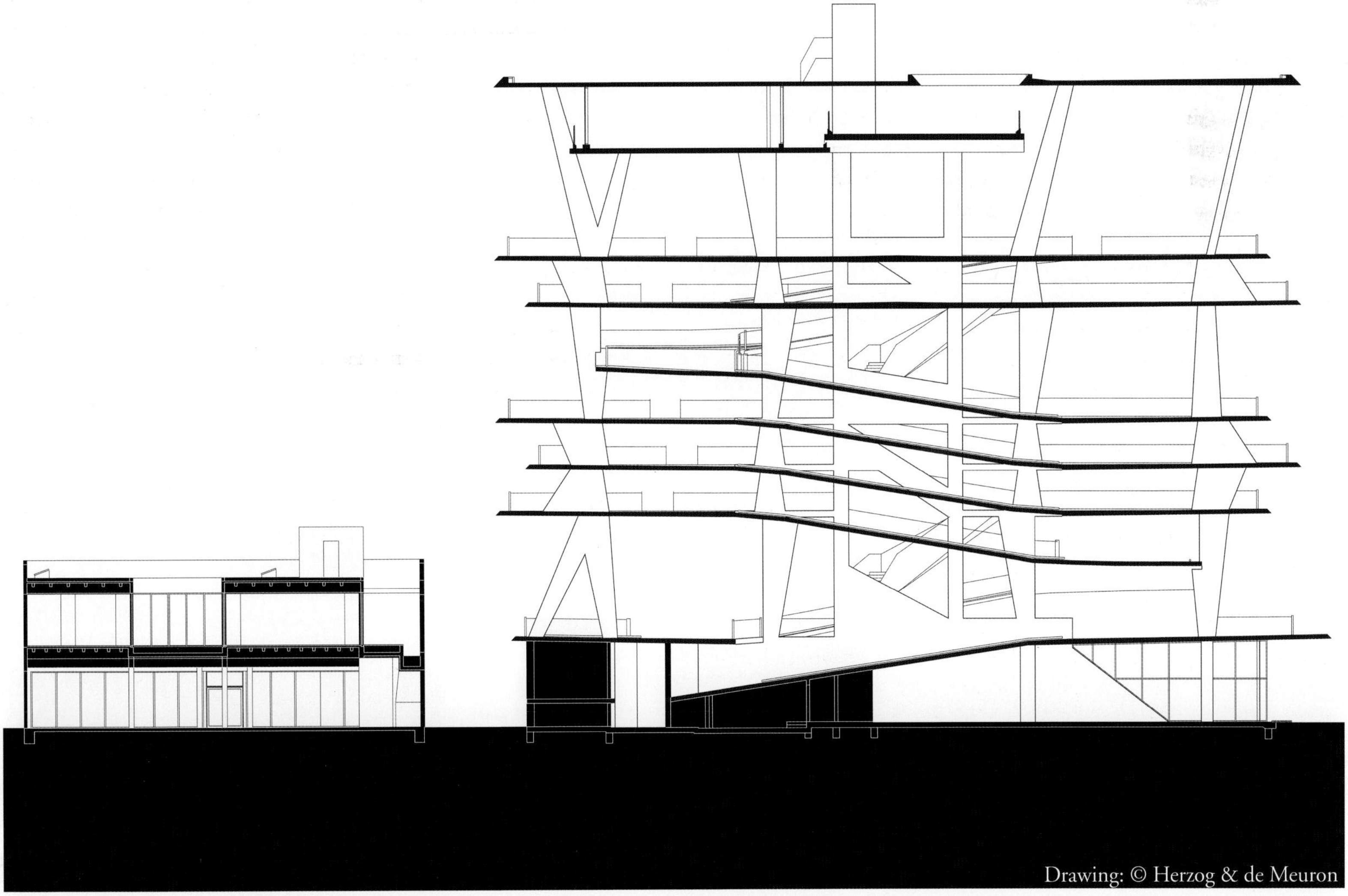
Drawing: © Herzog & de Meuron

Beam Grid and Lighting Effects

Trumpf Canteen, Stuttgart, Germany (2008)
Architect: Barkow Leibinger
Structural Engineer: Werner Sobek
Model: Veronica Guzman + Hyemin Jang + Andrew Moorman

© Christian Richters

The cellular, honeycombed form of this roof structure reflects the overall polygonal plan configuration of the pavilion that serves as the canteen for employees of the Trumpf machine company outside Stuttgart. Nine groups of slanting columns are used to hold the roof aloft; these columns' inclinations effectively also provide horizontal stability, a design solution that eliminates the need for shear walls and thus allows the roof to perceptually "float" above the varying terrain and mezzanine level below. Such an articulated cellular roof structure also provides splendid opportunities for exploiting the system's daylighting, artificial lighting and acoustical advantages.

The roof structure is in fact a composite of steel and glulam timber beam systems, with primary steel beams arranged in a triangular plan layout on which the secondary, smaller-scale glulam cellular systems are supported. These timber structures work as unique two-way beam grid systems, with the cells effectively producing a number of zigzagging timber beam lines spanning between adjacent steel beams. For the sides of the timber polygon cells to work as segments of a beam running continuously from one cell to the next, the cell-to-cell joints must be made bending moment-resistant. This is achieved by means of two multi-armed steel plates that connect the top and bottom of the multiple glulam elements that come together at each joint; these plates are discreetly hidden from view within the thickness of the timber.

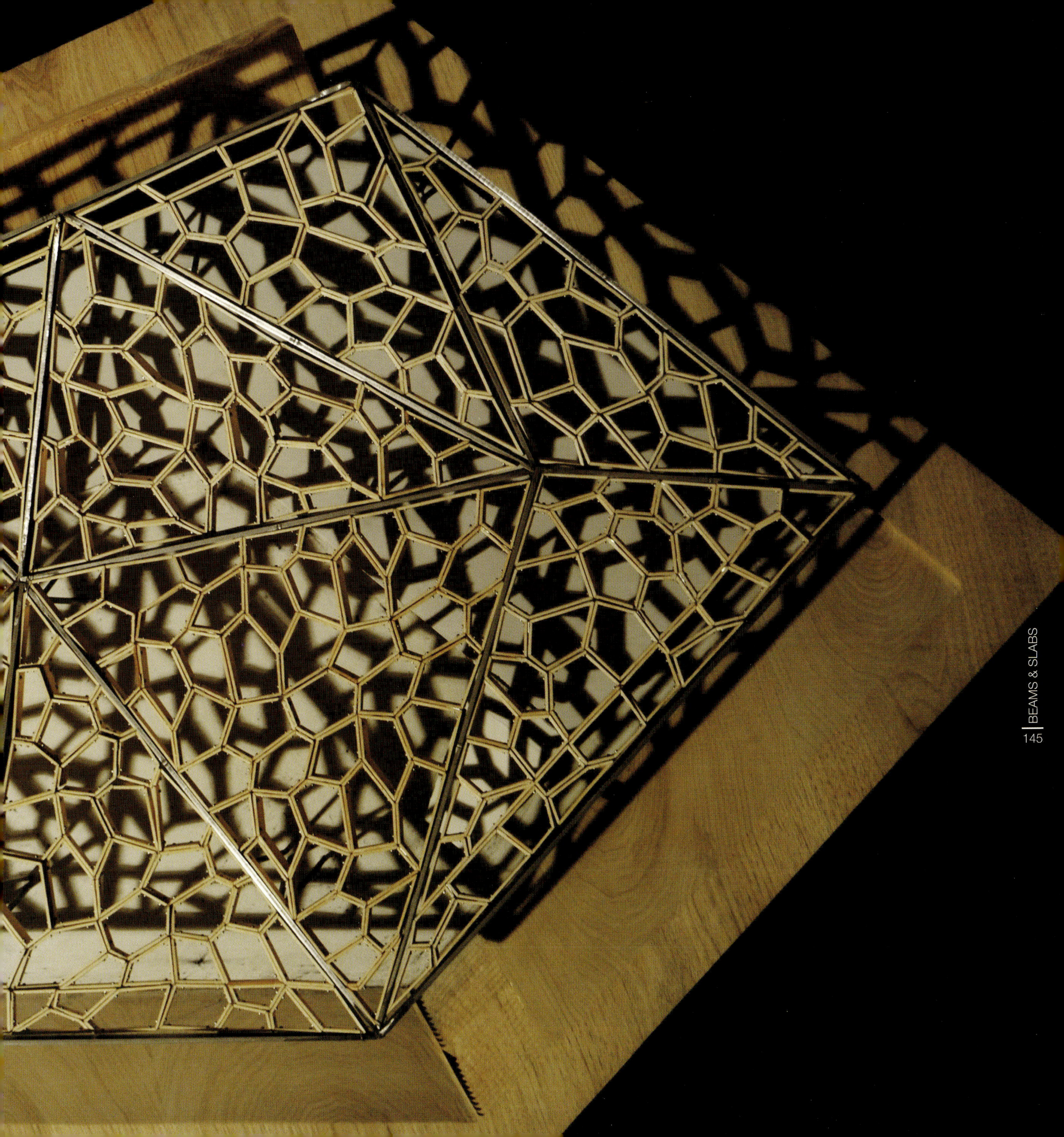

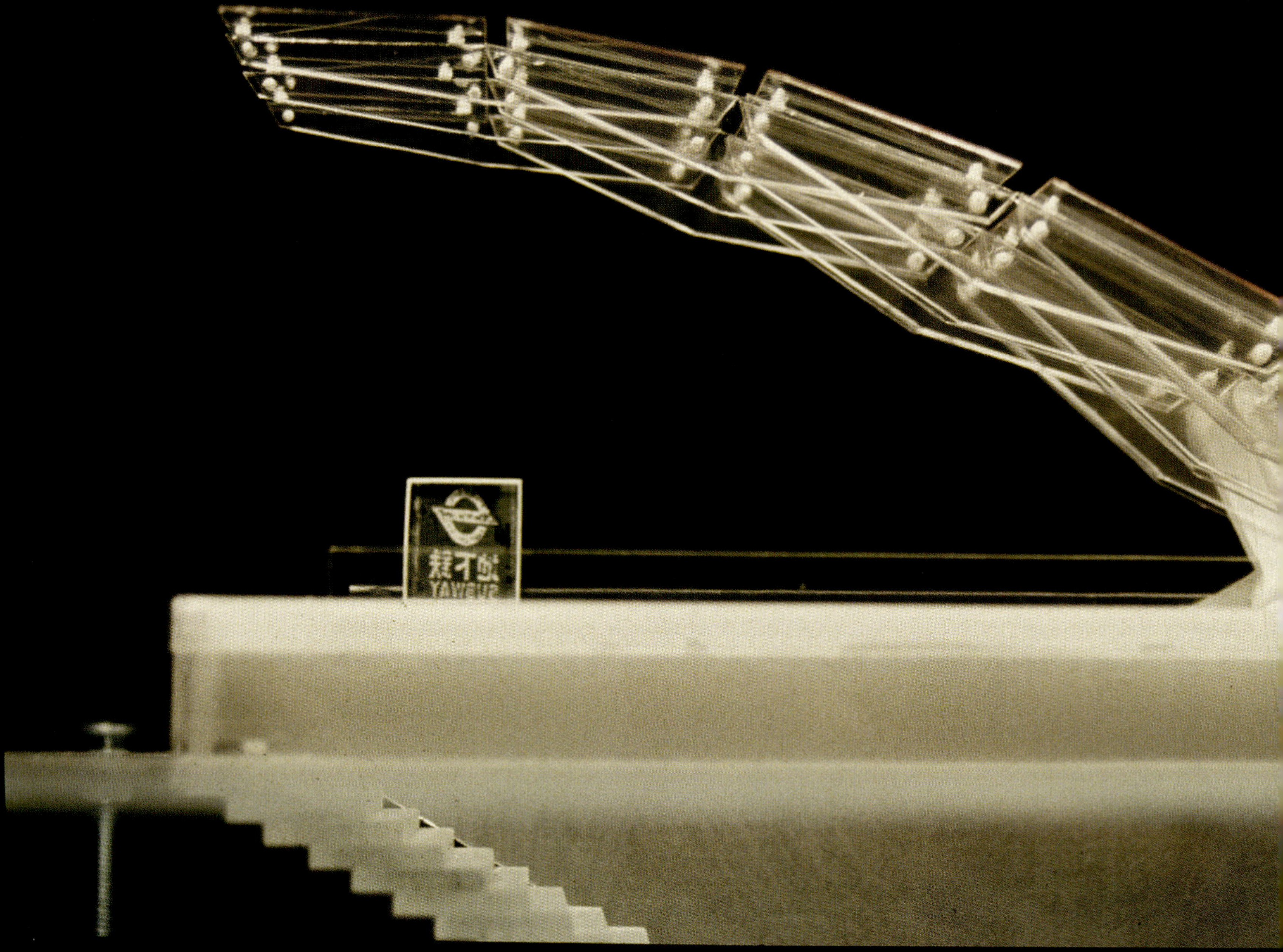

Variable-Depth Cantilever

Yurakucho Subway Station, Tokyo, Japan (1996)
Architect: Rafael Viñoly Architects
Structural Engineer: Dewhurst Macfarlane and Partners
Model: Maki Kawasaki

Nicholas Bruscia

The all-glass canopy for the staircase entrance to a Tokyo subway station is a structurally daring and groundbreaking piece of urban architecture. Springing from a single line of support, three glass support beams covered with glass sheets for the roof cantilever out 10.6m (32ft) in a curved arc that protects commuters and invites them into the subway system. Transparency and light reflections give the structure a distinctive appearance; certainly it is more than effective in announcing the presence of a station hidden deep underground. Production limitations on the maximum length of toughened glass resulted in the beams being constructed by four overlapping segments of near-triangular components, or so-called "blades", connected to each other by being pinned at their middle and end points. The one-sided, asymmetrical support condition results in dramatically increasing bending moments and shear forces as the structure approaches the base, and the depth of the cantilever varies accordingly. Moreover, where the cantilevering beams are fixed to the steel tube that supports them four blades comprise the cross-section of each beam, reducing to three, two and one as the tip of the cantilever is reached. Each such blade segment typically consists of two 19mm (3/4") thick toughened and laminated glass panels; in the most highly-stressed portion of the structure blades of acrylic glass (PMMA) are used, acting as a safety measure in case the glass should be damaged.

Beams Spanning Space

Museum of Anthropology, Vancouver, BC, Canada (1976)
Architect: Arthur Erickson
Structural Engineer: Bogue Babicki Associates Ltd.
Model: Cayley Lambur

Joseph Goldberg

The post-and-beam form that characterizes the University of British Columbia's Museum of Anthropology can be seen as a modern tribute to the building traditions of the region's First Nations' cultures, whose rectangular longhouses were roofed lengthwise by the trunks of the huge cedar trees that grow in the area. In the museum's great hall, below the long-spanning concrete beams, are exhibited the art work and cultural artifacts of the northwest coastal people, while the portal structures frame exterior views of the spectacular natural environment that is so closely connected to this culture. The building is entered under a low roof into a compressed, dark space holding accessible archives and small-scale displays; gradually the ground drops away and the roof rises up to orient one toward views of mountains and saltwater straits. Totem poles stand vertically within the tallest of these framed structures, addressing the coastal landscape.

The inverted U-shaped cross-sections of the concrete beams have significant depth to deal with the large bending moments resulting from the long spans. To further help counter these, the beams are post-tensioned into an overall state of pre-compression in order to make the most of a construction material that is notoriously weak with respect to the tension stresses that accompany bending; moreover, the cantilevered ends beyond the column supports are also an effective means of reducing the beams' maximum bending moments and stresses.

© Béka & Partners

Wall as Beam

Bordeaux House, France (1998)
Architect: Rem Koolhaas/OMA
Structural Engineer: Cecil Balmond/Arup
Model: Dan J. Choi

A heavy-looking top floor of mostly enclosed living space hovers with seemingly little support over the transparent, glass-enclosed ground level of this house. In fact, the exterior concrete walls of the upper level serve as story-height beams, and both a visual and physical tension is created as these are supported on a transverse rigid frame on one end and by an exposed rooftop steel beam at the other that hangs the wall-beams from above. In turn, a circular core provides one asymmetrical support for this steel beam while its other end is anchored in tension to the ground, thus providing the necessary balancing bending moment that ensures equilibrium. [see also p. 257]

Timothy Hursley

Inclined Beams: The Rafter

Cook House, Oxford, MS, USA (1991)
Architect: Mockbee Coker Howorth Architects
Model: Michael Barnoski

Experimental in form, this house is inspired by the vernacular architecture of the rural American South. Prominent concrete block volumes provide lateral stability and contrast with a wood- and steel-framed structure. Sloping rafters work as inclined beams to carry the roof loads; these meet at the ridge without vertical support being provided there, resulting in their balanced pushing against one another. The rafters also tend to thrust outward at their lower ends, but this is countered by the cross-bracing that makes the overall roof structure resemble a scissors truss. Placing this bracing relatively high contributes to the spatial opening of the top-floor living space.

Stealth Beam Grids

Burnham Pavilion, Chicago, USA (2009)
Architect: UN Studio, Garofalo Architects
Structural Engineer: Rockey Structures
Model: Cole Phoenix Skaggs + Lisa Yun Zhu

© Christian Richters

While completely hidden in the finished pavilion, two irregular beam grid systems are nevertheless instrumental in the realization of this temporary structure that celebrated the centennial of the 1909 Plan of Chicago (called the Burnham Plan). Inspired by the cantilevering roof eaves of Frank Lloyd Wright's Robie House, built in Chicago that same year, the Burnham Pavilion emphasizes strong horizontal lines and large projecting roof overhangs, but in a distinctively contemporary fashion. The 0.3m (1ft) uniform thickness of the roof swoops down in places to meet a similar floor plate lifted slightly off the ground, in each instance concealing inverted-tripod-like groupings of steel tubular columns – which effectively carry both gravity loads and by means of their inclination provide lateral stability to the pavilion in all directions.

Both roof and floor structures are constructed from a mix of metal and wood beam systems, in which rolled steel sections are used as primary beams with wooden beams filling the gaps between them. For increased versatility of form, ribs of cut plywood sheets replace regular wooden beams in the roof structure, enabling the secondary beam system to be shaped into upward and downward projections. Openings in the pavilion roof direct views outward and frame the cityscape of surrounding tall buildings, while a lighting system in the floor provides night-time color to the smooth plywood skin coated with white reflective paint. [see also p. 40]

Beams Articulating Floor and Roof Planes

Ruth Lilly Pavilion, Indianapolis, IN, USA (2010)
Architect: Marlon Blackwell Architect
Structural Engineer: Guy Nordenson and Associates
Model: Lily Chung + Stephanie Yao Zhao

Luke Zhen Han

A visitors' pavilion provides educational and service spaces along the pathways of the 100 Acres Art & Nature Park of the Indianapolis Museum of Art. Built on a raised deck that stretches out in three directions on a site protected against occasional floodwaters by earthen berms, the pavilion touches the ground relatively lightly. The floor deck, sidewalls and roof surface are made of spaced-apart slats of ipé wood, a durable Brazilian hardwood; together these form a surface that folds back upon itself and conceptually connects ground, pavilion and sky.

The lines visible through the partially open roof reveal the traces of the structural beams above that form the planar roof system, for which a grid of H-profile steel beams are simply connected to each other by bolts and splice plates. A secondary layer of lighter steel T-sections is supported by the primary steel framework, to which are attached the wooden slats of the roof canopy; light filters through these layers, mimicking the way sunlight penetrates through leaves and branches in the surrounding forest. An analogous steel beam system supports the floor structure that is lifted up off the ground, but which in plan has a different configuration than the roof. Moment-resisting frames brace the pavilion against horizontal loads; these are created by rigidly connecting certain steel beams of the floor and roof systems to the columns that support them.

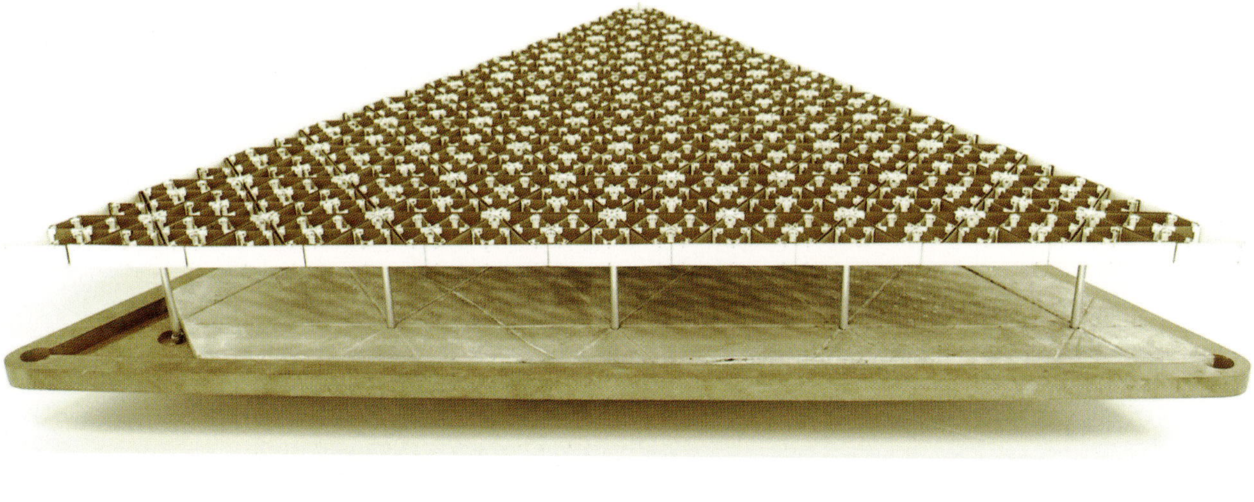

Hiroyuki Hirai

Beam Grid Non-Directional Space

Nemunoki Children's Art Museum, Shizuoka, Japan (1999)
Architect: Shigeru Ban Architects
Structural Engineer: Minoru Tezuka, Van Structural Design Studio
Model: James Nguyen + Sean Wen

Equilateral triangles form the ruling geometry for this children's art museum. With a hierarchy of modules, from the 30m (100ft) side of the overall plan down to the smallest structural unit of 1m (3ft), the triangulated roof structure is the dominant feature in this building. The beam grid is made of vertical sheets of 0.6m (2ft) deep corrugated and honeycombed paper material whose short segments are effectively made continuous by the unique connectors at each of the points of intersection. This roof is supported by 15 uniformly spaced tubular steel columns, resulting in an overall structural system that is at once functionally, visually, and spatially omni-directional. [see also p. 164]

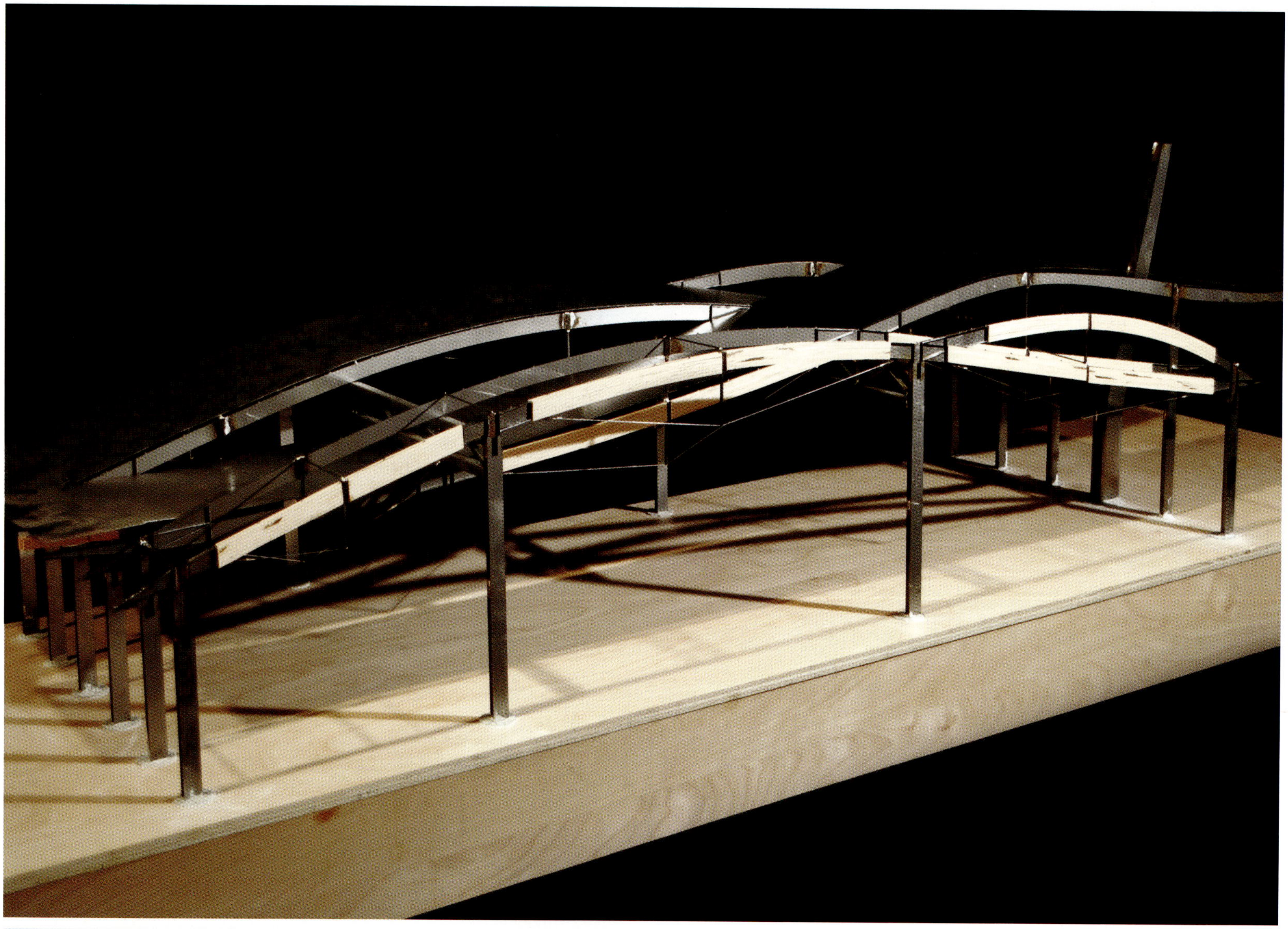

Tension Rod-Stiffened Beam

Raleigh-Durham Airport Terminal 2, NC, USA (2008)
Architect: Fentress Architects
Structural Engineer: Arup
Model: Peter Gudonis + Andrew Herington

The undulating form and material of the long-span roof of this airport is inspired by the nearby hills and wooded countryside of North Carolina, while the glulam timber beams' natural color also gives the large terminal space a warm and welcoming atmosphere. These slender, curved beams also signal technological competency: they span up to 49m (160ft) with the help of expressive steel compression struts and tension rods in an arrangement that forms inverted king-post structures. Said the legendary engineer Robert Le Ricolais about such structures: «It's a glorious device, to create fictitious supports; the paradox of columns suspended in the air.» [see also p. 165]

01. Uniform-depth continuous beams – Galzigbahn Cablecar Station, Innsbrucke, Austria, 2006; Driendl Galzigbahn (arch.); Brandner Ingenieurbüro and Bernard Ingenieure ZT GmbH (eng.); model by Yenny Hsieh & Camille Vélez **02. Double-sided roof-beam system; braced against buckling** – Abedian School of Architecture, Bond University, Brisbane, Australia, 2013; CRAB Studio / Peter Cook and Gavin Robotham (arch.); Arup (eng.); model by Christopher Andras & Stephanie Cheung **03. Radiating roof-beams** – Camera Obscura Pavilion, Greenport, NY, USA, 2005; Gary Paul (arch.); model by Sheyen Ikeda & Jimmy Shi **04. Spiraling beams support stair** – Scholzberg Tower, Liberec, Czech Republic, 2006; e-Mrak (arch.); model by Mariya Tsvetkova **05. Varying depth cantilevering arms for shading canopy** – Kuwait Pavilion, Seville, Spain, Expo 1992; Santiago Calatrava (arch., eng.); model by Heera Gangaramani **06. Varying depth for roof-beams reflects continuous frame behavior** – Gymnasium, University of Shiga Prefecture, Hikone, Japan, 1995; Itsuko Hasegawa Architectural Design Studios; Umezawa Structural Engineers; model by Adela Kalenja **07. Multi-directional, angled beams activate canopy** – El Bosque de Acero, Cuenca, Spain, 2010; Moneo Brock Studio (arch.); Jesus Jimenez, NB35, Cristina Alcazar (eng.); model by Joshua Carrelo Mendez & Nicholas Dareau **08. Finger joints ensure glulam beam continuity** – RPBW studio/offices, Genoa, Italy, 1991; RPBW (arch.); P. Costa (eng.); model by Saira Aktar & Juan Marcos Rodriguez Lopez **09. Cantilevering Vierendeel-style beams; propped on wall, anchored at back end** – Porche Pavilion, Wolfsburg, Germany, 2012; Henn Architekten (arch.); Schlaich Bergermann und Partner (eng.); model by Haydee Casellas & Arista Jusuf **10. Floor beams carry gravity loads, transmit lateral forces to bracing** - Gates Hall, Cornell University, Ithaca, NY, USA, 2014; Morphosis Architects; Thornton Tomasetti Group, Inc. (eng.); model by Jessica Jiang & Liam Martin

05

06

07

08

09

10

11

12

13

14

15

16

17

18

19

20

11. Two-way beam grid relies on top and bottom connections to transmit bending moments – Metropol Parasol, Seville, Spain, 2011; Jürgen Mayer H. (arch.); Arup (str. eng.); model by Greg Gyulai & Simin Wang **12,14. Multi-directional moment connections ensure continuity of beam grid** – Nemunoki Children's Art Museum, Shizuoka, Japan, 1999; Shigeru Ban Architects; Minoru Tezuka, Van Structural Design Studio; model by James Nguyen & Sean Wen **13. Two-way beam grid provides physical and spatial continuity** – Francis Gregory Library, Washington DC, USA, 2012; Adjaye Associates (arch.); ReStl Designers, Inc. (eng.); model by Iroha Ito & Whitney Liang **15. Glulam edge beam continuity ensured by full-depth connection** – Highway Support Center, Assen, Netherlands, 2014; 24H Architecture (arch.); Constructie Adviesbureau Geuijen, Woodteq Houtconstructies (eng.); model by Jerry Xuan Yu Liu & Andrew Wong **16. Roof rafters as continuous beams; multiple points of support** – Archery Hall and Boxing Club, Kogakuin University, Tokyo, Japan, 2013; FT Architects; model by Yichen Jia & Ji Eun Lee **17. Hierarchy of one-way framing system emphasized by angled roof** – Inca Public Market, Inca, Majorca, Spain, 2011; Chermaine Lay + Carles Muro (arch.); GMK Associats, BOMA (eng.); model by Shinhyuk Kim & Piotr Nowakowski **18. Tension-rod-strengthened glulam beam** – Terminal 2 RDU Airport, Raleigh-Durham, NC, USA, 2011; Fentress Architects; Arup, Stewart Engineering; model by Peter Gudonis & Andrew Herrington **19. Minimal depth roof-beam system enabled by many columns below** – KAIT Workshop, Kanagawa, Japan, 2010; Junya Ishigami + Associates (arch.); Konishi Structural Engineers; model by Jordan Berta & Henry Gao **20. Undulating roof-beams are continuous and carry load in bending & shear** – California Academy of Sciences, San Francisco, CA, USA, 2008; RPBW, Stantec Architecture (arch.); Arup (eng.); model by Beatrice Goh & Daphne Shen

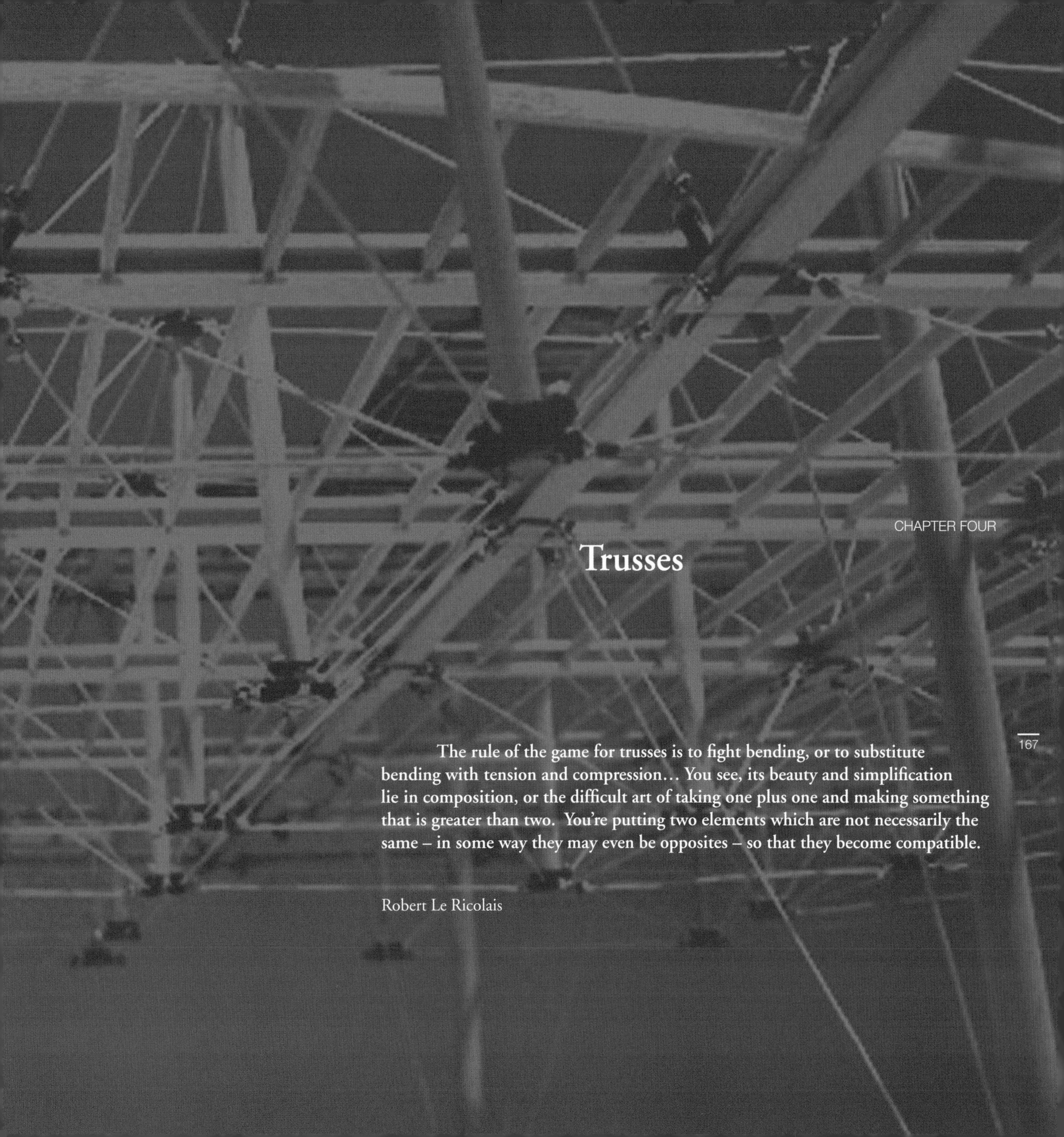

CHAPTER FOUR

Trusses

> The rule of the game for trusses is to fight bending, or to substitute bending with tension and compression… You see, its beauty and simplification lie in composition, or the difficult art of taking one plus one and making something that is greater than two. You're putting two elements which are not necessarily the same – in some way they may even be opposites – so that they become compatible.
>
> Robert Le Ricolais

View from the Quai du Louvre down the Seine. Photo: Ed Clark / The LIFE Picture Collection / Getty Images

At its most prosaic, a truss is nothing but a beam with holes cut out of it – or, as in the words of Robert Le Ricolais (p. 167), it is merely an assembly of tension and compression elements. Just like a beam, a truss can serve to carry transverse loads, span between supports, open up space for occupation, cantilever outward, act in one direction or two, and so on. And yet, there is so much more to the truss – Le Ricolais hinted as much when he added to his initial observation that unaccountable benefit can be derived from composing its various pieces to act together as one.

Can there be any more convincing proof of this assertion than the Eiffel Tower? Literally, of course, this structure is nothing but a truss cantilevering vertically into the air. Like any tower, it carries the gravity loads of its occupants and of its own self-weight, and it resists horizontal wind forces by flexing sideways – preventing excessive deflections by means of the tension and compression forces that develop within its myriad components. The structural engineer readily recognizes in the tower's elegant profile the telltale shape of a bending moment diagram – narrow at the free end (top), wide at the support (base), with a curved profile in between. And yet, the Eiffel Tower is so much more than these things, whether seen on the skyline from afar or experienced from within, whether understood as a symbol for a city, indeed, a whole country, or sensed as a looming presence even when unseen. Roland Barthes' classic 1964 essay *La Tour Eiffel* conveys all of these things and more; surely the truss has had no better interlocutor…

La Tour Eiffel: A Truss, and More…

The Eiffel Tower
Roland Barthes
translated by Richard Howard

'Writers, painters, sculptors, architects, passionate lovers of the beauty, until now unspoiled, of Paris, we come to protest, with all our strength, with all our indignation, in the name of disregarded French taste, in the name of art and French history presently in danger, against the erection, in the very heart of our capital, of the useless and monstrous Eiffel Tower. … Will this city of Paris continue to listen to the baroque, mercantile fancies of a builder of machines, and irreparably lose its honor and beauty? For the Eiffel Tower, which even the commercial America would reject, means, without any doubt, a Paris dishonored. Everyone feels this, everyone says it, everyone is deeply hurt, and we are only a weak echo of the universal opinion, so legitimately alarmed. Indeed, when the people of other countries finally come to visit our Exposition, they will cry in astonishment: "What?—is this horror what the French have brought forth to give us an idea of their famous taste?" They will be right in mocking us, for the Paris of sublime Gothic art, the Paris of Jean Goujon, of Germain Pilon, of Puget, of Rude, of Barye, etc., will have become the Paris of Monsieur Eiffel.'[1]

— E. Meissonier, Ch. Gounod, Charles Gamier, W. Bouguereau, A. Dumas, Francois Coppée, Leconte de Lisle, Sully Prudhomme, and Guy de Maupassant, among other signers

Maupassant often lunched at the restaurant in the tower, though he didn't care much for the food: *It's the only place in Paris,* he used to say, *where I don't have to see it.* And it's true that you must take endless precautions, in Paris, not to see the Eiffel Tower; whatever the season, through mist and cloud, on overcast days or in sunshine, in rain—wherever you are, whatever the landscape of roofs, domes, or branches separating you from it, the *Tower is there*; incorporated into daily life until you can no longer grant it any specific attribute, determined merely to persist, like a rock or the river, it is as literal as a phenomenon of nature whose meaning can be questioned to infinity but whose existence is incontestable. There is virtually no Parisian glance it fails to *touch* at some time of day; at the moment I begin writing these lines about it, the Tower is there, in front of me, framed by my window; and at the very moment the January night blurs it, apparently trying to make it invisible, to deny its presence, two little lights come on, winking gently as they revolve at its very tip: all this night, too, it will be there, connecting me above Paris to each of my friends that I know are seeing it: with it we all comprise a shifting figure of which it is the steady center: the Tower is friendly.

The Tower is also present to the entire world. First of all as a universal symbol of Paris, it is everywhere on the globe where Paris is to be stated as an image; from the Midwest to Australia, there is no journey to France which isn't made, somehow, in the Tower's name, no schoolbook, poster, or film about France which fails to propose it as the major sign of a people and of a place: it belongs to the universal language of travel. Further: beyond its strictly Parisian statement, it touches the most general human image-repertoire: its simple, primary shape confers upon it the vocation of an infinite cipher: in turn and according to the appeals of our imagination, the symbol of Paris, of modernity, of communication, of science or of the nineteenth century, rocket, stem, derrick, phallus, lightning rod or insect, confronting the great itineraries of our dreams, it is the inevitable sign; just as there is no Parisian glance which is not compelled to encounter it, there is no fantasy which fails, sooner or later, to acknowledge its form and to be nourished by it; pick up a pencil and let your hand, in other words your thoughts, wander, and it is often the Tower which will appear, reduced to that simple line whose sole mythic function is to join, as the poet says, *base and summit*, or again, *earth and heaven*.

This pure—virtually empty—sign is ineluctable, *because it means everything*. In order to negate the Eiffel Tower (though the temptation to do so is rare, for this symbol offends nothing in us), you must, like Maupassant, get up on it and, so to speak, identify yourself with it. Like man himself, who is the only one not to know his own glance, the Tower is the only blind point of the total optical system of which it is the center and Paris the circumference. But in this movement which seems to limit it, the Tower acquires a new power: an object when we look at it, it becomes a lookout in its turn when we visit it, and now constitutes as an object, simultaneously extended and collected beneath it, that Paris which just now was looking at it. The Tower is an object which sees, a glance which is seen; it is a complete verb, both active and passive, in which no function, no *voice* (as we say in grammar, with a piquant ambiguity) is defective. This dialectic is not in the least banal, it makes the Tower a singular monument; for the world ordinarily produces either purely functional organisms (camera or eye) intended to see things but which then afford nothing to sight, what *sees* being mythically linked to what remains *hidden* (this is the theme of the voyeur), or else spectacles which themselves are blind and are left in the pure passivity of the visible. The Tower (and this is one of its mythic powers) transgresses this separation, this habitual divorce of *seeing* and *being seen*, it achieves a sovereign circulation between the two functions; it is a complete object which has, if one may say so, both sexes of sight. This radiant position in the order of perception gives it a prodigious propensity to meaning: the Tower attracts meaning, the way a lightning rod attracts thunderbolts; for all lovers of signification, it plays a glamorous part, that of a pure signifier, i.e., of a form in which men unceasingly put meaning (which they extract at will from their knowledge, their dreams, their history), without this meaning thereby ever being finite and fixed: who can say what the Tower will be for humanity tomorrow? But there can be no doubt it will always be something, and something of humanity itself. Glance, object, symbol, such is the infinite circuit of functions which permits it always to be something other and something much more than the Eiffel Tower.

In order to satisfy this great oneiric function, which makes it into a kind of total monument, the Tower must escape reason. The first condition of this victorious flight is that the Tower be an utterly *useless* monument. The Tower's inutility has always been obscurely felt to be a scandal, i.e., a truth, one that is precious and inadmissible. Even before it was built, it was blamed for being useless, which, it was believed at the time, was sufficient to condemn it; it was not in the spirit of a period commonly dedicated to rationality and to the empiricism of great bourgeois enterprises to endure the notion of a useless object (unless it was declaratively an *objet d'art*, which was also unthinkable in relation to the Tower); hence Gustave Eiffel, in his own defense of his project in reply to the Artists' Petition, scrupulously lists all the future uses of the Tower: they are all, as we might expect of an engineer, scientific uses: aerodynamic measurements, studies of the resistance of substances, physiology of the climber, radio-electric research, problems of telecommunication, meteorological observations, etc. These uses are doubtless incontestable, but they seem quite ridiculous alongside the overwhelming myth of the Tower, of the human meaning which it has assumed throughout the world. This is because here the utilitarian excuses, however ennobled they may be by the myth of Science, are nothing in comparison to the great imaginary function which enables men to be strictly human. Yet, as always, the gratuitous meaning of the work is never avowed directly: it is rationalized under the rubric of use: Eiffel saw his Tower in the form of a serious object, rational, useful; men return it to him in the form of a great baroque dream which quite naturally touches on the borders of the irrational.

This double movement is a profound one: architecture is always dream and function, expression of a utopia and instrument of a convenience. Even before the Tower's birth, the nineteenth century (especially in America and in England) had often dreamed of structures whose height would be astonishing, for the century was given to technological feats, and the conquest of the sky once again preyed upon humanity. In 1881, shortly before the Tower, a French architect had elaborated the project of a sun tower; now this project, quite mad technologically, since it relied on masonry and not on steel, also put itself under the warrant of a thoroughly empirical utility; on the one hand, a bonfire placed on top of the structure was to illuminate the darkness of every nook and cranny in Paris by a system of mirrors (a system that was undoubtedly a complex one!), and on the other, the last story of this sun tower (about 1,000 feet, like the Eiffel Tower) was to be reserved for a kind of sunroom, in which invalids would benefit from an air "as pure as in the mountains." And yet, here as in the case of the Tower, the naïve utilitarianism of the enterprise is not separate from the oneiric, infinitely powerful function which, actually, inspires its creation: use never does anything but shelter meaning. Hence we might speak, among men, of a true Babel complex: Babel was supposed to *serve* to communicate with God, and yet Babel is a dream which touches much greater depths than that of the theological project; and just as this great ascensional dream, released from its utilitarian prop, is finally what remains in the countless Babels represented by the painters, as if the function of art were to reveal the profound uselessness of objects, just so the Tower, almost immediately disengaged from the scientific considerations which had authorized its birth (it matters very little here that the Tower should be in fact useful), has arisen from a great human dream in which movable and infinite meanings are mingled: it has reconquered the basic uselessness which makes it live in men's imagination. At first, it was sought—so paradoxical is the notion of an empty monument—to make it into a "temple of Science"; but this is only a metaphor; as a matter of fact, the Tower is *nothing*, it achieves a kind of zero degree of the monument; it participates in no rite, in no cult, not even in Art; you cannot visit the Tower as a museum: there is nothing to see *inside* the Tower. This empty monument nevertheless receives each year twice as many visitors as the Louvre and considerably more than the largest movie house in Paris.

Then why do we visit the Eiffel Tower? No doubt in order to participate in a dream of which it is (and this is its originality) much more the crystallizer than the true object. The Tower is not a usual spectacle; to enter the Tower, to scale it, to run around its courses, is, in a manner both more elementary and more profound, to accede to a *view* and to explore the interior of an object (though an openwork one), to transform the touristic rite into an adventure of sight and of the intelligence. It is this double function I should like to speak of briefly, before passing in conclusion to the major symbolic function of the Tower, which is its final meaning.

The Tower looks at Paris. To visit the Tower is to get oneself up onto the balcony in order to perceive, comprehend, and savor a certain essence of Paris. And here again, the Tower is an original monument. Habitually, belvederes are outlooks upon nature, whose elements—waters, valleys, forests—they assemble beneath them, so that the tourism of the "fine view" infallibly implies a naturist mythology. Whereas the Tower overlooks not nature but the city; and yet, by its very position of a visited outlook, the Tower makes the city into a kind of nature; it constitutes the swarming of men into a landscape, it adds to the frequently grim urban myth a romantic dimension, a harmony, a mitigation; by it, starting from it, the city joins up with the great natural themes which are offered to the curiosity of men: the ocean, the storm, the mountains, the snow, the rivers. To visit the Tower, then, is to enter into contact not with a historical Sacred, as is the case for the majority of monuments, but rather with a new nature, that of human space: the Tower is not a trace, a souvenir, in short a culture; but rather an immediate consumption of a humanity made natural by that glance which transforms it into space.

One might say that for this reason the Tower materializes an imagination which has had its first expression in literature (it is frequently the function of the great books to achieve in advance what technology will merely put into execution). The nineteenth century, fifty years before the Tower, produced indeed two works in which the (perhaps very old) fantasy of a panoramic vision received the guarantee of a major poetic writing (*écriture*); these are, on the one hand, the chapter of *Notre-Dame de Paris (The Hunchback of Notre Dame)* devoted to a bird's-eye view of Paris, and on the other, Michelet's *Tableau chronologique*. Now, what is admirable in these two great inclusive visions, one of Paris, the other of France, is that Hugo and Michelet clearly understood that to the marvelous mitigation of altitude the panoramic vision added an incomparable power of *intellection*: the bird's-eye view, which each visitor to the Tower can assume in an instant for his own, gives us the world to *read* and not only to perceive; this is why it corresponds to a new sensibility of vision; in the past, to travel (we may recall certain—admirable, moreover—promenades of Rousseau) was to be thrust into the midst of sensation, to perceive only a kind of tidal wave of things; the bird's-eye view, on the contrary, represented by our romantic writers as if they had anticipated both the construction of the Tower and the birth of aviation, permits us to transcend sensation and to see things *in their structure*. Hence it is the advent of a new perception, of an intellectualist mode, which these literatures and these architectures of vision mark out (born in the same century and probably from the same history): Paris and France become under Hugo's pen and Michelet's (and under the glance of the Tower) intelligible objects, yet without—and this is what is new—losing anything of their materiality; a new category appears, that of concrete abstraction; this, moreover, is the meaning which we can give today to the word *structure*; a corpus of intelligent forms.

Like Monsieur Jourdain confronted with prose, every visitor to the Tower makes structuralism without knowing it (which does not keep prose and structure from existing all the same); in Paris spread out beneath him, he spontaneously distinguishes separate—because known—points—and yet does not stop linking them, perceiving them within a great functional space; in short, he separates and groups; Paris offers itself to him as an object virtually *prepared*, exposed to the intelligence, but which he must himself construct by a final activity of the mind: nothing less passive than the *overall view* the Tower gives to Paris. This activity of the mind, conveyed by the tourist's modest glance, has a name: decipherment.

What, in fact, is a panorama? An image we attempt to decipher, in which we try to recognize known sites, to identify landmarks. Take some view of Paris taken from the Eiffel Tower; here you make out the hill sloping down from Chaillot, there the Bois de Boulogne; but where is the Arc de Triomphe? You don't see it, and this absence compels you to inspect the panorama once again, to look for this point which is missing in your structure; your knowledge (the knowledge you may have of Parisian topography) struggles with your perception, and in a sense, that is what intelligence is: to reconstitute, to make memory and sensation cooperate so as to produce in your mind a simulacrum of Paris, of which the elements are in front of you, real, ancestral, but nonetheless disoriented by the total space in which they are given to you, for this space was unknown to you. Hence we approach the complex, dialectical nature of all panoramic vision; on the one hand, it is a euphoric vision, for it can slide slowly, lightly the entire length of a continuous image of Paris, and initially no "accident" manages to interrupt this great layer of mineral and vegetal strata, perceived in the distance in the bliss of altitude; but, on the other hand, this very continuity engages the mind in a certain struggle, it seeks to be deciphered, we must find signs within it, a familiarity proceeding from history and from myth; this is why a panorama can never be consumed as a work of art, the aesthetic interest of a painting ceasing once we try to recognize in it particular points derived from our knowledge; to say that there is a beauty to Paris stretched out at the feet of the Tower is doubtless to acknowledge this euphoria of aerial vision which recognizes nothing other than a nicely connected space; but it is also to mask the quite intellectual effort of the eye before an object which requires to be divided up, identified, reattached to memory; for the bliss of sensation (nothing happier than a lofty outlook) does not suffice to elude the questioning nature of the mind before any image.

This generally intellectual character of the panoramic vision is further attested by the following phenomenon, which Hugo and Michelet had moreover made into the mainspring of their bird's-eye views: to perceive Paris from above is infallibly to imagine a history; from the top of the Tower, the mind finds itself dreaming of the mutation of the landscape which it has before its eyes; through the astonishment of space, it plunges into the mystery of time, lets itself be affected by a kind of spontaneous anamnesis: it is duration itself which becomes panoramic. Let us put ourselves back (no difficult task) at the level of an average knowledge, an ordinary question put to the panorama of Paris; four great moments immediately leap out to our vision, i.e., to our consciousness. The first is that of prehistory; Paris was then covered by a layer of water, out of which barely emerged a few solid points; set on the Tower's first floor, the visitor would have had his nose level with the waves and would have seen only some scattered islets, the Étoile, the Panthéon, a wooded island which was Montmartre and two blue stakes in the distance, the towers of Notre-Dame, then to his left, bordering this huge lake, the slopes of Mont Valérien; and conversely, the traveler who chooses to put himself today on the heights of this eminence, in foggy weather, would see emerging the two upper stories of the Tower from a liquid base; this prehistoric relation of the Tower and the water has been, so to speak, symbolically maintained down to our own days, for the Tower is partly built on a thin arm of the Seine filled in (up to the Rue de l'Université) and it still seems to rise from a gesture of the river whose bridges it guards. The second history which lies before the Tower's gaze is the Middle Ages; Cocteau once said that the Tower was the Notre-Dame of the Left Bank; though the cathedral of Paris is not the highest of the city's monuments (the Invalides, the Panthéon, Sacré-Coeur are higher), it forms with the tower a pair, a symbolic couple, recognized, so to speak, by Tourist folklore, which readily reduces Paris to its Tower and its Cathedral: a symbol articulated on the opposition of the past (the Middle Ages always represent a dense time) and the present, of stone, old as the world, and metal, sign of modernity. The third moment that can be read from the Tower is that of a broad history, undifferentiated since it proceeds from the Monarchy to the Empire, from the Invalides to the Arc de Triomphe: this is strictly the History of France, as it is experienced by French schoolchildren, and of which many episodes, present in every schoolboy memory, touch Paris. Finally, the Tower surveys a fourth history of Paris, the one which is being made now; certain modern monuments (UNESCO, the Radio-Télévision building) are beginning to set signs of the future within its space; the Tower permits harmonizing these unaccommodated substances (glass, metal), these new forms, with the stones and domes of the past; Paris, in its duration, under the Tower's gaze, composes itself like an abstract canvas in which dark oblongs (derived from a very old past) are contiguous with the white rectangles of modern architecture.

Once these points of history and of space are established by the eye, from the top of the Tower, the imagination continues filling out the Parisian panorama, giving it its structure; but what then intervenes are certain human functions; like the devil Asmodeus, by rising above Paris, the visitor to the Tower has the illusion of raising the enormous lid which covers the private life of millions of human beings; the city then becomes an intimacy whose functions, i.e., whose connections he deciphers; on the great polar axis, perpendicular to the horizontal curve of the river, three zones stacked one after the other, as though along a prone body, three functions of human life: at the top, at the foot of Montmartre, pleasure; at the center, around the Opéra, materiality, business, commerce; toward the bottom, at the foot of the Panthéon, knowledge, study; then, to the right and left, enveloping this vital axis like two protective muffs, two large zones of habitation, one residential, the other blue-collar; still farther, two wooded strips, Boulogne and Vincennes. It has been observed that a kind of very old law incites cities to develop toward the west, in the direction of the setting sun; it is on this side that the wealth of the fine neighborhoods proceeds, the east remaining the site of poverty; the Tower, by its very implantation, seems to follow this movement discreetly; one might say that it accompanies Paris in this westward shift, which our capital does not escape, and that it even invites the city toward its pole of development, to the south and to the west, where the sun is warmer, thereby participating in that great mythic function which makes every city into a living being: neither brain nor organ, situated a little apart from its vital zones, the Tower is merely the witness, the gaze which discreetly fixes, with its slender signal, the whole structure—geographical, historical, and social—of Paris space. This deciphering of Paris, performed by the Tower's gaze, is not only an act of the mind, it is also an initiation. To climb the Tower in order to contemplate Paris from it is the equivalent of that first journey, by which the young man from the provinces went up to Paris, in order to conquer the city. At the age of twelve, young Eiffel himself took the diligence from Dijon with his mother and discovered the "magic" of Paris. The city, a kind of superlative capital, summons up that movement of accession to a superior order of pleasures, of values, of arts and luxuries; it is a kind of precious world of which knowledge makes the man, marks an entrance into a true life of passions and responsibilities; it is this myth—no doubt a very old one—which the trip to the Tower still allows us to suggest; for the tourist who climbs the Tower, however mild he may be, Paris laid out before his eyes by an individual and deliberate act of contemplation is still something of the Paris confronted, defied, possessed by Rastignac. Hence, of all the sites visited by the foreigner or the provincial, the Tower is the first obligatory monument; it is a Gateway, it marks the transition to a knowledge: one must sacrifice to the Tower by a rite of inclusion from which, precisely, the Parisian alone can excuse himself, the Tower is indeed the site which allows one to be incorporated into a race, and when it regards Paris, it is the very essence of the capital it gathers up and proffers to the foreigner who has paid to it his initiational tribute.

From Paris contemplated, we must now work our way back toward the Tower itself: the Tower which will live its life as an object (before being mobilized as a symbol). Ordinarily, for the tourist, every object is first of all an *inside*, for there is no visit without the exploration of an enclosed space: to visit a church, a museum, a palace is first of all to shut oneself up, to "make the rounds" of an interior, a little in the manner of an owner: every exploration is an appropriation; this tour of the *inside* corresponds, moreover, to the question raised by the *outside*: the monument is a riddle, to enter it is to solve, to possess it; here we recognize in the tourist visit that initiational function we have just invoked apropos of the trip to the Tower; the cohort of visitors which is enclosed by a monument and processionally follows its internal meanders before coming back outside is quite like the neophyte who, in order to accede to the initiate's status, is obliged to traverse a dark and unfamiliar route within the initatory edifice. In the religious protocol as in the tourist enterprise, being enclosed is therefore a function of the rite. Here, too, the Tower is a paradoxical object: one cannot be shut up within it since what defines the Tower is its longilineal form and its open structure: How can you be enclosed within emptiness, how can you visit a line? Yet incontestably the Tower is visited: we linger within it, before using it as an observatory. What is happening? What becomes of the great exploratory function of the *inside* when it is applied to this empty and depthless monument which might be said to consist entirely of an exterior substance?

In order to understand how the modern visitor adapts himself to the paradoxical monument which is offered to his imagination, we need merely observe what the Tower gives him, insofar as one sees in it an object and no longer a lookout. On this point, the Tower's provisions are of two kinds. The first is of a technical order; the Tower offers for consumption a certain number of performances, or, if one prefers, of paradoxes, and the visitor then becomes an engineer by proxy; these are, first of all, the four bases, and especially (for enormity does not astonish) the exaggeratedly oblique insertion of the metal pillars in the mineral mass; this obliquity is curious insofar as it gives birth to an upright form, whose very verticality absorbs its departure in slanting forms, and here there is a kind of agreeable challenge for the visitor; then come the elevators, quite surprising by their obliquity, for the ordinary imagination requires that what rises mechanically slide along a vertical axis; and for anyone who takes the stairs, there is the enlarged spectacle of all the details, plates, beams, bolts, which *make* the Tower, the surprise of seeing how this rectilinear form, which is consumed in every corner of Paris as a pure line, is composed of countless segments, interlinked, crossed, divergent: an operation of reducing an appearance (the straight line) to its contrary reality (a lacework of broken substances), a kind of demystification provided by simple enlargement of the level of perception, as in those photographs in which the curve of a face, by enlargement, appears to be formed of a thousand tiny squares variously illuminated. Thus the Tower-as-object furnishes its observer, provided he insinuates himself into it, a whole series of paradoxes, the delectable contraction of an appearance and of its contrary reality.

The Tower's second provision, as an object, is that, despite its technical singularity, it constitutes a familiar "little world"; from the ground level, a whole humble commerce accompanies its departure: vendors of postcards, souvenirs, knicknacks, balloons, toys, sunglasses, herald a commercial life which we rediscover thoroughly installed on the first platform. Now any commerce has a space-taming function; selling, buying, exchanging—it is by these simple gestures that men truly dominate the wildest sites, the most sacred constructions. The myth of the moneylenders driven out of the Temple is actually an ambiguous one, for such commerce testifies to a kind of affectionate familiarity with regard to a monument whose singularity no longer intimidates, and it is by a Christian sentiment (hence to a certain degree a special one) that the spiritual excludes the familiar; in Antiquity, a great religious festival as well as a theatrical representation, a veritable sacred ceremony, in no way prevented the revelation of the most everyday gestures, such as eating or drinking: all pleasures proceeded simultaneously, not by some heedless permissiveness but because the ceremonial was never savage and certainly offered no contradiction to the quotidian. The Tower is not a sacred monument, and no taboo can forbid a commonplace life to develop there, but there can be no question, nonetheless, of a trivial phenomenon here; the installation of a restaurant on the Tower, for instance (food being the object of the most symbolic of trades), is a phenomenon corresponding to a whole meaning of leisure; man always seems disposed—if no constraints appear to stand in his way—to seek out a kind of counterpoint in his pleasures: this is what is called comfort. The Eiffel Tower is a comfortable object, and moreover, it is in this that it is an object either very old (analogous, for instance, to the ancient Circus) or very modern (analogous to certain American institutions such as the drive-in movie, in which one can simultaneously enjoy the film, the car, the food, and the freshness of the night air). Further, by affording its visitor a whole polyphony of pleasures, from technological wonder to haute cuisine, including the panorama, the Tower ultimately reunites with the essential function of all major human sites: autarchy; the Tower can live on itself: one can dream there, eat there, observe there, understand there, marvel there, shop there; as on an ocean liner (another mythic object that sets children dreaming), one can feel oneself cut off from the world and yet the owner of a world.

Photo: Emi Yasuda

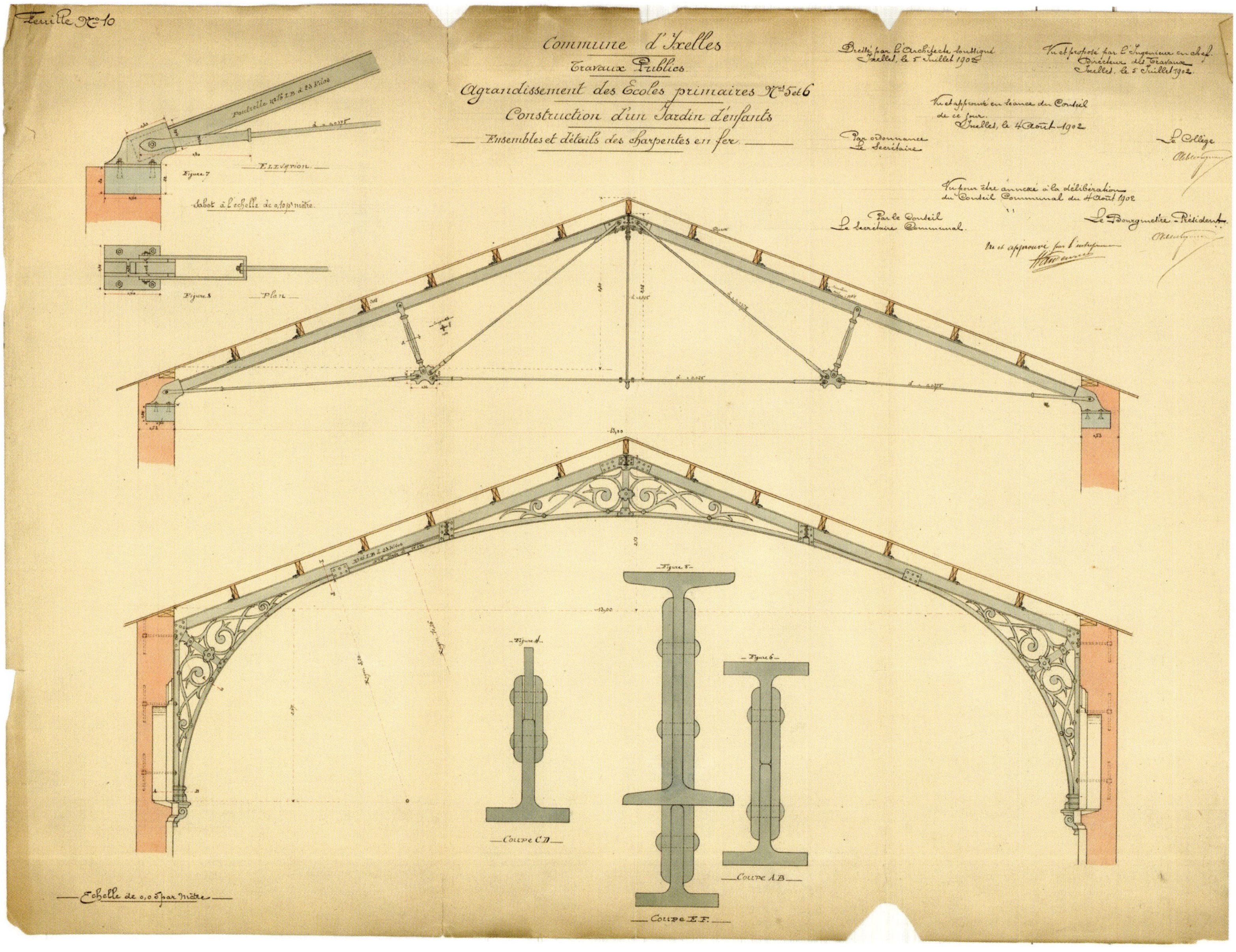

Agrandissement des écoles primaires n° 5 et 6. Construction d'un Jardin. Ensembles et détails de la charpente en fer. 1902 (By permission of the Municipal Archive of Elsene)

The debate that Roland Barthes lays bare in the preceding essay between those who saw the Eiffel Tower as the embodiment of a new age of technological and societal development versus those who were horrified by its exposed structural skeleton in the midst of aesthetically "dignified" Paris, is echoed here at the much more intimate scale of Belgian model schools. Built in communities nationwide over a forty-year period that straddled 1900, the schools each incorporated, for progressive health reasons, a central covered courtyard – thus requiring a long-span structural system, something the truss is exceptionally well-suited for. This group of schools thereby created the equivalent of a controlled experiment on the development of truss forms at that time between the highly efficient, "industrial", still-today-renowned Polonceau truss and the much less rational, "artistic", now-somewhat-obscure Ardant truss. Belgian society sometimes demonstrated a certain ambivalence between these two forms, and variations of both types were sometimes drawn up and carefully detailed as alternates for a single project (left; for the school in Ixelles, adjacent to Brussels). In a rather ironical denouement to this particular story, the authors clearly demonstrate that advances in methods of structural analysis led away from the more contemporary, rational truss form; it is left for the reader to draw potential parallels between this and the structural forms that today's digital technologies have enabled.

Truss Forms and Style Battles

The Ardant Truss: A Forgotten Rival of the Well-Known Polonceau Truss

Michael de Bouw, Ine Wouters, Leen Lauriks,
Quentin Collette, Abdelrahman Hussein Younes

Notwithstanding the inspiring iron and steel witnesses to the 19th and 20th century that still persist today, in the beginning, iron and steel were used in industrial buildings only. The introduction of this new material into non-industrial architecture was not accepted without striking a blow and many heated but also in-depth discussions. Some prominent figures such as the Belgian engineer Arthur Vierendeel (1852-1940) advanced the thesis that iron had already emerged from the shadow of stone and timber as a fully fledged building material by the mid-19th century and that it would inevitably triumph eventually. [1,2]

Yet many of his contemporaries thoroughly disagreed, or only agreed on the potential of iron, clearly stating that it had a long way to go and maybe would never reach the grand realizations of the traditional building materials because of its technical drawbacks, lack of (architectural) expression and limited mouldability.[3,4] Nevertheless, this new material would soon be used in industrial buildings on a large scale. Applications in industrial construction were mainly driven by cost-cutting measures: iron and steel had some advantageous material characteristics that enabled engineers to create long spans, unencumbered interiors, and to use prefabricated components that could be easily assembled on site. According to the prominent Belgian professor Paul Combaz (1845-1920), iron had become the basic material for industrial buildings by 1897.[5] Yet he immediately points out that it was not acceptable from a structural and aesthetical point of view to reveal this material openly to the public; architects had not yet found a suitable aesthetic language for this new material and in the public's perception iron constructions were extremely slender and light compared to the accustomed looks of stone and timber designs. Therefore, they judged them to be less stable and less safe, which is not surprising at all as even many contemporary engineers were not completely convinced of the stability of iron structures.[5]

Notwithstanding the ongoing discussions between the camps for and against these new materials, the 19th and early 20th century would become the golden era of iron architecture thanks to advances in calculation methods, production techniques, chemical insights and the perseverance of some great engineers and architects. Despite the fact that iron was not yet accepted in everyday constructions, some engineers, architects and authoritative persons were convinced of its originality and rationality. Consequently, they tried to find a new architectural language matching this material's properties, and apply it to prestigious public edifices, such as numerous intriguing bridges, glasshouses, railway stations, covered marketplaces, department stores, etc.[2]

At that time, people were clearly in two minds about the aesthetics and the efficiency of iron architecture. In Belgium this new iron architecture and the contrast between efficiency and aesthetics found virtue in the Brussels model schools. These (semi-) public building types were used by some prominent architects to acquaint the youth with the material and architecture of the future: iron frame structures. Looking at the state model schools, it will be noticed that iron components were indeed widely used for stairs, (cantilever) galleries, columns, beams and roof trusses.[6]

The Brussels model schools and their roofs

The idea of the Brussels model schools was developed between 1860 and 1875 by the pedagogical pressure group Ligue de l'Enseignement, the Mayor of Brussels Karel Buls and the architect Ernest Hendrickx.[6] The first model school, the École Modèle, was built in 1875.[7,8] More than 55 schools were built in Brussels solely according to this layout. Soon it would become a national and international icon that would be copied on a large scale all over Belgium and even in other countries such as France and Spain.[6]

These school buildings were very innovative in several respects, such as their heating and ventilation systems, the pedagogical ideologies, the sanitary facilities, etc., which gained international recognition.[9] Their main characteristic, however, is the presence of a central covered courtyard, the "préau", flanked by two stories of classrooms.

Many different roof constructions are used to span the préau. The analysis of the Brussels model schools revealed that architects used solid roof constructions as well as frame structures. In the case of a solid roof construction, brick barrel vaults or concrete slabs were used. For the frame structures, timber or iron was employed to create a duopitch roof. Analysis of the iron roof trusses over the préau of the model schools reveals that these trusses are sometimes hidden and sometimes openly visible. It is remarkable that the hidden iron roof trusses always consist of industrial bar roof trusses such as the German, English or Belgian type. These were not considered aesthetically beautiful and as a consequence were concealed behind by a false ceiling. On the other hand, just like one finds two imports of the Art Nouveau, i.e. the geometrical and pure one (Paul Hankar, Henri Jacobs, Paul Hamesse, etc.) versus the natural and organic trend (Victor Horta, Gustave Strauven, Ernest Blérot, etc.)—one finds two similar imports with regard to the visible metal roof trusses: the plain and straightforward Polonceau truss versus the decorated and smooth Ardant truss. Some 25 model schools made use of visible iron roof trusses: 14 of them used Ardant trusses, 11 preferred Polonceau trusses.

Polonceau versus Ardant, or efficiency versus aesthetics

The Ardant and Polonceau trusses of the model schools reflect well the aforementioned ongoing debate on the aesthetics and the efficiency of iron architecture. Both truss types were used to span the 9 to 15 m wide préau of the model schools, yet the idea behind both trusses was completely different.

Origins and setup

The Polonceau truss originated from the idea of using all of its components in an optimum way. In order to achieve this, in 1839 the French engineer Camille Polonceau invented a gable roof that used two inclined trussed beams and a central tension tie.[10,11,12,13] The Polonceau truss became one of the first roof trusses to be simple, efficient and economic at the same time. After all, in the second half of the 19th century, the cost of iron structures was merely determined by the amount of iron or steel used because the cost of labour was very low compared to the cost of materials.[10,14,15] As a consequence, engineers focussed on the weight-to-span ratio in order to determine whether a structure such as a roof or bridge was efficient/economic or not. For example, to prove the superiority of his truss, Polonceau states in his 1839 publication in the French journal "Revue Générale de l'Architecture et des Travaux Publics" that the necessary amount of material in his configuration was very limited, resulting in a very light and thus cheap truss.[10,16] Together with the ease of calculation (by means of a small simplification with regard to the principal rafters and the use of graphical statics), this resulted in a frequent use of this truss typology until the 1890's.

Polonceau trusses have many advantages; however, many architects criticized its lack of architectural expression and rather industrial looks. Consequently, architects started to experiment with curved roof trusses to create a larger interior volume and a more aesthetical solution.[17] Yet, in addition to the fact that these curved structures were less stable than triangular systems, one of the major initial disadvantages was the unavoidable presence of the tension ties to resist the lateral arch thrusts induced by the curved form. In order to resolve this problem, the military engineer Paul-Joseph Ardant—a teacher at the École d'Application de l'Artillerie et du Génie at Metz—published his work "Études théoriques et expérimentales sur l'établissement des charpentes à grande portée" in 1840, which provided the results of a vast series of experiments he had carried out on 14 curved roof truss types.[17,18] His objective was to determine the laws of the resistance of arches to bending and rupture, as well as the magnitude of their thrust on the supports. His conclusions state that the arch is the most flexible of truss forms and that all arches exert some horizontal thrust on the walls, although, theoretically, the semi-circular arch should not. In order to stiffen this form, he recommended the spandrel arch, which is tangential and framed to the principal rafters of a gable frame. Being the precursor of the de Dion truss and the three-hinged arch—both used for the first time during the Paris World Expositions of 1878 and 1898—the Ardant truss would become very popular.

The duality within the model schools

The difference in efficiency—according to the historic definition of their weight-to-span ratio—between both trusses is proved by the examples of the model schools. Analysis has indeed revealed that the mean weight-to-span ratio of the Polonceau truss (0.33 kN/m) is much lower than that of the Ardant truss (0.79 kN/m). Taking into account the truss distance, this trend is confirmed: the Polonceau's mean weight-to-surface ratio (0.08 kN/m²) is 2.5 times lower than the Ardant's (0.20 kN/m²). Still, one can see [next page] that from 1900 onwards engineers switched from the Polonceau truss to the less efficient Ardant truss to span the central covered courtyards of the schools. This raises some questions because it would be reasonable to believe that they were always seeking to improve the efficiency of their structures.

The reason is not straightforward and it is clear that architects and engineers were of two minds. In some cases drawings of two fully developed solutions have even been found: one for the established and easy calculable Polonceau truss and one for the more aesthetical Ardant truss. For example, for the school P6/13 "Les Marronniers" (1902), there exists an original drawing of the préau and its Polonceau truss, whereas in reality an Ardant truss was erected. The opposite choice was made in school No. 12 "Les jardins d'Elise" (1906): here, the drawings show a richly decorated Ardant truss, but a Polonceau truss was built on site. For school No. 5&6 "des Etangs" (1880-3), two fully developed truss designs have been found. The drawings specify the global geometry, sections and dimensions of all components for both the Polonceau and the Ardant truss. In the end this school's préau was spanned by means of the Ardant solution.

This evolution and ambiguity can be explained by the continuous interplay between the evolution of the calculation methods, the aesthetics and the aims of standardization.[6]

Whereas during the time of the model schools the Polonceau trusses could already be calculated accurately using graphical statics, this was not the case for the Ardant trusses. By 1840 Ardant had already determined, by way of extensive tests, that rigid connections between the principal rafters and the tangential arch were essential for the working of the Ardant truss.[18] Nevertheless, it was not until 1902 that a suitable calculation method was explained by Vierendeel.[15] This was the first time in Belgium that engineers could dimension the curved decorative web members of the Ardant truss and assure their appropriate behaviour. From that date onwards the Ardant trusses took the lead in the model schools.

However, in addition to the calculation problem, the aesthetics and the search for a new architectural language certainly played an important role. It is clear that the industrial bar roof trusses were not regarded as beautiful and therefore were hidden behind a false ceiling in the model schools. The only exception was the Polonceau roof truss. Although it was often criticized because of its industrial looks and the loss of uninterrupted space due to the multitude of triangulation members,[15,16] it was often employed because of its efficiency and the ease of calculation. Nevertheless, the curved form always appealed to architects' and engineers' imagination and many experiments were performed.[19] Yet because of the lack of a suitable and efficient solution, prior to 1900 most of the architects of the model schools had to resort to the Polonceau truss. But in order to embellish the (rather industrial-looking) Polonceau truss and imitate the curved form they were striving to achieve, some of the architects applied richly decorated spandrels at the side springings as [is the case], for example, in the case of the Royal Athenaeum "Victor Horta". Apparently, these decorative bearings represent a typical attempt to improve the aesthetics of the Polonceau truss when used for prestigious public buildings, e.g. the main railway station in Budapest (1877).

Finally, a third argument was the rise of standardization. After 1900 steel production was in full swing. As production costs and prices dropped, forges started to publish catalogues with standard sections. As by that time the cost of a structure would mainly be determined by the labour input instead of the materials, the production of special pieces to fit all the components of the Polonceau trusses together (e.g. the compression struts and the connection parts) would be a major disadvantage.[16] The use of Ardant trusses would solve these problems. After all, the Ardant truss did not need annoying tension ties, it created a larger interior volume, standard iron sections could be used and the connections were simply created by plates, flat irons or smaller standard section irons, thus avoiding difficult connection pieces that needed to be forged or cast for each specific situation.

Conclusion

In the age of the World Expositions and Art Nouveau, lightness, brightness, transparency, elegance and daring creations served as guiding principles when creating iron architecture. Many of the impressive filigree designs at the successive (inter)national exhibitions in Europe of that time provide a good picture of the fascination of and interest shown in finding a new architectural language for the new building materials iron and steel. The introduction of these materials in non-industrial buildings, however, was not accepted without striking a blow.

This article was written from the standpoint of the (semi-) public Brussels model schools in order to illustrate the struggle and the search of architects and engineers in Belgium during the period 1875-1920. It has been clearly shown that the architects and engineers of that time were of two minds. Prior to 1900 overriding importance was mainly given to efficiency and they resorted to the well-known and efficient Polonceau truss.

Still, they were clearly struggling with the aesthetics and the search for an appropriate architectural expression. At first they tried to resolve that problem by embellishing the Polonceau truss by means of decorative spandrels. Yet, after 1900 when the calculation methods were known and standardization took over, its aesthetical counterpart ... [Ardant] truss would take the lead within the model schools.

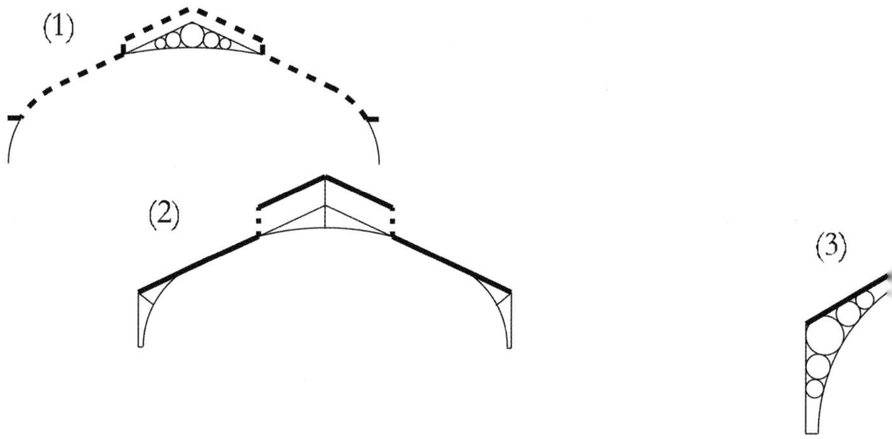

(1) School no.13 “Cooremans” (1878-80)
(2) School no.5&6 “des Étangs” (1880-3)
(3) School no.6 “J.J. Michel” (1891-2)
(4) School no.2 “Gallait” (1895-7)
(5) School no.7 “Baron Steens” (1896-7)
(6) School P6/13 “Marronniers” (1902)
(7) School no.10 “Karel Buls” (1902-6)
(8) Athenaeum “Verwée” (1903-4)
(9) School no.19 “Alfred Mabille” (1904-7)
(10) School P9/10 “Carrefour” (1906-9)
(11) School “Dachsbeck” (1910-4)
(12) Athenaeum “Bracobs Lambert” (1911)
(13) Athenaeum “Bracobs Lambert” (1911) (gym)
(14) Athenaeum “Serge Cruz” (1920)

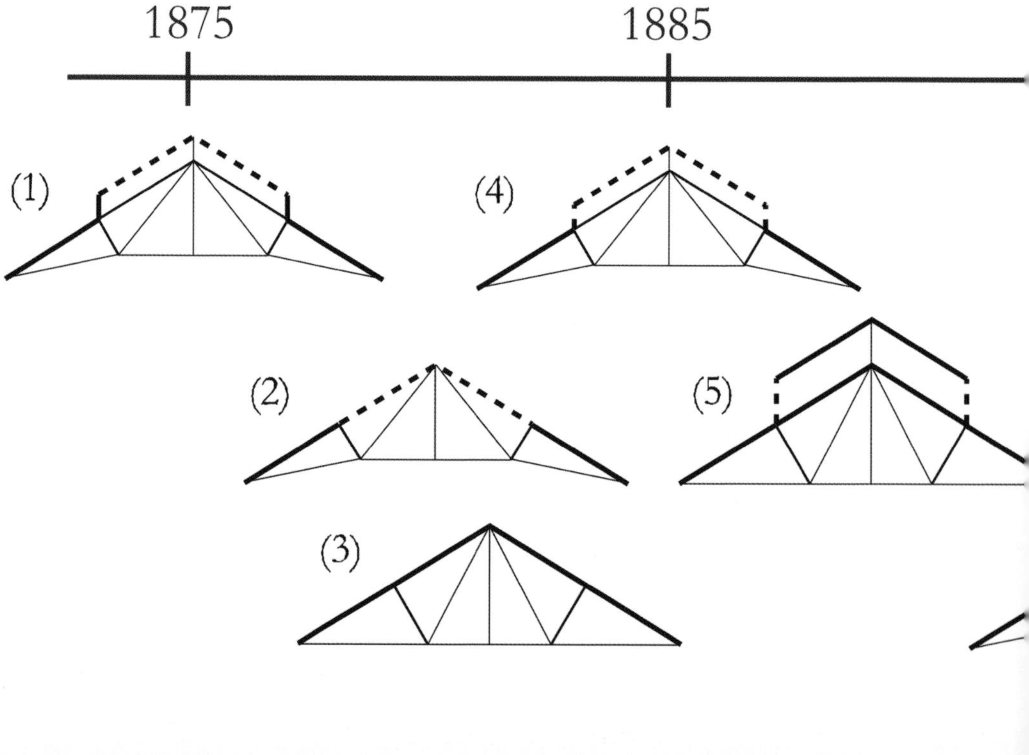

(1) École Modèle (1872-5)
(2) Athenaeum “Victor Horta” (1880)
(3) School no.5&6 “des Étangs (1880-3)
(4) School no.7 “Arc en Ciel” (1885-90)
(5) Mission Locale (1888)
(6) School no.6 “J.J. Michel” (1891-2) (gym)
(7) School P8 “Tourterelles” (1897)
(8) School no.10 “Trapèze” (1898)
(9) School no.4 “Betlehem” (1899-1905)
(10) School no.4 “Betlehem” (1899-1905) (gym)
(11) School no.12 “Jardins d’Élise” (1906)

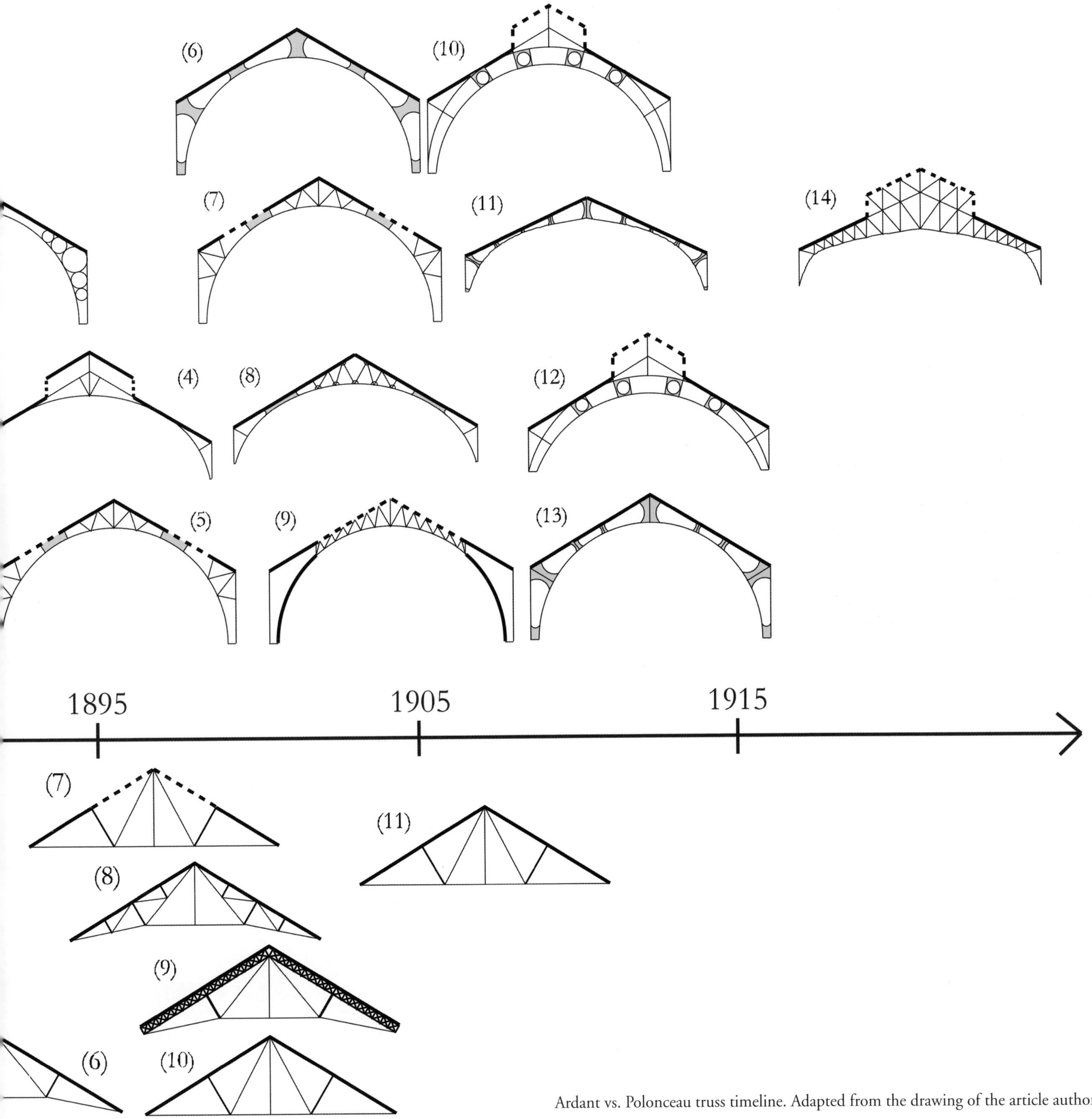

Ardant vs. Polonceau truss timeline. Adapted from the drawing of the article authors

Pompidou Center. Photo: Marc Petitjean

Comparing a handful of remarkable building designs from the second half of the twentieth century that have resulted from close collaborations between renowned architects and structural engineers, Christian Penzell's essay features a discussion of the highly distinctive truss forms that were developed for two art museums. One is the iconic built reality that is the Pompidou Center designed by Renzo Piano and Richard Rogers with Peter Rice/Arup, while the other – the ZKM (Center for Art and Media Technology) designed by Rem Koolhaas/OMA with Cecil Balmond/Arup – was only ever constructed in model form. In both cases, sets of trusses have essential floor-supporting structural roles, even if their final configurations are quite different. In the Pompidou, rows of exposed, simply-supported, rather conventional-looking Warren-type trusses are clearly part of this building's rational, industrial and then-controversial High Tech design aesthetic. The trusses of the ZKM, on the other hand, are by design intent much harder to discern, being of the full story-depth Vierendeel variety; i.e., they are composed of vertical and horizontal members that look like nothing so much as conventional columns and floor beams (although these "columns" also manage to somehow change shape, spacing, skip floors, etc.). The ZKM trusses thus support the design of a building intended to "generate density, exploit proximity, provoke tension, maximize friction, organize in-betweens, promote filtering, sponsor identity and stimulate blurring." (S,M,L,XL) and whose irregular forms were enabled by significant advances in computation methods. Clearly, one truss form does not suit all design intentions; indeed, trusses can be as distinctive as their collaborating designers intend them to be.

Truss Forms and Design Collaborations

The Culture of Construction: Examples from the Last Fifty Years of Remarkable Development
Christian Penzel

Technology does not primarily ask what is, but what can be. In this spirit, any truly technical achievement has the character of the discovery as revelation: an existing fact per se is thus extracted, as it were, from the region of the possible and transplanted into that of the real. [1]
— Ernst Cassirer

Collaborations between architect and engineer always appear interesting at first glance if a design makes use of exceptional structural means or methods. Development of the technical prerequisites is above all incumbent upon the engineer, who devises the structural systems—supposedly independent of design influence—from the inherent necessity of material and purpose, and brings these into view in independent, engineered structures. Inspired by these buildings, architects seek to use the opportunities they generate in structure and appearance, appropriating them for their own purposes. Since the beginning of industrialization, since the impressive appearance of the first large industrial structures, our concept of that which is built has been repeatedly modified by that which is technically feasible, in a continuous process of acquisition and reshaping. New positions in architecture are generated by the driving force of technical progress, in the constant search for cultural appropriation of the formal potential contained therein.[2]

Upon closer inspection, however, this self-evident observation could perhaps be turned around, the consequence then being the unexpected assumption that certain achievements in the field of construction and technology will not be conceivable without first changing the cultural context. The technical achievement would also consequently always be based on a creative stance, without which it could not become reality. A look back at some of those vicissitudes might illuminate some of today's issues and reveal a few basic patterns in the relationship between engineer and architect. …

Individual Orchestration – Renzo Piano, Richard Rogers, Peter Rice, and the Drama of Construction

With his polemics on contemporary building culture, the American engineer and innovator Buckminster Fuller now explicitly opposes this outlined process of coalescence, in which modern technology is to be integrated in an established architectural canon and thereby loses its autonomy.[3] All efforts to that effect taken by architects are seen by him as attempts to uphold a traditional system of form and design and to deny acknowledgement of the real power of technology based on constant mutation and renewal. This criticism is taken up and translated to good effect by the technology movement of the 1960s, most notably by architects like Cedric Price and the Archigram group, who, with their visions of technologically determined building structures in a state of constant change, fundamentally call into question the image of a completed form in the Classical sense.[4]

The most important built manifesto that emerged from this euphoria is the Pompidou Center, (1971-77) by Renzo Piano and Richard Rogers. The machine for culture, located in the center of Paris, is a multifunctional building that derives its outward appearance above all from the architects' idea of creating a completely flexible building, a kind of freely usable framework.[5] At any point in the building, each one of the diverse uses should be conceivable, so that one can imagine the building's inner life in constant flux. The consequence of this is the accumulation of maximum requirements: an enormous multi-level building that doesn't have a single column inside—to be able to install large exhibitions unhindered—and whose load-bearing structure must be capable, at every point, of taking the heavy load of a library. This stipulation ultimately leads to a complete inversion of the building, in which all the customary 'innards' are exposed on the outside—from the structure to the mechanical system and the pedestrian circulation—to obtain a completely purified footprint, free of any built limitations. The span needed for this purpose—nearly 45 meters—is surmounted by a series of trusses 3 meters high, hung from an exterior structural framework. As a representative of the idea, this work of course expresses the intrinsic visual message of the building. Its effectiveness comes from the complete fragmentation of the structure into discrete elements, each of which fulfills a very specific function. Tubes as columns for the compressive forces, vertical and diagonal rods for the tensile forces, and as the most prominent structural element, the so-called gerberettes, specially formed members for transmitting loads. The gerberettes (they owe their name to Gerber beams) direct the internal loads from the trusses, thanks to their hinged support condition, without transmitting any bending moments into the very slender columns, which are themselves not in the plane of the facade, but are instead in front of it to maintain the purity of the concept—a quite elaborate solution to a self-made problem. For ordinary load transfers and bracing of the prismatic building form, something that can usually be managed in one plane, the architects thus establish a construct several meters high.

At the center of this arrangement is precisely that cast-iron gerberette, an invention of the engineer Peter Rice. The artistically designed chunk of steel, needed for conveying loads from truss to column and external tension bracing, enables customized detail connections and can be adapted to the expected flow of forces. The didactic content of this visualization finds its counterpart in the expressive use of materials. Here, for the first time since the advent of rolled sections, cast steel is again employed at a large scale for building construction. In so doing, Rice seeks an explicit connection to the historical works of engineering from the nineteenth century.[6] With the notion of the tactile in construction, however, Rice is not only concerned with the material expression, but in essence about individualization of the form, which represents the spirit of its creator like a signature.[7] The recognizable hallmark of the designer is meant to make the machine-made components accessible to the attentive viewer. Whereas Mies's efforts would have been precisely to extract cultural significance from the anonymous industrial product, Rice eschews standardized common products such as the continuous profiles of double T-beams, and insists on the individual form of the cast part. The engineer takes a stance against the dictate of using industrially premanufactured components through a masterly exploitation of building materials, his formative idea represents human appropriation of material with the help of technology. Innovation is thus elevated to a humanistic principle.

The repetitive use of visibly pinned and bolted components does not lack a certain irony, yet it is also reminiscent of Joseph Paxton's Crystal Palace, a key building of Modernism that, like no other, forced architecture to engage with the new possibilities presented by functional buildings. Over a hundred years later, it seems the time has now come in which its technological, non-tectonic expression—albeit now equipped with a touch of romance and yearning for simple mechanics—is suitable for representing one of the most important cultural buildings of the twentieth century. Contrasted with the Miesian order, the decisive shift now no longer lies in representing the technology with genuine architectural means, but in bringing the untransformed technology into view as directly as possible. With this in mind, the gerberette is no longer necessarily understood as a tectonic element obligated to provide stability; instead, it has much more the character of a machine component. With its dynamic form, milled out joints, and pinned axes, it can be associated more with the image of a rocker arm, and in fact, a considerable degree of its effectiveness is based on the possible movement, which is prevented, however, by various precautions and which allows an optically precarious balance to emerge. Using these means, Piano and Rogers orchestrate the drama of a structure as a balancing act—the glorification and exploitation of technology as image. This, conversely, is consistent with Rice's intention to exaggerate the structural circumstances enough for a spectacle of the lines of force to emerge from them—a performance for the amusement of the viewer. Like theater directors, the designers thereby highlight certain details and connections and de-emphasize others, in order to create a precisely calculated image on the edge of instability.[8] The skillful hallmark of the engineer plays a decisive role in the process. His suggestive power and individuality contributes significantly to an architecture that, as High-Tech and recently also as Bio-Tech, to this day operates formally by always transforming new building technologies into brands. But even more important than elevating technology to a fetish is no doubt the accompanying dissolution of customary tectonic relationships. The classic aspiration toward repose and strength as resistance to gravity, only briefly interrupted in the early Modernist era by experiments in their symbolic conquest, is now replaced by the precisely constructed game for the amusement or irritation of the viewer. In the battle for attention, the temptation to orchestrate such a spectacle and to refine it with the art of the engineer, now belongs to the fixed repertoire of architecture.

Partial Collages – Rem Koolhass, Cecil Balmond, and the Informal Patchwork

With various innovations in connection technology and the use of materials, including his research on structural glazing, among other things, Peter Rice has subsequently significantly broadened the scope of the constructible. Despite an obvious tendency toward orchestration, Rice nevertheless remains tied to the engineering tradition that is committed to optimizing the means and which sees the beauty of a thought represented in the form of a closed and harmonious system. With the strategy of the informal, Cecil Balmond—who follows shortly after Rice as directing engineer at Ove Arup—now puts up for negotiation exactly that very core of the engineering tradition. Similarly to Rem Koolhaas on a formal level, Balmond is engineering tradition.[9] Similarly to Rem Koolhaas on a formal level, Balmond is concerned with fundamental revision of the rationalist reflection of Modernism with regard to structural design.

In the designs for the libraries in Paris (1992-93) and for the ZKM media center in Karlsruhe (1989), they experiment together with the goal of overcoming the constraints of regular and ostensibly optimized systems and freeing themselves from the logic of grids and repetition. Thus the ZKM, a stacked hybrid with different uses, is to be understood as a polemical reckoning with the Pompidou Center.[10] The building typology is nevertheless by and large identical: an outer layer, which serves as a circulation zone and carries the vertical loads, encompasses the large, internal spaces with the main uses. The enormous trusses from the Pompidou Center, which take up a proportionately large amount of space in each of the levels, are in this case, however, replaced with the much more efficient, story-high Vierendeel trusses, allowing every other level to function as a beam thanks to vertical, rigid connections between floor and ceiling slabs. In this way, even though only half of the levels are in fact column-free, the volume can be used without restrictions.

But efficiency constitutes merely the ostensible goal. Koolhaas and Balmond are concerned above all about eliminating a recognizable and dominant structure. To avoid the idea of uniformity, the Vierendeel trusses are replaced to some extent by trusses, reinforced in other locations by individual columns, and the individual elements of each of these structural members are formed differently—from dissolved bracing structure to double-T sections and solid-walled tubular sections. These elements are combined with exhilaration, and in so doing, the readability of their precise function—upon which Rice was absolutely dependent—is intentionally undermined. The artistically formed detail, which is meant to give a visual impression, in sinewy or beefy form, of the nature and strength of the acting forces, is replaced here by a series of ad-hoc solutions.

In so doing, Balmond explicitly distinguishes his attitude from High-Tech architecture inasmuch as he recognizes the elegance of their elaborated details, but declares the essence of the repetition and the multitude of structural elements as being a formal problem.[11] In place of the closed system, a discernible order of parts corresponding to one another, he uses an open collage of loosely connected structural fragments. In one fell swoop, not only is the didactic communication of stability rejected, but at the same time, the regulatory effect of a building structure based on proportion is also eliminated. The dismissal, in other words, is not only ostensibly directed against High-Tech architecture, but in fact against the cumulative modern canon of an abstract rationale that expresses itself in geometric orders and structural hierarchies, and which found its culmination with Mies. The concept of the informal, in contrast, follows a series of vaguely defined generators—local, hybrid, and juxtaposition—that are meant to lead to the dissolution of an unequivocal order, beginning at the structural level. Accordingly, the local event has primacy over the universal solution (local), the overlap over clarity (hybrid) and the parallelism of orders over the singularity of one system (juxtaposition).[12] In the first step, this methodology enables the relatively free combination of structural interventions. For example, the Kunsthal in Rotterdam (1987-92), one of the early projects done in collaboration with Rem Koolhaas, has individual segments utilizing different load-bearing structures that correspond to distinctions in the program and which often appear to be pieced together without a clear system.[13] Columns of different shapes and dimensions, walls, sloped floors, and trusses are structurally connected to one another, without resulting in an overall system. In contrast, the sub-orders constitute something like a pluralism of disparate elements, which constantly produce new irregularities in zones of transition. As with a collage, the fragments of the structure, such as the large, arched lateral bracing in the roof, always remain as discrete interventions within the state of tension between autonomy and integration in the whole. In the manner of the bricoleur, who Claude Lévi-Strauss established as a counterpart to the engineer,[14] the structural elements are taken like found objects from an imaginary repertoire, selected according to the task, and then assembled. Balmond does not meet structural challenges with inventions—specifically developed solutions like in the case of the gerberette—but with more or less existing and generally well-known means. The structural fragments thus represent neither a particular innovation, nor do they intend to didactically communicate their precise function. Balmond breaks with the obligation to legibility as well as with the optimization logic of an engineering ethic that directs its ambition toward reducing dimensions and minimizing the use of materials.

In reaction to the elegance of Rice's hybrid structures, such as the one he developed for the IBM Pavilion (1960-84)—delicately machined and tapered wooden struts, which are connected together with elaborately formed, polished steel nodes and deep-drawn polycarbonate pyramids into a self-supporting, barrel-shaped building shell[15]—Balmond responds with the ad-hoc system of boards, bent rebars, rolled sections, and metal decking as the roof structure for the Congrexpo in Lille (1990-94).[16] At the scale of the systems as well as at the level of detailing, Balmond succeeds, in a very pragmatic and direct way, at responding to the varied circumstances and requirements. In other words, the real achievement is paradoxically in abandoning the search for an optimal solution, in order to begin a process of finding that ends with partial solutions of limited consequence. Instead of an elaborated tracery—Rice continually identified the Gothic as a reference[17]—the integration of disturbances, randomness, and dissonant elements then produce more a kind of artistic patchwork. As opposed to exaggerated eloquence, Balmond relies on the formal exploitation of his pragmatism, a disinterest in the 'good form' in favor of using found elements and systems.

The compulsion to practice formative design, as is ostensibly the case with Rice, admittedly appears at first glance to be clearly mitigated, but upon closer inspection it reappears at another level and to a vastly greater extent inasmuch as the regime of the grid is eliminated and a superordinate organizing structure is thereby destroyed, the entire process of design gains an increasing dynamic in which architectural and structural elements are decreasingly distinguishable from one another. The formation of load-bearing structures in the form of local centers, their rhythmization into partial orders, and the orchestration of overlapping zones are operations of great consequence, in spatial as well as conceptual terms. By eschewing the overly explicit perceptibility of his computational actions and thereby camouflaging his instruments, the engineer, beneath the cloak of the bricoleur, thus succeeds in substantially expanding his influence far into the architect's area of expertise.[18] Not unexpectedly, the question of authorship between engineer and architect can, in this case, only be answered very imprecisely.

What ... Piano and Rogers opened up with their focus on the technology, ... Koolhaas continues with his manner of surrealistic assembly: they all open up possibilities at the architectural level that literally appear to provoke a complementary reaction in structural thinking—congenial responses that coalesce to yield an independent reality and the autonomy of the engineer.

Epilogue

The ... cases presented here may be viewed as paradigms for developments in architecture in which the formal expression and the structural form coalesce in an exceptional way. An initial conjecture would be that the contributions in both of their disciplines—the artistic as well as the technical—each constitute an autonomous achievement that would also be measured in their respective categories. Developing an architectural concept is something fundamentally different than working out techniques and methods for construction. Even so, it appears that crucial developmental steps take place in both disciplines in a similar manner, following cycles of rejection and reinterpretation. A consequence of this observation is that the art of engineering, contrary to all expectations, does not develop in the scientific sense of a linear and constant increase in knowledge, but is instead equally subject to the changing positions of its protagonists and the conditions of a cultural setting. Accordingly, it would in no way be like what is commonly assumed, that the engineer merely places the tools at the architect's disposal. Rather, certain shifts in the architectural culture evidently first lead to new approaches in the art of thinking about a structure, and thereby to achievements that ultimately achieve independent significance in the field of technology. From there, they subsequently have a reflexive effect on architecture, which, for its part, is always prepared to seize the formal potential of new insights. Thus progress in the applied sciences appears less autonomous than commonly presumed and the interdependency of both disciplines seems considerably more complex than expected.

ZKM Model. Photo: © OMA

Casa Cavanelas. Photo: Andres Otero/Luz

If, as was just seen for the ZKM building, full-story-height trusses can be made deliberately hard to read in support of a design intent to convey formal and spatial complexity, in Oscar Niemeyer's 1954 Cavanelas House we encounter a version of the converse: small-scale, light-weight trusses that are seemingly quite ordinary and relatively easily discerned but that in reality are no less deceptive in terms of what their form conveys. At first glance the roof of this house appears to be suspended; among other characteristics its gently curved profile suggests the effect of the downward pull of gravity between points of vertical support. The small-scale trusses under the roofline accentuate this desired visual effect, their delicacy enhancing the impression of an ultra-light, flexible roof surface. From a structural perspective, moreover, the trusses seem to be working in tension as "suspension cables", anchored by the angled buttress-like piers at the sides of the house. And yet, as Dal Co and Trombetti describe in their subtle and detailed analysis of the Casa Cavanelas' minimal structural system, impressions can sometimes be deceiving… [n.b.: The trusses are identified in the text as "beams", their load-carrying equivalent.]

Niemeyer's Subtly Deceptive Trusses

Playing the Instrument of the World: A Minimal Masterpiece by Oscar Niemeyer and Roberto Burle Marx
Francesco Dal Co and Tomaso Trombetti

Oscar Niemeyer and Roberto Burle Marx were contemporaries: Niemeyer was born in Rio de Janeiro in 1907, Burle Marx two years later, at Treviri, the city of Rhineland-Palatinate that was also the birthplace of another famous Marx, Karl. Their paths crossed in 1936 when they joined forces with Jorge Moreira, Ernani Vasconcelos, Alfonso Eduardo Reidy, Carlos Leão, namely the best Brazilian architects of the time, guided by Lucio Costa and advised by Le Corbusier to construct the Ministry of Education and Health in Rio de Janeiro, a work that was to become a manifesto for contemporary architecture in their country. After that Burle Marx and Niemeyer worked together on many other occasions, but their relationship was abruptly interrupted when the construction of Brasilia was almost complete. In 1954, when they completed the Edmundo Cavanelas house at Pedro do Rio (Rio de Janeiro), they had solid experience and had already produced several joint masterpieces. They had worked together on the recreational complex of Pampúlha, the residence at Belo Horizonte of Juscelino Kubitschek (the future president of Brazil, and the man behind the construction of Brasilia), the Parque Ibirapuera in São Paulo, and the house Niemeyer had designed for himself at Canoas (Rio de Janeiro) in 1953. After that date, and for another 25 years or so, Niemeyer and Burle Marx worked side by side on many other projects during the course of their successful careers. In this context the construction of the Cavanelas house is a minor episode, but one that is so expressive that it must be included among the small masterpieces of 20th century architecture.

To appreciate the originality of the architectural idea developed by Niemeyer for this project, further proof of his fertile way of using varied compositional registers, it is useful to compare the Cavanelas house to his other works in the same period. If, for example, we examine the house built at Pedro do Rio, the residence at Canoas, from two years earlier, and the Catetinho, the temporary dwelling made for President Kubitschek in Brasilia two years later, we see that it is impossible to combine them in terms of formal similarities or structural conceptions. While the house at Canoas might suggest the validity of the friendly remark of Le Corbusier, who called Niemeyer one of the "last exponents of the Baroque", the Catetinho and the Cavanelas house demonstrate the partial inadequacy of this nevertheless ironic, penetrating viewpoint.

The Cavanelas house, in fact, is further proof of how the meaning of the experience of Niemeyer is hard to grasp, because it is marked by sudden shifts: the length of his career makes them seem like passages, but they are not. The villa at Pedro do Rio is also a clear demonstration of how his best works are not the result of disciplined exercises in rigor on the level of structural conception, but instead of the empirical knowledge with which Niemeyer uses materials, disguising the extenuated exploitation to which he submits them to obtain formal and spatial effects apparently freed from the constraints of static laws. From this point of view, too, the Cavanelas house is exemplary, because the entire construction is actually reduced to the configuration of the roof and the refined, elusive display of the correspondence of its form to the structure. If, however, we analyze the behavior and the making of this structure, we can understand that its conception aims to achieve a purely visual effect, aside from its intrinsic coherence.

The construction seems similar to a tent, suspended between four vertical uprights, positioned on the ground to protect a space that is, to a great extent, transparent. The roofing is like a flat, continuous curve, and its profile seems to have been naturally designed by its own weight. Observing it for the first time, one has the impression that its form was defined by a reversed catenary. But upon closer examination it is clear that in spite of the purity of the line that concludes it, the structure is more complicated than it seems. The photographs taken during construction allow us, though only roughly, to explain its functioning and its formal implications.

From a structural viewpoint the roof is supported by a reticular framework composed of four main longitudinal beams, two inside, two outside, and fifteen secondary crossbeams. The internal longitudinal beams, bearing a greater load at relatively small intervals, are configured as beams with three spans, resting on four supports. The two central supports are structural walls, while the ones at the ends are formed by crosswise border frames. The external longitudinal beams, which give the construction its optical effect and represent its formal signature, have just two spans on three supports: and consequently their spans are significantly larger than those of the corresponding internal beams. The smaller load placed on these outer beams, which due to their geometric placement support about half the weight supported by the internal beams, permits them to cover these larger spans with structural dimensions which are substantially similar to that of the central beams. So the roof is composed of a structural system formed by beams with two spans on the outer portion of the building, and beams with three spans in the central portion. Using this solution, Niemeyer was able to use smaller intervals for the beams bearing the greatest loads, namely those inside, while giving the observer the illusion, produced by the fact that the added supports are practically hidden from view, of a roof composed of two larger spans, with a very slim profile.

The crosswise ribbing, or the secondary beams, has three spans: the intervals and thicknesses are smaller than those of the longitudinal elements on which it rests. The two external crossframes that bear loads half as large as those of the internal parts, instead of resting on the four longitudinal beams, rest directly on pillars located at the corners of the construction, and function as support for the extremities of the central longitudinal beams. This solution is made possible by a significant adaptation of the static scheme, given the fact that these perimeter elements behave like single-span beams and must support larger loads than those of the beams with three supports. To deal with these greater strains in an adequate way, the external crossbeams, in spite of their apparently smaller span, have heights and thicknesses equal to those of the longitudinal border beams. In this way, they ensure continuity of sizing at the external perimeter of the roof, contributing in a decisive way to define the most evident characteristic of the entire construction. This continuity, then, is the result of the inner, non-linear functioning of the structure of the roof, demonstrating that the Cavenelas house represents one of the most successful among the many attempts made by Niemeyer to associate the spatial and formal virtues of his compositions with the apparent daring of their structural solutions. The roof of the Cavanelas house offers explicit confirmation of this consideration. As we have seen, its slope reflects the form of a catenary curve. This impression is reinforced if we observe the triangular form of the pillars supporting the longitudinal beams at the edge, positioned at the four corners of the construction. As we know, a catenary generates great horizontal thrust *H* on its supports, causing a tension directed toward the center of the catenary itself. This thrust increases the more the curve is flattened, which in our case would force the four corner pillars on which it rests to assume, for optimization of the structure, the above-mentioned triangular form. But in our observation of the configuration of the pillars we need to go beyond their appearance, which tends to disguise the ways in which the simplicity of the structural intuition has been compromised to achieve the formal effects sought by Niemeyer on this occasion, and many others. In the light of all this, it is clear that the central longitudinal beams of the roof of the house are not configured like a catenary, given the presence of the intermediate supports and those at the extremities composed of the border crossbeams, which are not capable of performing the required horizontal actions. Therefore these beams are configured as inflected elements. Equally stimulating reflections can derive from observation of the more complex, perhaps intentionally "mysterious" functioning of the external longitudinal beams. Quite probably they represent a rare example, the result of an intuition developed empirically by the architect, that induced Niemeyer to make use of a mixed beam/catenary system (or "arch/beam", as Mario Salvadori describes it). In fact, we know that every inflection and lowering necessarily leads to a lengthening of the axis of a beam*. If this elongation is prevented by a suitable horizontal reaction *H* at the supports, then together with the "bending" action of the beam, a "catenary" behavior is also developed (or an inverted arch). One of the two effects ("beam" or "arch") will prevail over the other as a result of the characteristics of the section of the beam and those of the

* As an example, the lowering at the center of a beam with two supports subjected to a uniform load q is equal to:

$$\frac{5\,ql^4}{384\,EJ}$$

with l, E and J respectively indicating span, elasticity modulus and moment of inertia of the beam.

connection at the extremities. In the case of the section of the beam, the higher the moment of inertia *J* of the frame, the less lowering there will be of the beam itself, with reduction of the horizontal reactions *H* at the supports and the resulting "arch effect". Where the extremities are concerned, the more the connection is prevented from moving horizontally, the more the arch effect will prevail; the "weaker" the support, in horizontal terms, the smaller the horizontal reaction *H* and the greater the beam effect. Taking the characteristics of the most common structures into account, it is seldom possible to create supports that are rigid enough to prevent any horizontal movement: the arch effect prevails only in the cases of very slender frames (so that the value of the moment of inertia *J* is reduced), characterized by noteworthy rises, i.e. by significant lowering at the center. But if we observe the Cavanelas house, we see that the rise of the roof beams is small, and the type of support at the extremities (the connection is guaranteed by the top of the pillars that in spite of their optimized triangular form are necessarily marked by an intrinsic horizontal "weakness") contributes to simulate a mixed beam/arch configuration and functioning. Moreover, the relationship between height and span of these elements, equal to about 1/27, is congruent with functioning as a beam, even in the light of the limited vertical loads bearing on the roof (the waterproofing is quite light, and the risks of snow, given the characteristics of the site, can be eliminated from our calculations).

Apparently simple, the result of the composition of a few movements and an equally small range of materials, the Cavanelas house, then, is the result of a series of structural compromises, or perhaps we should say a mixture, skillfully disguised and resolved by the essential quality of the form (or the sign, we are tempted to say, looking at the profile of the roof).

Nevertheless, the structural functioning of the roof is very coherent with respect to the layout of the house. In fact, the straight portion of the roof shelters a large living area and contiguous patio, while the other portion covers the more fragmented spaces and facilities. The wall segment separating the living area from the patio, open to the garden, is not weighed down by the two longitudinal border portions of the roof that it crosses, because the chimney is contained inside it. On the opposite side, the living area is bordered by a second wall, also in reinforced concrete covered with stone, bearing three of the longitudinal beams. Given its role of separation between the living area and the bedroom/bath area, and proving how the structural adaptations are coherent with the functional layout, this second wall almost entirely crosses the volume and continues into the garden. Though of different proportions, as one is extended vertically, the other horizontally, the two walls form a sort of perspective tube that frames the views of the garden surrounding the house. The two flatter portions of the garden function as backdrops for each other, and are offered as alternative scenes for the view from the living room.

The sagaciously pragmatic construction solution we have described above makes the house seem like a curtain, light and temporary, stretched in the middle part of the garden, between the two slopes that border the flatter area on which Burle Marx concentrated his work. The slopes of the valley at the center of which the Cavanelas house was built are densely wooded, covered with flourishing vegetation. At the sides, where the slopes finish, Burle Marx exploited the coverage capacity of *Alternanthea tenella*, installing a row of palms, and positioning bushes of *Plumbago capensis*, groups of *Hemerocallis flava* with a vivid yellow hue, and *Lantana camara*, as well as *Cassia macranthera*, whose trunks emerge from this composition designed as a frame. The frame separates an eloquent interval between uncontaminated nature and the refined flat surface set aside for the house. As simple as a tent, shaped like a timeless construction, thanks to the skill with which the nature around it has been organized, the construction appears as something unexpected and surprising. Grasping its meaning, Burle Marx has set it on an expanse of carpets that contrast their refined, rarefied patterns with the random density of the natural vegetation of the backdrops.

To underline this contrast Burle Marx utilized decisive chromatic effects, shifts of volume and figures that seem to have been borrowed from the paintings of Klee and Arp adding consistency

Construction Photographs of Casa Cavanelas

through painstaking care in the composition of different types of plants. On one side of the garden they are arranged to form a reddish wave, making use of the dark heart-shaped leaves of *Iresine herstii*; this band of shrubbery emerges from a green meadow (*Stenotaphrum secundatum*) that is surrounded by an earthen path, connecting to the patio. On the opposite side the footprint of the house is placed in direct contact with a checkerboard formed by gramineae, amaranths and asteraceae of different colors and sizes. Here, as can also be seen in the house at Canoas and in other gardens he designed for constructions by Niemeyer, Burle Marx has placed a sculpture; in our case it is a bronze of a female figure, resting on one side, set on a concrete pedestal before the geometric incision in the ground to insert the swimming pool. The surface of the pool corresponds to that of the equal squares subtracted from the checkerboard plantings. To design it Burle Marx utilized *Stenotaphrum secundatum* and *Stenotaphrum secundatum variegatum* for the squares of different green tones, below, and *Iresine herbstii* and *Helichrysum petiolatum* for the squares leaning toward red and yellow, standing out with respect to the others. This composition, whose colors adapt to the passage of the seasons, at first glance might resemble the garden made by Gabriel Guévrékian at the Villa Noailles in Hyeres, in 1925. Though intriguing, this similarity is misleading. At the villa in Hyeres, Guévrékian's garden is simply decor, and as its nickname "the cubist garden" indicates, it is simply a further, bizarre addition that Charles and Marie Laure de Noailles wanted to insert in their art collection at the seaside villa. The garden of Burle Marx at Pedro do Rio, on the other hand, is a complete work of architecture. It is not decor, nor is it a completion of the work built by Niemeyer, with which it coexists in a dialogue. Made by using what nature offers to those who understand its behavior, appreciating the mutual attractions of the botanical world, grasping their hidden possibilities, the garden of Burle Marx is the result of a lengthy exercise in abstraction. This exercise has a purpose shared by that of Niemeyer in the construction of the house, and it is the premise for the dialogue the two architects continued for so many years. The objective that united them, in fact, was to demonstrate that natural and artificial can be combined only by avoiding any procedures of imitation, countering the charms with which nature seduces the fantasy of men with the power of abstraction, the adaptation of reason – that reason whose reasonable but strenuous exercise allows the great architects to "play the instrument of the world", as Burle Marx and Niemeyer did on this occasion.

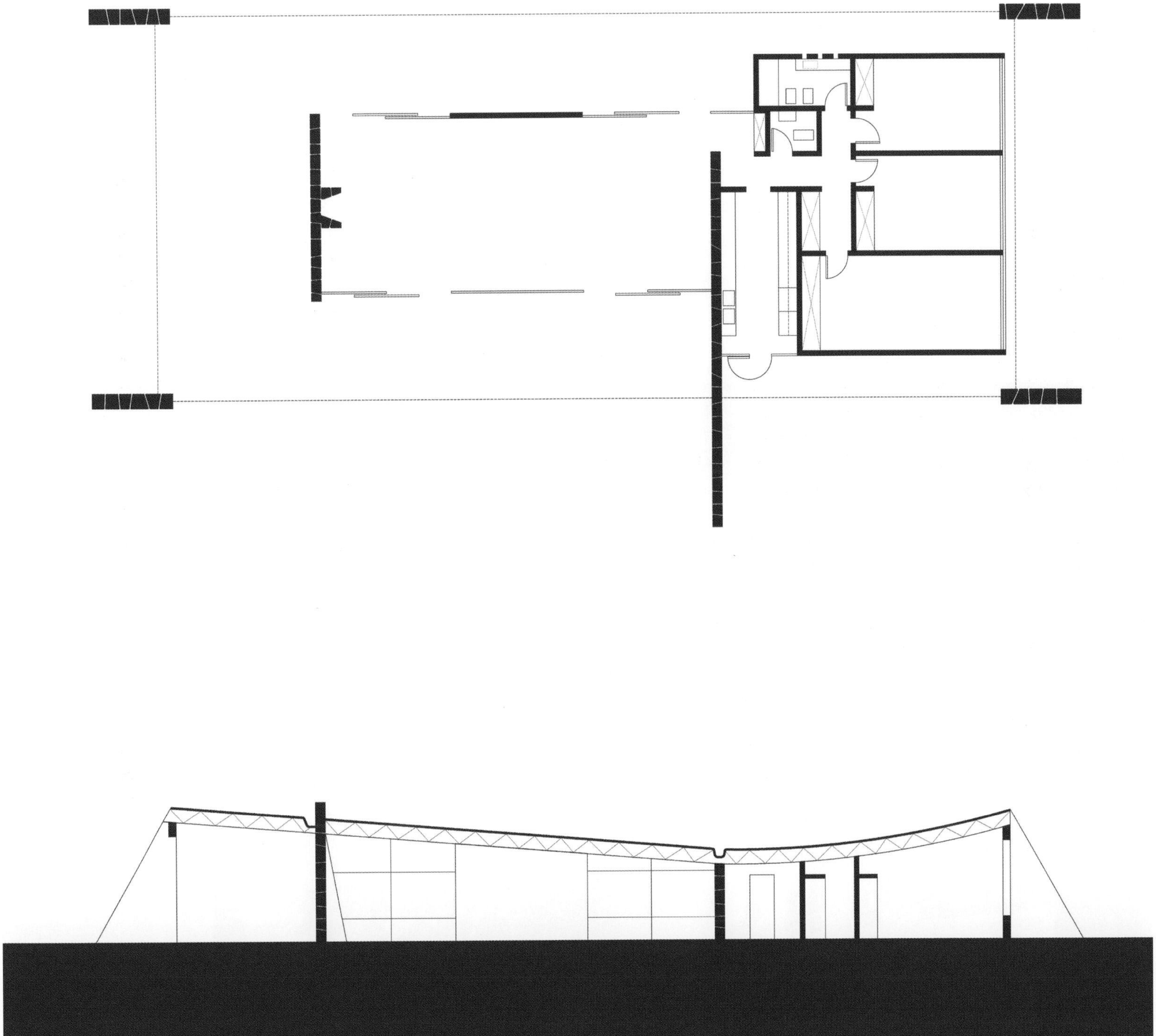

Section and Plan of Casa Cavanelas. Drawing adapted from original

Festival Plaza, Expo '70, Osaka by Kenzo Tange

It is perhaps surprising to associate the industrial aesthetic of the truss with the organic-growth-inspired stylistic and cultural movement of post-war Japan known as Metabolism, but the example of the Osaka World's Fair of 1970 provides perhaps no better illustration of such a concept-to-form relationship. Several of the Metabolists' guiding principles were applied here at all scales – from the "stem-and-branches" axes of the master plan for the Expo site to the design of mega-structure public pavilions built to accommodate the modular capsules intended to showcase new living strategies for an increasingly urban and dense living environment (presaging, perhaps, today's ongoing concerns and a rekindled interest in "microhousing").

As part of this all-encompassing strategy, Kenzo Tange designed the Expo's main public pavilion, the mega-scale Festival Plaza. Here the simple 2D truss can be seen to have evolved into its 3D counterpart known as the space frame – still "only" an assembly of compression and tension elements, albeit one which has rather remarkable space-spanning and place-defining characteristics. From a structural perspective, just as the planar truss can be thought of as analogous in certain respects to a beam, so too can the space frame be considered the equivalent of the two-way continuous slab; i.e., large loads can be carried, open spaces covered, and perimeter cantilevers projected outward to engage even more space. Moreover, because of its inherently open quality, the space frame lends itself well to being both relatively "transparent" (notwithstanding its mega-scale) as well as occupiable by the Metabolists' living capsules and circulation systems. At Osaka, the truss became a truly all-embracing structural form.

Metabolism and the Space Frame

from *Kenzo Tange and the Metabolist Movement: Urban Utopias of Modern Japan*
Zhongjie Lin

The Plan and Pavilions

Expo '70 set a grand stage for the Metabolists. In addition to his post as the chief planner, [Kenzo] Tange designed the main pavilion called the Festival Plaza. Kurokawa, Kawazoe, and Maki designed the experimental capsules installed in the roof over the plaza. Kikutake was the architect of the Expo Tower; Otaka designed the main gate; Kurokawa designed two of the most eye-catching pavilions, Takara Beautilion and Toshiba IHI Pavilion; and Isozaki created the giant robots on the Festival Plaza. Moreover, Sumitomo Pavilion was designed by Sachio Otani, Tange's colleague at the University of Tokyo who had also been influenced by Metabolism. Ten years after the founding of Metabolism, these architects gathered again to show the world Japan's creative energy. As the Osaka Expo opened, articles about its master plan and the pavilions appeared in leading architectural journals throughout the world, and many journals covered the event with an entire issue.[1] These articles brought tremendous international visibility to the Metabolists' works.

The master plan for the 330-hectare site completed under Tange's supervision demonstrated the structuralist approach to planning that the architect had developed in the plans for Tokyo and Skopje. It provided a basic structure and allowed individual constructions to happen in an autonomous manner. The infrastructure and main facilities of the Expo were organized around a linear axis known as the Symbol Zone. Running north-south across the entire site, the Symbol Zone consisted of two sections connected by the Main Gate plaza. The northern part of Symbol Zone included the Festival Plaza, the Museum of Fine Arts, and a Japanese Garden in the north end. The southern part extended to the Expo Club and terminated at Kikutake's Expo Tower and the South Gate.

The entire zone was bound together with spacious promenades and moving walkways, forming the spine of the Expo city. Reiterating Nishiyama's concept of an urban core, which had been included in the official document of Osaka Expo, Tange claimed that this spine would become the heart of a future city that would eventually grow from the Expo site. He articulated this vision at an interview with Kawazoe:

> *I imagine that the trunk elements can remain and that a new city can grow up in the areas where the pavilions now stand. When this happens, what is now the Expo site will become either the heart of a city with a population of 500 thousand or will become that city in its entirety. Some of the factors contributing to the future usefulness of the site are its proximity to Osaka, Kyoto, and Kobe; its direct connections with the express highway running from Tokyo to Kobe, and its position as the starting point of the new Chugoku through highway.* [2]

To Tange, the northern section of the Symbol Zone, an area about 1,000 meters long and 150 meters wide also known as the Trunk Facility, would serve as the "trunk" of the whole Expo site, which he conceived of as a "tree." He elaborated on this organic analogy:

The trunk facilities organize the entire grounds in the master plan. If we compare them to a tree, the Symbol Zone, located in the center of the grounds, is the trunk. The moving walkways, leading in four directions from the Symbol Zone, and the service areas, or Sub-plaza, at the end of each walkway, can be compared to branches and leaves; and the pavilions grouped around the seven Sub-plazas, to the individual and colorful flowers blooming on the tree. [3]

This made clear Tange's Metabolist strategy in planning. The trunk and the branches set a basic pattern and provided a structure of growth for a "city with a daytime population of 400,000." From the trunk, the circulation system branched out in different directions with escalators, moving walkways, and monorail lines connecting individual pavilions to the trunk. With this structure fixed, a variety of pavilions should be able to "grow" freely and provide sufficient room for individual creativity. In fact, there was hardly any restriction on building design. Even the height control of 100 meters was in the end ignored by architects designing the pavilions, such as the Soviet Union Pavilion. The result was a great variety of structures and forms that Tange described as "colorful flowers."

The layout of Osaka Expo bore similarities to the pattern of Tange's Plan for Tokyo. They both featured a linear axis that accommodated the circulation spine and the public urban components. Where there had been the "gate" to Tokyo Bay City – the port – there was the main entrance to the Expo. Residential blocks spreading randomly in Tokyo Bay were replaced by a variety of national and corporate pavilions on the Expo site. Monorail lines and moving walkways connecting the Trunk Facility to individual pavilions at the Expo played the same role as the freeways that linked the central spine to residential blocks in the Tokyo Bay Plan. In both cases, all the elements were organized in a hierarchical manner, and both layouts testified Tange's faith that centralized power could foster individual freedom and creativity.

The focal point of the entire Expo site was the Festival Plaza designed by Tange and his associates Isozaki and Koji Kamiya. Reflecting the theme "Progress and Harmony for Mankind," it served as the main space for exhibitions or major events for up to 30,000 people. Tange echoed Nishiyama's original idea about the plaza in his statement:

The Expo must be more than a display of past traditional achievements and present technological progress of the people of the world. It must also be a festival where human beings can meet, shake hands, and accord minds. Furthermore, the entire exposition ground must be a plaza contributing to the development of this festival of human harmony. [4]

To build such a place for mass gatherings and great events, Tange employed one of the most recent technologies: the space frame construction. An engineering marvel of the twentieth century introduced to architecture by Buckminster Fuller, the space frame and its structural potential were well explored by German-born American architect Konrad Wachsmann, who invented a system using prefabricated elements for large-span buildings like aircraft hangers. The tetrahedral frame and universal joint details of the hanger that Wachsmann designed for the US Air Force circulated widely and inspired many avant-garde architects including the Metabolists. In 1958 Wachsmann offered a two-week seminar at Tokyo Institute of Technology, which informed the Japanese architects of the recent development of space frame structure.[5] The seminar was organized by Takashi Asada, and among the participants were lsozaki and Keiichiro Mogi, both from Tange's laboratory. Tange used a steel space frame structure in the design of a stupendous roof over the Festival Plaza. This roof measured 290 meters long and 110 meters wide, and was lifted 38 meters above the ground by four gigantic posts also built as space frame structures. With the long span of nearly 300 meters, the roof was hailed as the largest single structure in the world. It could alone shelter exhibits and activities of an international exposition. And, theoretically, the structure was capable of infinite extension to cover an even larger area, making possible a miniature city under a single roof.

For visionary architects, the space frame's capacity of expansion, usage of a modular system, utmost flexibility, and openness to programs made it a perfect tool for creating a universal environment. French architect Yona Friedman and his *Groupe d'Études d'Architecture Mobile* (GEAM) developed a number of schemes called *La ville spatiale* (the Spatial City) in the 1960s, presented as collages showing endless space frame structures floating over European cities or landscapes.[6] These Spatial Cities provided enormous space frameworks, within which inhabitants could build homes according to their needs and ideas. Tange's giant roof for Osaka Expo appeared to be a realized version of Friedman's Spatial City. The roof not only sheltered exhibitions and ceremonies on the Festival Plaza, but also had a number of capsules installed within its space frame. Tange must have been fascinated by the space frame structure not only for its capacity of constructing large space, but also for its universal adaptability and infinite extendibility, qualities in accordance with the primary concept of the Festival Plaza – an open and universal space for the gathering of people from throughout the world.

The exhibitions at the Festival Plaza were organized in three sections: Past, Present, and Future. The space under the plaza level housed exhibitions of past civilizations. The plaza level, dedicated to the present and becoming the site of various ceremonies, was dominated by a gigantic sculpture named "Tower of the Sun," a creation of artist Taro Okamoto.[7] The tower took the form of a tapering white column with outstretching arms, adorned by two faces at its midpoint, white and black, front and back, with a golden, concave face at its top. Over seventy meters tall, the sculpture pierced through Tange's mega-roof and became the symbol of the entire site. On the plaza there were also a few large electronic devices operated by robots. These robots, designed by Isozaki, were cybernetically controlled by means of human feedback, showcasing the technology of creating and manipulating spaces based on human activities. The Future section was hung high above in the space frame, only accessible through ramps and escalators within the Tower of the Sun. Visitors could walk through a number of capsules installed within the space frame, suggesting environments of a future aerial city. These capsules were designed by several young architects of Tange's choice, including both Metabolists and Western avant-gardes like Archigram, Hans Hollein, Yona Friedman, Giancarlo de Carlo, and Aleksei Gutnof. Kurokawa and Kamiya designed a few "Capsules for living;" Archigram presented a "Dissolving City;" and Giancarlo de Carlo created a "City of Participation." [8]

The capsule was the theme of many pavilions in the Osaka Expo, an influence attributable to the 1967 World Exposition in Montreal. The most memorable architectural work in this exposition was Moshe Safdie's experimental collective housing project Habitat '67. This building, stacking numerous prefabricated concrete boxes one upon another to form an extraordinary "hill town," explored the future form of housing. A more substantial idea of capsule architecture, however, came from Archigram. Since its emergence in 1961, this British avant-garde group had developed the design concept of capsule in several projects, drawing inspiration from various areas such as space travel, minimal living, and atypical materials. In particular, Peter Cook's 1964 project "Plug-in City" envisioned mass-prefabricated capsules for dwelling and office clipped on a vast diagonal space frame to form a whole city. Futuristic schemes like this, celebrating flexibility, expandability, and mobility, became enormously influential in the 1960s.

One of the structures that confirmed Archigram's influence at Osaka Expo was the Expo Tower designed by Kikutake. It stood at the south end of the Symbol Zone's main axis and offered views of the entire Expo city. Visitors could ascend in two high-speed lifts that took them to capsules and overlook platforms on different levels. The architect was apparently inspired by Peter Cook's unbuilt project of Montreal Tower submitted to the 1967 World Exposition. Like Montreal Tower, Kikutake's design consisted of a tower-shaped megastructure with a number of capsules attached to the main structure. The capsules on both towers took the form of geodesic spheres, an invention of Buckminister Fuller in the late 1940s that had become well known when Fuller used it to build the US Pavilion at Expo '67. While Cook's main structure was a solid tower with Brutalist imprint, Kikutake's tower was a space-frame structure composed of steel pipe struts and cast steel ball joints. This design made the Osaka tower appear lighter and suggestive of the capacity for future extension.

It was Kurokawa who made the capsule his iconic form at the Osaka Expo. In addition to one of the capsule houses suspended over Festival Plaza, Kurokawa designed two corporate pavilions, Toshiba IHI Pavilion and Takara Beautilion. Both of them were based on three-dimensional frameworks used as open structures to organize capsule units. Sponsored jointly by an electrical and a heavy industrial company, Toshiba IHI Pavilion featured a 500-seat dome theatre clad with orange steel panels. The theatre was lifted above ground by an expressive space-frame structure consisting of six giant columns and a gigantic canopy built of 1,500 black metal tetrapods. Underneath the theatre was a reception hall. A 50-meter tower, assembled using the same tetra-pieces, stood on the main approach to the theatre. The other pavilion Takara Beautilion was one of the most successful technological fantasies at the Osaka Expo. It was characterized by a three-dimensional framework made up of steel pipes that stretched out in all directions. A number of cubic capsules clad with stainless steel, housing displays of the company's beauty products, were installed in the framework with connectors. In both pavilions, the frameworks terminated at opened joints, giving the buildings unusual silhouettes and strongly suggesting incompleteness and expandability. Kurokawa extensively employed the technology of prefabrication, allowing instant assembly of the structure and installation of capsules. In fact, Takara Beautilion was put together on site in only six days. The pavilions could also be dismantled with ease and transported elsewhere for reconstruction.

Kurokawa continued to develop his capsule architecture after the Expo. The Nakagin Capsule Tower, built in 1972, gave this concept its most pronounced form and became arguably the most notable building of the Metabolist movement. The concept of capsule substantiated Metabolism's original idea of distinguishing interchangeable elements from permanent structure. It was also emblematic of Metabolism's somewhat naive faith in technology in changing the urban formation as well as social structure. The fast-developing and by then readily available industrial technology of prefabrication and standardization seemed to offer a direction for contemporary architecture and urbanism. In reality, however, just like Tange's Yamanashi Press and Broadcasting Center and Safdie's Habitat '67, the Metabolist concept of capsule never became a successful model for the mass-production of living or work spaces. The individual designs built turned out to be heavy, inflexible, and over-deterministic with regard to the megastructure. Overemphasized industrialization made them yield to a culture of consumerism.

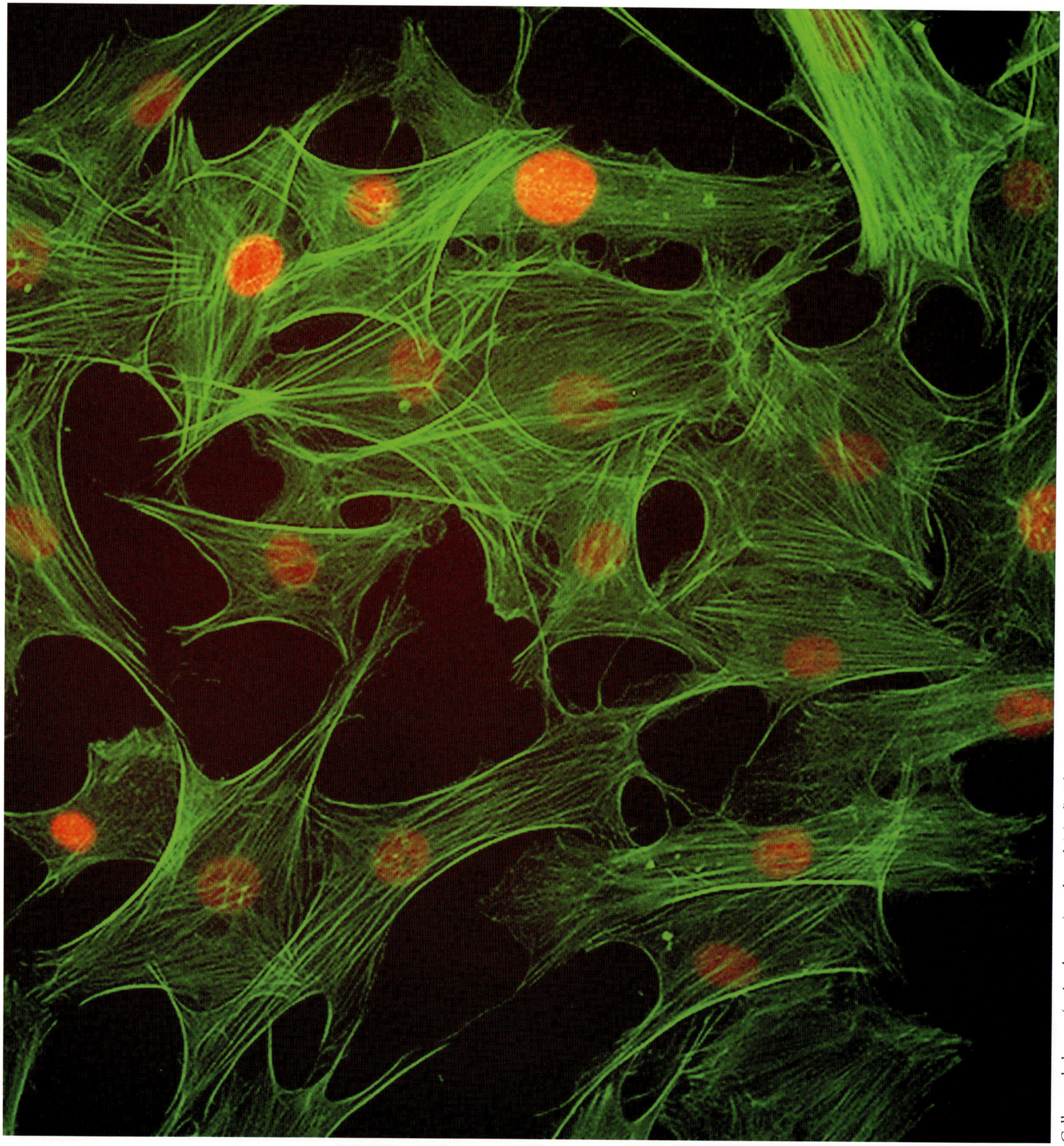

Cell cytoskeletons (stained green) and nuclei (red). Photo: Tom Polte and Donald Ingber

Connections between biological topics and trusses and architecture are not limited to the large-scale projects of the Metabolists. In this article, the microscopic world of cell structures – cytoskeletons – is explored. In doing so, cell biologist and bioengineer Donald Ingber rather astonishingly brings to light living cells' natural trussed structures of the so-called tensegrity variety – a structural configuration identified, developed and made famous by the sculptor Kenneth Snelson and by the architect, inventor and theorist Buckminster Fuller. Tensegrity structures are, like all basic trusses and true to Le Ricolais's words, made up only of tension and compression members; their key distinguishing feature, however, is that no two compression members touch each other – i.e., they are tied together only by means of pre-stressed tension elements. (Fuller would famously observe by analogy that "Nothing in the Universe touches anything else.")

Reserving yet another surprise, Ingber also demonstrates that certain cell structures incorporate the classic geometrical configurations of Fuller's geodesic domes! All of this is conveyed here in remarkably accessible fashion even for those relatively uninitiated in the arcane world and terminology of cell biology; certain passages toward the middle may be a bit of a tough slog – those sections can be skipped over and/or read and reread to understand more each time. In the end, though, one can only be left to marvel at the amazing interconnectedness of the seemingly disparate topics of structure and architecture and life…

Tensegrity and the Architecture of Life

The Architecture of Life
Donald E. Ingber

Life is the ultimate example of complexity at work. An organism, whether it is a bacterium or a baboon, develops through an incredibly complex series of interactions involving a vast number of different components. These components, or subsystems, are themselves made up of smaller molecular components, which independently exhibit their own dynamic behavior, such as the ability to catalyze chemical reactions. Yet when they are combined into some larger functioning unit—such as a cell or tissue—utterly new and unpredictable properties emerge, including the ability to move, to change shape and to grow.

Although researchers have recognized this intriguing fact for some time, most discount it in their quest to explain life's fundamentals. For the past several decades, biologists have attempted to advance our understanding of how the human body works by defining the properties of life's critical materials and molecules, such as DNA, the stuff of genes. Indeed, biologists are now striving to identify every gene in the complete set, known as the genome, that every human being carries. Because genes are the "blueprints" for the key molecules of life, such as proteins, this Holy Grail of molecular biology will lead in the near future to a catalogue of essentially all the molecules from which a human is created. Understanding what the parts of a complex machine are made of, however, does little to explain how the whole system works, regardless of whether the complex system is a combustion engine or a cell. In other words, identifying and describing the molecular puzzle pieces will do little if we do not understand the rules for their assembly.

That nature applies common assembly rules is implied by the recurrence—at scales from the molecular to the macrocopic—of certain patterns, such as spirals, pentagons and triangulated forms. These patterns appear in structures ranging from highly regular crystals to relatively irregular proteins and in organisms as diverse as viruses, plankton and humans. After all, both organic and inorganic matter are made of the same building blocks: atoms of carbon, hydrogen, oxygen, nitrogen and phosphorus. The only difference is how the atoms are arranged in three-dimensional space.

This phenomenon, in which components join together to form larger, stable structures having new properties that could not have been predicted from the characteristics of their individual parts, is known as self-assembly. It is observed at many scales in nature. In the human body, for example, large molecules self-assemble into cellular components known as organelles, which self-assemble into cells, which self-assemble into tissues, which self-assemble into organs. The result is a body organized hierarchically as tiers of systems within systems. Thus, if we are to understand fully the way living creatures form and function, we need to uncover these basic principles that guide biological organization.

Despite centuries of study, researchers still know relatively little about the forces that guide atoms to self-assemble into molecules. They know even less about how groups of molecules join together to create living cells and tissues. Over the past two decades, however, I have discovered and explored an intriguing and seemingly fundamental aspect of self-assembly. An astoundingly wide variety of natural systems, including carbon atoms, water molecules, proteins, viruses, cells, tissues and even humans and other living creatures, are constructed using a common form of architecture known as tensegrity. The term refers to a system that stabilizes itself mechanically because of the way in which tensional and compressive forces are distributed and balanced within the structure.

This fundamental finding could one day have practical applications in many areas. For example, new understanding of tensegrity at the cellular level has allowed us to comprehend better how cellular shape and mechanical forces—such as pressure in blood vessels or compression in bone—influence the activities of genes. At the same time, deeper understanding of natural rules of self-assembly will allow us to make better use—in applications ranging from drug design to tissue engineering—of the rapidly accumulating data we have about molecules, cells and other biological components. An explanation of why tensegrity is so ubiquitous in nature may also provide new insight into the very forces that drive biological organization—and perhaps into evolution itself.

What is Tensegrity?

My interest in tensegrity dates back to my undergraduate years in the mid-1970s at Yale University. There my studies of cell biology and also of sculpture led me to realize that the question of how living things form has less to do with chemical composition than with architecture. The molecules and cells that form our tissues are continually removed and replaced; it is the maintenance of pattern and architecture, I reasoned, that we call life. Tensegrity structures are mechanically stable not because of the strength of individual members but because of the way the entire structure distributes and balances mechanical stresses. The structures fall into two categories. Structures in one category, which includes the geodesic domes of Buckminster Fuller; are basically frameworks made up of rigid struts, each of which can bear tension or compression. The struts that make up the framework are connected into triangles, pentagons or hexagons, and each strut is oriented so as to constrain each joint to a fixed position, thereby assuring the stability of the whole structure.

The other category of tensegrity structures encompasses those that stabilize themselves through a phenomenon known as prestress. This type of structure was first constructed by the sculptor Kenneth Snelson. In Snelson's elegant sculptures, structural members that can bear only tension are distinct from those that bear compression. Even before one of these structures is subjected to an external force, all the structural members are already in tension or compression—that is, they are prestressed. Within the structure, the compression-bearing rigid struts stretch, or tense, the flexible, tension-bearing members, while those tension-bearing members compress the rigid struts. These counteracting forces, which equilibrate throughout the structure, are what enable it to stabilize itself.

Tensegrity structures of both categories share one critical feature, which is that tension is continuously transmitted across all structural members. In other words, an increase in tension in one of the members results in increased tension in members throughout the structure—even ones on the opposite side. This global increase in tension is balanced by an increase in compression within certain members spaced throughout the structure. In this way, the structure stabilizes itself through a mechanism that Fuller described as continuous tension and local compression. In contrast, most buildings derive their stability from continuous compression because of the force of gravity.

The tension-bearing members in these structures—whether Fuller's domes or Snelson's sculptures—map out the shortest paths between adjacent members (and are therefore, by definition, arranged geodesically). Tensional forces naturally transmit themselves over the shortest distance between two points, so the members of a tensegrity structure are precisely positioned to best withstand stress. For this reason, tensegrity structures offer a maximum amount of strength for a given amount of building material.

From Skeleton to Cytoskeleton

What does tensegrity have to do with the human body? The principles of tensegrity apply at essentially every detectable size scale in the body. At the macroscopic level, the 206 bones that constitute our skeleton are pulled up against the force of gravity and stabilized in a vertical form by the pull of tensile muscles, tendons and ligaments (similar to the cables in Snelson's sculptures). In other words, in the complex tensegrity structure inside every one of us, bones are the compression struts, and muscles, tendons and ligaments are the tension-bearing members. At the other end of the scale, proteins and other key molecules in the body also stabilize themselves through the principles of tensegrity. My own interest lies in between these two extremes, at the cellular level.

As a graduate student working with James D. Jamieson at Yale, I focused on how the components of biological systems—especially of cells—interacted mechanically. At this time, in the late 1970s, biologists generally viewed the cell as a viscous fluid or gel surrounded by a membrane, much like a balloon filled with molasses. Cells were known to contain an internal framework, or cytoskeleton, composed of three different types of molecular protein polymers, known as microfilaments, intermediate filaments and microtubules. But their role in controlling cell shape was poorly understood.

Another mystery in those days concerned the way isolated cells behave when placed on different surfaces. It had been long known that cells spread out and flatten when they attach to a rigid glass or plastic culture dish. In 1980, however, Albert K. Harris of the University of North Carolina at Chapel Hill showed that when affixed to a flexible rubber substrate, cells contract and become more spherical. This contraction bunches up, or puckers, the underlying rubber.

It occurred to me that a view of the cell as a tensegrity structure could easily explain such behavior. I modeled a cell as such a structure; it consisted of six wood dowels and some elastic string. I arranged the dowels—which bore the compressive stress—in three pairs. Each pair was perpendicular to the other two, and none of the wood struts actually touched one another. A tension-bearing elastic string connected to the ends of all the dowels, pulling them into a stable, three-dimensional form. I also placed a smaller, spherical tensegrity model, representing the nucleus, within the larger one that represented the rest of the cell. Then, to mimic cytoskeletal connections between the nucleus and the rest of the cell, I stretched elastic strings from the surface of the large tensegrity structure to the smaller one inside.

To understand how my experiment worked, it is necessary to know that pushing down on a tensegrity model of the kind I built forces it into what appears to be a flattened pile of sticks and string. As soon as the pressure is removed, the energy stored in the tensed filaments causes the model to spring back to its original, roughly spherical shape. To simulate how cells behave when placed on a surface, I mimicked a solid culture substrate of glass or plastic by stretching a piece of cloth taut and pinning it firmly to a piece of wood below. I affixed the tensegrity model to the substrate by flattening it and sewing the ends of some of the dowels to the cloth. These attachments were analogous to the cell-surface molecules, now known as integrins or adhesion receptors, that physically connect a cell to its anchoring substrate.

With the dowel ends sewed to the tightly pinned cloth, the model remained flat, just as a real cell does on a hard substrate. When I lifted the pins to free the cloth from the wood, however, thereby making the cell's anchoring surface flexible, the tensegrity model popped up into its more spherical form, puckering the cloth underneath. Furthermore, I noticed that when I stretched the model flat by connecting it to the cloth substrate, the cell and nucleus inside it extended in a coordinated manner. The nucleus model also moved toward the bottom of the simulated cell. Soon thereafter, I showed experimentally that living cells and nuclei spread and polarize in a similar manner when they adhere to a substrate. Thus, with my highly simplified construction, I showed that tensegrity structures mimic the known behavior of living cells.

Hard-Wiring in Cells

In the years since my modeling experiment, biologists have learned a great deal about the mechanical aspects of cells, and their findings seem to confirm that cells do indeed get their shape from tensegrity. Further, just as the models predict, most cells derive their structure not only from the cytoskeleton's three major types of filaments but also from the extra-cellular matrix—the anchoring scaffolding to which cells are naturally secured in the body.

Inside the cell, a gossamer network of contractile microfilaments—a key element of the cytoskeleton—extends throughout the cell, exerting tension. In other words, it pulls the cell's membrane and all its internal constituents toward the nucleus at the core. Opposing this inward pull are two main types of compressive elements, one of which is outside the cell and the other inside. The component outside the cell is the extracellular matrix; the compressive "girders" inside the cell can be either microtubules or large bundles of cross-linked microfilaments within the cytoskeleton. The third component of the cytoskeleton, the intermediate filaments, are the great integrators, connecting microtubules and contractile microfilaments to one another as well as to the surface membrane and the cell's nucleus. In addition, they act as guy wires, stiffening the central nucleus and securing it in place. Although the cytoskeleton is surrounded by membranes and penetrated by viscous fluid, it is this hard-wired network of molecular struts and cables that stabilizes cell shape.

If the cell and nucleus are physically connected by tensile filaments and not solely by a fluid cytoplasm, then pulling on receptors at the cell surface should produce immediate structural changes deep inside the cell. Recently Andrew Maniotis, who was in my group at Children's Hospital of Harvard Medical School, demonstrated this directly. By binding micro-pipettes to adhesion receptors on the surface of living cells and pulling outward, Maniotis caused cytoskeletal filaments and structures in the nucleus to realign immediately in the direction of pull. Thus, as my early experiments suggested, cells and nuclei do not behave like viscous water balloons.

How Mechanics Controls Biochemistry

Tensegrity can be invoked to explain more than the stabilization of cellular and nuclear form. For example, Steven R. Heidemann, working with Harish Joshi and Robert E. Buxbaum of Michigan State University in the mid-1980s, found that tensegrity can explain how nerve cells extend long, thin projections called neurites, which are filled with microtubules and transmit electrical signals in the nervous system. This growth is required for repair of nerve damage.

Heidemann's group found that microtubules are compressed at their ends by the pull of surrounding contractile microfilaments inside the neurites. More important, the researchers discovered that microtubule assembly (elongation)—and, hence, neurite extension—is promoted by shifting compressive loads off the microtubule and onto the cell's attachments to its extracellular matrix. In other words, the existence of a tensegrity force balance provides a means to integrate mechanics and biochemistry at the molecular level.

Very recently, Andrew Matus of the Friedrich Miescher Institute in Basel added a vivid footnote to this story. By making cells that produce fluorescent microtubules, Matus actually viewed those microtubules buckling under compression.

The tensegrity model suggests that the structure of the cell's cytoskeleton can be changed by altering the balance of physical forces transmitted across the cell surface. This finding is important because many of the enzymes and other substances that control protein synthesis, energy conversion and growth in the cell are physically immobilized on the cytoskeleton. For this reason, changing cytoskeletal geometry and mechanics could affect biochemical reactions and even alter the genes that are activated and thus the proteins that are made.

To investigate this possibility further, Rahul Singhvi and Christopher S. Chen in my group, working with George M. Whitesides, also at Harvard, developed a method to engineer cell shape and function. They forced living cells to take on different shapes—spherical or flattened, round or square—by placing them on tiny, adhesive "islands" composed of extra-cellular matrix. Each adhesive island was surrounded by a Teflon-like surface to which cells could not adhere.

By simply modifying the shape of the cell, they could switch cells between different genetic programs. Cells that spread flat became more likely to divide, whereas round cells that were prevented from spreading activated a death program known as apoptosis. When cells were neither too extended nor too retracted, they neither divided nor died. Instead they differentiated themselves in a tissue-specific manner: capillary cells formed hollow capillary tubes; liver cells secreted proteins that the liver normally supplies to the blood; and so on.

Thus, mechanical restructuring of the cell and cytoskeleton apparently tells the cell what to do. Very flat cells, with their cytoskeletons stretched, sense that more cells are needed to cover the surrounding substrate—as in wound repair—and that cell division is needed. Rounding indicates that too many cells are competing for space on the matrix and that cells are proliferating too much; some must die to prevent tumor formation. In between these two extremes, normal tissue function is established and maintained. Understanding how this switching occurs could lead to new approaches to cancer therapy and tissue repair and perhaps even to the creation of artificial-tissue replacements.

Making Cells Do the Twist

The next level up in the hierarchy of self-assembly is the formation of tissues, which are created from the joining of cells to one another and to their extracellular matrix. One emergent property of tissues is how they behave mechanically. Many different types of tissue, including muscle, cartilage, blood vessels and skin, exhibit a response known as linear stiffening. If you pull on your skin, for example, you will feel the resistance increase as you tug harder. An increasing external force is met with increasing resistance. Recent studies show that even isolated molecules, such as DNA, exhibit linear stiffening, yet until we examined this phenomenon in the context of tensegrity, there was no mechanical or mathematical explanation for this behavior.

In 1993 my co-worker Ning Wang, working with James P. Butler of the Harvard School of Public Health, developed a device that allowed us to twist individual molecules on the surface membrane of living cells while simultaneously measuring the cellular response. We found that when we increased the stress applied to integrins (molecules that go through the cell's membrane and link the extracellular matrix to the internal cytoskeleton), the cells responded by becoming stiffer and stiffer—just as whole tissues do. Furthermore, living cells could be made stiff or flexible by varying the prestress in the cytoskeleton by changing, for example, the tension in contractile microfilaments.

Although the exact details of the interaction are not all known, we showed, using a stick-and-string tensegrity model, that the gist of the response can be discerned from the way in which tensegrity structures respond to stress. Essentially, all the interconnected structural elements of a tensegrity model rearrange themselves in response to a local stress. Linear stiffening results because as the applied stress increases, more of the members come to lie in the direction of the applied stress.

Working with Dimitrije Stamenovic of Boston University, we developed a mathematical model based on these principles. It predicts, for the first time, the linear-stiffening response of tissues, living cells and even molecules. We hope to use this model to help design advanced materials that have the linear-stiffening property and that may be useful in such applications as protective clothing and artificial body parts. The same mathematical approach may also be incorporated within computer programs as a shortcut to accelerate molecular modeling and drug design.

In Wang's magnetic-twisting studies and in Maniotis's micropipette-pulling experiments, we found that applying stress to cell-surface receptors involved with metabolism—rather than adhesion—did not effectively convey force to the inside of the cell. Thus, these studies confirmed that mechanical forces are transmitted over specific molecular paths in living cells, a finding that provided new insight into how cells sense mechanical stimuli that regulate tissue development. This insight, in turn, may help us better understand a wide variety of phenomena, from the growth of muscle in response to tension to the growth of plant roots in response to gravity.

Molecular Geodesic Domes

Although the tensegrity models predicted many cell behaviors, one disparity needed explaining. Many cells can spread and flatten without microtubules—the most important compression struts in the model. If living cells can change from spherical to flat without these struts, how can tensegrity apply? Again using an uncomplicated modeling approach, I found that, incredibly, the microfilament network itself is a tensegrity structure.

In the cytoskeleton of a living cell, contractile microfilaments form a lattice that reorganizes locally into different forms, such as large bundles or networks of triangles. To explore the mechanism behind this reorganization, I modeled the microfilament lattice as a polyhedral framework of soda straws that contained six triangles and four squares. The straws were held together by a single elastic string that I threaded through all the straws and tied to itself. I assumed that each soda straw in the model represented a single contractile microfilament that could generate mechanical tension by shortening itself. It is known that contractile microfilaments get stiffer when they shorten. Thus, the internal elastic thread in the model would then mimic the continuous tension in the whole structure that results from the shortening of all these stiffened filaments.

I assumed that this soda-straw model represented one modular cytoskeletal unit that interconnected in all directions with other similar modules in a round, unattached (suspended) cell. The question I was trying to answer was, What would happen to this framework if the cell it supported were to attach to a rigid surface?

Cells attach by binding to surface-bound molecules in the extracellular matrix. But cells are not evenly "glued" to the matrix; rather they are "spot welded" in localized sites known as focal adhesions. Contractile microfilaments respond to anchorage by shortening and increasing isometric tension within the lattice. The soda-straw models suggested that the increasing tension produced by attachment would cause the individual contractile microfilaments that formed the squares in the model to self-assemble into linear bundles stretching between these focal-adhesion sites where integrin receptors anchor the cell to the matrix. In fact, when living cells spread on a surface, individual contractile microfilaments align in a nearly identical manner to form bundles called stress fibers.

In contrast, at the top of the cell, there is no adhesive substrate to resist the pull of the shortening microfilaments. In these regions the contraction of each microfilament can be resisted only by the pull and stiffness of its neighboring filaments. Fuller showed many years ago that inward pulling and twisting causes this type of polyhedral structure to undergo what he called a "jitterbug" transformation: the highly flexible framework of squares and triangles converts into fully triangulated octahedral or tetrahedral forms—or, in other words, into fully triangulated tensegrity structures.

When I interconnected many similar soda-straw models, I found that the individual modules progressively contracted, resulting in the formation of a geodesic framework composed of alternating octahedral and tetrahedral forms, closely packed. In a cell, contraction of surrounding microfilament networks that interconnect with the cell base would bend this framework down over the spherical nucleus, thereby transforming it into a highly triangulated dome—specifically, a geodesic dome.

Elias Lazarides, then at Cold Spring Harbor Laboratory in New York, and Mary Osborn and Klaus Weber of the Max Planck Institute in Gottingen, Germany, observed these very transformations in the region of the cytoplasm above the nucleus in spreading cells. Significantly, the existence of a geodesic dome within the cytoskeleton at the molecular level demonstrates conclusively that cells can and do use the architecture of tensegrity to shape their cytoskeleton.

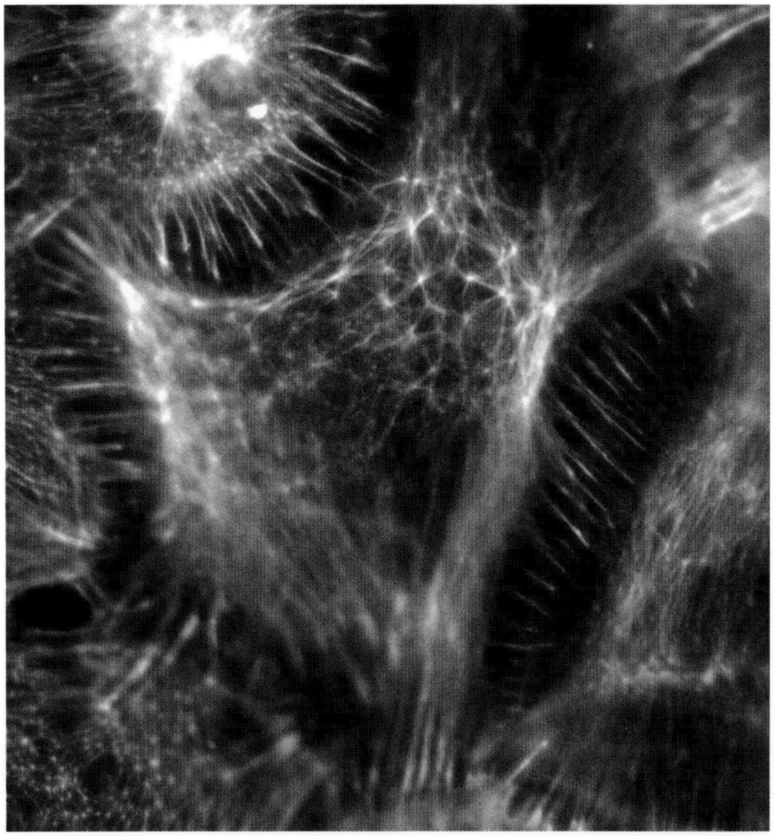

Geodesic dome within cytoskeleton of a living cell.
Photo: Julia Sero and Donald Ingber

A Universal Pattern

The geodesic structure found within the cytoskeleton is a classic example of a pattern that is found everywhere in nature, at many different size scales. Spherical groups of carbon atoms called buckminsterfullerenes or buckyballs, along with viruses, enzymes, organelles, cells and even small organisms, all exhibit geodesic forms. Strangely, few researchers seem to have asked why this is so. My view is that this recurrent pattern is visual evidence of the existence of common rules for self-assembly. In particular, all these entities stabilize themselves in three dimensions in a similar way: by arranging their parts to minimize energy and mass through continuous tension and local compression—that is, through tensegrity.

The assembly of viruses, the smallest form of life on the earth, involves binding interactions between many similar proteins that come together to form a geodesic viral coat that encloses the genetic material. During virus formation, linear extensions of the proteins overlap with similar tails that extend from neighboring proteins to form a triangulated geodesic framework on the nanometer scale. Each joint in this framework self-stabilizes as a result of a balance between the pull of intermolecular attractive forces (hydrogen bonds) and the ability of the individual protein tails to resist compression and buckling.

The same basic scheme is apparent in buckyballs, except that the building blocks are atoms instead of proteins. In buckyballs, 60 carbon atoms form a geodesic sphere covered by 20 hexagons interspersed with 12 pentagons: the pattern on a soccer ball. In effect, the 90 carbon-carbon bonds in a buckyball are the struts in a tensegrity sphere.

It is more difficult, however, to see that the same building rules also apply to irregular structures, including many biological molecules, that do not exhibit geodesic forms. Proteins, on which cells depend for structure, catalysis and many other functions, are long strings of amino acids. Small regions of the protein's amino acid backbone fold into helical forms that stabilize themselves through a balance between the attractive force of hydrogen bonds (pulling together different regions of the molecule) and the ability of the protein coil to resist shortening, or compression. In other words, these helical regions stabilize themselves through tensegrity—as does any helical molecule, such as DNA.

Protein organization also involves hierarchical assembly. The small regions of a protein that are helically stiffened are separated from one another by parts of the same amino acid backbone that act as if they were flexible hinges. These strut-like regions fold back on themselves (because of tensile hydrogen-bonding forces) in order to stabilize the entire molecule. The stiffened helices may be extremely compressed locally, even though forces are equilibrated across the whole prestressed molecule.

Because a local force can change the shape of an entire tensegrity structure, the binding of a molecule to a protein can cause the different, stiffened helical regions to rearrange their relative positions throughout the length of the protein. For example, when a signal-bearing molecule binds to a receptor that goes through the membrane and into a cell, the attachment can cause conformational changes at the opposite end of the receptor. These conformational changes, in turn, alter the shape of adjacent proteins and trigger a cascade of molecular restructuring inside that cell. Indeed, this is how cells sense and respond to changes in their environment.

Thus, from the molecules to the bones and muscles and tendons of the human body, tensegrity is clearly nature's preferred building system. Only tensegrity, for example, can explain how every time that you move your arm, your skin stretches, your extracellular matrix extends, your cells distort, and the interconnected molecules that form the internal framework of the cell feel the pull—all without any breakage or discontinuity.

Remarkably, tensegrity may even explain how all these phenomena are so perfectly coordinated in a living creature. At the Johns Hopkins School of Medicine, Donald S. Coffey and Kenneth J. Pienta found that tensegrity structures function as coupled harmonic oscillators. DNA, nuclei, cytoskeletal filaments, membrane ion channels and entire living cells and tissues exhibit characteristic resonant frequencies of vibration. Very simply, transmission of tension through a tensegrity array provides a means to distribute forces to all interconnected elements and, at the same time, to couple, or "tune," the whole system mechanically as one.

Implications for Evolution and Beyond

Although changes in DNA generate biological diversity, genes are a product of evolution, not its driving force. In fact, geodesic forms similar to those found in viruses, enzymes and cells existed in the inorganic world of crystals and minerals long before DNA ever came into existence. Even water molecules are structured geodesically. The relevant question is, How did organic molecules and cells evolve from inorganic components? After all, in terms of how emergent properties arise, self-assembly of molecules into organelles or cells into tissues is not very different from the self-assembly of atoms into compounds. For example, sodium, an explosive metal, and chlorine, a poisonous gas, combine to form sodium chloride, whose emergent property is that it can be used as table salt. The important principle here is the manner in which a structure shapes itself and holds its subcomponents together in three-dimensional space; this characteristic is what defines the way the structure as a whole will behave.

More broadly, all matter is subject to the same spatial constraints, regardless of scale or position. Thus, given these constraints, tensegrity is the most economical and efficient way to build—at the molecular scale, at the macroscopic scale and at all scales in between. It is possible that fully triangulated tensegrity structures may have been selected through evolution because of their structural efficiency—their high mechanical strength using a minimum of materials. The flexibility exhibited by prestressed tensegrity structures would be advantageous because it allows structures to take on different shapes. For example, if a molecule or cell were able to transform into a shape that was more stable at a certain temperature or pressure, or more efficient metabolically, then its lifetime would have been extended. It would have been more likely to interact with other, similar entities and then to self-assemble once again.

Researchers now think biological evolution began in layers of clay, rather than in the primordial sea. Interestingly, clay is itself a porous network of atoms arranged geodesically within octahedral and tetrahedral forms. But because these octahedra and tetrahedra are not closely packed, they retain the ability to move and slide relative to one another. This flexibility apparently allows clay to catalyze many chemical reactions, including ones that may have produced the first molecular building blocks of organic life.

Over time, different molecular collectives self-assembled to form the first structures with specialized functions—the forerunners of present-day organelles—which then combined with one another to create the first simple cells. These cells then produced proteins that self-assembled to form extracellular matrix–anchoring scaffolds that, in turn, promoted self-assembly of multicellular tissues. Organs developed from the self-assembly of tissues, and complex organisms arose through combination and progressive remodeling of different organs. Indeed, the development of an embryo from a sperm and an egg recapitulates all these stages of self-assembly.

The emergence of DNA and genes gave rise to a new mechanism for generating structural diversity that accelerated evolution. Yet throughout all this time the rules guiding the process of hierarchical self-assembly remained essentially unchanged. So it is no surprise that the basic arrangement of bones and muscles is remarkably similar in *Tyrannosaurus rex* and *Homo sapiens*; that animals, insects and plants all rely on prestress for the mechanical stability of their bodies; and that geodesic forms, such as hexagons, pentagons and spirals, predominate in natural systems.

Finally, more philosophical questions arise: Are these building principles universal? Do they apply to structures that are molded by very large-scale forces as well as small-scale ones? We do not know. Snelson, however, has proposed an intriguing model of the atom based on tensegrity that takes off where the French physicist Louis de Broglie left off in 1923. Fuller himself went so far as to imagine the solar system as a structure composed of multiple nondeformable rings of planetary motion held together by continuous gravitational tension. Then, too, the fact that our expanding (tensing) universe contains huge filaments of gravitationally linked galaxies and isolated black holes that experience immense compressive forces locally can only lead us to wonder. Perhaps there is a single underlying theme to nature after all. As suggested by early 20th-century Scottish zoologist D'Arcy W. Thompson, who quoted Galileo, who, in turn, cited Plato: the Book of Nature may indeed be written in the characters of geometry.

Needle Tower by Kenneth Snelson. Photo: Onderwijsgek

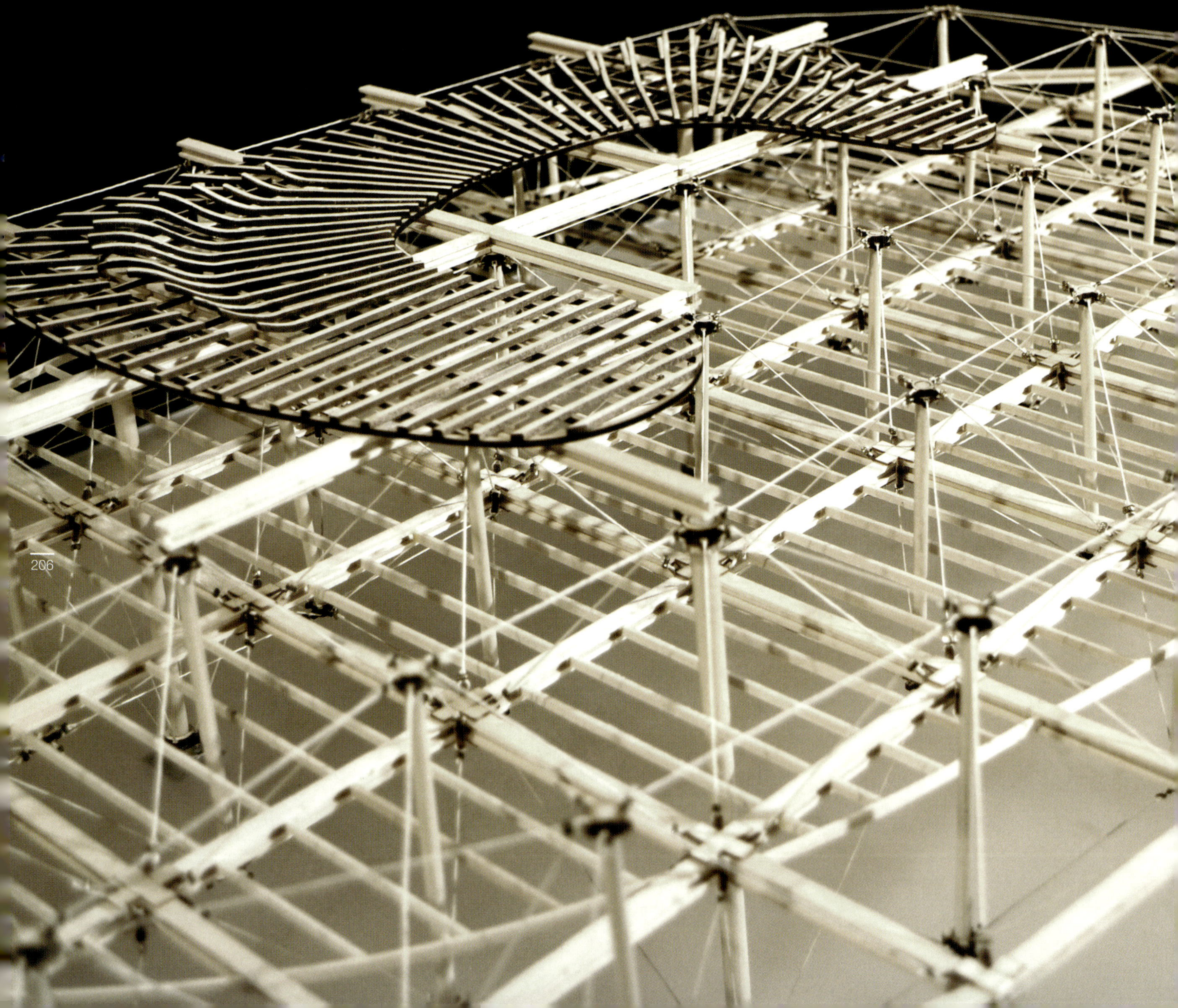

Blurring Structure

Blur Building, Yverdon-les-Bains, Switzerland (2002)
Architects: Diller Scofidio + Renfro
Structural Engineer: Passera + Pedretti, Emch + Berger
Model: Juan Carlos Artolozaga + Mia Kang

© Beat Widmer

"Immaterial design" and feature-less, scale-less, space-less, mass-less and surface-less building – these are words that have been used to describe the temporary structure built over Lake Neuchâtel. Filtered lake water was shot as a fine mist through fog nozzles placed on the open structural framework that measured roughly 91m x 61m x 20m (300ft x 200ft x 65ft) – thereby creating a spectacular artificial cloud. The visual and physical lightness of the tensegrity structural system plays an essential role in furthering the dematerialization concepts that are central to the design of Blur; in this case all the vertical struts in the structure can be seen to be held in position by angled tension rods at their top and bottom ends – thus allowing the struts to seemingly "float" in mid-air. The overall structural system cantilevers outward in all directions from four central column supports, and by pulling the vertical supports inward these tend not to be seen from the sides – thus helping to visually disengage the "mist cloud" from the water's surface. Moreover, the trussed quality of the tensegrity system provides the structural depth that is necessary to handle the overall bending moment demands by means of an assembly of structural elements that are individually subject to either pure axial tension or compression, thereby minimizing their cross-sectional dimensions and providing an overall openness and lightness of form. [see also p. 41]

Trusses Spanning Space

Zenith Concert Hall, Limoges, France (2007)
Architect: Bernard Tschumi Architects/Architect Atelier 4
Structural Engineer: Jaillet-Rouby; Technip TPS
Model: Davin Stamp + Ziyin Zhou

© Christian Richter

This large, multi-purpose concert hall is situated in a forest clearing; the context is referred to by the curved wooden structure that supports the building's translucent polycarbonate panel outer skin; a series of glulam ribs and irregularly positioned diagonal bracing elements further distinguish the building envelope. Just behind this layer is an interstitial foyer, and a second enclosure (this one surrounding the central concert hall) provides acoustical and visual separation for the events inside.

Within the hall itself, unobstructed sightlines for up to 8000 spectators are achieved by relying on several steel roof trusses whose material capacity and overall structural depth allow these to clear span the required 80m (240ft) distance. Left exposed in the ceiling, the trusses are aligned according to the configuration of the functions below: from the back wall of the stage they run out parallel to each other before abruptly angling out radially, following the seating arrangement. At their outer ends these trusses are supported on a row of steel columns that follow the curved outer perimeter of the space. The ends of the trusses angle down to meet the columns at a point, effectively creating a structural hinge and ensuring that no bending moments are transferred to the columns. This configuration also "softens" the visual transition from the ends of the deep trusses to the smoothly curved building enclosure just beyond.

Long-Span Truss Variations

Four Sports Scenarios, Medellín, Colombia (2010)
Architect: Mazzanti Arquitectos and Felipe Mesa/Plan:b Arquitectos
Structural Engineer: Nicolás Parra and Daniel Lozano – CNI Ingenieros
Model: Jose Ibarra + Cristina Medina-González

© Iwan Baan

An international competition for this sports hall was won by turning a brief that called for a group of four independent sports venues into the design of a single building, albeit one that is visually and spatially "broken up" by being composed of several parallel bands, each having distinctively bent roof forms. Indeed, from the surrounding hillsides the green metal roof appears as an iconic, yet vaguely familiar-looking undulating surface topography.

Roof trusses span across the full width of the building, rising up to different heights according to the needs of particular sports below. Gymnastics, basketball, boxing and volleyball can thus receive individualized consideration while under a unifying structural system. Trusses have greatest depth where it is most needed to resist overall bending moments; i.e., near mid-span. The significant structural depth also means that individual truss member dimensions can be minimized, allowing relatively slender steel members to be used to maximize the amount of natural daylighting in the space. Solid steel plates are necessary at the ends of the trusses, on the other hand, where the largest shear forces govern their detailed design. The whole trussed roof assembly is lifted into the air on a series of tripod-like groupings of inclined columns that are aligned along the sides of the building and that together are capable of resisting the building's gravity and lateral loads alike.

Hiroyuki Hirai

Enveloping Space Frame

Imai Hospital Daycare Centre, Akita, Japan (2001)
Architect: Shigeru Ban Architects
Structural Engineer: TIS & Partners
Model: Suemin Jeon

The interior of this small pavilion has the inviting-yet-protective qualities of a barrel-vaulted space, something especially appropriate given the primary users. In contrast, the outside takes the form (in section) of a rotated square. These two layers, one made of bent sheets of laminated veneer lumber (LVL) assembled in an *adjiro* (wicker work) pattern, and the other of skeletal timber construction (clad with steel and polycarbonate panels), are connected by diagonal steel struts, thereby unifying the assembly into a composite space frame that both stiffens the structure and creates a double-layer barrier to maintain the thermal comfort of the interior. It also creates wonderful light and shadow effects.

Space-Defining, Cantilevering Trusses

Institute of Contemporary Art, Boston, USA (2006)
Architect: Diller Scofidio + Renfro
Structural Engineer: Arup
Model: Gabriel Hohag + Spencer Lapp

© Iwan Baan

Situated right at the water's edge in Boston harbor, this museum seems to defy gravity by having its upper volume precariously balanced on a much smaller base and by cantilevering out 25m (82ft). This elevated part of the building houses the main art galleries, which are designed to be column-free and of multi-story height, thus ensuring maximum curatorial flexibility. On the underside of this projecting volume and partly suspended from it is a 325-seat auditorium that is renowned for its downwardly-angled framed view of the water's surface.

What makes this whole arrangement feasible is a system of four large-scale cantilevering steel trusses; these have to resist especially large overall bending moments given the museum's high occupancy live loads, which helps to explain their exceptional depth of 6.85m (22.5ft). Each of the trusses is asymmetrically supported on pairs of columns located within the lower part of the building. Equilibrium is established by the trusses' pushing down against the columns closest to the water while being anchored against tension uplift by the columns furthest away from the water. Between the primary trusses, much smaller-scale transverse trusses carry the gallery floors and roof (not shown). In spite of the main trusses' remarkable proportions and fundamental load-carrying and space-defining functions, however, this system is hidden from view in the finished building, doing its work anonymously but no less importantly.

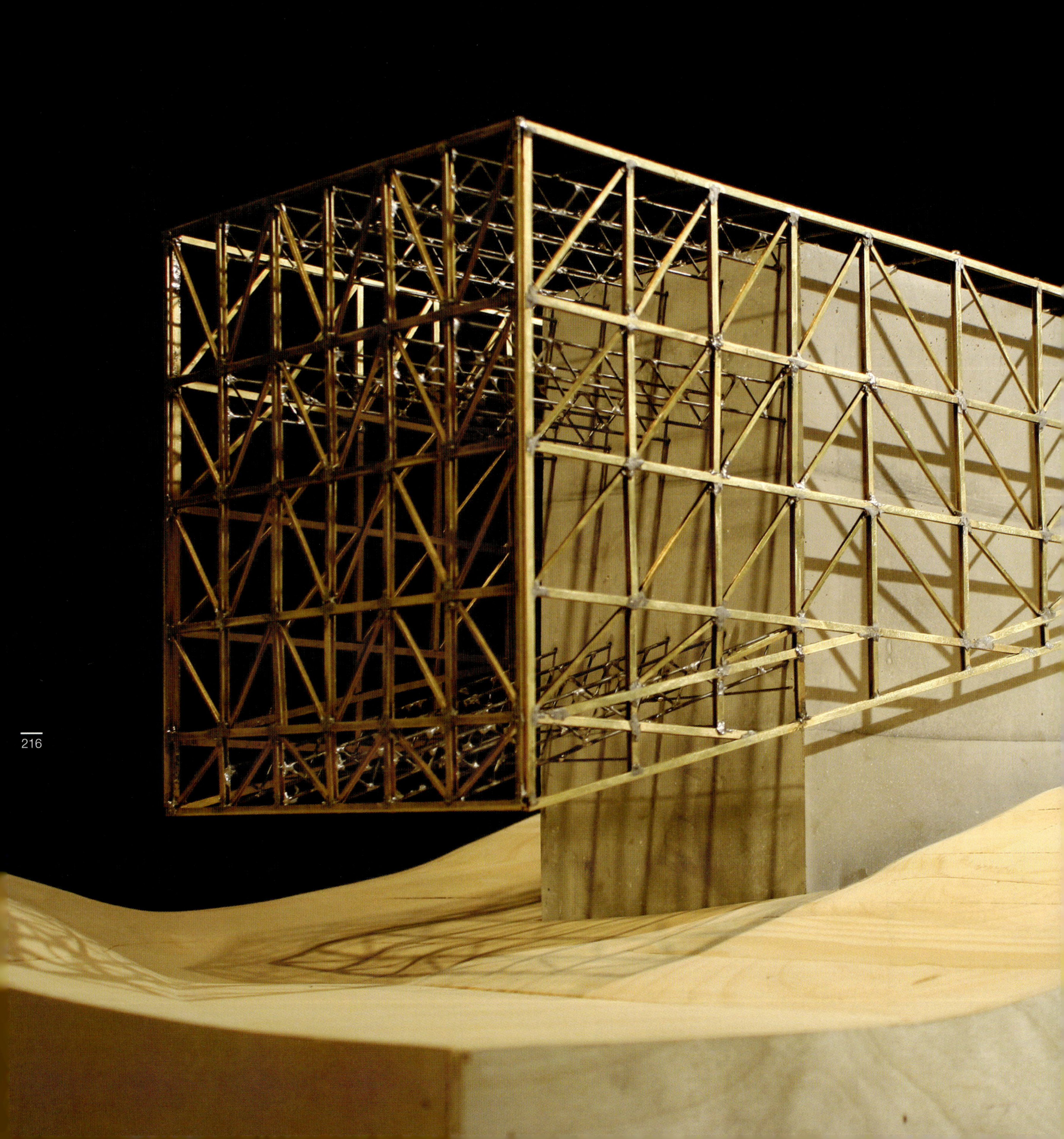

Multi-Story Trusses

Seoul National University Museum of Art, Seoul, South Korea (2005)
Architect: OMA
Structural Engineer: Arup
Model: Ji Young Chung + Ga-In Sim

Yoshinori Kuwahara

The basic form of this university museum is that of a rectangular box held aloft on a central core, except that the bottom of this lifted volume is cut along a diagonal running roughly parallel with the sloping site. This overall form is certainly visually distinctive; it also helps to establish the use of interior and exterior spaces; e.g., the sloped underbelly of the building suits well the need for inclined seating in the auditorium, and keeping the ground beneath the building accessible enables the site to mostly remain open, with walkways passing directly underneath the building.

The primary structural elements that make this form possible are self-evident: deep, multi-story steel trusses can be seen through the semi-transparent façades. Their impressive overall depth convincingly addresses the large bending moments produced by the cantilevering building volumes; conveniently, the sloped underside leads to a logical correspondence between overall truss height and the magnitude of loads (and resulting overall bending moments) that need to be resisted, with the deeper truss located on the downhill side where more floor levels are carried. More illogically, however, the cantilevered trusses at that end also get deeper with distance from the supporting core; even highly efficient trusses are not always subject to "purely" rational logic. Much less noticeable at first glance is the fact that the building façade trusses run right by the central concrete core that ultimately supports them; multiple transverse connectors are therefore necessary between these, with heavy shear forces needing to be transferred by brackets composed of inclined tension diagonals and compression struts.

Sergio Gómez

Place-defining Space Frame Canopy

Orchideorama; Medellín, Colombia (2006)
Architect: Plan B Architects + JPRCR Arquitectos
Structural Engineer: Ménsula Ingenieros S.A.
Model: Alberto Embriz de Salvatierra + Maria Paula Villarraga

Within Medellín's Botanical Gardens is a grove of constructed "trees" that both shelters and defines an informal, open-air public space. The Orchideorama takes certain of its design cues from the surrounding natural context: structural modules consist of tall, partly trussed trunk-like sets of columns that branch out in all directions into a horizontal canopy. Hexagonal space frame modules cantilever outward in a balanced, self-equilibrating fashion – mimicking the roughly symmetrical arrangements of branches on a tree or petals on a flower. The details of the canopy's space frame structure demonstrate the system's intrinsic qualities of visual openness and structural efficiency.

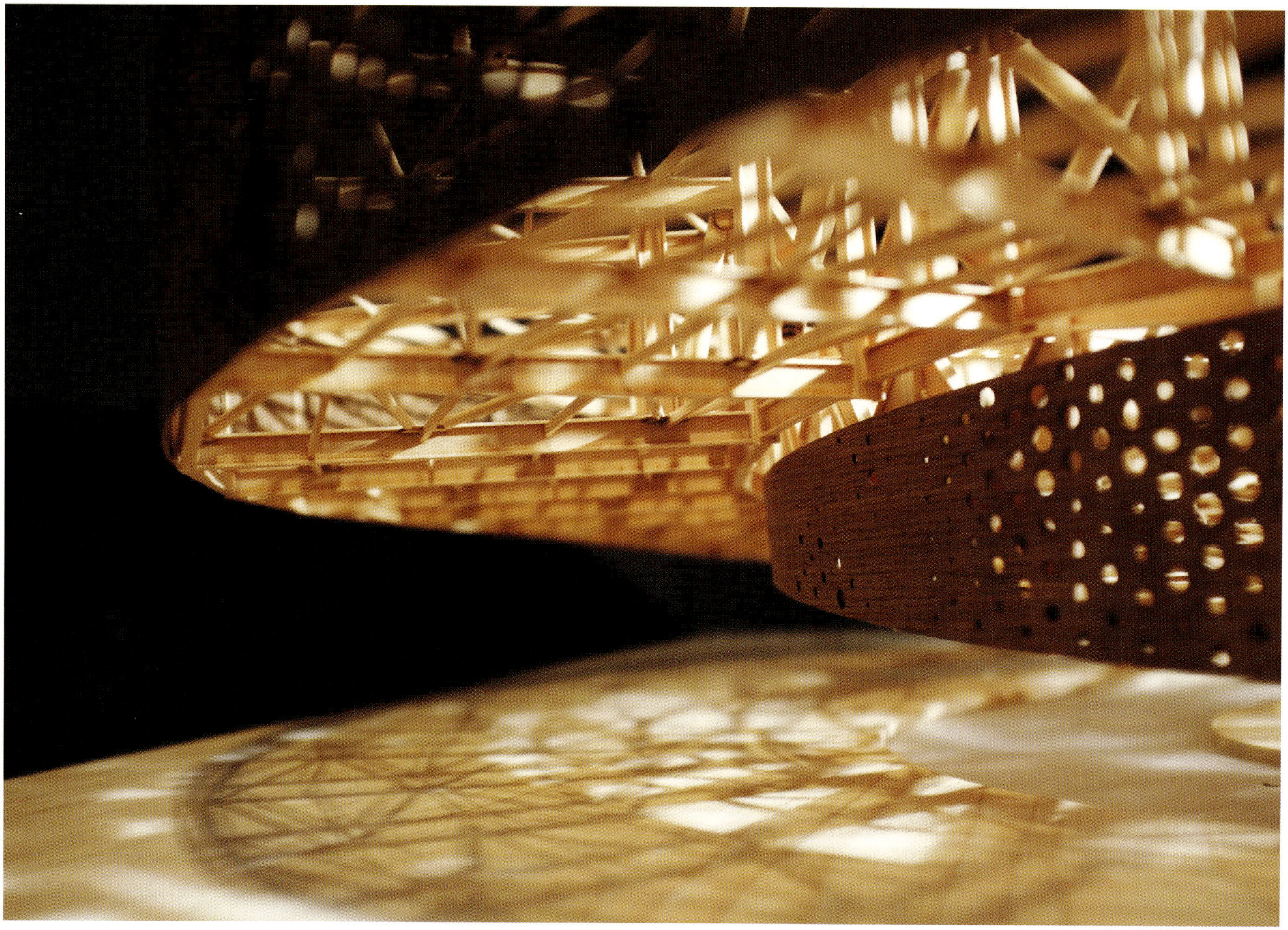

George X. Lin

Curving Tubular Trusses

Danish Pavilion, Shanghai Expo (2010)
Architect: BIG, Structural Engineer: Arup
Model: Daniel Toretsky + Allison Wills

Intended to showcase sustainable aspects of Denmark's urban lifestyle, this pavilion was conceived as a loop in which visitors could bicycle or walk in a continuous circuit. While this basic idea is conceptually simple, its geometrical and structural realization are not. A rectangular tube of 4.5m (15ft) depth curves around/over/under itself; all four sides work together as a "box-beam", a structural form highly efficient in resisting transverse and torsional loads, thus enabling the pavilion's dramatic cantilevers. The inner façade of the tube is visually closed and hides a truss behind it, while the outer one consists of an 8mm (3/8") thick, stiffened steel plate; perforations admit light and subtly vary according to structural demand.

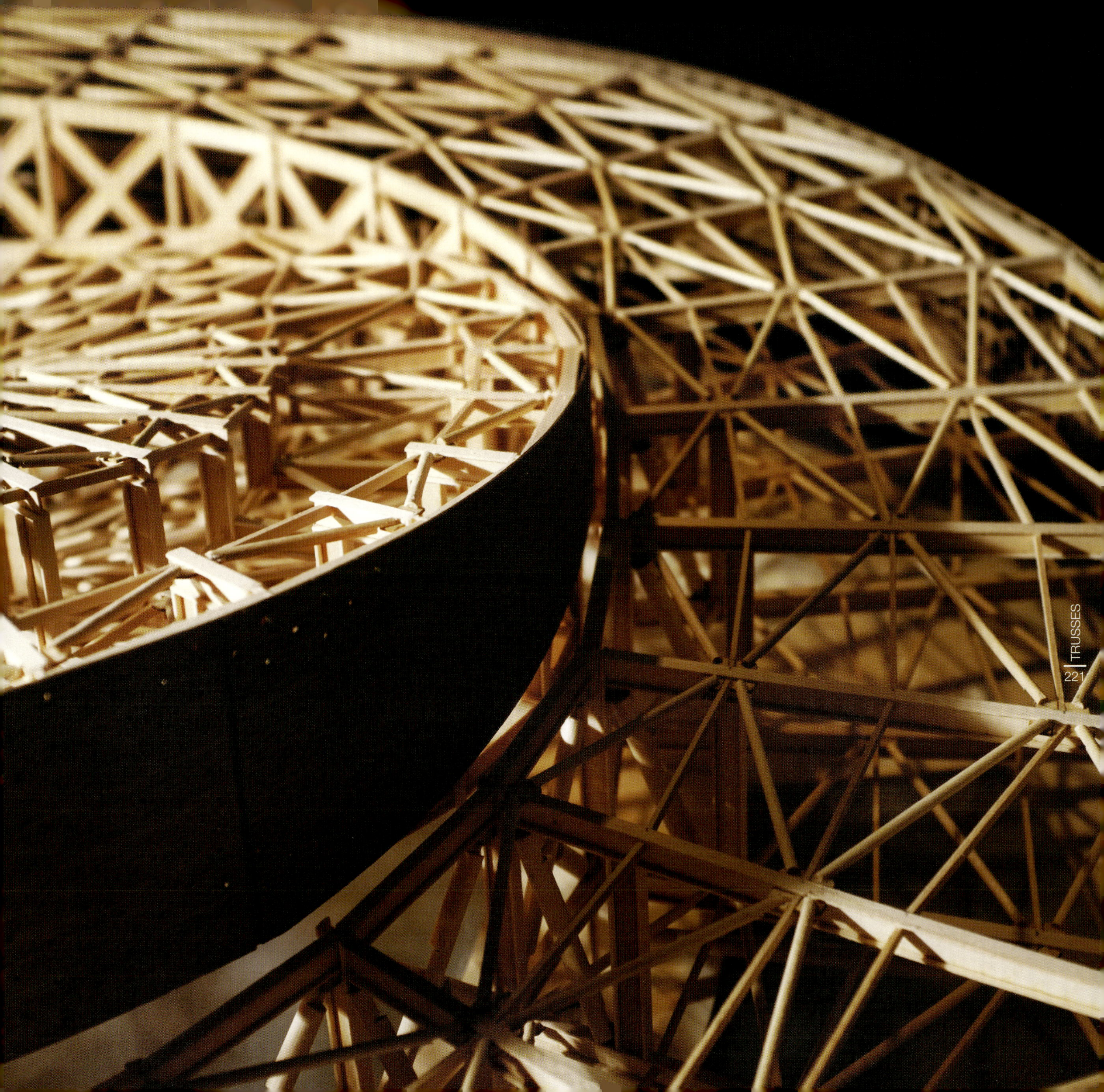

01

02

03

04

05

06

01,02 Vierendeel truss carries one side of roof, opens wall – Archery Hall, Kogakuin University, Tokyo, Japan, 2013; FT Architects; model by Yichen Jia & Ji Eun Lee **03. Truss diagonals change inclination to remain in tension** – Excavation canopy, Cartagena, Spain, 2011; Amann Cánovas Maruri Architects; José Cerezo Ingeniería; model by Catie Ely & Ruby Kaur **04. Radial truss arrangement** – Congress Center, Badajoz, Spain, 2006; SelgasCano (arch.); José Romo - Fhecor (eng.); model by Tyler Barker & Heidi Schmitt **05. Trusses enable long-span roof; braced frames stabilize pavilion** – Franch Pavilion, Seville, Spain, Expo 1992; Jean-Paul Viguier et Associés (arch.); ARCORA (eng.); model by Matt Davitt **06. Trussed canopy supported by asymmetrical buildings** – Inter-Junction City Housing, Yokohama, Japan, 1993; Riken Yamamoto & Field Shop (arch.); Imai Consulting Structural Engineer, Plus One Structural Des. & Eng. Firm; model by John Noe **07. Trusses support ends of one-way beams** – Inca Public Market, Inca, Majorca, Spain, 2011; Chermaine Lay + Carles Muro (arch.); GMK Associats, BOMA (eng.); model by Shinhyuk Kim & Piotr Nowakowski **08. Angled wooden roof trusses and braced frames open workshop space** – GMIT Letterfrack Furniture College – Machine Hall, Co. Galway, Wales, 2001; O'Donnell + Tuomey Architects; model by Katie O'Regan **09. Light space frame roof contrasts with heavy masonry walls** – Primary School, Gando, Burkina Faso, 2001; Diébédo Francis Kéré (arch.); Eddy Widyaya (eng.); model by Aaron Goldstein & Colin Stratford **10. Space-frame-supported residence** – Bentham House, Almere, Netherlands, 1984; Bentham Crouwel Architekten bna; Ingenieursburo Starsman (eng.); model by Colin Sieburgh **11. Small-scale-trussed floor joists; diagonals stabilize frame and support balcony** – Schulitz House, Beverly Hills, CA, USA, 1976; Schulitz Architects; Kurily and Szymanski (eng.); model by Jonathan Arnold

12

13

14

15

12. Cantilevering trusses – diagonals angled to be in tension – International Garden and Horticultural Exhibition Pavilion, Shizuoka, Japan, 2004; Kengo Kuma and Associates (arch.); Norihide Imagawa (eng.); model by Sean Steed & Andrew Wong **13,17. Composite glulam and steel trusses; bowed profile varies with bending moment** – Parco della Musica Auditorium; Rome, Italy, 2002; RPBW (arch.); Arup (eng.); models by Anna Grohn and Michael Esposito, respectively **14. Story-height truss hung off core; tension diagonals change orientation at mid-span** – ArtsQuest Center, Bethlehem, PA, USA, 2011; Spillman Farmer Architects; Barry Isett & Associates (eng.); model by XiaoXaio Li & Ying Xu **15. Occupiable trussed tube; side walls, roof & floor are trussed** – Sifang Art Museum, Nanjing, China, 2011; Steven Holl Architects; Guy Nordenson and Associates (eng. consultants); model by Kenneth Chow & Stefan Krawitz **16. Cantilevering trussed building; gusset plate connection detail represents effective pin joint** – Willian J. Clinton Presidential Library, Little Rock, AR, USA, 2004; Polshek Partnership/Ennead Architects; Leslie E. Robertson Associates (eng.); model by Alexandra Lima & Taylor Stollbert **18,20. Cardboard tube space frame roof canopy** – Information Center, Singapore Biennale 2006; Shigeru Ban Architects; model by Alex Iida **19. Trussed "reciprocal frame" system; cable propped off top helps resist uplift** – Bibracte excavation canopy, Mont Beuvray, France, 2008; Paul Andreu (arch.); RFR Group / TESS (eng.); model by Lingbo Fan & Yilia (Willow) Hong **21. Trusses enable long spans; few points of support allow roof to "float" above ground** – Aquatics Centre, London, UK, 2011; Zaha Hadid Architects; Arup (eng.); model by Alvaro Alvares & Benjamin Waters **22. Variable depth roof trusses follow bending moment demand; trussed columns; knee brace creates rigid frame** – Carraro Residence, Kyle, TX, USA, 1990; Lake|Flato Architects; model by Cyrus Dochow

16

17

18

19

20

21

22

CHAPTER FIVE

Frames

The rational clarity of planar framework must have had an enormous effect, even on the compositional aspects of architecture. Not only because it was natural to build with the planes that construction technology provided, but also because its incipient rational clarity gave the plane a peculiar force that, on the other hand, coincided with formal investigations that were at the root of the Modern Movement. This plane that vibrates with a kind of religious fervor, can be seen in the works of Le Corbusier, Gropius and Mies van der Rohe.

Eladio Dieste

The Fair Store by William Le Baron Jenney, Chicago, 1892

At its most fundamental, the structural building frame is a two- or three-dimensional combination of beams and columns that opens up space for occupation, for circulation, for viewing things, or for things being viewed. Thus, diverting ever-present gravity loads "sideways" via its beams and then transferring them vertically downward through the columns is a primary function of the frame. But frames also can serve an essential role in stabilizing buildings against lateral forces, perhaps by means of bending behavior and rigid connections between the column and beam elements – in which case we label it a rigid frame – or else by incorporating diagonals and then calling it a braced frame instead. Frames can have a wide range of sizes from micro- to mega-scale, they can be a single portal or multi-bay and/or multi-story, and they can be made from virtually the full range of materials available for construction. No matter what their overall configuration, though, the key to how frames function is also to be found in their details, including members' cross-sectional shapes and orientations, their sometimes-varying dimensions, as well as in the design of their connections.

In his classic essay *The Chicago Frame*, architectural historian/theoretician/critic Colin Rowe elaborates on the remarkable impact on design resulting from the development of the metal building frame in Chicago during the late 1800s/early 1900s. But Rowe also somewhat unexpectedly debunks the commonly-held view that Frank Lloyd Wright's equally exceptional Chicago-based architecture was derived from the innovation of the skeletal frame; on the contrary, Rowe argues that it was as a result of his distinct lack of interest in the frame that Wright was able to develop his contrasting approach. The frame, then, can also act as a foil for design; in Wright's case, at least, this is demonstrably no less important a role for it to have played…

To Frame – or not to Frame…

The Chicago Frame
Colin Rowe

The skeleton of the steel or concrete frame is almost certainly the most recurrent motif in contemporary architecture and is surely among the most ubiquitous of what Siegfried Giedion would have designated its *constituent elements*. Perhaps the role of the frame is most aptly summarized in the drawing by which Le Corbusier illustrated the structural system of his experimental Domino House; but, while its primary function is evident, apart from this practical value, the frame has obviously acquired a significance that is less recognized.

Apparently the neutral grid of space that is enclosed by the skeleton structure supplies us with some particularly cogent and convincing symbol, and for this reason the frame has established relationships, defined a discipline, and generated form. The frame has been the catalyst of an architecture, but one might notice that the frame has also become architecture, that contemporary architecture is almost inconceivable in its absence. Thus, one recalls innumerable buildings where the frame puts in an appearance even when not structurally necessary; one has seen buildings where the frame appears to be present when it is not; and, since the frame seems to have acquired a value quite beyond itself, one is often prepared to accept these aberrations. For, without stretching the analogy too far, it might be fair to say that the frame has come to possess a value for contemporary architecture equivalent to that of the column for classical antiquity and the Renaissance. Like the column, the frame establishes throughout the building a common ratio to which all the parts are related; and, like the vaulting bay in the Gothic cathedral, it prescribes a system to which all parts are subordinate.

It is the universality of the frame and the ease with which it has apparently directed our plastic judgment that has led to the focusing of so much attention on the Chicago commercial architecture of the 1880s and early 1890s. In Chicago, seemingly, our own interests were so directly anticipated that if, as we apparently sometimes conceive it to be, the frame structure is the essence of modern architecture, then we can only assume a relationship between ourselves and Chicago comparable to that between the High Renaissance architects and Florence, or the High Gothic architects and the Île-de-France. For, although the steel frame did make occasional undisguised appearances elsewhere, it was in Chicago that its formal results were most rapidly elucidated.

For some ten years, the architects of Chicago devoted themselves to the solution of typical problems of the frame; and, before the end of this time, they had achieved results that are still today unsurpassed for their elegance and economy. But, admiring these results and acknowledging this great achievement, one is still disposed to ask of these Chicago buildings whether they are indeed representatives of a "modern" architecture. Certainly the process of their design was as rational and as direct as that of any modern building is supposed to be. Certainly these buildings are lacking in both rhetoric and sentimental excess; but, also, there is about them a quality of rudimentary magnificence, a flavor at once more heroic and more brutal than is to be found in any building of the present day. These structures make no compromise with the observer; they are neither capricious nor urbane, and they display an authenticity so complete that we are disposed to accept them as facts of nature, as geological manifestations rather than as architectural achievements. "In Chicago," says Louis Sullivan, "the tall building would seem to have arisen spontaneously in response to favourable physical conditions.... The Future looked bright. The flag was in the breeze." [1] In Chicago we are led to believe that the slate was at last wiped clean, the break with "the styles" was made, and the route of future development defined.

The alleged debacle that overwhelmed these Chicago architects of the 1880s is common knowledge. The World Columbian Exhibition cut short their development; public taste no longer endorsed their decisions; and, although for some few their principles remained luminous, it was not until comparatively recently that their figures reemerged, sanctified and established in the pantheon of architectural progress.

Still, the disaster was never quite so complete as our sense of myth requires that it should have been; and, as we know, pockets of resistance survived which eclecticism could not obliterate, so that it was again in Chicago that a second and equally decisive contribution to present-day architecture was made. Montgomery Schuyler, one of the most devoted apologists of the Chicago School, writing of the city in the 1890s, noticed that its architectural expressions were twofold: "places of business and places of residences." The image of Chicago that remained in the mind he found to be "the sum of innumerable impressions made up exclusively of the skyscraper of the city and the dwellings of the suburbs. Not a church enters into it," he says, "Scarcely a public building enters into it.... Chicago has no more a Nouvel Opera than it has a Notre Dame." [2] It was a relatively uncomplicated situation which Schuyler recognized, a situation dominated by two building types—the commercial structures of the Loop and their suburban complement. With the 1890s, the spirit of experiment may be said simply to have transferred itself from one of these types to the other, so that it became in Oak Park that Frank Lloyd Wright was to conduct those researches into architectural form whose results now seem to have been preeminently superior to any other achievement of that day. The much-publicized contributions of van de Velde, of Horta, Olbrich, Hoffmann, Loos, Perret, Mackintosh, and Voysey can only appear as irresolute and undirected when compared with the astonishing finality of these early works of Wright's, which although less implacable than the office buildings of the Loop, are every bit as conclusive. These houses are the monuments of an unerringly consistent development, and to informed observers of the time it was apparent that here a plastic statement of the very highest relevance was in process of delivery, that here a definite answer had already been given to those questions that many of the most advanced buildings of the day seemed to exist merely to propose.

The international impact of this early phase of Wright's career is a matter of history; and, if the exact influence that the publication of his work exerted in Europe may remain a matter of dispute, it can scarcely be denied that in such a building as the Gale House of 1909 Wright had already defined principles of form that at least very closely parallel those enunciated ten years later by van Doesburg or Rietveld in *de Stijl's* major architectural monument, the Schroder House of 1924. In each case the vision of an architecture as a composition of sliding planes predominates; and Wright's anticipation of this idea seems to have been as complete as Chicago's earlier anticipation of the formal role that the frame structure was destined to play.

This priority of Chicago's contribution need not imply a dependence elsewhere on it. Obviously both van Doesburg and Rietveld could claim a legitimate descent from the innovations that Cubism had introduced; obviously too, Le Corbusier's preoccupation with problems of the frame structure derives not from the steel skeleton of Chicago but from the reinforced concrete frame of Auguste Perret. But neither of these observations can obscure the apparent evidence that Chicago did seem to experience a prevision of two of the major themes of twentieth-century architecture—the frame structure and the composition of intersecting planes.

This apparent insight of Chicago's is widely recognized; but its recognition has created certain acute critical problems. Wright's achievement was scarcely likely to pass into oblivion, but the renewed consciousness of Chicago's earlier contribution, which has been stimulated by the later work of Mies van der Rohe, is responsible for a conspicuous interpretative embarrassment. Thus, although we know it to be different in kind, we are apt to feel that Mies's campus of the Illinois Institute of Technology is the polished culmination of a rationalism identical with that displayed by Jenney in the second Leiter Building, but, equally, we are obliged to believe that at least a partial explanation of the intuitive certainty, which so early distinguished Wright's work, was provided by his own personal relationship with the older masters of the Chicago School. We can understand that his own audaciousness was reinforced by their daring, his own sense of order by theirs, his own precocity by those qualities which have led so many observers to see in the commercial buildings of Chicago the most complete adumbration of contemporary forms.

It is at this point that the judgment of the present day discovers its dilemma. We may assert that the architects of the office buildings in the Loop clarified a basic disposition of twentieth century architecture, yet for the structural skeleton that their achievement exposed, it can only be said that Wright (who might be considered their most illustrious pupil) seems to have shown a most marked distaste.

With the exception of the Larkin Building in Buffalo and the S.C. Johnson Company's Administration Building at Racine, Wright has, of course, built no large office buildings; and it might therefore be claimed that he had no reason to employ the frame structure. Even in the Larkin Building, the cathedral-like internal space suggests a certain aversion to those conclusions of the Chicago School whose relevance is so enthusiastically acclaimed today, while in the Johnson Administration Building an entirely different conception of structure is entertained. Admittedly a number of early skyscraper projects, including the Luxfer Prism Skyscraper and the Abraham Lincoln Center, are for steel-frame buildings; and, in 1912, the Press Building for San Francisco shows a concrete frame. But in all of these designs, a Sullivanian influence is to be detected, and in none of them are we made aware of that inimitable world of Wrightian form which characterizes the domestic designs of the same years. We can believe that, in all these instances, Wright was struggling with a problem that he felt to be intractable and found to be unsympathetic. It is not until the National Life Insurance Company Skyscraper project of 1924 that this problem seems to become clarified and we find the sharp revelation of the differences in outlook that identify Wright's development as something apart from that of his predecessors in Chicago.

The classic Chicago office buildings, like the classic palaces of Renaissance Italy, were conceived as single volumes, or when situation did not permit the appearance of a volume, as single facades. Like Italian *palazzi* they overwhelm the observer by their economy of motif and consistency of theme, while, as architectural expression, they present no more than an unmodified surface exhibiting a rationally integrated and well-proportioned structure. But Wright's building is distinguished by the observance of quite contrary principles. Rather than a single structurally articulated block, it displays a highly developed composition of transparent volumes, while rather than the "static" structural solution of the frame, it presents the more "dynamic" motif of the cantilever, which had already been employed in the Imperial Hotel. Thus, while conceptually this building is radically distinct from Chicago's earlier contributions to skyscraper design whose architects had attempted neither such elaboration nor such openness, technically it is also distinct, since both its construction and its curtain wall constitute an innovation in the Chicago tradition.

According to Henry-Russell Hitchcock, "Wright has likened the special construction used in the [Imperial] Hotel to the balance of a tray on a waiter's fingers,"[3] and the structural members both in that building and in the 1924 project do seem to have been conceived in that way as a series of nuclei generating around themselves intelligible volumes of space. This preference, already presumed by Wright's old preoccupation with the central chimney stack, must explain some of his reluctance to use a regular skeletal frame, which scarcely permits such an interpretation of structure. But the indivisible fusion of structure and space, which Wright has designated "organic," is scarcely realized in either the Tokyo building or the National Life Insurance Company project, and it is not until the St. Mark's Tower scheme of 1929 that it first becomes explicit at a major scale.

The spaces created by the St. Mark's Tower are at last of an unmistakably Wrightian order, and, understandably, the tower has been the prototype for all the tall buildings by him that have followed. Aggregations of St. Mark's Towers are the basis for the 1930 apartment-house project and again for the Crystal Heights Hotel design of 1940, while the tower appears in condensed form as the laboratory building at Racine, Wisconsin, before being finally transcribed as the Price Office Building at Bartlesville, Oklahoma.

Conceptually all these structures present the nucleus of a gigantic mushroom column supporting a series of trays, which, as shown by the apartment-house and hotel projects, is implied to be systematically extensible by approaching column to column until the circumferences of their trays impinge or even overlap. Like the central core of the chimney and the real mushroom columns of the Johnson Administration Building, the idea of the St. Mark's Tower may seem to derive from the "organic" demand for the integration of space and structure; and, as fulfilling this demand, the building becomes a single, complete, and self-explanatory utterance.

As an extension of the domestic theme, the St. Mark's Tower is among Wright's most brilliant and ingenious achievements, and the virtuosity with which it is organized can only arouse the greatest admiration. Its vitality and coherence are undeniable, its plastic control little short of awe inspiring. Admitting the basic premises on which its inspiration depends, the tower is a superbly logical development, but for very many observers, both it and its derivatives can only stand as a series of enlarged question marks. Admiring it as an individual achievement, recognizing it as a highly suggestive exception, these observers are still disposed to ask whether after all it is not a most elaborate evasion of a normal and standard structural fact. The frame, by so many modern architects, has been received almost as a heaven-sent blessing. Why, one inquires, has it been so distinctly rejected on the part of Wright? Did he consider it a merely adventitious shortcut to unimportant solutions? Did he consider it too great a restriction of a "creative" freedom? Just why did he remain so very unbeguiled by Chicago's first great architectural discovery?

The question is so pressing that one may be justified in proceeding with speculation, and a number of immediate answers suggest themselves. The answer that Wright's career has been largely in the field of domestic architecture considers the problem only superficially. The use of the steel or concrete frame in domestic architecture may not be necessary, but many conspicuous monuments of the modern movement survive to prove it not abnormal. The answer that America had already discovered an alternative structure in the balloon frame is more convincing, but not completely so. Economy in America recommended the balloon frame, but in Europe economy equally recommended a brick or masonry structure, and by the more significant innovators economy's recommendations were frequently disregarded.

A partial answer has already been suggested in the notice of Wright's highly developed and individual demand for "organic" space, and here one of the most obvious differences between him and his predecessors in Chicago may be found. Louis Sullivan, for instance, was by no means typical of the Chicago School in general, but a major and unnoticed distinction between Wright and Sullivan, as also between Wright and his other Chicago predecessors, may be found in their feeling for the plan.

For Wright, as for Le Corbusier, the plan has always been a generator of form. If the plans of his earliest buildings are in no way remarkable, by the Blossom House of 1892 it is quite clear that a disciplined orchestration of spaces had become one of his primary interests, while almost any of his houses of the next thirty years will reveal how intensively this interest was sustained. Wright's *partis* (architectural schemes) develop without apparent effort. There are few lapses in his plans, few volumes where his basic rhythms are not experienced, and, in all this, he is very definitely to be distinguished from Sullivan, whose most ardent admirers have never claimed for him any highly developed interest in the formal possibilities of the plan. Sullivan's buildings may often be superb assertions of the primacy of structure, but one finds it hard to believe that for him the significance of their plans was other than a negative one. The plans of the Wainwright and Schiller buildings, for instance, are hardly those of a master, while such a plan as that of the National Farmer's Bank at Owatonna, Minnesota, will scarcely bear analysis.

Sullivan was not primarily a planner. Indeed, there was little in his practice that could prompt him to any sophisticated evaluation of the plan. Sullivan was primarily an architect of commercial buildings; and, of all buildings, the office block is obviously that without the need of any but the minimum of planning. It requires elementary circulations and a well-lit floor area; but apart from these, it neither can nor should present any spatial elaboration. Thus, the unobstructed evenly lit floor and the indefinite number of floors that it permitted recommended the steel frame to the architects of Chicago as the answer to a practical dilemma; but also, by the nature of the context in which they explored it, they were necessarily inhibited in the exploration of its spatial possibilities.

With a lack of stylistic prejudice and with a discretion, which seem remarkable to us today, the Chicago architects projected onto their facades the neutral structure that they felt to be the reality of the frame behind. If, as was the case with Sullivan's Wainwright Building in Saint Louis and his Guaranty Building in Buffalo, it was considered aesthetically desirable that the frame should be modified, this process was rationalized in terms of the need for psychological expressiveness in the facade rather than in any need for internal spatial excitement.

With little occasion to use the frame for any other program than that of the office building, it is not surprising that the Chicago architects remained unaware of certain of its attributes, so that some explanation of Wright's unwillingness to employ it may possibly be found here. To repeat: unlike Sullivan, who had approached architecture primarily with the object of realizing an expressive structure, Wright was, from the first, abnormally sensitive to the demands of an expressive space. These demands (one might surmise) he was compelled to satisfy, and it was only later (one might believe) that his Sullivanian training reasserted itself to demand a rationalization of this spatial achievement in terms of a generating structure. The monumental construction of the Hillside Home School suggests that a rationalization of this kind was already underway around 1902, and, by 1904, in the Martin House, this process had taken on unmistakable definition. By then, and supposing Wright to have wished a predominantly structural rationale, his space compositions were already of a richness that would scarcely permit their accommodation within any system so austere as that provided by the Chicago frame.

However, an answer along these lines, suggesting that a cause for Wright's rejection of the frame may be discovered exclusively in the nature of his formal will, can at best provide only a partial explanation of the problem, and a further reason must be offered that may, perhaps, be found to lie in the varieties of significance with which the frame has been endowed.

At the present day, Chicago's failure to arrive at any statement of the frame as a vehicle of spatial expression seems to be curious. We are now completely accustomed to regard the skeleton structure as a spatial instrument of some power, since it is, after all, some considerable time ago that a formula was evolved permitting the simultaneous appearance of both structural grid and considerable spatial complexity, and most of modern architecture, the so-called International Style, may be said to have been dependent on this formula.

In order to arrive at an equation of the demands of space and structure, Le Corbusier and Mies van der Rohe had been led to postulate their functional independence, for example, the independence of partitions from columns. In contrast, Wright's development, which may be said to proceed from a conviction as to the "organic" unity of space and structure, the International Style may be seen to issue from an assumption of the separate existence of both according to distinct laws. Wright's structure creates space or is created by it, but in the International Style an autonomous structure perforates a freely abstracted space, acting as its punctuation rather than its defining form. There is thus in the International Style no fusion of space and structure, but each in the end remains an identifiable component, and architecture is conceived not as their confluence but, rather, as their dialectical opposition, as a species of debate between them.

That a solution in these terms was possible for European innovators of the 1920s derives, among other reasons, from a particular concept of the frame which they entertained—that such a concept was neither possible, nor to be envisaged, in Chicago of the 1890s must be partly explained by a different significance which was there attributed to the skeleton structure. In Chicago it might be said that the frame was convincing as fact rather than as idea, whereas in considering the European innovators of the 1920s one cannot suppress the supposition that the frame to them was much more often an essential idea before it was an altogether reasonable fact.

In order to clarify these too-general observations, a classic Chicago building, Holabird and Roche's McGlurg Building of 1899-1900, might be paralleled with an almost contemporary European building of 1897, Horta's Maison du Peuple in Brussels. Both of the projects, though different in function, are comparable as advanced buildings of their day. Both show preoccupation with problems of the frame, but it is the contrast between the rather quiet elegance of the first and the frenetic restlessness of the second which is immediately apparent. The McGlurg Building is a subtle and uncomplicated statement. The Maison du Peuple is an oblique and a highly involved reference. In the McGlurg Building it is possible to suppose that certain practical requirements have been accommodated; in the Maison du Peuple it is impossible not to deduce that certain theoretical desiderata have been stated. In the first, the steel frame presents itself as the solution of a specific problem, while in the second, a cast-iron prevision of the steel frame is exposed apparently as the manifesto of an architectural program. Holabird and Roche's structure is primarily a building; Horta's is predominantly a polemic.

There is little doubt that Horta's building cost the greater aesthetic effort, but there is almost complete certainty that Holabird and Roche's is more generally pleasing to the taste of the present day. Of Holabird and Roche's self-consciousness, however, the McGlurg Building offers no assurance, while of Horta's sophistication the Maison du Peuple is indisputable evidence. In Horta's case one can guess at a hyperawareness of the response his building was likely to evoke. One can sense the anticipation of extended controversy, critical explanations, avant-garde delight, conservative horror. The Maison du Peuple is a building offered to a society, and whether society will accept or reject it, Horta still assumes its participation as an audience. That is, Horta invites reaction, and, accordingly, the Maison du Peuple exhibits a humanity that the McGlurg Building does not display. For there, rather than any subject for the discussion of a coterie, Holabird and Roche have attempted to provide no more than the rational envelope for the activities of their clients' tenants.

Indeed, if the methods followed by Holabird and Roche at this time were in any way typical of the Chicago School in general, it might safely be assumed that they were definitely not anxious that their building should involve them in any of the excitements of artistic notoriety. In the word of the French novelist Paul Bourget, whose appreciations of the Chicago School have been constantly quoted, the Chicago architects had "frankly accepted the conditions imposed by the speculator" [4]—they had limited themselves to producing buildings that should be no more than the logical instruments of investment. In other words, being in no position to make manifestos in the cause of rationalism, they were simply obliged—and within the strictest terms—to be as rational as they might.

This distinction between two styles of argument (it is really a question of the idea of mechanization versus the fact) would seem to crystallize the basic differences of approach signified by the two buildings, and it is a distinction that might be extended further. "I asked one of the successful architects of Chicago what would happen if the designer of a commercial building sacrificed the practical availableness of one of its floors to the assumed exigencies of architecture as has often been done in New York," writes Schuyler. "His answer," he continues, "[was] 'Why the word would be passed around and he would never get another one to do. No, we never try tricks on our businessmen, they are too wide awake.'" [5] The businessmen of Chicago, then, were not prepared to make sacrifices for the idea, did not require the overt architectural symbolism that was apparently necessary in New York, did not even require those fantasies on mechanistic themes that could be obtruded on the citizens of Brussels; but the Chicago architects (or some of them) were still quite aware that symbolic meaning had ever been among the necessary attributes of architecture; and if, as Schuyler infers, they were compelled to be utilitarian, they were not always unconscious of the social significance of their utilitarianism. John Root, for instance, required that the modern office building should by its "mass and proportion convey in some elemental sense an idea of the great, stable, conserving forces of modern civilization." [6]

But, even in this demand, one might continue to notice a difference between Chicago and Brussels. In Belgium, Siegfried Giedion tells us, it had been discovered that architectural *forms* were impure, that the atmosphere was "infected," and that, in consequence, architectural "progress" was there conceived as a kind of "moral revolt." [7] But the Chicago architects had been scarcely allowed to subject *forms* to so detached a scrutiny, and had they enjoyed the leisure to do so, if their conclusions had conflicted with the requirements of the speculator, it is to be doubted whether they would have been enabled to put them into practice. "The great, stable, conserving forces of modern civilization" (or, perhaps, the great, expanding forces of a *laissez-faire* economic system?) represented for Root a power which it was desirable to express. But for Horta? One must doubt if Horta recognized any such imperative. He, one suspects, had arrived at certain critical conclusions as to the nature of contemporary society and had come then to envisage his work as the architectural manifestation of these judgments.

In Belgium, it is evident, the *art nouveau* was one of those revolutionary movements essentially dependent on a highly developed program; but in Chicago, it should be clear that the structural revolution was largely without any such theoretical support.

"The Chicago activity in erecting high buildings (of solid masonry) finally attracted the attention of the local sales managers of

Eastern rolling mills," Sullivan tells us, and it was *they*, he says, who conceived of the idea of a skeleton that would carry the entire weight of the building. From then on, he continues, the evolution of the steel frame "was a matter of vision in salesmanship based upon engineering imagination and technique," and, in this manner, as a *product for sale*, "the idea of the steel frame was tentatively presented to Chicago architects." Sullivan asserts:

> *The passion to sell is the impelling power of American life. Manufacturing is subsidiary and adventitious. But selling must be based on a semblance of service—the satisfaction of a need. The need was there, the capacity to satisfy was there, but contact was not there. Then there came the flash of imagination which saw the single thing. The trick was turned and there swiftly came into being something new under the sun.* [8]

The Chicago structural revolution therefore was the result of a certain combination of ruthless open-mindedness and imaginative salesmanship. On Sullivan's admission, the architects of Chicago did not *demand* the frame; it was *presented* to them, and this simple fact may explain both the rapid and dispassionate manner in which they contrived to rationalize the frame structure and the way in which so many of them were able to abandon their method for another and different one. "The architects of Chicago," Sullivan adds, "welcomed the steel frame and did something with it. The architects of the East were appalled by it and could make no contribution to it." But from Schuyler we learn the opposite, that the architects of Chicago were not very different from architects elsewhere. "They are," he writes, "different on compulsion.... [They have] frankly accepted the conditions imposed by the speculator, because they really are imposed, and there is no getting away from them if one would win and keep the reputation of a 'practical' architect." [9]

Taken together, these two statements are confusing, but they are not perhaps as contradictory as at first they may appear. They describe a situation; they suggest a lack of theoretical awareness; they indicate a responsiveness to the new; and they illustrate a willingness to defer to the client. And the clients, Schuyler continues,

> *the men who project and finance the utilitarian buildings [are not] the most private spirited [but] they are the most public spirited body of businessmen of any commercial city in the world. [They are] the same men who are ready to incur expenditures for public purposes with a generosity and a public spirit that are elsewhere unparalleled. They are willing to make the most generous sacrifices for their city to provide it with ornaments and trophies which shall make it more than a centre of pig sticking and grain handling. They are willing to play the part of Maecenas to the fine arts, only they insist that they will not play it during business hours.*

The candor of these contemporary observations goes a long way to dispose of a critical scheme to which nowadays we pay our respects. It disposes of the dichotomy between the virtuous Chicago of the Loop and the depraved Chicago of the Fair. Magnificently undisguised, the office buildings of the Loop owe something of their authenticity to their being no more than the rationalization of business requirements, and although they are social documents of the highest importance, in spite of Root's endeavors they are scarcely, in any deliberate and even sense, cultural symbols. They were conceived as the means to achievement, and for what was thought to be that achievement itself, it is necessary to look elsewhere, presumably both to the suburban residential development and to "the ornaments and trophies," the unparalleled expenditures, and "the generous sacrifices," of which those lavished on the World Columbian exhibition can only appear the most outstanding.

Thus, seen in terms of the admirable pragmatism that actually reared the buildings of the Loop, which was responsible for their directness and lack of gesture, both these and the structures of the Fair, like opposite sides of a coin, come to appear as complementary phenomena. Because business and culture were conceived of as distinct activities, because the commercial magnates of Chicago were not willing "to play the part of Maecenas to the fine arts ... during business hours," it was possible for the architects of Chicago to proceed with the most audacious innovations; and, because in doing so they offended no expressed social or artistic preference, no check was offered to their remorseless evolution of a basic structural logic. As Schuyler tells us, this rationalization could not have been effected in New York. It could not, as we know, have been effected in Europe. It was possible in Chicago because there *business* was without inhibition; but unhappily, as the World Columbian Exhibition proves, *business* was not for this reason irresponsible.

Thus, what to us appears to have been Chicago's success and Chicago's failure were implicit in the same conditions. A primary architectural achievement was determined by the urgency of a physical need and by the lack of a specifically architectural program, and as a result an apparently complete architectural revolution was made possible.

But just this lack of program in the end made it not possible for this revolution to become decisive. The office buildings of the Loop were undoubtedly admired by contemporaries, but, however rational their structure and however immaculate their form, it is hard to represent them as the response to any very adequately acceptable notion of society. They invoked no completely receivable public standards; they stipulated only private gain; and for the taste of the time, which had not yet sufficiently expanded, or contracted, to be able to envisage the machine with a poetic bias, they were not so much architecture as they were equipment. Stimulating facts they might be, but they were scarcely to be received as facts of culture.

Distinctions such as these which go some way to clarify the other than technical and formal differences between a McGlurg Building and a Maison du Peuple, necessarily elicit questions of attitudes and mythologies. Such questions might possibly be brought into sharper focus by the brief analysis of a further pair of buildings that, in *Space, Time and Architecture*, Siegfried Giedion was led to compare: Daniel Burnham's Reliance Building of 1894 and Mies van der Rohe's Glass Tower project of 1921.

It is the similarity of these buildings with which Giedion is concerned; and, in terms of a Wölfflinian background such as his, which tends to ignore problems of content (implying that roughly identical forms suppose roughly approximate meaning), it is the common likeness of the American building and the German project which will command attention. But, if we have here, very obviously, two extensively glazed office towers, it is fundamentally not their similarity but their unlikeness which should most seriously involve us—and particularly so since to emphasize their unlikeness need not involve any great exercise of critical acuity.

Reliance Building by Burnham and Root, Chicago, 1890

Thus, we have a building and a would-be building—the concrete result of a particular problem and the abstract solution of a general one—a building that services an existing requirement and a proposal that relates to a possible future need. We have something that answers and something that anticipates. The Reliance Building rises above the streets of a commercial capital; the Glass Tower soars against a background of wooded hills and above an agglomeration of Gothic roofs, and if we can scarcely believe the Glass Tower to be a necessity in this toy city of an older Germany, then also we may know it to be not only the project for an office building but also the advertisement for a cause. For, if the Reliance Building, very largely, *is what it is*, the Glass Tower, like the Maison du Peuple, very patently, *is something which it does not profess to be—a highly charged symbolic statement.* While the Reliance Building is almost devoid of ideological overtones, the Glass Tower is not only a presumptive building but also an implicit social criticism.

From these differences of innuendo both building and project derive their weakness and their strength: if the one lacks poetry, the other lacks prose. Burnham, one might guess, is someone optimistic about the present, who accepts the prevailing ethos and who envisages the future as its continuance, while Mies, one could suppose, is someone not able to collaborate with the existing, who is constrained to reject the established and who insists only on the justifications of time. Which is, of course, grossly to simplify. But, if Burnham's complicity and Mies's protestation may be equally respectable, they do impose on their respective products a quite different significance; and, while the Reliance Building remains a direct answer to a technical and functional problem, the Glass Tower, by inferring an altruistic order of society, continues to be both much less and much more than this. For, unlike the Reliance Building, the Glass Tower engages both the moral and the aesthetic interests of our Utopian sentiment.

In Europe in the 1920s it might be said that the tall building such as Mies had here projected presented itself primarily as a symbol rather than as any object for use. It was a symbol of a technologically oriented future society and, to a lesser degree, a symbol of an America which seemed to anticipate that future development; and thus, by circumstances, the idea of the tall building in Europe became imbued with an ultimate persuasiveness that in America it could not possess. In Europe the idea of the tall building was apt to be the substance of a dream, but in America the idea become fact was prone to be little more than an aspect of a too-emphatic reality. "The American engineers," wrote Le Corbusier, "overwhelm with their calculations our expiring architecture." They are not, he asserts, "in pursuit of an architectural idea"; rather they are "simply guided by the results of calculation."[10] And although this may have been as true of the Chicago architects of the 1880s as Le Corbusier felt it to be of the engineers of a later date, it is only too obvious that the skyscrapers of the *Ville Radieuse* are not the results of any comparable calculation. Rather they betray a mind preoccupied with the ideal order of things. They exude what Dr. Johnson described as "the grandeur of generality." They are rational abstractions on the theme of the American skyscraper rather than what the American skyscraper itself was—a rational calculation (with trimmings if necessary) as to the worthwhile investment in a given speculation.

We are here at the place where different conceptions as to what is real, rational, and logical exist side-by-side and to stigmatize any as being radical or conservative, irrelevant or relevant, is not to be very useful. Simply, it is best to say that, while in Chicago certain things (the culmination of an unbridled empiricism?) were done, there was an incapacity and/or refusal to conceive of them in other than specific terms, that they were construed without any regard for their proper enormity, that one has to look to those European skyscrapers that existed only in the imagination to discover any even slightly plausible, public rationale for what Chicago had produced, and that, just as the European innovators of the 1920s related the skyscraper not simply to commerce but to a notion of society as a whole—even implying that the skyscraper might be an agent of social salvation—so these same innovators also ascribed an ideal, a general, and an abstract function to the structural frame. In America, the skeleton structure, conceived to be of utilitarian value, had been rationalized by the predominantly utilitarian tone of a Chicago business community, but in Europe, where simple issues of utility could not assume such prominence, it was given a logical form only by the sustained volition of an architectural intelligentsia. For these avowed protagonists of revolution the frame became something other than what it had been for Chicago: it became an answer not to the specific problem—office building—but to the universal problem—architecture.

Le Corbusier's drawing for the Domino House represents precisely such an evaluation and is perhaps the perfect illustration of the meaning of the frame for the International Style. What we have here is not so much a structure as an icon, an object of faith which is to act as a guarantee of authenticity, an outward sign of a new order, an assurance against lapse into private license, a discipline by means of which an invertebrate expressionism can be reduced to the appearance of reason.

Disposed to accept the frame as much for reasons of dogma as utility, the International Style was therefore led to envisage it as enforcing a system with which the architect was *obliged* to come to terms, and, for this reason, the exponents of the International Style felt themselves under the necessity of evolving an equation between the demands of space and the demands of the skeleton structure. In Chicago, a comparable obligation could not exist, and, therefore, no comparable equation could be reached. There, where the frame served as no more than empirical convenience, it was scarcely to be invested with ideal significance. It could predicate no city of tomorrow. Indeed, by the 1890s, it predicated a city of yesterday; its overtones were not so much prophetic as they were historical. Since it soon became increasingly possible to see the frame structure as the nakedly irresponsible agent of a too-ruthless commercialism, so it became—not around the office building conceived as paradigmatic and normative, but around the alternative program of the residence—that idealist and progressivist sentiment was able to effect a coherent expression.

It is by such inferences that Wright's continual unwillingness to use the frame may possibly be explained. He was too close to it to be able to invest it with the iconographic content that it later came to possess, too close to the Loop to feel other than its abrasiveness and constriction, and too undetached from Chicago to see the city as the idea that it so nearly is and that the reforming mind of the 1920s might have wished it to become.

To attribute an iconographic content to the frame was, for better or worse (and unknowingly), the prerogative of the International Style. If one can understand how for Mies, preoccupied with anonymity—again with the idea and not the fact—his own self-willed and classical anonymity could be equated with the empirical anonymousness of the Chicago School, one may also perceive how for other exponents and apologists of the International Style, unacquainted with the sociopolitical detail of the Loop, its technical and formal effects must often have been seen as derived from the same details as had comparable effects in Europe. That is, because structural renovation was unconsciously associated with the will to complete social reform, the Loop could be seen as some surreptitious adumbration of a *Ville Radieuse* and that therefore an intention could be ascribed to its architects that they did not possess.

But in the Loop, unlike the *Ville Radieuse*, the world was accepted as found, and while it remains ironic that, in terms of forms, this midwestern acceptance should be so comparable to the discoveries of European protest, it should not be curious that for Wright the forms conceivable as representing protest should have to be sought elsewhere.

Freiderichstrasse Skyscraper project, Berlin. Drawing by Mies van der Rohe, 1921

The Propylaia to the Acropolis, Athens. Photo: Braun, Clément & Co., 1890. The J. Paul Getty Museum, Los Angeles

The Parthenon prominently features classical post-and-beam frame structures: surrounding the temple's central walled *cella*, for example, are multiple stone portals consisting of closely spaced columns capped by horizontal stone blocks that are pushed to their spanning limits as beams, all to support the original pedimented roof while opening up the space below to occupation. But elsewhere on the Acropolis one can also find frames that serve other, more symbolic purposes.

Martin-McAuliffe and Papadopoulos begin their essay about the Athenian hilltop citadel with a curious but seemingly minor observation: the Parthenon has been and is to this day typically photographed from an odd, skewed approach angle. This anomaly is at first explained as the result of the off-axis placement of the Great Propylaia, once an equally glorious framed structure that served as the "entry" portal into the Acropolis' walled upper precinct. Thus one is led to conclude that the Propylaia's location and alignment are likely the result of necessity for gaining access to this difficult hilltop site and thereby establishing, quiet by accident, the Parthenon's unusual photographic framing phenomenon. But another, more unexpected reason eventually emerges for this arrangement, for upon exiting the precinct through the Propylaia the visitor is confronted with a carefully framed view in the distant landscape of the site of a key Athenian military victory! In other words, this portal's specific alignment was anything but accidental; rather, it ensured that when leaving the Acropolis Athens' citizens were reminded of their city-state's preeminence one last time and in no uncertain terms. Frames, it turns out, can serve many functions.

Framing Views, Framing Victory

from *Framing Victory: Salamis, the Athenian Acropolis, and the Agora*
Samantha L. Martin-McAuliffe and John K. Papadopoulos

As the monumental ceremonial gateway to the Acropolis, [the Great Propylaia] structure frames the entrance to the citadel and sanctuary of Athena. Significantly, it was also the primary approach for all visitors in antiquity, as it is today. That the Propylaia is one of the most iconic buildings of ancient Athens and of Greek architecture in general is an understatement. Designed by the architect Mnesikles, and constructed from Pentelic marble between 437 and 432 BCE, the name refers to "gateways"—Propylaia—in the plural on account of the five doors of different sizes that pierce the cross-wall of the central hall.[1] So admired was this building that the central portion of the Mnesiklean Propylaia was copied in the second century CE by the architect of the Great Propylaia at the Sanctuary of Demeter and Persephone (Kore) at Eleusis.[2]

Straddling as it does the boundary between the sacred precinct within and the secular space outside, the Propylaia is topographically liminal. Jeffrey Hurwit refers to it as both a termination and a prelude.[3] For Hurwit, as for most scholars of Greek art and architecture, the Propylaia serves two primary functions. First of all, it provides a monumental setting for the culmination of the Panathenaic Way—and thus the ceremonial passage up to the Acropolis at the time of the festival of the Panathenaia.[4] Robin Rhodes elaborates on this, contending that the western elevation of the gateway articulates the procession of the Panathenaia itself; its two pediments step upward, as if echoing the passage of people up the slope of the citadel.[5] Secondly, the gateway prepares the visitor for what will be found within the sanctuary. In this latter respect, the interior of the Propylaia should be understood as more than a transitional space or geometrically defined boundary. Importantly, it serves as a "viewing prelude"—what Donald Preziosi would call a *theatron*.[6] This particular situation is well captured in the reconstructed perspective view by Gorham Phillips Stevens.[7] Furthermore, a reconstruction of the procession of the Great Panathenaia passing through the Propylaia is offered in a watercolor by Peter Connolly.[8]

Both perspectives—that of termination and that of viewing prelude—stress the relation of the Propylaia with the interior of the Acropolis, and there has been much discussion on the position and alignment of the Great Propylaia in relation to the Parthenon and other buildings of the Periklean building program.[9] The issue is well summarized by John Camp, who begins by noting that although many Greek sanctuaries developed in a haphazard fashion,[10] this was not the case with the Acropolis, and he goes on to present three connections between the Propylaia and the Parthenon that are among the easiest to appreciate: (1) The Propylaia, as laid out, was intended to be *almost* exactly as wide as the Parthenon is long [emphasis ours]. (2) The ratios used in the Propylaia (3:7) are *almost* identical to those of the Parthenon (4:9) [emphasis ours]. (3) The two buildings, though not on the same axis, are set on the same orientation.[11]

Most scholars agree that these and similar associations among the buildings of the Acropolis must have been part of the overall design of the entire program: a wondrous and well-conceived ensemble, supervised by the hand of Pheidias. The Classical Acropolis thus has a symetry, a tidiness, that several scholars stress.[12]

For many modern visitors, the Parthenon has come to be the crowning pinnacle of the Periklean building program, eclipsing the Propylaia and other buildings on the Acropolis, but this was not the case earlier on. For Plutarch, who lived during the first and second centuries CE, it was the program as a whole that was important. In his *Life of Perikles*, he underscores this by stressing that Pheidias directed all the projects on the Acropolis and was the overseer of everything for Perikles.[13] His language is clear and precise, recording the awe and astonishment that he experienced in confronting the buildings of the Acropolis that still stood intact in his day:

> *As the works rose, shining with grandeur and possessing an inimitable grace of form, and the workmen strove to surpass one another in the beauty of their workmanship, the rapidity with which they were executed was especially marvelous. For the projects, each of which they thought would require several successive generations to reach completion, were all being completed together in the prime of one man's administration.... For that reason the works of Perikles are even more admired—though built in a short time they have lasted for a long time. For, in its beauty, each work was, even at that time, ancient, and yet, in its perfection, each looks even at the present time as if it were fresh and newly built. Thus there is a certain bloom of newness in each work and an appearance of being untouched by the wear of time. It is as if some ever-flowering life and unaging spirit had been infused into the creation of these works.*[14]

Referring to a specific building, Pausanias, writing in the middle of the second century CE, describes the roof of the Mnesiklean Propylaia in the following terms: "The formal entrance has a roof of white marble, which down to my own times is still incomparable for the size and beauty of the stone."[15] The much-admired ceiling had marble coffers decorated with gold or gilded stars against a blue background, and traces are still preserved on the east cornice of unfinished, but clearly outlined floral patterns.[16]

The sheer magnificence of the Great Propylaia is echoed in earlier accounts of the fourth century BCE, closer in date to the time of construction. Demosthenes, for example, in describing the great monuments of Athens, twice lists the Propylaia first and the Parthenon second, while elsewhere he mentions the Propylaia without any reference to the Parthenon.[17] In a similar vein, Aeschines, when urging the Athenians to recall the great achievements of their ancestors, singles out the Propylaia, not the Parthenon.[18] And Cicero, citing Demetrios of Phaleron (born ca. 350 BCE), provides a critique of the sumptuousness of the Propylaia.[19] Whatever later generations thought of the Periklean building program, the ancient Athenians themselves valued the Propylaia. Like all ancient monuments, the building embodies meanings and messages that are now obscured or entirely lost to us. However, it may be possible to recover aspects of the wider significance of this ceremonial gateway by reassessing its topographical situation. ...

A Monumental Exit

The predominant modern interpretation of the Propylaia has remained one of termination and prelude. Yet, in contrast to the Parthenon, which has a clear front (a curtailed pronaos and the main cella, which housed the chryselephantine statue of Athena Parthenos) and back (the opisthodomos), the Propylaia is an opening that served both as entrance and exit. It is this dual aspect of the Propylaia that has featured surprisingly little in the modern literature. The importance of the Propylaia as an exit is, however, brought to the fore in a remarkable carbon print, dating to 1890, but from an earlier negative, by Braun, Clément et Cie, a French firm active 1877-1928.

The firm was founded by Adolphe Braun (1812-1877), a textile designer who began by using photographs of plants in his fabric designs. Sometime after 1853, he produced an album of views of his native Alsace; later, by employing other photographers, he published views of Switzerland, Austria, Belgium, and France.[20] The studio he established in Paris was able to produce large, durable, rich, and very detailed prints through the carbon printing process. In addition to large-scale works of art from various European collections, the company had amassed a sizable inventory of drawings, paintings, and sculpture, as well as views of European cities and Classical sites. The massive scale and the clarity of these reproductions were so good that they were frequently sold to educational institutions and museums. As the firm expanded, it commissioned stereoscopic views of tourist destinations and added new, even larger-scale prints.[21] The company was successful because of the burgeoning tourist trade, and many of the large-scale prints featured "must-see" sites. Although many of the views were conventionally touristic in nature—like the romantic views of the Giza plateau in Egypt with the pyramids in the distance, or the Roman forum—others, like that of the passageway of the Propylaia, were far from conventional.[22]

The clarity of the classic Braun view of the Propylaia can only be described as stunning; the photograph is massive (77.5 x 61 cm). As with many Braun views, there is a figure providing scale, in this case a short-skirted guardian who leans against a pillar. However, rather than adopting the standard viewpoint toward the Parthenon, Braun's image captures a symmetrical view through the Propylaia and away from the Acropolis. In the center, at a distance, is a sliver of the Saronic Gulf, glimmering below the mountains of "Divine Salamis."[23]

Just as it forms the ceremonial gateway into the Athenian Acropolis, the monumental passageway *out* of the citadel provides every visitor a reminder of what was a watershed event in the history and topography of Athens: the defeat of the Persian armada in the Battle of Salamis on a late September day in 480 BCE.[24] A fundamental change in Athenian topography was brought about in the aftermath of the Persian sack. Having twice defeated the might of the Persian military machine—once at Marathon by land in 490 BCE, and again at Salamis a decade later, by sea—virtually single-handedly and in their own territory, the Athenians did much more than come of age. They emerged as a major power, ready to take on the Spartans—and all of the Peloponnesians for that matter—on their own terms, ready to dispel the Persians from Europe (as they did in the later Battle of Eurymedon in 466), ready to embark on an empire, and ready to provide their city with an architectural presence that would ensure its perpetual visibility. In the period immediately following Salamis, the social, political, and architectural reforms of Kimon and Perikles irrevocably transformed the landscape of central Athens, sweeping away much that went before.

In 480 BCE Athens was essentially an unfortified city, relying on the Mycenaean wall around the Acropolis built almost a millennium earlier, which enclosed an area that could not accommodate, let alone protect, its population.[25] After the Battle of Plataia in 479 BCE, Themistokles inspired the Athenians to construct a new city wall, which was completed in record time; at the same time, he also persuaded the Athenians to complete the fortification of the Piraeus.[26] The development of the Piraeus as the main harbor of Athens has been linked with the archonship of Themistokles in 493/2 BCE, but it was precipitated and brought into fruition by the realities of the Persian attack after 480 BCE.[27] The completion of the two Long Walls (*ta makra teiche*)—that is, the Phaleric and the North Long Walls that linked Athens with the Piraeus—occurred under Kimon, and the plan protected not only the passage to the new harbor of the Piraeus, but also the old harbor at Phaleron.[28] Slightly later, in 445 BCE, the so-called South Wall (or Middle Wall) was built between the Phaleric and North Walls, largely on the advice of Perikles.[29] The topographic and architectural ramifications of this change of primary harbor from Phaleron to the Piraeus for the city of Athens were profound.[30] Moreover, the incorporation of the new harbor at Piraeus within the overall fortification scheme expanded—both physically and conceptually—the city of Athens exponentially, signaling its maritime outlook and naval might, encapsulated in the term *thalassocracy*: "empire of the sea."[31]

The sheer physicality of the Themistoklean Wall was balanced, and in a sense matched, by the new building programs in the heart of the city. The wall provided the clearest expression of what the city builders took to be their domain: it was the border between town and suburb.[32] As Yi-Fu Tuan elaborates, the "city is a place, a center of meaning, par excellence. ... The traditional city symbolized, first, transcendental and man-made order as against the terrestrial and infernal nature. Second, it stood for an ideal human community. ... It was as transcendental order that ancient cities acquired their monumental aspect. Massive walls and portals demarcated sacred space."[33]

It was in the period immediately following Salamis that the need for a new Agora—a market place and civic center—was not only felt, but also realized, as it was during this period that the grandeur of the building program on the Acropolis was conceived. This is reflected in the passage in which the Athenian historian Thucydides becomes, albeit for a brief moment, an archaeologist in his comparison of Sparta and Athens. At 1.10.2, Thucydides states:

> *For if the city of the Lakedaimonians should be deserted, and nothing should be left of it but its temples and the foundations of its other buildings, posterity would, I think, after a long lapse of time, be very loath to believe that their power was as great as their renown. (And yet they occupy two-fifths of the Peloponnesos and have the hegemony of the whole, as well as of their many allies outside: but still, as Sparta is not compactly built as a city and has not provided itself with costly temples and other edifices, but is inhabited village-fashion in the old Hellenic style, its power would appear less than it is.) Whereas, if Athens should suffer the same fate, its power would, I think, from what appeared of the city's ruins, to be conjectured double what it is.*[34]

It was in this context that both the Parthenon and the Propylaia were conceived and constructed. Whereas the Parthenon housed the gold and ivory cult statue of Athena Parthenos (the Virgin), the Propylaia did something totally different. For an Athenian exiting the Acropolis, the Propylaia framed Salamis itself. Mnesikles designed the building to face and to view the island and mountains of Salamis. But there is something more: If one follows the passage directly out of the Propylaia, the sight line would skirt just to the north of the Kantharos harbor of Piraeus, and more or less between the Kynosoura Peninsula of Salamis—on the north side of which the Athenians stationed their fleet from Ambelaki Bay in the south to Paloukia Bay and the islet of St. George to the north—and the islet of Psyttaleia, where the Persians stationed troops.[35] It was on the Kynosoura Peninsula that the Athenians erected a trophy in the form of a marble column commemorating the Battle of Salamis.[36] Upon exiting the Propylaia Salamis was in your face.

By framing the site of Salamis, the process of moving through the Propylaia from east to west becomes experiential, the object being framed coming into clearer and clearer view. Upon entering the Propylaia from the east, it is the mountains in the central portion of the island that are visible; by the time one exits the Propylaia on the west side, virtually all of Salamis is in view. While the stages of this process can be recorded through photography, it is important to understand that the camera's lens cannot replicate first-hand experience and perception. Nonetheless, Braun's image is especially instructive because it reminds us of what may transpire when we look through, rather than solely toward, buildings.

Photo: Vassilis D. Gonis

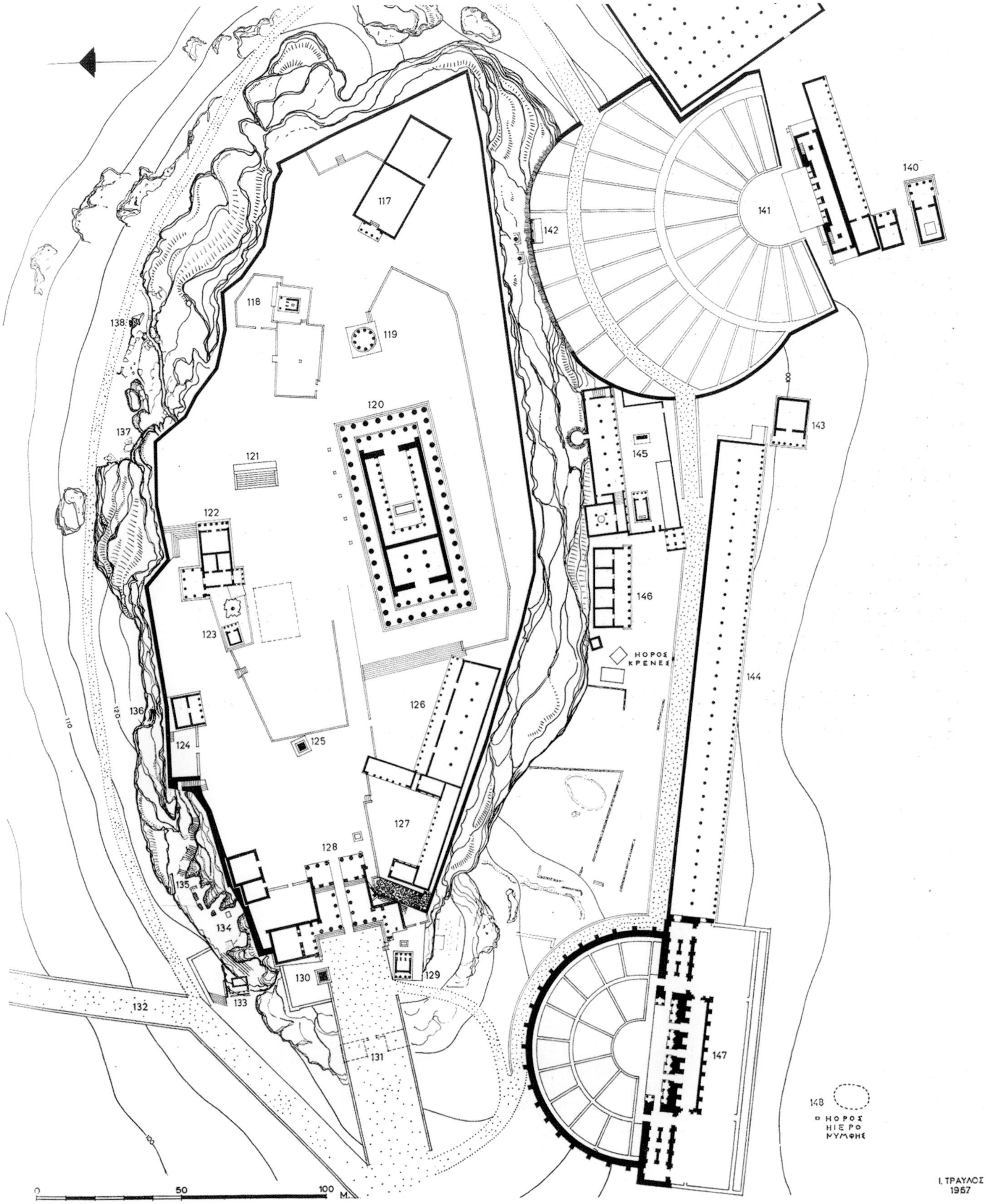

Drawing reproduced from *The Pictorial Dictionary of Ancient Athens* by John Travlos

UNESCO Headquarters. Photo: Lucien Hervé

Frames can sometimes take unexpected forms and initially be difficult to recognize, even when the structure is in full view. But, as is often the case, this ends up being more of a matter of perspective – visual and otherwise. In extracts from an essay by architectural historian Barry Bergdoll, two frame buildings are discussed here – Marcel Breuer, Bernard Zehrfuss and Pier Luigi Nervi's iconic UNESCO Assembly Building in Paris and St. John's Abbey in Minnesota, USA (on which Breuer and Nervi also collaborated) – that have clear formal similarities to each other but that are also not so easily associated with the conventional skeletal frames that Colin Rowe described at the start of this chapter.

With both the UNESCO and St. John's Abbey buildings, the lasting impression when seen from up close or experienced from within is of the spectacularly folded concrete walls and roof surfaces. From a certain distance and exterior vantage point, however, and especially when the enveloping concrete structure is considered as one entity at the scale of the whole building, it becomes clear that in terms of overall *section* this folded structure does indeed form a frame – one that creates a large open space in which people can congregate for various purposes. The folded surfaces provide the effective sectional thickness needed to replicate the bending resistance of column and beam elements in a more conventional frame; moreover, the folds of the roof merge into those at the top of the walls to effectively become rigid "joints", thus ensuring the continuity needed to develop a moment connection between the two, whereas the flattening of the walls toward their base provides the equivalent of a "pin" connection. These two buildings, then, in terms of both overall form and detailed resolution can be seen to present remarkable yet recognizable variations on the theme of frame forms.

Breuer and Nervi's Folded Frames

from *Into the Fold: Nervi, Breuer and a Post-War Architecture of Assembly*
Barry Bergdoll

Nervi's most important contribution to the [UNESCO] complex came in the structural system for the Conference-Assembly building, which houses under a single great span two differently sized halls and a delegates' lobby in between. Inside and out the form is given by the great folded concrete space beams. These are intersected by a curved slab "whose gentle wave follows the lines and stresses". Breuer had been interested for many decades in different materials in finding architectonic form from a transcription of the structural laws at play; but never before had the precise mathematics of lines of forces been put into play. Little wonder that almost overnight the French press championed the design — in counterpoint to the polemic against the first monumental modern building intra-muros in Paris — and grasped an analogy with the rational structural aesthetics of the Gothic. But unlike the Gothic cathedral where the interior vaults and the pitched roof were entirely independent, here the startling rhythm of the exterior facade, and the sweep of the roof seen from the upper levels of the Secretariat, and in particular from the Delegates' restaurant on the top floor, were nothing but the outer surface of the same great ribs that gave such a powerful unity and dynamics to the interior of the halls, almost the belly of the whale. [Mario] Salvadori, who had begun teaching structure to architects at Columbia University's School of Architecture a few years earlier, heralded this milestone as an all-too-rare collaboration between architecture and engineering. "The Conference-Assembly Building is an extraordinary and imposing structure which looms larger than its size would suggest. It consists of a solid corrugated front wall which folds at the top to become a slanting roof. The roof slopes down to a set of columns and rises again to the top of the back wall. The structure is monolithic and gives a feeling of tremendous strength and lightness. I consider this particular structure one of the masterpieces of the concrete age. ... The corrugated front wall and roof give a plastic definition of space to the Assembly hall which is entirely new in concept, completely correct structurally and extremely exciting visually."[1] [Photographer Lucien] Hervé captured it in a single image when he turned his camera to the north, aligning the furrows of the Assembly Buildings roof with the open iron work of the Eiffel Tower, a photographic gesture often repeated but never with the same tautness. The French architectural critic and philosopher Francoise Choay noted that UNESCO "has probably aroused more strong feeling than any building since the Eiffel Tower, for it upsets preconceived notions and disturbs conventional ways of seeing, thinking and living".[2] Salvadori continued his analysis with a precision worth quoting: "The lowest point of the roof is supported by columns which have an elliptic cross-section at the bottom and a rectangular cross-section at the top. This extraordinary shape is enhanced by the wooden forms into which columns were poured. The forms were lined with parquet wood and the stripes in the concrete have the marking of the wood. Because of the tremendous concern for detail on the part of the architects Breuer and Zehrfuss and of the grandiosity of conception of the entire project, the UNESCO buildings in Paris are one of the landmarks of concrete construction in Europe today. Never before has the human eye looked at these logically shaped structures. But, the theoretical concepts developed by architect and engineer could have been completely ruined by slipshod execution".[3] As much as the Secretariat building brought a steel curtain wall more closely associated with post-war American office building, the concrete work of the Assembly building in particular set a new standard, one of the singularly most influential aspects of the project.

The other achievements of the UNESCO building derive less from the collaboration of the three architects than from the shared desire of the new UN agency and its architects to make the "Palais de l'UNESCO" a showcase for the synthesis of the arts that was being theorized, debated, and longed for on both sides of the Atlantic after the Second World War. This had been a central theme of the "Nine Points for a New Monumentality" drawn up in 1943 by José Luis Sert, Fernand Léger and Sigfried Giedion in New York, as well as the call for a "Synthèse des arts", voiced in 1949 by Le Corbusier and André Bloc. At UNESCO it took the form of myriad works of art — Alexander Calder, Joan Miró, Picasso and others — inside and out which made the project for a number of years a focus of art criticism and pilgrimage. One of the most successful expansions of this intention to merge space making and art making came with one of the final commissions, as the building was all but complete, for a garden from the Japanese-American sculptor Isamu Noguchi set before the elegant raised cube of Breuer, Nervi and Zehrfuss's "Bâtiment 3", overall office space in a building originally conceived to house the International Civil Aviation Organization.[4]

The controversy and tensions that had accompanied the awarding of the UNESCO commission in 1952-53 did not subside with the inauguration of the building in 1958, after five intensive years in which the day-to-day work of construction and small scale design decisions were increasingly handled by Zehrfuss. Much of the debate centered on the issue of whether a break with the masonry tradition of post-Haussmanian urbanism ran the risk of breaking the much admired urban harmony of Paris's streetscapes. But the most vitriolic of all attacks came from the homelands of the two chief designers: the United States and Italy. Lewis Mumford, who had already been a vociferous critic of the United Nations building in New York for its failure to achieve a humanistic modernist symbol, was no less scathing of the Parisian counterpart which ought to have been "a providential opportunity for the Modern Movement to pause and sort out its gains and reckon with its failures ... The moment had come, in short, for the modern architectural leaders, no longer a group of hot rebels, to accept the responsibilities of government". But instead he found the building a collection of clichés: "The result is a Museum of the Antiquities of Modern Art and Architecture". But even Mumford, in a tour-de-force deployment of his fears of technocratic modernism, reserved praise for the Assembly building, which "deserves scrutiny and a large measure of commendation ... all the more because it suggests, in addition to its own architectural merits, what could have been a sounder setting and a handsomer design for the whole UNESCO group".[5] Translated into Italian, fellow defender of the organic Bruno Zevi offered up much of Mumford's critique in *L'Espresso*,[6] even quoting Mumford before his article appeared, revealing the extent to which the two were working together to formulate a powerful critique of what they viewed as the mainstream of post-war modernism against the possibilities of more "organic" research and expression. Nervi wrote discreetly, as always, of his dismay on these articles to Breuer, but was perhaps granted the last word in 1966, when UNESCO commissioned him to contribute the article on "Architecture as it serves the human requirements of our time", in *The Arts and Man: A World View of the Role and Function of the Arts in Society* (UNESCO, 1969). The building in turn served as a model for a new horizontal modernism, its influence and effects to be witnessed not only in other Paris buildings but in horizontal national capitals across the globe as well — from London to Washington, DC....

Saint John's Abbey, Collegeville, Minnesota

The closest immediate cousin of UNESCO's Assembly hall is the great Benedictine Abbey Church of Saint John's at Collegeville, Minnesota, which Breuer was working on in parallel in the early 1950s to the UNESCO commission. Here he had a free hand to work on his own, developing a building style for an entire college campus, one of the most comprehensive commissions of his career and, along with UNESCO, the project that transformed his career from an architect of single-family houses to one of the form givers of the American post-war commercial building, particularly in its structural concrete expression. The two commissions were developed in Breuer's New York office in the early 1950s in close juxtaposition, even in tandem; these two idealist and ideologically charged institutions of supranational governance afforded Breuer a virtually unprecedented opportunity to give form to the recent calls for a new monumentality. The challenge was to seek forms which would not betray modernism's fear of empty symbols and historical rhetoric in design and composition, even as they helped recuperate what were perceived as the lost communitarian and psychological depth of traditional design. Opening a letter from a Benedictine monastery in Collegeville, Minnesota in mid-March 1953, Breuer could scarcely have imagined that within the next five years the design of a monastery church for the world's largest Benedictine order would make the Catholic Church, along with the United Nations, the mainstay of his burgeoning practice. If in 1953 the non-practicing Hungarian Jewish Bauhaus master thrice removed from his homeland had never heard of Saint John's, the monks had done their homework when they decided to include Breuer's name among the "twelve outstanding architects" who received a letter from Abbot Baldwin Wilfred Dworschak asking "whether you would be interested in preparing a comprehensive building plan and report for Saint John's Abbey".[7] Throughout 1952 and early 1953 Breuer was in the limelight for the on-going saga of UNESCO. Once he was chosen as Saint John's architect, the Paris and Collegeville commissions would develop in Breuer's mind and in his office in extraordinary interchange, the one serving as the laboratory for the other. They were secular and sacred conjugations of Breuer's first opportunities to design monumental complexes of buildings charged with providing a center for organizations with both an international meaning and spread of influence, buildings in short which were as expressive of the old desires of the universalist ambitions of the modernism of Breuer's student years and of the new trajectories of an emerging global order of the post-war period. Abbot Baldwin's letter to twelve architects made it clear not only that "The Abbey is one of the largest Benedictine communities in the world at this time... but that the design would need to be addressed not only to a community resident at Saint John's but to the far-flung set of parishes and monastic foundations the Abbey is in charge of in the Bahamas, Mexico, Puerto Rico, Kentucky, and Japan".[8]

The twelve modern architects interviewed attest to the conviction of the monks to depart from the austere neo-Romanesque style of their existing buildings: Thomas Sharpe of Oxford, Barry Byrne, a former employee of Frank Lloyd Wright, Joseph Murphy of St. Louis, a leading designer of Roman Catholic churches, the Austrian Robert Kramreiter, the Germans Rudolf Schwarz and A. Boslett and the Swiss Herman Bauer. Here was a spectrum, from the highly traditional revivalist designs of Murphy to some of the most daringly abstract and modernist designs of Schwarz, a leading thinker in the German liturgical movement closely followed by many at Saint John's. Alongside these names with ecclesiastical credentials were a series of American modernists (mostly European émigrés) who had little or no experience building for the church, including Richard Neutra, Walter Gropius and Marcel Breuer. Abbot Baldwin's letter to the architects was a veritable manifesto of religious and aesthetic modernism and an open-ended invitation to enter into a period of mutual learning towards the creation of a new Benedictine architectural expression: "The Benedictine tradition at its best challenges us to think boldly and to cast our ideals in forms which will be valid for centuries to come, shaping them with all the genius of present-day materials and techniques. We feel that the modern architect with his orientation towards functionalism and honest use of materials is uniquely qualified to produce a Catholic work. In our position it would, we think, be deplorable to build anything less, particularly since our age and our country have thus far produced so little truly significant religious architecture".[9]

Breuer was by far the youngest and had the least experience with large scale building and planning; yet the monks voted by a substantial majority to entrust the planning of the next century's growth of their monastery and university to him as much for the qualities of his personality as for their sympathy with his architectural views: "He is a very quiet man who makes no attempt to impress the client, remains calm, although he was evidently very much interested, and speaks only when he has something to say...". When asked about religion he responded that although he was not a Catholic — he claimed to be a Lutheran though in fact he was born Jewish and in adult life practiced no creed — and had not built a church, "the modern in general has a great thirst for works of content, if you want, for the spiritual. He is looking for something that expresses more than pure functionalism, for a deepening of content.... He talked about the integration of engineering and architecture, especially about the possibilities of working with a really creative engineer. Engineering was not used enough today, he said 'as a demonstrative form'.... In explanation of what he meant, he said that in Gothic architecture, the way the weight was supported was actually the very form of the church, it demonstrated the engineering". When they asked him about concrete he replied that "Modern architecture has not yet exploited reinforced concrete as a form", and again referred to Gothic as an analogy, although he said he preferred the stronger, less fussy forms of the powerful Romanesque churches. "His statement that we should make use of as daring engineering as our theological and liturgical understanding demands, reveals an architect of the caliber we need".[10] The Abbey's desire to push liturgical reform towards a greater sense of community participation far in advance of the Vatican and Breuer's sense that the Modern Movement, in aligning itself with engineering, might take a step towards a new formal expressiveness were forming an alliance.

Breuer left it to his young designers Hamilton Smith and Robert Gatje in New York to work on translating Saint John's liturgical beliefs into a diagram for the layout of the monastery as the core of a master plan for planning Saint John's whole site."[11] By the time they finished this diagram, dated 2 July 1953, Breuer was back in Europe where the design of UNESCO was at a crucial juncture. UNESCO played a very real role in the evolution of Breuer's design for Saint John's over the next few months. Although he took a side trip to Germany to study liturgical arrangements in buildings along the Rhine from the great Romanesque Abbey of Maria Laach to the recently completed works of Rudolph Schwarz in and around Cologne, Breuer took, in the end, more cues from Nervi's great Assembly hall of UNESCO. It pointed the way towards giving form to the monks' desire for a wholly new space for worship which could bring the community of monks and the congregation into more direct connection, and in which the sacraments were brought out of the recesses of the apse into the focus of the space and the ceremony. Marking up Smith & Gatje's drawing, Breuer zeroed in on the shape and the spatial planning of the great church. Smith & Gatje had drawn a long thin longitudinal church, a sort of modernized Maria Laach nave, preceded by a separate baptistery. Responding at once to the desires for a new relationship between the monks and the congregation — which on Sundays would number some 1250 students and parishioners — and to the lessons he was learning about disposing large crowds, hierarchically arranged but in working harmony in the various size Assembly halls of UNESCO, Breuer sketched an emphatic equilateral triangle over the diagram. While Smith & Gatje had accommodated Saint John's long tradition of choral responses by having the monks face one another in a schematic monk's choir placed behind rather than in front of the altar, Breuer noted that in addition to facing one another the monks should also face the congregation and the idea emerged rapidly of placing the monks in the apex of a triangle and the congregation across its broad base, all of them facing an altar centrally placed: this way the monks faced not only one another for their choral responses, the heart of their offices, and the altar, but the congregation as well. By the end of the month the triangle had become a trapezoid, precisely the form used for the Assembly hall at UNESCO. As at UNESCO, this form had the advantage of holding large numbers of people with, at the same time, the illusion of intimacy and with a central focus. Seen from the monastic choir, the nave appears much shorter than it is in reality; from the nave the monks choir is splayed into a panoramic view. This effect would be further enhanced once the three-dimensional form that could house this great broad figure without compromising interior supports was worked out in an intense period of collaboration between Breuer and Nervi — whom the monks had endorsed as a collaborator for the structural questions during Breuer's August 1953 visit, and who immediately extended his experiments in the great spanning capacity and great strength of large folded plates of concrete used in both elevation and to span the space, the whole tied together as an integral cage of buttress-like trusses.

With Nervi's advice[12] Breuer imparted many of the most successful aspects of the UNESCO Assembly halls to the church, where a dynamic space of diagonals in all planes was effected. The ten great serrated buttresses of the Assembly hall in Paris were translated, at Collegeville, into twelve. This was perhaps symbolic of the twelve apostles, but also echoed the planning module of twelve that Breuer would use in the monastic wing. These twelve pleated folds increase in all dimensions — width, depth, and wall thickness as they cross successively broader segments of the bell-shaped plan. The longest fold, immediately inside the front door accomplishes a clear span of over 135 feet, soars 15 feet from top to bottom and has walls which vary in thickness between 6 and 8 inches. The effect of all this diagonal movement, enhanced by the floor which slopes downwards towards the altar, is a subtle telescoping of the space and a great dynamism of movement which is impossible to read from the diagrammatic plan, and rather inadequately captured in photographs. In Paris Breuer emphasized the sense of organic wholeness and of enclosure of this integral structural system by connecting it to the Secretariat by a low passage so that a sudden transition of scale takes place upon entering the Assembly hall. Indeed this is one of the most remarkable elements of the UNESCO plan, its feature of a kind of meandering landscape over which the buildings emerge but in which movement runs through and beyond each individual element. In Paris the great transition of scale is accomplished by a deliberately informal asymmetrical juncture, a perhaps somewhat tense result of a lack of resolution between the formal gestures required by the site and by Breuer's Bauhaus belief in asymmetrical planning. In Minnesota, guided by liturgical requirements and decorum, Breuer achieved a much greater richness of effects and embraced for the first time axial planning which he was to use over and over again in his most monumental works of the 1960s: the Whitney Museum in New York and the IBM headquarters at La Gaude in the South of France, with its almost neo-Egyptian entrance sequence. Indeed by then Breuer had penned the introduction to a photographic essay on Egyptian architecture celebrating the lessons to be learned from the Egyptian sublime scale for an aesthetic of modern concrete and institutional expression.[13]

In his aspirations to create a system of modern religious architecture, this multidirectional canting and subtle diminution of the great folded concrete plates — the equivalent for a modern concrete architecture of the column or the vault in classical temples or gothic cathedrals but also endowed with something of the power of the battered walls of Egyptian architecture — were given visual refinements which not only made them more structurally efficient but which echoed the magnificent system of visual refinements in the Athenian Parthenon then much studied by American archaeologists and engineers. The result was trumpeted by *The Architectural Record*: "Breuer ... has gone into an expression new to him — sculptural form of structure. Checked out by the brilliant Italian engineer Pier Luigi Nervi — whose career had begun in the 1920s in stadium architecture, notably with his municipal stadium in Florence — Breuer will bend a thin cowl of concrete into walls and roof over this monastic church, creased into fold for structural stiffness".[14] As with Le Corbusier's Dominican church at Ronchamp, the architectural press found itself resorting to pictorial analogies for the first time in decades in an effort to explicate the form giving of modern architecture in a new phase. For years to come Nervi and Breuer would echo one another expressing in almost identical phrases their joint conviction that it was the role of a new synthesis of technology and art to carry the incomplete miracle of Gothic further: "They were the real forerunners of modern technology, replacing the equilibrium achieved by heavy masses of masonry with the equilibrium of forces created by the interplay of thrust and counterthrust of slender ribs built with very good materials", as Nervi put in his 1961-62 Charles Eliot Norton lectures at Harvard.[15] Breuer added the synthesis of architecture and sculpture, the fluid ways in which concrete both was made and in turn made manifest the play of structural forces. As he explained in a 1963 lecture at the University of Michigan entitled "Matter and Intrinsic Form", "it can reflect the stresses working in the structure with photographic truthfulness".[16]

One of the most extraordinary features of this collaboration, and the vital feature which distinguishes the earth bound UNESCO Assembly hall from the sacred space of Saint John's Abbey church was the decision to lift the folded plates in the air on a system of concrete buttress-piers that at once call to mind the buttresses of the Gothic cathedrals, but is in essence a brilliant reversal of the system of loads in a Gothic cathedral. Bringing the clerestory of Gothic to the ground, Breuer extends the interior space of the church to the modernist cloister gardens on either side, a horizontal complement to the vertical expansion of space. The transfer of the structural loads is accomplished through a continuous hollow edge beam which also carries concealed up-lights that make the dramatic capacity to hold heavy concrete aloft as awe-inspiring at night as during the day. ...

St. John's Abbey interior. Photo: Eric Sutherland

Reliance Controls Factory by Foster + Partners

Another type of frame, frequently used for resisting lateral loads on buildings, stands out because of its visual distinctiveness. As its name would imply, the braced frame has a diagonal member (or two, in an "X" configuration) that is incorporated into the typical beam-and-column frame assemblage; the system thereby becomes much more efficient, resisting loads by means of axial tension and compression forces in its members (instead of relying on their much more inefficient bending behavior.) Of course, such diagonal members do impose certain aesthetic consequences and spatial pros and cons in terms of design, and so such frames have been both embraced as a sign of technological progress as well as critiqued for a lack of artistic grace.

The expressive aspect of the diagonally braced frame has been considered emblematic of the British High Tech movement, an architectural style represented here by the Reliance Controls Factory built in the 1960s (but dismantled in 1991). Prominently featured, even accented, were the braced frames along the building's exterior perimeter; much less widely recognized was the stunning degree of interior openness made possible by the efficiency of this external bracing system. Two of the Reliance Control Factory's Team 4 architects, Norman Foster and Richard Rogers, are widely recognized as having been at the vanguard of development of the British High Tech movement; what is generally less well known is that these two individuals were heavily influenced in this regard by their earlier shared experiences attending graduate school and travelling in the USA, a story partly retold here in an extract from Murray Fraser's remarkable book on the topic of transatlantic exchange and, in particular, of American influence on post-war British architecture.

Braced Frames and High Tech Dreams

from *Architecture and the "Special Relationship": The American Influence on Post-War British Architecture*
Murray Fraser with Joe Kerr

The writings of Reyner Banham and the avant-garde visions of Cedric Price and Archigram influenced a younger generation of architects passing through British schools of architecture at the turn of the 1960s. Most significant were Norman Foster and Richard Rogers, who trained at Manchester University and the Architectural Association in London, respectively, and who became friends in the USA in 1961-62 as postgraduate students at Yale University.[1]...

The story of how Foster and Rogers met has often been told. It all began in London at a glittering reception in mid-1961 for those lucky enough to win scholarships at American colleges for the forthcoming academic year. Foster, in fact, had a choice of scholarships, including the most prestigious – a Fulbright – but he turned that down in favour of a Henry fellowship to Yale, since the latter permitted him to work in architectural practice while studying. It also meant he had to forego the chance to study under Louis Kahn at the University of Pennsylvania in Philadelphia, to his great regret. Rogers too had been offered several scholarships, including a Fulbright of his own, which he accepted; he also could have joined Louis Kahn in Philadelphia, but opted for Yale because his wife, Su Rogers (née Brumwell), had a place there to study urban planning...

Like other students over on American scholarships, Foster and Rogers realized this was their best chance to travel around and see the architecture and landscapes of the USA – indeed, they had already been doing this whenever they got breaks from their studies. As an example, accompanied by Su Rogers and a fellow American student, they had done a tour of the work of Frank Lloyd Wright and Mies van der Rohe in and around Chicago. Richard Rogers recalls: 'America enthralled us with its scale, energy, optimism and openness. We travelled by thumb, by car and by Greyhound bus, voraciously absorbing the culture, both of the massive open spaces and of the tall, taut, energetic cities.'[2] At the end of their studies, Richard and Su Rogers drove over to San Francisco – again apparently at James Stirling's suggestion – where Richard Rogers managed to get a job with Skidmore, Owings & Merrill, just as John Winter had before him. And like Winter, Rogers visited classic modernist icons such as the Eames House, or the villas of Craig Ellwood, during his time on the West Coast. Rogers and his wife might even have stayed longer in San Francisco – visas permitting – but an unmissable opportunity arose to design a couple of houses in Britain, one for Su Rogers's mother and step-father. So they drove back across the USA and sailed to Southampton in time for Christmas that year. Norman Foster returned from the States a touch later, in mid-1963, having worked first for an urban planning firm in New Haven and then motoring over to the West Coast to experience life there. He greatly enjoyed a stint with Anshen & Allen, designing a segment of the University of California campus at Santa Cruz.[3] Foster, in common with Rogers, was thoroughly impressed by the Southern

Californian Schools Construction System prototype, which ... had just been designed by Ezra Ehrenkrantz as a flexible, highly serviced modular system. On arriving back in Britain, Foster was contacted by Rogers to see if their tentative plans to set up in practice might turn into reality, along with Su Rogers and another colleague. Team 4 was duly born, although the intended fourth member, Georgie Cheeseman (later Georgie Wolton) – who herself had travelled widely in the USA, and was the only qualified architect among them – dropped out immediately. She went on to design a number of superb steel-and-glass Americanized houses with her own practice, including one in 1969 using Cor-Ten steel, for which she visited the Cummins Engine plant in Darlington to examine Kevin Roche's detailing.[4] In the meantime, her sister, Wendy Cheeseman – then training to be an architect – took over the vacant fourth jersey in Team 4; she subsequently married Norman Foster...

The impact of the USA on Team 4, and on the later careers of Rogers and Foster, cannot be emphasized enough. This is not to say they were not also deeply influenced by modernism in continental Europe, such as Pierre Chareau's Maison de Verre in Paris (1931), or the work of Jean Prouvé, or the dramatic 1960s lightweight structures of Frei Otto (a disciple of Bucky Fuller). Victorian engineering was another crucial source of inspiration, as was a Puritanical emphasis on drawing out building details carefully by hand, hinting at a link back to Arts and Crafts architects like Philip Webb. This mixture of British and European influences was part of the hybridization of architectural culture then taking place, but even so, it should be stressed that it was always their US experiences that underpinned Team 4's vision. Although historical traces from Britain and continental Europe added certain inflections, it was the spark provided by America that ignited the High Tech engine. Foster and Rogers did not undertake special journeys together across Europe to find the future of architecture; that was just something they did in the USA. And now, on their return home, their task was to import the same positive thinking and can-do philosophy to Britain. As Brian Appleyard has noted, Rogers and Foster 'were still fresh from Yale and they shared a determination to bring the intensity of their experience of America to little England.'[5]

Norman Foster has always been frank about his reverence for the USA, later telling the American Institute of Architects:

> *When I first came to America as a student more than thirty years ago, it was the land of my heroes and it still is. I had great expectations and they were fulfilled beyond the dreams that I dared not dream ... It is no exaggeration to say that I discovered myself through America ... I have come to love, admire and respect what your country has to offer. It has given me more than I can ever pay back – it will remain a lifelong debt which goes beyond architecture.*[6] ...

According to Colin Davies... the first building to be designed in the High Tech manner was that by Team 4 – largely by Foster and Rogers – for the Reliance Controls Electronics Factory (1966; demolished 1991).[7] It sat in an industrial estate on the edge of Swindon, and embodied a desire to match up to the Americanizing lead set by Eero Saarinen and Kevin Roche. Appropriately, the factory was for an Anglo-American parent company, of which the head of the British arm happened to be Jock Campbell (soon to be made chairman of Milton Keynes Development Corporation). The job came to Team 4 after first being offered to James Stirling, but he felt it was too small for his practice and so he recommended Foster and Rogers, his friends since Yale. Reliance Controls employed mostly female labour in the making of precision electronic equipment, and hence the client wanted a nongendered atmosphere in the building – far away from the traditionally macho image of industry, and explicitly along the lines of the latest American factories. Team 4's solution for Reliance Controls was an instant success, winning the inaugural *Financial Times* award for the best British industrial building that year. The actual design consisted of a stark, single-story rectangular box of uninterrupted profile. It was clad with a double skin of insulated profiled-steel decking, plastic-coated on the outer face, which was used not only for the external walls, but also wrapped over to form a roof that acted as a structural diaphragm in the horizontal direction. Steel was in plentiful supply once again, now that the mid-1950s shortages produced by the Korean War were a thing of memory. Indeed, in the 1960s the annual output of steel in Britain rose steadily to a peak of 28,000 tons in 1970, and there were plentiful imports from abroad especially from US Steel – that helped to keep prices down. Steel had thus become a viable material for architects like Team 4 to use as external cladding in place of more usual materials such as brick, tiling or concrete. The layout of Reliance Controls was organized on a repeated 12m x 12m grid, four bays across and five bays in length. A total of 2,880m^2 of accommodation was created, and the building was designed so it could be expanded four-fold if needed. It was to do so along a central linear spine, with the services distribution networks concealed in a trench under the floor slab; but in the event this expansion never happened.

The exterior facades of the Reliance Controls factory made overt reference to the temple-like ordering of Kevin Roche's Cummins Engine Components Plant. Hence the lateral steel beams which formed the fascias in Reliance Controls, along with the stunted projecting I-beam sections welded onto the outer structural columns, could be read visually as a pseudo-entablature. As in the Cummins factory, these outermost steel columns were placed slightly outside the actual volume, giving again a peristylar effect. Yet what was most distinctive – and novel – about Reliance Controls was the fact that the structural forces acting on the building were expressed by a series of slender (and soon widely imitated) steel diagonal cross-braces between the external columns on the two main façades. In this way, tensile forces naked to the eye were made visually explicit. The diagonal braces operated in tension against the natural tendency of the structural frame to lozenge, preventing it from lateral collapse and enabling the steel columns to be made slimmer. The idea of diagonal tie bracing had its first outing over a century before, in Joseph Paxton's Crystal Palace of 1851. More pertinently, there were also a number of post-war American precedents, far closer in age and spirit, such as the Eames House and Ehrenkrantz's SCSD school in Palo Alto – both visited by Foster and Rogers. However, the most obvious influence was the use of tie-rod bracing in a sumptuous steel-framed house by Paul Rudolph in Lido Key in Sarasota, Florida, in the mid-1950s.[8] Its proper title was the Philip Hiss Residence, but because of its steel bracing struts and extensive roof louvres to shade the dwelling against the sun, it was popularly referred to as the 'Umbrella House'; as such, it was one of the earliest US experiments in the overt display of tensile forces. As well as being their head of school at Yale, Richard Rogers has admitted his interest in the houses of Paul Rudolph from that period, and Norman Foster had of course worked in Rudolph's office, so a direct influence is more than plausible. Indeed, Foster now describes Rudolph as 'the single most formative force in my life', adding:

> *In 1961 Paul Rudolph was the main reason that I chose to go to Yale University for the Masters course in architecture. As a student I was familiar with his early works through illustrations in the magazines of the time ... The architecture to me was fresh, radical and unconventional. I am thinking of those early houses in Florida with brise-soleils like white, abstract sculptures.*[9]

Team 4 naturally made tweaks to this precedent. In the 'Umbrella House', Rudolph had let one in each pair of diagonal bracing rods cross behind its twin, bending fractionally out of line to achieve this. But in the Reliance Controls Factory, Team 4 designed a distinct component with threaded connections into which each diagonal strut could be screwed; this placed all the members in the same plane, obviating the need for any rod to pass behind another. Also in their design for Reliance Controls, Team 4 took the idea of expressing the tie-rod bracing a step further. In fact, only one bay on each of the long façades needed to be braced to stabilize the frame against lateral collapse, but Team 4 deliberately opted to have every bay braced, for aesthetic effect. The result was a continuous arcade of St Andrew's (Saltire) crosses along the main elevations, thereby making something of a structural nonsense of the expressed detail. Tony Hunt was again the engineer, and he pointed out this structural anomaly – as well as others – but visual styling won the day. Hence the Reliance Controls scheme also marked the point at which the structural rationality proclaimed by High Tech architects lapsed into exaggeration and expressionism – i.e. at its very birth.

Internally, as in Roche's Cummins Engine plant, the Reliance Controls Factory contained simply a single space and a shared entrance for all staff. Some service cores for toilets and suchlike were divided off with aluminium stud-walls or painted blockwork, but otherwise the volume was undifferentiated. This open arrangement again implied a democratic informality in use, through the forced mixing of managers and workers – a feature widely commented upon in coverage of Reliance Controls at the time. 'It is not just an instrument of productivity ... for the linear pattern so established has gone on to break down the traditional division between one entrance for manual workers and another for those with white collars,' wrote the *Architectural Review*. 'So the pattern of change here is ultimately one of social change, of behaviour between one man and another.'[10]

And even more so than at Cummins Engine, the Reliance Controls Factory wished to set a tone for a new type of building that would banish forever the harsh, dirty environment of the typical factory in the typical industrial estate, replacing it with a cleaner, softer and carpeted workplace. Such conditions were believed to be better suited to the increasingly computerized labour practices being invoked by Prime Minister Harold Wilson in his speeches in the mid-1960s. Most famous of all, in October 1963 had come his mantra that a new-look Britain was 'going to be forged in the white heat of this (scientific) revolution'.[11] According to Wilson, 'those charged with the control of our affairs must be ready to think and speak in the language of the scientific age'; this was precisely what Foster and Rogers were so eager to do.[12] Less remembered now is that Wilson adopted this tone because of the inroads being made by American technology and management techniques in Britain. As noted previously, by the mid-1960s the plentiful US multinational subsidiaries – of which Cummins Engine was a classic example and Reliance Controls a hybrid version – accounted for nearly 14 per cent of British manufacturing output, and this proportion was palpably higher in fields such as electronics. Indeed, in the year that the Reliance Controls Electronics Factory opened, Wilson warned Britain that if the USA was allowed to continue to set the tempo, 'we will turn into wood cutters and water carriers in the industrial society while they ... will enjoy an increasing monopoly in the technologically advanced sectors of production.'[13] A building such as Reliance Controls was thus both part of the trend towards American economic domination, and at the same time part of the hope that US subsidiaries were finally spurring the modernization of British industry. By the late-1960s, British companies were investing in the region of £610 million each year in industrial buildings, a not inconsiderable sum.[14] But what was most urgently needed were exemplars like Reliance Controls to show how the stimulus provided by US capital and technology could actually lead to architectural innovation.

Hence the goal of Reliance Controls was not merely to create a cleaner, better designed 'serviced shed' – in the tradition ever since Behrens and Gropius to ennoble factories as symbolic icons – but also to revolutionize and modernize the labour conditions inside. The aspiration was to transform British working practices in holy conjunction with the manufacturing spaces that housed them. As an ensemble, Reliance Controls was suitably lightweight in the direction that Bucky Fuller was urging architects to travel, and its ethos was undeniably crisp and simple. The design was subtly handled to give maximum aesthetic impact to the repetitive components and cladding sheets which encased the frame. However, the building's relative lightness and its use of minimum-section steel members meant that shear forces and the prospect of twisting became pathological issues which needed to be tackled in the design, prompting the visual exaggeration of cross-bracing between the external columns. But all things considered, it proved astonishingly cheap, working out at even less than the Cummins Components Plant, at just under £45 per m^2. And it was extremely fast to build, with only nine months between starting on site and the factory going into operation. In this regard, too, Reliance Controls harked back to the rapid assembly process of the Crystal Palace in the previous century. Since it embodied all these positive feel-good attributes, Reliance Controls ushered in an era in which young British architects vied with each other to produce the most technologically advanced factory designs, inspired by the latest US practices but always adapted to suit native conditions. Curiously enough, a small factory that was designed in part by Marcel Breuer – now based in the USA – was erected on another site on the same Swindon industrial park, also around the same time as Reliance Controls. But it proved a poor rival, being easily upstaged by Team 4's new kid on the block.[15] Was this perhaps an indication that in just a few short years, British industrial architecture had become more innovative than that in the USA?

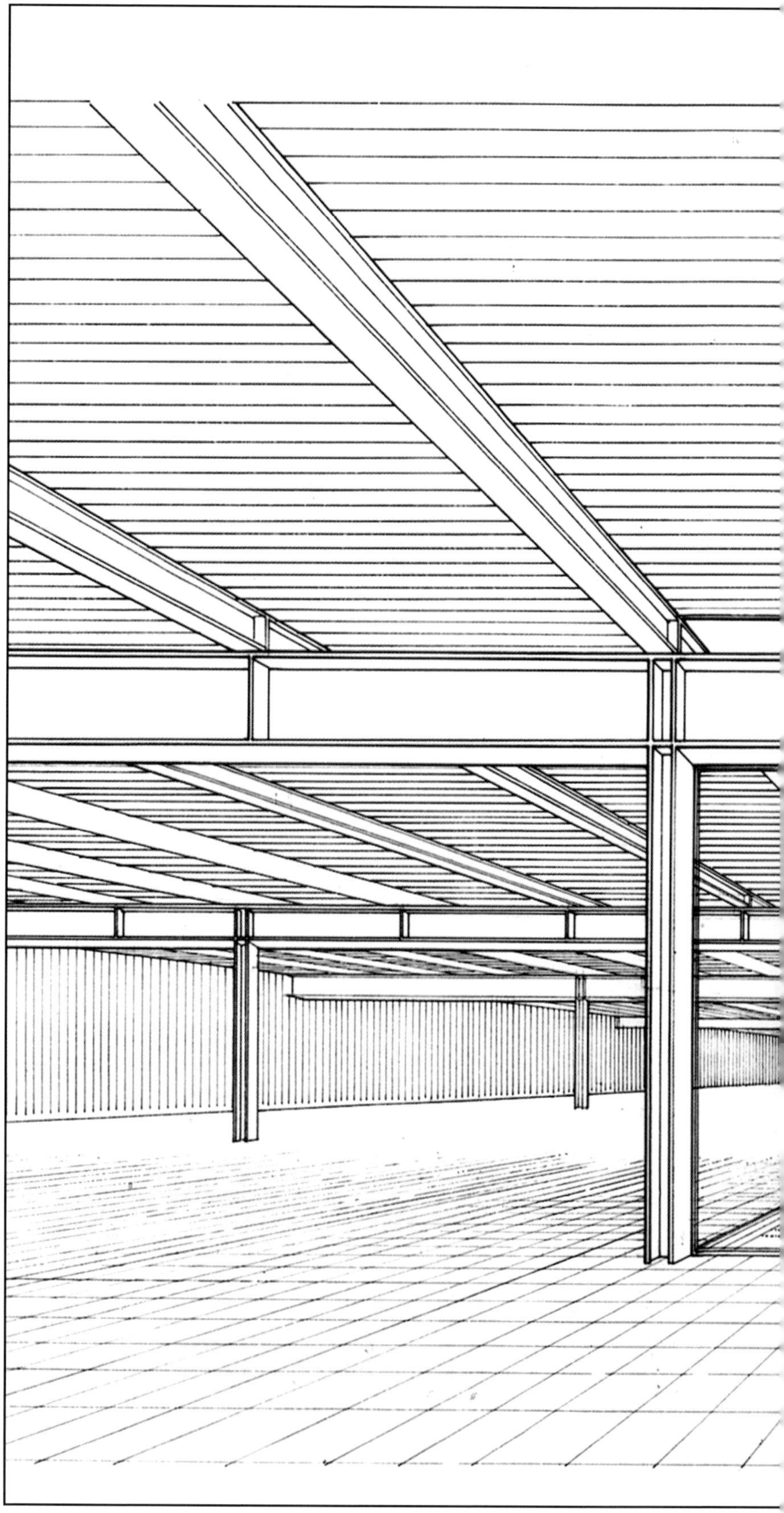

Reliance Controls Factory interior by Foster + Partners

FOSTER ASSOCIATES

Frames structurally support and spatially define the iconic *Maison à Bordeaux* and its views of the surrounding landscape. The architect Rem Koolhaas and structural engineer Cecil Balmond collaborated closely on the design of this house, as recounted here by Balmond himself. The format of this retelling is uniquely made accessible and informative: written in diary-like fashion, the first person story-telling reveals the many stages of the iterative process as well as the alternative framing strategies that were considered and then rejected or refined. Even more unique is the format of the presentation, with conceptual sketches and diagrams intermixed with detailed construction drawings and photos, all interwoven with the text in an interactive and *informal* fashion – in just the manner of the rest of the book from which this entry is reproduced. The process of design, so often rendered arcane and inaccessible, is here made human.

Informal Frames

from ***Informal***
Cecil Balmond

BORDEAUX VILLA

Some people keep a diary.

Others, like me, find the daily minutiae too meaningless to record with its small traffickings up and down. But if one looks back over time and runs a memory record of a project through one's mind, a diary of sorts takes shape. In serial fashion, key events milestone the project – changes, dead-ends, parallel lines of enquiry, the conclusion and the ambitions of that first inception – moments of importance that turn into only a few days of recollection. Looking back on the Bordeaux project, I remember only Eight Days. And with each day the long hours of criticism, the short seconds of inspiration, the tug of all those movements that push and pull each way as what we call 'The Project' ticks on.

DAY ONE

Rem Koolhaas phones me. As usual the voice is urgent, full of convictions and ambitions, the language poised beautifully on extreme polarities. He has an unusual request, to make a villa in Bordeaux 'fly'.

The project is on a fantastic site with panoramic views over the rich, wine-laden city stretching along the river.

Rem says the client is seriously disabled from a recent car accident but is fighting back, determined to have a new life. And the house has to be a special one that can accommodate his needs with those of his wife and two children. They have a large town house, but now under different circumstances the family wants a new villa, up on the cliff edge, overlooking the city.

And I had that reaction when one first hears of a project – the immediate excitement, a new challenge and with it the start up fear – will it succeed?

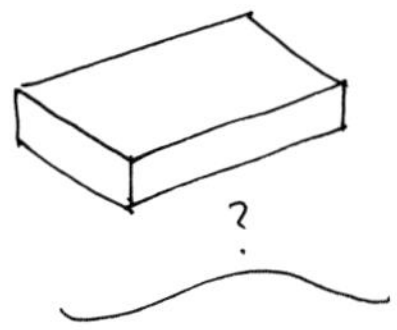

In the event, the answer was quite unexpected.

Generic Issues

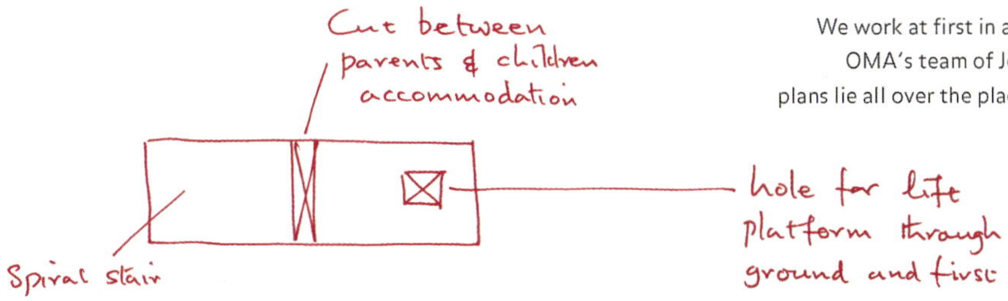

We meet in Bordeaux. The setting is something else – a hotel designed by Jean Nouvel overlooking the fields of Floriac, just a few miles outside the city.

We work at first in a ground floor reception room. No one seems to be about. OMA's team of Jerry and François are here and sketches of the site and ground plans lie all over the place. They outline the brief to me.

A family house, for husband and wife, plus two children. The design must give access to the disabled person, to release the full potential of the house. The principle tectonic is to be a box, up in the air, where the bedrooms will be located. Below this are the living spaces, surrounded by glass. The glass may open out onto the landscape and vanish; below the living space is a partial basement, cut into the earth on one side but open to an entry courtyard on the other. There is to be a special lift, a moving part of the house really to reach all levels.

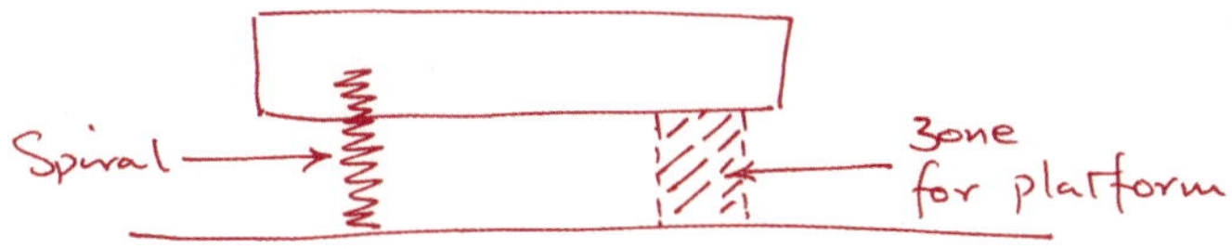

INTERROGATION:

To ask a mass to levitate is not a new question; there is always an architectural demand for a lightness of being, *tabula rasa* visions with nothing to account for gravity. Structure in these situations simply gets in the way, becoming an enemy of promise.

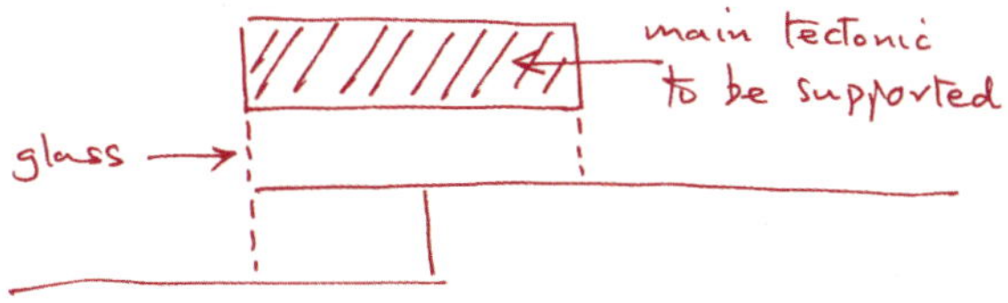

But gravity is a tyrant. Its pull cannot be avoided, and the usual response for supporting a load in the air is to configure legs to hold the weight up from below. There is a directness of purpose to this configuration but there is also a complacency to look for nothing else.

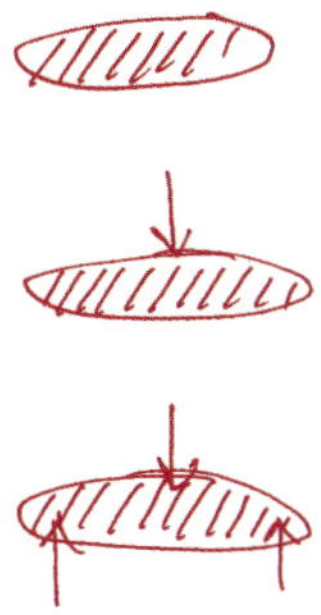

And the paradigm of 'table' brings with it implicit acceptance of a static symmetry.

A classic reference to this assumption in modern architecture is the Villa Savoye, Le Corbusier's pristine vision of a white box of light floating over the fields of Savoye.

Pilotti, concrete rods of a machine-like elegance, staple the form into the earth and anchor it, unmoving. Perhaps that is what the architect wanted, an altar forever fixed in space. Its mnemonic is temple. Such icons of form exert a stranglehold on future perception.

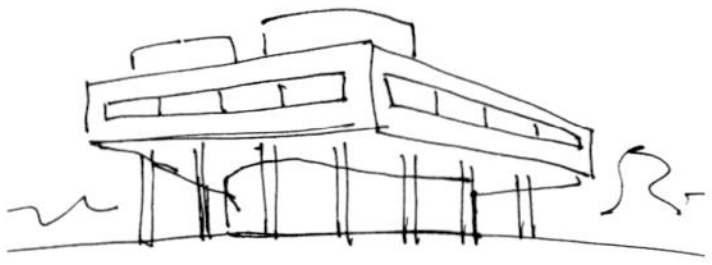

Countless imitations kill off speculation.

Now the question was being asked again, how to make a tectonic mass elevate, even fly. But did it need to? We went up to the site to have a look.

We cut through the heavy growth, finally emerging at the top. The views were terrific. The sun was going down, flooding the river with colour. Lights came on in the distance; it was that time of the day when cities turn into fairylands. If this were my house, I too would want a magic carpet up here, to look out on a twinkling land – the word 'hover' came to mind.

If a weight suspended above the earth should somehow levitate, the risk-answer must lie in the breaking of symmetry.

I sketched out various solutions, trying to set the mass 'free'.

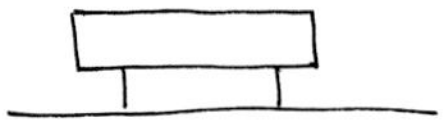

Columns were stuck well underneath to give a feeling of free edge:

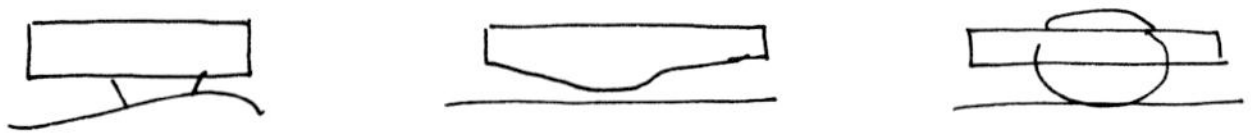

In some cases the ground came up to disguise the support:

In other instances raking columns initiated oblique lines to take away the feeling of direct support.

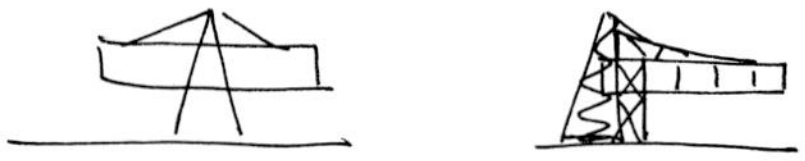

I tried top hung support as well but that felt alien and inappropriate for the site.

None of the ideas really satisfied. I still felt confined. The picture of the site kept imposing its own dynamic, challenging a better solution. No matter how the columns were placed beneath the load the generic concept of table came back, and with it the imprint of an 'anchor' killing off the ambition.

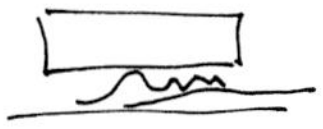

Something else was needed.

The idea of *launch* came to mind, to energise the building as momentum. Two lateral moves broke with symmetry.

Move one:

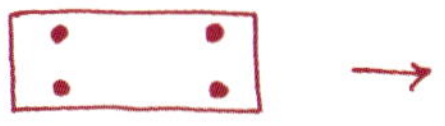

what if the supports in plan are displaced beyond the boundary, well outside the box?

Move two:

what if the supports 'flip' in elevation, one top hung, one bottom fixed?

Suddenly we had the dynamic we wanted. The side-way shifts in plan and jumps in elevation brought a skewed tension to the solution. They stretched the concept of balance to the edge of the predictable, towards a moment of instability, setting up a precise danger point.

26

At one end the box sits on a shelf beam. At the other end its weight hangs off a roof girder, precarious and scary. The cable that restores balance is placed outside the plan, mimicking the movement of the displaced column at the shelf support end. Each cross-section is the reverse of the other.

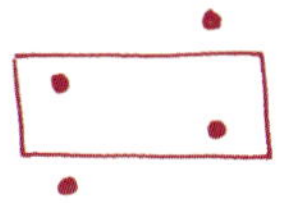

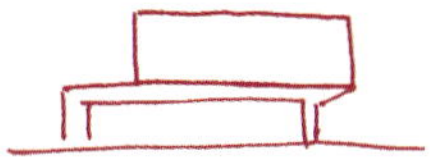

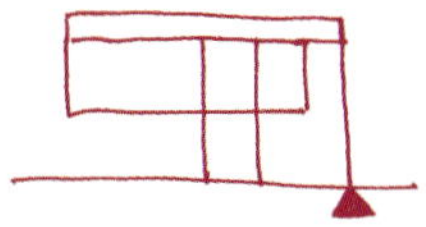

A contradiction is offered in how the load is perceived. The solution pulls one way and then the other. The weight of the box is both supported from the ground and hung up in the air, in plan and elevation the exaggerations deny any conventional reading of balance.

The idea of a table is destroyed. Instead, the dynamic is *launch.*

In my mind's eye I already saw the villa flying.

27

DAY THREE

Imagine a ball at the bottom of a concave curve. It nestles securely, unmoving. That is the pragmatic response to the support of load – a secure base, a stable configuration.

The reverse of this is a moment of insecurity at the top of a curve, inherently a position of instability. A slight push at the summit, one way or the other and the ball moves off and away.

The two diagrams serve as a metaphor for design; tried and tested, or new?

At the bottom of the valley, there is the point of tradition and solid reference. No matter how far we experiment and get away from that location and move up the slope, we fall back to the bottom and settle at the origin. Analysis always brings us back to the zero point. The solution cannot get away from its original reference. The Villa Savoye belongs to the valley diagram in its configuration of structure.

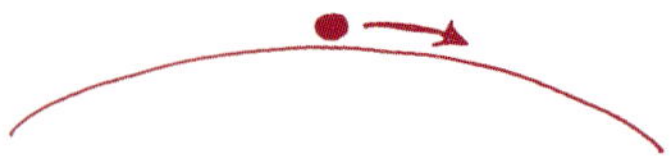

But at the summit of a hill the point is one of departure, the outcome unpredictable. There is no way back to the origin. We roll into the unknown to chart a new course. In the cliff top scenario there is not the safety of past reference, only the certainty of unfamiliar territory ahead.

The Bordeaux Villa belongs to this second category of diagram – its future interpretation yet to come.

28

DAY FOUR

This day was one of balance, working out the top support which picks up the wall beams.

At one end, the villa has a core running through it, a shaft that encloses a spiral stair. It is deliberately offset to add drama.

Such an eccentric support would cause a mass to tip over.

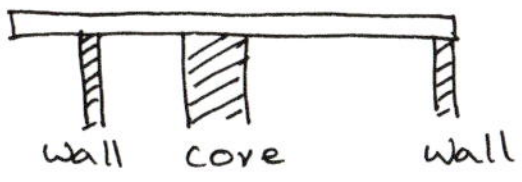

The diagrammatic is:

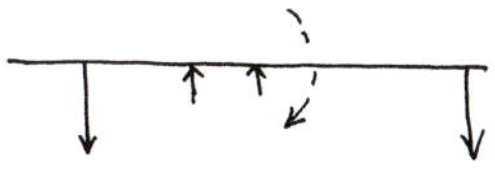

A tie down is needed at the extreme end to restore stability.

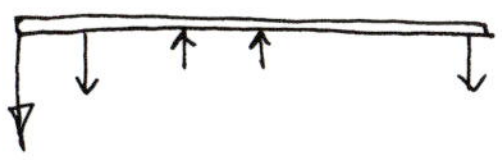

In the Bordeaux Villa this is given by a cable, providing tension through a counter weight buried in the ground. The trick is to keep the cable under tension all the time. A hot day, for example, will increase the length of the tie due to thermal expansion, slacken it, and tend to tip the box over to one side. So the cable is over tensioned to compensate and be taut under this condition keeping the mass to the horizontal. Asymmetrical loading of snow, or wind, or people can also induce slackness in the cable; and for each of these conditions calculations were made to ensure tension, at all times.

What happens if the cable is cut?

The box will tilt to one side; but the deflection is calculated and the material proportioned in such a way as to keep the structure stable in this extreme condition. Due to the elastic nature of materials (even concrete) once the cable force is reinstated the structure will ease back to the horizontal!

30

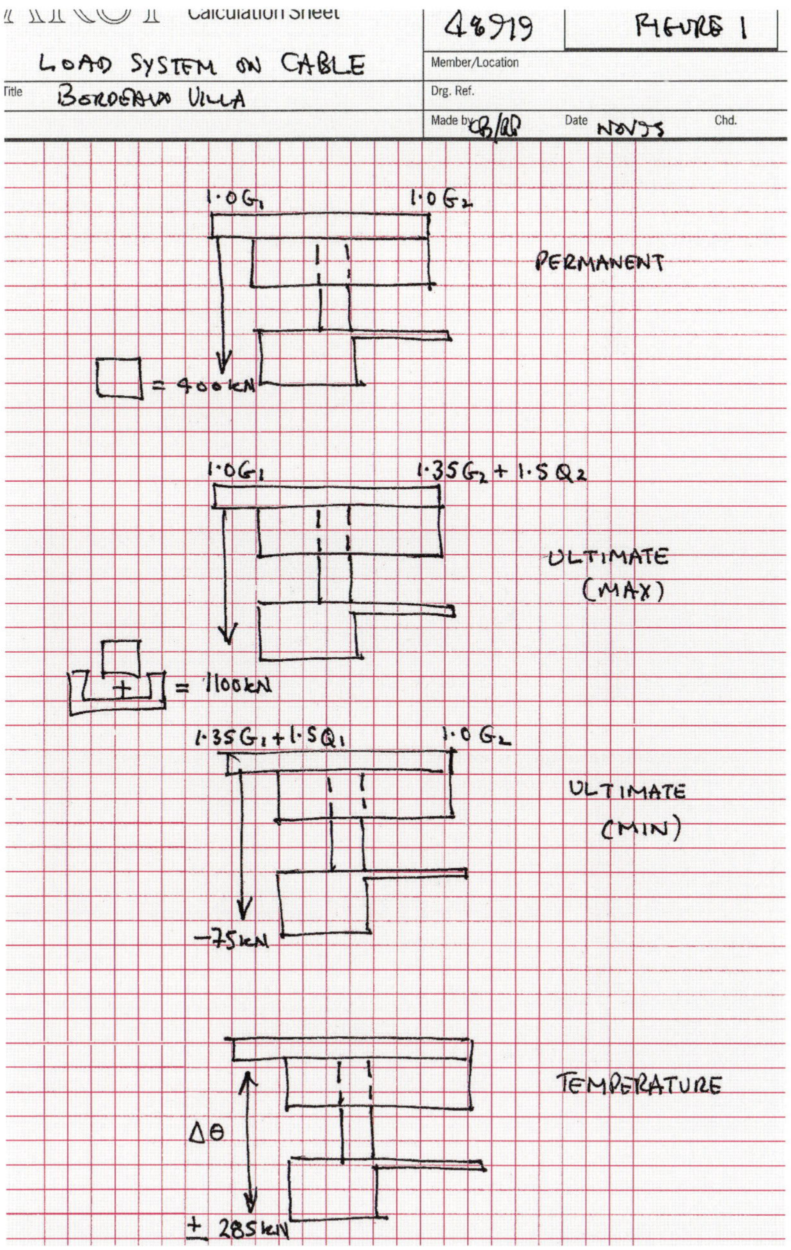

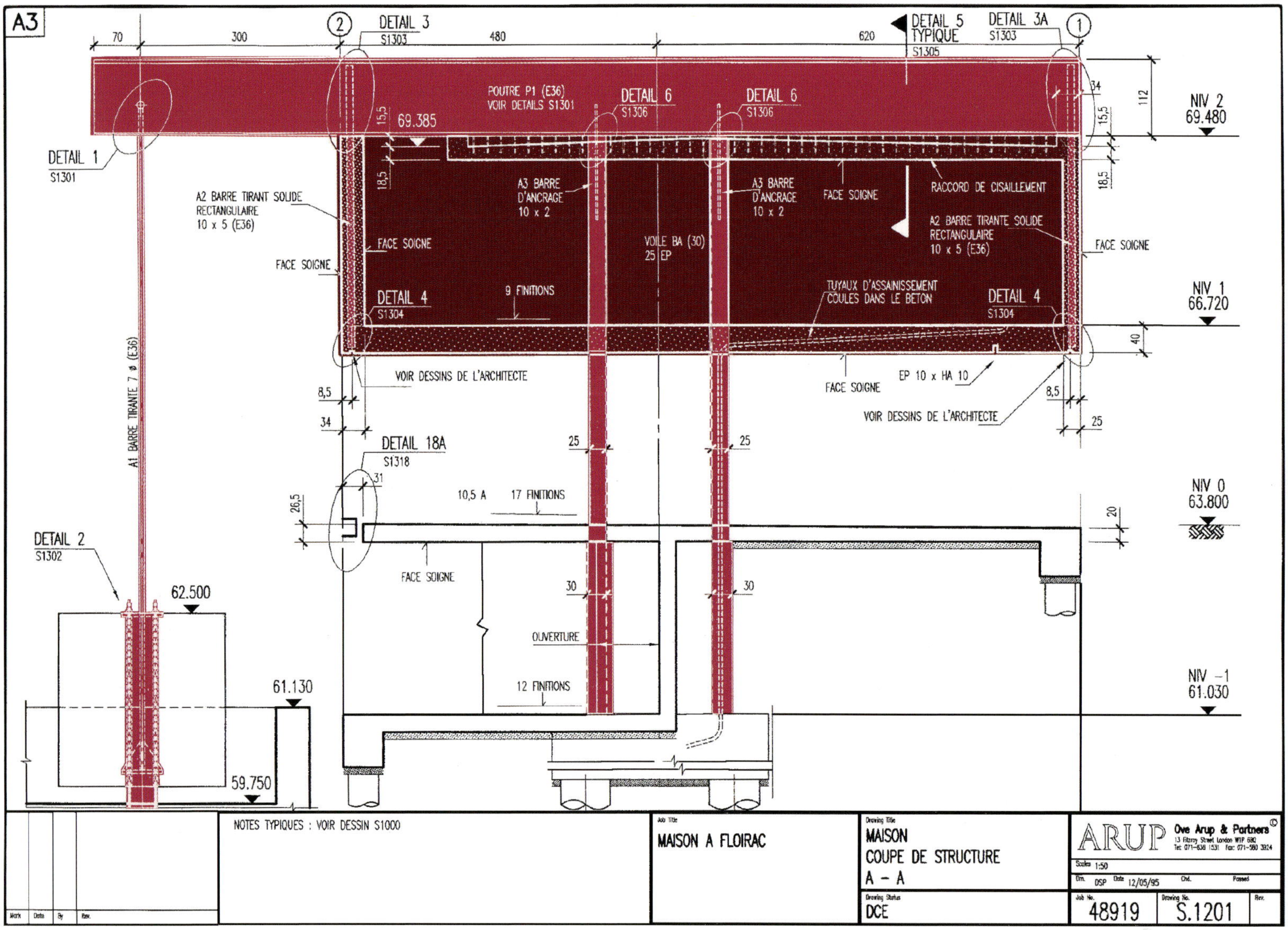
A3
DETAIL 3
S1303
DETAIL 5
TYPIQUE
S1305
DETAIL 3A
S1303
POUTRE P1 (E36)
VOIR DETAILS S1301
DETAIL 6
S1306
69.385
NIV 2
69.480
DETAIL 1
S1301
A2 BARRE TIRANT SOLIDE
RECTANGULAIRE
10 x 5 (E36)
A3 BARRE
D'ANCRAGE
10 x 2
FACE SOIGNE
RACCORD DE CISAILLEMENT
A2 BARRE TIRANTE SOLIDE
RECTANGULAIRE
10 x 5 (E36)
VOILE BA (30)
25 EP
DETAIL 4
S1304
9 FINITIONS
TUYAUX D'ASSAINISSEMENT
COULES DANS LE BETON
NIV 1
66.720
VOIR DESSINS DE L'ARCHITECTE
EP 10 x HA 10
A1 BARRE TIRANTE 7 ø (E36)
DETAIL 18A
S1318
10,5 A
17 FINITIONS
NIV 0
63.800
DETAIL 2
S1302
62.500
OUVERTURE
12 FINITIONS
61.130
NIV -1
61.030
59.750
NOTES TYPIQUES : VOIR DESSIN S1000
MAISON A FLOIRAC
MAISON
COUPE DE STRUCTURE
A - A
DCE
ARUP Ove Arup & Partners
13 Fitzroy Street London W1P 6BQ
Scales 1:50
DSP 12/05/95
48919
S.1201

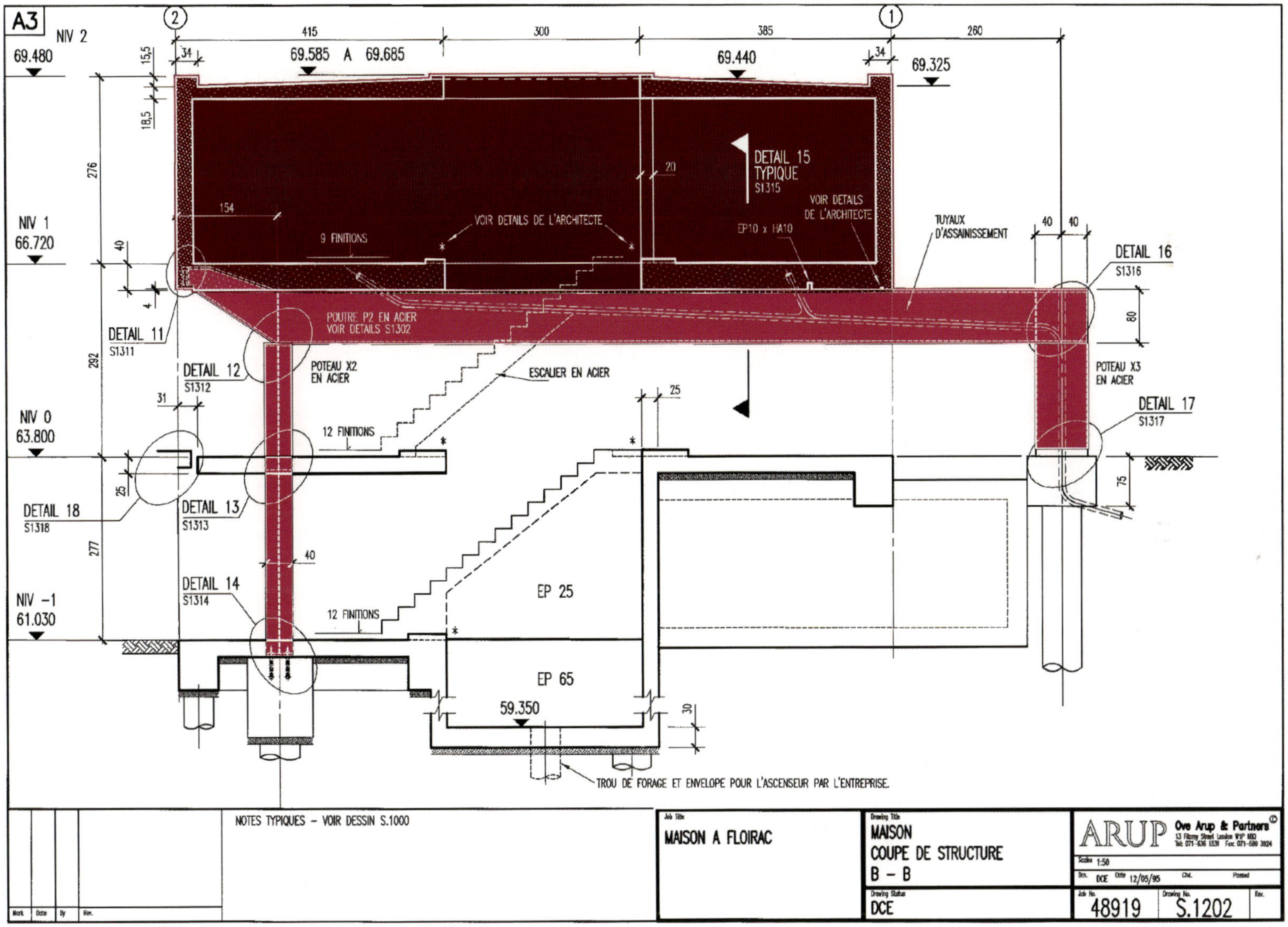
A3
NIV 2
69.480
415
300
385
260
69.585 A 69.685
69.440
69.325
DETAIL 15
TYPIQUE
S1315
VOIR DETAILS
DE L'ARCHITECTE
VOIR DETAILS DE L'ARCHITECTE
9 FINITIONS
EP10 x HA10
TUYAUX
D'ASSAINISSEMENT
NIV 1
66.720
DETAIL 16
S1316
POUTRE P2 EN ACIER
VOIR DETAILS S1302
DETAIL 11
S1311
DETAIL 12
S1312
POTEAU X2
EN ACIER
ESCALIER EN ACIER
POTEAU X3
EN ACIER
DETAIL 17
S1317
NIV 0
63.800
12 FINITIONS
DETAIL 18
S1318
DETAIL 13
S1313
DETAIL 14
S1314
EP 25
NIV -1
61.030
12 FINITIONS
EP 65
59.350
TROU DE FORAGE ET ENVELOPE POUR L'ASCENSEUR PAR L'ENTREPRISE.
NOTES TYPIQUES - VOIR DESSIN S.1000
MAISON A FLOIRAC
MAISON
COUPE DE STRUCTURE
B - B
DCE
ARUP
Ove Arup & Partners
1:50
12/05/95
48919
S.1202

DAY FIVE

I proposed a seamless winding of material for the elevated box, a concrete culvert.

Specification: 40 cm floor; 20 cm roof; 25 cm walls.

The roof and floor spanned 11 metres onto longitudinal wall beams. These beams in turn had two supports, and cantilevered beyond them at each end. Though thin in section the depth of these walls gave adequate stiffness and the gable ends of the box could be kept open if needed. On the wall beams, lines of principal stress were marked so that holes could be cut out without complications to the structural action.

Keep it simple – that was the aim.

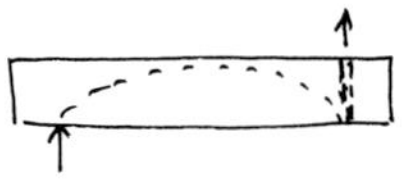

A grid was plotted on the wall elevation to allow a random solution. Rem speculated that small porthole-like windows scattered throughout the elevation would look terrific. We floated small circles, like soap bubble experiments, through the elevation as we tried various punctuations – low level portholes for the client in a wheelchair, and high level vista points for the others. Views were calculated and prescribed. A beautiful drawing, like a wind rose, took shape in OMA's office.

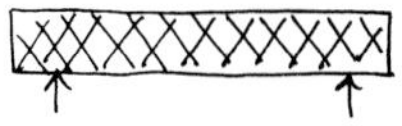

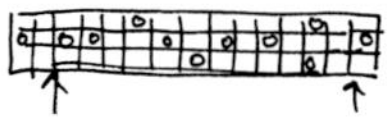

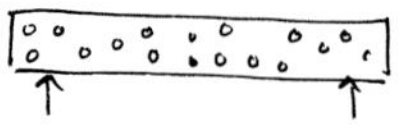

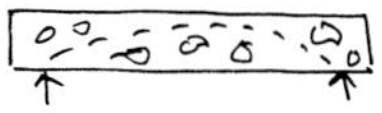

The design, we thought, was progressing well. The shape, size and configuration were solved, the materiality agreed: we were into the 'Avant Projet Détaillé' stage of design, prior to tender.

Then came the problems.

The floor slab looked too heavy, the roof too light. The free edges along the cuts in the slab were deflecting significantly and the walls were felt to be too thin.

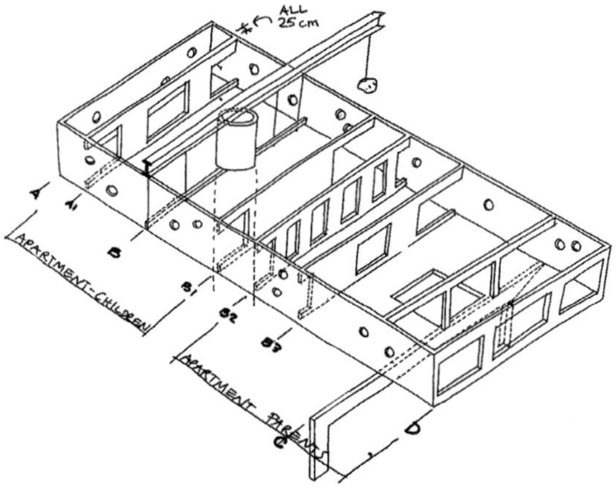

Strategies were looked at to lighten the floors; conventional beam and slab framing methods/void formers in polystyrene/rib systems/etc. Use of the stairs from ground to first floor as a prop was even considered so that all key dimensions could be maintained; but the stair was too weak and located badly, to take any significant load.

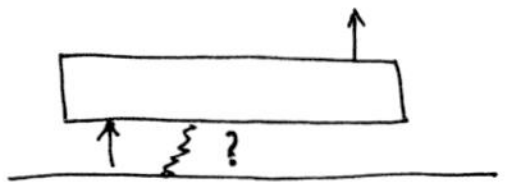

Various initiatives by our respective teams grew, challenging the concept.

Suddenly it all seemed too difficult. That uneasy moment arrived when the initial idea began to turn into a grave doubt. The culvert form was abandoned. Internal Vierendeel type beams were introduced to stiffen the roof and floor, allowing more slender dimensions for slab elements, but the Vierendeel solution meant intrusions below the soffit, reducing headroom and a consequent heightening of the vertical dimension of the box. Did we want to do this?

If a few more millimetres were added to the height of the wall we saw the suspended form, from being 'heavy and just right', turning into 'massive and ugly'.

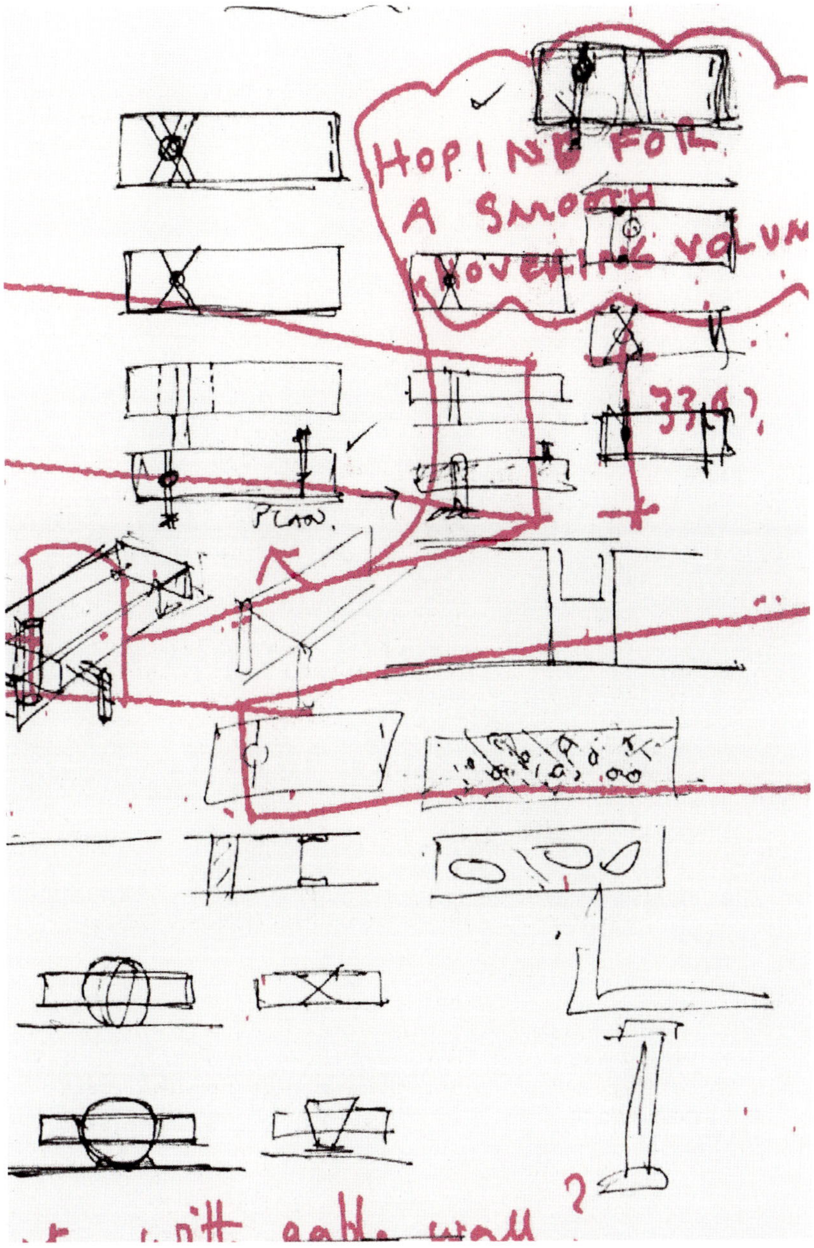

There were other technical problems as well.

The physical cut in both roof and floor slabs, gave a major discontinuity to the transmission of lateral loads. Normally the slabs would be considered as braced diaphragms, but now the walls had to act as horizontal ties, passing stability load between the core and slender verticals of the portal type shelf beam.

One side of the basement opened onto the landscape, the other side remaining buried against the cut earth . . .

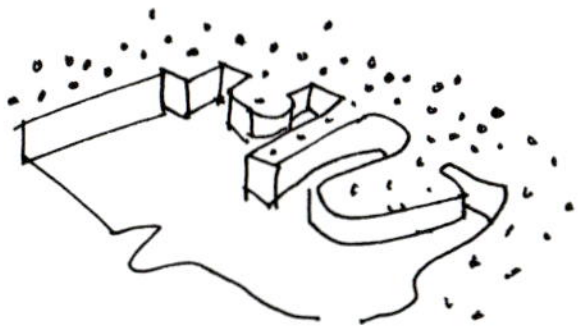

. . . this gave a horizontal force from the retained earth face that had to be resisted. Again, a problem of lateral stability.

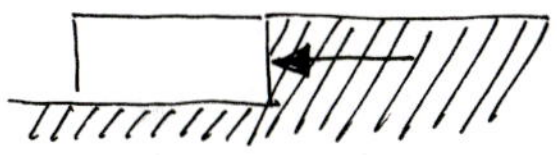

Other questions were asked such as how to make the glass walls at ground level 'vanish', and what chases and slots should be cut into the concrete slab to accommodate sliding rails? The very interventions that gave freedom to the people in the house, eroded the concrete section and weakened it, threatening more support or thicker dimensions. A meeting was called for.

It is the insanity of design 'rightness' that makes one stick to stubborn judgements and we returned to the initial concept despite the uncertainties. No one can account for such dictates but they dig in, convinced of their own *a priori* logic.
We decided to start afresh, drawing the simple culvert shape again; I restated the dimensions as if the questions against it had never been. Perhaps it was just the renewed focus that helped, for things quickly fell into place. The slabs worked, the beams worked. Conduits, slots for door slides, drainage falls, free edge deflections, were somehow all solved. We were back on track. What had the fuss been about? Impossible to say: how does a collective nervousness work to destroy a confident starting point? Reassertion of the concept seemed to steady the hand of the possible and work a minor miracle. The day looked good again.

39

DAY SIX

The main tectonic of the box solved, attention turned to the design and proportioning of the two main lines of support. If a mass has momentum, it should not be 'pinned' or held back. The supporting beam lines should not restrain, they must just touch.

TOP HUNG:

Rods buried in the concrete walls took the load up into the top steel beam. This girder was made to accommodate a double web so that the rod fixing passed between the web plates in secret. Similarly, the tension cable departed through a slot cut in the bottom flange. The roof connected via shear studs buried in a concrete plinth to give a seamless feeling between beam and slab.

The aim was to declare 'look no hands'; the apparent lack of 'nailing' or gussetting adding to a perceived moment of danger.

BOTTOM SUPPORT:

Here the proposal was for a portal type frame. Initially concrete was considered, but the dimensions of the beam grew, reducing headroom at ground level drastically. Transferring the wall load at the tip of the cantilever also produced a high shear stress. Steel with its greater strengths seemed more appropriate. A hollow section could also be developed for this beam, allowing a path for drainage pipes from the floor above. And steel provided sharp edges in contrast to the seamless wrap of concrete – a hard precision could be brought to the solution

A special feature was made of starting the taper from the centre of its supporting column, to emphasise an exact point of balance. The idea was to stress this coincidence against the more distributed aspects of the overall configuration.

40

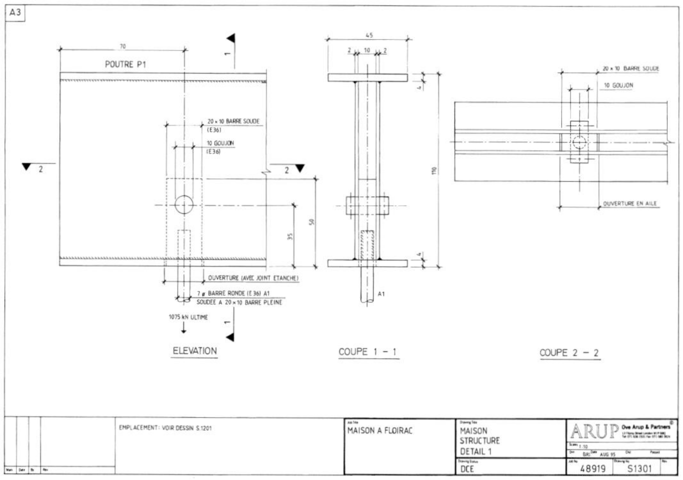

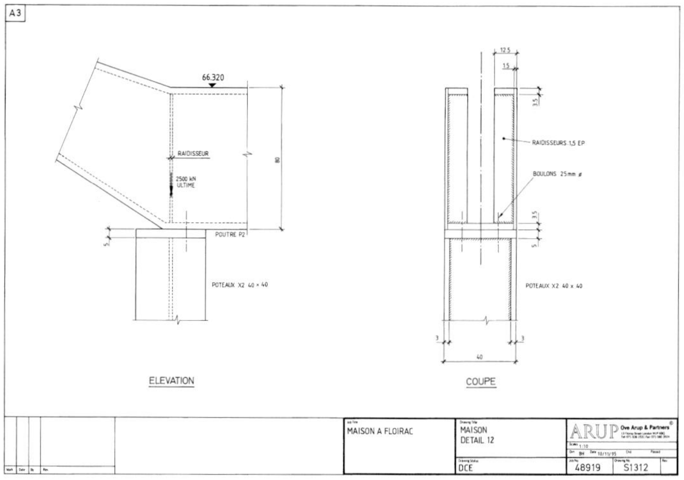

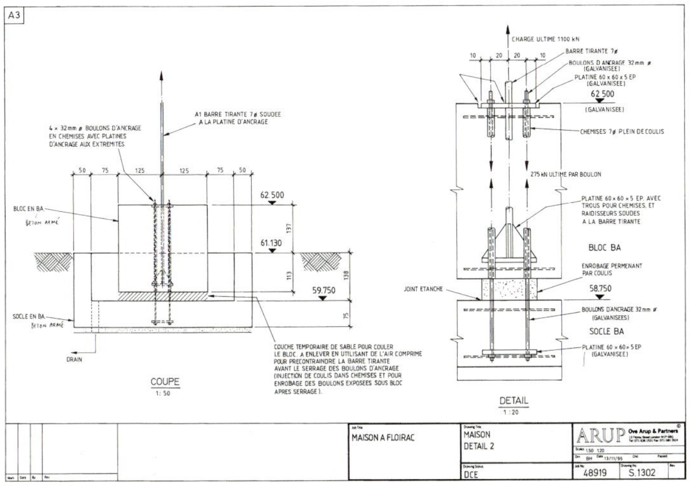

DAY SEVEN

No one wants a day like this, but every project seems to have one – savings had to be made! The project was over budget and despite our attachment to the solution, some key features had to be redesigned.

Two cost reductions were agreed to.

1: Reduce the weight of the steel roof beam by making it much deeper, from 1.0 m to say 1.4 m.

We had spent a lot of time minimising the size of this top girder, keeping volume and bulk down, and every millimetre had been guarded jealously. If we accepted the contractor's proposal for a change, there would be a 40% increase to the vertical height of a key element. This was hard to swallow.

But the dramatic increase in height exaggerated the idea of 'beam', moving it towards another definition in Koolhaas' mind, of 'fascia'. The OMA team thought it would actually work better, and not for the first time in our work, out of a forced brutality a new inspiration was improvised.

2: Get rid of the counterweight.

Conceptually we wanted a very visible reading of 'anchor', a rock hanging freely from a cable. Through design development and concerns for safety the rock had turned into a concrete dead weight, located in a pit and held down further by a buried foundation. This was now too expensive. It was cheaper to bury the anchor they said, and have the cable tie disappear into the ground, fastened onto a lump of dead concrete.

This was a pity. The visible counterbalance underlined the drama of tipping over. But savings had to be made, and we reluctantly agreed to the change. Only a plate on the surface would denote passage through to the subterranean holding. It was expedient but not poetic, not our daredevil vision of a hung weight in space denoting a danger moment.

43

DAY EIGHT

Construction was over. The shutters had been taken off, slabs depropped; walls were sustaining their design load and transmitting stress around the various window apertures. The thin box culvert spanned and cantilevered. Would the mental picture we had of the box 'flying' as it were, be there? Would the analogue of the actual building take shape and leap out at us?

The day I went to see the work, by luck, Rem was there. François and Jerry were there as well. The same people assembled in Bordeaux as on Day One.
Was this the conclusion?

We compared notes. The skew supports gave configurations such that one end of the box literally seemed to launch itself off into space. Being released from the traditional securing of a centre of gravity, the mass seemed to power itself. We saw that symmetric supports would have been terrible, giving a static feel.

Wrenching the supports apart, moving them outside the plan, gave a degree of release.

Flipping the supports in elevation, one top and one bottom, added the second release.

The two movements taken together allowed the mass its own momentum – from tremendous to terrific. Almost scary at one angle, like a missile pointing over the edge, at another angle it looked a monster trapped against its will. Either way, the configuration worked. It was dramatic, brutal and exciting.

For Rem and I this was raw hypothesis made real, no adornment, no finish, just *structure*.

Ursula Litschi

Expressing Moment Frames

Buchholz Sports Hall, Uster, Switzerland (1998)
Architect: Camenzind Evolution
Structural Engineer: Geilinger Stahlbau
Model: Miriam Roure

This glass-enclosed building with its exposed steel frames refers to the architecture of Mies van der Rohe from some thirty years earlier. Spaces for sporting events and seating for 1000 spectators are spanned and contained by frames whose profiles stand out against the brightly daylit interior.

The frames are of the "rigid" variety that depends on the bending stiffness of its elements and on certain rigid beam-to-column connections in order to resist gravity and lateral loads and be stable. This is expressed by the variation of the member dimensions; i.e., the shape of their bending moment diagram is clearly legible, with the in-plane dimension of the members varying quite distinctively. Locations of maximum flexure correspond to maximum dimension, while elsewhere the section tapers to hinge points corresponding to zero bending moment.

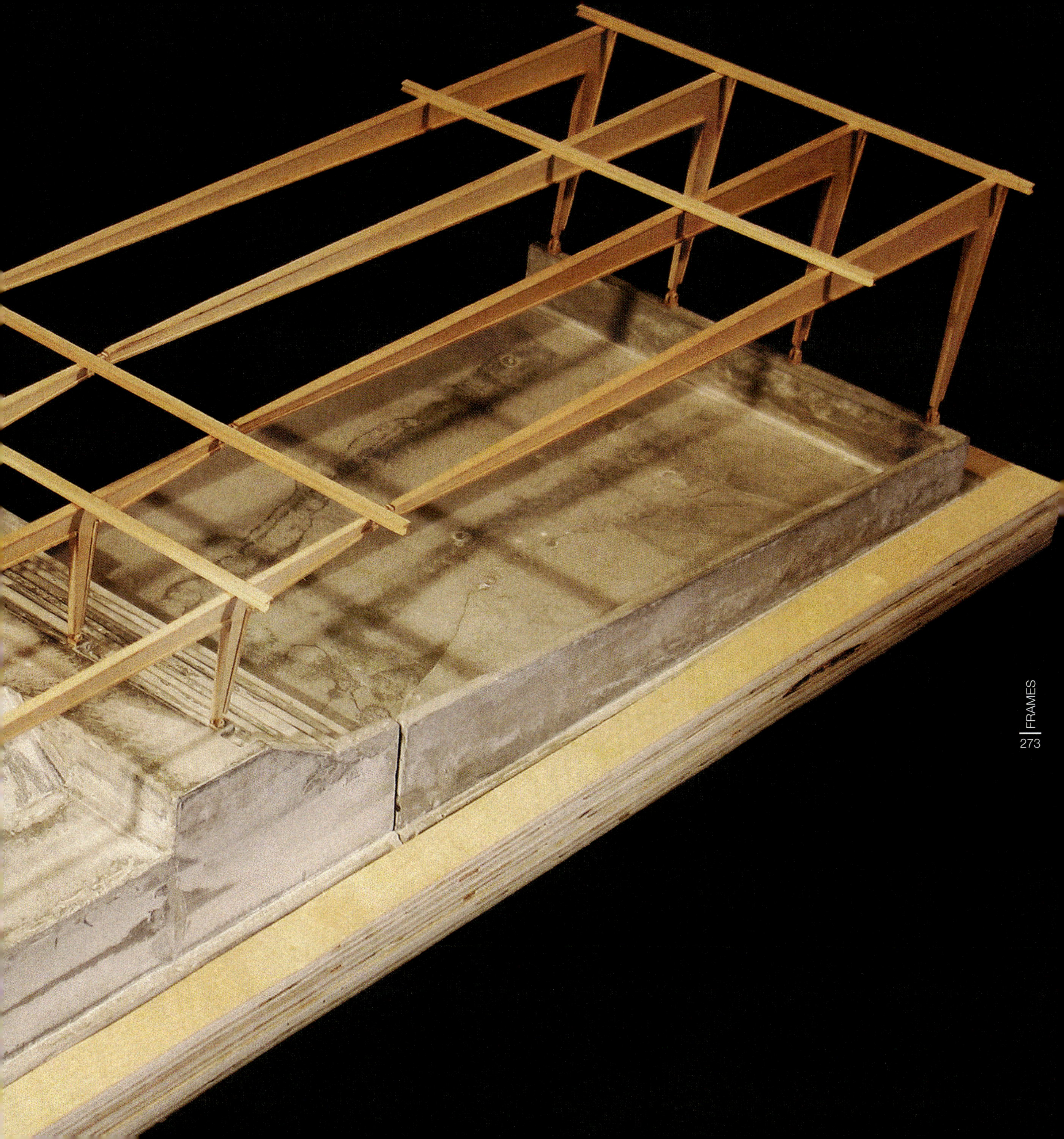

© Mini Yu Sun/Arup

Trussed Rigid Frames

Beijing National Stadium, Beijing, China (2008)
Architect: Herzog & de Meuron, Arup Sports, China Architectural Design & Research Group. Structural Engineer: Arup
Model: Mandy Chen + Hana Svatoš-Ražnjcevic´

This seemingly random array of crisscrossing steel elements disguises quite a recognizable structural system: 48 planar rigid frames span at skewed angles over the stadium seating, each tangential to the roof's central opening. These frames intersect with one another, and in so doing provide stability and share loads. Also, the vertical and horizontal segments of the frames are trussed, which suggests they have to resist large internal bending moments. Each rigid frame is of the two-hinged configuration: the trussed columns have pinned connections at their bases but their dimension increases toward their top corner connection to the trussed beams, where the bending moments are largest. [see also p. 295]

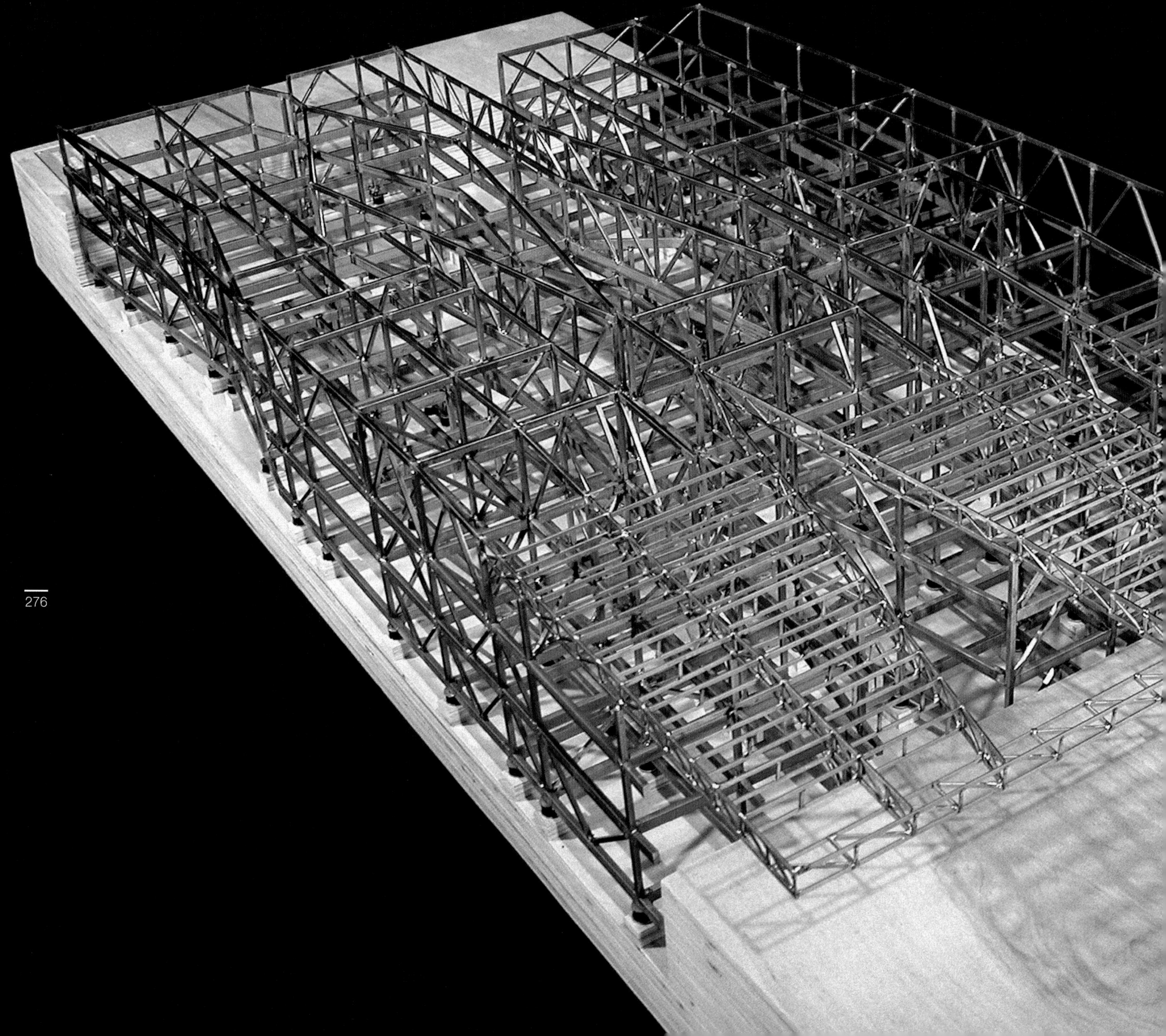

Frame Articulations

de Young Museum, San Francisco, CA, USA (2005)
Architect: Herzog & de Meuron
Structural Engineer: Rutherford & Chekene
Model: Kumar Sebastian Coors Atre + Reilly Hogan

© Michael Layefsky

The de Young Museum is located in San Francisco's Golden Gate Park, not far from the eponymous bridge. It replaces an earlier museum building built there in 1894 in the Egyptian-revival style whose cast concrete ornamentation had all fallen off or been removed by 1949 and which was completely destroyed in 1989 by the Loma Prieta earthquake. These historical facts are reflected in its replacement building's design: e.g., the park's trees inspired a contemporary "ornamental" façade made of perforated copper sheeting whose patterning mimics sunlight passing through leaves; also, the building is partially isolated from earthquakes by seismic bearings at the base of its columns that absorb kinetic energy and allow the building to "float" independently above the ground motion.

The visual massiveness of this 27,000m^2 (293,000ft^2) multi-story steel-framed building is diminished by partially sinking it below grade; also by having openings that penetrate deep into the sides of the building and courtyards that bring light down to its lower levels. From a structural perspective such "carving up" of the overall building results in a collection of effectively separate "buildings", each of which needs to be stabilized. The consequence is a remarkable density of many braced frames of the "V", inverted-"V" and single diagonal configuration that are strategically dispersed throughout the overall structural system. Ironically, the "opening" of the building in one sense requires it to become more "closed" in another. [see also p. 293]

Peter Buteÿn

Frame Variations

Water Pavilion, Neeltje Jans Island, Netherlands (1997)
Architect: NOX/Lars Spuybroek
Structural Engineer: Ingenieursbureau Zonneveld
Model: Nathan C. Friedman

Located on an artificial island constructed as part of the system of water-level-control dams along the Dutch shoreline, this pavilion features an interactive display of water technologies that change by means of visitor-activated sensors. The building is of a highly innovative form for its time, having continuously curving geometry in which floors, walls and roof merge into each other; digital computation was instrumental for both the overall design and fabrication of component parts. A set of curved steel moment-resistant frames define form and space alike, with shapes that vary according to complex changes in plan and section geometry; e.g., to accommodate the twisting form the frames are radially oriented towards two imaginary focal points, while the continuous change of section requires all of the frames to be different (and rather dramatically so).

© Iwan Baan

Frames Bracing 3D Space

Makoko Floating School, Lagos, Nigeria (2013)
Architect: NLÉ/Kunlé Adeyemi
Structural Engineer: Pieters Bouwtechniek; Roel Bosch
Model: Jing Liu + Yongxiao Liu

This floating school in the Lagos Lagoon is built as a prototype that can adapt to varying water levels – whether tidal or climatic; it is carried on 256 buoyant plastic barrels. The lower level serves as an open communal gathering/work space; above are enclosed classrooms and an observation area at the top. Five wooden A-frames made from offcuts support these levels and give the building its distinctive form; critically, this configuration also maintains a low centre of gravity. Diagonal bracing stabilizes the frames in both orthogonal directions, but is not needed in every bay; rather, it is positioned strategically according to both structural and occupancy/circulation needs.

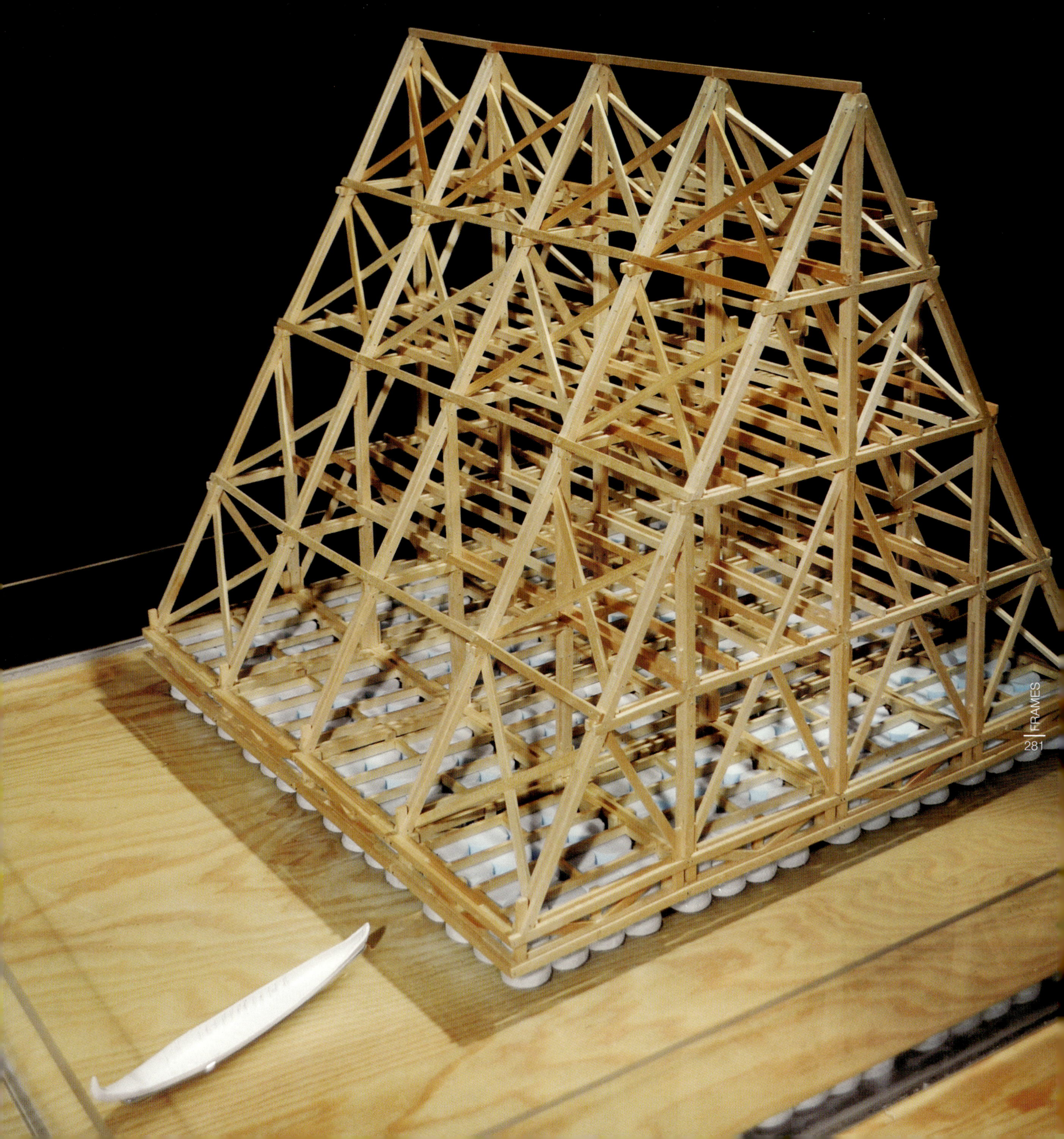

Inclined-Strut Bracing

Steilneset Memorial, Vardø, Norway (2011)
Architect: Peter Zumthor Architect
Structural Engineer: Finn-Erik Nilsen/Oslo and
Akershus University College of Applied Sciences
Model: Kevin Alexander + Jackie Krasnokutskaya

© Andrew Meredith

Located on the rugged shoreline facing the Barents Sea, the so-called Witch Burning Memorial Museum commemorates the 91 native people who were put to death in the 17th century for practicing witchcraft. Inspired by the vernacular timber trestles used in the region for air-drying fish, the Memorial's relentless length makes its presence felt in the expansive landscape. A full-length boardwalk is contained within the fabric membrane volume that is stretched taut between the ribs of the structure; small window openings admit/emit light and account for the life of each of the victims. At the end of this linear sequence is a steel and glass contemplative pavilion designed with the artist Louise Bourgeois; a chair at its center burns in perpetuity while angled overhead mirrors reflect the flames and the charged history of the place.

A long series of simply-connected transverse frames composed of exterior vertical columns and floor- and roof-level beams are stabilized by inward-leaning angled struts on either side of the rectangular opening that defines the central spatial axis. These struts provide the necessary resistance for the frames to be braced against the lateral loads that are applied to the structure by both the strong ocean winds as well as by the inward pulls from the many cable anchorages that are needed to stretch and stabilize the fabric membrane. [see also p. 292]

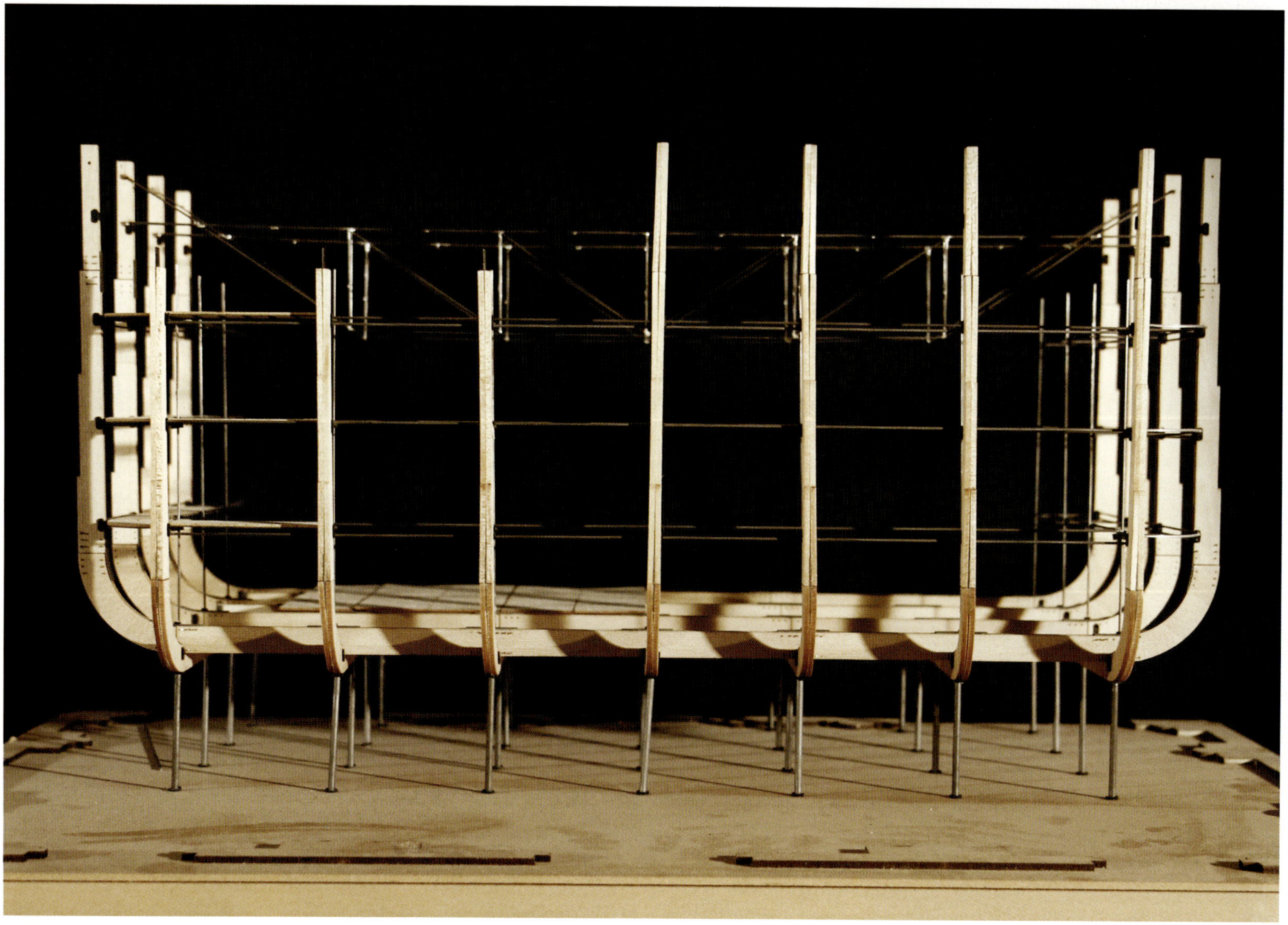

Gianni Berengo Gardin

Rigid Frame Inverted

Prometeo Musical Space, Venice and Milan (1983-84)
Architect: Renzo Piano Building Workshop
Structural Engineer: Favero & Milan
Model: Dorota Anna Niedzwiecki

Built inside a deconsecrated church and later in a warehouse, this musical performance space was specially designed for an innovative opera production. The audience was seated at the center, surrounded by the musicians on the scaffold-like perimeter platforms carried by the curved, boat-like wooden ribs. These cantilevering, vertical ribs have profiles that vary according to bending moment demand and are bent at the base to become floor beams. For ease of transport and assembly, the structure was built in modular fashion and bolted together on site – the exposed details at once a testament to the structure's impermanence, but also to its raw power.

Masuda + Otsubo Architects

Flexible Braced Frames

Little Hilltop Wind Tower, Yamagushi Prefecture, Japan (2011)
Architect: Shingo Masuda and Katsuhisa Otsubo, with Yuta Shimada
Structural Engineer: Jun Sato Structural Engineers
Model: Anamika Goyal + Alex Jopek

A commission for a place to view wind turbines in the landscape was reconceived as the design of a structure that allows visitors to "see" the wind at close quarters. This tower interacts with shifting winds by visibly swaying back and forth; i.e., for wind speeds of 8m/s (18mph) there is 150mm (6in) movement at the top. Acting as a vertical cantilever, the 7.5m- (25ft-) tall tower accomplishes this by having its steel X-braced frame structure made of very light, thin components and by incorporating specially detailed sliding connections at the ends of the bracing elements; moreover, a flexible double-layer skin made of vulcanized rubber sheets permits the movement to occur without damage.

Aalto Arts / Anne Kinnunen

Diagrid Bracing Structure

Korkeasaari Lookout Tower, Helsinki, Finland (2002)
Architect: Aalto University, Wood Studio/Ville Hara
Structural Engineer: Hannu Hirsi, Lauri Salokangas/Nuvo Engineering
Model: Megan Lund + Cassidy Viser

Designed and built by a group of students, this 10m-tall (30ft) wood structure offers views from an island zoo back toward Helsinki harbour. Two observation decks are contained within the basket-like, grid-shell structure that both supports the floors and braces the tower against lateral loads. The structure consists of 72 long, pre-bent timber battens crisscrossing each other diagonally to form a lamella grid. The necessary twisting of the 60 by 60mm (2.5 by 2.5in) glulam members to accommodate the doubly curved shape was achieved by on-site steam bending, an eco-friendly technique well known in traditional boat building. The wood is treated with a linen oil-based wood balm that provides UV-protection.

John Linden

Shape- and Space-Defining Frames

Chanel Mobile Art Pavilion, Paris (also New York, Hong Kong, Tokyo) (2008-2010)
Architect: Zaha Hadid with Patrik Schumacher
Structural Engineer: Arup
Model: Hong Yeol In + Sida Zhang

Although designed as a mobile structure, after a world tour this building was situated next to Paris's Institut du Monde Arabe. Its exterior form and internal spaces are irregularly curved, demonstrating what 3D computer modeling and CNC machining enable in architecture; the building skin is similarly innovative, made of white, shiny panels of fiber-reinforced polymer (FRP).

The hidden steel structural system is a kit of parts that could fit into standard shipping containers; upon arrival at a site, the system was assembled in a week. A set of ribs, each one different, establishes the pavilion's curved overall form and varying internal spaces. In plan, these rib-frames are arranged "radially" (with respect to the building's roughly triangular configuration), spanning the distance from the outer "wall" to the edge of the internal courtyard. Braced frames surround the courtyard and stabilize the pavilion against lateral loading in any direction.

01

02

03

04

06

05

01,02. Braced frames and trusses form series of rigid frames – Les Grandes Tables de l'île Seguin temporary restaurant, Paris, France, 2011; 1024 Architecture; model by Justin Foo & Aya Mears **03. Inclined compression struts stabilize frame in orthogonal directions** – Fleetguard Factory, Quimper, France, 1981; Richard Rogers Partnership (arch.); Arup (eng.); model by Awymarie Riollano **04. Multi-bay, multi-story rigid frame; provides compression ring for suspended ceiling** – Sandra Day O'Connor Courthouse, Phoenix, AZ, USA, 2000; Richard Meier & Partners (arch.), James Carpenter (glass ceiling, main courtroom); Arup (eng.); model by Justin Roznowski **05. Varying angles of rigid frame suggest motion; openness allows through passage** – Mediopedana Station, Reggio Emilia, Italy, 2013; Santiago Calatrava (arch., eng.); model by Stephany Amasifuen & Andreea Gulerez **06. Inclined compression struts stabilize wooden frame** – Steilneset Memorial, Vardø, Norway, 2011; Peter Zumthor (arch.); Finn-Erik Nilsen/Oslo and Akershus University College of Applied Sciences (eng.); model by Kevin Alexander & Jackie Krasnokutskaya **07. Bracing stabilizes multi-story, multi-bay steel frame; base-isolation diminishes seismic sidesway** – de Young Museum; San Francisco, CA, USA, 2005; Herzog & de Meuron, and Fong & Chan Architects; Rutherford & Chekene (eng.); model by Kumar Sebastian Coors Atre & Reilly Hogan **08. X-bracing stabilizes steel frame** – Parking Stack, Sindelfingen, Germany, 1999; Petry + Wittfoht Architects; A.Kannemacher, J.Rath, R.Sturm (eng.); model by Rosangela Roque **09. Braced frames and trusses form overall rigid frames; open interior space** – Biblioteca Vasconcelos, Mexico City, Mexico, 2010; Alberto Kalach (arch.); Enrique Arriaga, EMRSA (eng.); model by Walmir Luz & Isidoro Michan Guindi **10. Cross-bracing stabilizes timber frame, opens central aisle, creates shadow effects** – Thorncrown Chapel, Eureka Springs, AR, USA, 1980; Fay Jones Architects; model by Eric Ross Bernstein

11

12

13

14

15

11,12. X-braced frames in orthogonal directions; pin connection detail – International Garden and Horticultural Exhibition Pavilion, Shizuoka, Japan, 2004; Kengo Kuma and Associates (arch.); Norihide Imagawa (eng.); model by Sean Steed & Andrew Wong **13. Sidewall bracing of timber frame** – Bird-Watching Tower, Graswarder, Germany, 2005; von Gerkan, Marg and Partners (arch.); model by Dillon Pranger & Mary Esther Palumbo **14. Diagonal members resist vertical shear** – Peak Lab Research Station, proposal for Klein Matterhorn, near Zermatt, Switzerland, 2004; HTA Luzern, Richard Horden (arch.); model by Joseph DeSense **15. Inclined bamboo columns provide stability** – German-Chinese House, Shanghai, China, Expo 2010; Markus Heinsdorff (arch.); Mike Sieder/University of Technology, Munich (eng.); model by Jason Freedman & Elizabeth Saleh **16. Inclined columns stabilize expandable house** – Zirl House, Zirl, Austria, 1997; Ernst J. Fuchs (arch.); Christian Aste (eng.); model by Justine Yovava Cheng **17. Exterior columns carry gravity, lateral loads** – Edificio BIP, Santiago, Chile, 2008; Alberto Mozó (arch.); Juan Lopez Engineers; model by Jina Kim **18. X-bracing stabilizes adjacent open frames** – Parrish Art Museum, Water Mill, NY, USA, 2012; Herzog & de Meuron (arch.); S.L. Maresca & Associates (eng.); model by Karim Daw & Relique Lott **19. Braced frames stabilize building, support truss from which floors are hung** – Media-TIC Building, Barcelona, Spain, 2010; CLOUD 9, Enric Ruiz-Geli (arch.); BOMA, Augusti Obiols (eng.); model by Michael Jefferson & Suzanne Lettieri **20. Inclined columns support, stabilize building overhang** – Rutgers Business School, New Brunswick, NJ, USA, 2013; TEN Arquitectos; WSP Cantor Seinuk (eng.); model by Paul Fuschetti & Amy Wood **21. Trussed rigid connection** – National Stadium, Beijing, China, 2008; Herzog & de Meuron (arch.), Ai Weiwei (design consultant); Arup (eng.); model by Mandy Chen & Hana Svatoš-Ražnjevi

16

17

18

19

20

21

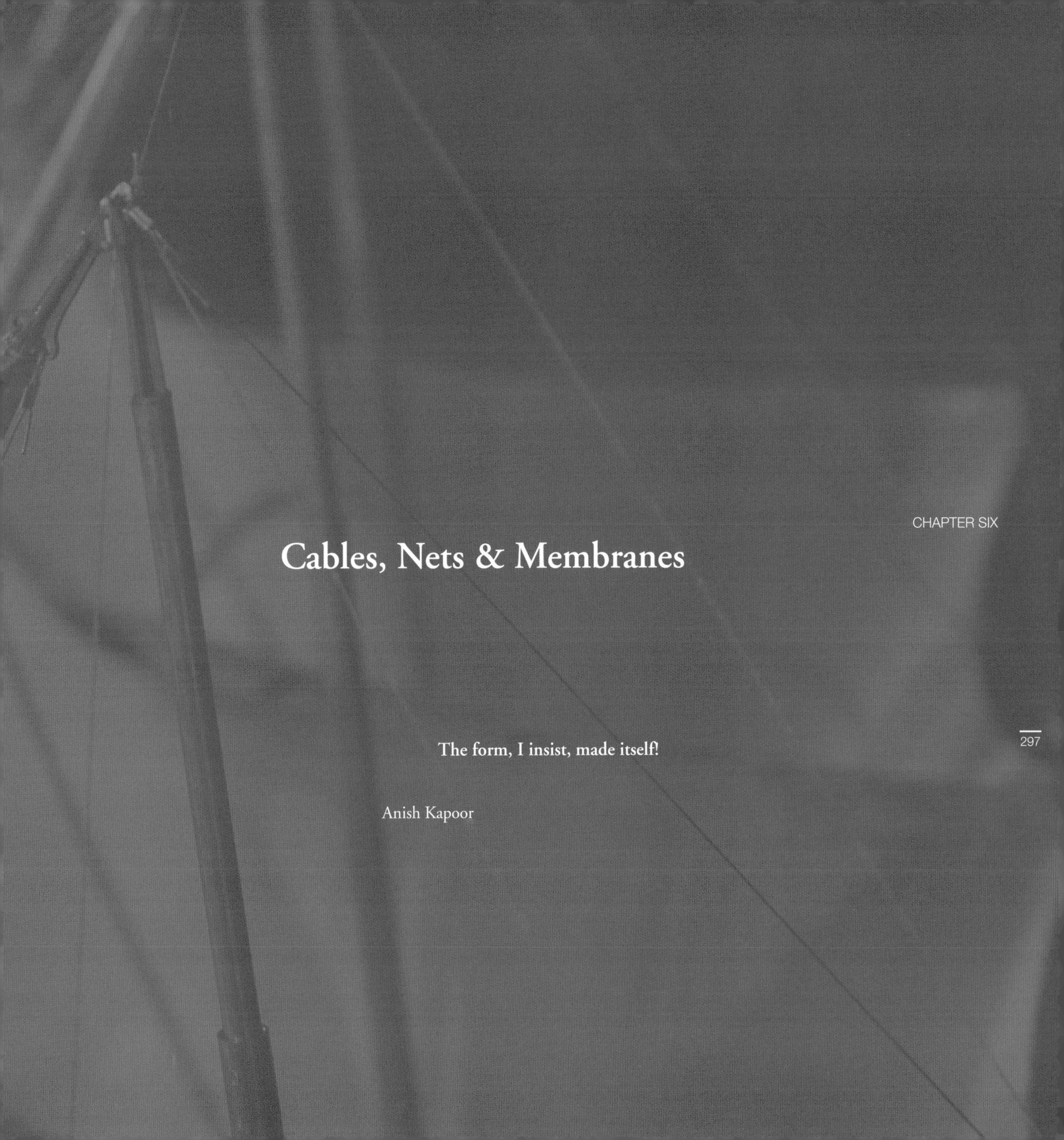

CHAPTER SIX

Cables, Nets & Membranes

The form, I insist, made itself!

Anish Kapoor

Munich Olympic Stadium

Structures that in various ways embody *tension* are the focus of this chapter; structures, that is, that emphasize and/or somehow exploit the unique material and spatial qualities associated with this load-carrying mechanism. Tension members carry load axially and typically exhibit the efficiency of doing so; not having to be concerned with buckling or bending, their cross-sectional dimensions can be kept to a minimum and the structure relatively light and transparent if desired. A tension structure, however, must be anchored to other structural elements (such as columns, walls, beams, trusses, and ground anchorages) and these are often visually prominent. Furthermore, tension structures deform easily and need to be stabilized, often by means of secondary structural systems. Thus, it is with some irony that this most efficient of structures is often among the most visually distinctive and that their frequent curvilinear forms, perhaps assumed to be "free" of constraint, have a geometry that is in fact tightly prescribed by force-balancing necessity.

Two iconic tension structures are the German Pavilion for Montreal's Expo '67 and the Olympic Stadium for the Munich Games of 1972. The sweeping forms of their cable-net canopies remain remarkable today, let alone when they were first built, and much has been written about their revolutionary impact on architecture. The text extracts reprinted here, drawn from Philip Drew's book about the work of Frei Otto, bring attention to other aspects of these structures, however, including the relationship of the roofs to the constructed landscapes beneath them, the careful choreography needed for fast-tracking construction in Montreal, and an unexpectedly frank discussion about design compromises made for the Munich stadium on behalf of a then-nascent television culture. Such seemingly "secondary" storylines, however, take nothing away from the overall narrative of two of the past century's quintessential "free-form" structures; indeed, they only serve to enrich it.

Seemingly Free Form Structures in Montreal and Munich

from *Frei Otto: Form and Structure*
Philip Drew

The summation of a decade of intensive research into lightweight structures was incorporated in the design of the German Pavilion at Expo '67, Montreal. Possibly to the detriment of architectural unity, Frei Otto attempted to convert the pavilion into an exhibition of lightweight building technology.

Time was an important factor in the design and realisation of the Montreal pavilion. Between the adjudication of the second stage of the competition on June 15, 1965 and the onset of the Canadian winter fourteen months later (September–October, 1966) the pavilion had to be designed, prefabricated, shipped to Montreal and erected. This was a formidable undertaking considering that an input of 20 000 man-hours was needed to develop the form and clarify the construction details.

The intimate relationship and interdependence of human culture and the earth alluded to by the Montreal exposition theme "Terre des Hommes" supplied Frei Otto with the inspiration of creating a series of related, overlapping landscapes which blended with the terraqueous setting. It was intended to create a large open canopy to span an artificial man-made landscape which freely extended into the environment. The structural systems provided the means for forming the pavilion's three constituent, layered landscapes: the sculptured earth platform; the raised deck of exhibition terraces which skirt the pavilion enclosure and snake around the mast high points and the funnel low points; and the free curvaceous roofscape generated by hoisting the roof onto eight masts and tugging it down at three low points. The asymmetrical placement of the high and low points, the varied moulding of shape and the orchestration of the sub-landscapes induced an empathy between these artificial landscapes and the setting.

Entering the pavilion at the ground floor level, a diversified terrain of platforms climbed in a gradual clockwise spiral around a central low court and returned to the entrance foyer at a level one story higher. The ground floor level entrance served as the foyer of the lecture hall and a wide spiral staircase connected it with the upper entrance level which led off onto the footbridge. The restaurant, kitchen, administration and mechanical service rooms were tucked under the main exhibition terraces which reached their highest elevation near the tallest mast. An elevated lattice deck constructed from modular steel units surrounded the main terraces.

The insertion of this intermediate platform between the roof and floor terrains added considerably to the dynamic character of the interior and permitted people to flow about and through the homogeneous pavilion space. The prohibitive cost of full air-conditioning, to dissipate the large thermal load captured by the translucent roof with 30 to 50 percent light transmission, was avoided by resorting to natural ventilation. Except for the 2.25 m high glazed wind-deflector walls which were designed to contain a large "cool-air basin", the pavilion was left open around its perimeter. This ensured adequate ventilation of the pavilion interior throughout the warm summer. The spontaneous convection circulation of air was reinforced by cold air blown into the main space at low points and allowed to spill out behind the wind-deflector wall dam, whence it gently rose to the roof peaks where it was drawn off by fans. In winter the space between the wind-deflector walls and the roof membrane was closed to facilitate heating.

The prefabrication of the masts, net and skin in Germany enabled the roof structure to be erected in a comparatively short time. The cable net was completely prefabricated by the firm of Stromeyer in Constance and shipped to Montreal in 9.5 m wide rolls. Except for the 38 m long mast which was delivered in two pieces and welded together on the Montreal site, the galvanised tubular steel masts (wall thickness 18-25 mm) made in Berlin by Steffens & Nölle were shipped in one piece as deck cargo. The erection procedure in Montreal followed the trial run at Vaihingen very closely. Although the gradual approach to the final prestressed state occupied five weeks, the most spectacular phase, involving the assembly of the net sections on the ground, its raising and attachment to the anchorage and system points, took a team of about fifteen men three and a half weeks. The erection procedure followed a carefully detailed sequence:

— The masts were lifted into position on previously prepared sand drums and stabilised by a temporary guyed rigging between the mast heads.

— The prefabricated net sections were then assembled and hauled up to the loops on the pulleys fixed to the mast heads.

— After the net had been lifted, new net sections for the internal areas were added.

— When the net was suspended from the heads of all the masts, it was pulled outwards or inwards (for peaks and valleys) and secured to the anchorages. After the net had been fixed between the masts and the anchoring points, the rough final shape became apparent.

—The mast height and initial prestressing of the net was accomplished by jacking up the mast and filling the space between its base plate and the sand, with more sand. A rubber bearing under the pole ensured an even distribution of the mast load.

— The main cables were tensioned by an iterative procedure in two trips around the roof using prestressing jacks. During the entire period of bracing the cable net, a four-man team was busy making corrections to the net. This was carried out by shifting edge clamps and cross clamps and by constructing new net cables in isolated cases.

— The membrane skin was pre-assembled on the ground and part sections were then raised. As soon as the roofing skin was close to the cable net, it was attached to the cable net.

— After installation of all the individual skin sections and eye glazings, uniform tension (average value 100-150 kP/m^2) was applied to the entire skin in a series of operations. Beneath the west prow of the Montreal pavilion, two snug lattice domes which sheltered an irregularly shaped lecture hall (17 m x 13 m with seating accommodation for 250 persons) and entrance foyer (20 m x 4.5 m) bore a strong kinship with the prestressed cable net. Prior to their clothing in protective membranes the structural affinity of the cable net and the lattice domes was highly visible. Both are variations on the theme of spatially deformed plane networks. They differ in that the cable net is a pure tension anticlastic shape and the lattice domes are pure compression synclastic shapes.

The essential features of the final design accepted for the main stadium roof at the Twentieth Olympic Games, Munich, was anticipated in an earlier design (1967) undertaken on behalf of the architects Brückner, Klement, Duve, for the grandstand roof over the football stadium at Gelsenkirchen-Bergerfeld. The arrangement of gentle saddle surfaces stretched between open loop ridges, supported by a system of flying guyed masts and tall stayed exterior masts, closely resembled the solution finally adopted at Munich. The individual petal-shaped saddle surfaces were threaded around a heavy edge cable which picked up all the interior system points on its journey over the playing field. The stadium seating was dug into the earth and the rear of the seating ramp was camouflaged with humped earth berms. This was preferable to the exposure of the ugly seating ramps on the west side of the main Munich stadium.

Fresh from his Montreal triumph, Frei Otto agreed to collaborate with the Stuttgart architects Behnisch & Partner on the Munich Olympic Games architecture. The success of the Behnisch submission in carrying off first prize and the commission to develop the Olympic architecture provided Frei Otto with his first real opportunity to implement the Futurist aspirations of lightweight construction. The Munich roofs were the climax of Frei Otto's evolution of light tension loaded surface structures. As chairman of the competition jury, Egon Eierman was able to stay conservative opposition to the roofs which wanted a safer and less controversial solution, and so kept the roofs alive.

The assonance of skyscapes and landscapes is the essence of the competition design (October 1967) for the Munich Olympics. The Olympic architecture was conceived as two spatially separate interweaving landscape terrains. Guarded by the hollowed shells of the main stadium and the athletics and swimming arenas sunken below the broad deck of the raised earth platform, the Olympic plateau is crowned by the salient peaks of a single magnificent roof which collects all the dispersed Olympic functions under its generous protectorate. Overlooked by the rubble mound, a poignant reminder of Munich's resurrection from the ruins of war, the Olympic stadium and arenas circle round a great Olympic Plaza which subsides into an artificial lake.

The Olympics Executive prevaricated over the feasibility of the roofs for some twenty-two months between October 13, 1967, and August 18, 1969. The Executive's indecision contributed to the escalation of costs for the roofs because it left far too little time to finalise details and complete building work. The deletion of a number of features impaired the practicality and aesthetic unity of the original proposal. The low roof skirt behind the west ramp of the main stadium and continuity of the roof cover over the main entrance assured a degree of weather protection which was sacrificed in the final roofs. The flying wing of roof which soared above the expressway over the main entrance bridge would have provided a dramatic and fitting introduction to the Olympics.

A further casualty in the later development of the scheme was the assonance of the two Olympic landscapes. The sensitive integration of the roof and landforms proffered in the original scheme was betrayed by a picturesque landscape which trivialised the heroic proportions of the roofs.

Somehow the shape and transparency of the giant hovering roofs manages to survive all the atrocities committed against them. The most remarkable quality of the roofs is seen even from some distance — their relatively low profile, peaked silhouette and non-assertiveness. The conflicting requirements of large, visually unobstructed interiors and sufficient curvature of the prestressed net surface to limit deformation decisively affected the final arrangement and shape of the roofs. Where there is sufficient height to ensure adequate curvature of the net surfaces so that no unnecessarily high prestressing forces are required to contain deformations, prestressed cable net structures have advantages over other structures for wide spans. The dual requirement of uninterrupted spans and adequate surface curvature was met by the duplication of masts outside the roof and the introduction of interior flying guyed masts. The roof surface was partitioned into individual saddle-shaped petals stretched between open loop ridges in a typical undulating configuration. The generally gentle curvature and high prestress of the undulating saddle surfaces, which are particularly noticeable in the main stadium canopy, resulted from the economic compromise between high curvature and wide spacing of the masts.

The belligerent intrusion into the Munich Games of television justifies their appellation as the 1972 Colour Television Olympics. The vast revenue which the German television system anticipated from the world colour television rights was used as a lever for important planning decisions which increased the cost of the structure and services engineering and all but wrecked the architecture. Any architect suffering from an infatuation with services expressionism is recommended to visit Munich for an instant cure. The provision of lighting and ventilation to carry off the enormous heat loads generated by the high intensity lighting intrudes with startling violence and crudity into the enclosed arenas. The essential presence and involvement of the spectators was disturbed by great trussed lighting and services grids hung from the tall masts. Next time it may prove more satisfactory to hold the Olympics in a giant television studio — *sans* spectators, of course! The original proposal by Behnisch for a PVC-coated polyester fabric roof similar to the one used for Montreal had been rejected on the grounds of insufficient durability. It in turn had been supplanted by the architects' idea of constructing a wood deck on the cable net or covering it with lightweight concrete or an insulating material. However, this was invalidated by the demand from the German colour television system that the stadium roof should be translucent enough to avoid any formation of shadow. The maximum allowable light ratio between the covered and open sections of the stadium was to be no greater than one in three.

Of the three alternatives tested (translucent PVC-coated polyester fabric, transparent acrylic glass panels, and translucent glass-fibre-reinforced polyester panels), a standard 2.90 m x 2.90 m acrylic glass panel, attached at single points to the cable net intersections, was decided upon. Since the original angles between the mesh cables vary up to 6° under loads and temperature changes, the glass panels were supported on Neoprene pedestals which assured freedom of movement. The joints between the panels were sealed with a continuous Neoprene profile clamped to the edges of the panels, wide enough and thin enough to allow wrinkles to form; a truly ugly detail.

One of the effects of the transparent covering is that it behaves like a chameleon, mirroring any change in the skyscape. Under a dark and threatening sky the roof assumes a heavy, turgid aspect. In the prevailing greyness of Munich, the roof acquires a silvery grey sheen almost indistinguishable from the surrounding sea of greyness. Had a more heavily tinted Plexiglass been used the contrast between the shiny cicada-skinned shell of the external sculptured form and the ethereal transparency of the interior would have been heightened. In addition, the spectators would have been shielded from solar glare.

An enumeration of the architects' and engineers' atrocities against the roofs — veritable crimes against tension — would prove so extensive that the reader ought to be spared the ordeal. Some of the choice offences which come to mind are the tall towers which lean over the main stadium and support the floodlighting, the twin bank of floodlights balanced insensitively on the main cable; the officials' and journalists' observation deck mounted obscenely on the seating ramp of the main stadium; the heavy glazed screens enclosing the athletics and swimming arenas. The detailing of the glass walls was so crudely done that it seems inconceivable that an architect who had lived through the last two decades could make such a hash of so conventional an architectural exercise. The top profile of the screen is so heavy and unsympathetic that it obliterates the beautiful edge profile of the roof. The sheer visual weight of the wall-framing competes with the delicate lightness of the roof. The attachment of the roof low points inside the swimming arena, a point at which the excitement of the roofscape is most easily appreciated, was mutilated by heavy pipe mullions which obstruct the spatial flow of the interior space up through the funnel spilling onto the roof. Such a dramatic occasion as the meeting of the roof and floor should have been handled with the utmost delicacy and transparency. The connection of the stadium with the athletics arena by means of a series of dancing ebullient saddle shapes is a major disappointment. The architectural pleasure engendered by the close proximity and smaller scale of the roofs is dampened by the discovery that they are purely decorative and do not provide a functional weatherproof entrance corridor.

In spite of these disappointments the verve of the roofs survives intact. They are cogent reminders that Frei Otto has released architecture from the unendurable burden of heavyweight technique. The Munich roofs represent a free architecture which outstrips even the most ambitious vaulting ventures found in the architectural past. The roofs convey the sense of effortless grace which is so much a feature of a great athlete's performance.

German Pavilion, Expo '67, Montreal

Snowdon Aviary, London Zoo

As important as the Montreal and Munich cable structures were in signaling the advent of innovative structural forms and spatial possibilities, they certainly had precursors; notable among these is Cedric Price's London Zoo Aviary built in 1964. This structure fully exploits the qualities of tension as a load-carrying strategy and enclosure system: it is hung from masts by angled cables, incorporates overall flexible stability by means of its tensegrity system (Bucky Fuller's abbreviation for "tension integrity") so as to "float" the four open pyramidal frames that establish the building's volume and shape, and uses cable mesh nets to provide the necessary "enclosure" that prevents the birds from flying away. These techniques combine to produce an open air, visually transparent and lightweight structure that fulfills its programmatic function while metaphorically as well as physically embodying the qualities of flight itself. This tensile lightness would have been in sharp contrast to other structures at the zoo such as the Picturesque artificial landscapes of the nearby Mappin Terraces but also the sweeping reinforced concrete ramps of the Penguin Pool (Chapter 3). As will be seen in the text below by Hadas A. Steiner, however, this did not prevent the Aviary from itself being subject to criticism, reflecting the inherent conflicts between expectations for minimalist architecture, the realities of construction, and the counter-realities of aesthetic decision-making.

What is perhaps more unexpected is to be reminded by Steiner about the context for Price's design for this structure in terms of developments at the time in cyber-technology, forms of energy exchange, and a then-nascent electronic culture. Seen in this light, the Aviary was a harbinger of things to come not only in terms of tensile structures but also for today's ongoing design explorations that seek to connect the realities of physical form with those rendered possible by virtual technologies.

Cybernetic and Lightweight Dreams

from *For the Birds*
Hadas A. Steiner

In place of industrial materials arranged in structurally conventional ways, [the renowned architectural critic Reyner] Banham shifted his hopes to the emerging domain of consumer-ready digital products and services. Banham was always on the lookout for contemporary avant-gardism, which for him had always meant true architectural applications of state-of-the-art technology. By 1964 Banham's critical allegiance had turned to the environmental pursuit of digital technology, or a milieu in which every part of the social experience that was in some way about exchange—of energy, of goods, of services—was architecture. In practices that took on this agenda the model of communications exchange superseded the extant criteria of circulation. Architecture would be that which circulated not what was circulated around, or even through. In the theory of the "global village," information was the primary substance of form. In fact, architectural expressions of this agenda began as a focus on the newfound possibilities of tension distribution and nonpoint load compression. Conceiving architecture as a dynamic distribution of energy within a structural system, then, was among the earliest interpretations of the material environment under the fluctuating conditions of electronic culture.

Migration

The milestone of this stage of technological thinking was ... an ornithological pavilion for the London Zoo.[1] As part of Casson's redevelopment scheme the Zoological Society commissioned Lord Snowdon to design a large free-flight birdcage to replace the Great Aviary of 1888.[2] Snowdon, not himself an architect, chose Cedric Price as a collaborator. In turn, Price solicited the support of Frank Newby, the investigative structural engineer who had taken over the firm of his mentor, Felix Samuely, and had already collaborated with Konrad Wachsman, Charles Eames, and Eero Saarinen.[3] When Price approached Newby, the latter was at work on the Leicester Engineering Building (1964) for Stirling and Gowan.

Samuely's approach to structures as dynamic entities had inspired Price during his student years at the Architectural Association, and this highly public commission would reflect that influence.[4] Starting from a brief prepared by Price, Newby proposed a tension structure using the concept of tensegrity, or discontinuous compression, that he had learned from Buckminster Fuller. The alliance of Snowdon, Price, and Newby yielded the distinctive peaks of this walk-through aluminum aviary on the steeply sloping north bank of the Regent's Canal.[5] The unusual choice of metal for the structure followed from the zoo's request for minimal structural upkeep, despite the fact that aluminum required chunkier structural members than was thought aesthetically ideal.[6] The resultant cage is an unobstructed volume of 150 by 63 feet in plan, with a height of 80 feet at its highest points. Pretensioned steel cables sheathed in plastic carry a mesh skin of black, anodized, welded aluminum netting. The cables support an unequal pair of tetrahedrons at either end. These tetrahedrons are made of aluminum tubes that measure one foot in diameter. Each pair flanks diagonal, aluminum shear legs that fix the skeleton in place. The fifty-four-foot legs had to be specially made by welding together curved extrusions to achieve the necessary diameter of two feet. Computer models, a technology not then in widespread use, were built to analyze the distribution of forces within the framework. As an experimental technology, the evolution of this structure entailed continual and time-consuming invention.

In contrast to the façadism of the Mappin Terraces, the crystalline structure of these four peaks was intentionally frank. Compared with the International Style of the Penguin Pool, the formal aesthetics of the aviary derived from the structural configuration and the materials suited to their functional task, not from a preference for a smooth white finish. Neither could the dematerialized effect, "all structure, services and air,"[7] have been less like the contemporary Brutalism of the Elephant and Rhinoceros Pavilion, even if both have a creature quality. But most significant for this story, the tensegrity habitat carries the trail of the garden right inside, along its main axis even. The pedestrian path zigzags through the rectangular plan of the aviary, crossing through the middle as a dogleg cantilevered bridge so that visitors have multilevel views of birds flying, nesting, and drinking from the waterfalls. The challenge for the project, as Banham assessed it, was the "taming of a piece of the existing topography and covering it with an enclosure high enough and broad enough for large birds to fly convincingly—and yet keep the public close enough."[8] Because of the steep incline, the ramp had to create traversable ground; as a result, "landscaping is integrated with the circulation system."[9] The sense that the ramp is a piece of terrain is again reinforced by its status as a link in the overall zoo circuit.

The ramp is integral to the pavilion as the mode by which circulation takes place and the function—proximity to the birds—is fulfilled. At the same time, the ramp is a cantilevered exercise in its own right, apart from the structure of containment. The dynamic combination of the "around and through" of Mappin with the technological rationalism of the Penguin Pool emphasizes the innovation of this early walk-through aviary. Any suspension of disbelief that an allegiance to naturalism had required, through disjunction from, and simulation of, a world outside, applied here to the appearance of floating structure. Indeed, it was the look of this structure that was subject to a myriad of criticisms, especially from purists who expected ultimate thinness of members in a tensile structure. Also, a cantilever without intermediate support brought about inevitable comparisons to Tecton's pool, despite the difference in span and loading conditions, and complaints were registered about the thickness of the aviary ramp. But unlike the total revelation of structure here, Arup had either concealed the massive abutments that really support the ramps below ground level or camouflaged them as a landing or by the diving tank.[10] As Banham retorted: "the aesthetic neatness of Lubetkin's ramps had to be bought at the cost of making their springings almost solid reinforcing-rod with barely enough concrete to cover." Banham continued with a phenomenological justification: "In any case, the user of the bridge does not see its supporting musculature, only a flat ribbon of footpath zig-zagging off into space and protected by handrails and balustrades of no more than domestic strength. It all looks more perilous than it really is."[11] This experiential quality is the very effect that is the heart of the Sublime.

The dream of lightweight, transitional, even ephemeral, architecture, incorporated circulation—and with it the very landscape from which it had been extracted—into its structural conditions. Indeed, Banham called the aviary "a very belated contribution to the Arcadian tradition in British architecture. But within that tradition, it does not belong to the gimcrack wing that gave us so many fake ruins and other collapsed objects among trees; rather, it belongs to the tough-minded stream whose triumphs are the palm stove at Kew Gardens, or Paxton's Victoria Regia house at Chatsworth."[12]

There is, it follows, a truly technological tradition in Arcadia—to be found in Burton's Palm House, not in his zoological follies—a corollary to Giedion's observation that the use of new materials has always been most avant-garde in architectures of display.[13] The experimentalist tradition of the World's Fairs could just as well be described by Charles Jencks's declaration that the aviary design did away "with enclosure, monumentality, stasis and even imagery. Price... tried to jettison *all* the traditional categories of architecture that even Brutalism had held on to such as identity and place. He put forward an idea of "servicing" instead of architecture; he placed primary value on all structures capable of quick change and response."

It is, however, with Jencks's final point that the description of Price's agenda breaks away from the past and picks up on a contemporary social agenda: "he envisioned a kind of nonbuilding activity which would liberate man from all the constraints and categories of the past; in short, he sensed the idea of absolute freedom."[14] The emphasis, not on the inevitability of technological forms or functions but on how choice plays a role—like the fact that tubes were a preference, not the only structural alternative—implies an understanding of the consequences of selection at both material and immaterial levels. In the aviary, as if to keep the obvious appropriation and mastery that a zoo connotes at a distance, the circulation was structurally separated from the cage.

When Ulrich Conrads and Hans Sperlich reflected on the Penguin Pool from their postwar perspective in the popular *The Architecture of Fantasy* (1960), they spoke of it nostalgically as the emancipation of a sequestered, earthbound form.[15] By liberating the ramps "to cut through the air with the sweeping weightlessness of a ribbon," Conrads and Sperlich explained, Tecton allowed the hermetic labyrinth to open into a "garden terrace." Modern urbanism had eliminated the intentional ambiguity of ambulatory planning for the sake of order, putting greenery and circulation into distinct compartments, separating garden from path, leisure from travel. Through the architectural eyes of the sixties, the garden and the path were reunited by spiraling arcs in the leisurely illusion of freedom through the spectacle of abstraction.

David Greene would (retroactively) describe the project of his own group, Archigram, as one that set "a new agenda where nomadism [was] the dominant social force; where time, exchange and metamorphosis replace stasis; where consumption, lifestyle and transience become the programme; and where the public realm is an electronic surface enclosing the globe."[16] Indeed, the crux of the matter is that the nomad moves with a freedom denied to the commuter, with no set itinerary or ultimate destination.[17] But as Fuller, the advocate of tensegrity, pointed out again and again, the lightest of architectures is still fixed in place by the infrastructural network. It is a major logistical and conceptual task to liberate structure from the predetermined anchor of infrastructure, or from the confines of the scenographer's panorama. Even nomadic peoples tread migratory paths with their stories and feet. Circulation, however dematerialized the route, encompasses that which the act of passage leaves behind. Panoramas, however total in the completeness of their vista, are always local in the sense that they occlude, even block, that which they cannot contain, just as the garden's perimeter denies the encroaching city. Moreover, the articulation of buildings as transmitters for transient entities, such as energy or information, takes on a decentralized, closed form by necessity. Networks may be infinitely extendible and they may be endlessly adaptable, but ultimately they must be complete. Cybernetic open-endedness requires a closed circuit. Virtual environments depend on a net of cables. The question remains of how an architectural instance could be, not a point on a map, but rather an event on the axis of time.

Destination

An affinity for tubes and the metaphor of the conduit ran its course in "High Tech" aestheticism. The other, less tangible implication of the birdcage—the diminishing of structural intervention in favor of transient program—continues to play itself out within digital discourse as an Arcadian form. That idealistic primitivism accompanies evolving technology is far from new: the affirmative connection between the "State-of-Nature" and a lost mobile culture has been theorized as the sacrifice of urban civilization from Thoreau and Rousseau to Leroi-Gourhan and Deleuze. Arcadia as a technologically driven spatial proposition emerged with the pictorial process through which industrialized topography came to be understood through the management of movement, whether of bodies or objects in the landscape, or of the landscape itself. With the dominance of the digital model over the industrial after World War II, the shift from the architectures of transition to that of transitional, even ephemeral, architectures accompanied technological development.

The circuit became the heart of the modernist design program, evolved into the way the avant-garde sought to transcend the corporeality of industrial engineering, and finally melted into the landscape of digital investigation. From the gardens of Sensationalism to those of adaptive algorithms, circulation engaged technological potential with natural processes to overcome the limits of buildings as artifacts. Still responsive to sensory input, structure sinks back into the landscape. The dissolution of the artifact into a landscape of indeterminate systems and the return of the Picturesque in the representation of ephemeral and virtual environments has been a consistent feature of the digital interpretation of the material world.

And so began the lightweight dreams in which people, and animals, were to be liberated from the constraints of shelter and the dynamic forms in which free-flight was, by necessity, tethered to the boundaries of freedom.

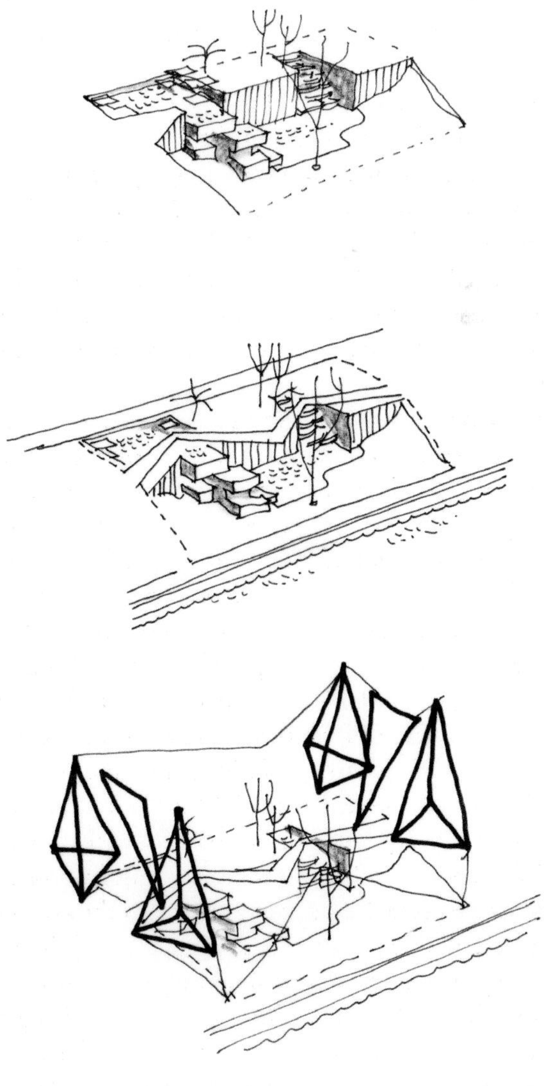

Cedric Price sketches

Renault Distribution Center by Foster + Partners. Photo: Richard Davies

Straight, taut, and angled *tension* members attached to tall masts are characteristic of the stayed system, a name having Old Norse origins and nautical associations (historically, thick ropes were used to stay boat masts and spars, or make them "stay" in place; today, thin steel cable wires do the same on sailboats.) This was a structural system favored by engineers for the reconstruction of Europe after the Second World War to support the decks of medium-length bridges; as often happens, the technological development became appropriated for the design of building structures. Correspondingly, tension stays in buildings are sometimes used to support long-span roofs from above, thus freeing the interior space from columns; given their angles of inclination and attachment to masts, stays are typically left exposed and are thus visually distinctive, often further emphasized by brightly-colored paint – to the extent that the geometry of stayed structures can become the iconic image for a building. Indeed, stayed systems together with braced frames and connection detailing became emblematic for an entire architectural movement – British High Tech – during the latter part of the 20th century.

The text below, which is a second entry from Murray Fraser's book, published in 2007, on American influence on post-war British architecture (see Chapter 5 for the other), cites several examples of industrial buildings designed by Norman Foster and Richard Rogers that feature this structural system. The photograph and section drawing of the Renault Distribution Centre serve to represent the type in terms of the visual impact of the exterior structure and the internal spatial openness that it affords. Murray continues with a rationale for why this flamboyant structural style came to be adopted on one side of the Atlantic and not the other; it is a story that incorporates cultural, economic, and national identity issues along with symbolic reasons for emphasizing such structural prowess.

Stayed Roof Systems and High Tech Identity

from *Architecture and the "Special Relationship": The American Influence on Post-War British Architecture*
Murray Fraser with Joe Kerr

A failure to thrive

[It is curious that]—for all of the adulation of the United States by Norman Foster and Richard Rogers—until recently neither had more than a handful of unbuilt projects in America, and they had completed virtually no buildings there. So why then were Foster and Rogers for many decades so unsuccessful in pushing their approach in the USA? The causes are worth exploring. It certainly couldn't be down to lack of competence or experience on their behalf. Frank Duffy has observed, for instance, of Foster's professional achievements; 'He has created a practice that is quite as powerful and technically at least as competent and sophisticated as the best of the great American practices of the 1950s and early 1960s.[1] Nor was it that their talents were unknown across the Atlantic. Norman Foster was awarded the Gold Medal of the American Institute of Architects (AIA) in 1994, only the fourth British architect to receive that honour. He subsequently won the prestigious Pritzker Prize in 1999—awarded privately by the Hyatt Foundation of Chicago to the world's top architects—even though not a single one of his most esteemed projects by that point, such as the Renault Warehouse and Distribution Centre in Swindon (1983) or the Hong Kong and Shanghai Bank in Hong Kong (1985-86) or Stansted Airport in Essex (1981-91), had been built in the States. Many of the materials and components for his buildings continued to be purchased from American factories, and there were the seeds of some work emerging. Of the few unbuilt Foster designs in the USA, easily the most remarkable was that produced in the late-1970s with Derek Walker, former head of the Milton Keynes architectural team, for a 30-story steel-framed extension to the Whitney Museum in Manhattan. They proposed a dramatically splaying base to house a new museum wing, all cross-subsidized by a sleek office tower above; it never stood a chance of going ahead.[2] Foster finally completed a real project in the USA with a decidedly modest extension to the Joslyn Art Museum in Omaha, Nebraska, well off the beaten track, from 1992-94. He got this commission because the director of the gallery at the time was an Englishman who had previously run the Sainsbury Centre at the University of East Anglia, one of Foster's seminal works. 'Naturally, everyone in the practice is proud that this is our first American building,' declared Norman Foster, although it was impossible to talk the project up any more than that.[3] Also in the mid-1990s his practice were designing a couple of medical and biological research buildings for Stanford University in Palo Alto; the first opened in 2000, the second a few years after. But again these were small beer compared to the Foster output elsewhere in the world.

Richard Rogers was made an Honorary Fellow of the American Institute of Architects in 1983, but (so far) has not been given their Gold Medal. He served as the Eero Saarinen Visiting Professor of Architecture at Yale University in 1985, being nominated by Kevin Roche, who finances that chair in memory of his mentor. Roche had previously also recommended Richard Rogers to J. Irwin Miller as architect for a factory building for a Cummins Engine Company subsidiary, the Fleetguard Manufacturing and Distribution Centre. The result was duly erected at Quimper in Brittany (1979-81), but that of course happened to be in France, not the USA.[4] This plant manufactured oil filters, and part of it served as a massive warehouse depot. It was in fact the first project that the reshaped Rogers office did after the departure of Renzo Piano, and for their design they came up with a low-cost, externalized structure consisting of a steel mast and tensile cables, superbly engineered by Peter Rice. All the structural elements were highlighted in bright red to animate what was otherwise the completely neutral box they supported. Here then was yet another overt case of the expression of tensile forces, as triggered by Bucky Fuller and the quest for ultimate lightness. A greater Rogers triumph, the Inmos Factory in Newport in South Wales (1982), had an indirect link to the USA in the sense that the job resulted from a decision by the British Government to fund microprocessor research in an effort to keep up with California's 'Silicon Valley'. It proved a futile aim, of course, and so the factory was of little use. Inmos was even more fetishistic in terms of tensile forces: a veritable spider's web of steel tension cables hung down from a raised central services zone, the latter containing also a linear corridor along the spine of the building. The suspension cables seemed as if they were there to hold up the external tubular steel roof trusses, but in fact their task was much less glamorous. An outer line of columns were introduced along both flank walls to pick up the roof trusses at those points; hence the purpose of the cables was simply to reduce deflection in the trusses, such that a larger span could be achieved between the central spine and the peripheral columns. The raised service spine was linked to a network of rooftop servicing points for the dust-and-dirt controlled research laboratories and production areas below, in which state-of-the-art silicon chips were to be manufactured. Tony Hunt's firm acted as the structural engineers. Reyner Banham and other critics lauded the building to the skies for its structural bravura, neatly skipping over the fact that the Inmos Factory was not an actual tension structure; it just looked like one. Inmos was yet again meticulously detailed and prefabricated, meaning it could be erected in just 15 months. The job had another clear benefit for Rogers, in that it became the prototype for the first American building by his firm; indeed, their only completed one until recently. This was for a second PA Technology Laboratory, or Patscenter, this time in an enormous industrial park close to Princeton, New Jersey. It was built in 1984-85. Even by High Tech standards the design was over the top, this time engineered by Peter Rice. A row of A-frame central supports held up a genuine suspension structure which allowed impressive 25m spans out sideways from the linear spine. The steel supports tethering the roof were held in place by exaggerated steel rings which resembled nothing so much as a surrealist array of giant floating Polo mints. A fellow High Tech enthusiast asked rhetorically: 'The choice of the Polo ring at the top of the masts is interesting for, although it is a functional means of jointing the tension rods, it also appears as a slightly stylized piece of expressionism, but why not?'[5] Or to put it another way, the building was trying much too hard to wow the USA. Even the Rogers office admitted to the client that the structural solution was going to add $170,000 onto the budget. They argued it would be worth the extra cost in terms of promotional advertising, given the building would become a landmark.[6] Why a New Jersey industrial park might need a landmark was never explained.

Around the time of the Patscenter in New Jersey, the Richard Rogers Partnership had a few other putative projects in the United States: a speculative office building in New York; a vast mall in Houston, Texas; an office tower in Seattle; American offices for Saatchi & Saatchi in Hudson Street in Manhattan; and some houses on Long Island, including one for Ruth Rogers's parents and another—as these things happen—for the film comedian Steve Martin. In the 1990s, Richard Rogers and his team designed a project for the Christopher Columbus Marine Research Centre in Baltimore, as well as a speculative scheme for prefabricated stainless-steel-and-glass diners based on Airstream caravans, and a mast-hung house in Los Angeles for his brother-in-law by his second marriage. Again, none were built. From the same era, the rust-red highlights created by the external steelwork in the Channel 4 Headquarters in Victoria, London (1990-94) was supposed, for some reason, to replicate the colour of the Golden Gate Bridge—try telling that to the marines, or anyone who has been to San Francisco for that matter.[7] More recently, Richard Rogers has been made a member of the American Academy and Institute of Arts and Letters, and in 1999 was awarded the Thomas Jefferson Memorial Foundation's architectural medal. He has just been awarded the Pritzker Prize as well. Yet as with Norman Foster, these signs of recognition were not matched until recently by tangible building commissions in America. This lack of interest in High Tech in the USA—a situation which has literally only changed in the past few years—is worth scrutinizing for its wider cultural insight.

The trouble with High Tech

High Tech is widely regarded as the most distinctive British contribution to global architecture over the past three decades, although it continues to be a problematic categorization. Things are not helped by the fact that the British architects usually identified as belonging to the High Tech camp passionately dislike the term.[8] The reasons why they hate the High Tech attribution is that it implies a rigid aesthetic style (expressed structures, exposed services, plug-in modules, glass fins, planar glazing, etc.), as opposed to a design method based on a fundamental exploration of technology, and also because the term is still associated in the public mind with industrial architecture built on suburban or out-of-town sites, hardly the most environmentally friendly image today. There is indeed a difficulty in defining the High Tech ethos as a whole. Reyner Banham had embarked on research for a major book about High Tech—it would surely have been brilliant—but was then diagnosed with terminal cancer in mid-1987, meaning he was unable to complete the project. However, some glimpses of his thoughts can be traced in a book he did manage to write in his final months about his long-term friend, Ron Herron of the Archigram group. Banham had evidently been delving into the writings of Martin Heidegger, the German existentialist philosopher, on the essence of technology. The intention of Heidegger had been to uncover a deeper reading of what mechanical tools and technological processes meant in industrialized societies; in particular, he wished to peel away the superficial, masking structures of rationalist and positivist thought, which in his view were imposed, tendentiously, by Enlightenment ideals of modernity. In the writings of Heidegger—especially his earlier work—he argued that mankind's use of tools and the creation of new technologies were not activities engaged upon once human consciousness had emerged in early societies. Rather, the development of tools and technologies had from the outset been part and parcel of the formation of individual and social consciousness, occurring simultaneously and in close dialectical relationship with ideas about the world. So by extension, the growth of modernized technology under capitalism—including phenomena like High Tech architecture—should not be seen as the manifestation of a prefigured 'modern' consciousness, but rather a means by which modernity was itself conceived and constituted. In other words, a critique of the techniques and technologies of production was essential to understand the very nature of modern life. With characteristic vivacity, Banham wrote:

> *Heidegger ... proposed that we would never really understand technology as long as we considered it only in instrumental terms, as a mere means of getting things done; even 'the correct instrumental definition of technology still does not show us technology's essence'. Several knotted paragraphs later he almost blows the whole proposition by announcing that 'The essence of technology is in a lofty sense ambiguous'. (Thanks a bunch, Martin!) Such ambiguity points to the mystery of all revealing, i.e., of truth.* [9]

Taking this problem—which Banham did not get a chance to develop further—then what can be said to be the revelation, the 'truth', which High Tech aims at through its exploration of steel-and-glass fabrication? Martin Pawley suggests that the term 'High Tech' had a complex provenance from the USA, beginning with its use in the early-1970s to describe an outré urban style of interior decoration which was:

> *... based on the use of wall-painted supergraphics, alloy car wheels as tables, industrial lighting and storage fittings, and other nondomestic items. From there it leaped across the Atlantic to describe the kind of structurally expressive lightweight architecture that had succeeded the heavy steel frame style introduced by Mies van der Rohe.* [10]

Probably the first conscious use of the term in architectural criticism came in 1972 in a book by Robert Maxwell, entitled New British Architecture, in which he called the projects of Richard Rogers 'an assembly of high-technology components'.[11] But once again the problem arises from defining High Tech as a specific technique of construction. Clearly it cannot be just a matter of technology—High Tech has to involve a deeper cultural proposition, or else, following Heidegger's analysis, it is nothing at all. In the mid-1980s, Alan Colquhoun tried tentatively to locate High Tech as a product of cultural difference between Britain and the USA, in which the former's feelings of inadequacy about its loss of industrial supremacy and imperial prestige were the trigger:

> *It is at least possible that the current enthusiasm there [Britain] for high-tech architecture is a compensation for lack of success on a commercial and political level. An architecture that aims at a transcendental and utopian vision of technology can, perhaps, be seen in Freudian terms, as a displacement.* [12]

But given that High Tech has dominated British architecture consistently over the last three decades—including a long stretch of economic confidence and prosperity from the mid-1990s—this interpretation cannot possibly hold water. Other observers such as Rick Mather, a leading American architect based in London, have suggested that the relative technological backwardness of Britain in the 1960s and 1970s, compared to the USA, prompted British High Tech architects to focus on continuing the Arts and Crafts tradition of designing and making refined, one-off elements—even if now using industrialized materials such as steel.[13] But that argument doesn't stack up either. The countries of continental Europe were just as economically and technologically behind the USA—in most cases, more so—yet did not develop the High Tech approach, plus this view also forgets how much America had been a locus for the Arts and Crafts in the early-twentieth century. The outcome of the latter was that the USA possessed its own romanticized, precious and craft-based approach to technology; how else might one describe the fantastical 1950s Cadillac designs by Harvey Earl?

So what is needed is a more nuanced interpretation. Thus it is the proposition here—as a broad cultural definition—that High Tech was at root a British dream of what US post-war architecture could have become, indeed should have become, if only American architects hadn't lost their nerve and succumbed to pessimism and post-modernism. Indeed, it was a commonplace observation in British architectural circles by the mid-1960s that the supremacy and degree of innovation that the USA so clearly enjoyed in the first two decades after the Second World War, and which Reyner Banham and others had been trumpeting, were being lost. A contributor to Architectural Design in August 1965 said that after a visit to the USA, he had 'come to the conclusion that American architecture is in a state of absolute regression. Having given up research for increasing productivity, it has succumbed to a baroque that is ... a purely decorative variety.'[14] British architects now spotted the chance to step into the breach. In this sense, High Tech can be seen as part of a tendency among many elite groups in post-war Britain to regard the USA in mythical terms, as the only positive model that offered a means to modernize British society.[15] This also explains why British High Tech exponents could so easily dismiss manifestations of architectural 'regression' in the USA, preferring to invoke the continuum of Anglo-American engineering interchange that had begun in the nineteenth century with railways, bridges, tunnels, prisons and exhibition buildings. In the case of Reliance Controls, Team 4 could use Paul Rudolph as a source of inspiration but ignore altogether Rudolph's latest quasi-Brutalist exercises in heavyweight concrete, like the Arts and Architecture Building at Yale. Instead they went back to his earlier, 'better' stuff—the lightweight steel houses in 1950s Florida, with diagonal tie-bracing alluding to the Crystal Palace. Norman Foster was in the late-1960s more than happy to hop onto a plane to Pittsburgh to work with an American company on glazing innovations not for use in the USA, but in Britain—thereby beginning to put the latter in advance. Indeed, what unites the British High Tech architects..., and what differentiates them from a previous generation who went to America, was that they didn't regard the United States as the fount or source of knowledge to be copied, but as a space for creative invention. Whereas those enamoured in Britain by post-war Miesian design were fanatical about applying a predetermined system, a proven method from a 'master', the dream merchants like Foster and Rogers—and their spiritual guides like Reyner Banham, Cedric Price and Archigram—wanted to absorb the spirit of the USA and come up with British hybrids. If a distinction can be drawn between an 'Americanized' and a 'Free Americanized' architectural style, then the latter is the High Tech approach. It is irrelevant that High Tech would probably not have been the approach adopted by American architects if they indeed hadn't become pessimistic and turned to post-modernism. High Tech was a cultural hybrid that made sense from the British perspective, when viewing the USA, even if it was not in America itself.

To dig deeper into this ideological context, it is vital to appreciate just how much British architects such as Archigram turned into icons the most technologically advanced structures in the United States, i.e. those at the forefront of the arms-and-space race. Totems like the Vertical Assembly Building (VAB) at Cape Kennedy, built by NASA in 1965 and so high that Saturn rockets could be fabricated upright, became the architectural equivalent of urban myths. The VAB building measured 218m by 158m in plan, and was 160m in height, giving it an internal volume of 3.7 million m^3. It had doors on four sides that were each a mind-blowing 140m tall, so that the rockets could slide out once built. Of the skyscraper towers in Britain at the time, the Post Office Tower was the only one that couldn't fit inside; just imagine a space that was 20 per cent higher than Centre Point, and much fatter. In the 1970s, Reyner Banham described the Vertical Assembly Building as the largest single room built by man, 'big enough to contain its own weather as well as fully assembled space rockets upright on their transporters'; another writer likewise claimed that 'the VAB, "the largest building in the world" ... is so large that it creates its own internal weather conditions, including an occasional thunderstorm.'[16] The part about it having its own weather system appears to be pure hokum, with no real evidence of this ever being the case. But what such comments did was to perpetuate the belief that America alone possessed the means to create the most advanced architecture, and hence it was this technological promise that was being shaken by the first stirrings in the mid-1960s USA—just at the moment when the Vehicle Assembly Building was being built—of 'negative' cultural forces like early post-modernism that would in time stop America from realizing its destiny. This interpretation by British High Tech architects existed not just on an ideological level, since it has been pointed out that there were a number of paradoxes within American technological supremacy which complicated matters at a deeper level. An unforeseen result of transatlantic collaboration in the post-war decades was that the United States found it ever harder to maintain its monopolistic position over scientific and technological knowledge. 'Indeed from the mid-1960s, its [America's] lead began to diminish,' notes one account.[17] This arose because of the sheer volume of experts that America had sent over to help countries like Britain, and also because of the presence in Britain of specialists who had been part of the 'brain drain' to the USA, but then returned home with enhanced skills and knowledge of the latest innovations. In this sense, figures such as Norman Foster and Richard Rogers were the equivalent within British architecture. Without perhaps realizing at the time they were engaged on a similar process in terms of building technology, it would explain why zealous Brits—like Foster and Rogers and those after them—felt confident enough by the late-1960s to pick up the baton that America appeared to have dropped.

Acknowledging this change suggests also why the cultural projection imagined by High Tech architects made little sense within the American construction climate at the time. For those living in a hegemonic nation like the USA, one so manifestly self-sufficient in economic and cultural terms, why even listen to this critique by outsiders from a less developed country? Economic realities in the US building industry were such that contracts became more geared towards 'fast track' design-and-build methods of procurement, meaning that detailed design fell to the contractor rather than the architect. Apart from centres of cosmopolitan culture on the eastern and western seaboards, plus a few isolated inland showpieces such as Chicago, the bulk of American construction was predicated on normative practice, rather than on the specialized methods of High Tech. This explains why there was for so long in the USA almost no examples of High Tech architecture, and why those built were so atypical and quirky.[18] It is also noticeable just how little attention American architectural critics and theorists gave to British High Tech, tending either to ignore it altogether or dismiss it. One critic, however, who dealt openly with High Tech is the New-York-based critic, Michael Sorkin; he admires the work of Foster and Rogers, while remaining cagey about the rarefied status of their projects.[19] Sorkin in his writings also encapsulated two of the standard lines against High Tech as deployed by architects in America, and so it is useful to spell these out.

The first, and most obvious, of American criticisms of High Tech is that it is a very expensive way to build—and hence is unsuited to the economics of the USA—due to its unique, highly crafted and perpetually innovative detailing. All of this increases the time that goes into designing and fabricating components. Kevin Roche has said:

> *High Tech is absolutely the most expensive form of architecture. Nobody in America would build the Hong Kong and Shanghai Bank; you just couldn't do it. It would be absolutely impossible. In fact you couldn't even suggest it, because you would never even get to first base. There is a reality, which is driven by the dollar, by economics, by cost-effectiveness, in American architecture, which actually is not a bad thing to have. The economy of means in a way, is one of the essential elements of architecture.* [20]

Likewise, Frank Duffy observed in the 1990s that, because of the cost and the amount of time to design it, 'an office building of the quality of Lloyd's would be inconceivable in North America'.[21] Colin Davies echoes this interpretation, noting:

> *High Tech is actually very foreign to the most deep-seated American instincts: keeping it simple, respecting the bottom line, moving fast, not getting obsessed with details, appealing to popular as well as professional taste, etc. High Tech is too uptight to be American.* [22]

The second objection to High Tech by US architects is that it is really only interested in creating a self-referencing aesthetic system, a beautiful style, that is too narrowly based on the relationship of steel and glass elements. The charge is that it fails to deal with the investigation of technology as a genuinely progressive aspiration. John Johansen, while sympathetic to Rogers and Foster, spots an obvious difference from his own method:

> *Their work [Rogers and Foster] is about the exquisite relationship of parts. Now that is a field in itself, almost, but one which is not specifically to do with the investigation that I am involved in. My view about anything is: 'Let's look for the whole field' ... So I am dealing with the essential things, and not the exquisite things. High Tech is almost a different school. The use of the word high is almost hype, almost outré. I do not think that I am connected with that so much. I don't expect technology to be high or low, or anything.* [23]

But it is too simplistic to accuse High Tech architecture of being anti-functional, of reducing technology to mere representation, of being obsessed with final products at the expense of process, or of continuing the costly and refined Arts and Crafts tradition. All are true to some extent, but it has to be acknowledged that these are also the characteristics of every contemporary British architectural approach, from neo-vernacular to neo-classical—negating the notion they are unique to High Tech. Architecture is always about a wide body of cultural ideas, and so cannot avoid inheriting much from the past. And within the cultural baggage of British architecture, this means for High Tech not only the Arts and Crafts inheritance, but also an industrialized mindset that sees design as generated through a diagrammatic plan and extruded section. It is why there is such affinity between High Tech architects and Joseph Paxton's Crystal Palace or the Victorian railway sheds or the industrial vernacular of the late-eighteenth and nineteenth centuries. The practitioners of High Tech equally insist their attitude is a progression of concerns voiced by modernists in 1920s Europe, who wanted to create a new architecture that was tailored to contemporary life, not only functionally, but also in social and cultural terms. However, to say all this is to reveal precisely why High Tech pioneers like Norman Foster and Richard Rogers were so intent in updating modernism to incorporate America's contribution after the Second World War. The USA from 1945 offered the primary cultural and social locus for modernism, and British architects had to wake up to the fact. And within this American post-war context, issues of environmental performance and building services were becoming all important. This is why a consistent theme for High Tech architecture since its emergence in the late-1960s was how to address issues about the use of natural resources. In spirit it harks back to the romantic critiques of modernization from Ruskin and Morris, but now expanded to ask how mankind might create a more sustainable form of consumer-driven capitalism across the globe. Out of this stance, the evolving proposition was that High Tech architecture needed to break away from merely improving the design of factories and offices on marginal sites, and become applicable to any building type in any urban location.

The first sign that High Tech might have a broader remit than as a stylish variant of suburban industrial architecture was of course Piano and Rogers's scheme for the Pompidou Centre, whatever criticisms were made of the outcome. In the wake of Pompidou, the salient history of High Tech has in fact been less about innovation in building technology—which if truth be told, has deviated little from its original steel-and-glass idiom. There has to be a diminishing number of ways to minimize the amount of steel required to hold glazing in space, or of imagining how glass can mutate into a structural material. Instead, the creative drive has been more about efforts to pursue High Tech within historically sensitive urban sites, and to adapt it to increasingly diverse forms of commercial or cultural buildings. For Foster, examples of this switch would include the aforementioned Hong Kong and Shanghai Bank headquarters in Hong Kong (1985-86) or the sublime Mediathèque in Nimes (1991-93). Typical in the case of the Richard Rogers Partnership would be the Lloyds Building in the City of London (1985-86, with Peter Rice as engineer), the European Court of Human Rights in Strasbourg (1992-95), or the Bordeaux Law Courts (1996-98). The Lloyds Building was particularly representative in that the client, Lloyds of London, insisted initially on a transatlantic shortlist for the invited competition, precisely because it believed the quality of British office building had fallen behind the USA, where it did a lot of its trade. Richard Rogers won the job in the end, but appropriately enough, his practice turned to two American precedents for inspiration. The first was the soaring, top-lit central atrium captured in surviving photographs of Frank Lloyd Wright's now demolished Larkin Building in Buffalo (1904-06), and the other was Louis Kahn's concept of 'served' and 'servant' spaces, which led to the idea of perimeter service towers for Lloyds, as an update of Kahn's organization for the Richards Research Laboratories in Philadelphia (1958-61). Frank Duffy sees the Lloyds Building as a classic hybrid of Anglo-American practice, noting the way in which its arrangement—like the Larkin Building—managed to invert the usual Manhattan arrangement of a solid service core and occupied periphery, by turning the centre into a light-filled void in which the movement of people was made visible and by pushing servicing elements to the exterior walls.[24] More symbolic still, Lloyds was the first major British application of stainless steel cladding, and hence was intended as a bold declaration of Americanized modernity—with connotations of NASA space missions—right in the stuffy heart of the City of London. Its use was argued on the basis of being a durable, self-cleaning surface that could preserve its looks—although of course there was no actual proof this would be the case. It came at a price, with the whole scheme in the order of £225 million. The building's showy appearance has raised the hackles of conservative observers ever since.

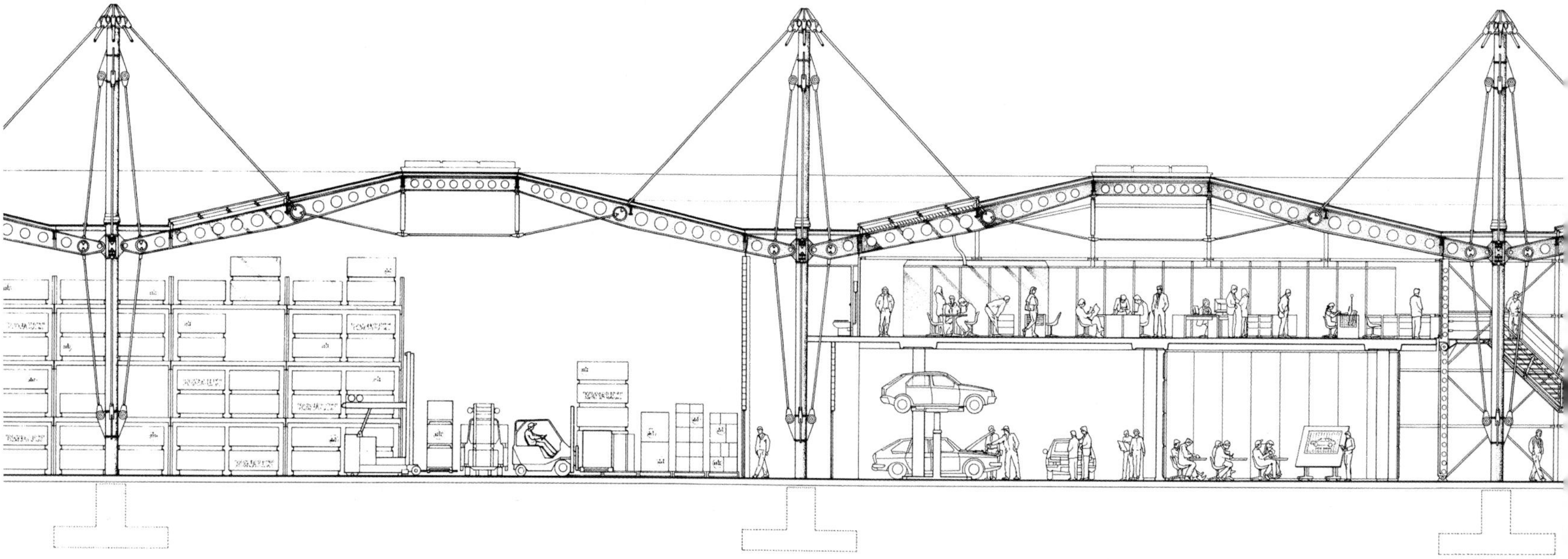

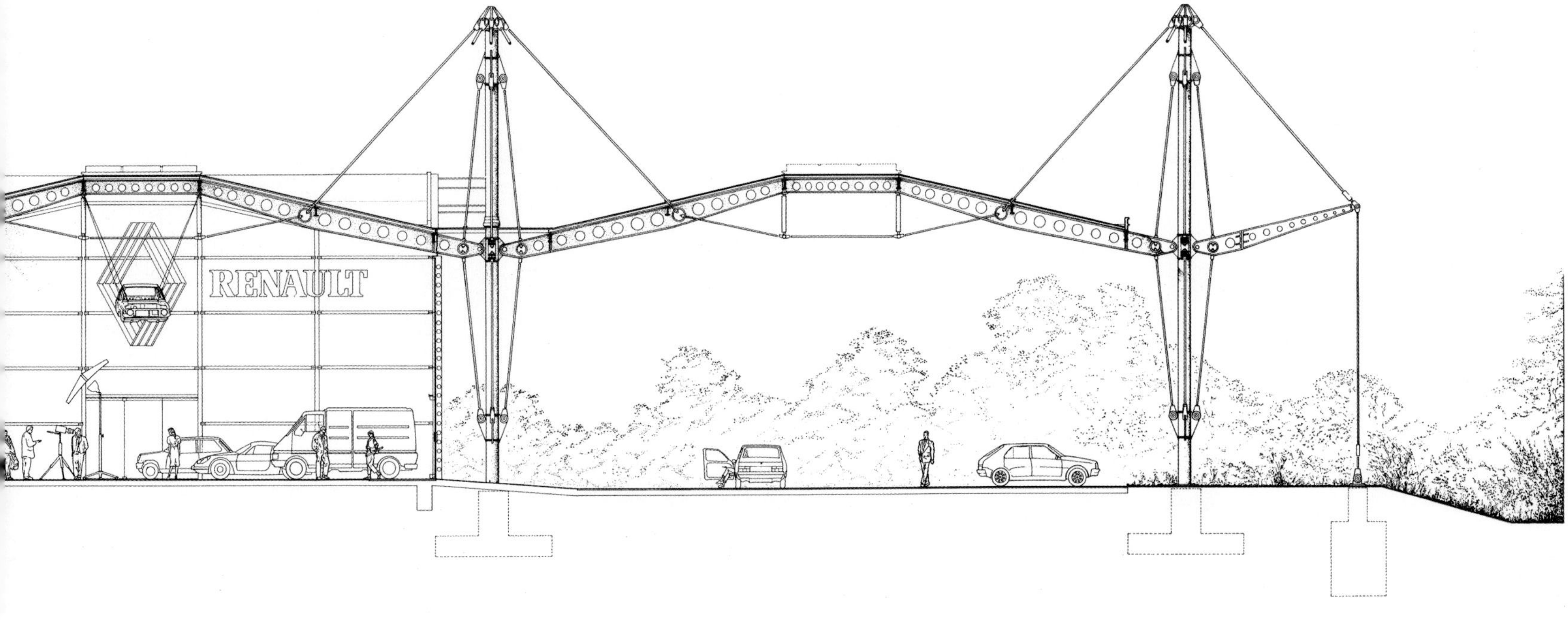

Section drawing of Renault Distribution Center. Photo: Richard Davies

Photos: Sundeep Bali

Another signature type of tension structure is the *suspension* cable system, easily identified by its distinctively curved profile. We are most familiar with this structural system from bridges that spectacularly defy gravity in terms of length of spanning distance or especially challenging siting conditions: from Inca rope bridges to Swiss stressed ribbons and from the Golden Gate to the Great Belt. Upon further reflection, we also readily associate the type with such iconic 1960s buildings as Eero Saarinen's Dulles airport terminal in Washington, DC and Kenzo Tange's Yoyogi athletic facility built for the Tokyo Olympics or, more recently, with the Portuguese pair of Alvaro Siza's national pavilion for Expo '98 in Lisbon and Eduardo Souto de Moura's 2003 Braga football stadium.

In the present case, however, the focus is on a much more modest example of the structural type – albeit no less spectacular and memorable – in the form of a shading (and, at night, lighting) canopy constructed on the outskirts of New Delhi as an installation for the 48°C Public Art Festival in 2008. As retold here by its architect Sanjeev Shankar, this canopy is both high- and low-tech, relying on primary load-carrying steel wire suspension cables in combination with a stabilizing system made of recycled cooking-oil cans. But the story of this structure is about so much more than simply its structural system or even its obvious aesthetic appeal – just as important is the community's intensive involvement in its construction and, moreover, the unexpected appropriation of locally sourced materials. Here the globally urgent issues of ecology and sustainability are made relevant to local need and context. The Hindi term *Jugaad* refers to attaining any objective with the resources at hand; certainly this goal was achieved in a most memorable manner by this suspension structure.

Jugaad: Suspending a Communal Canopy

from *Jugaad: An architectural installation for 48°C*
Sanjeev Shankar

What happens when a thousand oil cans decide to fly?

Jugaad explored this idea through a celebratory and constantly evolving process of re-purposing and redefining the cooking oil can, a ubiquitous feature of Indian life. The project borrows its name from a hindi term which refers to attaining any objective with the available resources at hand. By combining this attitude with an open-source, inclusive process, the project took recycling and reuse beyond a simple utilitarian measure into an exciting adventure of defiance and collective will. This journey is the result of a unique engagement with the residents of Rajokri, an urban village on the outskirts of New Delhi in India. Over a period of three months, Sanjeev Shankar used the discarded oil can as a vehicle to explore ideas of sustainability, recycling and re-purposing with 90 other residents from the village. Using grass root ingenuity, *Jugaad* reincarnated 945 such cans into an incredible free-standing shade canopy spread over 70 square metres.

This story celebrates the practice of jugaad and the collective spirit of India and its people.

The Journey:

What happens when people are inspired, challenged and encouraged to work together for a cause? What happens when constraints become triggers for innovation?

Along with these triggers, the journey in New Delhi began with the recurring image of the oil can. Initial resistance within the village to work with an outsider and explore the discarded oil can, a common symbol of 'waste', was an important challenge for us. It was crucial to appreciate that the main priority of the local community was survival and earning their daily bread. Global issues of environment, sustainability and recycling can inspire them only if they are linked to their daily lifestyle. Through deep human level engagement, there was a gradual change in perception and the community saw the merits of this project and the potential in transforming mundane, discarded domestic objects. Gradually, the entire community was inspired. The oil can soon became an object of desire and value. Hundreds of oil cans were scavenged from different parts of the city and cleaned in large cooking vessels which are usually used for local weddings. After washing the cans, the lids were cut-out and their edges bent to create metallic tiles. As the word spread, more village families participated in the process. The can lids were hand-painted with *gulal*, a deep pink pigment used in *holi*, an Indian festival of colour. The painted lids were drilled along the edges and stitched together using thin metal wires to create a pixelated pink metal fabric. 20 volt halogen fittings were then placed in the existing apertures to provide illumination at night. The top layer of the canopy with 945 can lids was now ready. To make the bottom layer, empty can bodies were perforated to admit light and allow air circulation. 692 such cans with each can weighing up to 700 gms were joined together using bolts which acted as shear connectors. The result was a sculptural honeycomb which acted as a reflector for the pixelated pink skin above. The two layers were suspended by pulleys using 12mm and 6mm steel cables, fastened to a pair of supports anchored into the ground. The fabrication process and vision of *Jugaad* became an integral part of village life and its people. There was song, dance, food, laughter and an overall spirit of celebration through the journey. These were as critical to the final result as was the unorthodox challenge of using scavenged materials to fabricate a magic carpet.

During day, *Jugaad* floated gracefully, gently, defiantly and improbably above the ground with light dappling through its skins, providing shade for the meeting place below. At night, the entire assemblage emerged from the darkness like a sparkling, other-worldly vessel on the brink of breaking free from its tethers. Each oil can, with its original colour, texture, labels and scars echoed an individual history and journey, and yet lent to a new beginning. Thousand oil cans did indeed fly!

The journey of *Jugaad* is a testimony to the combined human spirit of creativity and improvisation in a culture of scarcity and survival. It marks a humble beginning for a radical way to design community places and bring democratic design to the fore.

Marsyas at Tate Modern by Anish Kapoor. Photo: © Dennis Gilbert / VIEW

An altogether different tension-defined art installation was designed by sculptor Anish Kapoor in close collaboration with structural engineer Cecil Balmond: *Marsyas*, shown at the Tate Modern in London in 2003. Here a spectacularly sized, claret colored, swooping structural fabric membrane was set in stark contrast to the industrial skeletal structure of the former turbine hall; the visual statement thereby produced being so strong that photographs of the project remain familiar more than a decade later, and no less compelling. What is generally less well known is the cultural inspiration for the installation: a morality story founded in Greek mythology that has since had many retellings and artistic reinterpretations – some of which we are reminded about in an extract from Joanna Burton's essay contribution to the comprehensive monograph *Anish Kapoor*.

It is with this inspiration in mind that Balmond's subsequent description about the design options that he and Kapoor considered for the piece becomes all the more meaningful. Notwithstanding that *this* Marsyas was built as an exceptional art installation, it also serves to highlight some of the typical design considerations for more "conventional" tension membranes, including selecting the fabric material according to stress capacity and other physical qualities, finding the double curvatures necessary to stabilize the membrane's form, establishing the anchoring structures needed to produce such geometry as well as resolving relatively complex connection details. Moreover, the remarkable lightness of the overall structural system in comparison to its gargantuan size and volume of enveloped space are also easily recognized. Having duly noted such familiar "technical" characteristics, it is all the more enriching to be reminded that at the Tate this heavily "engineered" and "naked" structural form had an equally strong cultural reference guiding it throughout the design process. With *Marsyas* then, all was membrane and membrane was all – structurally and metaphorically.

Marsyas: Structure and Metaphor

from *Namely, What is Called Love*
Johanna Burton

Flayed

> *How lovely that thing you are playing is! I wonder did Chopin write it at Majorca, with the sea weeping round the villa, and the salt spray dashing against the panes? It is marvellously romantic. What a blessing it is that there is one art left to us that is not imitative! Don't stop. I want music to-night. It seems to me that you are the young Apollo, and that I am Marsyas listening to you.*[1]
> — Oscar Wilde, *The Picture of Dorian Gray*

During the last interaction they will have before Dorian Gray takes his own life, Lord Henry, praising his friend's musical abilities, likens him to Apollo while assigning himself the role of Marsyas. An odd compliment, which can be paraphrased as: 'Your talents awake in me the desire to surpass you.' Or perhaps it is more a heady request for the inevitable: 'Flay me.' A parable of narcissism, an allegory of desire, a meditation on beauty, Wilde's *The Picture of Dorian Gray* is also, of course, a cogitation on art; the preface to the story comprises a succinctly biased account of someone's — the author's? the protagonist's? — ideological proclivities toward art, criticism and a particular breed of decadent connoisseurship. But the central art object of the story may not be the clandestine portrait (the surrogate aging in place of its 'original') at all. Perhaps, instead, the truly pivotal artwork is Gray's final performance of a nocturne at the piano, whose notes surge as an unspeakable kind of exchange between player and receiver, filling the bodies of both with its sway, and temporarily rendering them vessels precariously united.[2]

[Anish] Kapoor, it should be noted, probably didn't have Wilde's Marsyasian moment in mind when he was conceptualizing his 2002-03 project for Tate Modern's vast Turbine Hall. Rather, he was reflecting on Titian's enormous canvas from the mid-1570s, in which the famous colourist rendered the satyr Marsyas's grisly fate.[3] As the story goes, having found Athena's cast-off flute (she was too self-conscious about puffing out her cheeks to continue playing it), Marsyas became so adept an instrumentalist that he challenged the lyre-strumming god Apollo to a musical competition, to be judged by the Muses. The competition was surprisingly close (some say Apollo resorted to trickery in order to win), but, finally awarded the prize, Apollo opted to flay Marsyas alive to punish him for his audacity. Titian's *Flaying of Marsyas* shows not the tale's pregnant moment but instead its most carnal one — Marsyas hanging upside down from a tree with Apollo rather daintily peeling ribbons of flesh from the satyr's muscular body. Yet, like Wilde, Titian tells a story with both visual and aural dimensions: on the basis of notes we will never hear, the god flays the lowly half-beast with a paintbrush, a clever commentary on the corporeal potency of music and the bloody immediacy of paint. It is such immediacy — of both colour and sound — that Kapoor takes from the Marsyas myth for his contemporary retelling. And, like Titian's and Wilde's before, Kapoor's version marries the seductive and the sadistic by focusing on the infra-thin medium of skin.

Kapoor's *Marsyas* was all membrane — a positing of an inside and an outside in the mode of the Möbius (where such binary terms become inherently irresolvable). Indeed, what Kapoor presented was a shared skin — one operating in the mode of the cave, the cone, the orifice, the opening, yet asserting all of these as forceful presences rather than spaces waiting to be filled. For anyone entering the Turbine Hall, a site so vast as to be inconceivable even while standing in it, *Marsyas* performed a strange function: rendering intimate the monstrous and confusing scale by exacerbating it. Was this a magnification of something smaller, or merely a portion of something even more gargantuan? Here was an eardrum, an anus, a conch-like spiral whose three headless necks beckoned with the promise or threat of deeper access. Nearly filling the hall's 160-metre-long, 23-metre-wide, 35-metre-high expanse, *Marsyas* nonetheless utilized materiality in such a way that, while undeniably taking up space, it simultaneously created an alternative one.

The Flaying of Marsyas, Titian (1490-1576)

Constructed using one immense sheet of claret-coloured PVC and three circular steel rings, *Marsyas* spanned the length of the hall, barely touching down on the east and west vectors, as though the piece itself were nearly weightless, suspended and floating. Thoroughly impossible as it was to get a holistic view of the work, one was forever traversing its surface, covering ground around and under it. The body (your body, my body), made its way around another body (that body, *its* body), reaching out to touch its skin or uttering some low hum (returned by the other body, whose capacity for sound was startling). Marsyas, as the story goes, was flayed, but in Kapoor's hands, he keeps on making music.

Yet, as much as *Marsyas* produces a kind of shared space that we might recognize as coming out of a tradition begun with Minimalist sculpture, there is an added ambivalence here. For, if, say, one of Donald Judd's works drew attention to the body phenomenologically, the viewer took the cube to be nonetheless inanimate in the end, a kind of stable, material thing around which she moved. Kapoor's *Marsyas*, on the other hand, while undeniably made of plastic and metal (though it is read as flesh, just as we would read the paint in Titian's work), evokes a relationship that suggests an exchange in two directions, not a rumination by one. You feel, as you are trying to comprehend *Marsyas*, that *Marsyas* is trying to comprehend you. There is a push and pull, something between you and it.[4]

And 'between-ness' is how one most succinctly describes a membrane, no matter how large or small: that which binds while also holding apart. *Marsyas*, furthermore, can be described as a quite particular kind of membrane, and one with innate musical ties. The work can be thought of, receiving and returning the strokes and utterances of its viewers as it does, as playing a kind of visual/aural hymeneal.[5]

from *Skinning the Imagination*
Cecil Balmond

Structure and Metaphor

As Kapoor's sculpture at Tate Modern takes shape and turns and climbs into space, narrowing only to expand again and widen, the form invokes the action of arch, wall, slab, even that of column and massive beam. The archetypes of structure — the imperative to span, leap the void, resist the elements and come down to earth in a collective surge at the foundation — are there. But no elemental line outlines an edge or frames the object, the undulation absorbs all. Surface bends into structure. Assemblies of lines and planes now merge in one confluence and spread over the surface of a warp. The discrete flows into the continuum. Structure runs in hidden currents; its vanishing provokes ambiguities, for which fold is now sinew or muscle? The guessing game is between structure and metaphor.

To build something, even to develop an argument, there is a particular logic of connection, structure realises meaning. But in buildings a structure usually buried beneath bricks and mortar behaves secretly, transmitting wind and gravity forces to the foundation, its actions not necessarily understood apart from that of somehow providing stability. Structural diagrams are also removed from reality; a line serving as the sign for a beam or column, an arrow indicating the action of a load, a dot is the centre of gravity of an object, and so on. Structure works like a ghost behind the scenes. This secret ambition to establish a transference from the real to the abstract resonates readily with the idea of a metaphor, to an action of shifting meanings. When we use a metaphor we assume the transfer, between words, of pattern — and a structure with its anatomy of line, zigzag brace, or contoured wave is already part of pattern. Either way the imagination is primed; structure and metaphor can act like twin poles of a magnet, each field of thought flowing into the other. And as structure gets buried in surface there is a tendency for that surface to maximise itself, to extend and grow in volume — one early idea was to do just that, expand the form, pumping up the shape to push against the sides of the Turbine Hall. Other models of a bean-like shape hung dangerously over the mezzanine platform, the surface again wanting to swell and fill out the available cross section. In each case the work sought to be the principal conduit of the building. That a piece of cloth could fabricate this is remarkable, stitching surface and volume, the ideal and the pragmatic into one smooth unravelling; structure is forgotten, even sculpture in the conventional sense is lost. Unvoiced metaphors disturb the air. …

Like a giant ear the construction is open to our whispers. There are no unknowns — everything shapes itself between the end anchors and centre annulus depending on the bias, cut, and warp of the chosen fabric. The computer realisations looked fantastic.

Finding the right shape though is painstaking. With fabric a particular geometry cannot be easily predetermined. A special computer program begins by assuming a profile, then loading it and allowing it to move, adding pre-stress to stiffen the form. While the structure searches for equilibrium to balance deflection against applied force, the position alters. And the iterations go on. What is sought is convergence. Once that is achieved, small alterations to the physical model cause significant computer time in checking out the stability of the cycle again — load — deflection — pre-stress — load — deflection... etc. Once the geometry is fixed, the shape is then fabricated as a series of longitudinal strips, cut in a specific way, so that when stretched the form would have no wrinkles, no ridges, only a smoothness. That is the theory. In practice fabric structure needs tolerance or 'give' in its fastenings so that if unwanted wrinkles do appear, after the cloth is stretched, there is room for adjustment.

But these factors alone — of material and form-finding, though complex and sophisticated — do not make the work. Colour adds life. Kapoor chose a deep red that had darker coagulations in it, viscous, blood-like. The problem is that colour lacquer has to be applied as a film in a particular way with structural PVC fabric, without that layer 'lifting' off and laminating. Special trials are needed.

The trials could not yield the varying dark tones we wanted; but a sample of another deep red hung in the studio produced different colour shades, as the cloth changed its curvature. The skin seemed to grow flesh beneath the red lacquer. I could see the technical abstractions we had struggled with — of warp, cutting patterns, and tension trajectories — materialise and thicken into muscle and bone and sinew. Strange that colour, that slightest vibration to the eye, should apply the strongest force.

Skinning the Imagination

As a 28m-diameter hole sucks you in, the circle pulls away and climbs up rapidly, narrowing, the seams of the fabric move onto a small passageway high on the cusp of a sweeping curve. That red orifice, like a throat, swallows the eye and squeezes it past into a vanishing. As the visitor escapes the suction and runs into the Turbine Hall the story unfolds of an arch that leaps and dips down to hover threateningly over a far land of the mezzanine. Again, a gaping hole is the only horizon. This time is it mouth or giant ear? Another arch leaps from the platform to come down on the other side towards earth, foreshortened, flaring into a circle as a mighty steel ring pulls it down and tensions the fabric. Through the open passageways, flying arcs and saturated colours, another force stretches our preconceptions and startles us with intense pictures. Something tough and resolute yet deeply disturbing pulls at our minds. Somewhere between memory and what we see, a hidden structure acts on our emotions with phantoms that shape visceral feelings. Nothing can be talked about, only felt. The imagination is exposed — raw, vibrant. Here at Tate Modern, with Anish Kapoor's work, preconceptions are stretched and warped into altogether another reality.

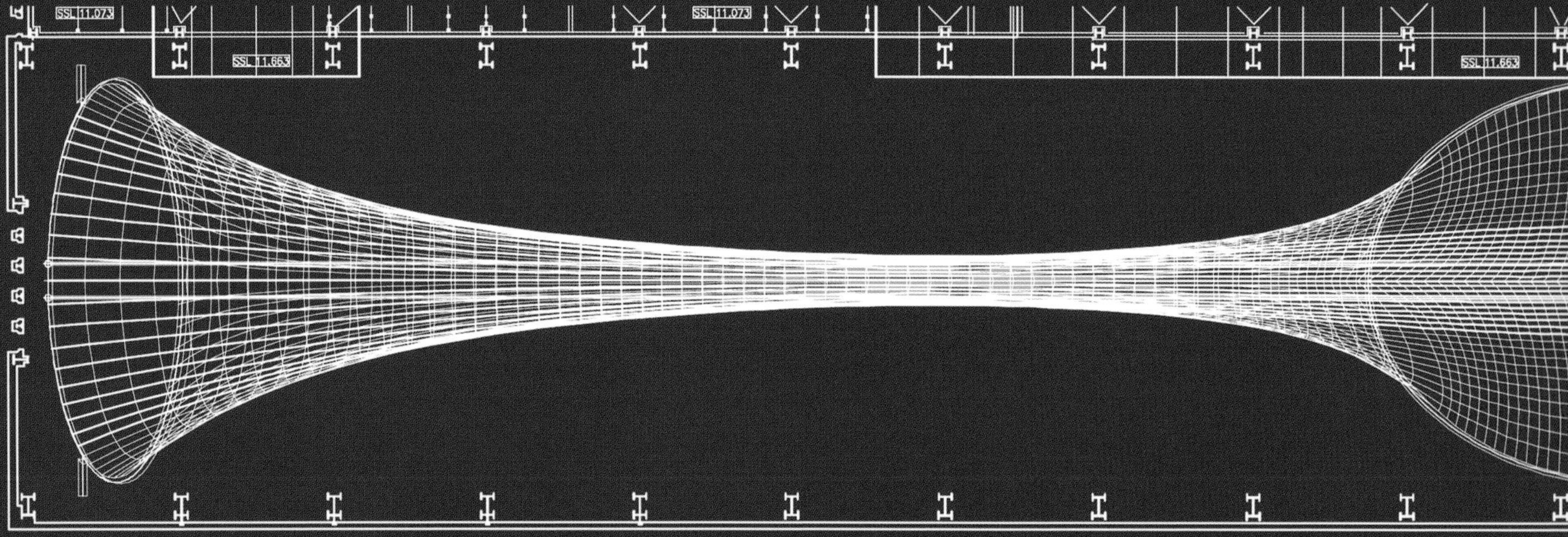
SSL 11.073
SSL 11.663
SSL 11.073
SSL 11.663

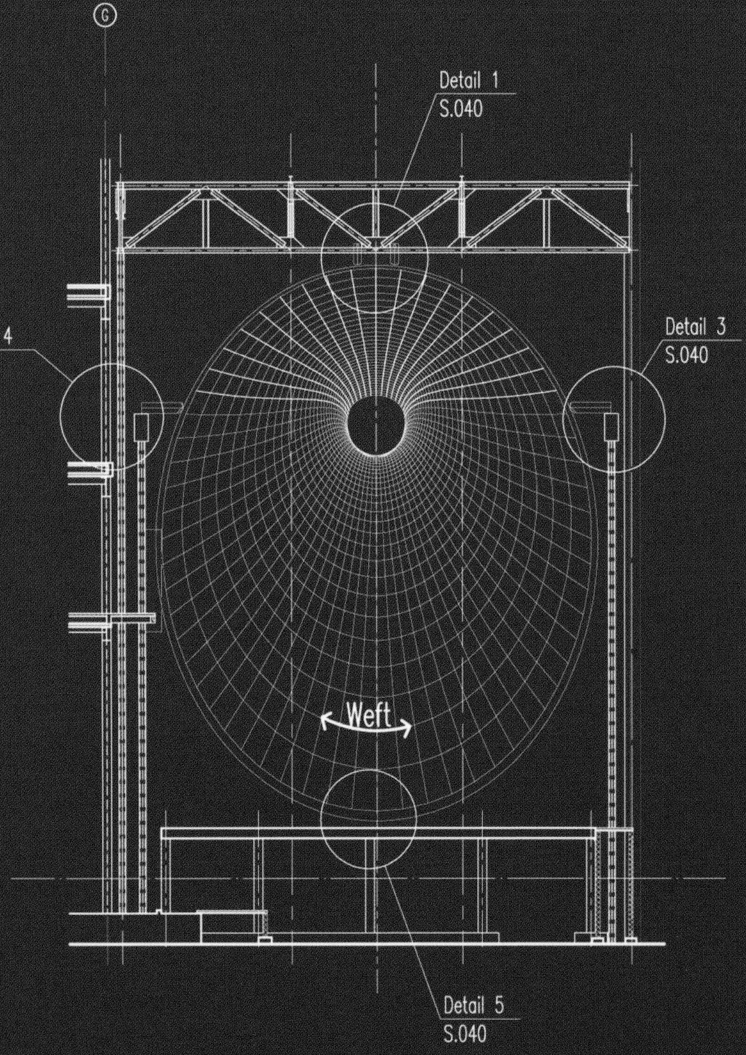
G
Detail 1
S.040
Detail 4
S.040
Detail 3
S.040
Weft
Detail 5
S.040

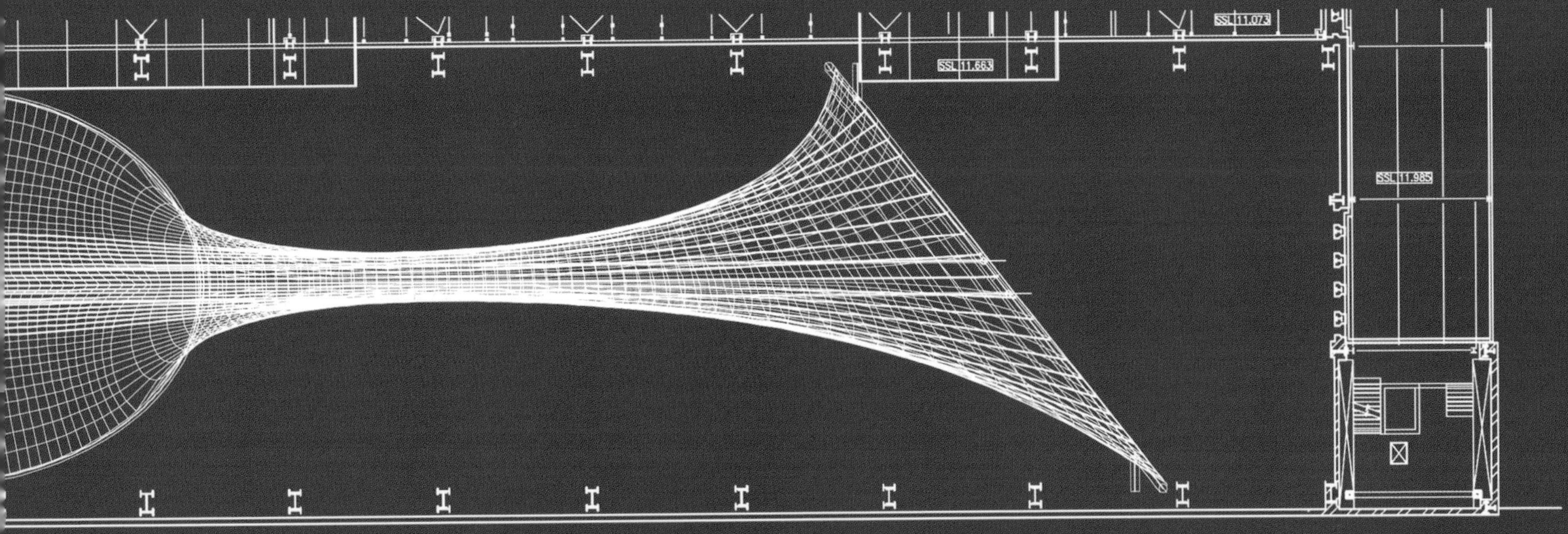
SSL 11.073
SSL 11.683
SSL 11.985

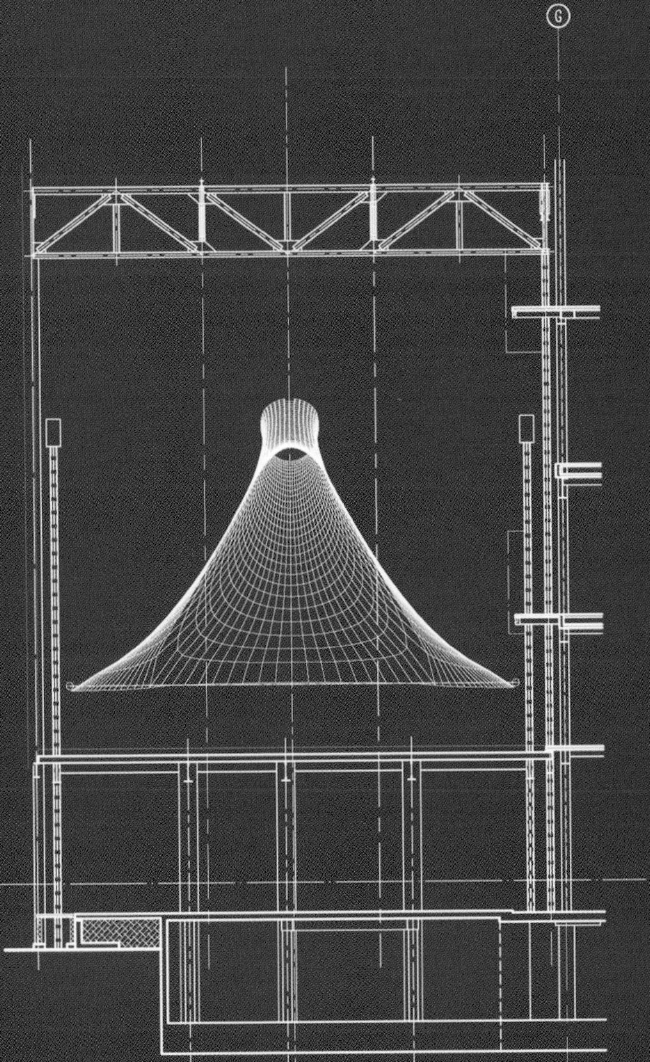

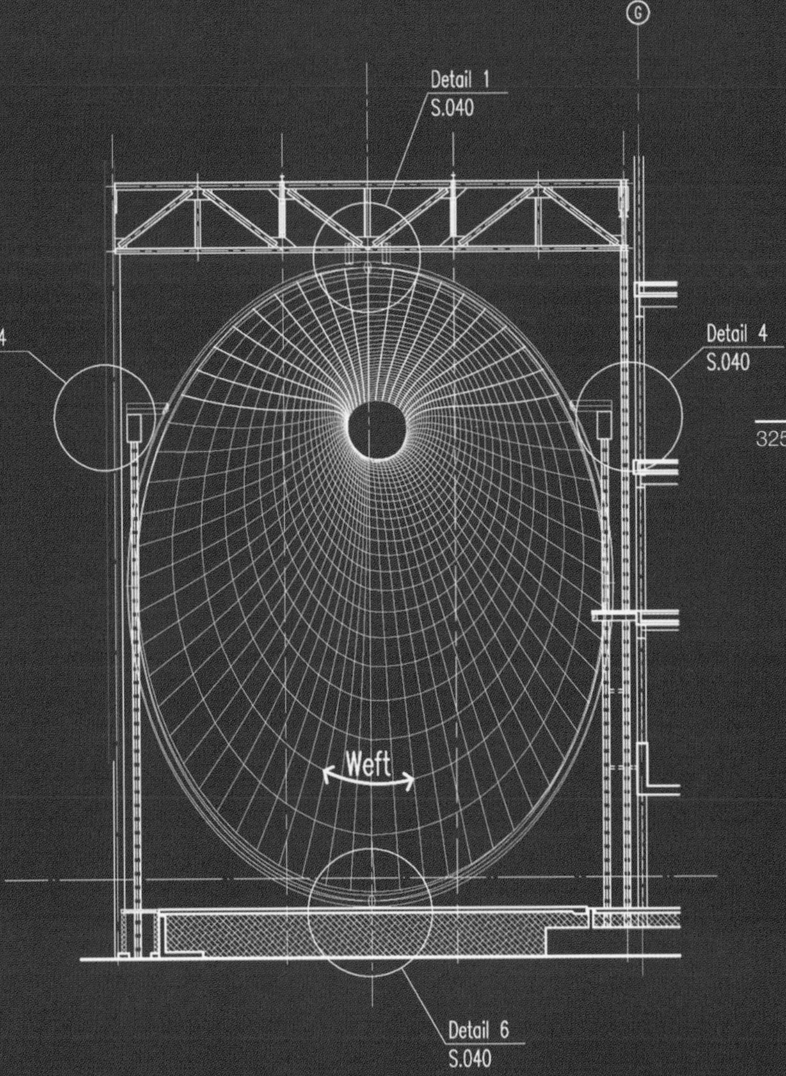
Detail 1
S.040
Detail 4
S.040
Detail 4
S.040
Weft
Detail 6
S.040

zacarious

"Floating" Stayed Roof Plane

PA Technology Center, Princeton, NJ, USA (1984)
Architect: Richard Rogers and Partners
Structural Engineers: Arup, Robert Silman Associates
Model: Sean J. Kim + Yen-Ju Timothy Tai

This first example of High Tech architecture built in the US prominently features a row of red-painted steel A-frames carried on portal frames; these serve to carry most of the loads, and to concentrate circulation and service functions along a central spine. To either side, 24m-long (75ft) roof beams span the interior spaces and leave them column-free, thus maximizing flexibility of occupancy. These beams are supported at mid-span by inclined tension rods anchored to the tops of the A-frames via distinctive O-shaped connectors. Tie-down columns at the beams' end prevent uplift of the large roof while also being able to carry compressive gravitational forces. [see also pp. 42, 43, 338]

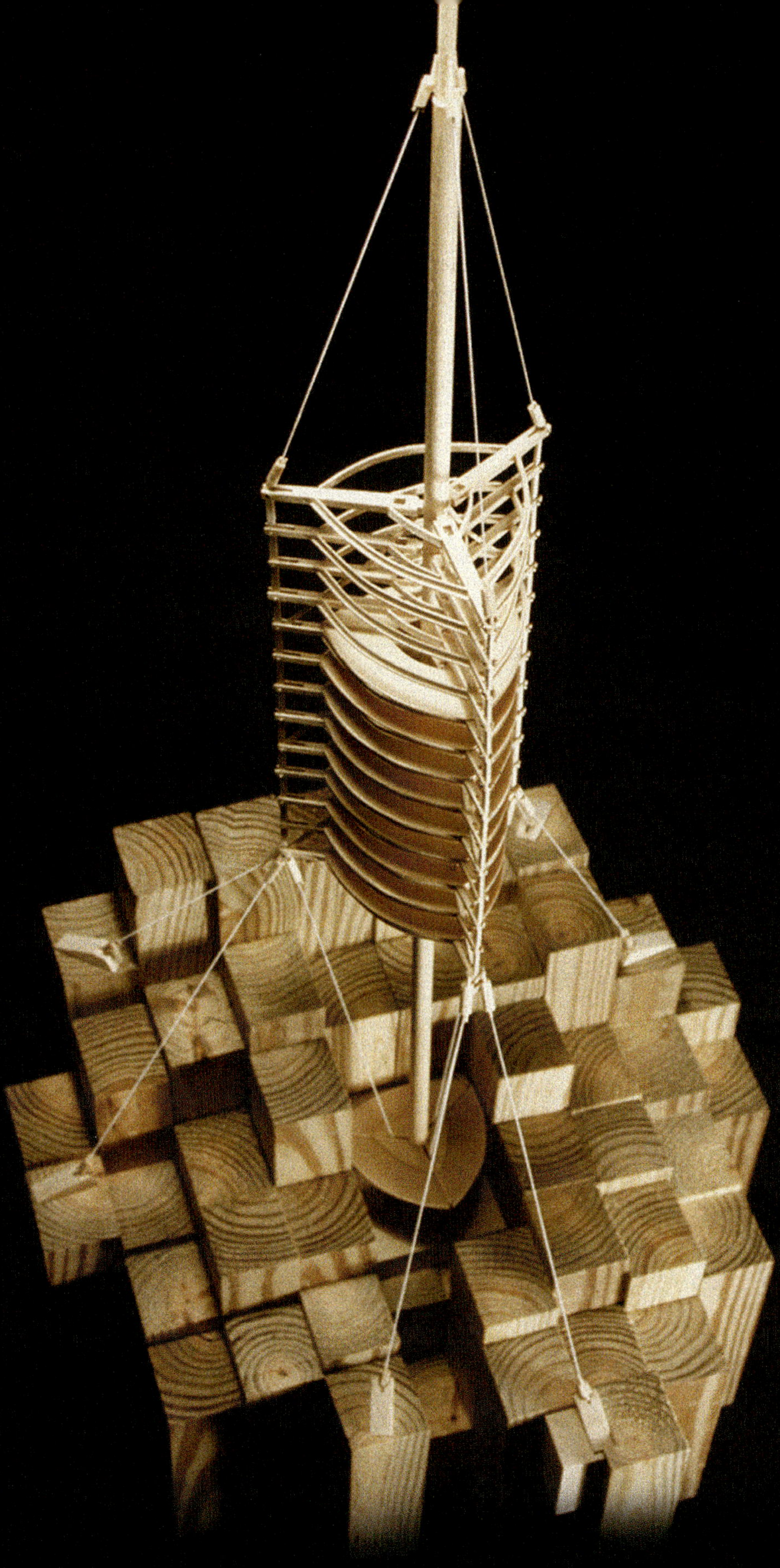

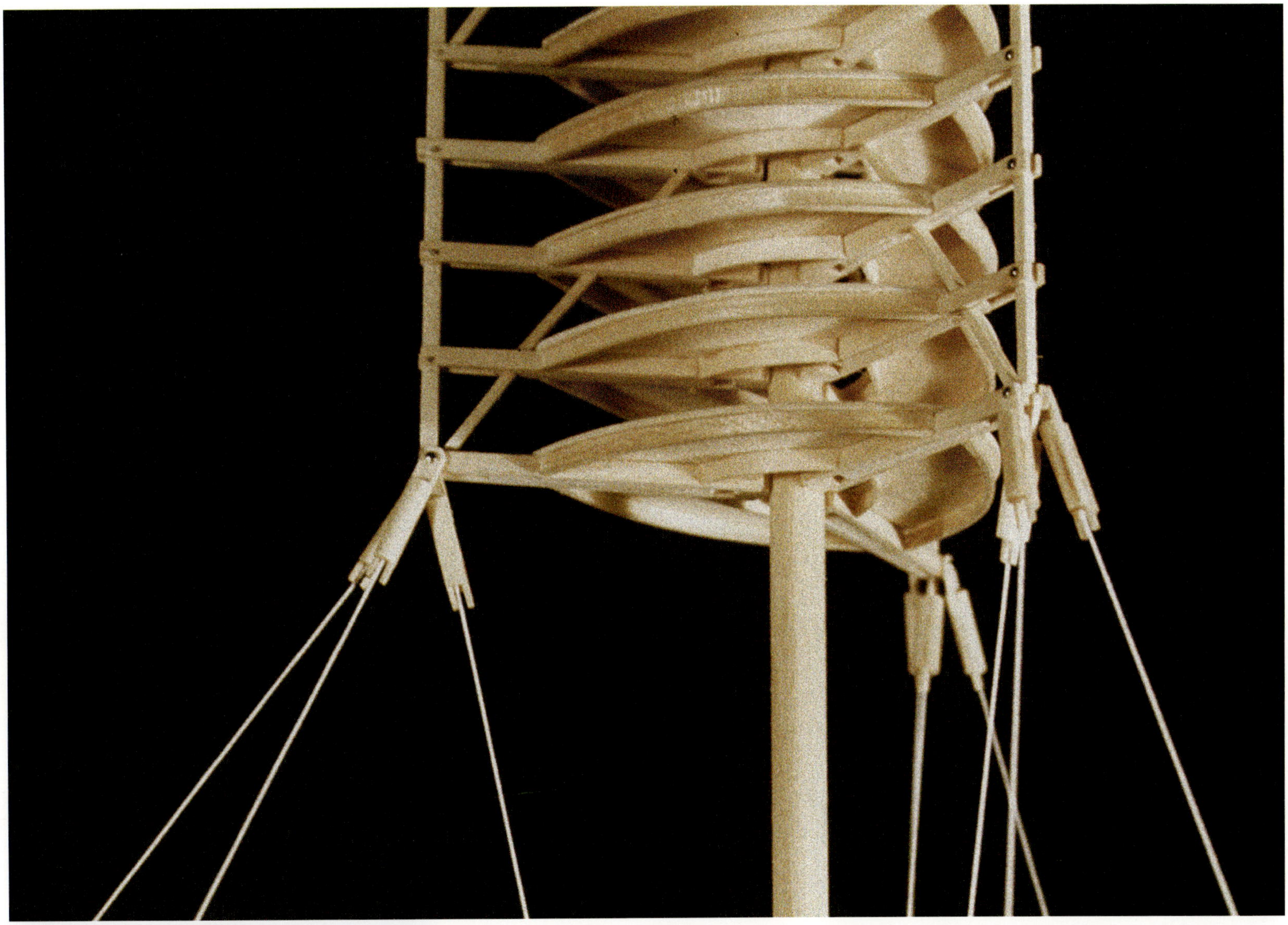

Ramón Etis

Stays and Guys: Transparency of Form

Torre de Collserola, Barcelona (1992), Architect: Foster + Partners
Structural Engineer: Arup; Julio Martínez Calzón and Manuel Julià Vilardell
Model: John Tsai

Reaching a spectacular height of 288m (864ft), this communications tower has a remarkably slender core measuring only 4.5m (13.5ft) in diameter; such apparent height-to-width proportions set the Barcelona tower well apart from other such structures. In reality, the reinforced concrete tube is braced sideways by an almost invisible multi-directional array of anchoring tension cables, effectively making this structure a guyed mast rather than a freely-cantilevering core (which would have required a 25m- (75ft-) wide base). This cable system stabilizes the mast against local buckling while also bracing it against wind loads. The detailed design of the bracing system also acknowledges the technical requirements for wireless transmission while simultaneously making possible a tower of remarkable visual transparency and material efficiency: i.e., the three upper stays are made from aramid fibres which are transparent to broadcasting signals because the material is not an electrical conductor, while the lower sets of cables consist of pre-tensioned high-strength steel.

Anders Sandberg

Stayed Structural System

Oxford Ice Rink, Oxford, UK (1984)
Architect: Nicholas Grimshaw and Partners
Structural Engineer: Arup
Model: Edsel Perez

With its spectacular structural system left exposed, the Oxford Ice Rink remains one of the signature buildings of the High Tech era. The cable-stayed system, with its two 33m- (100ft-) tall masts, gives visual identity to the one-story building; its physical lightness is also justified by the site's poor ground conditions. The system enables the 72m x 38m (250ft x 125ft) interior space to be column-free: transverse rigid frames are supported at their mid-spans by a twinned central spine beam which is, in turn, carried every 15m (50ft) by two pairs of stays that angle up to the masts and then are back-stayed to an anchorage in the ground. This structure can be "read" in both its force-equilibrating form and detailed member design; i.e., the tension cables are thin; the spine beam and masts are expressively configured to resist buckling in compression; and the transverse frames have member profiles and corner connections intended to resist bending moments.

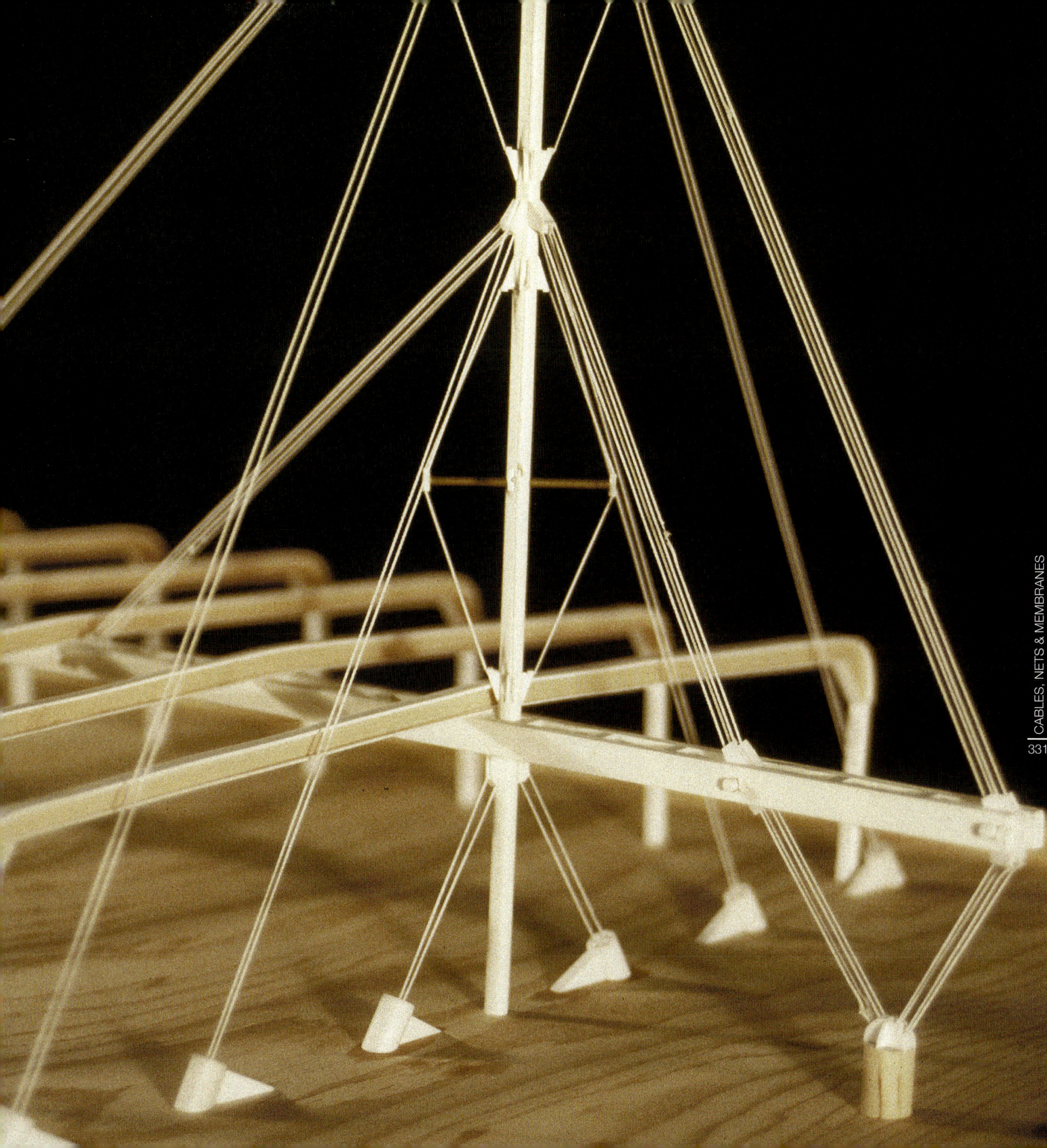

Threaded Structure

ICD/ITKE Research Pavilion, Stuttgart, Germany (2013-14)
Designers: Institute for Computational Design – Prof. Achim Menges,
Institute of Building Structures and Structural Design – Prof. Jan Knippers
Model: Charisse Foo + Hanxi Wang

Annual research pavilions designed and built at the University of Stuttgart explore the potentials of digital fabrication methods while adhering to the ideals of lightweight structures long associated with the institution. In this instance, an open, double-layered structure covers an area of $50m^2$ ($538ft^2$) in a biomimetic form inspired by the protective shell for beetles' wings. Carbon and glass fibres are stretched and interwoven between two light steel frames by multi-axis robots to create 36 doubly curved, polymer-stiffened modules, each having unique 3D geometry; these were then manually connected together. The efficiency and lightness of tension structures is here extended into novel building forms and fabrication techniques.

Doubly Curved Cable Net

Olympic Velodrome, London (2011)
Architect: Hopkins Architects
Structural Engineer: Expedition Engineering Ltd;
Schlaich Bergermann und Partner (cable net)
Model: Karl Pops + Aleks Stojkovic

Richard Davies

The exterior of the London Velodrome alludes to the cycling track inside, with its curved red cedar plank cladding and a roof that follows the track's iconic form, rising up dramatically at the ends and swooping down low in the middle, thus providing the ideal perimeter geometry for anchoring a cable net roof. Pairs of 36mm (1.5in) diameter cables form a 3.5m (10.5ft) orthogonal grid; those in the long direction drape down in the middle, working as suspension cables, while those running perpendicularly pull downward against the first set and are highest in the middle and lower at the sides; i.e., the cables thus define an anticlastically curved surface and work together to carry the roof loads and maintain its stability and stiffness. A steel truss along the perimeter counters the inward pull of the cables by working as a compression ring. The cable net system thus efficiently provides a huge column-free space of 12.000m^2 (130.000ft^2) for cycling events and their spectators.

Nigel Watts

Tension-Defined Form and Space

Munich Olympic Stadium, Munich, Germany (1972)
Architect: Günther Behnisch & Partner, Frei Otto
Structural Engineer: Leonhardt & Andrä
Model: Rich Tong

Working with tension forces is an effective strategy when designing a structural system that is both materially efficient and relatively transparent. A consequence, however, is that the structure has a highly distinctive shape and identity, necessitated by the requirements of physical equilibrium. In this iconic stadium, pre-tensioned steel cable nets cover the seating area, clad with transparent acrylic panels. Tall guyed masts, flying struts, and stay and anchoring cables establish the necessary connection points in 3D space to appropriately shape the cable nets and provide overall equilibrium – as well as visual distinctiveness and transparency – for what is largely a tension-force-defined system. [see also p. 299]

01

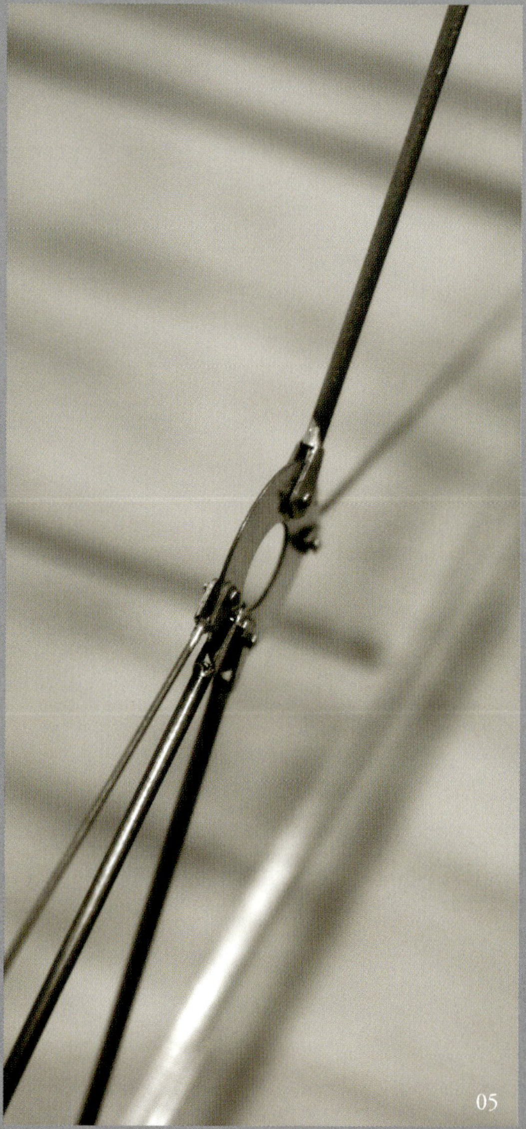
05

02

04

03

06

07

08

09

10

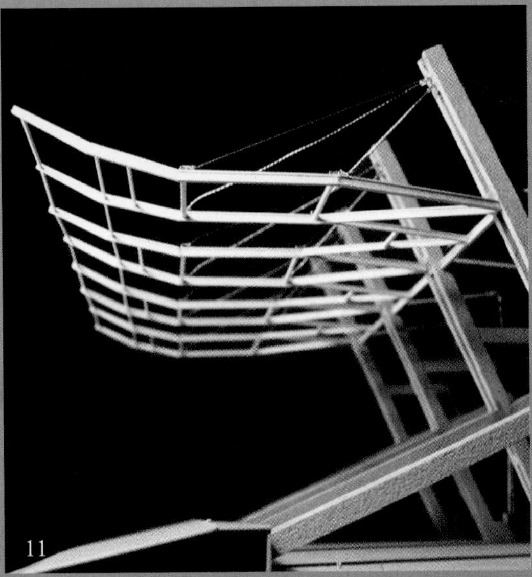
11

01,04,05. Long span achieved due to multiple stay supports; connection detail for intersecting tension rods – PA Technologies Center, Princeton, NJ, USA, 1982; Richard Rogers and Partners (arch.); Arup (eng.); model by Sean J. Kim & Yen-Ju Timothy Tai **02,03. Radial suspension cables; tension ring at center, compression ring at perimeter; representation of glass panels' weight reproduces cables' parabolic curvature** – Sandra Day O'Connor Courthouse, Phoenix, AZ, USA, 2000; Richard Meier & Partners (arch.), James Carpenter (glass ceiling, main courtroom); Arup (eng.); model by Justin Roznowski **06. Spring anchorage for pre-stressing rods allows for drying/shrinking of stacked wood** – Swiss Pavilion, Hanover, Germany, Expo 2000; Peter Zumthor (arch.); Conzett, Bronzini, Gartmann (eng.); model by Garrett Knoll & Adrianne Ngam **07. Ramp walkways supported by hangers on one side, attached to deep truss on the other** – Lerner Hall, Columbia University, New York City, NY, USA, 1999; Bernard Tschumi Architects; Severud Associates (eng.); model by Ian Klein **08. Pre-tensioned guy cables stabilize tower in all directions** – Scholzberg Tower, Liberec, Czech Republic, 2006; e-Mrak (arch.); model by Mariya Tsvetkova **09. Anchorage for fabric membrane at top of mast prevents overstressing fabric; membrane's double curvature evident** – Rosa Parks Transit Center, Detroit, MI, USA, 2009; Parsons Brinkerhoff (arch.); FTL Design and Engineering Studio (eng.); model by Hallie Black & Ainslie Cullen **10. Thin stays in tension, mast & roof trusses configured to resist buckling and bending** – Exhibition Centre, Sydney, Australia, 1988 (demolished 2014); Philip Cox Richardson Taylor Partners (arch.); Arup (eng.); model by Bryant Lu **11. Stayed roof opens space to views; thin tension cables, relatively thicker mast and roof beams** – Loubriel Stadium, Bayamón, Puerto Rico, 1973; Reed, Torres, Beauchamp et al (arch.); model by Elisabeth Warlop

12

13

14

15

16

12,13. Angled pylons provides vertical and horizontal support for highly stressed, relatively flat suspension cables – Millenium Bridge, London, UK, 2000; Foster + Partners (arch.), Anthony Caro (collab. arch.); Arup (eng.); model by Chris Green **14,17. Water-filled parachute fabric bags provide ballast to anchor cable to counter uplift of light roof** – Bibracte excavation site canopy, Mont Beuvray, France, 2008; Paul Andreu (arch.); RFR Group, TESS (eng.); model by Linbo Fan & Willow Hong **15. Site-specific asymmetrical anchorage of suspension cable roof canopy** – Municipal Stadium, Braga, Portugal, 2003; Eduardo Souto de Moura (arch.); AF Associados (eng.); model by Patrick Delahoy **16. Equally spaced tension cable hangers support roof beams from parabolic arch** – Olympic Velodrome, Athens, Greece, 2004; Santiago Calatrava (arch., eng.); model by Patrick Fraher **18,19. Tensegrity system for fabric canopy; lower end of "flying" columns supported by thin tension cables** – Cutty Sark Pavilion, London, UK, 2007; Youmeheshe Architects/ Alastair Townsend (arch.); Toby Mason, David Dexter Associates (eng.); model by Hong Ji Chen & Jennifer Wang **20. Hangers support mezzanine within vaulted space; arched ribs have depth to resist bending** – Fortabat Collection Museum, Buenos Aires, Argentina, 2008; Rafael Viñoly Architects; Soubie Fernandez y Asociados (eng.); model by Catherine Kim & Roberto Soto **21. Bookstacks hung from rooftop truss & within mega-frame for building** – Biblioteca Vasconcelos, Mexico City, Mexico, 2007; Alberto Kalach (arch.); Enrique Arriaga, EMRSA (eng.); model by Walmir Luz & Isidoro Michan Guindi **22. Vertical hangers support end of walkway support beams** – Tree Tower, Neuschonau, Germany, 2009; Josef Stöger (arch.); WIEHAG GmbH (eng.); model by Johanna Grazel Mejia & Jose David Pagan

17

18

19

20

21

22

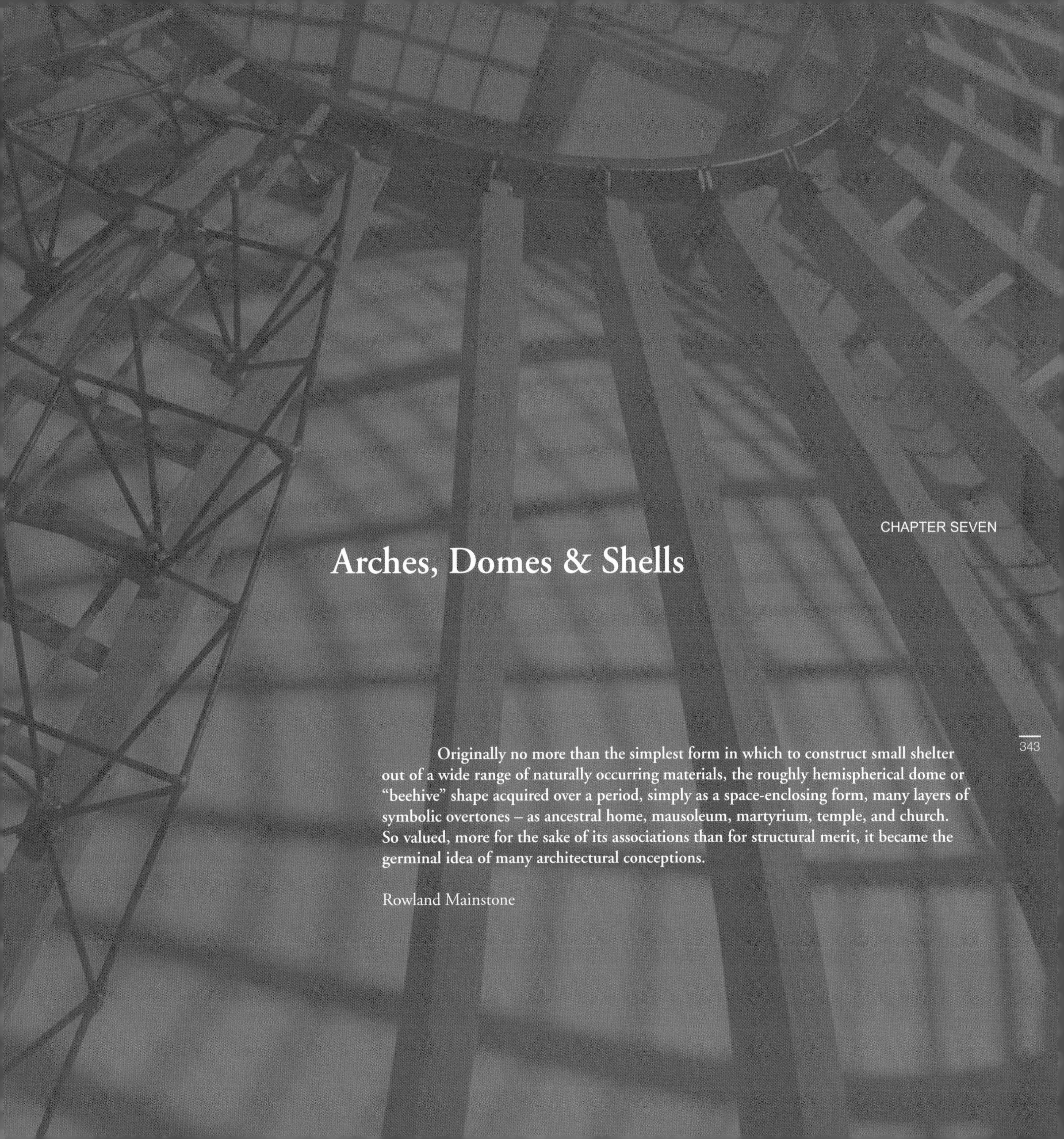

CHAPTER SEVEN

Arches, Domes & Shells

Originally no more than the simplest form in which to construct small shelter out of a wide range of naturally occurring materials, the roughly hemispherical dome or "beehive" shape acquired over a period, simply as a space-enclosing form, many layers of symbolic overtones – as ancestral home, mausoleum, martyrium, temple, and church. So valued, more for the sake of its associations than for structural merit, it became the germinal idea of many architectural conceptions.

Rowland Mainstone

Gateway Arch. Photo: Keith Dotson

Arches, vaults, domes and shells are structures that work in compression to divert gravity loads to the sides in order to create occupiable spaces; moreover, they are generally characterized by having iconic downward curvatures whose shape on the inside envelops space while on the exterior heralds the communal activities that they frequently shelter. Carrying loads by means of compression, of course, results in the need for a certain "thickness" of structure to counter the tendency to buckle out of alignment; in fact, for anything but an "ideal" arch/dome/shell having funicular profile (that is, whose inverted shape corresponds exactly to that of a flexible tensile structure loaded in just the same manner) there will always be a state of compression *and* bending through the thickness – resulting in the structure's needing to be even thicker, or having flanged or hollowed or trussed section profiles best able to counter such demands. Thus, notwithstanding their apparent simplicity and familiarity of form, arches, domes and shells can be somewhat more involved in terms of behavior and design than might at first appear to be the case. Even so, as a group these are structures that are of remarkable overall slenderness relative to spanning distance and loads carried; it is no accident that the form has been with us for so long.

Such considerations have direct visual consequences, of course, as are discussed here by the renowned mathematician Robert Osserman in connection with the Gateway Arch in St. Louis. Certainly one of the world's tallest and most widely recognizable commemorative arches (dedicated to the westward expansion of the United States), this structure's signature shape has long been debated as to whether it is derived from pure structural necessity or whether it is an architect's aesthetic tour de force. Osserman addresses the topic in a particularly accessible manner, even as he incorporates some of the relatively complex mathematics underpinning his arguments; for those for whom these parts are too heavy slogging, it is suggested to skip ahead a few lines to where the descriptive text resumes.

Informing Arch Form

from *How the Gateway Arch Got its Shape*
Robert Osserman

Much has been written on the subject of Eero Saarinen's most widely known creation and architectural landmark, the Gateway Arch in St. Louis. Nevertheless, it is difficult to find complete and authoritative answers to some of the most basic questions:

1. What is the shape of the Arch?
2. Why is it the shape that it is?
3. Of the various decisions that had to made, which were based on esthetic, and which on structural considerations?

These questions raise issues of a purely mathematical nature that are of independent interest. A number of them have been treated elsewhere and will be referred to as needed. Here we focus on the basic questions that are our central concern.

The Shape of the Arch

The terms most often used in describing the shape of the Gateway Arch are *parabola, catenary,* and *weighted catenary.* We shall discuss each of those terms in some detail later on, but let us note that they all represent mathematical idealizations of physical phenomena. A parabola, as Galileo demonstrated, is the shape of a path traversed by a projectile subjected only to its initial impetus together with the force of gravity, in the absence of air resistance. A catenary is the shape assumed by a hanging chain or a flexible cord of uniform density. A weighted catenary is the shape assumed by a hanging chain whose links vary in size or weight, or by a flexible cord of variable width, or variable density material.[1]

An equally basic feature of the shape of the Arch is what we shall call, borrowing a term from computer, television, and movie screens, its "aspect ratio": that is, the ratio of width to height of the inside dimensions of the smallest picture frame that can hold the full frontal view of the Arch; or, in architectural drawing terms, a front elevation of the Arch. Aspect ratios are usually expressed in a form such as "3-to-2" or "3:2."

An occasional source of confusion stems from the fact that both the parabola and the catenary extend to infinity. In both cases there is, up to scaling, a single curve, but arcs of a single parabola or catenary can look very different from each other, depending on the part that one chooses, and the corresponding aspect ratio of the given arc. In fact, in both cases, one may choose arcs with any aspect ratio one wishes. Fig. 2 illustrates how to obtain a variety of aspect ratios from a single catenary.

A further potential source of confusion is that Saarinen changed the aspect ratio of his Arch design between the time that he originally won the competition, and the final design used in the construction. The original design was for an arch that was 630 feet wide and 590 feet high, whose aspect ratio was therefore approximately 21:20, or just shy of square. By the time the arch was built, Saarinen had kept the original width, but raised the height to 630 feet, exactly matching its width.

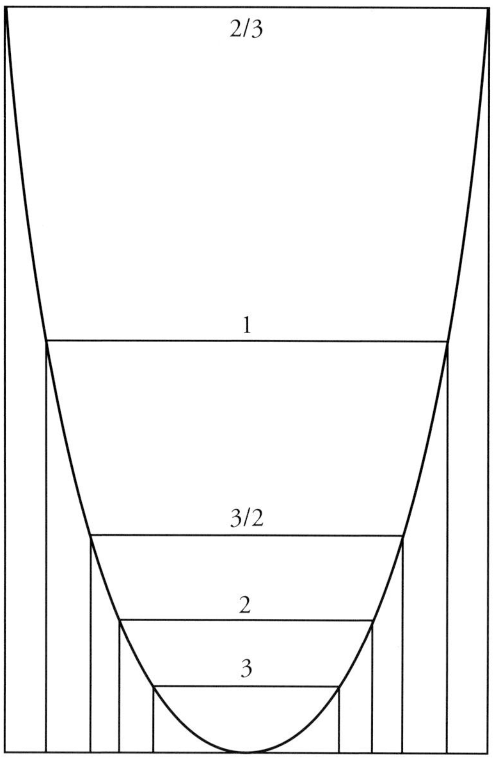

Fig. 2 Aspect ratios for a catenary

Fig. 3 Parabola and catenary with aspect ratio 1:1

According to architect Bruce Detmers,[2] who worked with Saarinen on the Arch, it was typical of Saarinen to favor simple geometric figures, such as a square, and therefore not surprising that he would modify his design to obtain the 1:1 aspect ratio. According to other sources, the principal reason that Saarinen increased the height of the arch was that between the time that he won the original competition in 1948, and the beginning of construction in the early 1960s, new and higher buildings had been added to the surrounding landscape, which forced Saarinen to modify his own plans so that the Arch would clearly dominate its surroundings. It is undoubtedly the case that both of these factors played a role in his final choice of the exact 1:1 aspect ratio.

It may be worth noting that the 1:1 aspect ratio is a very old tradition in architecture. In medieval times it was known as *ad quadratum*. The original 1386 specifications for the cathedral of Milan is an example.[3]

The contrast between the shape of a parabola and a catenary is clear if we choose segments of each with a 1:1 aspect ratio (Fig. 3).

In Fig. 3, the parabola is the pointier inner curve and the catenary the rounder outer curve.

History of the problem

Commemorative arches designed to be lasting monuments date back thousands of years, with a number still standing from the days of ancient Rome. However, it does not appear to have been until 1675 that the question was raised—at least in print—of what shape an arch *should be*, from a mathematical and structural point of view. At that time, one of the leading scientists of the day,[4] Robert Hooke, provided his answer to the question in the form of an anagram of the Latin phrase: *ut pendet continuum flexile, sic stabit contiguum rigidum inversum,* or, "as hangs the flexible line, so but inverted will stand the rigid arch." Hooke was famous for his ability to devise physical demonstrations and experiments illustrating both old and newly discovered scientific principles, and was specifically commissioned to do that for the recently created Royal Society. In the case of the ideal shape of an arch, he realized that what one wants is that the slope of the arch at each point exactly match the combined horizontal and vertical forces acting on that part of the arch—the vertical component being due to gravity from the weight of the portion of the arch lying above the point, and the horizontal force being simply transmitted unchanged along the arch. At the apex of the arch, there is no weight above it, hence no vertical component, and the force is simply the horizontal one of the two sides of the arch leaning against each other. As a result, the slope at that point is zero. As one moves down along the arch, the vertical force keeps increasing, and the slope of the arch must increase accordingly.

One simple consequence of this general reasoning is that at the base of the arch, the horizontal force continues to be present—a fact well known to builders who created flying buttresses and other devices to counter that force—and as a consequence, the bottom of the arch should never be strictly vertical, but rather, angled outwards. As it happens, probably not by chance, Hooke recorded his dictum at the time when both he and Christopher Wren were among the chief architects in charge of surveying the damage, and of rebuilding London after the disastrous fire of 1666. Hooke shared his insight with Wren, who immediately applied it to his design of St. Paul's cathedral, which features an interior dome that is the first to be angled out at its base, rather than vertical.[5]

But the main thrust of Hooke's observation was that the exact shape of an ideal arch could be obtained by simply hanging a chain (or "flexible line") and recording the form that it takes. The equilibrium position would be determined by a balance of vertical and horizontal forces that are the mirror image of what they would be in the case of the arch, with the role of gravity reversed: the vertical component at each point is determined by the weight of the chain below it that needs to be supported, while the horizontal component is simply transmitted unchanged along the chain.

Left unanswered by Hooke is the obvious mathematical question raised by his purely physical solution to the ideal shape of an arch: "what is the equation of the curve that is formed by a hanging chain?" Wherever this subject is mentioned in print, one is likely to find a statement to the effect that Galileo was the first to raise the question, and that he answered incorrectly that the shape that the chain would take was a parabola. Both of those statements merit a closer look.

Galileo's discussion of the shape of a hanging chain appears in print in his last, and in the opinion of many, his best, book, *Two New Sciences.* The book takes the form of four days of dialogue on a wide array of subjects. The first day introduces the first "new science": the analysis of the strength of beams and columns from a scientific and mathematical point of view. It is often considered as the incubator of the modern fields of structural engineering and strength of materials. During the second day, Galileo has his chief protagonist, Salviati, propose two practical methods of drawing a parabola.[6] The first is by rolling a ball along a tilted metal mirror, and the second is by hanging a fine chain, and marking points along it. In other words, he does not pose the question of the shape taken by a chain, he simply assumes that it takes the form of a parabola, based on both theoretical reasoning, using the decomposition of the forces acting on it in the vertical and horizontal directions that led him to deduce the parabolic path of a projectile, as well as on experimental evidence: drawing a parabola on a vertical board, and observing the shape of a hanging chain that seems to follow the same curve.

Few commentators note that Galileo returns to the same question on the fourth day of his dialog, and explicitly states that the similarity is only approximate. He also explains the analogy between the forces acting on a projectile, and those on a hanging chain. Here is the exact quotation:

> *Salviati: The curvature of the line of the horizontal projectile seems to derive from two forces, of which one … drives it horizontally, while the other … draws it straight down. In drawing the rope, there is [likewise] the force of that which pulls it horizontally, and also that of the weight of the rope itself, which naturally inclines it downward. So these two kinds of events are very similar. ...*
> *But I wish to cause you wonder and delight together by telling you that the cord thus hung, whether much or little stretched, bends in a line that is very close to parabolic. The similarity is so great that if you draw a parabolic line in a vertical plane … and then hang a little chain from the extremities … , you will see by slackening the little chain now more and now less, that it curves and adapts itself to the parabola; and the agreement will be the closer, the less curved and the more extended the parabola drawn shall be. In parabolas described with an elevation of less than 45°, the chain will go almost exactly along the parabola.*[7]

In short, Galileo never poses the question of precisely what shape is taken by the hanging chain, and he contents himself with noting that it provides a close approximation to a parabola, especially when the parabolic arc that one draws is near to the vertex where the shape is relatively flat. For example, a 45° parabola would be represented by the equation

$$y = \tfrac{1}{2} x^2, \quad -1 \le x \le 1,$$

which fits in a rectangle of width 2, and height ½, so that its aspect ratio is 4:1. Fig. 4 shows the parabola together with a catenary having the same aspect ratio.

Fig. 4 Parabola and catenary with the same aspect ratio: 4:1

It is often pointed out that unlike the case of a freely hanging cable which will take the form of a catenary, when a cable supports a roadway that is much heavier than itself and whose weight is distributed evenly along the horizontal rather than equally along the cable, the cable will take the shape of a parabola. That will be the case for the cables joining the two towers of a suspension bridge.

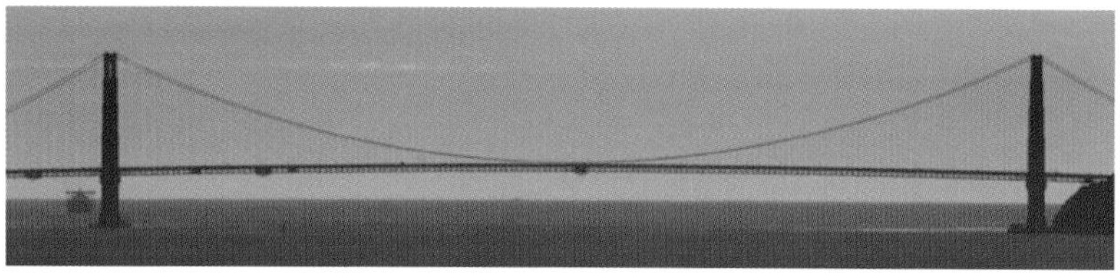

Fig. 5 The Golden Gate Bridge

Fig. 6 30° parabola and corresponding catenary

In the case of the Golden Gate Bridge, shown in Fig. 5, the central cables form curves that make an angle of almost exactly 30° with the horizontal at the points where they leave the towers. However, as Fig. 6 makes clear (or as one can show by a direct calculation), the parabola and approximating catenary are virtually indistinguishable in this case.

The fact that the overwhelming number of references to Galileo's treatment of this subject declare him to have been in error, and ignore the fact that he ends up getting it exactly right, would seem to reflect an extra degree of pleasure in catching him out in any perceived slip-up. In fact, the first page to come up on a Google search of "Galileo wrong" starts with an item from NASA entitled "Was Galileo wrong?" and ends with a NOVA television program entitled "Galileo's battle for the heavens: his big mistake." The first of these entries questions whether the acceleration of gravity is the same for all varieties of materials—a fundamental tenet of science ever since Galileo, and certainly true within the limits of measurements available to him (and many subsequent generations). The last has to do with an actual mistake: his theory that tides were caused by the rotation of the earth. In between these two items are a series of references to a book entitled "Galileo was Wrong: The Church was Right," devoted to proving that the Earth in fact *is* motionless and at the center of the Universe, just as Galileo's opponents asserted at the time.[8]

Of course we now know that had Galileo posed the question of finding the exact shape of a hanging chain, he could not have answered it, since the basic tool needed had not yet been invented: the calculus. It was not until the end of the seventeenth century that the problem was explicitly formulated and solved, the curve in question being dubbed a "catenary" since it was formed by a chain—a *catena.*[9] The brilliant but cantankerous Bernoulli brothers, Jacob and Johann, produced a series of derivations of the equation for the catenary along with a series of barbs at each other's reasoning, such as Jacob's parody of an argument of Johann that he describes as somewhat like proving that a pebble is stone by reasoning that "every man is stone; every pebble is a man; therefore every pebble is stone."[10] Whatever the shortcomings of the reasoning, they did indeed arrive at the correct conclusion. The equation for the catenary can be written in the form we now call the hyperbolic cosine,

$$y = \cosh x = \tfrac{1}{2}(e^{x} + e^{-x})$$

in suitable choice of coordinates.[11]

The design of the Arch

The Gateway Arch was only one component—although clearly the most dramatic one—of Eero Saarinen's winning entry in the 1947 open competition for the design of a "Jefferson National Expansion Memorial," dedicated to Thomas Jefferson—to his vision of an America stretching across the continent, and his Louisiana Purchase, which roughly doubled the size of America at the time. By a truly strange coincidence, the first use of "catenary" recorded in the Oxford English Dictionary is by the future President Thomas Jefferson, in a letter dated December 23, 1788 to Thomas Paine, recommending the use of a catenary arch rather than a circular one for a 400-foot span iron bridge that Paine is proposing to build. Jefferson would certainly have been inordinately pleased, as an architect himself, to know that the principle of the catenary would form the basis of what was to be the largest monument in America in the twentieth century, in honor of Jefferson himself.

The Jefferson Memorial competition attracted virtually all the major architects in America, including Eero's father Eliel, a much more famous architect at the time than his 37-year old son. At least one part of the confusion involving the shape of the Gateway Arch stems from the fact that the competition was held in two parts, first narrowing down to the top five contenders, and then—after significant revisions were made—choosing the winner among those five. In addition, there was a gap of 15 years between the time that Saarinen's proposal was chosen and when construction actually began, during which time still further changes were adopted. And even after construction had started, alterations were made, as one can see from different sets of blueprints in the Saarinen archives at Yale University. Further confusion arises from a certain degree of carelessness in terminology that can be seen, for example, in a dictionary of architecture where a picture of an arch is accompanied by a caption referring to it as a "catenary or parabolic arch",[12] not aware of, or not interested in, fine distinctions. Whatever the reason, newspapers and architectural journals that reported or commented on the shape of Saarinen's winning design for the Gateway Arch, referred to it without exception as a parabola.[13] By chance, among the letters that Saarinen received was one from H. E. Grant, head of the Department of Engineering Drawing at Washington University in St. Louis, asking for more details about the "parabolic arch," since Grant wanted to use it as an example in a book on descriptive geometry that he was writing at the time. In his response, dated March 24, 1948, Saarinen says:

> *The arch actually is not a true parabola, nor is it a catenary curve. We worked at first with the mathematical shapes, but finally adjusted it according to the eye. I suspect, however, that a catenary curve with links of the chain graded at the same proportion as the arch thins out would come very close to the lines upon which we settled.* [14]

In other documents Saarinen left considerable room for ambiguity. In 1959 he wrote:

> *The arch is not a true parabola, as is often stated. Instead it is a catenary curve—the curve of a hanging chain—a curve in which the forces of thrust are continuously kept within the center of the legs of the arch.* [15]

Whether by "catenary curve" he means an actual catenary, or is trying to hedge a bit, is not clear. In an unpublished transcript dating from 1958-59, he describes the Arch as "an absolutely pure shape where the compression line goes right through the center line of the structure directly to the ground. In other words, a perfect catenary".[16]

If one consults the Wikipedia entry for "catenary" one finds—at least at the time of this writing (June 2009):

> *The Gateway Arch in Saint Louis … follows the form of an inverted catenary. … The exact formula*
>
> $$y = -127.7\,ft \cdot \cosh(x/127.7\,ft) + 757.7\,ft$$
>
> *is displayed inside the arch.*

The equation given is indeed that of a catenary, and it has the desired dimensions of 630 feet in both height and width, but it is not the equation that was used in the construction of the arch, and that appears on all the blueprints and specifications.[17]

At the Arch itself, a sheet provided by the National Park Service, under whose jurisdiction the monument falls, is headed "Equation for the catenary curve of the centroid of arch cross-section." Below that is the same equation that appears on the blueprints. We shall return to the equation shortly, but it is definitely not a catenary.

In 1983, an article entitled "Is It a Catenary? New questions about the shape of Saarinen's St. Louis Arch," appeared in an architectural journal.[18] The author, Michael J. Crosbie, explained that despite widespread belief that the Gateway Arch is shaped like a catenary, it is not. Instead, it is a "weighted catenary," the form taken by a "weighted chain" in which the various links are of different weight, rather than all the same. In mathematical terms, it amounts to using a "flexible line" with a density that is variable rather than constant. It appears to be uniformly true that any description of the shape of the Gateway Arch that tries to be accurate will use the term "weighted catenary" or something similar.

We are now in a position to state precisely the mathematical questions that arise.

1. How much information is conveyed by the expression "weighted catenary"? More precisely, what range of curves may be obtained by suitable choice of a variable density?
2. What was the basis for the choice of the particular "weighted catenary" chosen by Saarinen? Was it primarily on esthetic or on structural/mathematical grounds?
3. The arch is designed so that its cross-sections are equilateral triangles. Again the question whether that choice was esthetic or structural.
4. The size of the cross-sections varies according to a precise formula, with the sides of the equilateral triangles growing from 17 feet at the apex to 54 feet at ground level. What determined those dimensions, and what is the significance of the specific formula used for the tapering? And once again, were those choices motivated by esthetic or mathematical considerations?

The answer to the first question can be formulated quite simply: the term "weighted catenary" conveys essentially no useful information; virtually any curve that one can picture as a possible candidate[19] for a weighted catenary can actually be reproduced by a suitably weighted chain.[20] Among those are, for example, a parabola and a circular arc, as well as the catenary-like curve of the actual arch. In all of those cases one can explicitly say how to distribute the weight so that the chain, or flexible line, will hang in exactly the desired shape. In other words, saying that the shape of the Gateway Arch is a weighted catenary is technically correct, but essentially devoid of content. Furthermore, it is not descriptive, in that it says nothing about the actual shape of the Arch, but only about the method used to produce it.

On the other hand, there is a very simple description of the precise shape of the Arch. It is what we call a "flattened catenary" and consists simply of a catenary that has been shrunk uniformly in the vertical direction by a given amount. It will have a vertical axis of symmetry, just as the catenary does, and if we choose that axis to be the y-axis, then the equation of a flattened catenary takes the form

$$y = A \cosh Bx + C, \qquad (1)$$

where $A,B > 0$. Note that if we take the catenary curve $y = \cosh x$, and scale it uniformly up or down in size, we get the equation $By = \cosh Bx$, while flattening it by a uniform compression in the vertical direction would give the equation $y = D \cosh x$, where

$$0 < D < 1.$$

In other words, equation (1) represents a catenary if and only if $A = 1/B$. The constant C corresponds simply to a translation in the vertical direction, and we if choose coordinates so that the vertex of the curve is at the origin, then $C = -A$. Putting all this together, we see that by setting $D = AB$, equation (1) takes the form

$$y = D(1/B)(\cosh Bx - 1) \qquad (2)$$

so that equation (2) represents a catenary with vertex at the origin that has been flattened vertically by the factor D.

The centroid curve of the Gateway Arch is of exactly this form, where A and B are specified numerical constants:

$$A = 68.7672,\ B = .0100333 \qquad (3)$$

so that the flattening factor D is given by

$$D = .69 \qquad (4)$$

In other words, the catenary is shrunk in the vertical direction by just under a third. The effect is to "round it out" somewhat more at the vertex. The y-coordinate in equation (2) for the Gateway Arch represents the vertical distance *down* from the vertex of the centroid curve. The numerical values given in (3) correspond to distances measured in feet.

It is worth noting that shrinking a curve in the vertical direction is exactly equivalent, up to uniform scaling, to expanding it uniformly in the horizontal direction—precisely what is often done to reformat a film done with one aspect ratio to fit it onto a wider screen with a different aspect ratio (Fig. 7).

It is also important to observe that since the flattening degree D for the Arch given by (4) is a little over 2/3, and since the centroid curve of the Arch is intended to have an aspect ratio of approximately 1:1 ("approximate" because it is the outer silhouette of the Arch that is designed to have aspect ratio 1:1, and the same will not be true of the centroid curve, as we discuss more fully below), we must start with a portion of the catenary having an aspect ratio of approximately 2:3 and either shrink it vertically by about 2/3, or stretch it horizontally by about 3/2 (Fig. 8).

It is ironic that Saarinen has been attacked from both sides, with some commentators criticizing the shape of the arch for being too purely mathematical to be taken seriously as a work of art, while others take him to task for not being "pure" enough. Michael Crosbie[21] notes

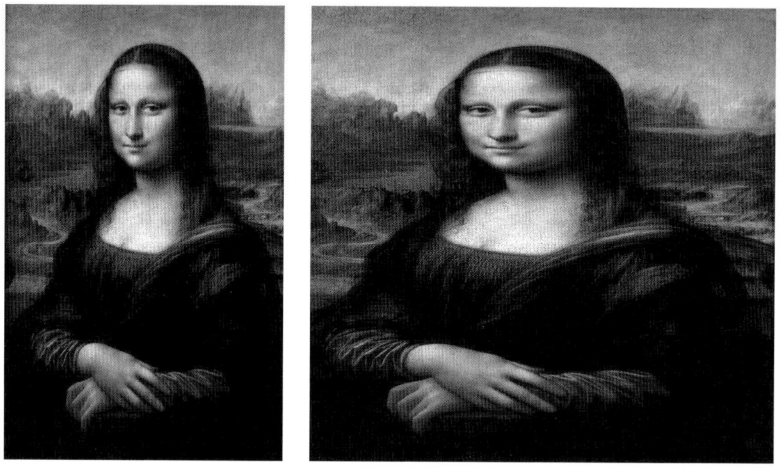

Fig. 7 Wide-screen Mona Lisa

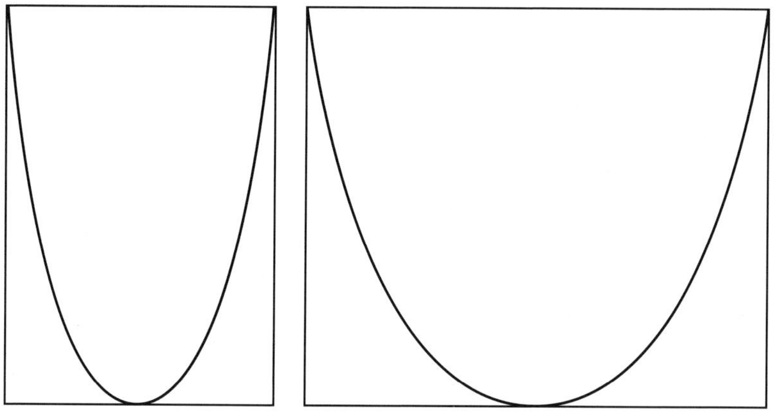

Fig. 8 Re-formatting to obtain a 1:1 aspect ratio

the fact that "the curve is not a perfect catenary," adding "—a pure form that would seem more attractive to Saarinen...". Hélène Lipstadt is more severe: "The purity is illusory and the explanation deceptive (if not deceitful), since he knowingly had his engineers calculate an impure, weighted catenary".[22]

Clearly, a catenary is no higher on the scale of purity than, say, a parabola or a circular arc, which are "weighted catenaries." The equation for the parabola is perhaps the simplest of all equations for a curve, consisting as it does of a polynomial with a single (quadratic) term. A circular arc is one step more complicated, involving square roots, and hence, algebraic functions. The catenary, built out of exponential functions, which are not even algebraic, but so-called transcendental functions, would seem to lie relatively far afield in the domain of mathematical purity. Presumably what is meant by the criticism is that the equation Saarinen used as a basis for his arch, on the suggestion of Hannskarl Bandel, one of his engineers, suffers from being *almost*, but not quite, a catenary, involving the insertion of rather arbitrary-looking numerical constants.

To criticize Saarinen for not using a perfect catenary, however, is to miss the point of Hooke's original insight. The catenary is the shape one obtains using a uniform chain or "line" and is therefore the shape one wants for an arch of uniform thickness. For a relatively small arch, uniform thickness would not be unreasonable, but for the kind of monumental structure proposed by Saarinen for his Arch, it would be almost unthinkable, both on esthetic and structural grounds. One would naturally want the cross-section of the arch to be the least near the apex, where it has little or nothing to support and where any additional weight adds to the strength requirements of everything below. Conversely, the parts of the arch closest to the ground have the most weight to support, and would naturally have the largest cross-sectional size. As a consequence, the correct shape would not be the mirror image of a uniform chain, but of a correspondingly weighted chain, as Saarinen points out in the quotation given above. That principle was clearly understood early on. A famous illustration from 1748 in a report by Giovanni Poleni on the cracks in the dome of St. Peter's shows a cross-section of the dome, together with the shape of a hanging chain that was weighted proportionally to the loads of the corresponding sections. Poleni used the result to deduce that the structure was basically sound, despite the cracks that had appeared.[23]

In short, a "pure catenary" is the ideal shape for an arch of uniform thickness, and a flattened catenary is the ideal shape for an arch that is tapered in a certain precise (and elementary) manner. In the case of a weighted chain, we may express the amount of weighting by a density function $\rho(s)$, where the weight of any arc of the chain is the integral of $\rho(s)$ with respect to arclength s over that arc. One can show[24] that a given flattened catenary of the form $y = f(x) = A \cosh Bx + C$ is obtained from a density function $\rho(s)$ which, when expressed in terms of x, takes the form

$$\rho(s(x)) = (ay+b)/(ds/dx) = (a\,f(x) + b)/\sqrt{(1 + (f\,'(x))^2)},$$

where the coefficients a and b are determined by the coefficients A, B, and C of $f(x)$, up to an arbitrary multiple (since multiplying the density by an arbitrary positive constant just changes the total weight, but not the shape of a hanging chain). What this means physically is that the weight of any portion of the chain lying over a segment of the x-axis, given by $\int \rho(s)ds$, is equal to $\int (ay+b)dx$ over the given x-interval.

That brings us to the answer to our fourth question: how the shape of the Arch—which is to say, the shape of its centroid curve—is related to the degree of tapering.

As we have noted, the centroid curve of the Gateway Arch is a flattened catenary whose equation is of the form (1), where the x-axis is horizontal, the origin is at the vertex, or highest point of the curve, and y represents the distance down from the vertex. We denote by h the height of the curve, and by w its width. The fact that y=0 when x=0 translates to the condition $C = -A$, so that the equation takes the form

$$y = A\,(\cosh Bx - 1). \qquad (5)$$

Then the fact that $y = h$ when $x = \pm w/2$ implies

$$h = A(\cosh Bw/2 - 1). \qquad (6)$$

If we introduce the notation

$$R = \cosh Bw/2,$$

then equation (6) becomes

$$A = h/(R-1) \qquad (7)$$

while from the definition of R,

$$B = (2/w) \cosh^{-1} R\,. \qquad (8)$$

The coefficients A, B that enter into the equation for the centroid curve given on the blueprints and all the official documents for the Gateway Arch have exactly this form (Fig. 9).

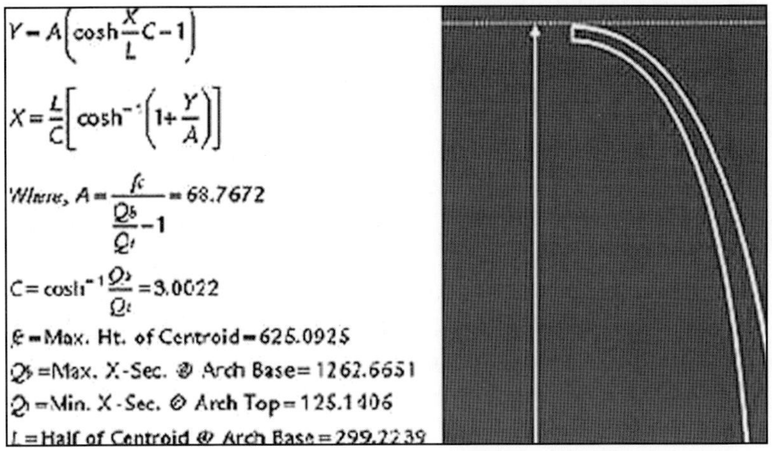

Fig. 9 Official equations for the Arch (National Park Service)

We see that their somewhat strange appearance arises simply from the condition that the curve pass through the points (0,0) and (w/2, h). The only question is the value of the constant R. By its definition, we have $R > 1$, and conversely, if we choose an arbitrary number $R > 1$, then equation (5) with coefficients defined by (7) and (8) represents a flattened catenary passing through the given points. We find further that the degree of flattening D of the curve is given by

$$D = AB = (h/w)(2 \cosh^{-1} R)/(R-1) \qquad (9)$$

Or, equivalently,

$$D = (1/r)(2 \cosh^{-1} R)/(R-1) \qquad (10)$$

where we have denoted by r the aspect ratio of the centroid curve,

$$r = w/h \qquad (11)$$

In other words, the flattening coefficient D is completely determined by the desired aspect ratio r and the—so far—arbitrary constant R.

We are finally in a position to spell out precisely the relation between the shape of the Arch and the basic geometric decisions that were made. In particular we see that the complicated-looking values of the coefficients A and B in the equation of the Arch are direct consequences of a few simple choices. Those choices are:

(i) the centroid curve be a flattened catenary;
(ii) the orthogonal sections be equilateral triangles with one vertex pointing inward;
(iii) the triangles at the top and the bottom be 17 and 54 feet on a side respectively;
(iv) the overall height and width each be 630 feet;
(v) the constant R in equations (7) and (8) be given by $R = Q_b/Q_v$, where Q_b is the cross-sectional area of the triangle at the base, and Q_v the corresponding area at the top.

From (ii) and (iii) it follows that the cross-sectional areas at the vertex and the base are

$$Q_v = 125.1406, \quad Q_b = 1262.6651, \qquad (12)$$

so that according to (v), the value of R is a little over 10. Also from (ii) and (iii) we can calculate the height h and width w of the centroid curve needed to make the outside dimensions of the arch satisfy (iv), and they in turn determine the aspect ratio r. Inserting all these quantities into the equations (7), (8), and (9), gives the numerical values of the coefficients A and B that we noted earlier, as well as the degree D of flattening of the curve.

The one remaining choice that must be made is a formula for the tapering from top to bottom of the Arch. The decision there was to make the cross-sectional area $Q(x,y)$ at the point (x,y) of the centroid curve a linear function of y, interpolating between the given values (12) at the top and bottom. In other words,

(vi) $Q(x,y) = Q_v + (Q_b - Q_v)\, y/h.$

Conditions (i)–(vi) together provide a complete mathematical description of the basic design of the Gateway Arch. Its actual construction, with an outside skin consisting of flat stainless steel plates, requires dividing this basic shape into sections,[25] each bounded by a pair of equilateral triangles, and replacing the curved surface defined by the equations by three flat pieces.[26] The result is also completely defined mathematically, but is an artifact of construction, intended to so closely approximate the curved surface that one is not even aware, for example, that the inner curve of the Arch, its intrados, is not a smooth curve, but a polygonal one. That is indeed the case, and we limit our discussion here to the curved surface of the Arch that underlies the construction.

What remains to answer is whether the choice of the shape itself was dictated largely by structural or by esthetic considerations. When this question was put to Bruce Detmers, who worked with Saarinen on the Arch, his answer was unequivocal: Saarinen's choice was purely esthetic. According to Detmers, Saarinen worked with a large variety of shapes, many of them made on the elaborated Hooke principle, by hanging a weighted chain, or a piece of rubber cut out with a varying width to gain the same effect. The resulting shapes were then used, upside down, to make sizeable models of the arch, and Saarinen would examine the models from all angles. He ended up rejecting them all, as either too flat or too pointed, or otherwise unappealing. He then turned to the engineer Hannskarl Bandel for further ideas, and it was Bandel who suggested the shape that Saarinen found to his liking and that was the one actually used for the design of the Arch. (As a parenthetical note, the key role of the engineers throughout the process, from design to completion, is all-too-often forgotten in accounts of the Arch and its construction.)

The question that arises, if one accepts that Saarinen chose the shape of the Arch on purely esthetic grounds, is "What role, if any, was played by mathematics?"

Bruce Detmers notes two such roles. First, mathematics was critical as a means of communication. It is one thing to draw a shape and to make models that are 10 or 12 feet high, but if one arrives at a pleasing design, then it is still necessary to convert that design into specific instructions to provide those who must manufacture and assemble the parts. There is no obvious way to make the transition from a sketch or a model that must be scaled up by several orders of magnitude and described with absolute precision in order to arrive at the full-sized structure. But as soon as the shape is defined by a mathematical equation, one may build it on any scale that the available materials and methods will allow.

Second, Detmers also alluded to Saarinen's predilection for perfect geometric shapes like a square or a circle. In the case of the Arch, as we have already noted, he decided that he would like its proportions to be such that it could be exactly inscribed in a square.

An additional, and crucial role of mathematics was to calculate the ideal shape of the fully three-dimensional structure whose central curve had the form decided on. That comes down to a process that is the reverse of starting with a hanging chain and adopting the form it takes in order to build an arch. Here one starts with a desirable shape, and has to determine the degree of tapering that would be structurally ideal to go with that shape. But as we have noted, to virtually any shape defined by a mathematical equation, one can assign a weighting that will produce exactly that shape.

The history of the particular equation suggested by Bandel for the Arch goes back to the mid-nineteenth century. It arose in trying to determine the ideal shape for an arch that supports an earth bridge—a bridge formed by simply piling up dirt above the supporting arch to make a flat road surface. The steepness of the arch at each point should be determined by the balance of the horizontal and vertical forces at the point; the horizontal force is just transmitted along the arch and is unchanged from point to point, while the vertical force results from the weight of the column of dirt directly above the point, and is therefore proportional to the height of the road above that point on the arch. From that one can show that the ideal shape must be a flattened catenary.[27]

In the case of the Gateway Arch, it does not support any other structure. However, the effect of the tapering is that the weight being supported by each cross-section increases steadily as one moves from the top to the bottom of the arch, just as it does for an earth bridge. What emerges then is a simple answer to our second and fourth questions regarding the shape of the Arch and the amount of tapering: the two are inextricably entwined, as are the esthetic and structural decisions that have to be made.

The reality is that far more comes into play than these basic considerations. In any project of the magnitude of the Gateway Arch, economic and political factors are inevitably going to be involved. One striking example is the appearance of the George Washington Bridge, with its two silvery towers of interlaced steel girders. According to the original design, those towers were to be covered in stone in the manner of the bridge's famous forerunner, the Brooklyn Bridge, and the steel framework one now sees were to be the invisible support. However, the money for the project ran out, and generations of New Yorkers, along with millions of out-of-town visitors, have engraved in their minds a very different-looking bridge than the one envisaged by its designers. The Eads Bridge across the Mississippi that now forms a backdrop to the Gateway Arch was as dramatic for its time as the George Washington Bridge across the Hudson several generations later. In both cases, the length of the bridges and the size of the river spanned broke new ground, and in both cases the bridges linked two adjacent states. In the case of the Eads Bridge, connecting Missouri to Illinois, powerful political factors entered in, affecting the final design of the bridge.[28]

Even on the structural level, many factors must be considered beyond the ideal shape for supporting the weight of the Arch itself. There are many forces besides gravity that must be taken into account, including those arising from potential gale-force winds, from earthquakes, and from uneven expansion and contraction as the sun heats up certain parts more than others. In addition, one must assure that the Arch is not susceptible to vibrations at certain resonant frequencies that might lead to structural failure, as happened in the famous case of the Tacoma Narrows Bridge.

Finally, there are many additional decisions that must be made, where esthetic and structural decisions are intermingled. For the overall effect, the most important was undoubtedly the choice of stainless steel for the outer surface, reflecting blue skies and clouds during the day, shining brilliantly against a dark sky when lit up at night. And right down to important details, such as the choice of whether to "brush" the steel horizontally or vertically, and what method to use for attaching adjoining steel plates.

That leaves us with one remaining question to be answered—question 3 about the choice of a triangular cross-section. The answer forms part of the subject of our final section.

Some controversial aspects of the Gateway Arch

No project as monumental as the construction of the Gateway Arch is apt to come to completion without arousing serious controversy. At the least, there are always matters of taste and a ready chorus of critics whose job it is to criticize. In the particular case of the Arch, there were four flags raised against Saarinen that are worthy of note.

The first was raised at the very outset, during the original competition: "What good is it?" A great deal of (public) money is to be spent on a structure with no "purpose" other than merely symbolic. (That is a criticism familiar to most mathematicians who engage in and teach "pure" mathematics, often with no practical applications in sight.)

It should be said that the Gateway Arch was designed with the express purpose of putting St. Louis back on the map after a long period of decline from its nineteenth-century glory as the second largest port in America and the "Gateway to the West." In that capacity, it has been wildly successful, attracting millions of visitors each year, and joining the Washington Monument and the Eiffel tower as among the most widely known symbols of their kind.

The unqualified success of the Arch, both symbolic and practical, as a draw of both attention and visitors to St. Louis, has pretty well answered this objection. Beyond that, many are struck by the beauty of the shape, and the issue then turns on the value of a piece of art or architecture that is admired and gives pleasure of a purely esthetic kind.

The second controversy arose during the construction of the Arch, when serious worries were expressed about its potential to fail and to collapse in what would have been a major catastrophe. That conflict and its resolution have been beautifully described by one of the principal figures involved, George Hartzog.[29]

The third regards our question about the choice of a triangular cross-section. Saarinen's original design for the Arch had a quadrilateral cross-section. Between the first and second phase of the competition, one of his colleagues, the sculptor Carl Milles, suggested that a triangular cross-section would be more attractive. Saarinen liked the idea and adopted it in his final designs, but he failed to publicly credit Milles with the suggestion, a failure that caused many hard feelings and much anger.[30]

The fourth controversy, and most interesting from many points of view, arose shortly after the proposal submitted by Saarinen and his team of co-workers was awarded the commission to build the monument. An article in the *New York Herald Tribune* displayed side-by-side pictures of the design submitted by Saarinen and a poster for an International Exposition that was planned for 1942 in Rome. The headline was "St. Louis Arch For Memorial Called Fascist." In fact, the Rome exposition was explicitly billed as commemorating the twentieth anniversary of Fascism in Italy, and Mussolini's "March on Rome" in 1922. The poster features an arch designed by the Italian architect Adalberto Libera that appears to be on much the same scale as that envisaged by Saarinen, and seems to resemble it strongly in shape. Saarinen vehemently denied knowing anything about the earlier proposed arch, which in fact was never built, due at least in part to the advent of World War II. He further noted that a "simple form, based on the natural laws of mathematics," could no more be co-opted by a political movement than the Washington Monument could be faulted for the fact that its design is that of ancient Egyptian obelisks that were built by slaves.

Ironically, Saarinen's defense—that the form of his Arch was a standard one that could well have been used by anybody—has the effect of diminishing the originality of his design. On the other hand, it provides fairly convincing evidence that he knew nothing about the earlier design. The resemblance on the poster turns out to be purely an artifact of the particular angle at which the Libera Arch is depicted. The actual plans submitted by Libera show that his proposal was for a strictly semi-circular arch, with no resemblance to Saarinen's, other than the overall similar scale, and of course the fact that both arrived at the same idea of a monumental arch as a symbolic gateway—in Libera's case, to the proposed Exposition and the associated newly rebuilt area of Rome, still known as EUR: Esposizione Universale Roma—and for Saarinen, to the broad Western expanse of America across the Mississippi River.

An additional irony is that when Saarinen's design acquired renown after he won the competition, Libera accused him of plagiarism, whereas Libera had himself been similarly charged, because another team of Italian architects had suggested much the same design for an entry arch to the EUR somewhat earlier than Libera.

The final irony is that even if World War II had not intervened, it is not clear that Libera's arch would have been built, or that if built, it would have been able to resist collapse. In fact, a semi-circle is far from an ideal shape for a monumental arch. Serious doubts were expressed at the time. Some of those doubts concerned the choice of materials and structural details of Libera's proposal. Others are intimately connected with Robert Hooke's original insight connecting the shape of an arch with that of a hanging chain. As we noted earlier, one consequence, put to use immediately by Christopher Wren, is that one wants the base of the arch to hit the ground at some angle, and not vertically, as is the case of a semi-circle. The larger the size of the arch, the more vital such considerations become. That is true for an arch of uniform thickness and the corresponding chain of uniform weight. But it is equally true for a weighted chain of any sort.

We have also noted earlier that although it may seem completely counter-intuitive, it is possible to weight a chain in such a manner that it will hang in the form of a perfect circular arc, provided only that it is less than a full semi-circle. That weighting will in turn indicate the ideal tapering of the arch for maximum structural stability. However, Libera's original specifications for his proposed arch give no indication that he was aware of the mathematics needed to determine the correct weighting or degree of tapering.[31]

Concluding remarks

The paintings and the book by Jasper Johns devoted to catenaries[32] make it clear that the shape of a hanging chain evokes an esthetic response quite apart from any attempt to analyze that shape by mathematical means.

In the case of architecture, the need to combine esthetic values with mathematical and structural principles is one that dates back to antiquity, and is certainly apparent in the surviving Greek temples. In some cases, mathematics and esthetics were viewed as interchangeable. As is apparent from our discussion here, in the case of the Gateway Arch they are, if not equivalent, then at least inextricable. It is clear from his letters and his various explanations, that Saarinen was aware at a very early stage that the structural requirement for maximal stability translated into keeping the line of thrust aligned as nearly as possible with the slope of the Arch, which in turn determined the relevant shape. Having begun with that principle, and tried out the resultant shape, he turned it around, modified the pure catenary shape "according to the eye," and then left it to his (superb) engineering team to apply the mathematical principles that would produce the desired shape and satisfy the structural needs.

Viewed more broadly, the role of the architect is one that has provoked a surprisingly wide range of responses. At one extreme, there is the assessment reported in the book *Brunelleschi's Dome* by Ross King,[33] that both ancient and medieval authors "assigned architecture a low place in human achievement, regarding it as an occupation unfit for an educated man." He cites both Cicero and Seneca in support of that view. At the other extreme, we have the view that "it is hardly surprising that, for the ancients, the image of the architect has demiurgic connotations".[34] The author, Edoardo Benvenuto, goes on to say:

> *In a famous dialogue of Paul Valéry* [35] *this "nearly divine" aspect is expressed in the following words of Phaedro to Socrates when speaking of his friend the architect Eupalinos:* [36] *"How marvelous, when he spoke to the workmen! There was no trace of his difficult nightly meditation. He just gave them orders and numbers."*

(To which Socrates responds, "God does just that".)

A twentieth-century version of this story is reported by Bruce Detmers, whose duties as a young architect working with Saarinen on the Gateway Arch included long hours spent translating the engineers' formulas for Saarinen's Arch into long columns of numbers generated, in the absence of a modern computer, on an old Marchand calculator borrowed from the accounting department. These numbers were then passed on to those responsible for manufacturing the various components needed in the construction of the Arch.

Detmers recounts one incident that may resonate as a distant echo of Phaedro and Eupalinos. He was working away at two or three o'clock in the morning, when Saarinen wandered in, and asked what he was doing. When Detmers explained, Saarinen's laconic response was, "Keep going."

Kashan's Great Bazaar. Photo: Mehdi Khansari

The planar arch, when extruded along a linear axis, becomes a spatial vault. Its shape envelops and contains space; inherently directional, the vault also encourages pedestrian circulation flow and is thus ideal for the commercial markets of the Iranian street bazaars discussed here. On the outside, the vaults' curved forms at once reflect the surrounding wind-carved natural terrain, while also serving to highlight the unique public spaces they foster within the context of the surrounding dense urban building environment. Their continuous form also lends itself well to other human needs in such a place, such as providing essential shading and climate control. To that end, a few strategically placed openings in the vaults admit carefully modulated light and promote ventilation – a recurring theme in the design of vaults (and of domes, for that matter, as will be seen in the next text entry.)

All of these aspects and more are beautifully revealed in the photographic essay contained in the book *The Persian Bazaar: Veiled Space of Desire.* A sense of that vision is provided by two introductory texts, in which the networks of vault-covered streets are described as hidden, ephemeral worlds of commerce, of making, of social exchange, indeed, of living itself. These vaults provide atmosphere – the air and space contained by them is thick with human activity.

Veiled and Vaulted Space

from Preface to *The Persian Bazaar: Veiled Space of Desire*
Gérard Grandval

Shaped unhurriedly, in wide spirals, with lines that reach from horizon to horizon in tiny increments; shaped by persistent abrasion, showing the wear of time and a sort of streamlined fluidity; that is how the Persian landscape appears to us.

Landscape or architecture?

It is an architecture where angles that were too sharp, textures that were too rough, ramparts that were too assertive seem to have been rubbed off or filed down. Unique and varied, it is beyond time, imparting to the dry clay and shards of silica an oceanic musicality that existed long before the inventors of the bazaar.

The God of whimsy, the great architect, the shaper of Persia, the mad master—is the wind, which has many names. The bazaar's architects are sons of the wind, and their fidelity is more remarkable in that the building of these cities, these vaults—this enclosed, protected, shady space—bears witness to the age-old battle against the wind, against the fire in the heavens, against desertification, abrasion, and burial.

By contrast, the architecture of the bazaar seems to represent the "within," the interior world—a container, a terra-cotta trunk, a spiral cavern that man has made and placed in the folds of the Persian landscape, in the larger architecture—yet it is curiously imitative.

There is combat, confrontation, and simultaneously alliance—a loving antagonism between the inherited landscape and this invented architecture. It takes place on several levels:

– Thus the opposition and alliance between the interior space—shaded, multicolored, fragrant—and the pale nakedness of the sands.
– Thus the straight line and the curve.
– In plan, the square is king: an abstract, invented box which was born of man and did not exist before him. In section and in volume, there is the curving line, the vault: the wave, the rhythmic dune—the mineral expression of great oscillations grounded in mother earth—no longer abstract but cosmic.
– On the inside, each time a narrow passage opens into a spacious hall with slanting shafts of light, it is like an in-drawn breath. From the outside, it is positively enchanting to contemplate; the curious continuity between man's architecture and the pre-existing space gives rise to the rather strange sensation of entering a world at once mineral and organic.

Cities buried, as if in suspension, by the sands, by the wind, the master wind; fragments of stranded giantesses seen somewhere else, at Bomarzo; unbelievably, exaggeratedly feminine. Like the nomads' tents, the vaults' inverted curves meet the horizon; the landscape is king. It is a compelling architectural landscape, seemingly unintentional and inevitable; repetitive, knitted, woven, yet still admitting infinite variations in the repetition; here everything is music.

Made up of basic elements, of dull sounds, of sub-multiples: the vault, the brick, the grain of sand. Each grain is different, for one who knows how to see. ...

from *Trade, Shopping and Architecture*
Oleg Grabar

For all those who have been in an Iranian bazaar, even in a relatively modern one like Tehran's, there lingers forever the memory of a wonderfully mysterious area in which known and unknown goods emerged from unexpected places, and people, dressed in many different ways, wandered under beautiful arches and domes of baked brick. It seemed like a remote and exciting world of its own, unique and changeless.

Cold reality and logic make one read it all quite differently.

The bazaars of Iran, it could be argued, are nothing but shopping centers. At first glance, they, of course, look different from our neatly compartmentalized and homogenized spaces enclosing pedestrians malls and surrounded by huge parking lots and delivery roads. But these differences are perhaps secondary and these ancient bazaars may just be like old clothes, quaint and perhaps no longer very comfortable, but covering the same bodies and the same actions as are part of the contemporary scene.

Let me pursue the point. The long spine of Isfahan's bazaar winds its way between two planned and constructed spaces which are partly open to the skies. One, the monumental ensemble of the *meydan-e Shah* (now the *meydan-e Imam*), is royal and religious; the other, the complex building known as the *masjed-e jame'*, is also religious but in a more civic and urban sort of way. One could enter this spine in many places, passing first through warehouses as one left the living quarters of private houses and small traders, generally related to each other through ethnic, tribal, family, or religious associations. People, in fact almost exclusively men, walked in this spine and goods were only occasionally brought in on the backs of donkeys, mules, and, more rarely, camels. At various intervals, there was a fountain to provide freshness and refreshments and a place for rest and for the exchange of news or gossip; someone, to be sure, also provided food. In all likelihood, there were times when entertainment, usually musical, was also available, and we know that an orchestra played at the *meydan-e Shah* entrance to the bazaar.

Isfahan was a capital and a show piece of Safavid wealth and patronage. Although lesser cities may not have received all the amenities found in the capital, among the striking features of Iranian (and other) bazaars are, nearly everywhere, the vastness, the expansiveness, of the spaces they occupy and the consistency of their arrangements, as though a basic, even if flexible, prototype had been invented or developed at some unknown time and then carried through the centuries.

So do our modern shopping centers give an impression of sameness in their arrangements: in such services as eating, drinking, and resting available in them; in the occasional appearance of entertainment; in the necessity for people to walk, while little carts or vans transport goods. Even the outlying areas of the spaces are comparable, as modern shopping centers have parking of private cars and trucks tying them to the daily life beyond. In heavily settled places, as with the Forum des Halles in Paris or with many reconverted garages and factories elsewhere, some of these elements of composition are placed underground with invisible parking places and subways, but the principle of a sequence going from the shopping center to the parking and then to means of access to various ways of local living is consistent in new shopping centers as they were in the bazaars of old.

We are less clear on whether traditional Iranian bazaars served as collective and family festive places, as happened outside of Iranian cities for the New Year or as transform our centers at Christmas time, but we can imagine that on major religious celebrations, like those of Muharram or of the end of Ramadan, the bazaars did play a role for larger urban groups than those who used them every day, even though it is safe to assume that a masculine environment always predominated.

Why not simply conclude that traditional bazaars were but the older equivalents of modern shopping centers with differences in life style and behavior expressed in multiple ways characteristic of each separate culture but without any fundamental alteration of comparable human behavior? There are, I believe, two reasons not to draw such a conclusion of universal sameness, even if one can easily admit that the same desires for material consumption and for acquisitiveness dominated both kinds of spatial organizations.

The first reason is both simple and important. In the modern world, manufacturing has disappeared from the shopping center. In the traditional world, things were made in bazaars. Everyone knows about streets with specialized artisans weaving baskets, making shoes, beating metal, transforming every conceivable raw material into all sorts of useful or decorative objects. Bazaars were noisy; some, like the streets of metalworkers, were overwhelming with the sounds reverberating on walls and vaults, so noisy in fact that in recent times apprentices were moved into open spaces around bazaars for the loudest operations affecting metals. Noises do not appear in photographs, but dust does, and all bazaars were filled with particles of work, the sawdust of woodworkers or the threads of textiles, mixed with the dust of architecture and of endlessly shuffling feet. This dust is like a veil which covers the visitor or like the filter through which he reaches whatever he sought, the object of his desires. And to the dust must be added odors, the sweet smells of candies and pastries, the rich scents of endless perfumes, the rough smell of leather or of paint, the hard odors of working bodies making things or carrying them around.

Making things was not simply a technical activity now gone from shopping centers; it was a continuous sensory experience for the eyes, the nose, the ears, at times the taste buds and even touch. That experience could be exhilarating and attractive or repulsive and depressing. But, when compared to the aseptic quality of our shopping malls, it always was a profoundly human experience, mixing in a uniquely rich combination everything that man can make and everything that exudes from the body. Both the inhabitants and the makers of the bazaar as well as visitors who came to it contributed all together to that concoction of noises, smells, and sights and imbibed it in ways which are quite different from those of our own shopping areas.

The other difference between traditional bazaars and contemporary centers lies in the nature and quality of their respective architecture. I shall restrict myself to two aspects of that difference. One is a technical one, at least at first glance. It involves the material of construction and the ways in which it was treated. Today steel beams or concrete blocks hold up two or three levels of shops connected by escalators or steps and end with a more or less translucent ceiling of glass or glass substitute, through which some sort of sky appears, even though one never quite knows whether it is the real sky or some image thereof. But, artificial or not, it is the source of light for most of the shopping center and that light always seems to be coming from the sun during the day, from artificial sources at night.

But something quite different happens with the construction of traditional bazaar spaces in Iran. Brick, the phonetic unit of construction, is always present, always visible, as though the whole atomic structure of the building was made apparent. Spaces are cut up into cubicles covered with vaults or domes, and the succession of cupolas, often with different decorative designs, seems to be an endless discovery of new treasures, of new ways to define space, of wondrous mysteries in richly designed zones of transition, in tactile walls whose bricks, and at times additional ornament (tiles or stucco), shine from obscured sources of light.

For, even though most domes have more or less the same opening at the top through which the light of the sun or of the moon comes down to the level of men, this light does not illuminate everything the same way but cascades down through a range of more or less mysterious volumes, as though endlessly searching for something it will never find in the continuous life of the bazaar. It is difficult to reconstruct in their fullness the ways of light in bazaars before the appearance of electricity. In addition to the round skylights, one should imagine thousands of small lights from candles or from oil lamps of different sizes. Just as with buildings transformed into their phonetic components, light must have appeared as a firework of flickering sources transfiguring people and things into sharply defined three-dimensional objects rather than illuminating them fully and almost cruelly.

The architecture of the bazaar was an experience of discovery; it created a mystery in which both men and things played a strange role, only partly defined through their specific function of selling and making or of buying and waiting to be bought. By its skillful manipulation of light and of built surfaces, this architecture sought to attract and to fascinate. Together with the noises, the smells, and the visual festival of colorful items on display, it proclaimed the complexity of life and something of its illusory quality. Everything may be possible and available, but perhaps nothing is real.

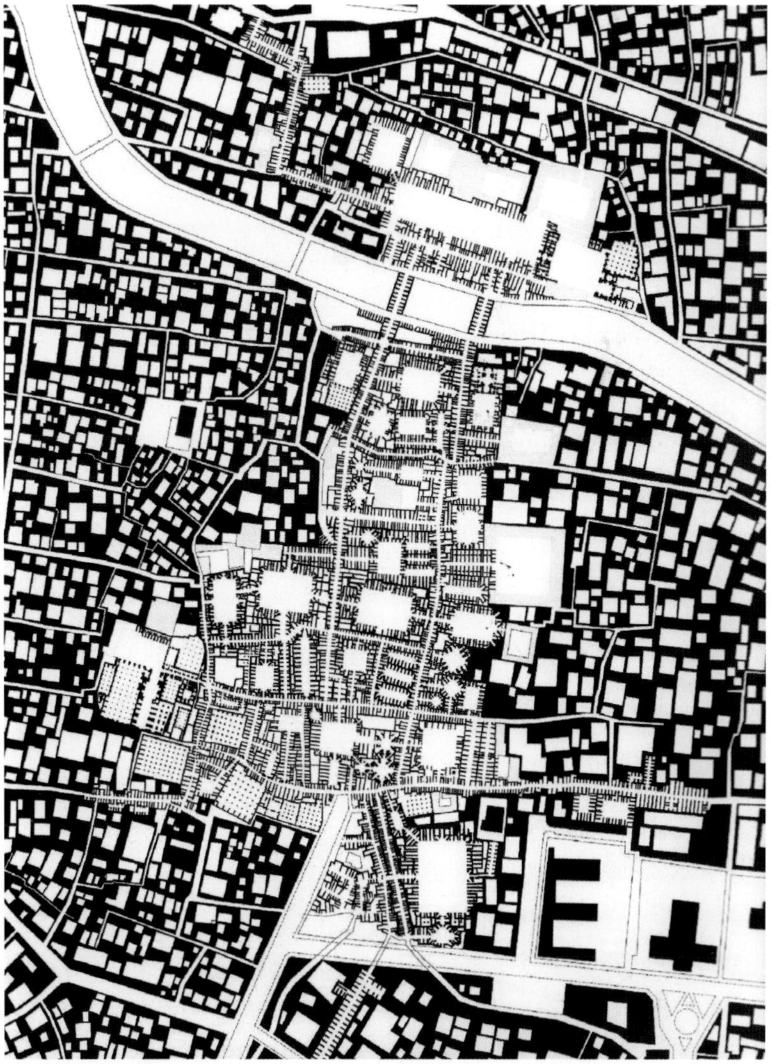

Rehabilitation plan for Tabriz Bazaar.
Photo: © ICHTO East Azerbaijan Office

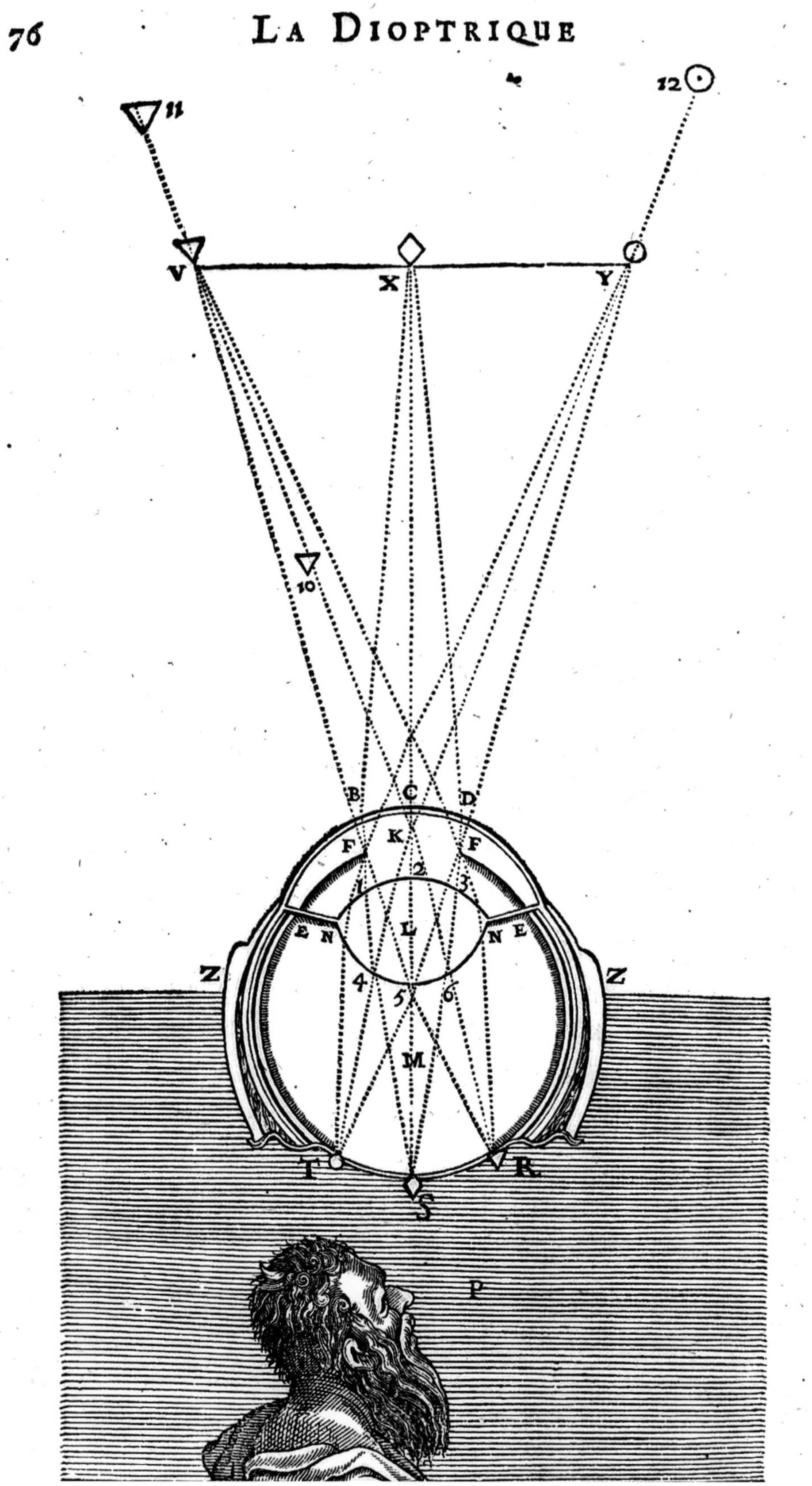

Fig. 1 Diagram of ocular refraction. René Descartes, 1637

Spatially and structurally, traditional masonry domes can basically be described as the form created when a planar arch is rotated about a central vertical axis. As with the arch and the vault, loads are mainly carried by means of compression, which again implies the need for significant thickness of form to deal with buckling as well as bending behavior, although as the advantages of dome shapes informed by funicular geometries became known the dome surface could be made thinner. Essential for any dome is the need to counter outward thrusts around the base – perhaps by means a series of radial shear walls or braced frames, or by a circumferential tension ring. At the apex there is also cause to relieve the concentration of compression forces where the many notional "arches" meet – something that is typically addressed by an annular compression ring, or oculus, which also just "happens" to be able to provide for the admission of light into the space below, as well as the evacuation of hot air.**

Aside from such "practical" considerations, the spiritual associations with the dome are longstanding, as attested to by the historical tradition of domes atop churches, mosques and temples. Their distinctive profile on the skyline beckons the faithful and signals power and influence – whether spiritual or otherwise – something only further reinforced by the frequently stunning decoration of their inside surfaces; the Renaissance and Baroque periods in Western architecture are renowned for this. It is also recognized that this was a period of many remarkable scientific discoveries, including the invention of optical instruments such as telescopes, camera obscura and magic lanterns (projectors). In the extract below, George Hersey describes the direct influence of such discoveries on dome design, and in so doing reminds us how architecture and structure can incorporate metaphysical and physical qualities alike.

Domes as Optical Instruments

from *Architecture and Geometry in the Age of the Baroque*
George Hersey

Our primary knowledge of light comes from our eyes.[1] And the eye is quite a piece of architecture. It is a hollow sphere or spheroid with a lens at one pole and a concave interior surface, the retina, at the other. The retina repeats images transmitted to it by the lens. Like a very flexible optical instrument, the eye absorbs, refracts, and otherwise manipulates the light that forms these images (Fig. 2).

In form and function the eye is a dome or sphere (light itself, of course, and especially projected light, radiates spherically). The eye-dome is framed by its retina (yellow in the picture), then successively by the choroid (pink: a vascular membrane containing large branched pigmented cells), then by the sclera (gray: a dense white fibrous outer coat).

At the dome's summit is the crystalline lens, an ellipsoidal solid, whose iris (pink) functions as a diaphragm, much as in a microscope. The lens is outwardly protected by its cornea (light gray). The cornea (transparent coat on the eyeball covering iris and pupil) arches out over a void called the anterior chamber. We need not concern ourselves with the eye's other parts – the muscles that move it, the nerves along which its images travel, its vessels of communication, and its wrappings of tissue and biochemical coatings. I will say, however, that many of these other properties and functions have equivalents in optical instruments.

Optical instruments, in short, were often thought of as enlarged or extended eyes. Sometimes the enlargement could be to colossal – that is, to architectural – scale, as with the 70-foot telescopes made by Newton's contemporaries.[2] In his treatise on optics (1637), Descartes illustrates a huge human eye oriented upward, along with a man staring up into it (Fig. 1). One purpose of the illustration is to show that exterior images (*V, X, Y*), when projected on the retina (*T, S, R*) are flipped. Thus the little triangle *V*, on the left outside the eye, turns into the little triangle *R*, inside the eye on the right. The diagram also shows that the lens, *L*, greatly refracts or condenses the outside image, reducing it to a tiny restatement of the exterior scene. Thus once again, by the way, we run into a phenomenon suggesting a self-similar graduated series. Note also, for future reference, that the visual rays are all of them cones – sources of the conic sections that will be so important in our study. But perhaps what is most important of all, at least for us, is that by changing its scale, Descartes makes his human eye into a dome or skylight. In Descartes's diagram, indeed, the eye is architectural in scale as well as design.[3]

Large or small, the eye has always been a key element in symbolic iconography. Often its meanings have clustered around the notion of the divine all-seeing eye. In the 1780s Claude-Nicolas Ledoux was making real and allegorical designs for a proposed theater of Besançon (Fig. 3). The theater is reflected in an eye looking out into an empty auditorium. What the eye sees, and what becomes its tiny inner projected image, is a circular theater all'antica, including a colonnaded seating area formed into a truncated cone, diminishing toward the stage.

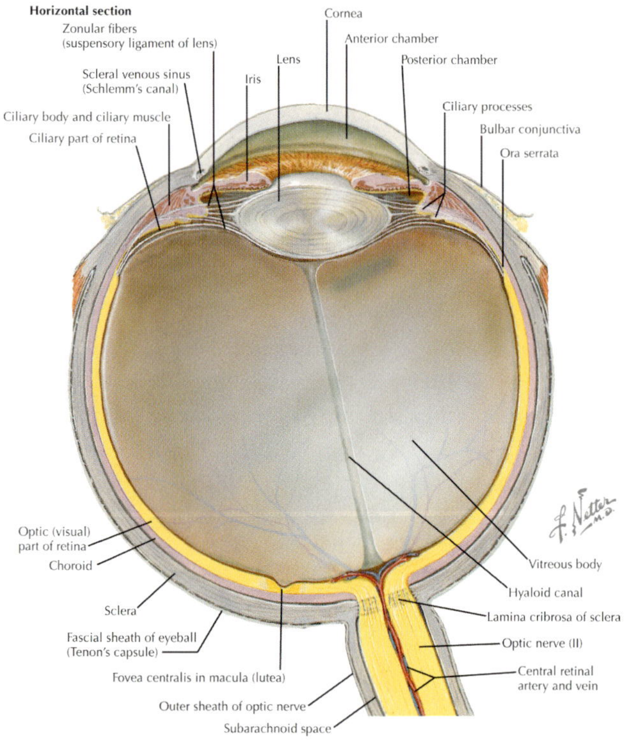

Fig. 2 Sagittal cross-section of a human eye

Then, from an unseen source above, a conical beam of light shines down on the colonnade, streaming out from the pupil onto the lower eyelid and on outward onto the actor's face. Ledoux thus also illustrates the old classical notion that the eye projects beams of light outward like a lantern.[4] (It is still common to speak of eyes this way.) And the beam projected by the eye in Ledoux's design, moreover, is at the same time a stage light, a spotlight. It illuminates part of the colonnade and shines down on a section of the seating. (The theatrical spotlight, with its lens, reflector, and narrow concentrated beam, became possible with the introduction of Argand lamps at the end of the eighteenth century.[5]) Ledoux's notion of a theater as a gigantic eye, as an optical projection instrument, is full of meaning for what I am saying. In Greek, *theatron* means "thing seen." One also thinks of Roman amphitheaters, which are often compared to great eyes, embedded in the earth, staring up at the sky.

It is worth looking at the structure of Ledoux's design. Just as sound and acoustics were thought of in terms of cones and conic sections, so were light and light-projected images. Ledoux's eye is a confluence of interpenetrating cones – the cone that comes from the eye itself, the cone of the spotlight shining on the auditorium, and the wider, truncated cone of the auditorium proper. We will be looking at the other iconic interpenetration later on, for example, in Wren's dome for St. Paul's – and indeed we will find these figures all through Baroque architecture.

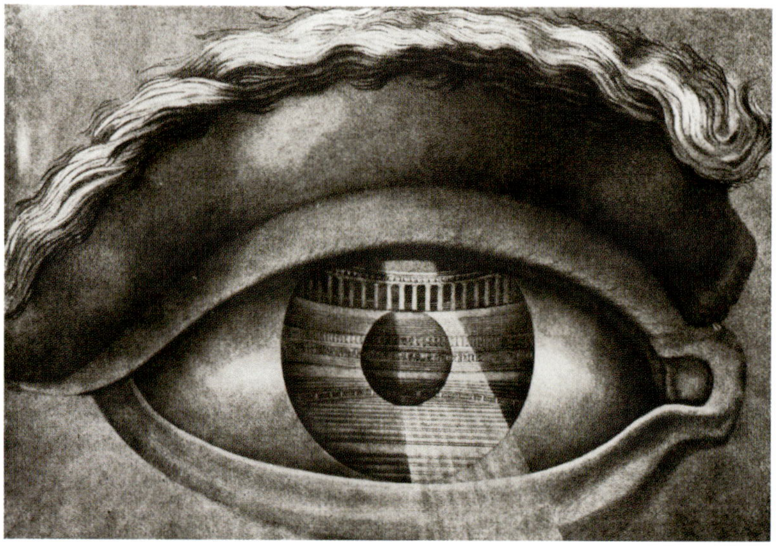

Fig. 3 Claude-Nicolas Ledoux, image of a theater for Besançon

Lenses and Reflectors

The eye is the model for three significant Baroque light-projectors: the telescope, the microscope, and – last but not least – the magic lantern. Optical or artificial lens are rigid versions of the eye's anatomical lens. The commonest type of artificial lenses is the plano-convex, flat on one side and spherical on the other. Other lenses are convex or concave sections of two similar or dissimilar spherical segments. The fact that astronomers studied what were thought to be the crystalline heavenly spheres, and studied them through lenses that were themselves segments of crystalline or at least glass spheres, was by no means lost on Baroque astronomers. (Nor was the fact that the globe-shape human eye included a crystalline lens and is filled with what was known as a vitreous or crystalline humor.) Still other lenses were ground and polished into hyperboloids, paraboloids, and ellipsoids (i.e., hyperbolas, parabolas, and ellipses that were rotated into solids).

In mechanical light-projection, lenses are often used together with reflectors. The latter – usually polished metal mirrors – also make use of spheroidal shapes as well as of paraboloids and the like. If the mirrors Archimedes used at Syracuse to burn the Roman fleet were parabolic – that is, shaped like huge cups – their effect would have been greatly enhanced.[6] He would also have approximated the effect of a reflector in a magic lantern, which maintains its focus as its perimeters revolve to make a complete 180-degree curve. This enormously concentrates the light it reflects (Figs. 4 and 7). As we shall see, the focus points used in drawing an ellipse or parabola, along with their three-dimensional forms, also constitute the focus point for light rays bounced into it.[7] ... Kircher used these ideas in discussing acoustics.

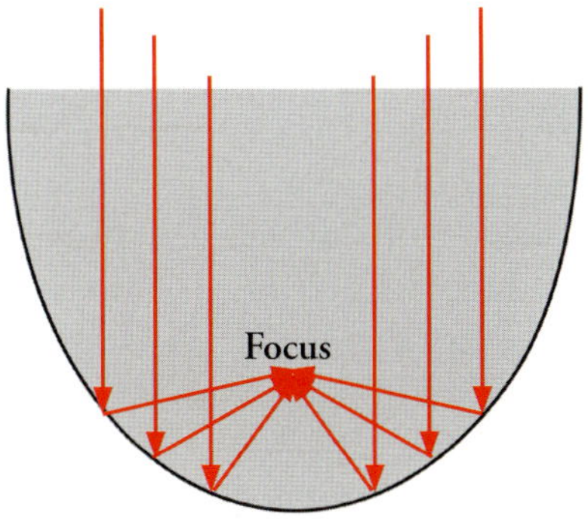

Fig. 4 Reflected light rays in a parabolic mirror

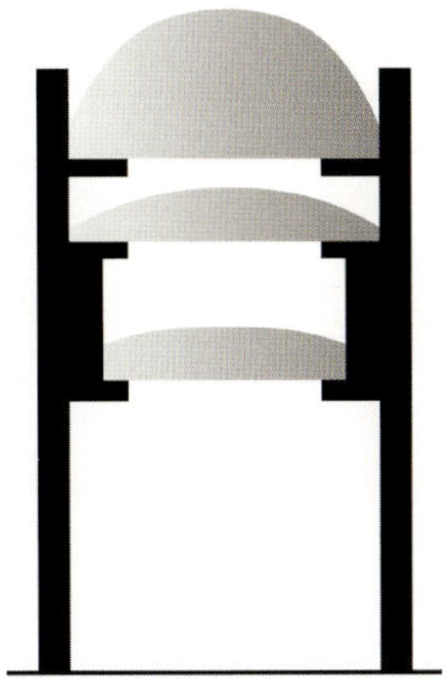

Fig. 5 Three plano-convex lenses set concentrically into a tube or stand

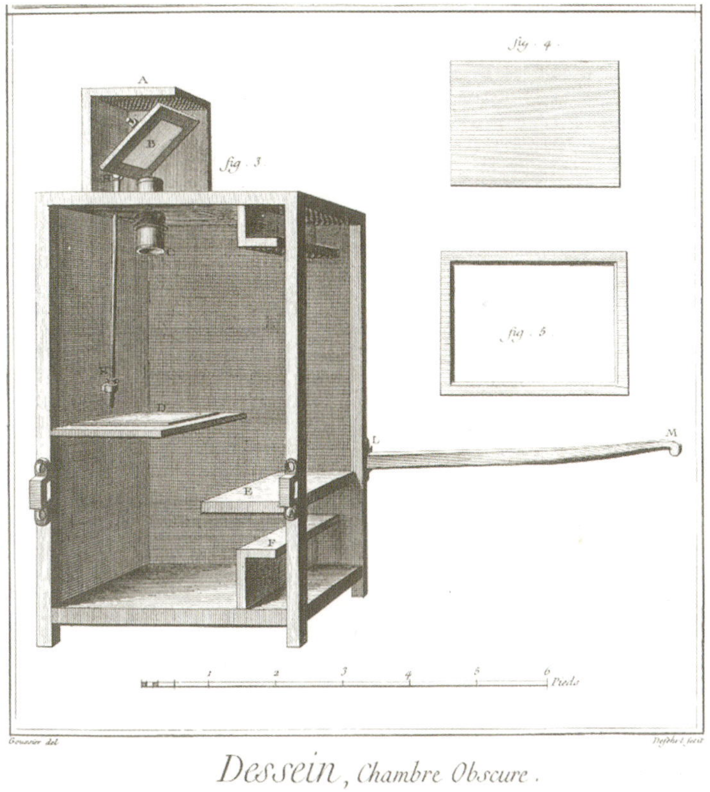

Fig. 6 Portable camera obscura illustrated in Diderot's *Encyclopédie*, 1751-72

Microscopes, Telescopes, and Magical Lanterns

The ancients, Seneca for one, knew that glass globes filled with water increased the apparent size of anything seen through them.[8] They also knew that similar devices could refract and condense rays of light. And, of course, it is this ability to bunch light rays into trajectories that leads on to the optical instrument proper.

But the true glass lens, like the eye's lens, not only condenses light but transmits images that are made out of light. It was apparently not until the thirteenth century that the image-transmitting lens came along, firstly in the form of eyeglasses. And not until Giovanni Battista della Porta, the sixteenth-century Neapolitan magician and philosopher, do we get descriptions of how lenses were shaped, ground, and polished – though he describes the technique itself as German.[9]

Then, early in the age of the Baroque, almost at one fell swoop, three optical instruments were invented: the telescope, the microscope, and the magic lantern. All three were virtuoso light-manipulators. They gathered it, filtered it, reflected it, condensed it, refracted it. And, more important, all three instruments projected images. With the microscope and the telescope, light gained new significance as the revealer of previously unsuspected worlds – with the microscope, worlds of unforeseen tininess; with the telescope, worlds unprecedentedly huge. Galileo reports in *The Starry Messenger* (1610) that through a telescope he had made for himself, "objects… appeared nearly one thousand times larger and over thirty times closer." [10]

The magic lantern, in turn, could import enlarged images from the microscope and telescope and then further reproduce, enlarge, shrink, and distort them. It could present them to audiences: put them in a theater (perhaps not unlike Ledoux's) so that many people – large crowds – could see the same image simultaneously.

The telescope seems to have been invented in Holland when in 1608 a certain Hans Lippershey applied for a patent.[11] More mystery surrounds the exact origin of microscopes, and they did not become prominent in scientific work for another half-century after they began to be built.[12] Thereafter, however, Anthoni van Leewenhoek and Robert Hooke made many important discoveries with microscopes.[13]

When lenses refract, bend, and concentrate light, the individual beams are gathered into cones and stellated or radiating bodies, like sunbursts. The individual beams are called "pencils," a term borrowed, appropriately, from projective geometry.

Lenses are mainly used in axial concentric groups, as in Figure 5. They are mounted at set distances from one another, depending on their focal length (the distance from them at which the image is sharp). Lenses may enlarge and enhance detail, but all sorts of aberrations usually come into play that need to be counteracted mostly with more lenses. The aberrations, which affect both the colors and the forms of images seen, can also be controlled with one or more diaphragms or adjustable apertures that act like the iris of the human eye. The diaphragms filter out stray pencils that diminish the image's brightness or otherwise distort it. It is the principle used in changing the f-stops on a camera.

Figure 6 shows a portable eighteenth-century wooden camera obscura (with lens as opposed to a pinhole) with its foreground and

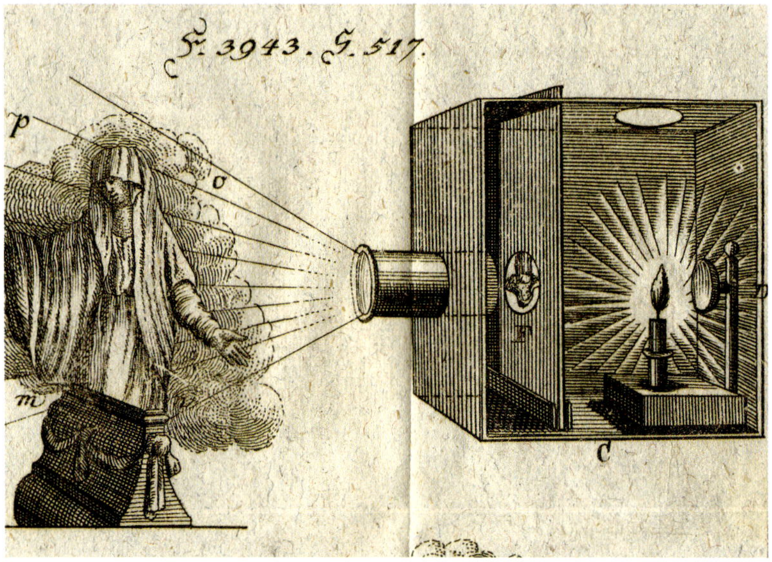

Fig. 7 A magic lantern. From J. G. Kruenitz, 1773

rear walls removed. The lens is in the hutch on top and is mounted vertically, which condenses and projects the image from the exterior view reflected in the mirror.[14] The artist sits on the bench and draws on a screen mounted on the desk, the last surface onto which the image is projected. As Philippe Comar points out, it only remained for early experimenters such as Nièpce and Daguerre to replace the screen with an emulsion-coated plate, and photography was born.[15]

A magic lantern does all these things in reverse and inside out. Inside the box is a light-source such as a candle or, later, an Argand lamp. Behind it is a reflector. This forces as much light as possible into a single narrow cone. A slide with a translucent image on it is located at the focusing center of the system, at the point where the image is flipped, and a set of condensing and objective lenses then projects the slide's image onto a screen some distance from the projector. Because the lenses are adjustable, the projection can be either smaller or larger than the original. Thus the projected image travels along the cone of light from the magic lantern, continuously being enlarged. Once again, in short, a self-similar progressive series.

We do not nowadays think of magic lanterns, those stalwarts of art-history lecturers, as scientific instruments. Figure 7 depicts a late-eighteenth-century specimen taken from J.G. Kruenitz's *Oikonomisch-Technologisch Enzyclopädie* of 1773. Indeed, in these early days magic lanterns tended to live up to their name. In the illustration, the slide (shown as a disk with an upside-down image inside the lantern at *F*), represents a heavily draped figure that is probably intended to be a ghost. Instead of a screen the image is projected onto a plume of smoke. As Gian Piero Brunetta makes clear in his book on the history of this instrument, the earliest proprietors of the devices were wandering entertainers. Even in the age of the Baroque, those who worked seriously with magic lanterns complained about their use by charlatans and entertainers.[16] On the other hand, Kircher, in his treatise on optics, seems to relish precisely these "magical" aspects of the magic lantern.[17]

Anyway, magic lanterns were used in science. And for us what was (and is) really important about them is what is also important about the microscope and the telescope: All three devices use projective geometry to transmit images. And these transmitted images may be understood as self-similar progressive series – series that get bigger and bigger or smaller and smaller. And, further, by refracting, condensing, and reprojecting light, all three instruments can warp, wrench, and bend their images. Most of the improvements later made in the instruments sought to control or eliminate such distortions. But at the same time the possibilities of distortion itself, as an artistic goal, came to the fore.

The magic lantern could have the same problems with spherical and chromatic distortion (turning straight lines into curves, or surrounding images with rainbow haloes) that telescopes and microscopes had. Yet the magic lantern, the slide projector, also came to be greatly improved.[18]

Optical Domes and Lanterns

Optics is more than a matter of lenses and diaphragms. It is the whole science of light – its creation, its transmission, its modification, and its use. So optics has always played a major role in architecture – which might be defined as the art of building adequately lit shelters. Windows, skylights, and the lanterns atop domes are optical devices. And, in architecture, light is not only propagated, directed, bounced, and diffused; it is used, almost as on the theater stage, to create emphases and special effects. In all these ways a building may be not only an acoustical but an optical instrument.

As noted (Fig. 5), cross-sections of microscopes, telescopes, and magic lanterns show us sequences of lenses enclosed in cylinders or boxes. We look, that is, at a set of spherical segments that are light-conducting, light-enhancing, light-gathering, and usually arrayed along a single axis. We see much the same thing in Baroque architecture. The crossing bays, pendentives, drums, and sequences of domes in churches, for example, are arrayed like lenses and reflectors. Throughout this period, axial sequences of concentric sphere-segments (and, occasionally, conic sections) emerge more and more into ecclesiastical and other architecture, just as they were doing, in these same years, in microscopes, telescopes, and magic lanterns.[19]

St. Peter's

As a point of departure, let us look at what is probably the most famous of all domes; Michelangelo's at St. Peter's (Fig. 8), 1546-64. Michelangelo created an inner hemispherical shell made of plaster – and marble-lined bricks. Just outside this inner shell is the familiar

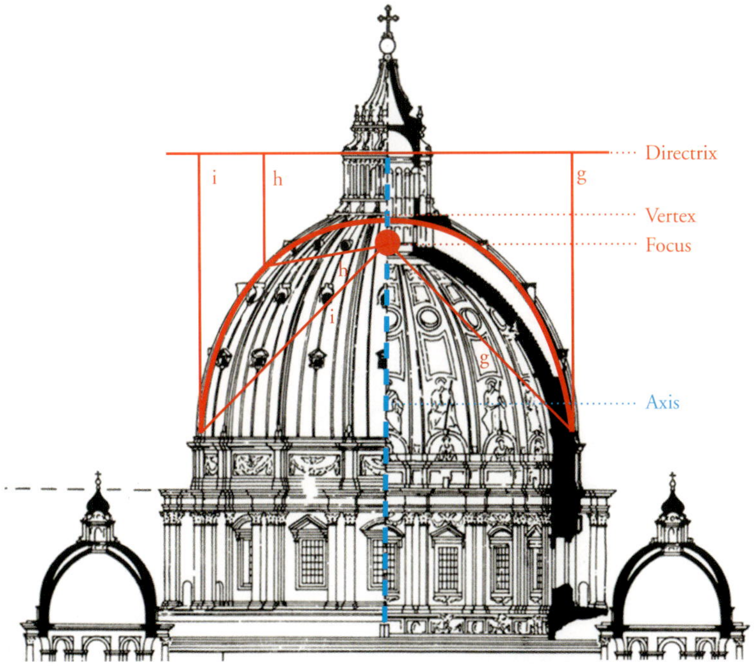

Fig. 8 Michelangelo and others, cross-section of St. Peter's dome, 1564

outer shell, concentric with the inner one and merged to it at the shells' two bases. The outer shell is also brick, but marble-clad and provided with a perimeter of oculi and a clustered radiating set of pronounced, molded vertical ribs. Let us call them pencils.

Though he had contemplated making the outer shell a paraboloid, Michelangelo decided in the end that it was to be a hemisphere like the inner one. But then, after Michelangelo's death, his assistant Giacomo della Porta returned to the earlier profile, raising the dome's outer shell into the gentle paraboloid we see today.[20]

In Figure 8 I have superimposed, in red, the diagram of a parabola, which determines the profile of the outer dome. The parabola's axis is shown in a blue dotted line. The focus, the directrix, and the vertex are labeled. The point where the axis cuts the parabola is the vertex. The chords *i*, *h*, and *g* within the parabola must all equal in length the corresponding lines or tangents *i*, *h*, and *g* running from the outside of the parabola up to the directrix. When the parabola is rotated through 360 degrees, the result is a solid known as a paraboloid.

A long series of paraboloid domes came into existence after the completion of Michelangelo's. They reappear on the churches of Italy, France, and Britain, on the U.S. Capitol and its many architectural progeny among the state capitals; and, back in Europe, in Moscow's St. Isaac's Cathedral and Turin's Mole Antonelliana. In these domes the paraboloidal shape is usually more pronounced than at St. Peter's. ...

Here I want to speak of [domes] as optical systems. Most are topped with lanterns or cupolas. The lantern is built on top of the dome's "eye," the opening at the center of the polar circle where the ribs join together around an oculus (note that word) or open ring. In geometry, this ring would be a torus. The lantern's weight helps keep the dome's ribs and curved plane forced into convex tensions. (As far as I'm concerned "lantern" is a better word than cupola – "small tub" – for these features.) Dome-lanterns function like the iris of the eye or like an optical diaphragm. They let in a set amount of light and then shunt it, diffuse it, or otherwise transmit it throughout the dome interior – much as with the eye's lens, iris, and retina. Sometimes even the minidome that tops off a lantern can act as a reflector, much like the domical reflector in a magic lantern.

These are some of the ways in which an architectural lantern, functioning together with its dome, is an optical instrument. And, furthermore, it comprises shapes reminiscent of, or identical to, those used in lens systems; sections of spheres and paraboloids. Images (usually of Heaven), more often than not, appear on the dome's inner surface. These would be the scenes that the optical system looks at.

The interior of the dome of St. Peter's, for example (Fig. 16), is just such a "telescoped" vision of Heaven and its chief inhabitants. Around the base are pendentive mosaics of the four Evangelists; above the drum, with its row of windows and paired pilasters, are further mosaics, all designed by the Cavaliere d'Arpino and executed in 1605 under Clement VIII. The lower tier of personages, in segmentally arched frames, presents busts of papal saints and Doctors of the Church. Then, higher, in free unframed space, comes a ring of large seated figures of the Redeemer, the Virgin, St. Paul, St. John the Baptist, and the Apostles. Higher still, a ring of angels carrying the instruments of the Passion; then come tondi filled with multiwinged cherubs and seraphs, then more angels with more attributes, and finally a tier of seraphs. At the center of everything, but also above everything, is the interior of the lantern. This is boldly set off with a ring of consoles and golden stars. Here, in this upper epidome, looking down upon us as though through an optical glass, is God the Father, blessing all who assemble below. One is reminded of Nicholas of Cusa, who, in his *De visione Dei* (1453), describes how God's eye, in a picture, sheds or projects its cone of "inaccessible Light" onto the viewer.[21]

And if God thus looks down at us through his lantern-spyglass, we look up at him through the vast eyeball of the dome and its upper lenses. Where, usually, we see him appropriately surrounded by his court, the chief citizens of Heaven, all basking in God's heavenly light. The contrast might have been intentional on the part of the designers. In St. Peter's this inner gilded globe is filled with an all-pervading luminousness very different from the light in the rest of the basilica. Note, too, that in many photographs of St. Peter's the drum windows act as spotlight, projecting pencils of brilliance onto parts of the molded annular entablature. These pencils would of course brighten, move, and dim throughout the day in accordance with the Sun's motion.

The divine optical system in St. Peter's is reinforced with inscriptions. Around the entablature's frieze are Christ's words to St.

Fig. 9 Hardouin-Mansart's engraving of the lantern of the Invalides, 1687

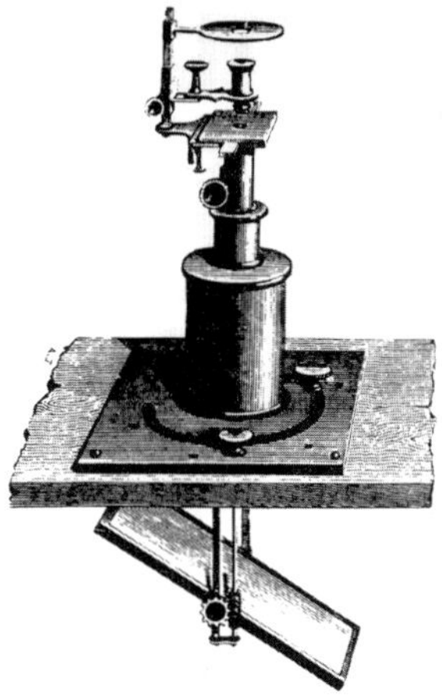

Fig. 10 (top) A solar microscope (c. 1750)
Fig. 11 (bottom) Plan of lantern stage for the Invalides

Peter: "*Tu es Petrus et super hanc petram aedificabo ecclesiam meam; et tibi dabo claves regni caelorum*" (adapted from the Vulgate, Matthew 16:18, "You are Peter [which means 'cornerstone' as well as 'rock'] and on this cornerstone [rock] I will build my church; and to you I will give the keys of the kingdom of Heaven"). And it is Peter, whose body was thought to lie directly below this dome in its original Roman tomb, who opens the gates – the apertures – to the cosmic kingdom.[22] It is a kingdom matched, above, by the kingdom of Earth that is below. In the cross-section of the dome and its supports we see this lower crypt area, beneath the floor of the high altar, acting as a final "lens" or "objective" in the whole of the optical/visionary system. These ideas were taken over in several important subsequent dome-and-lantern systems, and in at least one other dome-lantern-tomb system.

The Invalides

But for all its qualities as an instrument for viewing Heaven, Michelangelo's dome is not the sort of optically complex configuration we find in later, more Baroque structures. I have in mind, particularly, the Invalides, St. Paul's, and the Paris Panthéon. In section, Michelangelo's dome has only a partial double shell. And two such shells, being nested, do not in this respect suggest a lens system. If we move forward in time from St. Peter's, however, we do see domes arranged concentrically in non-nested vertical configurations. In other words, we find domical structures that actually do resemble cross-sections of microscopes or telescopes.

Let's jump to 1687 and to Jules Hardouin-Mansart's great dome complex at the church of the Invalides, Paris (Fig. 9 and 11).[23] Here, supported by a ring of consoles, the lantern complex, formed into a tempietto, rises from the tall molded rim of the great dome's eye. The plan of the complex maps the way the lantern's light floods down through a forest of wooden framing, and through successive lower diaphragms or irises, to fill the global volumes of the dome proper.

Note here the similarity between Mansart's lantern and a solar microscope – that is, one that uses a mirror to reflect sunlight through the slide (Fig. 10). It is true that this particular instrument dates from sixty years or more after Hardouin-Mansart's dome. But opticians had been making just such complexes of ribbed and molded cylindrical containers for decades, with the outer cylinders filled with linear series of lenses that were almost always segments of spheres or paraboloids.

By 1687 there was no longer anything new about all this. So let us look at something more interesting. In the Invalides, the entire system of domes expands, in section (Fig. 12), into a latticed paraboloid to form the church's main outer dome. Down through that lattice, moreover, there descends a central cylinder of open space. This

Fig. 12 Hardouin-Mansart's engraving of the dome system of the Invalides

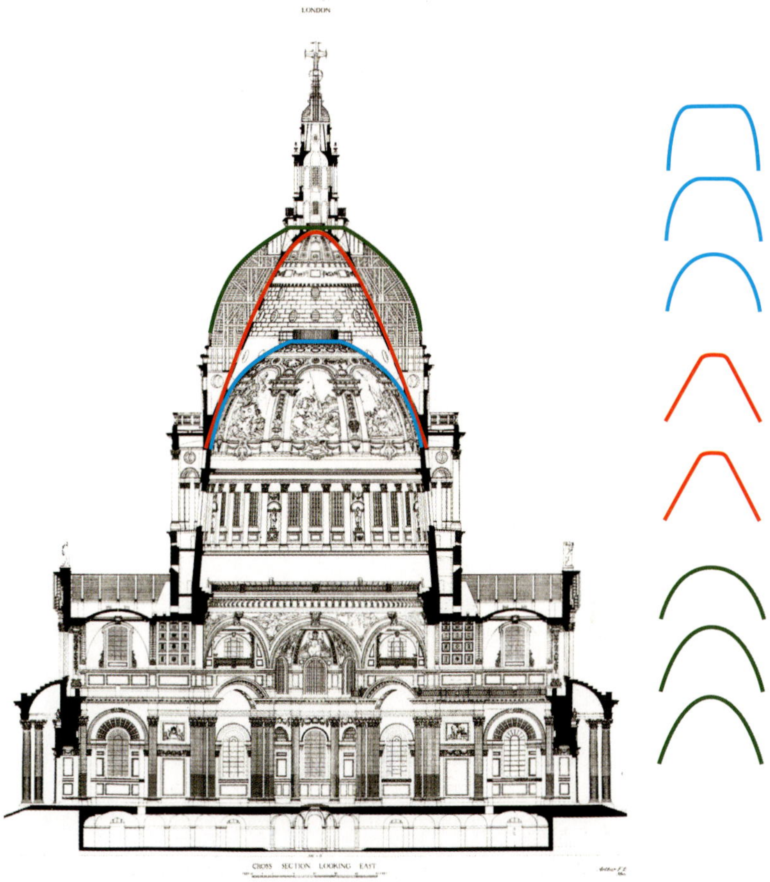

Fig. 13 Cross-section of the dome of St. Paul's Cathedral, 1710

cylinder ends up against the plane of a sphere-segment – a segment that like many plano-convex lenses is less than a full hemisphere.

Then – and this is the novelty – that dome-segment is fronted by another such segment, of even flatter profile. This consists of an enormous oculus, three times the diameter of the upper one. In other words, we view the church's painted Heaven, quite literally, through an iris or pierced lens. Using bounced and diffused sunlight or skylight, rather than artificial light, we see, through this aperture, a scene set in Heaven – Charles de Lafosse's dome painting, *St-Louis Giving Up His Sword to Jesus Christ*. The whole setup is strongly comparable to that of the magic lantern or camera obscura.

The dome system at the Invalides received a final "optical" element when Napoleon I's body was returned to France. For it in 1841 Ludovico Visconti designed a new crypt. This is a vertical cylinder open to the floor above and directly on axis with the center of the dome above it. The crypt became the outer "objective" lens for the system. The tomb of the hero became the final image that God, gazing down through the lantern, sees – much as, at St. Peter's, he looks down on the apostle's tomb. Of course it is equally easy to imagine Napoleon's earthly remains looking up to God from below. These systems, as with other optical systems like microscopes and telescopes, can work in both directions.

St. Paul's

As noted, paraboloid domes appeared all throughout Europe and on just about every continent visited by Catholic missionaries. And there are Protestant paraboloids – or, rather, paraboloid variants. Across the Channel is St. Paul's, the masterpiece of Sir Christopher Wren (1675-1710; Fig. 13).[24] There, however, one finds not a true paroboloid but a set of three domes. The outer dome is a flattened hemisphere – half an oblate spheroid, one might say, perhaps as a bow to Wren's colleague Newton. Then, within, are catenoids. These form the two inner domes supporting the outer. A catenary is the type of plane curve formed by a chain hanging from two points. A catenoid is a catenary curve revolved through 360 degree. Cubical catenoids and paraboloids have flattened apices. When Wren was designing the dome of St. Paul's, catenaries had just recently been distinguished from parabolas (they have different formulas), notably by Jacobus Bernoulli in 1691.[25] Wren's dome in its definitive from was begun some time after 1702.[26] In the illustration (Fig. 13) I show the outer dome as a cubical catenoid (in green), the middle dome as a paraboloid (in red), and the inner dome as a cubical catenoid (in blue). Next to the cross-section of the cathedral are other catenaries (blue), a cubical parabola and a truncated cone (both red), and more catenaries (green), the latter three not being cubical. All these shapes were generated mathematically, for which I

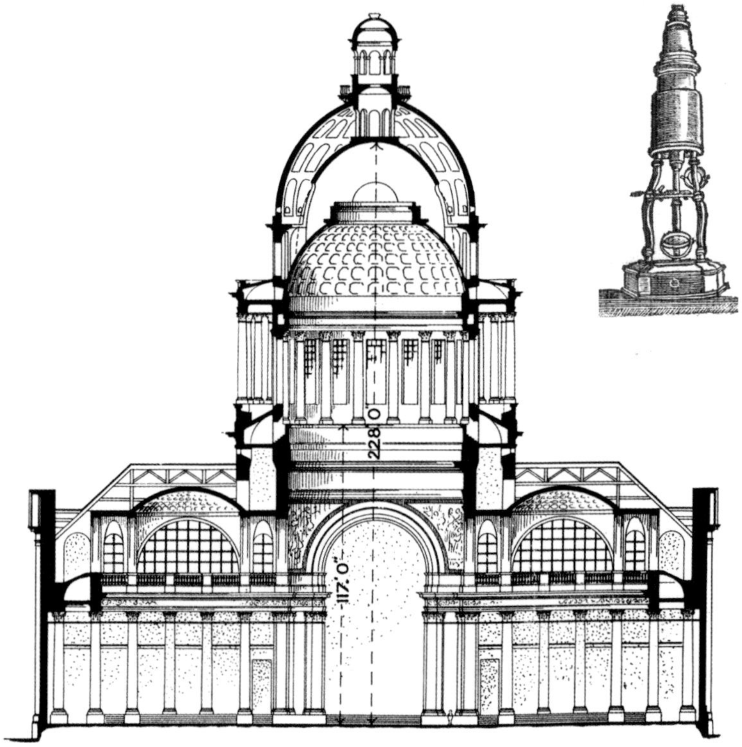

Fig. 14 (bottom) Partial cross-section of the Panthéon, 1790
Fig. 15 (top) Detail from John Cuff's trade card (c. 1750?)

thank Michael Frame. They provide a wider picture of the geometrical possibilities Wren was working with. The formula for a catenary, by the way, is

$$x = (a/2)(e^{x/a} + e^{-x/a}).$$

Both of Wren's inner catenoids are exactly 100 feet wide across their narrow axis and 120 feet long.[27] The inner catenoid cants the interior wall of the drum inward. This establishes the bottom section of the second catenoid, which has about a 10-degree slope. The effect is to build a theatrical forced perspective structure into the drum interior – making it seem higher than it is. In other words, Wren is achieving greater majesty through optical distortion. These same anamorphic projections are followed in the painted scene on the inner dome, which represents an arcaded rotunda through whose arches heroic scenes are glimpsed.[28]

Down through the center of Wren's system is the by-now-expected cylinder of oculi or diaphragms. These form the main course of the system's vertical illumination. The vertical cylinder is supplemented by the horizontal illumination coming in from the windows of the drum. Here the analogy would be not with the lenses but with an optical projector's canted reflectors. Wren had in fact designed a double reflector-telescope that exploited just this principle.[29] So far as I know, St. Paul's has the only catenoid domes erected in this period.

The Paris Panthéon

By 1715 Wren's dome was in place. In the years afterward the optical, and specifically telescopic/microscopic, character of these structures in domed churches only increased. Look at Jacques Soufflot's dome of the Paris Panthéon, completed in 1790 (Fig. 14).[30] Here, lantern, dome(s), and even the church's aisle vaults make for a setup that is extraordinarily "optical," complete with auxiliary "lenses" and "reflectors." Moreover, the section of each of Soufflot's lens-domes – those of the lantern and those served by it, including outer shell, middle shell, and inner shell – all have different paraboloidal or spherical sections.

For comparison I illustrate a microscope (Fig. 15) taken from the trade card of the British optician John Cuff (who also supplied the solar microscope we looked at earlier). Seen as a model dome system, Cuff's microscope, starting at the top and descending, consists of eyepiece (lantern), dome, oculus moldings, and drum. There, as in Soufflot's church, the structure separates into a set of legs around an opening. In the church we get the four crossing pier, in the microscope the three cabriole legs. Meantime, replacing the human observer who would stand at the church's crossing, the microscope has an adjustable mirror that bounces light upward through the slide and into the eyepiece. Here again is an equivalent in function (not position) to the sidelighting furnished by drum windows. The "lantern slide," meanwhile, is a painting by Baron Gros, The *Apotheosis of Ste-Geneviève*. One gazes up to Heaven, with all this optico-architectural assistance, to watch the saint being welcomed there.

Many other such domes were build in the Baroque era. Thus, in 1653-57, Borromini designed a paraboloid dome for Sant'Agnese in Agone. Some other Roman churches with such domes are Domenico Fontana's Cappella Sistina and Santa Maria Maggiore (begun in 1585) – like the St. Peter's dome a Renaissance predecessor of the Baroque paraboloids; Carlo Maderno's dome for Sant'Andrea della Valle (1622-25); Rosato Rosati's for San Carlo ai Catinari (1612-20); and the dome of Sant'Ignazio (begun in 1626) by Orazio Grassi, Carlo Maderno, and others. These paraboloids then led to others, including, as noted, the dome of the U.S. Capitol.

It is completely appropriate, optically, cosmically, and terrestrially, that Baroque domes should have these properties. The whole complex of ideas and forms, of lenses and lenslike devices, of reflectors and mirrors, and of seen and unseen worlds goes back to the concept of the sphere. We are returned to spherical segments, to spheres' behavior, and to the various luminous substances of which the planets, the planetary spheres, and perhaps even the planetary beings were supposedly made.

Fig. 16 St. Peter's dome. Photo: Scala / Art Resource, NY

Formwork for construction of hypar shell, Palmira Chapel

For over half a century Félix Candela's thin reinforced concrete shells have been celebrated for their structural and spatial daring by practitioners and academics alike. Established by a precise geometry, their seemingly "free" anticlastic double curvatures could amazingly be created using straight timber boards – which of course made these all the more legendary, with the traces of the formwork serving as a constant reminder of the seemingly impossible feat.

But these shells also embody deeper, cultural meanings when they are considered in the context of Candela's geopolitical thinking as a Spanish expatriate expelled from his home country after the civil war there. As conveyed here by María González Pendás, Candela's documented vision for free and open political spaces is consistent with and conceptually reinforced by the forms of his concrete shells. The revolutionary quality of his explorations of shell structures is thus not limited to technical proficiency but takes on more profound meaning; these forms were not only the product of structural virtuosity, but can also be seen as the projection of political objectives. As Pendás points out, however, a contradiction emerges to the social virtuousness that this line of thinking suggests: the structural and social emancipation that the forms so boldly announce was countered somewhat by the fact that their construction was dependent on cheap manual labor available in Mexico at that time. As is often the case, even the most celebrated of innovations (structural or otherwise) is not ever completely free of "controversy" if one looks hard enough. Does this cultural/economic blemish diminish the work, any more than the utopian political aspirations elevate it? Hardly. Such contradictions only serve to make these projects all the more "human".

The Politics of Candela's Shells

from *Félix Candela's Geopolitical Imaginary*
María González Pendás

On March 1, 1960, the architect Eduardo Robles wrote to his colleague and fellow-exile Félix Candela (1910-1997) to congratulate him on the publication of his work in the Spanish journal *Arquitectura*. "I was as moved as you might have been," writes Robles, by the affection and the treatment you get from those who considered you so annoying only a few years ago, when they could not publish a thing of yours." [1] After years of conflicted relations with, and censorship of, Félix Candela, *Arquitectura*, the official publication of the Chamber of Architects of Madrid, dedicated its October 1959 issue to him.[2] This included a brief essay by Candela, an extensive thirty-two-page review of his work, and a series of laudatory commentaries by several Spanish architects and critics.[3] What was of significance for Robles, though, was less what these commentators pointed out than what they failed to mention: "they intentionally leave out something that has always characterized you: your liberal 'political' strength, in which they never believed." For Robles, this aspect was not only of paramount importance to understanding Candela's work, but was also related "to what you have done with the theories on shell construction."[4]

Robles's comment points toward two intriguing aspects of Félix Candela: that his work cannot be fully comprehended without relating it to his political discourse, and that this relationship seems most significant in the context of looking at his work—which was conceived and built in Latin America—from the viewpoint of Spain. And yet, other than a quick biographical mention of his having fought against Francisco Franco and for the Spanish Republic during the Spanish Civil War (1936-1939) and his subsequent exile from Spain during the Franquista regime (1939-1975), Candela's politics and the way these relate to his architecture are, to this day, pretty much absent from interpretations of his work. The image of Candela as a pragmatic, know-how builder and structural virtuoso has predominated since Colin Faber's influential monograph *Candela, the Shell Builder* (1963).[5] A collaborator of Candela's, Faber gave detailed technical descriptions of his concrete shells with calculations of their statics, descriptions of structural details, and plenty of construction photographs—with no hint of concerns for a larger intellectual or political discourse. A previous but lesser-known book on Candela by Félix Buschiazzo put more emphasis on Candela's role as a writer, but still failed to assess a deeper intellectual or political drive.[6] Candela certainly supported this construal of his persona as a silent builder. Shortly before his death in 1997, he admitted to not having had many intellectual preoccupations throughout his career beyond technological and building issues, and not having suffered from that "complex of the savior of humanity so common among architects, that old trope that they are going to change society and the world through architecture." [7] Architectural scholarship has largely taken this statement at face value, emphasizing a strictly formalist and technical analysis of the work, and hardly questioning Candela's politics and his status as an intellectual.[8]

However, Candela's own writings of the 1950s and 1960s radically contradict his latter disdain for the utopian bent so dear to architects. Taking on the challenge suggested by Robles in his letter, in this chapter I reveal a part of Félix Candela's political imaginary as he articulated it from exile in Mexico, and suggest a relationship between his politics and his poetics of this period. Although Candela never very directly regarded architecture as a social catalyst, not only was he concerned with devising a discourse as a public intellectual, but he also envisioned a geopolitical model that was intrinsically related to his conception of technics—and of architecture—and he eventually engaged with activist publications and institutions of the Spanish political exile. Further, it was precisely the ambiguous location that Candela himself occupied, as he looked at Spanish politics from Latin America and thought of Spain and Latin America in relation to each other, that formed the basis of his understanding of the role and the specifics of technological development in the building industry, and by extension to both his political and his architectural projects in this period. Tellingly, the one political statement that Candela explicitly endorsed through drawing was the logo for the journal of the Agrupación Europíesta de México (AEM), *Intercontinentes*, in the mid-1960s. This depicts a world globe with two sweeping arrows: one that links South America to Spain, and another linking Europe to Central and North America. As a sub-group of the intellectual elite formed of Spanish Republican exiles in Latin America, the aim of the AEM was—as imagined in the map—to launch the recuperation of Spanish democracy in joint collaboration between Spain's former colonies and the European left. Ultimately, the attempt was to offer this transcontinental assembly as a response to the bipolar ideological and economic order prevailing during the Cold War. As we shall see, it was in this in-between territory where Candela not only imagined his built structures, but also where he posited an alternative model of economic and social progress.

Discourses of Idealism: From Pan-American Utopia to Spanish Democracy

> *I never grow tired of proclaiming myself a Spaniard. But I don't mind being a Spaniard from Mexico. I am convinced that the future of Spain, its next renaissance, resides in these Hispanic countries of America. I don't know how I got to believe that they constitute the foundation of the next great superpower, one the world so badly needs; a world desperate under the stupid domain of the two most obtuse and materialist countries.*[9]

Candela's intellectual persona was arguably born a decade after his flight from Franco's Spain to Mexico, when he simultaneously started to open up new venues for building and for writing.[10] In 1950, he built his first vaults and hypars (hyperbolic paraboloids) with his newly formed construction company Cubiertas Ala—the Experimental School in Ciudad Victoria and the acclaimed Rayos Cósmicos Pavilion in Mexico City—and published his first article—"Cubierta prismática de hormigón armado en la Ciudad de México" ("Reinforced Concrete Prismatic Shells in Mexico City") precisely in the journal that would later become *Arquitectura*, soon to be followed by his first public lecture in Mexico on the same topic.[11] These events led to very prolific years in the construction and structural development of his concrete shells, and in the presentation and publication of his lectures. These lines of work being fundamentally technical in scope, by the mid-1950s Candela started to broaden his discourse into politics more explicitly. Starting through exchanges of correspondence with colleagues in Spain and in exile, Candela began speculating about imperial power, the political and cultural future of Spain, and the relationship between Spain and Latin America. Moreover, he realized how his newly acquired status of famed architect who writes and is able to put forth his ideas in the public realm, called for rethinking his professional role by turning his discourse from technical specialism toward political commitment.[12]

The possibility to publically leap into politics came in late 1959, coinciding with the completion of some of his most famous structures—like the Church of San José Obrero in Monterrey and the lyrical free-edge hypar for the Palmira Chapel in Lomas de Cuernavaca—when the Mexican exile group of the Federación Universitaria Estudiantil (FUE) gave a dinner in his honor. The FUE, of which Candela had been a member during his student years in Madrid, was a secular student organization that supported the Republican educational reforms against the Falangist Sindicato Español Universitario (SEU) in the early 1930s; after the Civil War it had been declared illegal and many of its members were purged. In the speech that he worked on for the occasion, Candela decided to finally present what he termed his "Thesis on Pan-Americanism." [13] Attacking many of the event's conveners, in the talk Candela refused the nostalgia that pervaded exile discourses at large, calling instead for new solutions to the political situation in Spain. New models were needed, he argued, which he was already exploring both as form-maker and as an intellectual. As he put it: "To write, to design, in a word to create has no other alternative, no other way. Why not do the same in politics? One must not look backward with nostalgia, but look forward." [14] Candela thus spoke of the "hombre nueve" (new man) and presented a blueprint for a new geopolitical model that—just like the concrete structures that were bringing him international renown—sprang from speculation and idealism. ...

Shells of Idealism, or on Candela's Politics and Poetics

How did Candela's pervasive political thinking and his status as an intellectual imbue, and in turn become influenced by, his architectural work? In his letter of March 1960, as elsewhere, Robles was never very explicit as to the connections between Candela's work and politics.

Candela himself was quite cryptic on this difficult point. In the 1959 FUE talk, he specifically related political thinking and structural design, but only in terms of a common attitude of innovation and idealism. Just as he had reacted against traditional theories of structural design for the development of his signature shell construction system, he set himself "to do the same" in politics, and to develop a political project that sprang from a similar "critical spirit" and was a fight against the status quo of rationalist and nationalist ideologies.[15]

Besides a question of attitude, the connection between the poetics and the politics in Candela coalesced around two main points. One was his conception of technics, or what he termed technology, but went beyond mere utilitarian or material aspects and into a broader conception of social and cultural methods and dynamics. For Candela, no formal or stylistic a priori directed his architecture. Instead, technology led directly to the definition of the built object, with aesthetics and function alongside it. Following Mumford, for Candela technics also originated a social contract: "[Technics] implies a process of civilization, or just as much, a process of renunciation of freedom and individual rights when these are in conflict with social objectives." [16] Technics, in the form of concrete shell construction and geometric structural thinking, was for Candela not only a basis for his building system, but also a defining force in negotiating "political space," and eventually in providing a new model of progress. Moreover, the building industry—at least as he practiced it in Mexico in the 1950s—provided the ideal realm for that "intermediate technology" in which the new Hispanic superpower would base its progress. Architecture and construction in this context offered an 'underdeveloped' position of resistance to the "technology innovation and industrialization" rampant elsewhere.[17] They thus offered the disciplinary model for an economic development that favored material efficiency over consumption, intuition over reason, and humanism over materialism. His shell structures deployed all these qualities, he argued: efficiency in the sense of using the least amount of material possible or the thinnest concrete section, for the definition of the most space; intuition in the sense that the construction required more hands-on trials than mathematical calculation; and humanism in terms of a building industry close to craftsmanship, with a limitation on the mechanization that embodied the destructive and alienating power of mass technification. Just as his structures were governed by the "natural laws of balance and economy," he was hoping for sociopolitical balance through a technological and material economy of efficiency.

The contradictions inherent in Candela's vision become all the more evident here. The efficiency that he called for operated in the initial stages of design and calculations, and in the finished product. But the construction process entailed an extreme deployment of material—wood for the framework—and of labor. Economic efficiency was only a plausible argument while the cost of wood remained low, and because his shell construction method required large amounts of unskilled labor at a moment when minimum wages and unions were still not operative in Mexico. Thus Candela's idealization of humanist technology was close to man only to the extent that the particular man responsible for it—the worker—was not quite able to articulate his rights. On this point, Candela's discourse loops back to his rejection of *patria*, that is, to his statement that one could live without a fatherland and that a new sociopolitical order could be conceived without national boundaries. But it is a loop back that renders this element of his thought as inconsistent, and closer—if unwittingly—to the most reactionary claims of *casta* and politics of Hispanism. Candela's technical model was in the end overlaid with the politics of race and class, as non-unionized construction workers were largely of indigenous, pre-colonial ethnic origins. For all the intent to do away with nation-based identity, the class/race hierarchies operative in Mexico at the time—as in the majority of the technically "backward" countries he summoned—remained intact in Candela's vision.

A second point should be made on a more metaphorical level, and relates to his idea of territory. The structural rationale for Candela's concrete shells—mainly hyperbolic paraboloids, or hypars—was based on the static equilibrium acquired by geometrical form over the specifics of the material. That is, their stability came from the geometry: saddle-shaped, ruled surfaces with double curvature, ideally boundless, and generated by the succession of straight lines. These were static when thought of as abstract and extensive geometries, from which Candela would isolate a fragment. This was easily constructed by using wooden planks for the formwork of poured-in concrete. The result was 'limitless forms, forms in continuous expansion," as Fernado Chueca put it, in striking contrast to the Euclidean, limited, and finished forms more proper to orthogonal structures.[18]

Somewhat analogously, his political model was based on an "amplified patriotism." [19] Candela imported—arguably with little reflection—a spatial logic based on extensive thinking and universalism into his political model. As a result, Candela's spatial and formal referents are somewhat generic. Although these constructions were indeed only possible as products of the Mexican tradition of building with concrete, and of the construction costs and labor conditions of the time at a symbolic level Candela's shells specifically rejected localism. They were of Mexico, but not necessarily willing to represent it aesthetically or historically. This becomes clearer when compared with attempts by some of his contemporaries to define a locally grounded modernity. For instance, Juan O'Gorman was at the time calling for modern architecture to become "realist, national, and regional" through explicit links with "formal references and material usage," as well as with technique connected to pre-colonial times, in the same way claimed by Candela. In this way, "the people" would identify it "as their own ... and become a human manifestation of a distinct culture." [20] These linguistic and aesthetic aspirations for a local character and style were far from Candela's concerns. If one likened the stone mosaic murals of O'Gorman's Central Library for the Ciudad Universitaria to Candela's analysis of vaults, the disconnection of the latter with any particular culture, context, and site further comes to the fore. This was the point he was making in his FUE 1959 talk with his rejection of *patria* and folklorism, and with his new Hispanic federation, as flawed as this was. Ultimately, Candela attempted to avoid any symbolic representation of national or regional ideologies, in order to define an Esperanto-like architecture, a non-local, unifying, and universally valid space; just as he argued for his new Pan-American identity.

In addition, one of the most problematic aspects of Candela's shells was their weakness in connection to the ground, the discontinuity between the logic of the shell and the way it was supported. Candela himself admitted that the supports were key, but supplementary to his structures: "the success of most of my work stems primarily in the detailing of the legs or supports, and in how discreet and concealed they are ... something that has not much to do with the shell itself."[21] Added to the fact that the buildings were often located outside of the urban center, or at least did not require a relationship to other buildings, Candela's shells often seem disconnected from the site, like alien objects that have just landed on location. Could one see these placeless shells as the formal counterparts to Candela's political rejection of any link to a homeland?

Candela's eventual and much-resisted physical return to Franco's Spain—he finally visited the country in late 1969, some six years before Franco's death—and the symbolic acceptance of the fatherland this implied, marked in fact the end of his political commitment. This was also the twilight of his experimental constructions: in 1968, Candela had built his last structure, the Olympic Pavilion in Mexico City; in 1969, he withdrew from his construction company Cubiertas Ala; in 1971, Candela moved to the United States, shifted his career toward pedagogy and never again built large-span structures.[22] By then, Candela seems to have lost both his political and his poetic idealism. In fact, Candela lost his acute awareness of the bridge between technology and politics, since he agreed to return to speak at a congress for the International Shell Association due to the association's apparent lack of connection to the Spanish government.[23] In the end, and as Diaz-Marta predicted, Candela was received and celebrated by government officials. Along with the shifting economics of the 1970s, which meant a rise in the cost of wood and in workers' wages, which played a significant role in diminishing Candela's practice, the fact is that the endgame of his political discourse and of his experimental period in building came in tandem, and coincided with his eventual embrace of *patria* in Spain.

The *Intercontinentes* logo map that Candela supported at the height of his political and structural speculations was not only at the basis of his thinking. In a sense, he also embodied it. Whether he is to be considered a Latin American architect, a Spanish engineer, a Mexican building contractor, or none, or all, of the above is still a point of scholarly discussion. It has already been suggested that Candela's career must be analyzed in relation to the sense of *desarraigo* (uprootedness), provoked by the experience of exile.[24] Rather than fueling the debate on Candela's identity, or his longing for it, his lack of a secure location appears as the point of departure for reconstructing his full-fledged political imaginary. Candela's ambiguity regarding his identity was a constituent aspect of his architecture *and* of his political thinking, which this chapter reveals only in part. A close look at Candela's private and public writings of the time discloses an outspoken figure who extended the base of his architectural work into a political project. His rejection of fatherland was in essence a claim of statelessness that came from his location between Latin America and Spain; as consequence of his long-lasting refugee status in Mexico, and of his problematic relationship with and conflicted return to Spain and its architectural culture. As ambiguous as this point was in his thought, Candela folded it into his political project as much as into his architectural thinking. More than other prominent members of the Spanish architectural exile in Latin America, Candela consciously and intensively pursued politics, reacted to the current bipolar world order of the Cold War, and extended his thinking into larger social concerns. The relationship between form and politics in Candela, as elsewhere, is certainly complex and anything but binding. And yet, one could not have existed without the other. In many ways, Candela aimed for no less than Hannes Meyer's call in 1926 to "undermine the local concept of the 'homeland.' The fatherland goes into a decline. We learn Esperanto. We become cosmopolitan." [25] Both his built work and his writings in the 1950s and 1960s—in a word his discourse—read as a critique of the nation-state and of rationalism, as an unapologetic and quintessentially modern rejection of roots, if with humanist undertones, and as a need to envision a new model of identity and an alternative model of socio-economic progress. These ideas were intrinsically related to his particular take on technology and to his attitude toward structural design and form-building. This led to the conception of a new architecture—new in the sense that it was innovative in technological and aesthetic terms—that resisted anything symbolic and that strove for a certain spatial universality, and that his sociopolitical vision at one point likewise imagined.

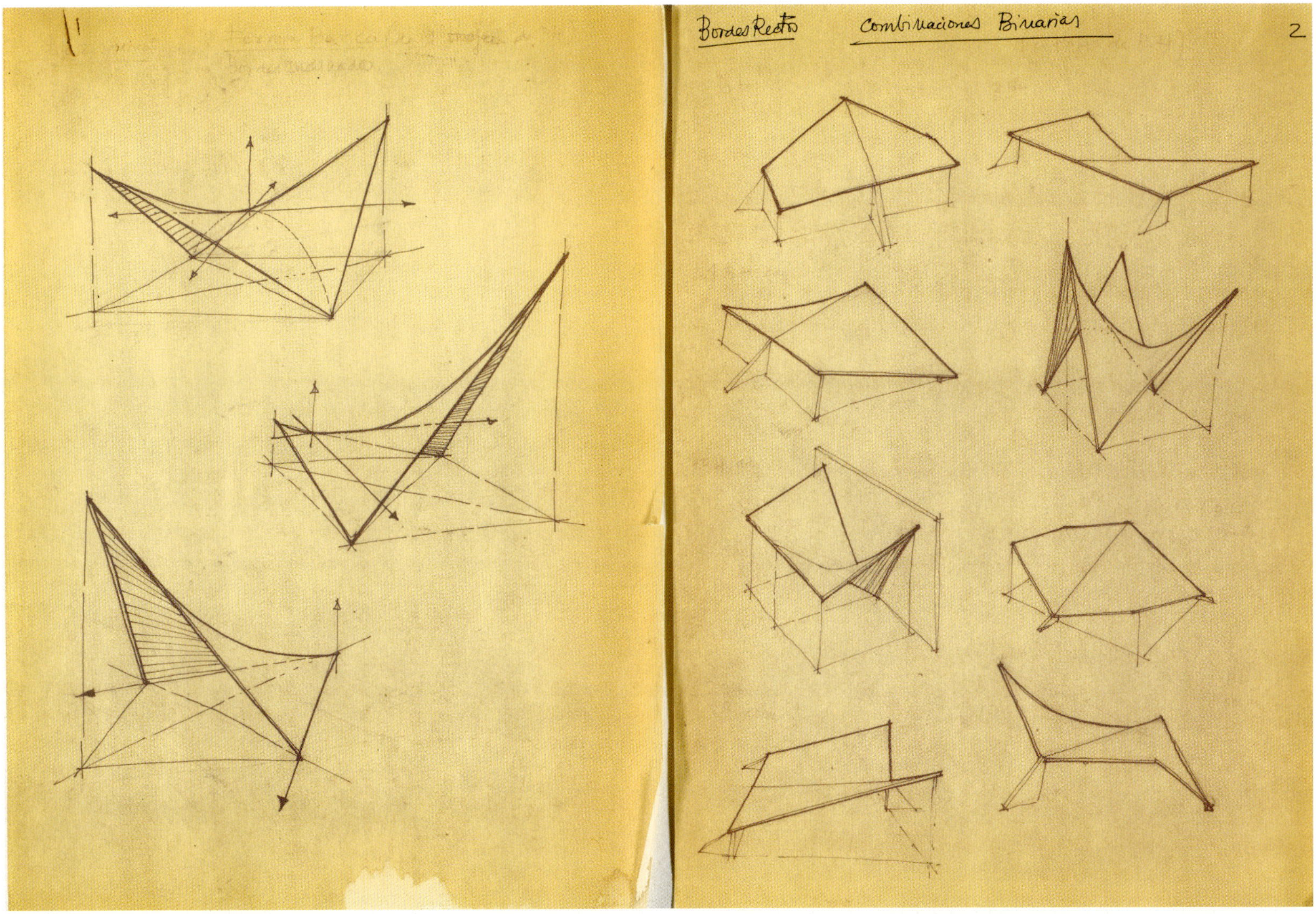

Félix Candela sketches of hyperbolic paraboloid shells

Serpentine Pavilion, 2009. Photo: Iwan Baan

Today the ceiling is all too often neglected in the design of buildings and their interior spaces. Certainly this was not the case with the underside of Baroque domes, seen earlier, whose designs explicitly established relationships between their ceilings and the skies above them. Just as clearly are such connections created by the plates and shells of the contemporary practice SANAA, even as their minimalist aesthetic approach could not be more different from that of their distant predecessors.

Authors Michael Holt and Marissa Looby explore this topic through a study of a trio of SANAA-designed ceilings. This begins with the mirrored underside of the ultra-thin roof plate of their Serpentine Pavilion, whose effect is to deliberately confuse the relationship between "inside" and out, between building and surrounding park, and between ground and sky. The essay moves on to discussing the openings and sense of space from under the undulating lower shell of the Rolex Learning Center. The thickness of this concrete shell (necessitated by heavy occupancy loads and flexural demands, as this is not a funicular form!) causes one to feel "underneath" a heavy surface; the sky is experienced as distant and removed. The Teshima Art Museum concludes the study, and here we return to the close interplay between ceiling and sky that was such an integral part of historical dome design. At Teshima the shell is relatively thin (although irregularly shaped, it needs only to support itself) and the openings to the sky dominate the space; here, in fact, the geometry is such that there are no walls and the ceiling created by the shell disappears because of the openings' strongly contrasting light. It is with some irony, then, that we conclude with a building that is all about sky; here architecture and structure are at once all *and* nothing…

SANAA's Ceilings and Skies

from *SANAA: Falling Upwards*
Michael Holt and Marissa Looby

In its treatment of the ceiling plane, the least developed element in modern architecture, SANAA establishes a zone of surrealist vertigo. ...

On first glance the eye rushes to analyze, it strives to comprehend objects, composition and meaning. In the foray into visual ordering and synaptic response the eye is led astray. Look again; objects disappear, expand, melt, figures are juxtaposed as objects; recognizable elements are left indescribable, rendered multiple and disoriented. The eye is left to contemplate a rich fabric of improbabilities and sequential alternations. At the point of recognition, the composition is thrust into a state of destabilized visual flux. Visual cues bring forth memories and associations, and yet it is precisely when these associations are made that the eye is met with a multitude of matches. Objectification liquefies. The image does not attempt at deceit, instead it provides a pure and unadulterated love of shocking the viewer through apparition and ambiguity. The image becomes exempt from aesthetic or moral concern—it becomes a pure creation of the mind.

In many of the works of the Belgian artist René Magritte, the ideas of disorientation, ambiguity and illogic are intertwined, complicating a question of representation. The image of reality is at once brought to the fore and coincidentally skewed back on itself. For Magritte, painting was nothing more than a visual riposte, not in representing the world per se, but instead it is an involuntary act of resemblance—a visual automatism.

Magritte constantly undermined perceived reality through compositional and conceptual dualities and puns, whether it is an asymmetrical collage of clouds in indoor space; material objects somewhat out of scale with their context; or, the simultaneity of objects being identifiable as items only to be simultaneously identifiable as something entirely different. He collated seemingly routine objects which covertly undermine a reality the viewer would normally take for granted. Magritte tinkered. He sabotaged the order of things—never altering the necessary shape of things—in order to falsify the consensus system. His work's most recognizable characteristic is to bring the sky from above into the room. Magritte made use of the sky, a familiar concept of what exists above us all, to disorient and disarm the viewer.

These prefatory observations converge to lobby here that SANAA, the collaborative practice of Kazuyo Sejima and Ryue Nishizawa, promote a similar sense of reverse vertigo—in the concept of falling upwards—through their use of an architectural element that exists above us all—the ceiling. An element that, almost by default, is perceptibly overlooked, aesthetically undervalued and although considered structurally essential it is a visual non-entity.

As one of a select few primary elements in the composition of a building, the ceiling has a primordial, basic function: to provide shelter. The ceiling can enclose a dwelling, more as a means to an end, so to protect the inhabitant from any inclement weather. Or, in Ecclesiastical typologies it can become dominant, awe-inspiring and fearsome, and yet the idea of shelter still remains. A ceiling maintains a position well out of reach, a component not to be meddled with, nor requiring tactility. It is simply a device in the creation of enclosure and by almost subservient consequence defines the volumetric space of a building. In much of contemporary architecture, the ceiling is such a device, it is stripped of ostentation and is instead left as a state of passive, altruistic reverie. No longer the emissary of the divine or rugged, it is jaded, an element fading into the background.

At one point, however, the ceiling was the devilish cad, the trickster of Modernism. The painted white ceiling as an honorable subterfuge allowing for the definition of the double-height space was a definable characteristic for the Modernist era—a case in point would be Le Corbusier's Villa La Roche-Jeanneret (1923), where the treatment of the ceiling as a reflective surface opened up spatial qualities that promote the notion of looking beyond. The ceiling becomes a truly passive non-entity—even when it is there, it is not there at all. The obverse of this is when a ceiling is deployed *proactively*. An element that is thrust into the visual *foreground* of the built object, it pronounces the spatial, structural or decorative order. More presciently, it focuses the attention upwards. A comparative example to that of Le Corbusier's is Louis Kahn's Yale University Art Gallery (1953), with its hollow concrete tetrahedral space-frame, which functioned perfectly as both the flooring of one level as it did the waffle-slab ceiling construction on another. It is not a question of whether Le Corbusier's ceiling visually functions as background or Kahn's ceiling as foreground, but whether a ceiling can function as both. Where it alternates from the foreground, to the background and back again, fueling the idea that it functions as the fluctuating protagonist, both seen and unseen simultaneously.

Enter SANAA

Three prominent projects have sparked such a question: the Serpentine Pavilion (SANAA, 2009); the Rolex Learning Center (SANAA, 2010); and, the Teshima Art Museum (Ryue Nishizawa, in collaboration with the artist, Rei Naito, 2010). The Serpentine Pavilion follows a simple post-and-plane arrangement. Slender stainless steel columns hold up a simple thin aluminum and ply-composite roof. The complexity comes

Rolex Learning Center. Photo: Marissa Looby

from the bending and curving both in plan and elevation. In plan the temporary structure reads as an organic flower or even a water drop, to proliferate the metaphor used by SANAA. In elevation, the roof continues this sense of the organic as it rises from flat plane ceiling, subtly undulating, and finally rising to its high point in one area so to open up views of London's Hyde Park. It is precisely this undulation that becomes characteristic. With the slope falling so low at one point that it becomes almost table height—viewed only from outside or by a small child from below—the ceiling allows for programmatic and spatial definition. It segregates. It is at once the provision of shelter and the divider of user and divider of space.

The surface of the roof begins to draw comparison with the work of Magritte. Its highly reflective aluminum creates a mirror on both the upside and underside plane, it is simultaneously recognizable as a ceiling plane and sheltering component in the structure but also comes as a visual continuation of the surrounding parkland. The sky and ground collide within this cosmetic application, in its reflection both sides of sky and ground are trapped, leaving the viewer a little bewildered as to where the structure begins or ends. The pavilion is a sheltered extension of the park; in paraphrasing the architects, it works as a field of activity with no walls. ...

In the Rolex Learning Center (Lausanne 2009), SANAA created a large single-story rectangular building that measures approximately 525ft x 245ft x 11ft (160m x 75m x 3.4m). Entry to the building, however, does not reinforce the rectilinear plan arrangement. Instead, the user is confronted with an undulating, shifting waveform with considerably large, abstract circular cut-outs which interrupt the uniformity of plan when viewed aerially. In what could easily be identified as a typical low-slung Mat building in plan is instead a rolling mass of expansive stressed structural arches, incisively punctured to produce program, external courtyards allowing light to flood into the deep floor plate. Internally, as a result of programmatic experimentation, SANAA seem to develop the open-plan concept used most notably in the works of Mies van der Rohe in a large-scale building. It is interesting to consider the SANAA installation at the Barcelona Pavilion (2008).

In the pavilion, originally designed in 1929, the ideas of distortion and transparency are palpable; Mies placed the eye-line of the viewer at exactly the mid-point of the floor and ceiling. In doing so he provided the user with an acute sense of enclosure, heightened by the use of the highly reflective Travertine non-load bearing wall that seems to disappear from sight. SANAA installed a semitransparent, imperfect circular-shaped acrylic curtain encasing the Travertine wall. What they tried to intensify was this idea of transparency by augmenting the openness of the space through slightly distorting the views. In doing so they reaffirmed the notion of ceiling and ground planes acting as the vice in which the user stands between. In a similar sense, the highly programmed Rolex Learning Center functions without any interior walls. By allowing the parallel ceiling and ground planes to undulate from a two-dimensional surface into three-dimensional topography they distort perspective. The floor-to-ceiling height (11ft) helps to control the definition of interior space and directs movement flow and circulation, creating diminishing views and hidden niches. Below the interior, notably at the building's point of entry, the user is forced to walk underneath the floor plate that rises from the ground to above head height, a feature that is somewhat disarming for the user. The concealed entry leaves the user with a sense of being swept under the carpet, establishing a visual hierarchy where the ceiling becomes the dominant feature. A heightened sense of *above*. The ceiling operates as a strange double agent. It shifts from a building component that is overbearing and intensely structural when walking underneath the floor plate; and, yet is by proxy a topographical ground plane that billows with no care for what lies beneath—the ceiling as a double entity.

Cue: Nishizawa

When embarking upon the design for Teshima Art Museum, Ryue Nishizawa made explicit reference to the previous projects although this time his collaborator was the artist Rei Naito (commissioned by Naoshima Fukutake Art Museum Foundation). The single volume gallery space is a cavernous dome that is entirely free of vertical support, the ceiling acting instead as both lateral, load-bearing support and shelter. The only apertures come from the two oval-shaped cavities that permit views skywards, creating a thoroughly unique art space. As a consequence, these ceiling vacuums allow the elements to penetrate the space, whether they be aural, visual or climatic. The ceiling is animated by the environment by the fact it is not entirely there; the sky becomes the foreground and enters the gallery space as the ceiling diminishes into the ground. In plan and section, the design for Teshima resembles a droplet of water. The globulous form is oppressive yet open, it stirs emotions of being outside and underneath at the same time. An overbearing Surrealist sense of being inside a droplet looking outward or viewing scalar objects from above. A removal of perspective and dimension. This project could well be likened to James Turrell's career-defining project Roden Crater, in the Arizona Desert, however, there is a reference that predates this. When viewing photographic imagery for Teshima there is an unmistakable, uncanny resemblance in the building's aesthetic appearance and disassociation of elements to the Surrealist works of René Magritte.

Cue: The Ceiling

In all three projects, the ceiling plays the leading part in the definition and organization of space. In an interview on SANAA's projects whilst the Rolex Learning Center was nearing completion, Nishizawa described an evolution of their projects by shifting dimensional organization, by stating that "[we are] now working on the Learning

Center project...here we have more three-dimensional changes, located outside of the two-dimensional wall."

At the Serpentine, the ceiling mirrors the ground aesthetically allowing it to fold into it at the sides. In the underbelly of the Rolex Learning Center the space is the residual effect of internal floor divisions through the topographical deviations, whilst the opposite is at play in the gallery space at Teshima, where the underneath becomes the inside. The Learning Center, however, acts as something of a conceptual bridge between the two projects that bookend it here. By allowing for the curvature to define the programmatic spaces, the building allows for what is in effect a double floor plate. The ceiling of exterior, 'underneath' spaces are crucial to the ground plane curvature of the internal, 'upside' spaces. There lies a duality of spatial definition, the floor and ceiling act separately, move organically and yet operate simultaneously. To label the Learning Center or Teshima 'natural', 'organic' or 'blob architecture', falling under the whims of contemporary architectural discourse, would be wholly inaccurate; they are referential to this type of terminology only by the fact that they are entirely *unnatural*. A continuous artificial entity. They are removed from their context yet entirely at ease with it. Furthermore, it is argued that SANAA have evolved Mies' Modernist concept of transparency and visual disappearance through the three-dimensional use of the open plan.

In addition to spatial trickery, there is a heightened notion of perceived structural *instability* provided by the relationship between light and heavy ceiling elements in each of the projects. The remarkably large spans of the Learning Center cultivate a sense of perilousness for the user standing underneath, an idea replicated in the Teshima Art Museum through the cantilevered structure that emanates from the ground plane. To achieve such large spans in the Learning Center, a laser cut formwork system was fabricated to cast the concrete. At Teshima, concrete was poured over a built-up mound of soil. Once the concrete had set, the earthen mound was excavated leaving a domed hole behind. The construction equivalent of displacement. Both methods of construction allow for a sheen or smoothness—almost a *softness*. The finishing is exquisite, deflecting notions of the sheer weight carried by these spanning structural arches as they suggest impossible weightlessness. The Serpentine is a prime example. Its flimsy ceiling becomes a projection of the sky in the foreground and the background, constantly changing, shifting and expanding. Moreover, the thinness of the ceiling structure at Teshima is so veiled it becomes removed from its heavy formwork, its concrete materiality. It is almost the definition of 'paper architecture' in the normative sense of the term. The fragility of the structure exemplifies the notion and importance of the interplay between the building and the vanishing point where it touches the ground.

Curtain Call

The ambiguity of the vanishing point facilitates a flux between what is perceived as foreground and that which is in fact background. Much in the same way Magritte subverts the order of things, SANAA have tampered with the sky. At the Serpentine the sky is a contextual collage as foreground, material objects are flipped and out of scale from their context; at the Rolex Learning Center the familiarity of the ceiling plane becomes a duality, functioning at once as sheltering element, planar component, and spatial divider in a large multi-programmed, open-plan building. SANAA are tinkering with more than just visual trickery, they are successfully experimenting through the programmatic play; and, at Teshima, Nishizawa falsifies the system of sky and building by amalgamating visual effects with the sky acting as foreground through the ceiling cavities, heightened by the diminishing planes. The sky, by puncturing the domed ceiling plane, is brought into the building, it becomes the alternating piece in the conceptual fluctuation between foreground and background. The idea of Magritte using the sky to disorient the viewer through using a recognizable pictorial image is akin to how SANAA make full use of the ceiling insofar as it promotes the concept of falling upwards—a notion of being at odds with perception and visual depth. Moreover, SANAA have evolved Mies' open-plan in the Rolex Learning Center, presenting a new role for the ceiling: a duality of functions, both the anterior and posterior element, simultaneously. In effect, the ceiling is functioning as Magritte's covert falsification of the order of things.

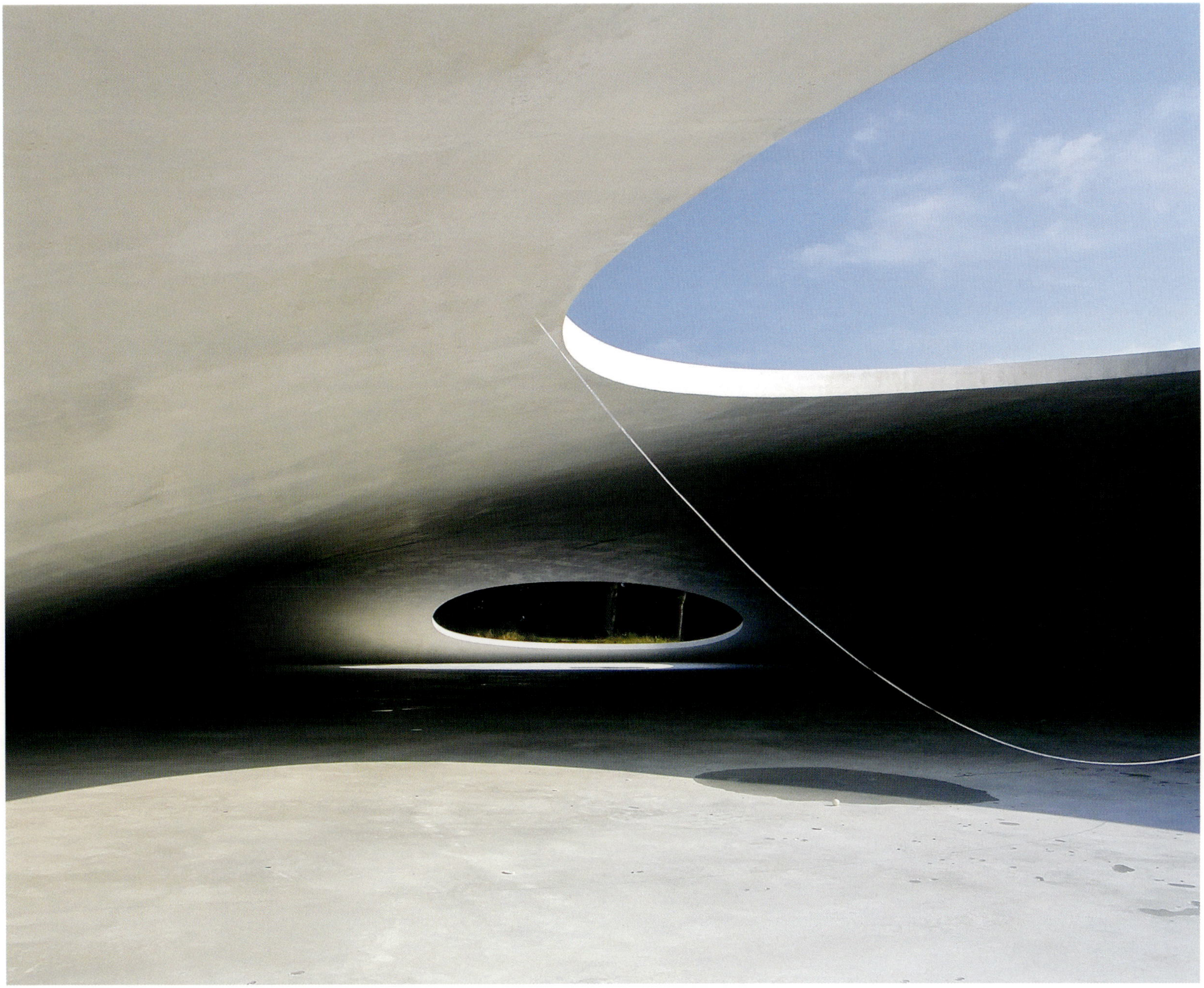

Teshima Art Museum. Photo: Ken Lee

Ribbed Dome

Stork Nest Farm; Dvur Semtín, Czech Republic (2010)
Architect: SGL Projekt s.r.o.
Structural Engineer: Nemec Polák s.r.o.
Model: Mary Bray Erickson + Janaya Hart

SGL Projekt

As a part of the redevelopment of an abandoned 19th century historic Czech farmstead and distillery into a contemporary hotel and conference center with attendant leisure facilities, this pony-riding arena also serves for other athletic and cultural events. Distinctively covered with haphazardly arranged oak log members, the exterior form of the building was inspired by the stork nest that has long sat atop the former distillery's chimney. The 34m (112ft) diameter and 12.5m (41ft) high domed interior space enclosed with translucent polycarbonate sheeting is at once visually dramatic but also programmatically ideal for riding ponies as there are no column obstructions.

The primary structure of the dome is provided by a series of glue-laminated timber ribs, each of which carries load by means of a combination of axial compressive force and bending behavior. The significant cross-sectional dimensions of the ribs attest to the need to prevent buckling caused by large compression forces; their varying depth reflects the changing magnitude of bending moments along their length, with clearly articulated zero-moment hinge connections at both top and bottom ends. The central 8m (26ft) oculus resolves the inward thrust of all the ribs into a ring of compression. Placed on top of the timber ribs, three-dimensional steel trusses define a different external profile for the building and provide support for the timber logs that give the building its distinctive stork-nest-like visual aspect.

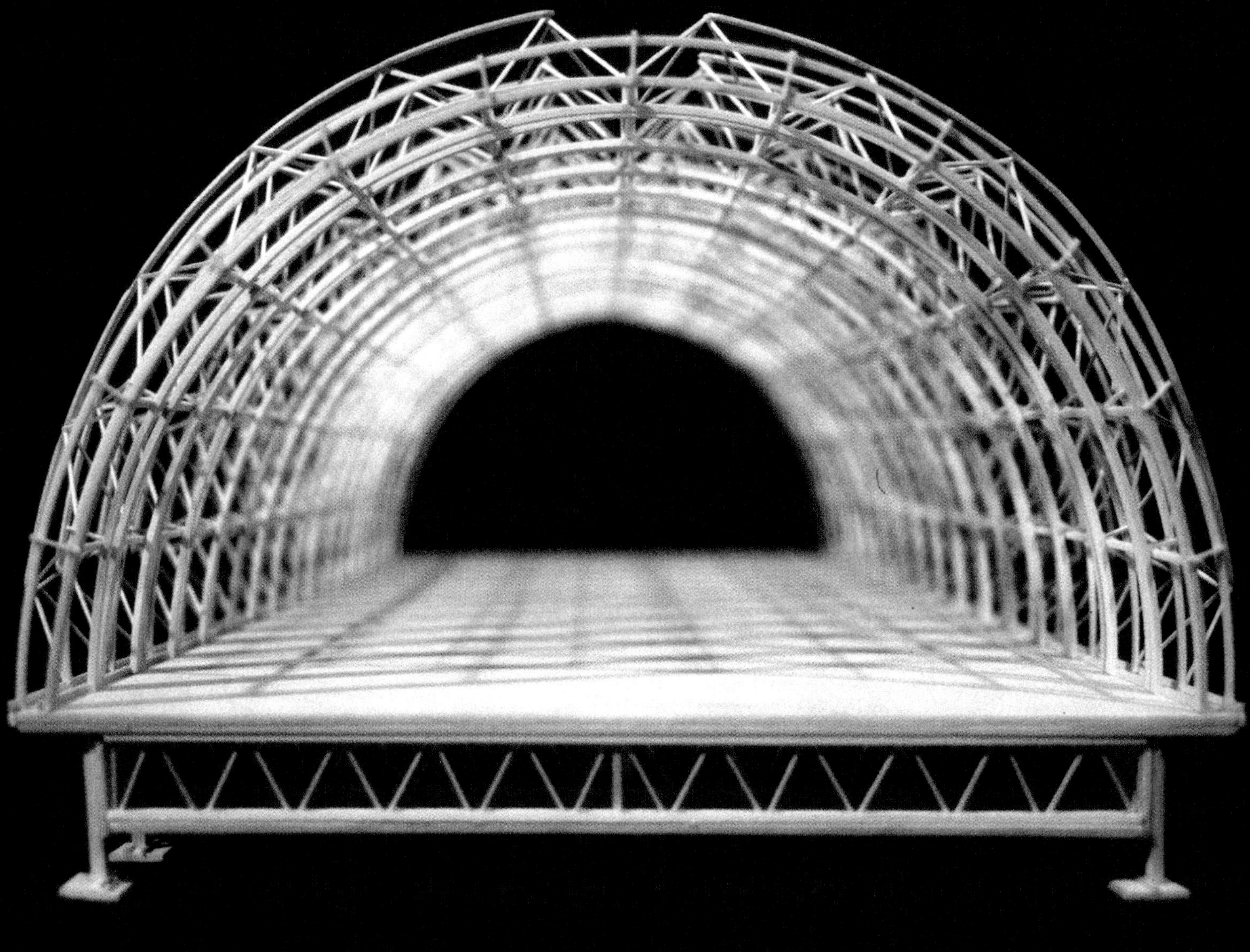

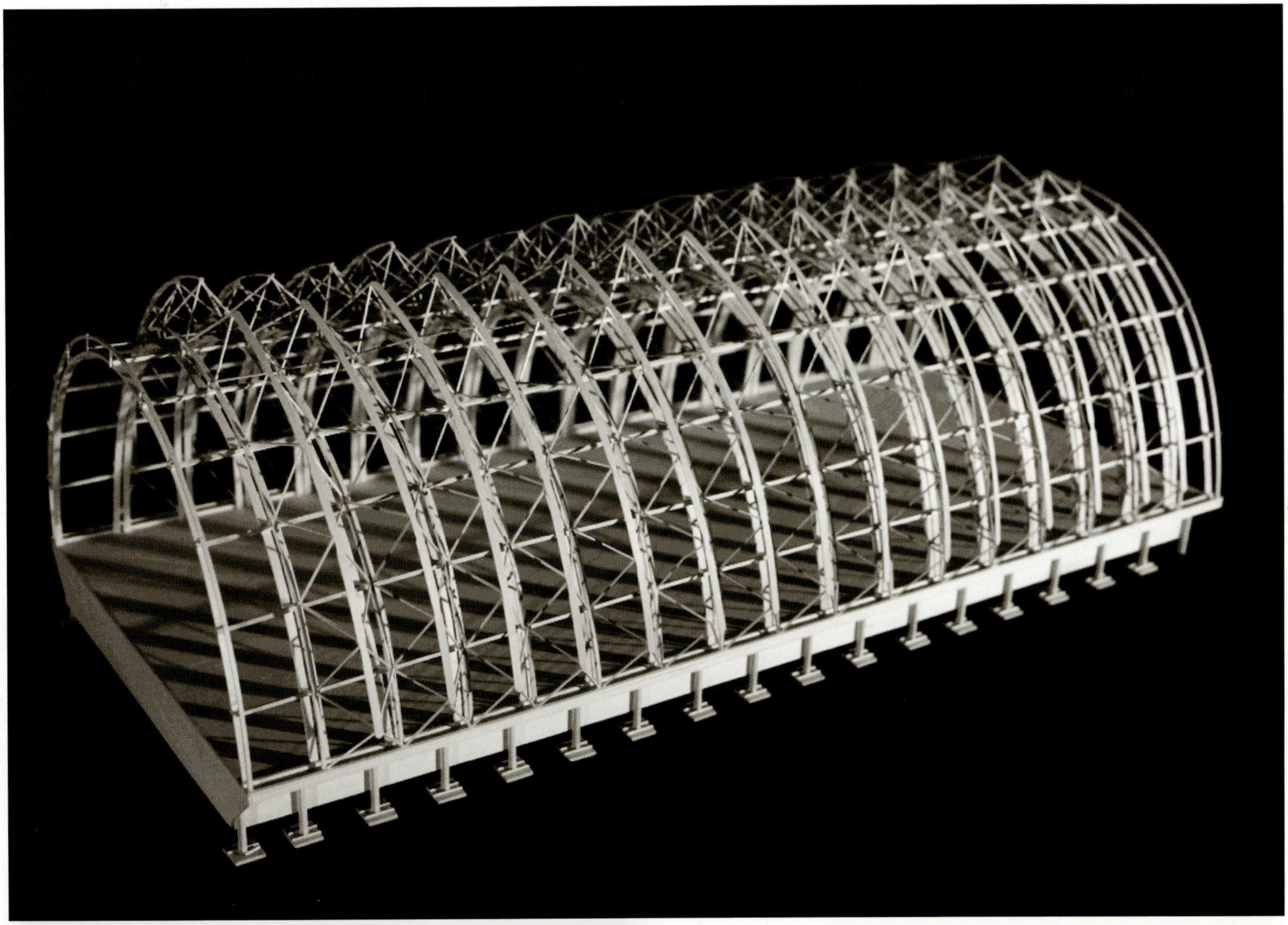

Gianni Berengo Gardin

A Trussed Deployable Vault

IBM Travelling Pavilion (1983-86)
Architect: Renzo Piano Building Workshop, Structural Engineer: Arup
Model: Emily Mueller

Within its vaulted space this travelling pavilion exhibited IBM's then-state-of-the-art computer technology for telecommunications. Intended to highlight this technology's mobile nature, the pavilion toured twenty European cities. Technical innovation was also the theme of the pavilion's structural system, with the vault created by a series of 36 trussed, three-hinged arched ribs, each a composite assembly of materials: segments of laminated beech wood for the outer chord members, 12 molded polycarbonate pyramids serving as the truss diagonal web members (and as the climate barrier), and finely detailed cast aluminum connectors and innovative glues. Lightness and transportability were also critical design parameters for this deployable structure.

Curved Ribs and Vaulted Space

Nature Boardwalk Pavilion, Lincoln Park Zoo, Chicago, USA (2010)
Architect: Studio Gang Architects
Structural Engineer: Magnusson Klemencic Associates
Model: Stephanie Gitto + Jonathan Negron

John W. Picken

This open-air pavilion highlights the redevelopment of an early 20th century park in the center of Chicago into a more "natural" ecological habitat and as a recreational and learning environment. Situated along a new boardwalk that meanders around the park, the structure was inspired by the geometric patterns and shape of a tortoise shell and is intended as an outdoor classroom and a living laboratory. Its light, open structural system offers occupants a direct visual and experiential connection to the natural cycles of the park's ecosystems.

The distinctively detailed vaulted canopy exhibits the essential qualities needed for providing strength and stability: in the transverse arched profile, loads are primarily resisted by a combination of compression force and bending action. Along the length of the vault the open diagonal pattern achieved by the curved rib segments not only stabilizes these ribs against buckling but also forms an effective network of diagonal bracing elements that can resist lateral forces acting along the length of the structure. The two-hinged, arched ribs are made up of a number of relatively short, modular, glue-laminated wood segments that are prefabricated and bent in two directions, rigidly joined to one another in the vertical plane. Two grade beams along the length of the bases of the vault are connected together by tension ties that resist the outward thrust of the overall arch form. [see also p. 396]

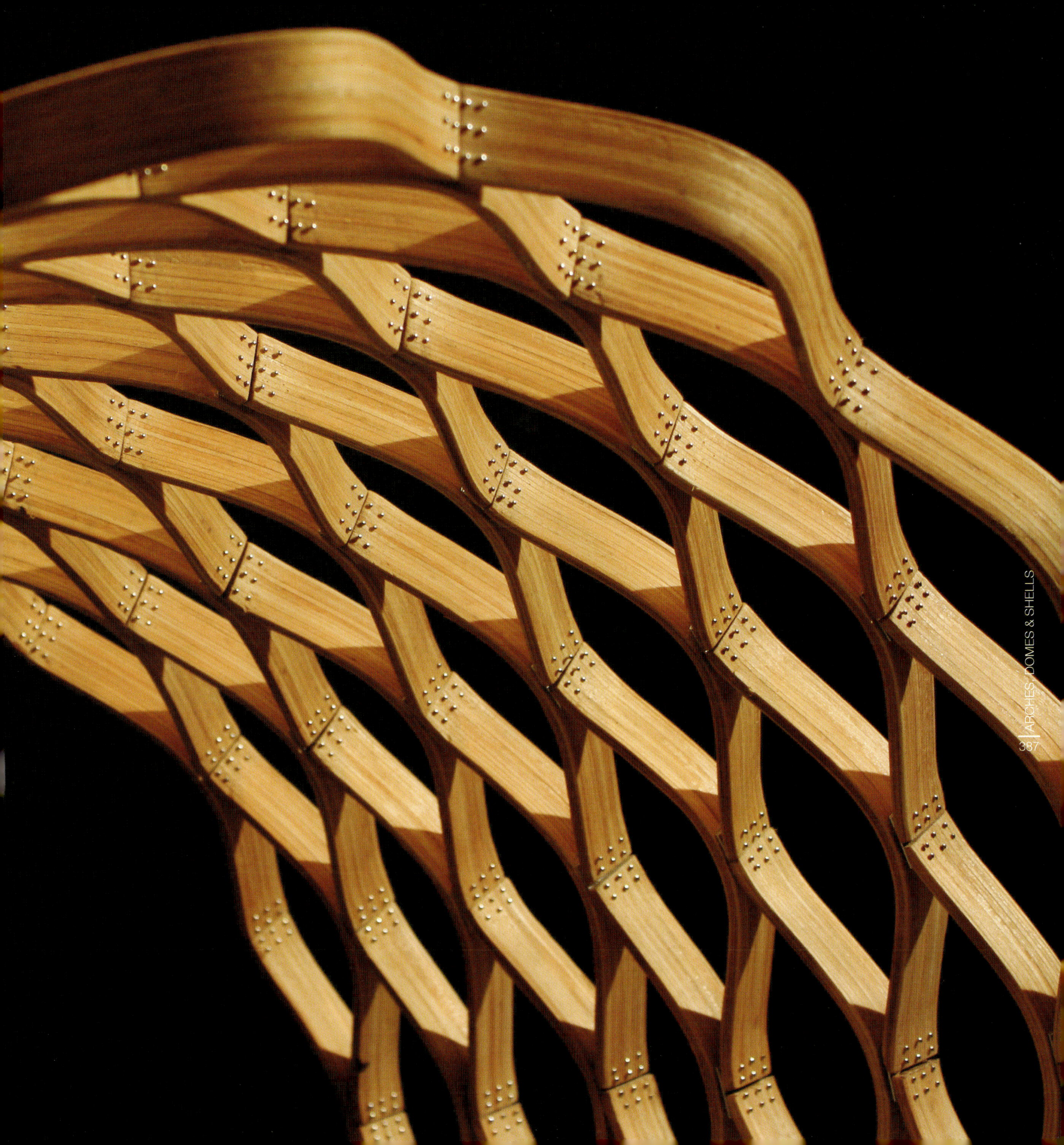

Catenary Curves Inverted

Church of Colonia Güell, Barcelona, Spain (started 1908)
Architect: Antoni Gaudi
Model: Katie Vitale

When Esebi Güell commissioned his friend Antoni Gaudi to design a church in 1898, the architect was given free rein. Gaudi envisaged an upper and lower nave, differing towers and a central dome; only the lower nave was constructed, however. This structure's unusual geometry was designed to build efficiently in masonry; to develop the form, Gaudi first experimented with hanging chains and textiles. Since structures made of materials having only tension stiffness change form with changing loads (so as to remain in tension), those with compressive strength benefit from having identical form turned upside down; i.e., a structure so configured will be subject to only axial compression forces (and no bending moments). "As hangs the flexible line, so but inverted will stand the rigid arch" is a dictum attributed to the 17th century's Robert Hooke; Gaudi extended this logic, experimenting some 200 years later with a complex 3D tension model in order to devise a unique compressive masonry structure.

David Cardelus

Lamella Grid-Shell Dome

Las Arenas, Barcelona, Spain (2011)
Architect: Rogers Stirk Harbour + Partners
Structural Engineer: Expedition Engineering and BOMA
Model: Emily Chang + Vincent Parlatore

The redevelopment of a late 19th century bullring gave rise to an intricate design for a mixed-use shopping and entertainment complex. Behind the circular historic façade, new structures contrast with and complement the preserved masonry wall. These are crowned by a wide-span, shallow glulam timber dome that, together with the steel-beam horizontal floor system just below it, create a large multi-purpose entertainment space carried high in the air on groups of inclined steel pylons. The stability of the lamella grid shell is assured by aligning its members to spiral out from the center, creating diamond-shaped openings that are braced against deformation by a set of concentric rings.

The Timber Grid-Shell Evolves

Haesley Nine Bridges Golf Club House, Yeoju, South Korea (2009)
Architect: Kyeong-Sik Yoon/KACI International + Shigeru Ban Architects
Structural Engineer: CS Structural Engineering/Creation Holz (timber)
Model: Henry Chuang + Papon Luengvarinkul + Rafael Martinez

Hiroyuki Hirai

The distinguishing feature of this 16,000m^2 (170,000ft^2) golf course clubhouse is its structural system, a striking example of contemporary developments in wood architecture and in design-to-production digital fabrication technologies. The 21 three-story-tall columns splay outward in tree-like fashion, their many "branches" seamlessly made to entwine and become an undulating, wooden grid-shell roof. As is the case with natural trees, the lower ends of these columns are relatively solid, and their fixed base connections provide lateral stability by means of vertical cantilever behavior. In contrast, at their upper ends the columns open up; circular skylights directly above them allow daylight to highlight their filigree quality as they merge into the roof system.

The hexagonal, wicker-like grid of the roof shell (whose pattern was similar to the traditional Korean bamboo "summer pillow" used for keeping cool at night) was prefabricated in panel segments in Switzerland and shipped to Korea for assemblage. It is composed of doubly-curved glulam members; the irregularly intersecting elements are joined together by the help of screws and glue used in precisely corresponding cuts made half-way through the wooden latticework; a certain oversizing of the cross-sectional dimensions also protects the structure in case of fire. Inspired by traditional Korean and Asian bamboo artifacts, but also bearing a certain likeness to the stone tracery of historical Western European ecclesiastical architecture, this contemporary structure has both multicultural and timeless qualities to it.

Shells – Real and Imagined

Rolex Learning Center/EPFL, Lausanne, Switzerland (2010)
Architect: SANAA
Structural Engineer: Bollinger + Grohmann
Model: Kao Onishi + Janice Rim

Hisao Suzuki

The Rolex Learning Center is a building that provides innovative spaces for multiple university functions and student activities. How this is accomplished is unique: two seemingly identical undulating white surfaces serve as floor and roof alike, with several large openings admitting light deep into the space.

But looks are deceiving, for these two surfaces could not be more different in terms of structural configuration and behavior. The lower surface is a reinforced concrete shell, connected to the ground in places and deriving most of its stiffness and strength from its curved shape, developing membrane-type axial stresses to carry the heavy occupancy loads. Universal access and other user requirements had to be reconciled with structural optimization, however, and the shell form is thus not "ideal"; i.e., more inefficient bending stresses are required within the surface in addition to membrane stresses, resulting in a thicker shell than would otherwise be the case. The roof, while appearing to be an identical shell, is instead built in "conventional" post and beam fashion, with the columns on a 9m x 9m (30ft x 30ft) grid, and the beams having typical one-way timber-and-steel beam hierarchy. It may seem ironic that such a spatially innovative building makes extensive use of such a traditional structural system; but the resulting roof has relatively little mass compared to a thick concrete slab, and so any seismic forces will thus be greatly reduced. [see also p. 377]

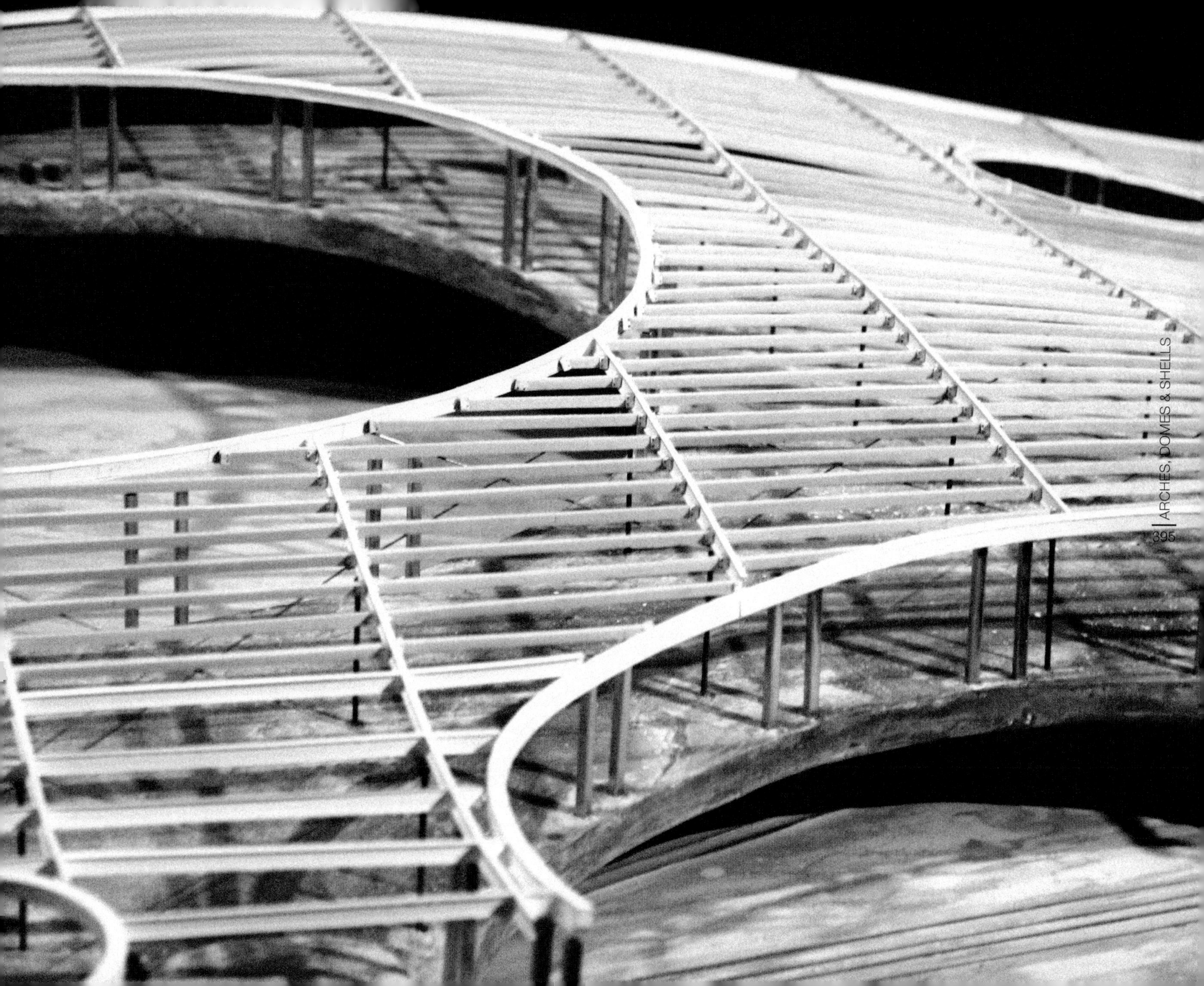

01

02

03

04

05

06

07

08

09

10

01. Lashed-together bamboo arches support pavilion roof – Mepantigan Auditorium, Sibang Kaja, Bali, 2007; Ibuku (arch., builders); model by Michael Raspuzzi & Max Vanatta **02. Four steel arches support floors of building, bridging over train tracks** – Broadgate Exchange House, London, UK, 1990; SOM (arch., eng.); model by Jennifer Miller **03,06. Arched glulam rib connections: moment resistant and hinged, respectively** – Lincoln Park Pavilion, Chicago, IL, USA, 2010; Studio Gang Architects; Magnusson Klemencic Associates (eng.); model by Stephanie Gitto & Jonathan Negron **04. Radial trusses create conical roof; compression ring at center, tension ring around base** – The Round Building, Mellor Cutlery Factory, Hathersage, UK, 1989; Hopkins Architects; Whitby and Bird (eng.); model by Mike Pritchard **05. Arched ribs create vaulted space; rib depth provides bending resistance** – Fortabat Collection Museum, Buenos Aires, Argentina, 2008; Rafael Viñoly Architects; Soubie Fernandez y Asociados (eng.); model by Catherine Kim & Roberto Soto **07. Overlapping straight wood segments create cylindrical vault, give it bending resistance** – Ultra Light Pavilion "Squarely Sphering", Shenzen, China 2011; Wang Shu / Amateur Architecture Studio; model by Nicholas DeMaio & J. Stuart Pidcock **08. Digital modeling and fabrication enable highly irregular geometry of wood modules for domed pavilion** – ICD, ITKE Research Pavilion, Stuttgart, Germany, 2011; ICD/University of Stuttgart/Achim Menges; IBSSD/ Jan Knippers; model by Kiril Bejoulev & Daniela Mourad **09. Light trussed arch ribs establish vaulted space, support for fabric membrane enclosure** – MOMI Pavilion, London, UK, 1992; Future Systems (arch.); Arup (eng.); model by Greta Stoyko **10. Schwedler-type wood shell-dome; membrane action develops by member axial forces** – Domaine de la Rive Theater, Biscarosse Lake, France, 2011; Nadau Lavergne Architects; Simonin (eng.); model by Sagar Karnavat & Samuel Ososanya

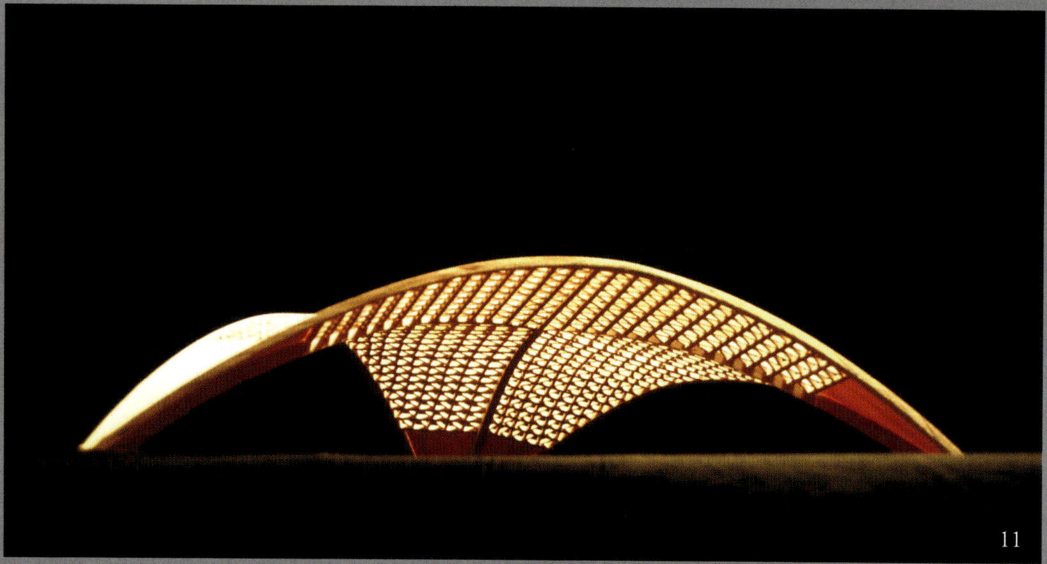

11

12

13

14

15

16

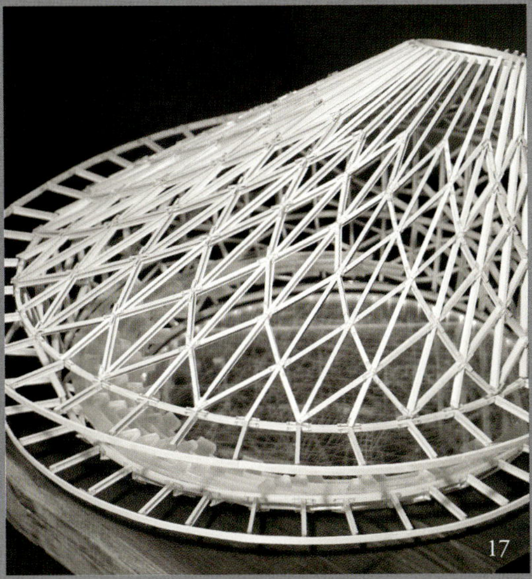

17

18

19

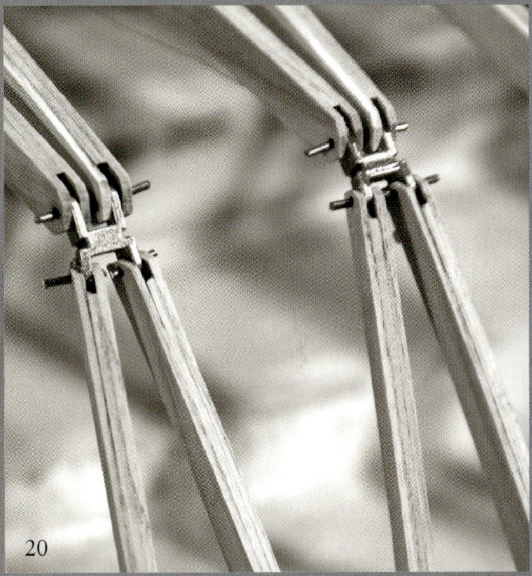

20

11. Concrete shell "lightened" by change to diagrid – CNIT / Centre of New Industries and Technologies, Paris, France, 1958; Robert Camelot, Jean de Mailly, Bernard Zehrfuss (arch.); Jean Prouvé, Nicholas Esquillan (eng.); model by Jonathan Doyle **12,15. Cardboard tubes define varying A-frame form; contain steel members** – Cardboard Cathedral, Christchurch, New Zealand, 2013; Shigeru Ban Architects; Holmes Consulting Group (eng.); model by Elie Boutros & Anders Izumi Evanson **13. Diagrid's curvature allows membrane action to be developed** – Nardini Research Center Auditorium, Bassano Del Grappa, Italy, 2004; Fuksas (arch.); Studio Sarti Engineering; model by Jeff Lodin & Kally Wu **14. Trusses define A-frame form; supports resist outward thrust** – US Air Force Academy Cadet Chapel, Colorado Springs, CO, USA, 1962; SOM (arch., eng.); model by Vincent Ahn & Calvin W. Liu **16. Diagrid form stiffened by transverse tension rods** – DZ Bank, Berlin, Germany, 2000; Gehry Partners (arch.); Schlaich Bergermann und Partner (eng.); model by Michael Curry **17. Eccentric conical roof** – Serpentine Pavilion, London, UK, 2007; Olafur Eliasson & Kjetil Thorsen (arch.); Arup (eng.); model by Jeremy Bilotti & Alexandra Donovan **18. Trussed three-hinged arch ribs; profile follows bending moment** – Waterloo Terminal, London, UK, 1993; Nicholas Grimshaw and Partners (arch.); Anthony Hunt Assoc. (eng.); model by Samuel Reilly **19. Three-hinged glulam arch ribs define vault** – Sea-Folk Museum, Toba, Japan, 1992; Naito Architects; Kunio Watanabe/Structural Design Group; model by Kate Chen & Sisi Yu **20. Hinge connection detail** – Palace of Water Sports, Kazan, Russia, 2013; SPEECH Tschoban & Kuznetsov (arch.); Arup (eng.); model by Sonya Mantell & Frank Wang **21. Arch ribs' change of material caused by curvature and bending moments** – Brentwood Skytrain Station, Vancouver, BC, Canada, 2002; Busby + Assoc. (arch.); Fast & Epp Partners (eng.); model by Betty Huang & Xi Zhang

21

Afterword

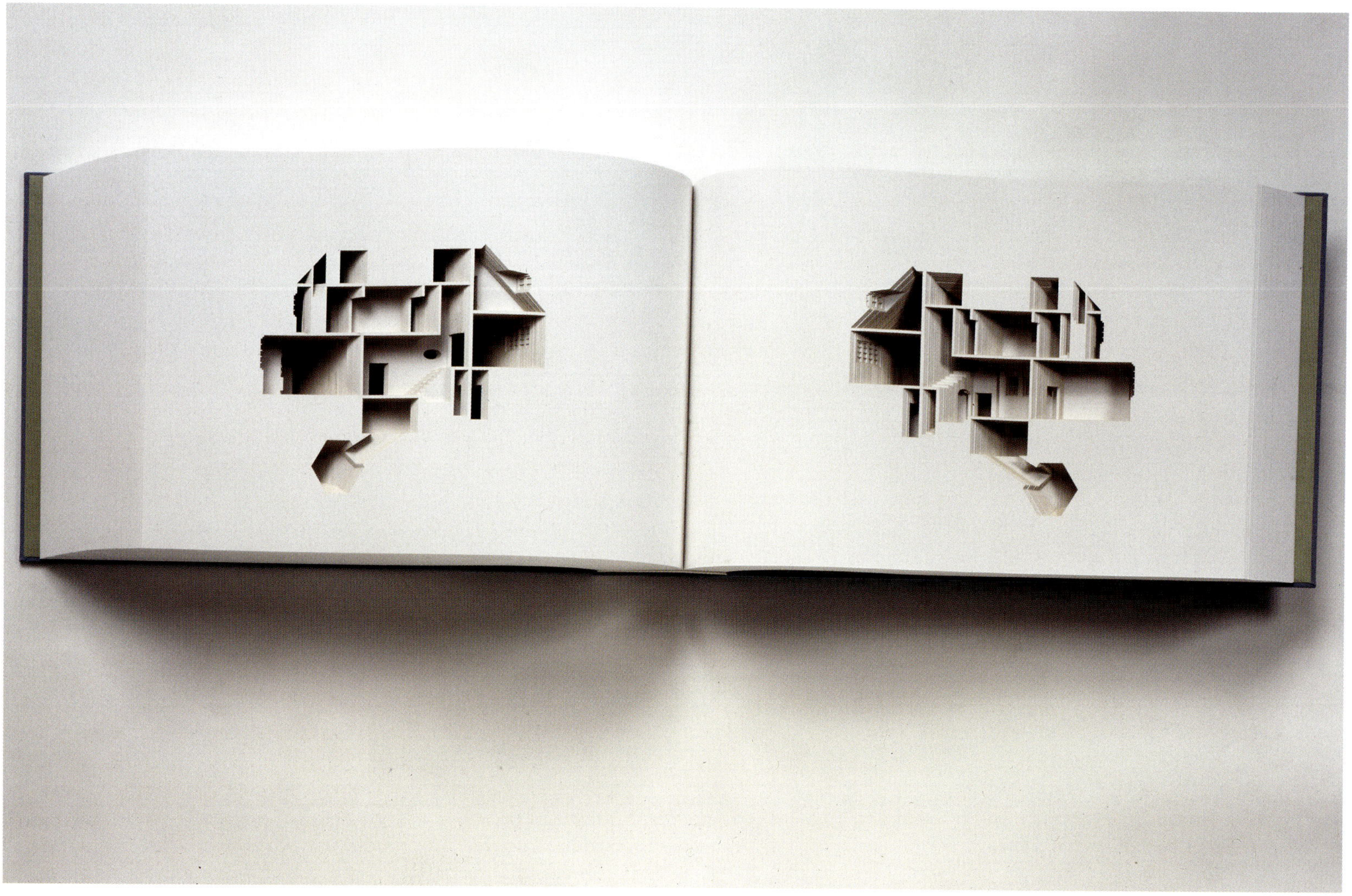

Your House. Reproduced by permission of Studio Olafur Eliasson

Models are Real

from *Models*
Olafur Eliasson

In order to understand, inhabit, and evaluate space, it is crucial to recognise its temporal aspect. Space does not simply exist in time; it is of time. The actions of its users continually recreate its structures. This condition is often forgotten or repressed, as Western society is generally still based on the idea of a static, non-negotiable space. Commercial interests also nurture this idea, as people have realised that static objects and objective spaces are more marketable than their relative and instable counterparts.

When surroundings are thought of as stable, we tend to lose a feeling of responsibility for the environments in which we move. Space becomes a background for interaction rather than a co-producer of interaction. But what takes place is, in fact, a double movement: the user's interaction with other people co-produces space, which in turn is a co-producer of interaction. By focusing on our agency in this critical exchange, it is possible to bring our spatial responsibility to the fore.

In the last forty years many artists and theorists have repeatedly criticised the static conception of space and objects. The idea of objecthood has, in part, been substituted with performative strategies, the notions of ephemerality, negotiation, and change, but today the criticism is, nevertheless, more pertinent than ever. It seems necessary to insist on an alternative that acknowledges the fundamental connection and interplay between space and time *and* ourselves. Because models possess two fundamental qualities, structure and time, one way of drawing attention to our co-production of space is a close examination of models.

As objects in general are not static, neither are artworks. These exist in a manifold of unstable relationships that are dependent on both the context in which they are presented and the variety of responses by the visitors – or users, another word I use to draw attention to the activity of the viewer. Since the early 1990s, when I was a student, artistic critical discourse has considered the museum visitor to be a constituent of the artwork, a conception that is essential to my practice today. To emphasise the negotiability of my works – installations and larger spatial projects alike – I do not try to conceal the technical means on which they rely. I make the construction accessible to the visitors in order to heighten their awareness that each artwork is an option or model. Thus, the artworks are experimental set-ups, and experiences of these are not based on an essence found in the works themselves, but on an option activated by the users.

Previously, models were conceived as rationalised stations on the way to a perfect object. A model of a house, for instance, would be part of a temporal sequence, as the refinement of the image of the house, but the actual and real house was considered a static, final consequence of the model. Thus, the model was merely an image, a representation of reality without being real itself. What we are witnessing is a shift in the traditional relationship between reality and representation. We no longer progress from model to reality, but from model to model while acknowledging that both models are, in fact, real. As a result, we may work in a very productive manner with reality experienced as a conglomeration of models. Rather than seeing model and reality as polarised modes, we now view them as functioning on the same level. Models have become co-producers of reality.

Models exist in various forms and sizes: objects such as houses or artworks are one variety, but we also find models of engagement, models of perception and reflection. In my artistic practice I work with analogue and digital models, with models of thought and other experiments that add up to a model of a situation. Every model shows a different degree of representation, but all are real. We need to acknowledge that all spaces are steeped in political and individual intentions, power relations, and desires that function as models of engagement with the world. No space is model-free. This condition does not represent a loss, as many people, deploring the elimination of unmediated presence, might think. On the contrary, the idea that the world consists of a conglomeration of models carries a liberating potential, as it makes the renegotiation of our surroundings possible. This, in turn, opens the potential for recognition of the differences between individuals. *What we have in common is that we are different.* The conception of space as static and clearly definable thus becomes untenable – and undesirable. As agents in the ceaseless modelling and remodelling of our surroundings and the ways in which we interact, we may advocate the idea of a spatial multiplicity and co-production.

Photo: Gareth Gardner. By courtesy of the Trustees of Sir John Soane's Museum

A Model Curriculum

Mark Morris

With the recent unveiling of the restored Model Room at Sir John Soane's Museum in London, a missing piece of an architectural puzzle fell into place. What had been one of the last showcase spaces Soane (1753-1837) created in his ever expanding house at Lincoln's-Inn-Fields was one of the first to be taken apart after his death. His will, leaving his house and its contents to the state as a museum along with an endowment for its perpetual operation, included a provision for a curator to be housed on-site. George Bailey, Soane's chief clerk and the museum's first curator, had the Model Room and Soane's adjacent bedroom largely dismantled for his own office and living space. Many of the models were relocated throughout the rest of the house. The tiered model stand – the centerpiece of the room – was eventually chopped in half, along with a large model of Pompeii that the stand had been built for, so it could be moved out of its room and fit elsewhere for display.

The stand now rebuilt with its far-flung models (some recreated) restored to their former positions, the Model Room is revived as a testament to an important shift in Soane's intense collecting. Whereas his model displays had been either focused on private recollections of his youthful architectural travels of 1778-80 (he was awarded a British version of the Prix de Rome by the Royal Academy) or his strategic intermingling of his own projects, realized or not, alongside representations of the Classical past, by the time Soane builds his Model Room in the 1820s he is using models as teaching aids to instruct his pupils/apprentices. This shift came gradually toward the end of his career, after being made a professor of architecture at the Royal Academy. Some models were used as evocative examples of historical precedent that could be synthesized or subtly redeployed by his students in new work; Soane was an expert at this cagey architectural quotation game. Others were meant to be instructive in the practice of building, models used a surrogates to show how buildings were put together. Soane had concerns over the growing professionalization of the architect, a trend he witnessed over the course of his own career, leading to "gentlemen-architects" distancing themselves from the building trades. The son of a builder, Soane himself was versed in construction and structural details from an early age. A year after his father died, his brother, William, a bricklayer, used his connection to a surveyor to arrange an introduction for John to architect George Dance the Younger (1741-1825), a founder of the Royal Academy, whom Soane would train under.

As part of compiling his instructive-type scale models, Soane purchased a group of twenty models by master model-maker François Fouquet intended for display in the Model Room. Unlike his previous acquisitions which focused on antique architectural sites shown in their contemporary states, mostly as ruins, the Fouquet models were of known Classical temples and monuments crafted as they would have looked the day they were finished; whole and pearly white, each model kept under a glass cloche dome. These are incredibly accurate models, many based on the measured archaeological drawings of Louis François Cassas (1756-1827); modeled brick for brick, tile for tile. These represented a key pedagogical component of his collection, a means to counter the sort of pure education in the art and history of architecture focused on drawing espoused at the École des Beaux Arts in Paris. For Soane the model represented a middle-way where architects-in-training could still tangibly experience, albeit in miniature, the construction process and gain an intuitive sense of statics and structures.

> *The business of the architect is to make the designs and estimates, to direct the works and to measure and value the different parts; he is the intermediate agent between the employer, whose honour and interest he is to study, and the mechanic, whose rights he is to defend. His situation implies great trust; he is responsible for the mistakes, negligences, and ignorances of those he employs; and above all, he is to take care that the workmen's bills do not exceed his own estimates. If these are the duties of an architect, with what propriety can his situation and that of the builder, or the contractor be united?*[1]

Between the ruin models of cork and the perfect plaster Fouquet ones, many construction details, interior and exterior, could be examined. The ruin models, not unlike the celebrated 1830 rendering of Soane's

Photo: Gareth Gardner. By courtesy of the Trustees of Sir John Soane's Museum

Bank of England as Ruin by Joseph Michael Gandy (1771-1843), reveal all manner of structural details – arches, piers, colonnades, sections of domes, etc. – normally hidden from view or simply not shown in a finished model. The ruin models could uniquely reveal a building's layers, the brickwork behind the marble facings. The Fouquet models, by contrast, were about exact proportions, numbers of parts and fastidious façade details. Soane's educational program (the drawings, models, casts and his house taken together) was not only intended for his pupils, but grew out of his life-long ambition to educate his sons, colleagues and clients regarding the aesthetic merits and historical context for his brand of architecture. In short, they offered a Grand Tour in miniature to anyone willing to take a walk around his house with opened eyes. Soane's effort with the Model Room was threefold: to bring a selection of specific models/precedents together in proximity for the visual and intellectual delectation of his colleagues and friends; to instruct his students and, at the same time, educate future educators; and to please himself.

> *As a collection, the models come to figure their collector's desire. Their yearning (and his yearning for them) is to be a complete series (even a series that may repeat some of its members). And so they commemorate the famous objects in which Soane traces his architectural ancestry not only item by item, but also as a totality, a paradigmatic classical heritage.*[2]

The Model Room's stand includes Soane's most extensive site model, a fragment of Pompeii complete with its hilly topography. Most of the models Soane displayed were minimally sited including just the immediate edge of a site beyond the façade given their "site" was really the room in which they were displayed; but a few of the ruin cork type, most notably Pompeii (still being uncovered in Soane's lifetime), cover a wider area and were seen as integral to the architecture being represented.

It is worth noting that the Model Room was previously the bedroom of Soane's wife who predeceased him by some 22 years. The displacement of her things, which had been kept as a kind of mausoleum, for the sake of the Model Room underscores the value he placed on this last great project. His wife claimed that she was made fatally ill by concern for her son, George, who had defied his father in not taking up architecture as a career, run up large debts, fathered illegitimate children and cruelly criticized his father's practice in newspapers under a pseudonym. Soane's bequeathing his home to the nation, which required an Act of Parliament in 1833, was his way of completely disinheriting his one surviving child. Had it not been for feckless George Soane, his father's house-museum would not exist today.

Soane was an oddball, an anomalous figure in many respects, not the least of which was his approach to architectural training. He was an upstart, a Royal Academician from the working class. His lectures at the academy reveal his mix of interests and skills, showcasing his background. Delivered as two courses of six lectures each, the first set focused on the history of Classical Architecture, the decline of Rome, the Renaissance and a nod to Inigo Jones (1573-1652); while the second was firmly focused on building techniques, bridge structures, details (for windows, doors and roofs), landscape architecture and urban planning. His finale lecture, the grand conclusion to his cycle, was on construction methods. Apart from his formal lectures at the academy, which were copiously illustrated, the day-to-day hands-on training he was devoted to at his house was exceptionally model-centric.

That physical scale models should persist in a Soanesque instructional mode nearly two centuries on at Cornell University's Department of Architecture, as part of Mark Cruvellier's Structural Systems course, is surprising given the sophisticated modeling software available and the rare appearance of the model in contemporary architectural education outside of the design studio. Yet there is persistent value in such models: in their crafting, a kinesthetic lesson is had in a university context, one that resonates and imprints itself deeply in the recollection of many graduates; and in their display as an ensemble of objects in a gallery setting forming a new sort of architectural totality from fragments of existing buildings recast. Both of these aspects have precedents in Soane's use of the model as a pedagogical tool. True, one could also find models used at the Bauhaus as heuristic devices or prototypes or in many post-war architecture programs influenced by the Bauhaus. The Texas Rangers – Colin Rowe et al – deployed the model as a diagram or means to formal abstraction; and some of Cornell's preoccupation with the model should be attributed to this group's influence. However, models of parts, not wholes, of existing (often famous) modern buildings crafted to learn something about their structural systems and then displayed with care, are more rooted to the precedent set by Soane than anyone else.

As part of the structures curriculum going on twenty years, the model assignment is held as a rite of passage by students; and an annual imposition on studio time by design faculty. Students generally work in pairs, a forced marriage of sorts that usually spurs on better and more work. These pairs decide their own case study, do some research (hunting for the best drawings and photographs of a given structure) and plan their approach to modeling; deciding, firstly, what engaging portion of the given architectural work to represent. This involves imagining the cropping of a complex three-dimensional object, not an easy task. Then there is the choice regarding scale which must be a flexible consideration, project to project, as the assignment mandates a given total volume for a model: 3ft wide by 3ft deep by 2ft tall. Typically, the goal is to maximize that volume to the closest conventional scale (1/8in = 1ft, for example). Metric scales are also permitted. Students then embark on a buying spree of materials, taking some time to test different fabrication techniques. They work in wood, metal, plastic, textiles, string, digitally fabricated and water jet-cut components, usually deciding on two or three materials to constructively limit their palette of options and repress any overly realistic or prettified representations.

This aesthetic agenda is largely unspoken, but meticulously followed. The models are complex, but rarely visually fussy; adhering to a vague notion of stark beauty. This restraint recalls Leon Battista Alberti's (1404-1472) dictums regarding the model:

> *I always highly commend the ancient custom of builders, who not only in drafts [drawings] and paintings, but in real models of wood or other substance, examined and weighed over and over again, with the advice of men of the best experience, the whole work and the measurements of its parts, before they put themselves to the expense or trouble. By making a model you will have the opportunity, thoroughly to weigh and consider the form and situation...*[3]

An early and forceful Renaissance advocate of using models as design tools, Alberti elaborated and crystallized the notion of the model not just as a medium of architectural expression, but as the primary vehicle of design development. He cautions against its fetishization:

> *I must not omit to observe, that the making of curious polished models with the delicacy of the painting, is not required from an architect that only designs to show the real thing itself; but is rather the part of a vain architect, that makes it his business by charming the eye and striking the fancy of the beholder, to divert him from a rigorous examination of the parts which he ought to make, and to draw him into an admiration of himself.*[4]

Having said that, there is a component of these models which does see an effusive level of creativity: the "site" upon which the structures model is set. It is as if the constraints of the architectural portion of the model have to be balanced by a degree of whimsy or one-upmanship relegated to the environment in which the structure exists. These include site models made in concrete, wax or resin cast from bespoke molds; chiseled slabs of marble or colored salt; wood bases carved with computer numerical control routers; water features with hidden pumps and drains; and so on. Students are encouraged to interpret site in open-ended ways that work as a foil to the structure inhabiting it. Each year the sites push the envelope a bit more and, in most cases,

By courtesy of the Trustees of Sir John Soane's Museum

do a fine job at complementing or extending themes of the structure being studied. Here one finds the individual expression, after Ruskin's conception of the Gothic craftsman, by the authors of the piece. Alberti might cringe, but this excess is what makes several of the models in any particular year more than the sum of their parts.

In the run-up to the assignment deadline, there is a frenzy of activity in the school's materials labs extending into the wee hours. The woodshop purrs, the metal shop clangs, laser-cutters catch fire occasionally, and the 3-D printers zip along. Students are bent over workbenches doing repetitive model-making tasks, checking minute measurements, and deftly putting elements together with tweezers. A dazzling layer of model detritus litters the floor; leftover sheets of basswood and sheet metal as complex and dainty, if not more so, as the things harvested from them. There is a palpable esprit de corps in this environment and a real seriousness in regard to getting these representations just right.

The end-of-semester exhibition of the structures models shifts the notion of site again where these fragments are reframed as a massive group displayed on trestle tables in the college's main gallery. There is even a well-attended exhibition opening to mark the occasion. More people jam into the gallery on this occasion than any other. Why? Because a new sort of city is formed, unintended juxtapositions can be marveled at, the clash of different scales makes what are in fact large structures small and vice versa and opens these objects up to productive misreadings that suggest other novel projects. This was Soane's ambition with his house: the group dynamic of diverse models in proximity to one another.

> *Models free us from literal constraints to make impossible comparisons with ease, Soane's models invite imaginary perambulations in which the eye is overwhelmed by one thing, then another, creating a phantasmagoric experience: the spatial art, which requires travel, has been internalized.*[5]

Whereas Soane meticulously choreographed his display over decades, structures teaching assistants have a weekend to set up their Lilliput. What is interesting here is the flip of retrospective models (models of existing structures) into speculative models that suggest structures or projects as yet unrealized.

Joseph Gandy's (1771-1843) exquisite 1818 rendering of "A selection of parts of buildings, public and private, erected from the designs of John Soane, Esq. R. A. in the metropolis and in other places

Photo: William Staffeld

of the United Kingdom between the years 1780 and 1815" shows over a hundred projects designed by Soane up until the year of his wife's death. A fictive room capped by Soane's trademark saucer-dome is filled with paintings and models at varying scales, arranged side by side as a model village lit dramatically by a lamp, a model sun. A large Bank of England model holds the mid-ground, while very small models are arranged over the architrave like a city on a Neoclassical cliff. The Bank of England appears again, as model of a model, on a desk in the foreground staffed by a tiny figure: Soane, dwarfed by his own genius. Model facades, sectional models as well as complete ones are featured. The effect is so unusual and distinctive that, of all the paintings Gandy did for Soane, only this one was directly attributed to the artist in the Royal Academy catalogues. As with the Cornell structures models, these models of Soane's work represent projects built. The rendering is technically a retrospective where Gandy has turned built works, executed buildings, back into models; in some cases where models did not exist for these in the first place. It was this watercolor that prompted Soane to create the Model Room.

> *In Gandy's drawing, as in Soane's Model Room, the monuments are displayed without any relation to their particular time or place. [...] They evoke a visionary and imaginative world where ideal, transhistorical, orders and forms may not only characterize buildings but may incorporate those buildings within other buildings.*[6]

For the structures models together in the gallery, chronological adhocism in terms of placement, alongside their individual cropping, helps confuse what are often well-known well-published projects. It reboots the projects as a whole and makes them new again for the gallery visitor.

Finally, there is a distinct pleasure to be had in viewing the displayed models. It is an aesthetic pleasure, pure and simple, available to anyone present. Much of this pleasure flows from scale and an immediate and intuitive grasp regarding the care, time and sacrifice represented in crafting detailed miniatures.

> *Now, the question arises whether the small-scale model or miniature, which is also the 'masterpiece' of the journeyman, may in fact not be the universal type of the work of art. All miniatures seem to have intrinsic aesthetic quality – and from what should they draw this constant virtue if not from the dimensions themselves?*[7]

This aesthetic experience is further enlarged by the density of models on display, curiously dwarfing the gallery visitor despite the fact that the models are themselves small scaled. The exhibition of the collective effort is instructive on two levels: it highlights a range of important real-world projects, their architects and engineers (the models are all labeled) as well as opening up these same projects to new interpretations. There is the combined aesthetic and instructive pleasure in what Claude Lévi-Strauss (1908-2009) locates in any miniature representation related to a sense of immediate understanding:

> *Being smaller, the object as a whole seems less formidable. By being quantitatively diminished, it seems to us qualitatively simplified. More exactly, the quantitative transposition extends and diversifies our power over a homologue of the thing, and by means of it the latter can be grasped, assessed and apprehended at a glance.*[8]

Such spring-loaded comprehension forms a large part of the models' appeal within and without the structures curriculum. For as time-consuming as they are to make, their effect is immediate. Everyone attending the exhibition thus takes away more than they bargained for. In the space of this temporary Model Room the models educate without effort, provide a pleasurable aesthetic experience and, together, often prompt fresh design work.

Soane would be pleased.

Hartell Gallery, Cornell University. Photo: William Staffeld

Endnotes

PREFACE

1. Fjeld, Per Olaf. *Sverre Fehn: The Pattern of Thoughts* (The Monacelli Press, New York, 2009), 22.

CHAPTER 1 | COLUMNS

Auguste Perret and the Concrete Column
1. *American Architect*, 1924, vol. 126, 249.
2. W.B. Dinsmoor, *The Architecture of Ancient Greece* (1950), 116, 117.
3. Gazette des Beaux-Arts, 1923, II, 199.
4. Le Corbusier, *Oeuvres Complétes (1910-1929),* 195; 199 (caption).
5. Le Corbusier, *Précisions* (1930), 51.
6. Ibid., 60.

Mies' Columns: Barcelona and Beyond
1. L. Mies van der Rohe, "Address to the Union of German Plate Glass Manufacturers, March 13, 1933." This text appears in English translation in Tegethoff, *Mies van der Rohe: The Villas and Country Houses*, 66.
2. See Jose Quetglas, "Fear of Glass: The Barcelona Pavilion," in *Architectural production,* ed. Joan Ockman and Beatriz Colomina (New York: Princeton Architectural Press, 1988), 144. Quetglas cites in the same essay one of the only firsthand critical accounts of the original pavilion, in *Cahiers d'Art* (1929) 8-9, by the Catalan critic N.M. Rubio Tuduri.
3. Robin Evans, "Mies van der Rohe's Paradoxical Symmetries," *AA files*, no. 19 (Spring 1990), 113.
4. Colin Rowe, "Neoclassicism and Modern Architecture," Part II, *Oppositions* 1 (September 1973), 18.

Villa Mairea's Columnar Variations
1. Aalto ridiculed the modular principles of the Finnish Constructivist of the 1960's by stating that the module he had used in his design for the Rautatalo Office Building in Helsinki (1951-57) was 'one millimeter or a fraction of it.' Nils Erik Wickberg, 'Finnish Architecture on the Early 1900s and Alvar Alto' in *Alvar Aalto vs. The Modern Movement*, ed. Kirmo Mikkola, 1st International Alvar Aalto Symposium, Jyväskylä (1981), 60.
2. This echoes the ideals of physical culture which were popular during the first decades of the century. The Aaltos had purchased a gramophone in the mid-1920s to practice the foxtrot at home, and the Gullichsens were also keen dancers.
3. Author's interview with Paul Bernoulli, Helsinki (May 21, 1989).
4. Göran Schildt, *Alvar Alto. The Decisive Years*. Rizzoli (New York 1986), 12.
5. The confusion of regular order is so complete that even Giedion mentions only the 'twin-columns' in his otherwise perceptive description, and recalls wrongly that the pattern of the tiled floor in the entrance lobby is diagonal, and one of the two photographs of the main staircase has been printed as a mirror image.

A Forest of Minimal Columns
Mark Wigley
1. Robert Smithson, 'Incidents of Mirror-Travel in the Yucatan,' *Artforum* (September 1969).
Giles Reid
none

The Sendai Mediatheque and its Tube-Columns
Andrea Maffei
none
Edzard Mik
none

CHAPTER 2 | WALLS

Barragán's Walls and Colour
1. Le Corbusier, in *Architecture d'Aujourd'hui,* special issue on Le Corbusier (April 1948), 11.
2. Like Ferdinand Bac, Barragán called himself a "landscape architect" (see interview by Elena Poniatowska, "Luis Barragán," November 1976, *Diario Novedades*, Mexico City, November 28 and December 5 1976).
3. The "red wall," which is no longer standing today.
4. "El arte de hacer ... " in Luis Barragán, *Luis Barragán: Ensayos y Apuntes Para Un Bosquejo Critico* (Museo Rufino Tamayo, Mexico City, 1985), 105.
5. The architect devised two variants for the colour of this wall—orange (contrasting with the greenery) and blue (hinting at the deep tones of the Mexican sky). See drawings (Barragan Foundation).
6. This residential neighbourhood is close to the French Riding Club, whose members it was designed to accommodate.
7. In older photographs, the wall and fountain are painted bright orange (See A. Salas Portugal Photograph Collection, Barragán Foundation.)
8. The sketches for the variants devised for Los Amantes show various layouts of vertical planes standing in the water. (See drawings in *Barragán: The Quiet Revolution,* Barragán Foundation).
9. Luis Barragán, interview by Elena Poniatowska, op. cit.
10. Originally, the tree was small and did not take up such a large amount of space.
11. The wall also plays a constructional role, as it bears the weight of the long portico.
12. Luis Barragán, interview by Elena Poniatowska, op. cit.
13. These works contain a design logic that has often been compared to diverse critical analyses with the spatial and planimetric methods of the De Stijl group.
14. Mathias Goeritz met Barragán as soon as he arrived in Mexico City, through Diaz Morales. The two men struck up an instant friendship, which led to them working closely together as of the early 1950s. Goeritz took part in the Pedregal venture, contributing to the overall artistic aspect of the work, notably by creating sculptures such as the *Animal del Pedregal* (1951)—the open-jawed snake (made of brightly painted concrete) that guards the entrance to the residential site. Goeritz wanted to make Pedregal "an experimental atelier for all the arts". See Mathias Goeritz, 'El Arte en el Pedregal', typed document, undated (FATLB Archives).
15. Mathtas Goeritz explored the theme of tower structures in his *Aquí y allá* sculpture in 1955, and in the scheme for the Toxmico Towers in 1957. He continued to draw on the theme in numerous works until the 1980s. See *Los ecos de Mathias Goeritz,* exhibition catalogue, Antiguo Colegio de San Ildefonso, Mexico City, 1997.

Inca Walls at Ollantaytambo
1. Jean-Pierre Protzen, "Inca Quarrying and Stonecutting," *Journal of the Society of Architectural Historians* 44, no. 2 (May 1985)
2. George E. Squier, *Peru: Incidents of travel and exploration in the land of the Incas* (London: Macmillan).
3. Reference is made here to Map 552, Bingham Collection, Yale Univ.
4. John Hemming, and Edward Ranney, *Monuments of the Incas* (Boston: Brown Little, 1982), 103.
5. Susan Niles noted that: "the term *kancha* has a broad range of meaning in the Quechua, but it seems to be based on the notion of an enclosure of some sort" (Susan Niles, *Callachaca: Style and status in an Inca community* (Iowa City: University of Iowa Press, 1987, 46.) Llanos, for example, uses *cancha* in the sense of enclosure. In his 1936 report on the excavation at Ollantaytambo, the word designates enclosed courtyards as well as buildings. It is Rowe who introduces the term *kancha* to refer to compounds of up to six buildings arranged around the sides of the enclosure facing into a courtyard (Rowe, John Howland, "An Introduction to the Archaeology of Cuzco," *Papers of the Peabody Museum of American Archeology and Ethnology*, vol 27, no. 2. (Cambridge, Mass.: Harvard University, 1944) 24; Inca culture at the time of Spanish conquest. In Julian H. Steward, ed., *Handbook of South American Indians*, vol. 2, 183-330; Bureau of American Ethnology Bulletin, no 143 (Washington, D.C. 1946), 223) More recently, it seems that the term is used to designate two or more buildings facing each other across a courtyard, whether or not the configuration of buildings is surrounded by a wall (Jean-François Bouchard, *Contribution à l'étude de l'architecture Inca: Etablissements de la vallée du Rio Vilvanota-Urubamba. Cahiers d'archéologie et d'ethnologie d'Amérique du Sud.* (Paris Editions, de la Maison des Sciences de l'Homme, 1983); Niles, 1987).
6. Susan Niles, *Callachaca: Style and status in an Inca community* (Iowa City: University of Iowa Press, 1987), 208-209.
7. Gasparini and Margolies, following Valcárcel, refer to this type of building as a *masma* (Gaziano Gasparini, and Luise Margolies, *Inca Architecture.* Translated by Patricia J. Lyon. (Bloomington: Indiana University Press. 1980)).
8. Gaziano Gasparini, 1980, 190, fig. 179.
9. Nuñez del Prado, Oscar, La vivenda Inca actual. *Revista universitaria* (Cuzco), nos. 130-133: 320-324. Reprint. (1966-1967), 322-323.
10. Gibaja de Valencia, Arminda, Sequencia cronológica de Ollantaytambo. In Ann Kendall, ed., *Current archaeological projects in the central Andes: Some approaches and results*, 225-243. Proceeding of the Forty-fourth International Congress of Americanists, Manchester 1982. BAR International Series 210. Oxford: B.A.R.
11. Nuñez 1966-1967, 322.
12. John Howland Rowe, *Inca culture at the time of Spanish conquest.* In Julian H. Steward, ed., *Handbook of South American Indians*, vol. 2, 183-330. Bureau of American Ethnology Bulletin, no 143. Washington, D.C. (1946), 223-224.
13. Guaman Poma de Ayala, Felope, *El primer nueva cronica y buen gobierno* [1615]. Critical edition by John V. Murra and Rolena Adorno. Coleccion America Nuestra, America Antigua, no. 31 Mexico City: Siglo Veintiuno Editores (1980), 123.
14. John Howland Rowe, An account of the shrines of Cuzco. Ñawpa Pacha (Berkeley), no 17 (1979-1980), 104.
15. It is noteworthy that, if indeed quality of construction and architectural details are an indicator of status, high status at Ollantaytambo was given to the southern part of town.
16. Susan Niles, 1987, 207-232.
17. Juan de Betanzos, *Summa y narración de los Incas* [1551]. Transcription, notes, and prologue by Maria del Carmen Martin Rubio. (Madrid: Ediciones Atlas, 1987), 173.
18. Bernabé Cobo, *Historia del Nuevo Mundo* [1653]. Edited, with preliminary study, by Padre Francisco Mateos. *Biblioteca de Autores Españoles desde la Formación del Lenguaje hasta Nuestros Días*, vols. 91 and 92. (Madrid: Ediciones Atlas).

Schindler's Metaphysical Walls
1. R.M. Schindler, "A Cooperative Dwelling," *T-Square 2* (February 1932): 21.
2. R.M. Schindler, "Shelter or Playground," in Dr. Philip Lovell's column, "Care of the Body," for the *Los Angeles Times,* 2 May 1926, 26-27, reprinted in Sarnitz, *Schindler*, 46.
3. R.M. Schindler, "Modern Architecture: A Program" (1913), translated by Harry Francis Mallgrave, in Lionel March and Judith Sheine, eds., *R. M. Schindler: Composition and Construction* (London: Academy Editions, 1993), 12.

Ando's Ephemeral Concrete Walls
1. Tadao Ando,. "Light, Shadow, and Form: the Koshino House," *Via,* no. 11 (1990), reprinted in Tadao Ando, *Tadao Ando: Complete Works,* ed. Francesco Dal Co (London: Phaidon, 1996), 458.
2. Tadao Ando, "The wall as Territorial Delineation," *Tadao Ando: Buildings Projects Writings,* ed. Kenneth Frampton (New York: Rizzoli, 1984), 129.
3. Tadao Ando, "From Self-Enclosed Modern Architecture towards Universality" *Tadao Ando: Buildings Projects Writings*, ed. Kenneth Frampton (New York: Rizzoli, 1984), 140-141 (my italics).
4. Here the term "objecthood" is borrowed from Fried's momentous criticism on minimalism. Objecthood is "the condition of non-art" and, thereby, the antithesis of an art object in which meaning should be entirely present in the instance of an experience. Meaning under the condition of objecthood is never present, but incessantly delayed and haunted by other. Michael Fried, "Art and Objecthood," *Art and Objecthood: Essays and Reviews* (Chicago: University of Chicago Press, 1998), 148-172.

5. Ibid, 165
6. Donald Judd, in his "Specific Objects" (1965), conducted as attack on Clement Greenberg's interpretation of modernist painting which sees the edge of the canvas as defining the "arrangement of whatever is on and inside it." Judd took what Greenberg regarded as the paradigmatic essence of painting merely as "a conventional limit, literally a frame to exceed," and thus as an object, which is neither painting nor sculpture. Unlike Judd, Robert Morris, in his "Notes on Sculpture, Parts 1 and 2" (1966), accepted Greenberg's position on the autonomous aspect of late-modernism and simultaneously contended the existence of the literal quality in late-modernism. This double-binding of minimalism between autonomy and literalism, however contradictory it was, lends itself as the ground for minimalism for Morris. For him, literal qualities in minimalist sculptures become the very artistic strategy by which Greenberg's claim on autonomy can be fully accomplished. Despite the differences as to the genesis of minimalism between Judd and Morris, they shared the vision on specificity and literalness of a minimalist object. The ideas of "the specific object" and "the literal object" endowed with wholeness, singularity, and indivisibility are opposed to the representational illusionism as the ideological locus of anthropocentrism. They also reject the "part-by-part" compositional logic which they saw as evincing anthropomorphism. Fried's aforementioned idea of objecthood is based on these conditions of minimalists' objects. Ibid., 166; Hal Foster, *The Return of the Real* (Cambridge: MIT Press, 1996), 44; Donald Judd, "Specific Objects," *Complete Writings 1959-1975* (New York: New York University Press, 1975), 182; Robert Morris, "Notes on Sculpture," *Minimal Art: A Critical Anthology*, ed. Gregory Battcock (New York: E. Dutton, 1968), 223.
7. Tadao Ando 1996, 458.
8. Tsuyoshi Hiramatsu. *Hikari no Kyokai: Ando Tadao no Genba* (Tokyo: Kenchikushiryo kenkyusha, 2000), 243.
9. Tadao Ando, 1996, 458.

The Sculpted Walls of Richard Serra
1. The first two works are inventorised, described and shown in: *Emanuel Hoffmann Foundation.* Exhibition catalogue Museum für Gegenwartskunst (Basel, Basel 1991), 150ff. and 351ff.
2. This ambivalence plays an important role in discussions about Serra, from a number of different angles. For example, Armin Zweite refers to the "dichotomy between latent panic and rational control." cf. Armin Zweite. 'Evidenz und Selbsterfahrung. Zu einigen raumbezogenen Skulpturen von Richard Serra.' In: *Richard Serra.* Exhibition catalogue Westf lisches Landesmuseum für Kunst und Kulturgeschichte Münster, (Stuttgart 1987), 8-28 (especially p. 12).
3. The associated methodological problems cannot really be discussed here. They require an art historical approach that disposes of analytical procedures for determining the relationship between fact and effect, that is capable of critically verifying the type of experience against the work.
4. The sculptural space is the space within a sculpture that exerts its effect. On the subject of its determination and the differences as compared with geometric or physical concepts of space cf. Gottfried Boehm. 'Plastik und plastischer Raum'. In: *Skulptur Ausstellung in Münster.* Exhibition catalogue Land-schaftsverband Westfalen-Lippe und Stadt Münster, Greven 1977, Vol. I, 23-44.
5. These remarks may nonetheless be hoped to correspond to Serra's thoughts. cf. his comments in: *Richard Serra. Recent Sculpture in Europe 1986-1988.* Exhibition catalogue m Bochum Art Gallery, Bochum 1988, p. 80. "However, I can record the history of art as a history of the particularization of weight. I have ... more to say about the monuments of death, more to say about the weight and density and concreteness of countless sarcophagi, more to say about burial tombs, more to say about Michelangelo and Donatello, more to say about Mycenean and Incan architecture, more to say about the weight of the Olmec heads."
6. Allusion to the book by Lars Olof Larsson. *Von allen Seiten gleich schön. Studien zum Begriff der Vielansichtigkeit in der europäischen Plastik von der Renaissance bis zum Klassizismus.* (Stockholm 1974).
7. Cf. the above-mentioned essay by Armin Zweite (as in note 2, p.12) and Yve-Alain Bois, "Ein pittoresker Spaziergang um Clara-Clara herum," *Münster Exhibition catalogue* 1987, pp. 51ff.
8. Richard Serra, as in Note 5, 78.
9. Cf. Christine Pries (ed.), *Das Erhabene. Zwischen Grenzerfahrung und Größenwahn.* (Weinheim 1989), and Christine Pries. 'Königsberger Avantgarde, oder: Wie modern war Immanuel Kant?' In: Wolfgang Welsch and Christine Pries (eds.), *Ästhetik im Widerstreit. Interventionen zum Werk von Jean-François Lyotard* (Weinheim 1991), 155ff.
10. Cf. John P. O'Neill (ed.), *Barnett Newman. Selected Writings and Interviews* (Berkeley/Los Angeles 1990), 174.
11. Regarding the category of the existential, cf. Armin Zweite as in Note 2, 12: "One will hardly be able to get this instant of existential self-experience out of one's mind, although Serra in no way intended to construct a psychologically dramatic, highly charged space."
12. Cf. Max Imdahl. 'Serra's *Right Angle Prop* and *Dead:* Concrete Art and Paradigms'. In: *Richard Serra. Works 66-77,* Exhibition catalogue Kunsthalle Tübingen and Kunsthalle Baden-Baden (Tübingen 1978), 164 ff.
13. In his *Critique of Judgement,* Kant linked the experience of human freedom with the process of limitation set in motion by the sublime. On the subject of how the work of art's inherent iconoclasm affects this experience in the realm of aesthetics cf. Gottfried Boehm. 'Die Bilderfrage'. In: Gottfried Boehm (ed.), *Was ist ein Bild?* (Munich 1994), 343.

CHAPTER 3 | BEAMS & SLABS

Arresting Cantilever Deflections
none

Nordic Pavilion - An Illuminating Beam Matrix
1. See Per Olaf Fjeld, *Sverre Fehn: The Thought of Construction* (New York: Rizzoli, 1983); *Progressive Architecture,* vol. 75 (Feb. 1994); *l'Architecture d'aujourd'hui,* no. 287 (June 1993).
2. Sverre Fehn, 'Nordisk paviljong ved Biennalen i Venezia' in *Byggekunst,* no. 6, (1962): 145 (author's translation).
3. Ibid., 145.

The Kimbell's Beam Variations
Patricia Cummings Loud
1. Simon Boussiron's 1910 Goods Station at Berey, outside Paris, used vaulted shells of concrete to span a large, relatively open interior. See Nikolaus Pevsner, *Sources of Modern Architecture and Design* (London: Thames and Hudson, 1968): 161. Perret used more sophisticated versions in Casablanca and in the Ateliers de Decors in Paris (1923). See Bernard Champigneulle, *Perret* (Paris: Arts and Metiers Graphiques, 1959); plates 16 and 17. For a more detailed consideration of possible and likely sources for the Kimbell, ancient and modern, including Le Corbusier, see Loud, "History of the Kimbell Art Museum", 31-39.
2. Neil Levine has pointed out an analogy with the entrance to the Bibliotheque Sainte-Genevieve in Paris, where one proceeds to the reading room through the vestibule with trees painted on the walls—the groves of academia—echoes of gardens Henri Labrouste wished actually could have been accommodated on the site of the library. Conversation with the author.
3. Parnassus inspired Ferdinando de Medici in the scheme for the gardens of his villa, later the French Academy, in Rome. See Glenn M. Andres, *The Villa Medici in Rome* (New York: Garland, 1976), 291- 95.
4. Kahn, "I Love Beginnings," *Architecture and Urbanism* 2, special edition (1976): 279, 285. The text was originally an address to the Aspen Design Conference in 1973.
5. "Conversation with William Jordy" in Richard S. Wurman, *What Will Be Has Always Been: The Words of Louis I. Kahn* (New York: Access Press and Rizzoli, 1986): 238.
6. Marlin transcription, Kimbell Art Museum files; see n. 154.
7. Donald L. Hoffmann, "Light, Space and Structure in the Kimbell Art Museum," *Kansas City Star,* October 8, 1972. Hoffmann authored several articles and a book on John Welborn Root, *Meaning of Architecture: Buildings and Writings by John Welborn Root* (New York: Horizon Press, 1967). His articles include "Frank Lloyd Wright and Viollet-le-Duc," *Journal of the Society of Architectural Historians* 28 (October 1969): 173-82.

Paula Deitz
none

The Iron and Steel Beam Evolves; Mies Follows Suit
Rowland Mainstone
1. H. G. Graves, "Further notes on the early use of iron in India", *Journal of the Iron and Steel Institute,* vol. 85 (1912), 187-202.
2. W. B. Dinsmoor, "Structural iron in Greek architecture", *American Journal of Archaeology,* 2nd series, vol. 26, (1922), 148-158.
3. The architrave blocks of the Temple of Zeus at Agrigento – Dinsmoor's chief example – are all now on the ground. Close inspection in 1969 of as many as were accessible failed to disclose even significant rust stains, and certainly none of the splitting that the rusting of solid embedded iron beams would have caused. And neither here nor elsewhere could the supposed beams have functioned as efficient reinforcements: they were incorrectly placed and inadequately anchored at the ends to act as ties. See also the comments by Hamilton, S. B., 'The structural use of iron in antiquity', *Trans. NS,* vol. 31, (1957-59), 29-47; and by Jewett, R. A., 'Controversy', *Technology and Culture,* vol. 9, (1968), 419-426. Choisy *Histoire,* vol. 1, 279, suggested that the cuttings at Agrigento were filled with *'un paquet de fers plates poses de champ'*.
4. The development of iron beams is outlined in Hamilton, S. B., 'The use of cast iron in building', *Trans. NS,* vol. 21, (1940-41), 139-155; and, more definitively, in Skempton, A. W., 'The origin of iron beams', *Actes du VHI Congres Internationale d'Histoire des Sciences,* (Florence, 1956), 1029-1039; and Jewett, R. A., 'Structural antecedents of the I-beam, 1800-1850', *Technology and Culture,* vol. 8 (1967), 346-362. Among the contemporary published sources see particularly Fairbairn *Application,* and the works by Tredgold and Hodgkinson cited in the next two notes. See also Swailes, T., '19th century cast-iron beams: their design, manufacture and reliability', *Proc. ICE: Civil Engineering,* vol. 114 (1996), 25-35.
5. Thomas Tredgold, *A practical essay on the strength of cast iron,* London, 1822.
6. Eaton Hodgkinson., 'Theoretical and experimental researches to ascertain the strength and best form of iron beams', *Memoirs of the Manchester Literary and Philosophical Society,* 2nd series, vol. 5 (1831), 407-544.
7. Two such collapses were of a beam in a cotton mill in Manchester described in Fairbairn, W., 'On some defects in the principle and construction of fire proof buildings', *ProcICE,* vol. 6 (1847), 213-224, and of a span of Robert Stephenson's Dee Bridge shortly afterwards. The latter led to the setting up of a Royal Commission whose report, *Report into the application of iron,* sets out in detail the views of many leading engineers of the time. See also Sutherland, R. J. M., 'The introduction of structural wrought iron', *Trans. NS,* vol. 36 (1963-64), 67-84.
8. S. Barlow and G. Foster, 'Universal beams and their application', *SE,* vol. 35 (1957), 425-440.

Peter Blake
none

Chinese Building Traditions Meet Modernism
1. This article was inspired by a 2003 conference, *The Beaux-Arts, Paul P. Cret, and 20th Century Architecture in China,* organized by Jeffrey W. Cody, Nancy S. Steinhardt, Tony Atkin, and Xing Ruan and held at the University of Pennsylvania. Professors Wu Hung and Katherine Fischer Taylor responded to the early draft of the paper with constructive criticism. Since then many friends and colleagues have helped me with revisions, especially those undertaken to prepare this English version. Among them are Mrs. Lin Zhu, Drs. Elizabeth Grossman, Swati Chattopadhyay, Stephanie Fay, Wei-cheng Lin, Seng Kuan, Wenming Fei, Yudong Wang, Tonia Eckfeld, Cary Liu, Sun-

Chang Lo, Tracy Miller, Chia-Ling Yang, Doris Wai, Mary Byers, Mr. Mark Giorgini, Ms. Mira Rai, Miss Tianjian Lai, and an anonymous reviewer. *My* study of Liang Sicheng and the design of the National Central Museum in Nanjing has also benefited tremendously from the support of the Asian Cultural Council in New York and Mr. Zhou Jianmin and Ms. Cheng Guihong at the Archives of Nanjing Municipal Consttuction in Nanjing. I take this opportunity to thank all of those who have helped make this paper's publication possible. Liang Sicheng (Liang Ssu-Cheng), preface to Liang Ssu-Cheng, *A Pictorial History of Chinese Architecture: A Study on the Development of Its Structure System and Evolution of Its Types*, ed. Wilma Fairbank (Cambridge, Mass.: MIT Press, 1984), vol. 8 of *Liang Sicheng quanji* (Complete works of Liang Sicheng) (Beijing: Zhongguo Jianzhu Gongye Chubanshe, 2001), 207.

2. The National Central Museum is a large building compound. But in most architectural-historical writings today, the term refers only to its main hall because this hall was the key building in the design that embodied all the requirements of architectural style in the competition program. It was also the part that the architects and Liang concentrated on in modifying the design. Because the focus of this paper is the form of the museum, my use of this term will also be limited to this hall.

3. Liang was repeatedly criticized for his revivalist ideas in China's political movements, from the 1950s until his death, and most Chinese still identify his work, and Liang himself, with the "big roof," even though they may not know of his involvement in the design of the National Central Museum in Nanjing in the 1930s.

4. Pan Guxi, ed., *Zhongguo Jianzhu Shi* (Hiscory of Chinese architecture) (Beijing: ZhongguoJianzhu Gongye Chubanshe, 2001), 382-83.

5. Yang Yongsheng and Gu Mengchao, eds., *Ershi Shiji Zhongguo Jianzhu* (Architecture of twentieth-century China) (fianjin: Tianjin Kexue Jishu Chubanshe, 1999), 207-8.

6. Liu Dingming, comp., "Guoli Zhongyang Bowuyuan Choubeichu 1933nian 4yue-1941nian 8yue choubei jingguo baogao" (The report of the Preparatory Committee of the National Central Museum on Its Work from April 1933 to August 1941), *Minguo Dang'an* (Republican archives), no. 2 (2008), 27-33.

7. "Guoli Zhongyang BowuyuanJianzhu Weiyuanhui ZhengxuanJianzhu Tu'an Zhangcheng" (the guidelines of the Architectural Committee of the National Central Museum for the design competition), in *Guoli Zhongyang Bowuyuan Jianzhu Weiyuanhui Jianzhu Tu'an Shencha Weiyuanhui Baogao* (the report on architectural design by the jury under the Preparatory Committee of the National Central Museum) (Nanjing: Guoli Zhongyang Bowuyuan Jianzhu Wciyuanhui, 1935), 1.

8. Ibid.

9. Wilma Fairbank, *Liang and Lin: Partners in Exploring China's Architectural Past* (Philadelphia: University of Pennsylvania Press, 1994), 23-30.

10. Liang Sicheng, *Qingshi yingzao zeli* (Qing structural regulations) (Beiping: SRCA, 1934), in *Liang Sicheng quanji,* vol. 6 (see note 1).

11. *Yingzao fashi (YZFS;* State building standards) is the oldest existing Chinese technical manual on building construction. It was compiled for Li Jie (Li Chieh) in 1100, published by the Northern Song government in 1103, and enforced in 1104. For a general introduction to this book, see Else Glahn, "Unfolding the Chinese Building Standards: Research on the *Yingzao fashi"* in *Chinese Traditional Architecture,* ed. Nancy Shatzman Steinhardt (New York: China Institute in America, 1984), 48-57. For biographical information on Li Jie, see Else Glahn, "Li Chieh," in *Sung Biographies,* ed. Herbert Franke (Wiesbaden: Steiner, 1976), 2:523-29. According to a study by the Chinese scholar Cao Xun, "Jie" should be "Cheng," which corresponds to Li's courtesy name. See Cao, *"Yingzao fashi* Chongning ben- Wei jinian Li Cheng *Yingzao fashi* kanxing 900 zhounian er zuo" (the Chongning edition of *Yingzao fashi*-In commemoration of the nine-hundredth anniversary of *Yingzaofashi* by Li Cheng*), fianzhushi* 108 (April 2004), 90-100. On Zhu Qiqian, his discovery and republication of *Yingzao fashi,* his establishment of the Society for Research in Chinese Architecture, and the study of *Yingzao fashi* by Liang Sicheng and his colleagues in the society, see Lin Zhu, *Koukai Lu Bandt damm: Zhongguo Ymgzao Xueshe shilue* (Opening the door of Lu Ban: A brief history of the Society for Research in Chinese Architecture) (Beijing, 1995); Shiqiao Li, "Reconstituting Chinese Building Tradition: The *Ymgzao fashi* in the Early Twentieth Century," *JSAH* 62 (December 2003), 470-89.

12. *Liang Sicheng, preface to Jianzhu sheji cankao tuji* (Pictorial references for architectural design), vol. 1 (Beping: SRCA, 1935)*,* in *Liang Sicheng quanji,* 6:233-36.

13. "Guoli Zhongyang BowuyuanJianzhu Weiyuanhui ZhengxuanJianzhu Tu'an Zhangcheng," in *Guoli Zhongyang Bowuyuan Jianzhu Weiyuanhui Jianzhu Tu'an Shencha Weiyuanhui Baogao, 8.*

14. "Guoli Zhongyang BowuyuanJianzhu Weiyuanhui ZhengxuanJianzhu Tu'an Shencha Weiyuanhui Baogao," in *Guoli Zhongyang Bowuyuan Jianzhu Weiyuonhui Jionzhu Tu'an Shencha Weiyuanhui Baogao*, 1- 7.

15. Ibid., 3. On Liang as "special member," see the text at n. 7.

16. These drawings are preserved in the archives of the museum (now Nanjing Museum) and Nanjing Chengshi Jianshe Dang'anguan (Archives of Nanjing Municipal Construction). For help in translating the Liao and Song architectural terminology from Chinese to English, I thank Nancy Shatzman Steinhardt and her pioneering work in her book *Liao Architecture* (Honolulu: University of Hawaii Press, 1997).

17. Chen Mingda, Cheng Mingda jianzhu yu diaoke shilun (Essays by Chen Mingda on ancient architecture and sculpture) (Beijing: Wenwu Chubanshe, 1998), 215-16.

18. Liang Sicheng, *Zhongguojionzhu shi* (A history of Chinese architecture), in *Liang Sicheng quanji,* 4:216.

19. Gin-djih Su (Xu Jingzhi), *Chinese Architecture-Past and Contemporary* (Hong Kong: Sin Poh Amalgamated, 1964), 136.

20. Lu Haiming and Yang Xinhua, eds., *Nanjing Minguo jiangzhu* (Architecture of the Republican period in Nanjing) (Nanjing: Nanjing University Press, 2001), 127-32.

21. Liang Sicheng, "Zhongguo jianzhu de tezheng" (Characteristics of Chinese architecture), *Jianzhu xuebao,* no. 1 (January 1954), 36-39, in *Liang Sicheng quanji,* 5:179-84.

22. As a matter of fact, this Beaux-Arts notion is also visible in Sir Banister Fletcher's *History of Architecture on the Comparative Method,* where the "comparative" part of each chapter discusses plans, or the "composition," and walls, openings, roofs, columns, moldings, and ornament, or the "elements."

23. Liang, "Jixian Dulcsi Guanyinge, Shanmen kao" (see n. 27), 88. Translation mine.

24. For more on the issue of classical orders and the analogy in Chinese architecture, see Zhao Chen, "'Minzu zhuyi' yu 'gudian zhuyi'-Liang Sicheng jianzhu lilun tixi de maodunxing yu beijuxing zhi fenxi" (Nationalism and classicism—An analysis of the contradiction and tragedy of Liang Sicheng's architectural theory), in *Zhongguo jindai jianzhu yanjiu yu baohu,* ed. Zhang Fuhe (Beijing: Tsinghua University Press, 2001), 2:77-86; Li, "Writing a Modern Chinese Architectural History," (sec n. 54); Lai Delin, "Liang Sicheng, Lin Huiyin Zhongguo jianzhushi xiezuo biaowei" (A historiographical study of Liang Sicheng and Lin Huiyin's writings on Chinese architectural history) *21st Century,* no. 64 (April 2001), 90-99.

25. Liang, *A Pictorial History of Chinese Architecture* (see n. 1), 225.

26. Liang, "Baodi Guangjisi Sandashidian" (see n. 26), 272. Translation mine.

27. Liang, "Jixian Dulesi Guanyinge, Shanmen kao" (see n. 27), 169. Translation mine.

28. For instance, Liang's Penn colleague Tong Jun (Tung Chuin), who received his master of architecture degree in 1928, held the view that material ingenuity is a positive value in architecture. He criticized "Chinese revival" architecture in 1945: "The only similarity between the Chinese wooden construction system and the reinforced-concrete method is their structural principle, which is frame-like rather than case-like. In terms of the cost-effectiveness of materials, however, the optimal span of a wooden frame is only half that of the steel one. Hence the proportions of all the elements will be totally different. Judging from the size of the elements alone, to imitate the palatial structure with reinforced concrete is a waste, and [the palatial structure thus] should not be taken as a model. Moreover, it will coat what is already a sufficient number of concrete beams and columns with paint, and cover what is already a sufficient number of roof terraces with tiles. Indeed, it can hardly be called rational." See Tong, "Woguo gonggong jianzhu waiguan de jiantao" (Rethinking the appearance of the public buildings in our country), *Neizheng zhuankan* 1 (October 1945), in Tong, *Tong Jun wenji* (Collected works of Tong Jun) (Beijing: Zhongguo Jianzhu Gongye Chubanshe, 2000), 1:118-21. Translation mine.

29. Liang, *Zhongguo jianzhu shi* (see n. 18), 107. Translation mine.

30. Liang, *A Pictorial History of Chinese Architecture* (see n. 1), 228.

31. Chen, Cheng Mingdajianzhuyu diaoke shilun (see n. 17), 215-16.

32. Liang and Liu, "Datong gujianzhu diaocha baogao" (see n. 23), 15:5-57. Translation mine.

33. Ibid., 157.

34. Ernst Boerschmann, *Chinesische Architektur* (Berlin: Verlag Ernst Wasmuth, 1925), 2:49, quoted in W. Perceval Yetts, "Writings on Chinese Architecture," *SRCA Bulletin* l, no. 1 (July 1930), 1-8.

35. Lin, "Zhongguo jianzhu de jige tezheng" (see n. 37), 163-79. Translation mine. Lin must have acquired this functional view of the roof in Chinese architecture from James Fergusson. See James Fergusson, *Illustrated Handbook of Architecture: Being a Concise and Popular Account of the Different Styles of Architecture Prevailing in All Ages and Countries* (London: John Murray, 1855), 140.

36. Lin, preface to Liang, *Qingshi yingzao zeli* (see n. 10), 23. Translation mine.

37. Liang, *Zho1lgguo jianzhu shi* (see n. 18), 216. Translation mine.

38. Su, *Chinese Architecture* (see n. 19), 136.

39. Hu Shih, *Chinese Renaissance* (Chicago: University of Chicago Press, 1934); Hu Shih, *Hu Shih koushu zizhuan* (An oral autobiography of Hu Shih), ed. and trans. Tang Degang (Taipei: Zhuanji Wenxuc Chubanshc, 1981), 165-79; Geng Yunzhi, *Hu Shi rinlun* (A new look at Hu Shi) (Changsha: Hunan Chubanshe, 1996), 66.

40. Zhao Shen, "Fakan ci" (Forward the journal), *Zhongguo jianzhu* (Chinese architecture), preview issue (November 1932), 1.

41. Lai Delin, "Zhezhong beihou de linian-Yang *T*ingbao jianzhu de bili wen ti yanjiu" (An ideal underlying eclectic design: A study on the proportions of Yang Tingbao's architecture), *Ytshushi yanjiu* 4 (2002), 445-64; Delin Lai, "Searching for a Modern Chinese Monument: The Design of the Sun Yat-sen Mausoleum in Nanjing," *JSAH* 64, no. 1 (March 2005), 22-55.

42. Chen Mingda once said that the goal of the society was "to find the [doctrines of] ancient Chinese architecture." Chen, *Cheng Mingdajianzhu yu diaoke shilun* (see n. 17), 215-16.

43. As a matter of fact, with the exception of Jianzhen Memorial (Yangzhou, 1963), which commemorated the Tang dynasty monk Jianzhen and was designed in the Tang style Liang had learned from his study of the main hall of Foguang Monastery, Liang's other designs did not emphasize stylistic purity. In 1954 he proposed the idea of "architectural translatability" *(jianzhu keyilun)* in the design of a Chinese-style architecture. He suggested that by substituting Chinese architectural elements for the corresponding Western elements of a Western-style building, the Western style could become Chinese. This idea, which demonstrated the influence of the Beaux-Arts dichotomy between "composition" and "elements," was exhibited in numerous designs after the 1870s. See Lai Delin, "Liang Sicheng 'jianzhu keyilun' zhiqian de Zhongguo shijian" (Architectural translation and the notion of architectural translatability in modern China), *Jianzhushi* 137 (February 2009), 22-30; "Goutu yu yaosu-xueyuanpai laiyuan yu Liang Sicheng 'wenfa-cihui' biaoshu ji Zhongguo xiandai jianzhu" (Composition and Elements: The Beaux-Arts origin and Liang Sicheng's "grammar and vocabularies" study of Chinese architecture and its influence on modern Chinese architecture), *Jianzhusi* 142 (December 2009), 55-64; Li Hua, "Cong Buza de zhishi jiegou kan 'xin' er 'Zhong' de jianzhu shijian" ("A 'new' and 'Chinese' architecture in relation to the Beaux-Arts tradition as a system of knowledge"), in *Zhongguo jianzhu 60 nian* (1949-2009): *Lishi lilun yanjiu* (Sixty years of Chinese architecture [1949-2009]: History, theory, and criticism), ed. Jianfei Zhu (Beijing: Zhongguo Jianzhu Gongye Chubanshe, 2009), 33-45.

Nervi's Isostatically Inspired Ribbed Floors

1. D. Friedman, *Historical Building Construction: Design, Materials, and Technology*, 2nd Ed (W.W. Norton & Co, 2010), 1-320.

2. B. Addis, *Building: 3000 Years of Design, Engineering and Construction* (Phaidon Press, 2007), 1-608.

3. T. Jori, *150 anni di storia del cemento in Italia: Le opere, gli uomini, le imprese*, (Gangemi Editore, 2011), 1-240.

4. R. Gulli, *Struttura e costruzione – Structure and construction* (Firenze University Press, 2008), 1-188.

5. S. Poretti, *Le plancher en poteries et béton dans le modernisme italien, L 'architrave le plancher la plate-forme: Nouvelle histoire de la construction,* Ed. Roberto Gargiani (Presses polytechniques et universitaires romandes, 2012), 703-709.

6. L. Sorrentino, "The Early Entrance of Dynamics in Earthquake Engineering: Arturo Danusso's Contribution," *ISET J. Earthquake Tech.* , Vol. 44, No. 1 (2007), 1-24.

7. F. Levi, and M.A. Chiorino, "Concrete in Italy. A review of a century of concrete progress in Italy, Part 1: Technique and

architecture," *Concrete Int*, Vol. 26, No. 9 (2004), 55-61.
8. C. Greco, Muggia e Nervi, Il Fecondo e Complesso Rapporto tra un Grande Maestro e un Discepolo Illustre, *Attilio Muggia: una storia per gli ingegneri*, Ed. Bettazzi, M.B. and Lipparini, (Editrice Compositori, 2010), 211-219.
9. C. Pourtois, Biography, *Pier Luigi Nervi: Architecture as Challenge*, Eds. C. Olmo, and C. Chiorino, (Silvana Editoriale, 2010), 201-209.
10. T. Iori, and S. Poretti, Pier Luigi Nervi's Works for the 1960 Rome Olympics. *Actas del Cuarto Congreso Nacional de Historia de la Construccion*, 2005, 605-613.
11. C. Chiorino, "Eminent Structural Engineer: Pier Luigi Nervi (1891-199) - Art and Science of Building," *Struct Eng Int*, No. 1 (2010), 107-109.
12. P.L. Nervi, *Structures*, Trans. G. Salvadori, and M. Salvadori, (F.W. Dodge Corp., 1956), 1-118.
13. P.L. Nervi, *Aesthetics and Technology in Building*, (Harvard University Press, 1965), 1-210.
14. T. Iori, Le plancher a nervures isostatiques de Nervi, *L 'architrave le plancher la plateforme: Nouvelle histoire de la construction*. Ed. R. Gargiani (Presses polytechniques et universitaires romandes, 2012), 755-760.
15. J.W. Dally, and W.F. Riley, *Experimental Stress Analysis*, 3rd Ed., (McGraw-Hill, 1991), 1-639.
16. H.T. Jessop, and F.C. Harris, *Photoelasticity: Principles & Methods*. (Dover Publications, Inc., 1950), 1-184.
17. C. Broniewska, and M.S. Mitra, Photoelastic Method for Stress Analysis, *Symposium on Industrial Failure of Engineering Metals & Alloys* (1953), 266-275.
18. R.B. Heywood, *Photoelasticity for designers* (Pergamon Press, 1969), 1-435.
19. A. Kuske, Photo-elastic Research on Plates in Transverse Bending, *Engineering* (1953), 20-39.
20. J.N. Goodier, and G.H. Lee, "An Extension of the Photoelastic Method of Stress Measurement to Plates in Transverse Bending," *Trans. Amer. Soc. Mech. Eng.*, Vol. 63 (1941), A27-A29.
21. H.M. Westergaard, and W.A. Slater, "Moments and Stresses in Slabs," *Proc. ACI*, vol. 17 (1921), 1-124.
22. S. Timoshenko, *Theory of Plates and Shells* (McGraw-Hill, 1959), 1-492.
23. C. Chiorino, "The Palazzo del Lavoro," *Pier Luigi, Nervi: Architecture as Challenge*, eds. C. Olmo, and C. Chiorino (Silvana Editoriale, 2010), 168-173.
24. P.L. Nervi, *New Structures* (Architectural Press, 1963), 1-167.

Maillart Minimalism: The Flat Slab Emerges

1. This investigation appeared in its original form in *Circle, International Survey of Constructive Art,* edited by J. L. Martin, Ben Nicholson, and N. Gabo (London, 1937), 220-236. It was published there under the title "Construction and Aesthetics" (English version by P. Morton Shand).
2. Although the first of his bridges have stood firmly up to the present day, and their adequacy for their purpose has long since ceased to be questioned, they still continue to arouse antagonism among local bodies, many of which regard them as positively hideous. It happened that most were built across remote Alpine valleys, where they were considerably cheaper to erect than other types and (an equally important consideration) where comparatively few people would see them. The stark, lean assurance of their construction belies the aesthetic lights of a wide section of the public through its elimination of emphasis on means of support and through the taut, weblike appearance of the arch-spans which results. "I am sick of these puff-pastry bridges" was the way the chairman of one of these local bodies expressed his aversion. This remark is worth mentioning, since it shows what an influence aesthetic feelings exercise alike on those who commission the building of bridges and those who merely chance to look at them, and how often these feelings are the secret determining factor of decisions apparently dictated solely by questions of cost and efficiency.
3. Early in his career Maillart was the engineer in charge of the construction of a sanatorium in ferroconcrete at Davos for which Hennebique was the contractor.
4. The first specifically architectural endorsements of this principle did not occur until twenty years after Maillart's initial experiments. Brinckmann and van der Vlugt's splendid van Nelle factory in Rotterdam (1927-28) is the outstanding example, although it embodies the ponderous American type of mushroom-headed columns.
5. The problem of bridging mountain gorges with curved spans occurs in every mountainous country. When girders and arches were used in the ordinary fashion the bridge must be held to a rigidly straight line. At most, a curve can be produced by building the approaches in staggered sections, as in the Rainbow Bridge near Carmel, California.
6. Cf. the strangely formed pillars of the Arve bridge.

Concrete Takes Flight

1. Even so, the casual accumulation of its masses has been cited—by the collaborators on the South Bank Center, for example—as the formal inspiration for other truth-to-materials complexes.
2. For a full description of the internal structure, see Peter Guillery, *The Buildings of London Zoo* (London: Royal Commission on the Historical Monuments of England, 1993), 58–63. Some of the interior caverns were suited as reservoirs to collect water that, after filtration, served the waterfowl below.
3. The *Essai* by Marc Antoine Laugier, published anonymously in 1753, was republished two years later with plates, including the famous frontispiece by Charles Eisen of the architectural "primitive hut" and its constituent elements: the column, entablature, and pediment. See Marc Antoine Laugier, *Essai sur l'architecture* (Paris: Duchesne, 1775; reprint, Los Angeles: Hennessey & Ingalls, 1977).
4. This structure has the distinction of being their very first commission as a firm. Despite initial satisfaction, there have since been problems with it for housing gorillas.
5. Originally an Antarctic breed, then the black-footed African "jackass" penguin.
6. John Allan, *Architecture and the Tradition of Progress* (London: RIBA Publications, 1992), 211.
7. The performative aspect of the pool was noted in *The Architects' Journal:* "The two cantilevered ramps have a theatrical quality and provide a suitable stage for the waddling gait of the penguins, who are shown to be able to hop as well as waddle. The pond, in fact, explains the characteristics of the penguins and 'produces' them effectively to the public." "Penguin Pool Zoological Gardens: Lubetkin, Drake and Tecton," *The Architects' Journal* 79 (14, June 1934): 856–858. See Pyrs Gruffudd, "Biological Cultivation: Lubetkin's Modernism at the London Zoo in the 1930s," in *Animal Spaces, Beastly Places: New Geographies of Human-Animal Relations,* ed. Chris Philo and Chris Wilbert (London: Routledge, 2000), 222–242.
8. "Animals served to animate [Lubetkin's] mathematically precise volumes connected by harmonious curves of concrete, a substance he mastered to perfection. ... Lubetkin favored animals that enhanced his aesthetic: the black and white of the penguins put the finishing touch to his dramatic composition, described by Paul Morand as a 'concrete island decorated with penguins.'" See Eric Baratay and Elisabeth Hardouin-Fugier, *Zoo: A History of Zoological Gardens in the West,* trans. Oliver West (London: Reaktion Books, 2002) 254.

Floor Plate–Defined Façades

none

CHAPTER 4 | TRUSSES

La Tour Eiffel: A Truss, and More...

1. The introductory quotation is an excerpt from the 'artists' protest', which was published in *Le temps* on 14 February 1887.

Truss Forms and Style Battles

1. S.C.A.B., "L'Emulation (9ième année)", 1884.
2. A. Vierendeel, *L'architecture métallique au XIXe siecle et L'exposition de 1889, à Paris*. (Bruxelles: Librairie Scientifique, Industrielle et Agricole E. Ramlot, 1890).
3. S. Giedion, *Building in France, building in iron, building in ferro-concrete*. (Canada: The Getty Center for the History of Art and Humanities, 1995).
4. S.C.A.B., "L'Emulation (18ième année)", 1893.
5. P. Combaz, *La construction: principes et applications* (Bruxelles: E. Lyon-Claesen, 1897).
6. M. de Bouw, *Brussels Model Schools - Structural Analysis of the Metal Roof Trusses*. (Brussels: VUBPress (doctoral thesis), 2010).
7. T. Demey, *Geschiedenis van de Brusselse scholen*. (Brussel: Ministerie van het Brussels Hoofdstedelijk Gewest, 2005).
8. R. Reyns, *De lagere school in België, van de middeleeuwen tot nu* (Brussel: ASLK- Galerij, 1987).
9. M. de Bouw, Wouters, I., Lauriks, L., Forty Years of de Dion Trusses in Nineteenth Century Brussels Model Schools. In: *Proceedings of the Third International Congress on Construction History*, Cottbus, 20-24 May 2009, ed. by K.-E. Kurrer, W. Lorenz and V. Wetzk (Berlin: NEUNPLUS1 Verlag+Service GmbH, 2009), 437-444.
10. G. Nieuwmeijer, Polonceau-spanten. *Monumenten* 11 (2001), 20-23.
11. C. Schädlich, Der Baustoff Eisen als Grundlage fiir die Herausbildung qualitativ neuer Baukonstruktionen im 19 Jahrhundert. In: *Zur Geschichte des Konstruierens*, ed. by R. Graefe, (Stuttgart: Deutsche Verlags-Anstalt (OVA), 1989), 138-151.
12. C. Holzer, "The Polonceau Roof and its Analysis," *International Journal for the History of Engineering and Technology*, Vol. 80 no. 1 (2010), 22- 54.
13. S. Holzer, Vom Einfluss des Analysewerkzeugs auf die Modellbildung - Zur statischen Analyse des Wiegmann-Polonceau-Trägers in der 2. Hälfte des 19. Jahrhunderts. Bautechnik 83 (2006), No 6, 428-434.
14. H. Dechamps, Les principes de la construction de charpentes métalliques, (Liège: Imprirnerie H. Vaillant-Carmanne, 1888).
15. A. Vierendeel, *La construction architecturale en fonte, fer et acier*. (Brussel-Leuven-Parijs, 1902).
16. B. Lemoine, *L'architecture du fer - France: XIXe siècle*. (Seyssel: Champ Vallon, 1986).
17. Steiner, F. H., *French iron architecture* (Michigan: UMI Research Press, 1984).
18. P. Ardant, *Etudes théoriques et expérimentales sur l'établissement des charpentes à grande portée*. (Metz: S. Lamort, 1840).
19. S. Holzer, "Der Bogen im Dach - Zur Entwicklung des weitgespannten Daches 1770-1840 unter dem Einfluss des frühen Bauingenieurwesens," *Bautechnik* 84 (2007), No. 2, 130-146.

Truss Forms and Design Collaborations

1. Ernst Cassirer, *Form and Technik* (Form and technology) (1930).
2. Diverse publications, beginning with: Le Corbusier, *Vers une architecture* (Paris: Cres, 1923); Werner Lindner, *Die Ingenieurbauten in ihrer guten Gestaltung* (Berlin: Wasmuth, 1923); Erich Mendelsohn, *Amerika—Bilderbuch eines Architekten* (Berlin: Rudolf Mosse, 1926).
3. Buckminster Fuller, quoted on Reyner Banham, *Theory and Design in the First Machine Age*, (Cambridge, MA: MIT Press, 1964), 114.
4. A synopsis of Buckminster Fuller's influence on the English technology movement is found in: Carsten Krohn, *Buckminster Fuller und die Architekten* (Berlin: Dietrich Reimer, 2004).
5. On design and structure of the Centre Pompidou, see: Renzo Piano. *The Renzo Piano Logbook* (London: Thames and Hudson, 1997); and Peter Rice, "Beaubourg," in: Peter Rice, *An Engineer Imagines* (London: Artemos, 1994).
6. Peter Rice, "Beaubourg," in: Peter Rice, *An Engineer Imagines,* 29f.
7. Peter Rice, "The Role of the Engineer," in: Peter Rice, *An Engineer Imagines,* 78f.
8. Peter Rice, "Instabile Strukturen," in: *Arch+,* no. 124/125 (1994).
9. Cecil Balmond, *Informal* (London: Prestel, 2002).
10. For design and structure of the ZKM, see: Rem Koolhaas, Bruce Mau, *S,M,L,XL*, (New York: Monacelli Press, 1995), 666ff.
11. "Musik als Ouelle der Inspiration—ein Gespräch mit Cecil Balmond," in: *Detail,* no. 12, (2005).
12. Cecil Balmond, *Informal,* 109f.
13. Cecil Balmond, "Informelles Konstruieren," in: *Arch+,* no. 117, (1993).
14. Claude Lévi-Strauss, *The Savage Mind* (Chicago: University of Chicago Press, 1968).
15. Peter Rice, "Glass and Polycarbonate," in: *Peter Rice. An Engineer Imagines* (London: Artemis, 1994).
16. Cecil Balmond, "Congrexpo—oder 'das Ei' on Lille," in: *Arch+* no. 124/125, (1994).
17. Peter Rice, "Sydney," in: *Peter Rice, An Engineer Imagines* (London, 1994), 63.
18. Some issues in the controversy over authorship are addressed in: Jennifer Kabat, "The Informalist," *Wired,* no. 9.04, (2001).

Neimeyer's Subtly Deceptive Trusses

none

Metabolism and the Space Frame

1. Coverage of the Osaka Expo can be found in *Architectural Review* (Aug. and Oct. 1970). *Architectural Record* (June 1970), *Architectural*

Design (June 1970), *Progressive Architecture* (Aug. 1970). *Architectural Forum* (Apr. 1970), *Bauwelt* (May 1970), *Architecture d'aujourd'hui* (Oct/Nov. 1970), *Canadian Architect* (July 1970), *Japan Architect* (Apr. 1969 and May/June 1970), among others.
2. Kenzo Tange and Noboru Kawazoe, "Some Thoughts about Expo '70," *Japan Architect* (May/June 1970): 34. *Chugoku* is the westernmost part of the main Japanese island, *Honshu.*
3. Takabumi Sasaki, "A Passage through the Dystopia of Expo '70," *Japan Architect (May/June* 1970), 145.
4. Kenzo Tange, "The Expo '70 Master Plan and Master Design," *Japan Architect* (May/June, 1970), 18.
5. This seminar was considered a significant event in postwar Japanese architecture, igniting young architects' enthusiasm in new building technologies. Hajime Yatsuka and Hideki Yoshimatsu, *Metaborizumu: 1960 nendai no Nihon kenchiku avangaruto (Metabolism: Japanese Architectural Avant-garde of the 1960s)* (Tokyo: Inax Publishing Co, 1997), 11. For Wachsmann's theory, see Konrad Wachsmann, *The Turning Point of Building: Structure and Design,* trans. Thomas E. Burton (New York, Reinhold, 1961).
6. Friedman founded the Groupe d'Etudes d'Architecture Mobile in 1958 to advocate his idea of mobile architecture. Among its members were David Georges Emmerich, Camille Frieden, Gunter Günschel, Oskar Hansen, Jean Pierre Pecquet, Eckhard Schulze-Fielitz, and Werner Ruhnau. For the latest study regarding Friedman and GEAM's works, see Larry Busbea, *Topologies. The Urban Utopias in France, 1960-1970* (Cambridge, MA: MIT Press, 2007).
7. Taro Okamoto created three sculptures for the Festival Plaza: the Tower of the Sun, the Tower of Motherhood, and the Tower of Youth. The Tower of the Sun is the only major piece preserved after the Expo when the site was turned into an Expo Park.
8. Mildred F. Schmertz, "Expo '70," *Architectural Record* (June 1970): 119.

Tensegrity and the Architecture of Life
none

CHAPTER 5 | FRAMES

To Frame – or not to Frame...
1. Louis H. Sullivan, *Autobiography of an Idea,* (New York, 1924), 314.
2. Montgomery Schuyler, "A Critique of the Works of Adler and Sullivan," *Architectural Record* (1895). Reprinted in Schuyler, *American Architecture and Other Writings,* ed. William Jordy and Ralph Coe (Cambridge, 1961), 377-79.
3. Henry Russell Hitchcock, *In the Nature of Materials,* (New York: Duen, Sloan and Pearce. 1942), 68.
4. Quoted in Schuyler, "A Critique," 381.
5. Schuyler, "A Critique," 381.
6. Harriet Monroe, *John Root* (New York, 1968). 107.
7. Siegfried Giedion. *Space, Time and Architecture* (Cambridge, 1941), 215.

8. Sullivan, *Autobiography of an Idea,* 312-13.
9. Schuyler, "A Critique," 382.
10. Le Corbusier. *Towards a New Architecture* (London, 1927), 33.

Framing Views, Framing Victory
1. For the building, see Tasos Tanoulas, "The Propylaea and the Western Access of the Acropolis," in *Acropolis Restoration: The CCAM Interventions,* ed. Richard Economakis (London: Academy Editions, 1994), 53-67; Tasos Tanoulas and Maria Ioannidou, Μελέτη ἀποκαταστάσεως τών προπυλαίων (Athens: Ministry of Culture, 2002); Tanoulas, Τά Προπύλαια*;* Jeffrey M. Hurwit, *The Athenian Acropolis: History, Mythology, and Archaeology from the Neolithic Era to the Present* (Cambridge: Cambridge University Press, 1999), 192. Plutarch in *Life of Perikles,* 13.7 names Mnesikles as the architect of the Propylaia; in the same passage he notes that the Propylaia was brought to completion in five years. For the Mnesiklean Propylaia, see William Bell Dinsmoor, Jr., *The Propylaia to the Athenian Akropolis, Vol. 2: The Classical Building* (Princeton: American School of Classical Studies at Athens, 2004). For Mnesikles, see Jens Andreas Bundgaard, *Mnesicles: A Greek Architect at Work* (Copenhagen: Gyldendal, 1957); see also Richard Allan Tomlinson, "The Sequence of Construction of Mnesikles' Propylaia," *Annual of British School at Athens* 85 (1990), 405-13.
2. See Demosthenis Giraud, "The Greater Propylaia at Eleusis, a Copy of Mnesikles' Propylaia," in *The Greek Renaissance in the Roman Empire: Papers from the Tenth British Museum Classical Colloquium,* ed. Susan Walker and Averil Cameron (London: University of London, Institute of Classical Studies, 1989), 69-75; Demosthenis G. Ziro, ʽΗ κύρια εἴσοδος τοῦ ἱεροῦ τῆς ʽἘλευσίνος (Athens: Athens Archaeological Society, 1991), 131-276; see also John Tavlos, *Pictorial Dictionary of Ancient Athens* (New York: Praeger, 1971), 482-93, with earlier bibliography. The general plan of the sanctuary at Eleusis in the second century CE is generally attributed to the Emperor Hadrian, though no explicit evidence associating him with the plan of the entrance forecourt survives. Pausanias's visit to the sanctuary at Eleusis in 160 CE provides a clear terminus post quem.
3. Hurwit, *The Athenian Acropolis,* 192.
4. For the Panathenaic festival, see Jenifer Neils, ed., *Goddess and Polis: The Panathenaic Festival in Ancient Athens* (Princeton: Princeton University. Press, 1992); Jenifer Neils, ed., *Worshipping Athena: Panathenaia and Parthenon* (Madison: University of Wisconsin Press, 1996); for the Panathenaic games, see Jenifer Neils and Stephen V. Tracy, ΤΟΝ ΑΘΕΝΕΘΕΝ ΑΘΛΟΝ*: The Games at Athens* (Excavations in the Athenian Agora, Picture Book 25) (Athens: American School of Classical Studies, 2003); see also Julia Louise Shear, "Polis and Panathenaia: The History and Development of Athena's Festival" (PhD diss., University of Pennsylvania, 2001).
5. Robin Francis Rhodes, *Architecture and Meaning on the Athenian Acropolis* (Cambridge: Cambridge University Press, 1995), 54.
6. Donald Preziosi, *Rethinking Art History: Meditations on a Coy Science* (New Haven: Yale University Press, 1989), 177- 78.
7. Gorham Phillips Stevens, "The Periclean Entrance Court of the Acropolis of Athens," *Hesperia* 5 (1936), facing 443.
8. Published in John M. Camp, *The Archaeology of Athens* (New Haven: Yale University Press, 2001), 83, fig. 76.
9. For succinct overviews, see Hurwit, *The Athenian Acropolis,* 192-97; Camp, *The Archaeology of Athens,* 82-90.
10. The presumption that Greek sanctuaries, as well as cities, grew haphazardly and without reference to a methodical plan is ripe for reappraisal. A highly organized site is not necessarily contingent upon formal, geometric planning, but instead can be orientated toward a higher, ethical order. For a fuller discussion, see Susan Guettel Cole, *Landscapes, Gender, and Ritual Space: The Ancient Greek Experience* (Berkeley: University of California Press, 2004), 67-85.
11. Camp, *The Archaeology of Athens,* 89.
12. See especially the discussion in Preziosi, *Rethinking Art History,* 168-79 (*summetria*); for a fuller discussion of *symmetria,* see Jerome J. Pollin, *Art and Experience in Classical Greece,* (Cambridge: Cambridge University Press, 1972) 72-78, 106-107. For the symmetry of the Parthenon see, among others, William Bell Dinsmoor, "The Design and Building Techniques of the Parthenon," in *The Parthenon,* ed. Vincent J. Bruno (New York: W.W. Norton, 1974), 171-98. In contrast, the pre-Periklean Archaic Acropolis is much less known. Thus, Hugh Plommer could state: "The literature on the [Archaic] Acropolis seems to me as untidy as the site." And William Bell Dinsmoor urged scholars to strive to place themselves "in the position of an Athenian, not in the right age of Perikles, but rather of 485/4 BCE, before the existence of the Parthenon and the Erechtheion." See W. Hugh Plommer, "The Archaic Acropolis: Some Problems," *Journal of Hellenic Studies* 80 (1960), 127; William Bell Dinsmoor, "The Hekatompedon on the Athenian Acropolis," *American Journal of Archiology* 51 (1947), 119.
13. Plutarch of Chaironeia (born before 50 CE, died after 120 CE), *Life of Perikles* (495-429 BCE), Section 13, translated by Jerome J. Pollitt, *The Art of Greece, 1400-31 BC: Sources and Documents* (Englewood Cliffs, N.J.: Prentice-Hall, 1965), 116. For Plutarch, the overview of Konrat Ziegler, "Plutarchos," in *Real-Encyclopädie der klassischen Altertumswissemchaft, Bd. 22.1,* ed. August Pauly, Georg Wissowa and Wilhelm Kroll (Stuttgart, *J.B.* Metzler, revised reprint 1964), 636-962, remains indispensable.
14. Plutarch, *Life of Perikles,* 13.
15. Pausanias 1.22.4.
16. For the remarkable unfinished anthemion patterns, see Tasos Tanoulas, "The Restoration of the Propylaea," in *Acropolis Restoration: The CCAM Interventions,* ed. Richard Economakis (London: Academy Editions, 1994), 151- 67, esp. 167.
17. Demosthenes *Against Androtion* 22.13, 76; *Against Aristokrates* 23.207. In the latter passage he notes that the great men of old—like Themistokles and Miltiades—lived in common houses, whereas their public buildings were "on such a scale and such quality that no opportunity of surpassing them was left to coming generations. Witness the Propylaia, docks, porticoes, and great harbor...." Perhaps the most critical passage is Demosthenes *Against Androtion* 22.76, to which we return at the end of this paper.
18. Aeschines 2.74.
19. Cicero, *De Officiis* 2.60.
20. See Lyons, Papadopoulos, Stewart, and Szedgy-Maszak, *Antiquity and Photography,* 201.
21. Ibid.
22. Ibid., 202, 205, pls. XIII, XVI.
23. For Divine Salamis, see Herodotus 7.141-43. Personifications of Salamis are rare; see Eleni Manakidou, "Salamis," in *Lexicon Iconographicum Mythologiae Classicae* (Zurich and Munich: Artemis Verlag, 1994), vol. VII: 1, 652- 53; the most relevant is that closest in date to the battle of Salamis, which depicts "Salamis" (inscribed), on an Athenian red-figure skyphos of about 460 BCE by the Lewis Painter, depicting Salamis on one side of the vase, Thebe on the other; see Manakidou, "Salamis," vol. VII: 2, 498 (Salamis 2); see further Karl Schefold and Franz Jung, *Die Sagen von den Argonauten von Theben und Troia in der klassischen und hellenistischen Kunst* (Munich: Hirmer Verlag, 1989), 86-87, figs. 68-69.
24. The Battle of Salamis is vividly brought to life by Barry Strauss in *The Battle of Salamis: The Naval Encounter that Saved Greece—and Western Civilization* (New York: Simon & Schuster, 2004).
25. In 490 BCE, the victorious Athenians returning to Athens from Marathon, and still perceiving the Persian threat, camped in open ground sacred to Herakles at Kynosarges, not behind a city wall.
26. See Travlos, *Pictorial Dictionary of Ancient Athens,* 158.
27. See Papadopoulos, *Ceramicus Redivivus,* 285-88, with figs. 5.5-5.6; see further Judeich, *Topographie von Athen,* 31, 430; Homer A. Thompson and Richard Ernest Wycherley, *The Athenian Agora Vol. XIV The Agora of Athens. The History, Shape and Uses of an Ancient City Center* (Princeton: American School of Classical Studies at Athens, 1972), 1, note 3; Klaus-Valtin von Eickstedt, *Beitriige zur Topographie des antiken Piriius* (Athens: Athens Archaeological Society, 1991).
28. The evidence that Phaleron was the principal harbor of Athens during the time of the Persian Wars is laid out in Papadopoulos, *Ceramicus Redivivus,* 285-88. The harbor was at the protected east end of the Bay of Phaleron.
29. John Travlos, Πολεοδομική ἐξέλιξις τῶν Ἀθηνῶν (Athens: Kapon & Aggelike Kokkou, 1960), p. 49, fig. 19; see also Travlos, *Pictorial Dictionary of Ancient Athens,* 158.
30. This is fully discussed in Papadopoulos, *Ceramicus Redivivus,* 285-88.
31. Henry George Liddell, Robert Scott, and Henry Stuart Jones, *A Greek English Lexicon* (Oxford: Clarendon Press, 9th edition, 1940), sv. *thalassokratia.*
32. Yi-Fu Tuan, *Topophilia: A Study of Environmental Perception, Attitudes, and Values* (New York: Columbia University Press, 1974), 230.
33. Yi-Fu Tuan, *Space and Place: The Perspective of Experience* (Minneapolis: University of Minnesota Press, 1977), 173.
34. Translation C. F. Smith.
35. For the respective positions of the Greek and Persian fleets before the battle, see Strauss, *The Battle of Salamis,* 74 and 126 (maps). For Psyttaleia, see Paul W. Wallace, "Psyttaleia and the Trophies of the Battle of Salamis," *American Journal of Archaeology* 73 (1969), 293-303. For the trophy, which is mentioned together with a similar marble column trophy at Marathon, see Menexenos 240 D, and 245 A; Plutarch, *Aristides* 16,4; and Nepos, *Themistokles* 5,3. The Kynosoura trophy was visible in the eighteenth and nineteenth centuries, see Eugene Vanderpool, "A Monument to the Battle of Marathon," *Hesperia* 35 (1946), 93-106, and especially 102-3, where the earlier accounts of James Stuart and Nicholas Revett (1762), Richard Chandler (1765), and Ludwig Ross (1839) are cited. For a related trophy on Psyttaleia, see Plutarch, *Aristides* 9; and see further Wallace, "Psyttaleia," 299.
36. Preziosi, *Rethinking Art History,* 175-78.

Breuer and Nervi's Folded Frames
1. M. Salvadori, "UNESCO Headquarters, Paris, France", in *The Architectural Record,* February 1958, 166.
2. F. Choay, introduction to *Le Siège de l'Unesco à Paris* (Paris: Vincent Freal, 1968). See also L. Hervé, *The Eiffel Tower.* Photographs by Lucien Hervé, Introduction by Barry Bergdoll (New York: Princeton Architectural Press, 2003), esp. p. 24.
3. Salvadori, 1958, 168.

4. On the Gardern see M. Trieb, *Noguchi in Paris: The UNESCO Garden* (San Francisco: William Stout, 2003).
5. L. Mumford, "UNESCO House: The Hidden Treasure", in *The New Yorker,* 19 November 1960, 213.
6. B. Zevi, "Incontro con Lewis Mumford. La Città Invisible", in *L'Espresso,* 15 May 1960, 20.
7. The best review remains W. Stoddard, *Adventure in Architecture Building the New Saint John's* (New York: Longmans, Green, 1958). See also V. Young, "Marcel Breuer: St. John's Abbey, Collegeville 1954", in *Casabella,* Vol. 67, no. 715 (October 2003), 28-39. See also "Building Committee, Comprehensive Plans and Reports 1952-54", Box 5/ Folder 4, in the Archives of the Abbey.
8. "Building Committee", in the Archives of the Abbey.
9. Quoted in Stoddard 1958.
10. "Building Committee", in the Archives of the Abbey.
11. See R. Gatje, *Marcel Breuer: A memoir* (New York: Monacelli Press, 2000).
12. Nervi's designs for Saint John's are kept in Breuer Archives; Special Collections Research Center, Syracuse University. The 1953 designs bear the title "Early sketches by Nervi for Church" and Nervi's own handwriting "Studi per Chiesa Arch. Breuer".
13. See Breuer's foreword to J.L. de Cenival, *Living Architecture: Egyptian* (New York: Grosset & Dunlap, 1964).
14. "A masterplan for the next one hundred years", in *The Architectural Record,* no. 130 (November 1961), 132.
15. P.L. Nervi, *Aesthetics and Technology in Building* (Cambridge, Massachusetts: Harvard University Press, 1965).
16. M. Breuer, *Matter and Intrinsic Form, Second Annual Reed and Barton Design Lecture,* presented at the University of Michigan, Ann Arbor, March 6, 1963 (Taunton, Massachusetts: Reed and Barton, 1963).

Braced Frames and High Tech Dreams
1. B. Appleyard, *Richard Rogers: A Biography* (London: Faber & Faber, 1986); *Foster Associates* (London: RIBA Publications, 1979); N. Foster, 'Personal Experiences', conference paper for 'The Special Relationship: American and British Architecture since 1945', Architectural Association/Paul Mellon Centre, London, 29-30 October 1998; N. Foster, 'Royal Gold Medal Address' (1983), reprinted in D. Jenkins (ed.), *On Foster ... Foster On* (Munich: Prestel, 2000), 483-503; N. Foster, 'With Wendy' (1989), reprinted in Jenkins, *On Foster ... Foster On,* 545-53; N. Foster, 'Pritzker Prize Address' (1989), reprinted in Jenkins, *On Foster ... Foster On,* 729-33; Y. Futugawa, 'Interview with Norman Foster' in *Global Architecture Extra* special issue (1998), reprinted in Jenkins, *On Foster ... Foster On,* 749-67; R. Rogers, 'Team 4' (1991), reprinted in Jenkins, *On Foster ... Foster On,* 271- 5; R. Stern, 'The Impact of Yale' (1999), reprinted in Jenkins, *On Foster ... Foster On,* 345-61; D. Sudjic, 'Foster Mark 3' (1996), reprinted in Jenkins, *On Foster ... Foster On,* 315- 16; D. Jenkins (ed.), *Norman Foster - Works 1,* (Munich: Prestel, 2002); D. Jenkins (ed.), *Norman Foster - Works 4,* (Munich: Prestel, 2004); *Foster: Catalogue 2001,* (Munich: Prestel, 2001); I. Lambot *et al., Norman Foster, Team 4 and Foster Associates: Buildings and Projects, vol. 1, 1964-73,* (1991), Godalming: Watermark; I. Lambot *et al., Foster Associates: Buildings and Projects, vol. 2, 1971-78,* 1989, Hong Kong: Watermark; I. Lambot *et al., Foster Associates: Buildings and Projects,* vol. 3, *1978-85,* 1989, Hong Kong: Watermark; I. Lambot *et al., Foster Associates: Buildings and Projects,* vol. 4, *1982-89,* 1996, Basel/Haslemere: Birkhauser/Watermark; *Norman Foster: Architect, Selected Works 1962/84* (Manchester: Whitworth Art Gallery, 1984); M. Pawley, *Norman Foster: A Global Architect.* London: Thames & Hudson, 1999; K. Powell, *Richard Rogers,* Munich: Artemis, 1994; K. Powell, *Richard Rogers: The Complete Works,* vol. 1 *(1961-88)* (London: Phaidon, 1999); K. Powell, *Richard Rogers: The Complete Works,* vol. 2 *(1987-92),* (London: Phaidon, 2001); K. Powell *Richard Rogers: Architecture of the Future,* ed. R. Torday, (Basel: Birkhauser, 2006); A. Powers, *Serge Chermayeff: Designer, Architect, Teacher,* (London: RIBA Publications, 2001), 209-10; M. Quantrill, *The Norman Foster Studio: Consistency through Diversity* (London: E&FN Spon, 1999); R. Stern, 'Britons at Yale in the 1960s', conference paper for 'The Special Relationship: American and British Architecture since 1945', Architectural Association/Paul Mellon Centre, London, 29-30 October 1998; D. Sudjic, *The Architecture of Richard Rogers,* (London: Fourth Estate/Wordsearch, 1994).
2. Rogers, 'Team 4' (1991), 272.
3. Stern, '*The Impact of Yale*' (1999), 345-61.
4. N. Jackson, *The Modern Steel House,* (London: E&FN Spon, 1996), 148-9.
5. Appleyard, *Richard Rogers,* 106. See also Rowan Moore, 'Norman's Conquests', *Prospect,* March 2002, 16-19.
6. N. Foster's acceptance speech for AIA Gold Medal on 1 February 1994, as reported in 'Saluting America', *Building Design,* 18 February 1994, 17.
7. K. Powell, *Richard Rogers: The Complete Works,* vol. 1, 50-7.
8. *Architectural Review,* May 1957, 378-80, special issue on 'Machine-Made America'; R. Boyd, 'Under Tension', September 1963, 324-34; I. McCallum, *Architecture USA* (London: Architectural Press, 1959), 199-200; J. McKean, *Crystal Palace: Joseph Paxton and Charles Fox (Architecture in Detail series)* (London: Phaidon, 1994), 52-3; P. Rudolph, *The Architecture of Paul Rudolph* (London: Thames and Hudson, 1970), 144-5.
9. Quote from Norman Foster in A. Donsajh, 'Foster Joins Campaign to Save Florida School', *Building Design,* 20 October 2006, 6; quote from Norman Foster in T. Monk, *The Art and Architecture of Paul Rudolph,* 4 (reprinted as N. Foster, 'Paul Rudolph' (1999), in Jenkins, *On Foster ... Foster On),* 745-7.
10. *Architectural Review,* January 1966, 10.
11. H. Wilson, 'Labour and the Scientific Revolution', *Annual Conferences Report,* (London: Labour Party, 1963), 140.
12. Quote from Harold Wilson in B. Pimlott, *Harold Wilson,* (London: HarperCollins, 1992), 302-4.
13. Quote from Harold Wilson in A. Grosser, *The Western Alliance: European-American Relations since 1945,* (London: Macmillan, 1980), 224.
14. 'Man Plan 3', *Architectural Review,* October 1969, 326-37.
15. Taylor, 'Made in Mid-Atlantic', 12, 22-3.

Informal Frames
none

CHAPTER 6 | CABLES, NETS & MEMBRANES

Seemingly Free Form Structures in Montreal and Munich
none

Cybernetic and Lightweight Dreams
1. As *Archigram* 4 commented next to an illustration of the aviary: "Many will say: this zoom stuff is all very well, but you could never build it ... it's for the birds." See *Archigram* 4 (1964), 13.
2. The prominent British photographer Tony Armstrong-Jones became the Earl of Snowden when he married Princess Margaret in 1960. While best known for capturing the spirit of London in the sixties and for his intimate portraits of artists, writers, actors, and designers, Snowden had studied architecture at Cambridge for two years and designed stage sets, furniture, and a birdcage at Mereworth Castle. His brother-in-law, the Duke of Edinburgh and the president of the Zoological Society, recommended him for the job.
3. In a conversation between Price and Newby, the transcript of which was printed in the *AA Files,* Price stated that the only options for an experimental structure of this kind were still Ove Arup's and Samuely's, the firms that had consulted on the Penguin Pool. See "Engineers and Architects: Newby+Price," *AA Files* no. 27 (Summer 1994), 28.
4. "I liked Samuely's lectures because he talked about weight, he talked about handling, he talked about movement. He was very much into pre-cast concrete but it didn't matter that it was concrete. He talked about buildings as dynamic structures. It was exciting." "Engineers and Architects: Newby+Price," 26.
5. For Samuely's recollection of the design process, see "Engineers and Architects: Newby+Price," 28–30.
6. Design and manufacture of aluminum parts, especially for a structure of this size, necessitated knowledge and skills learned outside of the construction industry.
7. Charles Jencks, *Modern Movements in Architecture* (London: Penguin, 1985), 285.
8. Reyner Banham, "Aviary, London Zoological Gardens," in *A Critic Writes: Essays by Reyner Banham* (Los Angeles: University of California Press, 1996), 119–121. First published in *Architectural Review* no. 138 (September 1965): 186.
9. Peter Guillery, *The Buildings of London Zoo* (London: Royal Commission on the Historical Monuments of England, 1993), 75.
10. John Allan, *Architecture and the Tradition of Progress* (London: RIBA Publications, 1992), 211.
11. Banham, "Aviary," 120.
12. Banham, "Aviary," 119.
13. Sigfried Giedion, *Building in France, Building in Iron, Building in Ferroconcrete,* trans. J. Duncan Berry (Santa Monica, Cal.: Getty Center for the History of Art and the Humanities, 1995), 120–121.
14. Jencks, 285–286.
15. Ulrich Conrads and Hans Sperlich, *The Architecture of Fantasy* (New York: Praeger, 1962), 72.
16. David Greene, "Prologue," in *Concerning Archigram,* ed. D Crompton (London: Archigram Archives, 1998), 3.
17. See Gilles Deleuze and Felix Guattari, *A Thousand Plateaus: Capitalism and Schizophrenia,* trans. Brian Massumi (Minneapolis: University of Minnesota Press, 1987), 351–423

Stayed Roof Systems and High Tech Identity
1. F. Duffy, C. Cave and J. Worthington, 'Systems Thinking Revisited' in *Planning Office Space* (London: Architectural Press, 1976), 194.
2. *Architectural Review,* January 1980, 14-15; *D. Walker Associates: The View from Great Linford,* (London: Academy Editions, 1995), 64-7.
3. Quote from Norman Foster in Quantrill, *The Norman Foster Studio,* 52. See also *Foster: Catalogue 2001,* 118-19; D. Jenkins (ed.), *Norman Foster - Works 4,* 404-25; R. Moore, 'Does it Matter What it Weighs?', *Building Design,* 17 September 1993, 12-14.
4. Interview by M. Fraser with J. Irwin Miller, Irwin Management Company Offices, 301 Washington Street, Columbus, Indiana, USA, 16 April 1997; Powell, *Richard Rogers: The Complete Works,* vol. 1, 214-19, 228-35.
5. C. Wilkinson, *Supersheds: The Architecture of Long-span, Large-volume Buildings,* 2nd edn., (Oxford: Butterworth Architecture, 1991/96), 89.
6. Appleyard, *Richard Rogers,* 298; Powell, *Richard Rogers: The Complete Works,* vol. 1, 242-7.
7. Powell, *Richard Rogers: The Complete Works,* vol. 2, 17, 164-5, 173, 210-11; Powell, *Richard Rogers,* 54-5, 120-5, 274-7.
8. This point is endlessly made, and was pointed out as long ago in Davies, *High Tech Architecture,* 6.
9. R. Banham, *The Visions of Ron Herron: AD Monographs No. 38,* (London: Academy Editions, 1994), 14. Reyner Banham's book was to have been entitled *Making Architecture: The Paradoxes of High Tech,* as is revealed in R. Banham, 'A Set of Actual Monuments', *Architectural Review,* April 1989, 89. For a succinct account of Heidegger's views on technology, see D. Cunningham, 'The Philosophy of Spatial Interface', PODNET Spatial Interface conference, Department of Architecture, University of Westminster, London, 3 April 2006.
10. M. Pawley, *20th Century Architecture: A Reader's Guide* (Oxford: Architectural Press, 2000), 15. See also J. Kron and J. Slesin, *High Tech: The Industrial Style and Source Book for the Home,* (New York: C.N. Potter, 1978); M. Pawley, *Terminal Architecture,* (London: Reaktion Books, 1998), 127-31.
11. Maxwell, *New British Architecture,* 29.
12. A. Colquhoun, *Modernity and the Classical Tradition: Architectural Essays 1980-1987,* (Cambridge, MA: MIT Press, 1989), 211.
13. 'Profile: Rick Mather', *Building Design,* 2 June 2000, 20. See also C. Davies, 'British Hi-Tech and America', conference paper for 'The Special Relationship: American and British Architecture since 1945'.
14. M. Ragon, 'An Architectural Journey: Notes on a Tour of the United States', *Architectural Design,* August 1965, 398.
15. D.W. Ellwood, 'American Myth, American Model, and the Quest for a British Modernity', in R.L. Moore and M. Vaudagna (eds), *The American Century in Europe,* (Ithaca, NY: Cornell University Press, 2003), 131-50.
16. Banham, *Megastructures,* 7; C. Jencks, *Architecture 2000: Predictions and Methods,* (London: Studio Vista, 1971), 22. For more level-headed accounts of the Vertical Assembly Building, with no mention of internal climate, see 'Space Frames', *Architectural Review,* March 1966, 215-16; Wilkinson, *Supersheds,* 33.
17. P. Duignan and L.H. Gann, *The Rebirth of the West: The Americanization of the Democratic World, 1945-1958,* (Oxford: Blackwell, 1992), 635.
18. Davies, *High Tech Architecture,* 140-7; Jackson, *The Modern Steel House,* 111-13.
19. M. Sorkin, 'Richard Rogers, Lloyd's, and After', in *Exquisite Corpse: Writing on Buildings,* (London: Verso, 1991), 321-6.
20. Interview by M. Fraser with Kevin Roche, Roche Architects, Hampton, Connecticut, 18 April 1997.
21. Quote from Frank Duffy in P. Hannay (ed.), *The Changing*

Workplace: Frank Duffy (London: Phaidon, 1992) 187.
22. Email correspondence from Colin Davies to M. Fraser, 23 March 2005.
23. Interview by M. Fraser with John Johansen, John Johansen Associates, Broadway, New York City, 14 April 1997.
24. Quote from Frank Duffy in P. Hannay (ed.), *The Changing Workplace,* 187-8. See also P. Buchanan *et al.,* 'Lloyd's', *Architectural Review,* October 1986, 43-79; Powell, *Richard Rogers: The Complete Works,* vol. 1, 174-209; Sounes, *Seventies,* 326-8; H. Wright, *London High: A Guide to the Past, Present and Future of London's Skyscrapers,* (London: Francis Lincoln, 2006), 151-3.

***Jugaad*: Suspending a Communal Canopy**
none

***Marsyas*: Structure and Metaphor**
Johanna Burton
1. In *The Complete Works of Oscar Wilde* (Harper & Row. New York, 1989), 162.
2. Roland Barthes, in his 1970 essay, 'Musica Practica', suggests that in taking on the role of the amateur musician (now an endangered, if not obsolescent, species) listeners felt stirred 'not satisfaction but desire—the desire to make such music'. Such desire renders listeners active, participatory, never merely receivers, as well as hinting that they are crucial to musical production rather than supplementary to it. Read this way, the scene between Lord Henry and Dorian Gray is particularly revealing: Gray's demise is immediately preceded by his first real desirous exchange. See Roland Barthes's 'Musica Practica', in his *The Responsibility of Forms,* trans. Richard Howard (University of California Press, Berkeley and Los Angeles. 1991). 262.
3. See Thomas Zaunschirm's discussion of Kapoor's uptake of Titian in his short essay, 'The Domain of *Marsyas*', in *Anish Kapoor: My Red Homeland* (Kunsthaus Bregenz, Bregenz, and Lisson Gallery, London. 2003), 148-51.
4. In another context, I have argued that Kapoor's *Marsyas* participates in what I've named 'urmateriality'—a mode of artistic production that takes as materials less the paint, plastics or photographs used in production, and more the psychic constructions attending them. In Kapoor's case, for instance, one can see his attention to the primal, the originary and the ancient as manifesting in works that hold out recognizable—but not articulable—content. I am particularly interested in Kapoor's engagement with the archetypes of sexuality (slits, bulges, protrusions) because they always, in his hands, invert themselves to reveal their own opposites. For more on 'urmateriality', see my 'The "Urmaterial" Urge', *Parkett.* no. 70 (2004). insert pp. 3-14.
5. The hymen is, of course, not only the fold partially closing the vagina but also the god of marrige in Greek mythology, and the hymeneal, the nuptial played at wedding ceremonies. I am not suggesting that Kapoor's piece reflects traditional unions such as marriage, but rather pointing to the ways in which the hymen, like *Marsyas,* brings together image and sound.

Cecil Balmond
none

CHAPTER 7 | ARCHES, DOMES & SHELLS

Informing Arch Form
1. One can also treat a cord from which are hung a series of literal weights, in which case the cord will take a kind of polygonal shape. However, we shall not consider that case here, since it is not too relevant to the curve of the Gateway Arch.
2. This and all further references to statements by Bruce Detmers come from conversations with him in March 2008.
3. Jacques Heyman, *The Science of Structural Engineering.* (London: Imperial College Press, 1999), 19.
4. Robert Hooke had the great misfortune to be a contemporary of Isaac Newton, and on two counts. First of all, Newton's brilliance and monumental achievements simply overshadowed any and all potential rivals among scientists. But perhaps even more so, because Newton developed one of his notorious lifetime grudges against Hooke, and did everything possible—which was quite a bit—to denigrate and belittle Hooke and his achievements.
5. Jacques Heyman, *The Science of Structural Engineering* (London: Imperial College Press, 1999), 40-41.
6. Galileo Galilei, *Two New Sciences*, trans. Stillman Drake, (Madison: University of Wisconsin Press, 1974), 143.
7. Galileo Galilei, *Two New Sciences*, trans. Stillman Drake, (Madison: University of Wisconsin Press, 1974), 256-7.
8. The issue here is that although Galileo is precisely correct in his great insight that one cannot scale up any structure an arbitrarily large amount, since the weight goes up as the cube of the scaling factor and the cross-sectional area of the supports—say columns for a building, legs of an animal, or trunk of a tree—increases by only the square, nevertheless he is "wrong" not to note that on the scale of normal buildings, strength is not the key issue, but stability, as in Hooke's dictum, and in that case what counts is the geometrical shape, invariant under scaling.
9. Strictly speaking, the term used was the Latin word, *catenaria*, and the English word "catenary" did not occur until somewhat later; this will be discussed shortly. An excellent and detailed history of the "catenary problem" is given by Clifford Truesdell in "The Rational Mechanics of Flexible or Elastic Bodies," 1638-1788; Introduction to *Leonhardi Euleri Opera Omnia*, Vol. X et XI Seriei Secundae, Lausanne, Orell Füssli Turici 1960; (Surprisingly, Truesdell also fails to cite Galileo's correct description of the catenary as an approximation to a parabola.)
10. "*Tout homme est pierre; tout caillou est homme; donc tout caillou est pierre.*" From a letter of August 11, 1697; Jacob Bernoulli, *Opera*, 829-839; reprinted in *Die Streitschriften von Jacob und Johann Bernoulli.* (Birkhäuser Verlag, 1991), 356-364 (see 361). See also pp. 1-114 of this volume for an overview in English of the contents, and pp. 117-122 for a list of "The Polemic Writings of Jacob and Johann Bernoulli on the Calculus of Variations" that are reproduced in the book.
11. Other names that should be mentioned in this brief history are Philippe de la Hire and David Gregory. De la Hire's *Traité de méchanique* from 1695 addresses the question of how to distribute weights along a chain to attain "a figure curved the way you wish it to be" (proposition 123), and he makes explicit the connection between arches and variably weighted chains. David Gregory discovered independently the relation between weighted chains and arches and described them in a letter later published in the Philosophical Transactions in August 1697. For more on both of these major contributions, see (Edoardo Benvenuto, *An Introduction to the History of Structural Mechanics. Part II: Vaulted Structures and Elastic Systems* (New York, Springer-Verlag, 1991) 321-329. Another good historical reference is (John Bukowski, "Christian Huygens and the Problem of the Hanging Chain," *College Mathematics Journal* 39, (2008) 1: 2-11] (the usual misleading statements about Galileo are repeated here, but it is instructive to see how early they originated and were propagated by successive generations).
12. *The Visual Dictionary of Architecture* (Lausanne: Ava Publishing, 2008) p 41.
13. At least that is the case for the dozens of articles, as well as congratulatory telegrams that are on file in the Saarinen Archives at Yale University.
14. Copies of Grant's letter and Saarinen's response are in the Saarinen archive. It is the only place I have found where Saarinen describes his winning design with as much specificity.
15. Quoted in [Michael J. Crosbie, "Is It a Catenary? New questions about the shape of Saarinen's St. Louis Arch," *AIA Journal* (June 1983): 78-79].
16. Eero Saarinen, *Shaping the Future*, eds. Eeva-Liisa Pelkonen and Donald Albrecht (New Haven: Yale University Press 2006) 343.
17. Whether this formula (or, for that matter, any other formula) is displayed inside the Arch as claimed, is something I have not been able to determine. It is not impossible, since the precise shape of the Arch was modified so many times during the planning process, but it is unlikely, because the decision not to use an exact catenary was made very early—long before construction began.
18. Michael J. Crosbie, "Is It a Catenary? New questions about the shape of Saarinen's St. Louis Arch," *AIA Journal* (June 1983).
19. The precise conditions for the graph of a curve to be representable as a weighted catenary are that it be convex, and that it makes a non-zero angle with the vertical at its endpoints. See [Robert Osserman, "Mathematics of the Gateway Arch," *Notices of the American Mathematical Society* 57, (2010) 2: 220-229].
20. Johann Bernoulli was already aware of the connection between arches and a chain of variable weight in 1698; see, for example, [Edoardo Benvenuto, *An Introduction to the History of Structural Mechanics. Part II: Vaulted Structures and Elastic Systems* (New York, Springer-Verlag, 1991), 327].
21. Michael J. Crosbie, "Is It a Catenary? New questions about the shape of Saarinen's St. Louis Arch," *AIA Journal* (June 1983).
22. Jayne Merkel, *Eero Saarinen* (London: Phaidon Press, 2005), 244, note 36.
23. Jacques Heyman, *The Science of Structural Engineering* (London: Imperial College Press. 1999), 38-39.
24. Robert Osserman, "Mathematics of the Gateway Arch." *Notices of the American Mathematical Society* 57, (2010) 2: 220-229.
25. There are 71 such sections on each leg of the arch, according to the specifications.
26. This is further complicated by a note on the blueprints that for the top 41 sections, the "exterior skin to be curved into a continuous smooth surface." This corresponds to roughly the upper half of the Arch, where the curvature is the greatest. It is also above the 300-foot level where there is another transition in the mode of construction, as we discuss more fully later on; below that level the stainless steel outer skin is backed by a layer of concrete.
27. Jacques Heyman, *The Masonry Arch* (Chichester: Ellis Horward Limited, 1982), 48-49.
28. Both of these examples are described in fascinating detail in the book *The Tower and the Bridge* [David Billington, *The Tower and the Bridge*, (Princeton: Princeton University Press, 1985).]
29. George B. Hartzog, Jr. was Director of the National Park Service at the time. See the chapter on the Gateway Arch in [George B. Hartzog, Jr., *Battling for the National Parks* (Kingston (Rhode Island): Moyer Bell, 1988).], especially 52-56.
30. See, for example, [Mark Coir, "The Cranbrook Factor," in Eero Saarinen, *Shaping the Future* (New Haven: Yale University Press, 2006) 29-4.]: "Milles strongly advised Saarinen to drop his initial plans to fashion the arch with a quadrilateral section in favor of a more sculpturally pleasing triangular section. Eero's failure publicly to recognize Milles's contribution to the monument angered the Swedish sculptor, who thereafter severed contact with Saarinen" [2006: p. 41 and footnote 40, p. 43].
31. On the other hand, some of Libera's sketches for the arch show a radical thickening near ground level, which would seem to indicate at least an intuitive understanding of the need for a suitable weighting to support the shape of a circular arc. From an esthetic point of view that thickening may be seen as producing a more dramatic effect for Libera's arch than for Saarinen's, or else as far less graceful. (Perhaps both.)
32. Jasper Johns, *Catenary* (New York: Steidel Publishing, 2005).
33. Ross King, *Brunelleschi's Dome: How a Renaissance Genius Reinvented Architecture* (Penguin Books, 2000) 157-158.
34. Edoardo Benvenuto, *An Introduction to the History of Structural Mechanics. Part II: Vaulted Structures and Elastic Systems* (New York, Springer-Verlag, 1991), Introduction xix.
35. Benvenuto is referring to Valéry's "Eupalinos ou l'architecte" [quoted in Paul Valéry, *Oeuvres*, Vol. 2, (Paris: Bibliotèque de la Pléiade/Éditions Gallimard, 1960) 83].
36. Eupalinos was the engineer to whom is ascribed (by Herodotus) the construction of the famous.

Veiled and Vaulted Space
none

Domes as Optical Instruments
1. Perkowitz, *Empire of Light*, 16ff. See also Lael Wertenbaker, *The Eye: Window to the World* (New York: Torstar, 1984).
2. Patrick Moore, *Eyes on the Sky: The Story of the Telescope* (London: Springer, 1997). Also see Richard Panek, *Seeing and Believing: How the Telescope Opened Our Eyes and Minds to the Heavens* (New York: Viking, 1998).
3. Kircher, without crediting Descartes, borrows much of this discussion, including the diagrams *(Ars magna,* 1: 112ff.). But he also carries it much further in applying conic sections to the theater machinery, solar clocks, and the like.
4. David Park, *The Fire within the Eye: A Historical Essay on the Nature and Meaning of Light* (Princeton, N.J.: Princeton University Press, 1997), 51ff.
5. Sidney Perkowitz, *Empire of Light: A History 4 Discovery in Science and Art* (New York: Henry Holt, 1993), 96ff.
6. I'll never know because Diodorus uses the expression *katoptron hetektenen,* translated as "hexagonal mirror." Those who have sought to re-create Archimedes' exploit have used ordinary flat mirrors, which worked. Park, *Fire within the Eye,* 23.

7. It is therefore perhaps relevant that Kircher writes in great detail both about Archimedes' instrument and about magic lanterns. *Ars magna,* 2:880ff.
8. Perkowitz, *Empire of Light,* 129; see also L. Sprague DeCamp, *The Ancient Engineers* (New York: Ballantine, 1974); Eugene Hecht and Alfred Zajac, *Optics* (Reading, Mass.: Addison-Wesley, 1979), 1.
9. Giovanni Battista della Porta, *Magia Naturalis Libri XX* (Frankfurt, 1591). See also G. B. Manzini, *L'Occhiale all'occhio: Dioptrica practica* (Bologna, 1660); and (the most complete treatise of the period) Chérubin d'Orleans, *La Dioptrique oculaire* (1671), which describes the making of telescopes and microscopes as well as lens design. For a modern view, see Marion Fournier, *The Fabric of Life: Microscopy in the Seventeenth Century* (Baltimore, Md.: Johns Hopkins University Press, 1996).
10. See Galileo Galilei, *Discoveries and Opinions of Galileo,* ed. Stillman Drake (New York: Anchor Books, 1957), 29.
11. Perkowitz, *Empire of Light,* 131.
12. Fournier, *The Fabric of Life,* 1. For the architectural importance of the telescope, see M. C. Donnelly, *Astronomical Observatories in the 17th and 18th Centuries,* book 34, fascicule 5, *Memoires* (Brussels: Académie Royale de Belgique, Classe des Sciences, 1964).
13. See the bibliography in Silvio Bedini, *Science and Optics in Seventeenth-Century Italy* (Aldershot: Variorum, 1994).
14. The first person to put a lens in a camera obscura seems to have been Giambattista della Porta. Park, *Fire within the Eye,* 137.
15. Philippe Comar, *La Perspective en jeu: Les dessous de l'image* (Paris: Gallimard, 1992), 106. I thank Benoit Mandelbrot for introducing me to this amusing and intelligent book.
16. Gian Piero Brunetta, *Il Viaggio dell'iconorwuta dalla camera oscura di Leonardo alia luce dei Lumiére* (Venice: Marsilio, 1997); see also Thomas J. Hankins and Robert J. Silverman, *Instruments and the Imagination* (Princeton, N.J.: Princeton University Press, 1995), 43ff., and bibliography, 241.
17. Kircher, *Ars Magna,* 1:177ff. ("De *proiectoionibus scenographicis geometrice expediendis,"* which deals not only with theatrical uses of projected light and images but with the anamorphic and barrel distortions that can be achieved by lens systems).
18. Hankins and Silverman, *Instruments and the Imagination,* 43ff., and bibliography, 241.
19. Lisa Jardine, in *Ingenious Pursuits: Building the Scientific Revolution* (New York: Doubleday, 1999), 76, 80, brings out this parallel.
20. See my *High Renaissance Art in St. Peter's and the Vatican* (Chicago: University of Chicago Press, 1993), 95ff.
21. Quoted by Alberto Perez-Gomez and Louise Pelletier, *Architectural Representation and the Perspective Hinge* (Cambridge: MIT Press, 1997), 17.
22. For the controversies about Peter's tomb, see Margherita Guarducci, *La Tomba di San Pietro: Una straordinaria vicenda* (Rome: Rusconi, 1989).
23. Pierre Bourget and Georges Cattaui, *Jules Hardouin Mausart* (Paris: Vincent, Freal, 1960); Bertrand Jestaz, *Hardouin Mausart et l'Hotel et église des Invalides* (Paris: Caisse nationale des monuments historiques et des sites, 1990).
24. John Harris, "Designing St. Paul's," *Country Life* 185 (1991): 80ff.; John Summerson, "J. H. Mansart, Sir Christopher Wren, and the Dome of St. Paul's Cathedral," *Burlington Magazine* 132 (1990): 32ff.; and Kerry Downes, *Sir Christopher Wren and the Designs of St. Paul's Cathedral* [exhibition catalog] (London: Trefoil, 1988). Lisa Jardine, *Ingenious Pursuits,* 72, quotes Robert Hooke, Wren's sometime collaborator and a mathematician-architect, saying that the dome of St. Paul's is "a cubical paraboloid conoid." According to Michael Frame this probably means "a cubical paraboloid that has been rotated around its axis 360°. A paraboloid is generated by rotating the parabola *y = x^2* around the *y* axis, so wouldn't it make sense to say a cubical paraboloid is generated by rotating a cubical parabola *y = x^3* around the *y* axis? A cubical parabola is flatter at its apex than a normal parabola." A conoid, meanwhile, is simply one type of revolved paraboloid.
25. See Galileo Galilei, *Dialogues Concerning Two New Sciences,* trans. Henry Crew and Alfonso de Salvio (1914; reprint, New York: Dover, 1954), 147; and Jardine, *Ingenious Pursuits,* 72, 331ff.
26. Jardine, *Ingenious Pursuits,* 333.
27. J. A. Bennett, *The Mathematical Sciences of Christopher Wren* (Cambridge: Cambridge University Press, 1982); Vaughan Hart, *St. Paul's Cathedral: Sir Christopher Wren* (London: Phaidon, 1995); and Peter Hurman, *St. Paul's Cathedral* (London: Bell and Hyman, 1987).
28. For the dome painting, see Carol Gibson-Wood, "The Political Background of Thornhill's Paintings in St. Paul's Cathedral," *Journal of the Warburg and Courtauld Institutes* 56 (1993): 229ff.
29. Bennett, *The Mathematical Sciences of Sir Christopher Wren,* 53. For drawings of the cathedral, see Arthur F. E. Poley, *St. Paul's Cathedral, London, Measured, Drawn, and Described by Arthur F. E. Poley* (London: the Author, 1927).
30. Adolf Max Vogt, *Boullees Newton-Denkmal: Sakralbau und Kugelidee* (Basel: Birckhauser, 1969), 157ff.; and Guilhem Scherf, "Pierre Julien et le decor sculpte de l'eglise Sainte-Genevieve a Paris," *Revue du Louvre et des musees de France* 38, no. 2 (1988): 127ff.

The Politics of Candela's Shells

1. Eduardo Robles to Félix Candela, March 1, 1960. Box 05.09, Félix Candela Architectural Records and Papers Collection, Avery Drawings and Archives, Columbia University, New York (hereafter FCA-CU). Original in Spanish. All translations from Spanish by the author unless otherwise noted.
2. I have fleshed out Candela's political vision as it developed in the 1950s and 1960s and in reaction to his conflicted relationship to Spain and to its architecture culture in "Geometría Extensiva también como proyecto político," in *Miradas Cruzados, intercambios entre Latinoamérica y España en la Arquitectura Española del siglo XX* (Pamplona: T6 Ediciones, 2008), and "Apátridas Architectures: Candela, Sert, and the Return of the Modern to Postwar Spain" in *Coming Home?* vol. 1, *Conflict and the Return of Spanish Civil War Exiles,* ed. Scott Soo and Alicia Pozo-Gutierrez (Newcastle: Cambridge Scholars Press, forthcoming).
3. Carlos de Miguel, ed., "Láminas de hormigón armada: Félix Candela," *Arquitectura* 10 (1959): 2-33.
4. Robles to Candela, March 1, 1960.
5. Colin Faber, *Candela, the Shell Builder* (New York: Reinhold, 1963). Similarly see Luigi Margani, *Le Superficie Rigate nelle Strutture Architettoniche* (Catania: Università di Catania, 1965).
6. Félix Buschiazzo, *Félix Candela* (Buenos Aires: Instituto de Arte Americana e Investigaciones Estéticas, 1961).
7. Félix Candela, "Discurso de aceptación al premio del Colegio de Arquitectos e Ingenieros de Madrid," *Arquitectura* 303 (1995): 46.
8. See David Billington and Marla E. Moreyra, *Félix Candela: Engineer, Builder, Structural Artist* (New Haven: Yale University Press, 2008); Enrique X. de Anda, *Félix Candela, 1910-1997: The Mastering of Boundaries* (New York: Taschen, 2008); Miguel Segui, ed., *Félix Candela, arquitecto* (Madrid: MOPU 1994); Miguel Segui, *Félix Candela y Emilio Pérez Piñero: Un dialogo imaginal* (Madrid: Rueda, 2004); Juan Antonio Tonda, *Félix Candela* (Mexico City: Consejo Nacional para La Cultura y las Artes, 2000). Salvador Perez Arroyo briefly mentions Candela's critique of Franco's regime during the 1960s, but otherwise insists on the image of Candela the builder: Salvador Perez Arroyo, *Los años críticos: 10 arquitectos españoles* (Madrid: Fundación Antonio Camuñas, 2003), 28. Two recent monographs start to open up Candela's personal and ideological history, but largely leave aside the specifics of his politics: Pepa Casinello, ed., *Félix Candela. Centenario 201: la conquista de la esbeltez* (Madrid: Fundacion Juanelo Turriano, 2010), and Juan Ignacio del Cueto, ed., *Félix Candela 1920-2010* (Madrid: Sociedad Estatal de Conmemoraciones Culturales, 2010). In the latter, Candela's activist role in Spain during the last years of the Republic is well addressed by Inés Sanchez de Madarlaga.
9. Félix Candela to Matilde Ucelay, August 7, 1957. Box 03.14, FCA-CU.
10. Cueto, ed., *Félix Candela 1920-2010,* 75-77. Lázaro Cárdenas's politics and policies made Mexico the preferred destination of exile for Spanish Republicans in Latin America. For an account of the architects who went into exile, see Henry Vicente Garrido, et al., *Arquitecturas desplazadas: Arquitecturas del exilio español* (Madrid: Ministerio de Vivienda, 2007); specifically for the case of Mexico, see Juan Ignacio del Cueto, "Arquitectos españoles exillados en México: Su labor en la Espana republican (1931-1936) y su integración en México" (PhD diss., Universidad Politécnica de Catalunya, Barcelona, 1996). Exile scholarship from the point of view of architecture remains biographical and contains little interpretation of the exiles' politics, which, as I argue elsewhere, comes more clearly to the fore when focusing on the figure of return over the experience of exile per se.
11. Félix Candela, "Cubierta prismática de hormigón armada en la Ciudad de México," *Revista Nacional de Arquitectura* 99 (1950): 126-32. For an account by Candela of the structures mentioned here, see *Arquitectura* 303 (1995): 46-56.
12. See correspondence with Enrique Segarra, Eduardo Robles, and Matilde Ucelay, former professional and political colleagues of Candela in Spain. Box 03 and others, FCA-CU.
13. The talk before FUE can only be reconstructed from schematic manuscript notes by Candela, hereafter FUE talk notes, FCA-CU. I was not able to find a formal, structured text prepared for the occasion. I date this event to late 1959 based on a series of letters between Eduardo Robles and Candela.
14. Candela, FUE talk notes.
15. Candela, FUE talk notes.
16. Candela, "Influencia de la tecnología," 60.
17. Ibid., 65.
18. Fernado Chueca, "Comentario," in *Arquitectura* 10 (1959): 22.
19. Candela, FUE talk notes.
20. Juan O'Gorman, "En torno a la integración plastica," *Espacios* (July 1953); rpt. in Ida Rodriguez Prampolini, *Juan O'Gorman: Arquiteco y pintor* (Mexico City: Universidad Nacional Autónoma de Mexico, 1982), 93.
21. Félix Candela, "Letter," *Arquitectura* 10 (1959): 2. Alberto Perez-Gómez has pointed toward a similar argument in Edward R. Burian, *Modernidad y arquitectura en Mexico* (Barcelona: Gustavo Gili, 1998), 46.
22. Cueto, "El ocaso de los cascarones," 104-106.
23. In letter from Manuel Sola-Morales to Félix Candela of January 30, 1968, Sola-Morales invited Candela to attend the colloquium "Industrialización de La Construcción" at the Colegio de Arquitectos in Barcelona, an invitation that Candela likewise rejected. For the details of Candela's trip to Spain, see the exchange of letters between Candela and Florencio del Pozo in 1968 and 1969, in the FC archives.
24. Miguel Angel Baldellou, "Desarraigo y encuentro," *Arquitectura* 303 (1995): 16-19; Ricardo Aroca, "A modo de presentación," in Miguel Segui, ed., *Félix Candela, arquitecto* (Madrid: MOPU, 1994),13.
25. Hannes Meyer, "The New World," in *Claude Schnaidt, Hannes Meyer: Bauten, Projekte und Schriften-Buildings, Projects, and Writings* (Teufen: A. Niggli, 1965), 91.

SANAA's Ceilings and Skies

none

AFTERWORD

Models are Real

none

A Model Curriculum

1. Spiro Kostof, ed., *Architect Chapters in the History of the Profession,* University of California, 2nd edition, 2000, p 194.
2. John Elsner and Roger Cardinal, eds. *The Cultures of Collecting,* Reaktion Books, London, 1994. p 171.
3. Leon Battista Alberti, *The Ten Books of Architecture* [1755 Leoni Edition], Dover, New York, 1986, p 22.
4. Ibid.
5. Robert Harbison, *Thirteen Ways: Theoretical Investigations in Architecture,* MIT Press, Cambridge, MA, 2001, pp 85-86.
6. Elsner, p 175.
7. Claude Lévi-Strauss, *The Savage Mind,* Weidenfeld and Nicolson, London, 1966, p 23.
8. Ibid.

Text Credits

Chapter 1 | COLUMNS

03. Collins, Peter, *Concrete: The Vision of a New Architecture*, © 2004 McGill-Queens University Press, by permission of the publisher. **09.** Frampton, Kenneth. Edited by John Cava., *Studies in Tectonic Culture: The Poetics of Construction in Nineteenth and Twentieth Century Architecture*, pp. 175-178, 188-190, © 1995 Massachusetts Institute of Technology, by permission of The MIT Press. **13.** Pallasmaa, Juhani. *Alvar Aalto: Villa Mairea*, pp. 80-82, 2005 RAM Publications, © Juhanni Pallasmaa, by permission of the author. **17.** Wigley, Mark, *SANAA: Serpentine Gallery Pavilion*, pp. 32-37, © Mark Wigley, by permission of the author. **19.** Reid, Giles, *SANAA, 2009 Serpentine Pavilion, Kensington Gardens, London, 2009* Architecture Today, © Giles Reid, by permission of the author. **23.** Maffei, Andrea, *Toyo Ito: Works Projects Writings*, pp. 232-236, 2001 Electa Magazine, © Andrea Maffei, by permission of the author. **25.** Mik, Edzard. *Interview with Toyo Ito*, ArchIdea Magazine issue 31, by permission of the magazine publisher.

Chapter 2 | WALLS

47. Pauly, Danièle. *Barragán: Space and Shadow, Walls and Colour*, pp.182-183, 199-214, © 2008 Birkhäuser, by permission of the publisher and the author. **51.** Protzen, Jean-Pierre. *Inca Architecture and Construction at Ollantaytambo* (1993), by permission of Oxford University Press. **57.** *The Architecture of R. M. Schindler* by Michael Darling and Elizabeth A.T. Smith. © 2001. Used by permission of Harry N. Abrams, Inc., New York. All rights reserved. **61.** Baek, Jin, *Nothingness: Tadao Ando's Christian Sacred Space*, pp. 89, 90-93, © 2009 Routledge. By permission of the publisher. **65.** Böhm, Gottfried, *Richard Serra: Intersection Basel*, pp. 47-69. 1997 Richter Verlag Düsseldorf, © Paul Böhm, by permission of the publisher and the author.

Chapter 3 | BEAMS & SLABS

91. Silman, Robert. *Strengthening Fallingwater*, pp. 262-271, contained in *Fallingwater* edited by Lynda Waggoner. 2011 Rizzoli, © Robert Silman, by permission of the author. **99.** Sandaker, Bjørn. *On Span and Space*, pp.151-155. © 2007 Routledge. By permission of the publisher. **103.** Kimbell Art Museum, *The Art Museums of Louis I. Kahn*, Patricia C. Loud, pp. 100-172. Copyright, 1990, Duke University Press. All rights reserved. Republished by permission of the copyright holder.www.dukeupress.edu. **106.** Deitz, Paula. reprinted by permission of the author from "Light and Space Artist" by Paula Deitz, ARTnews, May 2015. © 2015 by Paula Deitz. **109.** Mainstone, Rowland J. *Developments in Structural Form, 2nd ed.*, pp. 148-149. © 2001 Routledge, by permission of the publisher. **110.** Excerpt(s) from *The Master Builders* by Peter Blake, © 1960, 1996 by Peter Blake. Used by permission of Alfred A. Knopf, an imprint of the Knopf Doubleday Publishing Group, a division of Penguin Random House LLC. All rights reserved. **115.** Lai, Delin. *Idealizing a Chinese Style*, pp 61-66, 80-86, © 2014 University of California Press Journals, By permission of the publisher through the Copyright Clearance Center CCC. **123.** Halpern, Allison B., Billington, David P., Adriaenssens, Sigrid. *The Ribbed Floor Slab Systems of Pier Luigi Nervi*, pp. 127-136, Vol. 54 (2013) No. 3 September n. 177, Journal of the International Association for Shell and Spatial Structures (J.IASS). Reproduced by permission of the International Association for Shell and Spatial Structures (IASS). **131.** Reprinted by permission of the publisher from *Space, Time and Architecture: The Growth of a New Tradition, fifth revised and enlarged edition* by Sigfried Giedion, pp. 450-467, Cambridge, Mass.: Harvard University Press, © 1941, 1949, 1954, 1962, 1967, 1969 by the President and Fellows of Harvard College, © 1977 by William J. Callaghan, © 1982 by Andreas Gidean and Verena Clay-Giedion. **137.** Hadas A. Steiner, *'For the Birds'*, Grey Room, 13 (Fall, 2003), pp. 14-16. © 2003 by Grey Room, Inc. and the Massachusetts Institute of Technology. **141.** Holt, Michael. and Looby, Marissa. *Herzog & de Meuron: Beyond The Wall, The Floor.* © Michael Holt, Marissa Holt. By permission of the authors.

Chapter 4 | TRUSSES

169. "The Eiffel Tower" from *The Eiffel Tower and Other Mythologies* by Roland Barthes, translated by Richard Howard. Translation © 1979 by Farrar, Straus and Giroux, LLC. Reprinted by permission of Hill and Wang, a division of Farrar, Straus and Giroux, LLC. **177.** Michael de Bouw, Ine Wouters, Leen Lauriks, Quentin Collette and Abdelrahman Hussein Younes, *The Ardant Truss: A Forgotten Rival of the Well-Known Polonceau Truss*, pp. 83-88, Steel Construction – Design and Research Publication. © 2010 John Wiley & Sons, Inc. by permission of the publisher. **183.** Penzel, Christian. "The Culture of Construction: Examples from the Last Fifty Years of Remarkable Development", pp. 41-42, 46-54 of *Cooperation – The Engineer and the Architect,* Aita Flury, ed. 2011 Birkhauser. Reprinted by permission of the publisher and on behalf of the author. **189.** Dal Co, Francesco & Trombetti, Tomaso, "Playing the instrument of the world: a minimal masterpiece by Oscar Niemeyer and Roberto Burle Marx", pp. 109-110, 2009 Rivista Internazionale Di Architettura. © Francesco Dal Co, by permission of the author. **195.** Lin, Zhogjie, *Kenzo Tange and the Metabolist Movement: Urban Utopias of Modern Japan*, pp. 214-224, © 2010 Routledge, by permission of the publisher. **199.** Ingber, Donald E., *The Architecture of Life*, pp. 48-

57, Scientific American. Reproduced with permission. © 1998 Scientific American, Inc. All rights reserved.

Chapter 5 | FRAMES

229. Rowe, Colin, "Chicago Frame", published in *The Mathematics of the Ideal Villa and Other Essays*, pp. 86-101, MIT Press 1976. Reproduced with permission of copyright holder David Rowe. **239.** Martin-McAuliffe, Samantha L. and Papadopoulous, John K., *"Framing Victory: Salamis, the Athenian Acropolis, and the Agora."* in the Journal of the Society of Architectural Historians, Vol. 71, No. 3, September 2012, pp. 332-361. © 2012 by the Society of Architectural Historians. Published by the University of California Press. **245.** Bergdoll, Barry, "Into the Fold: Nervi, Breuer and a Post-War Architecture of Assembly" published in *Pier Luigi Nervi: Architecture as Challenge*, pp.101-104, 105-114, © 2011 Silvana Editoriale, by permission of the publisher. **251.** Fraser, Murray and Kerr, Joe, *Architecture and the 'Special Relationship': The American Influence on Post-War British Architecture*, pp. 301-308, © 2008 Routledge, by permission of the publisher. **257.** Cecil Balmond / Januzzi Smith, *Informal* © 2007 Prestel Verlag, München, in der Verlagsgruppe Random House GmbH.

Chapter 6 | CABLES, NETS & MEMBRANES

299. Drew, Philip, *Frei Otto: Form and Structure*, pp. 35-39, 1976 Westview Press, © Philip Drew, by permission of the author, independent architectural historian. **305.** Hadas A. Steiner, *'For the Birds'*, Grey Room, 13 (Fall 2003), pp. 20-27. © 2003 by Grey Room, Inc. and the Massachusetts Institute of Technology. **309.** Fraser, Murray and Kerr, Joe, *Architecture and the 'Special Relationship': The American Influence on Post-War British Architecture*, pp. 301-308, © 2008 Routledge, by permission of the publisher. **317.** Shankar, Sanjeev, *Jugaad: An architectural installation for 48°C by Sanjeev Shankar*, 2013 Sanjeev Shankar Website, © Sanjeev Shankar, by permission of the author. **321.** Burton, Johanna, "Namely, What is Called Love", pp. 167-169 of the book *Anish Kapoor*. 2009 Phaidon Press Limited, © Johanna Burton, by permission of the author. **323.** Balmond, Cecil, "Skinning the Imagination", contained in the book *Anish Kapoor Marsyas*, 2003 Tate Publishing, © Cecil Balmond. By permission of the author.

Chapter 7 | ARCHES, DOMES & SHELLS

345. Extracted from "How the Gateway Arch Got its Shape", Nexus Network Journal, vol. 12, no. 2 (2010), pp. 167-189. Reprinted by permission. **357.** *The Persian Bazar: Veiled Space of Desire*, Mehdi Khansari, Minouche Yavar, Mage Publishers © 1993, www.mage.com **361.** Hersey, George L., *Architecture and Geometry in the Age of the Baroque*, pp. 56-72, © 2002 University of Chicago Press, by permission of the publisher. **371.** Pendás, María González. "Félix Candela's Geopolitical Imaginary" contained in the book *Latin American Modern Architectures: Ambiguous Territories*, pp. 270-273, 279-287, © Routledge, reproduced by permission of the publisher. **377.** Holt, Michael and Looby, Marissa, "Sanaa: Falling Upwards", 2011 Domus, © Michael Holt and Marissa Looby, reproduced by permission of the authors.

AFTERWORD

403. Originally published as "Models are Real" pp. 18–25 in *Models,* Emily Abruzzo, Eric Ellingsen, and Jonathan D. Solomon, eds, 306090 Books 11 (New York, 2007). © Olafur Eliasson, reprinted by permission of the author. **405.** Morris, Mark. "A Model Curriculum" Original printing.

Image Credits

Chapter 1 | COLUMNS

02. CNAM/SIAF/CAPA/Archives d'architecture du XXe siècle/Auguste Perret/UFSE/SAIF/1936-1948. Fonds: Perret, Auguste et Perret frères. **08.** doublespace photography. **10, 11.** Ford, Edward R., The Details of Modern Architecture, Volume 1, figures 9.10 & 9.12, © 1990 Massachusetts Institute of Technology, by permission of The MIT Press. **12.** Darren Stewart Capel. **15.** Juhani Pallasmaa. **16.** Photo: Iwan Baan. **19.** © SANAA. **20-1.** Luke Hayes. **22.** © Tomio Ohashi. **25.** By courtesy of Toyo Ito & Associates, Architects. **27.** www.jonasadolfsen.no. **29.** Photo: Åke e:Son Lindman. **30.** Photo: Iwan Baan. **33.** Bamboo Wing, designed by Vo Trong Nghia Architects, photograph Hiroyuki Oki. **34.** © Wenzel Photography. **36.** Photo by Alex Fradkin. **39.** William Veerbeen, Netherlands.

Chapter 2 | WALLS

46. © 2015 Barragan Foundation, Switzerland / Artists Rights Society (ARS), New York. **50.** By Gvillemin CC BY-SA 3.0. **54, 55.** Oxford University Press. **56.** Grant Mudford Studio. **59.** Floor plan of the Schindler House, including gardens. Courtesy of Friends of the Schindler House, gift of Mrs. Richard Neutra. **60.** Mia Kang. **63.** By courtesy of Tadao Ando Architect & Associates. **64.** Photo by Peter Moore, Photo © Barbara Moore/Licensed by VAGA, New York, NY © 2015 Richard Serra / Artists Rights Society (ARS), New York. **69.** © 2015 Richard Serra / Artists Rights Society (ARS), New York. **71.** Alex Gaultier, image courtesy of Miralles Tagliabue EMBT. **73.** Daici Ano. **75.** Roland Halbe. **76.** Bart van Hoek. **79.** wakiiii. **80.** Paul Warchol. **82.** Richard Anderson.

Chapter 3 | BEAMS & SLABS

90. Photo by Peter Brian Klein, kleinphotographic.com **95, 96-7.** Robert Silman. **98.** Photo: Teigens Fotoatelier / DEXTRA Photo CC **100.** By permission of Prof. Per Olaf Fjeld. **101.** Sverre Fehn, Nordic Pavilion in Venice. Photo: Ferruzzi, 1962, The National Museum of Art, Architecture and Design, Norway. NMK.2008.0734.313.028. **102.** Kimbell Art Museum, Fort Worth, Texas. Constructed 1969–72. View from the southwest with Henry Moore's *Figure in a Shelter* (1983). Louis I. Kahn (1901–1974), architect. Photograph: Robert LaPrelle. © 2013 Kimbell Art Museum, Fort Worth, Texas. **105.** © Renzo Piano Building Workshop. **107.** © Nic Lehoux. **108.** Redrawn from/Adapted from Figure 8.4 in *Developments in Structural Form, 2nd ed.*, by Rowland Mainstone. **111.** Chicago History Museum, Hedrich-Blessing Collection, HB-13810-I. **113.** Andreas Levers. **114.** Mrs. Lin Zhu. **117, 119, 121.** Delin Lai, Ph.D. **122.** MAXXI Museo nazionale delle arti del XXI secolo, Roma. MAXXI Architecture Collection, Pier Luigi Nervi Archive. Courtesy Pier Luigi Nervi Project Association, Brussels. **124.** Photo: Fabio Mantovani. **125.** Public domain. Moody, W.T., and Phillips, H.B., Photoelastic and Experimental Analog Procedures, US Dept. Int. Bureau of Reclamation, No. 23 (1967) pp. 1-100. **127, 129.** (plots) Journal of the IASS. Vol. 54 (2013) No. 3 September n. 177. Reproduced with permission from International Association for Shell and Spatial Structures (IASS). **129.** (photos) MAXXI Museo nazionale delle arti del XXI secolo, Roma. MAXXI Architecture Collection, Pier Luigi Nervi Archive. Courtesy Pier Luigi Nervi Project Association, Brussels. **130.** ETH-Bibliothek Zürich, Bildarchiv / Fotograf: Unbekannt / Hs_1085-1912-1-547 / Public Domain Mark. **132.** © Chriusha (Хрюша) / CC-BY-SA-3.0 /Wikimedia Commons. **135.** ETH-Bibliothek Zürich, Bildarchiv / Fotograf: Unbekannt / Hs_1085-1924-25-1-24 / Public Domain Mark. **136.** © Crown copyright.EH **139.** RIBA Library Photographs Collection. **140.** Cora Visnick. **143.** © Herzog & de Mueron. **144.** Christian Richters. **147.** Nicholas Bruscia. **148.** Joseph Goldberg. **150.** Ila Bêka & Louise Lemoine © Bêka & Partners. **153.** Timothy Hursley. **155.** Burnham Pavilion, Chicago, 2009, by UNStudio. Photo: © Christian Richters. **156.** Luke Zhen Han. **159.** Hiroyuki Hirai. **160.** © Brady Lambert.

Chapter 4 | TRUSSES

168. Ed Clark/The LIFE Picture Collection/Getty Images. **175.** Emi Yasuda. **176.** Agrandissement des écoles primaires n° 5 et 6. Construction d'un Jardin. Ensembles et détails de la charpente en fer. 1902 (Municipal Archive of Elsene). **180-1.** By permission of the article authors. **182.** Marc Petitjean. **187.** © OMA. **188.** Andres Otero/Luz. **191, 193.** © 2015 Artists Rights Society (ARS), New York / AUTVIS, Sao Paulo. **194.** Architectural Press Archive / RIBA Library Photographs Collection. **198.** Tom Polte and Donald Ingber, Boston Children's Hospital and Harvard University. **203.** Julia Sero and Donald Ingber, Boston Children's Hospital and Harvard University. **205.** By Onderwijsgek (Own work) CC BY-SA 2.5 nl via Wikimedia Commons. **207.** © Beat Widmer. **209.** © Christian Richter/Courtesy of Bernard Tschumi Architects. **210.** Photo: Iwan Baan. **213.** Hiroyuki Hirai. **214.** © Iwan Baan. **217.** Yoshinori Kuwahara. **218.** Sergio Gómez. **220.** George X. Lin.

Chapter 5 | FRAMES

228. Chicago Historical Society, ICHi 21294. **235.** Library of Congress, Prints & Photographs Division, HABS ILL,16-CHIG, 30-2. **237.** Digital Image © The Museum of Modern Art/Licensed by SCALA / Art Resource, NY. **238.** Braun, Clément & Co. (French, active 1877-1928). The Propylaia to the Acropolis, Athens, negative 1869; print about 1890. The J. Paul Getty Museum, Los Angeles. Google Art Project. **242.** © Vassilis D. Gonis (2004) Athens, teNeues. **243.** John Travlos, *The Pictorial Dictionary of Ancient Athens,* fig 91. Reprinted by permission of © Ernst Wasmuth

Verlag Tübingen 1971. **244.** Photo: Lucien Hervé. By permission of Judith Elkan. Marcel Breuer Papers, Special Collections Research Center, Syracuse University Libraries. **249.** Eric Sutherland for Walker Art Center, Minneapolis, MN USA. **250.** Architectural Press Archive / RIBA Library Photographs Collection. **255.** Foster + Partners. **256-71.** Cecil Balmond and Prestel Munich · London · New York, 2002. **272.** Photograph by Ursula Litschi, courtesy of Camenzind Evolution. **274.** © Mini Yu Sun / Arup. **277.** © Michael Layefsky. **279.** Peter Buteÿn. **280.** Photo: Iwan Baan. **283.** © Andrew Meredith. **284.** Prometeo musical space. Photo: Gianni Berengo Gardin. By courtesy Fondazione Renzo Piano. **286.** Shingo Masuda + Katsuhisa Otsubo Architects. **288.** Aalto Arts / Department of Architecture / Anne Kinnunen. **291.** Photo: John Linden.

Chapter 6 | CABLES, NETS & MEMBRANES

298, 303. Institut für Leichtbau Entwerfen und Konstruieren, Universität Stuttgart, Bildarchiv. **304.** Architectural Press Archive / RIBA Library Photographs Collection. **307.** Cedric Price fonds. Collection Centre Canadien d'Architecture / Canadian Centre for Architecture, Montréal. **308, 314-15.** Richard Davies. **316, 318-19.** Sanjeev Shankar. **320.** © Dennis Gilbert / VIEW. **322.** Titian [Public domain], via Wikimedia Commons. **324-5** Courtesy and by permission of Cecil Balmond Studio. **327.** "IMGP7111" by zacarious is licensed under CC BY 2.0. **329.** Ramón Etis. **330.** "Building prow" by Anders Sandberg is licensed under CC BY 2.0. **332.** © ICD/ITKE Universität Stuttgart. **334.** Richard Davies. **337.** Nigel Watts.

Chapter 7 | ARCHES, DOMES & SHELLS

344. Photograph by Keith Dotson. **350.** By Leonardo da Vinci [Public domain], via Wikimedia Commons. **351.** National Parks Service. www.nps.gov/jeff/planyourvisit/mathematical-equation.htm **356.** Mehdi Khansari. **359.** IMG42837 © Courtesy of Architect / ICHTO East Azerbaijan Office (photographer). **360.** Wellcome Library, London. CC BY 4.0 **362.** (L) Netter Images. **362.** (R) By Claude Nicolas Ledoux [Public domain], via Wikimedia Commons. **363.** (R) Encyclopédie, ou dictionnaire raisonné des sciences, des arts et des métiers, etc., eds. Denis Diderot and Jean le Rond d'Alembert. University of Chicago: ARTFL Encyclopédie Project (Spring 2013 Edition), Robert Morrissey (ed), www.encyclopedie.uchicago.edu/. **364.** Fig. 3943, vol. 65, p. 518, "Lanterne" in: J.G. Kruenitz, Oekonomisch-technologische Enzyklopaedie, 2nd ed. 1803, (Universitätsbibliothek Trier, www.kruenitz.uni-trier.de). **365.** RIBA Library Photographs Collection. **366.** (L, R) DR1984:1407, DR1984:1408 Collection Centre Canadien d'Architecture/Canadian Centre for Architecture, Montréal. **366.** (R, top) A solar microscope (c. 1750). From Hankins and Silverman, instruments and the imagination (Berlin: Springer, 1995). Courtesy of the Magic Lantern Society of Great Britain. **367, 368.** RIBA Library Photographs Collection. **368.** (L, top) Science Museum / Science & Society Picture Library PD-1923. **369.** Scala / Art Resource, NY. **370, 375.** Avery Architectural & Fine Arts Library, Columbia University. **376.** Photo: Iwan Baan. **378.** Marissa Looby. **381.** Ken Lee. **383.** Courtesy of SGL Projekt s.r.o. **385.** IBM Travelling Pavilion. Photo: Gianni Berengo Gardin. Courtesy of Fondazione Renzo Piano. **386.** Photo: John W. Picken. **388.** In public domain. PD-1923 **390.** Photo: David Cardelus. **393.** Photo: Hiroyuki Hirai, Architect: Kyeong Sik Yoon/KACI + Shigeru Ban Architects. **394.** Hisao Suzuki.

AFTERWORD

402. By courtesy and permission of Olafur Eliasson. **404, 406.** By courtesy of the Trustees of Sir John Soane's Museum. **408.** By courtesy of the Trustees of Sir John Soane's Museum. Photo: Gareth Gardner. **409, 410.** William Staffeld.

Index

Italicized entries indicate images